**SUBURBAN AMBUSH**

Parallax  Re-visions of Culture and Society

Stephen G. Nichols, Gerald Prince, and Wendy Steiner, Series Editors

# SUBURBAN AMBUSH

THEY FIREBOMBED
THE DINNER TABLE
TAKING US COMPLETELY
BY SURPRISE.

WE EVACUATED
OUR CASUALTIES
FROM THE PATIO—
TRACERS SKITTERING
ACROSS THE SUMMER
SKY.

DAD IS A MEMORY
WE'RE TRYING TO KEEP
ALIVE.

WORDS BY RON KOLM
GRAPHICS BY ART RAVESON

# SUBURBAN AMBUSH

*Downtown Writing and
the Fiction of Insurgency*

## ROBERT SIEGLE

The Johns Hopkins University Press   Baltimore and London

The Johns Hopkins University Press,
701 West 40th Street, Baltimore, Maryland 21211
The Johns Hopkins Press Ltd., London

The paper used in this publication meets the minimum requirements of
American National Standard for Information Sciences—Permanence of Paper for
Printed Library Materials, ANSI Z39.48-1984.


*Library of Congress Cataloging-in-Publication Data*
Siegle, Robert.
    Suburban ambush : downtown writing and the fiction of insurgency/
Robert Siegle.
        p.    cm.—(Parallax : re-visions of culture and society)
    Bibliography: p.
    Includes index.
    ISBN 0-8018-3847-9 (alk. paper).—ISBN 0-8018-3854-1 (pbk. :
alk. paper)
    1. Experimental fiction—New York (N.Y.)—History and criticism.
2. American fiction—New York (N.Y.)—History and criticism.
3. American fiction—20th century—History and criticism.
4. Manhattan (New York, N.Y.)—Intellectual life.   5. New York
(N.Y.)—Intellectual life.   6. City and town life in literature.
I. Title.   II. Series: Parallax (Baltimore, Md.)
PS144.N4S54   1989
813'.540997471—dc20                                        89-33037
                                                                CIP

*for Jane*

# CONTENTS

# PREFACE

*Suburban Ambush* tells the story of the reinvention of American fiction. It draws its title from a piece by Ron Kolm which has appeared in several versions and nearly twenty magazines around the world: the conceit of a military strike on the heart of Suburbia has considerable resonance. The kind of raid we shall follow, however, is one from within by artists whose work has only slowly, if at all, moved into the more remunerative channels of the culture industry, but that has now achieved a critical mass which requires our close attention. However, before turning to those artists in general, and then to Kolm's work in particular, I think some initial words might be useful concerning this book's origins, the process of its construction, and its organization, because it claims a great deal for a group of writers who are well known only among those most involved in the making of new art. The project began out of my sense that the fiction published during the seventies by major commercial houses suffered in comparison with the narratives in nonacademic little magazines and small-press offerings. This phenomenon is national and involves generations on both sides of a birthday dividing line that falls around 1947. I have titled this project "The Unread Renaissance" in order to call attention to the comparative neglect with which we have treated those writers who are reinventing narrative form with a vigor we have not seen since the twenties. A companion study to *Suburban Ambush*, it includes writers from around America and some on the senior side of my dateline.

I found so intense a concentration of talent and productivity in the region stretching from Tribeca to the Lower East Side in New York, so strong a sense of community and interchange among those working in different art forms, and so significant a generational identity among those born postwar that I found it imperative to separate the writers treated here and to give them sufficient space to make their case to a national audience. Their work is less well known outside New York than it should be and is easily lost among the heavily hyped narratives of late modernists such as Raymond Carver and *Granta*'s "dirty realists," and of those who have sensationalized the downtown nightlife of Los Angeles (such as Bret Easton Ellis) or New York (such as Jay McInerney). We are noticing the wrong fiction when we look to what these writers have thus far produced. But even some who do read something from our strongest writers often show some difficulty recognizing its importance. When I shared a Kathy Acker novel with a colleague, the note that came back offered a response at best lukewarm: "Sometime you'll have to explain to me the value of this sort of thing." It was at least more tolerant than the reviewer who dismissed the whole movement as "the East Village, sexual-terrorism-and-real-estate-whining school."

It is quite distressing when intelligent readers grow intolerant, and it is difficult to resist accusing the nay-sayers of political or existential cowardice as they reject the constant change that marks cultural process. Not that all work is equal, of course. Tama Janowitz's *Slaves of New York* is a smarter book than Jay McInerney's *Bright Lights, Big City*, and both Janowitz and McInerney have a much better ear for language than, say, David Leavitt in *Family Dancing*. But none of these writers risks as profound a social anger as Kathy Acker, none passes so freely beyond the boundaries of univocal narrative as Constance DeJong, none reads the ideological details of American life so astutely as Lynne Tillman. The writers examined in detail in *Suburban Ambush* are writers who, as a feature of *this* age in fiction, connect their reflexive analysis of the possibilities of narrative with an equally penetrating awareness of the social realities beyond the realm of art. They would doubtless agree with Lucy Lippard's catalog comment about the artists involved in COLAB's (Collaborative Projects') MetaLanguages/Textual Venues exhibition at the B.A.D. (Bohemia After Dark) Museum in October 1987: "The social element of response, of exchange, is crucial even to the most formalized objects or performances. Without it, culture remains simply one more manipulable commodity in a market society where even ideas and the deepest expressions of human emotion are absorbed and controlled. I resist the notion that in modern times the task of image and symbol making should be relegated to one more frill on the 'quality of life'" (*The End of Art Panel*, 1987, 9).

A similar attitude rests behind the essay by John Carlin that accompanied the Pop Apocalypse exhibition at Gracie Mansion in June 1988 in which, writing about powerful artists such as David Wojnarowicz and Sue Coe, he opposes the Warholian pop art that made "comics and cans safe for museums" to work marked by "stylistic outrageousness, political and moral responsibility, and deliberate rudeness" (Carlin 1988). Although the work of most of the writers discussed in *Suburban Ambush* is outrageous and rude in rather more delicate ways than the hard-hitting work of Wojnarowicz and Coe, Carlin's comments are a fair description of Acker's work. More to the point, the apocalyptic visual art that he describes shares its politics and its double edge of appropriation and ideological exposure with the fiction that this book addresses.

The theoretical underpinnings of *Suburban Ambush* are in my earlier book, *The Politics of Reflexivity: Narrative and the Constitutive Poetics of Culture.* I have made no effort to counterpoint fiction and theory, except at points at which the latter's explanatory power seemed especially useful (to have done otherwise would have resulted in a quite different book), and so there are relatively few fireworks set off at the points of affinity between Acker and Jacques Lacan, Tillman and Michel Foucault. Nonetheless, *Suburban Ambush* in many ways carries forward my earlier book's contention that energetic reflexivity inevitably takes one deep into a critical engagement with the social, political, and economic structures of the culture. There are still those critics who think poststructural theory negates the possibility of taking political positions. I don't think so. I think such theory undermines our desire to claim that *our* position is grounded upon any authority with traditionally conceived truth claims. It should not be nearly so traumatic to accept that our politics must rest upon the consent of those who agree with us, and that those politics seek a society formed by the values that emerge from our collective social and historical experiences. Poststructural theory makes taking political positions unavoidable, because "philosophy" and "morality" and most everything else lose the privileged space of isolation and ahistoricalism which they often appear to assume for themselves. There is no resting upon categories or principles that are *a priori* self-evident, but this freedom should invigorate rather than dispirit. These writers' fluency in both new fictional practice and poststructural theory bears out my belief that poststructural ideas happen in the world and produce real effects that change the way people think about themselves and their society.

I've seen such effects in another origin of this book, the teaching that I have been doing for the last decade at a university dedicated to engineering, business, the physical and life sciences, and architecture as its primary pursuits. Many of these students already dream of leather brief cases, but many of them reject the consuming instrumentalism of the more monomaniacal of engineers and the ethical and spiritual vacuities of the next Ivan Boeskys. These students are looking for something, but they mirror in their architectural drawings, their creative writing, and the rock music of their

nightlife the same mix of late modernist and poststructural inclinations that make difficult their teachers' efforts at an accurate
critical sorting of new cultural productions. How do you tell the
slick commercial product from the cultural earthquake if both have
the same drugs, sex, and rock 'n' roll taking place center stage? What
is innovative and what is fashionable, especially when many works
are both? I repeatedly have watched classes of students approach this
fiction with late modernist assumptions about what fiction should
be, recoil, and then suddenly realize something very strange. As one
young man said in my office, "I thought all this political stuff was
way out until it started happening in my life." His first reality therapy revealed to him that the underlying cultural analysis behind
this new fiction spoke to his life, sorted out frustrations, blind angers, ennui, and a profound anxiety over what will happen to his
generation's curiosity and vitality when it encounters the professional world.

The test of fiction continues to be its capacity to lead readers
through language to a richer understanding of the difficult business
of living in the world. That business seems particularly difficult in
an age rethinking its ontology, its epistemology, its understanding
of language, and the approach that its collective survival myths take
toward the ideological stakes in every feature of daily life. And working through these issues is particularly difficult for readers away
from the art-making centers of New York, San Francisco, Seattle,
Los Angeles, and other such active intersections of different media
and ideas. We are a nation poorly trained as readers, let alone as
readers of new forms and difficult analytical texts. But exposure
cures, as I have found repeatedly with classes that are at first dazed,
then roused to debate, and then—quite crucial to the special qualities of this fiction—energized to go and take over for themselves the
art-making privilege and the license for cultural critique our academic system seems forever to defer until the arrival of Mastery.

*Suburban Ambush* grows out of these interests in narrative,
theory, and pedagogy, and it offers its readers one pathway through
the intersection of these three concerns in the particularly lively
arts scene of New York since the mid-seventies. Those who were
not present during the years of this fiction's emergence can follow
my own efforts as an outsider to catch up on what I could only
overhear long-distance, as if I were hearing half of another conversation with my AT&T calling card. I simply went to places such as
St. Mark's Bookshop, Printed Matter, Embargo Books Ltd., and
Spring Street Books and looked through the shelves for fiction that
"looked different" from that of John Updike or Saul Bellow. I bought
issues of *Bomb, Benzene,* and *Between C & D* and returned to Virginia to deduce what had been happening while I was busily working
out my ideas about narrative theory. My experience anticipated that

of my students, because the novels and stories began to make sense.

I approached these writers, explained my project, and interviewed
them, sometimes for hours at a sitting, at their studios, apartments,
or favorite bars or cafés. From the hours of tape I learned a great deal
about the minute interconnections among art forms, about the daily
texture of a community's intermingling lives, about its reading and
its literary prejudices, and about its own ideas about what those
within the community were attempting to do. The results of those
interviews dot the pages of this book and fill in the gaps that an
outsider such as myself would otherwise have had to struggle might-
ily to infer.

The organization of this book tries to lead readers quickly into
the heart of the communal vision that has inspired the distinctive
fiction of these writers. The first chapter, "Suburban Ambush," explores the energy and contradictions of the arts community of
which these figures are very much a part rather than, say, of the
academic world. It turns then to one representative figure, Ron
Kolm, whose varied activities as writer and small-press publisher
constitute an instructive prelude to the story of what these writers
have attempted. The three chapters that follow study writers who
have produced substantial bodies of work as important in influence
as in sheer quality. Kathy Acker, the most sensational of the downtown writers, also has been the most prolific and offers an extensive,
profound, and penetrating analysis of American society. Her fiction
can be a tough introduction to this new narrative—the first-time
reader must overcome the initial responses of confusion and of distaste for Acker's strong material long enough to recognize what
Acker is teaching through precisely those responses. But she was
among the first downtown writers, along with Constance DeJong,
and remains the most influential. DeJong's fiction returns to the
primary social relation of storytelling to reconsider the impact of
the collective nature of the narrative voice upon the individual.
Lynne Tillman appropriates realist narrative in order to explore
what it more typically leaves unsaid about representation and gender.

The chapter "Tanam Press: Fire over Water" looks at the distinctive group that Reese Williams gathered together in his Tanam
Press endeavor, a group extremely close to the visual arts (many are
crossover artists working in several media) and acute in its response
to life in a culture of electronic media. Clustered mostly in the
Tribeca and Soho areas, but not to be identified with the Soho of
gentrification and pricey galleries, Tanam Press's writers typify the
way that the specific culture to which they contribute cohabits the
same space with the commodity culture that they critique. The
chapter "Condensed Book: Performance Art and Fiction" examines
the crossover from performance art to fiction, its three main figures

shifting us from the Soho roots of Spalding Gray to the more East Village affiliations of Peter Cherches. Performance art's mingling of drama, stand-up comedy, song, and movement has had its impact upon much new fiction's quick cuts and general irreverence to the decorums of genre. The chapter "Between C & D" moves into the heart of the East Village sensibility by examining a trio of its strongest writers and the crucial magazine they produce together. The work of Joel Rose, Catherine Texier, and Patrick McGrath suggests three distinguishable narrative modes which nonetheless share the literary and social politics of a community working distinctly against the ideological grain of the Reagan era. The chapter "Village Voices" begins with a close look at the magazines that have been crucial to the literary culture of this arts scene, keeping its writers in close touch with one another and with developments in the adjacent arts. The chapter then turns to several writers whose fiction has emerged from those magazines into recent books that suggest the vitality, range, and energy of the new writing.

The final chapter, "Downtown Writing," contains general remarks about postmodernism and about this writing by way of tying its threads together loosely enough to leave plenty of growing room. I love literary history; I mistrust it, as I do critical theory, when it verges very far from what people who are not historians or theorists are actually doing. To some readers, this inductive inclination will seem an anachronism rather than the reality check it is for me. In any case, the plan of the book seeks to follow the shape of the new writing as it has emerged since bits of Acker's *Black Tarantula* and DeJong's *Modern Love* began showing up in readings in the mid-seventies, to describe briefly at appropriate moments points of contact with the adjacent arts, to help readers reflect upon its most important writers and texts, and to emerge at the end with some sense of the more radical postmodernism that this writing embodies. Critics from many points of view have claimed *postmodernism* for their favored kind of work, and it should not surprise us that so many postmodernisms have emerged as a result: history is always far too various to conform to totalizing definitions. But, as I shall suggest in the final chapter, the writers of *Suburban Ambush* work within a distinctly poststructural vein of postmodernism, which is quite different from the version we find, for example, in Charles Jencks's account. Perhaps the label is more trouble than it is worth and we should just call this *poststructural fiction*. But I think it is the first body of narrative to take a decisive step beyond modernist practice, and it is that step which this book is most concerned to describe.

My debts are many and begin with research funds provided by the Department of English and the Center for Programs in the Humanities at Virginia Polytechnic Institute and State University. An even greater debt is to the writers who took time out from their busy schedules to talk with me. Allan Bealy, Peter Cherches, Constance DeJong, Ron Kolm, Judy Lopatin, Patrick McGrath, Richard Prince, Joel Rose, Betsy Sussler, Catherine Texier, Lynne Tillman, Anne Turyn, Brian Wallis, and Reese Williams all undertook to educate a Virginian about their work and the cultural environment from which it arose. Many were very generous in supplying me with copies of out-of-print works, pieces published in periodicals outside the usual university-library holdings, manuscripts in progress, and all manner of tips, suggestions, and contacts for pursuing these matters. My prose would be much drier without their observations, my knowledge of the scene much more limited without their insights, my discussions much thinner without the range of material to which they gave me access.

Very special thanks must go to Ron Kolm, who has been my key contact ever since the day he looked over the huge stack of books and magazines I had gathered in a research raid on St. Mark's Bookshop and, instead of simply presenting the bill, also asked me, "Who are you, anyway?" One of those rare individuals both known and liked by, it seems, everyone, Ron opened many doors for me and saw to it that I did not miss any important materials. I feel fortunate to be able to call him a friend. Jerome Klinkowitz read the manuscript and was quite kind in his comments and suggestions—certainly any of us who work in the field of current fiction owe much to the Klinkowitz shelf in our own libraries. I also owe a great deal to Eric Halpern, whose encouragement and receptiveness have been important throughout this book's evolution. Jane Warth has saved the reader many unnecessary confusions with her remarkable editorial gifts, and I am very grateful to have benefited so much from her hard work on this book. My students over the last five years all deserve medals for their service in the reconnaissance corps under a squad leader who was making up his map as we moved across this territory. The intensity of their engagement with these works was a welcomed corroboration of that risky judgment we make browsing the shelves of the bolder bookstores—"Ah, this looks interesting." Finally, my wife, Jane, is the cocreator of this book. Active in the interviews, sharp-eared during our transcriptions, unwearied through every draft and revision, she is an enthusiast whose good spirits kept mine that way through a project that both pleased and instructed its makers.

# SUBURBAN AMBUSH

# SUBURBAN AMBUSH

Perhaps the most potent demystifiers of the illusions in which most of us live are the gritty streets from which the tactility of East Village writing takes its cue. Buildings burned out by junkies so that they can sell off the copper piping, boarded-up dead stores with their graffiti-laced steel shutters, postnuclear vacant lots, jumpy-eyed adolescent males and twelve-year-old girls with Mona Lisa smiles, scruffy winos and children exploding out of school into side-walk tag-team mayhem—all this still exists on the Lower East Side, where yet to conquer is the gentrification of lace-curtain ice-cream shops, antique stores with Aztec jaguars, Italian boutiques' akimbo mannequins, damask tablecloth dining salons, and designer shower-curtain shops. Writers, painters, musicians, performance artists, and the otherwise unclassifiably creative still live in this quarter of alphabet avenues and single-digit streets in refuge from the subur-banization carried into Manhattan by the bridge and tunnel set, an upscaling that inflates rents, average incomes among the new ten-ants, and self-satisfaction. To those who regard a community of difference as a source of vital energy for rethinking the American experience, gentrification is the face of the enemy.

This is the generation of writers about which the Right has been worrying. They schooled in the Velvet Underground, left their na-iveté on the streets when the generals' sons and daughters left the Pentagon demonstrations in time to get back out to McLean for supper, watched Nixon self-destruct too late for our collective good. They scattered, reassembled, wrote for small presses and even smaller magazines, balanced jobs copy-editing or programming or typing and filing against their commitment to an art that did not comply with the gallery system's need for collectors' editions or the writing workshops' ideal of the "well-made" story. Richard Prince *almost* called his important anthology of such work *Apartment*

*Writing* because so many visual artists would run out of materials, or even just room, before their ambitions for visual art could be realized. And so they wrote, or did graphic art they could share by photocopies, or put words and decals around the city on stickers, in stencils, next to the work of the Writers—subway-car spray-can artists—Mayor Koch was trying to arrest.

Prince called that anthology *Wild History* instead, and its wildness is the history of our age of simulation when thirty-minute press conferences require hours of retractions and "clarifications," when advertisements embody our apparent ideals as a culture, when Disneyland is coming more and more to look like the Real Thing, when nations bar the press so that their diners will not be "disturbed" by the evening news of regular beatings in the occupied territories. There is an edge to that wildness, and it shows in the incendiary titles of magazines such as *Benzene* and *Bomb*, which kept the work circulating for readers as this decade began, the opening of the eighties. It shows, too, in the metaphors invoked by titles of collections such as *Blatant Artifice* and *Blasted Allegories*. The histories chronicle our *Haunted Houses* from the era of our *Blood and Guts in High School* through the involutions of *Modern Love* to the eerie ironic distress of *Welcome to the Barbecue* that threatens us all one turn of the spit at a time.

These works corrode rather than conform to the commodity formulae toward which latter-day modernist fiction tends, just as the writers who create them have chosen *not* to live in the more comfortable academic and professional worlds in which late modernist fiction still prevails. They live enough out of phase with the prevailing norms of the professional managerial class to play the real against the realistic, the phenomenological against the media image, art against commodity. They are not trying to get rich at it unless they do so finally on their own terms; they are all smart enough and talented enough to have made plenty of money, if that is what they had been looking for in the first place. These writers live and write near Wall Street rather than commuting there; they clerk in the law firms rather than profiteering in the high-seas piracy we call the practice of law; they lampoon academics such as me rather than hustling for tenure; they satirize the gallery culture rather than conforming to its commercial formulae; they get a critical edge from the burnouts of the afterhour crowd rather than packaging them in bright lights for the big city readership that wants to cruise the downtown scene on the morning train.

In the mid-seventies the time arrived for a "fiction of insurgency," an appropriately double genitive marking its passage beyond liberationist illusions of free space and unmediated time, but also its guerrilla campaign against the imminent transformation of American consciousness into a shopping mall. Downtown writing *is* insurgent, but its alpha and omega reside in the other half of the double genitive—in its status as fiction rather than revolution. "Insurgency" in this context is absurd, that is, but not for the reasons supposed by those who like to dismiss the Left in this country as radical chic. Insurgency is a "fiction" in comparison with our metaphysically inspired liberationist politics, the utopian dream of liberation with full sensation. Our metaphysical heritage has conditioned us to expect revolutions to have fully articulated programs, governments to solve all problems, positions to be unambiguous, truths to be absolute, lives to be fulfilled, Being to be, at the very least, itself. The "good life," the golden age, exists somewhere, at least mentally diminishing our feeble approximations of their perfected forms, disciplining us for our failures to achieve them, normalizing us to the hidden agenda of their public formulations by schools, churches, states, and media.

Downtown writing seeks not liberation but liberty, real rather than full sensation, tactical critique rather than strategic game plan. It opens space—mentally, psychologically, semiotically—where simulation, repression, and convention have converged to predetermine our Being. It shakes up reified relations—roles, genders, social structures—so that at least momentary experiences of various sorts of Other might take place before the great culture machine swallows it up again. And it surrenders the dream of Utopia in favor of *utopian:* no structure will escape reification, no legislation fail to repress and normalize, no specification avoid replacing the "reality" it was intended to approach. Despite these odds, downtown writing persists in a sort of hit-and-run guerrilla action, or works at times as a mole in The Company, but is never to be found in anything quite like a five-year plan or a white paper. It is an alternative community, but not an alternative state.

"Community" is an important modifier, because these writers know one another, or know one another in heavily overlapping circles. They share more, besides. They have positioned themselves on the margins of the suburbanization of America. Many work unromantic jobs proofreading, keyboarding, waiting tables to maintain their energies not for the GNP but for writing books. They do not teach; most of them avoided writing programs or loathed their repressive, or formulaic, or actively reactionary teachers. Their friendships are formed with one another and more generally in the art world, not in the academic or other professional classes. They socialize not at Broadway shows or charity fundraisers or formal dinners, but at the Pyramid Lounge or the Performance Garage or Artists' Space or at any of the clubs and bars dotting downtown's increasingly sensationalized dreamscape.

The sixties for them was not the fabrication of *Time* or Allan Bloom or William Bennett, but a time of decisive break with the continuities wrought by the normalizing institutions of schools, popular culture, journalism, family, and gender, or by that great national drive for upward mobility. Less Christopher Cross, more Lou Reed. Less *Passages*, more fluidity. Less formalism, more engagement. Less genteel belles-lettres than politicized reflexivity, gritty social realities, disruptive and thought-jolting technical maneuvers, and a driving intensity of pace heard more in club bands than on MTV.

It is, then, an insurgency, but not one that expects to break free of some kind of specific corrupt institution. It is an insurgency against the silence of institutions, the muteness of the ideology of form, the unspoken violence of normalization. But it does not expect of itself the pure voice of the Other—it knows its own language is divided against itself, its every move a contradiction that marks the position of the speaking subject at the end of the twentieth century. To speak or act, even in the most ironically positioned intervention, is to risk becoming assimilated like a feedback loop in a self-regulating mechanism, discharging excess energy and occasioning minor adjustments in the social engineering. Or, even worse, to be used outright by precisely what we oppose. It is itself, after all, as part of the art world's "invasion" of the Lower East Side, in ironic alliance with the collusion between city government and big capital to displace the working-class residents of this area and to create chic living space for those who work nearby in the shadow of the twin towers to the south. Rosalyn Deutsche and Cara Gendel Ryan mount a devastating critique of the art world's complicity in this process of gentrification in a 1984 essay originally published in *October* and reprinted in Kurt Hollander's *Portable Lower East Side* in 1987. The sense of community fostered by the City Arts Workshop program set up almost twenty years ago by Susan Shapiro-Kiok, or by Carol Watson's organizing activities with the Catholic Charities' Housing Leverage Fund, or by the ministry of Father Joaquin Beaumont, is endangered by the same kind of city thinking that used its funds and money from Exxon not to train youths for jobs or even to clean up a city-owned vacant building, but to paint one side of Avenue C "like a movie set," a "series of store facades" that "would give the illusion of development" (Moore and Miller 1985, 189). Simulated "renewal" until the investors lined up for the Real Thing?

The area has survived some assaults in the past. At one point, the city started to build the Second Avenue subway, digging up the pavement and leaving mud streets and wooden sidewalks that fostered the illusion of a Wild, Wild West in which the drug trade took the outlaws' roles. Abandoned as the financial crisis was settling in, perhaps the subway will start up again after gentrification is complete. But even my own descriptions smack of the promotional tone Deutsche and Ryan criticize in their article. They quote, for example, the enthusiasm in the Summer 1984 *Art in America* special coverage of the "unique blend of poverty, punk rock, drugs, arson, Hell's Angels, winos, prostitutes and dilapidated housing that adds up to an adventurous avant-garde setting of considerable cachet" (Deutsche and Ryan 1987, 35).

Deutsche and Ryan are not the only ones to complain of the tone in the art world's treatment of their neighbors. One long-term resident of the area thinks "it's like a lot of bored people from good backgrounds getting into the *bad* of the neighborhood" (Moore and Miller 1985, 49). Richard Armijo, a poet, editor, painter, and owner of Embargo Book Ltd. on Rivington Street, took exception to ABC No Rio's Portrait show. Area residents were offered portraits for a dollar, but might, if they had strayed as far, have discovered themselves selling for good prices in a posh Soho gallery not too long afterward. Armijo asks: "Why do anonymous images of the so-called underclass elicit our interest and appreciation, even monetary patronage, while the people themselves are confined to ghettos, encouraged to concentrate in projects, restricted to mostly blue-collar jobs, their intelligentsia too late acknowledged, and their daily movements monitored by cops, sociologists, liberals, and now artists?" (ibid., 99). Lucy Lippard (of PADD—Political Art Documentation and Distribution) was disturbed by the Unforgettable Moments show, which displayed the personal stories of neighborhood residents: "Participants were found through social agencies in the ghettoes, where such experiences become public property, unlike the bastions of middle-class privacy further downtown" (ibid., 111).

Deutsche and Ryan, zeroing in on the catalog from the first museum exhibition of East Village art at the University of Pennsylvania's Institute of Contemporary Art (ICA), drive home the point with a vengeance:

> The Lower East Side enters the space of the ICA catalogue in three forms: mythologized in the texts as an exciting bohemian environment, objectified in a map delimiting its boundaries, and aestheticized in a full-page photograph of a Lower East Side "street scene." All three are familiar strategies for the domination and possession of others. The photograph, alone, is a blatant example of the aestheticization of poverty and suffering that has become a staple of visual imagery. (Deutsche and Ryan 1987, 51)

For several pages they analyze a photograph depicting a "bum" slouched beneath graffiti and a poster for the Pierpont Morgan Library's Hans Holbein exhibition and conclude that "the figure of the bum provides the requisite identification with marginal figures and social outcasts by which avant-garde and the bohemian glamour accrues to the East Village scene despite its embrace of conventional values" (ibid., 53).

The core of the argument is thus that the artists get their highs from others' misfortunes and, wittingly or not, function in a class alliance with the forces conspiring to eliminate the increasingly unsuitable blue-collar residents and replace them with information-age employees. Deutsche and Ryan have the statistics to illustrate the shrinking job pool for these workers, their exclusion from planning processes and thus also from the final products of "renewal" projects, the futility of any hope for the assimilation that shifted earlier populations of the area up the economic ladder, and the rising rents and evictions that drive them out of the neighborhood altogether. Artists, in contrast, seem to be the developers' vanguard for glamorizing an area prior to its marketing. Alan Moore and Marc Miller tell a paradigmatic tale: "One early center of activity was the so-called Fine Arts Building at 105 Hudson Street in Tribeca, a nearly vacant office building that, in a calculated strategy, was rented to artists for studios and fledgling art dealers for galleries. After two years of glamorous action had put the building and the 'Tribeca' (triangle below Canal street) area on the New York map, 105 Hudson Street was swiftly and completely co-oped to the affluent" (Moore and Miller 1985, 2). By its complicity in the eighties' episodes of this continuing plot, not to mention its commercial appetites, the art scene "participates in the dominant culture even as it poses as 'subcultural'" (Deutsche and Ryan 1987, 42).

This critique is vital, I think, because it comprises the most obvious of a whole series of contradictions within which the postmodern artist is caught. Is self-promotion and five-to-six-digit pricing a way of selling out to the commercial establishment? Is using paint or narrative form introducing dead languages, and languages of death, into works that seek to explore some kind of alternative voice, some alternative life? Is relying upon any sort of coherence and continuity and readability a lapse back into metaphysical nostalgia, phallogocentric habits that recolonize one's work as soon as it emerges? Does media assimilation of innovation transform the avant-garde into another corporate division producing forms of planned obsolescence? Does growing up in the suburbs make it impossible to speak outside the middle-class interest or to live apart from carport comforts of mind and body?

None of these questions has an easy answer. David Deitcher, in a reflection upon current art for a New Museum of Contemporary Art catalog, argues that "in what can be taken as a significant reversal of the conditions of the modernist past, it seems most effective when it refuses resolution, when it denies answers, and when it demonstrates the travesty that is the promise of continuous and easy access to meaning, or to now inaccessible cultural traditions. For these promises are the stock and trade of consumer culture itself" (Deitcher 1985, 21).

Deitcher's contribution is to remind us of the importance of postmodern openness resisting recognizable closures, playing them off against one another to win a little more time, a little more space, to work things out. Thomas Lawson provides another way to conceive the artist's role when he suggests the model of "Spies and Watchmen":

> Better the strategy of the spy, the infiltrator, the undercover agent, who can make himself acceptable to society while all the while representing disorder. Master of the double-bluff, he is able to infiltrate the centers of power in order to undermine the structure from within. An art of representation, a flirtation with misrepresentation. An ambiguous art which seems to flatter the situation which supports it while undermining it. Sweetly arbitrary, art which appears attractively irrational, but which turns out to be coldly rational; art which looks distant, but is deeply felt. (Lawson 1987, 139–40)

These arguments help us conceive of the aesthetic strategies these artists pursue in resisting dominant cultural forms, but Deutsche and Ryan are talking about existential strategies—action—and in many ways there simply is no response to make. They are right. But places such as the Lower East Side are also at the psychic heart of the American experience, a heart that is also literal for writers such as Joel Rose, who lives across the street from his grandfather's abandoned tailor shop. Returning to that heart is a way of recovering an unassimilated voice after suburban childhoods or interludes have processed it into precisely the class discourses that Deutsche and Ryan so effectively analyze. That voice has been sotto voce at best, heard perhaps in the gang sagas that Rose recovers in some of his stories, heard in the work of a Miguel Piñero or a Bimbo Rivas or an Amiri Baraka, heard also from the strong women who keep rising and shaping their community and who now all but dominate the writing scene. But usually it has been represented only in the telling pictures of Jacob Riis or their contemporary versions so criticized by Deutsche and Ryan.

No doubt much work fails to survive the formidable forces arrayed against anyone who would really speak in a nonhegemonic tongue: the mechanisms for "turning" an agent of difference are both micro and macro in scale, blatant and subtle in operation, external and internal in location, material and ideological in form. But the best work gives voice to a lost Other—one shaped by race, or class, or gender, or belief, or some combination of these—and articulates the experience of power from the perspective of a non-beneficiary, a phenomenon that Linda Kintz examines in interesting ways in the context of Jacques Derrida's comments on the "Other." For those a part of the scene, the ironies of privileged white artists living, writing, performing, and exhibiting on the Lower East Side (or on Rivington Street at ABC No Rio or in the South Bronx at Fashion/Moda) are indeed a subject of anxiety. But the same ironies are also a source of energy that does not necessarily serve the privileged or, perhaps with Lawson's point in mind, does not serve *only* big money. Ironies, after all, unravel univocality, and it is other voices that these writers, filmmakers, painters, sculptors, video artists want to hear and speak.

These city-dwelling suburban exiles and fortunate urbanites of the postmodern persuasion do share something quite profound with their black, Hispanic, or immigrant neighbors. The point is best introduced, perhaps, by "Richard," a longtime resident of East Thirteenth Street, where Group Material once had its gallery: "Anyways, people have all that experience but they never sit their asses down long enough to figure out what all those experiences were about. I don't know, maybe they were all about nothing. Most of us don't know what the fuck is hitting us at the time—we just go along. Vietnam, right?" (Moore and Miller 1985, 45). "Richard" has shifted quickly from those who have lived through *real* revolutions to the many for whom experiences "hit" inexplicably, inscrutably, part of some larger mechanism not apparent on the cultural surface: "When you eat day-to-day, you get a day-to-day brain. You get what you need now and worry about the consequences later. To tell the truth, you usually don't even know what the consequences will be until it's too late and you've fucked yourself" (ibid., 47).

Something that you can certainly feel but not see in the daily grind, something that precludes the possibility of naming it, something that cannot justify or make meaningful but can at least explain what all those experiences—of health costs, political corruption, police violence, the drug industry, the job trap—"were about." Do we want to call this something the social construction of consciousness, as did Marx? The structural determination of individuality, what "Richard" chafes against here, ranges in formulation from semiotic sedimentation to austere analyses of base and superstructure, from a sense of media imagery invading private spaces to Noam Chomsky's campaign against governing through disinformation, from appropriation exposing the implications of institutionalized (i.e., commodified) form to the desublimation of the cultural contradictions within art, gender, love, what have you.

The postmoderns know these things from ransacking poststructural theory. Their neighbors know it from the daily material experience of oppression in all its great and small forms. The *edge* to real postmodern writing, as opposed to late modernist lingerings in autonomously structured selves, comes from just what these experiences share. In their joint projects and shows we find a dimension of class interaction unthinkable in abstract expressionism, the fifties' beats, or the sixties' hippies who suffered greatly from what Lucy Lippard fears in the less rigorous exhibitions of our own age: "Lacking political analysis of the battle actually going down in these communities, art that doesn't mean to do so simply reinforces the oppression it pictures" (ibid., 111).

Lippard is suggesting, it would seem, an analysis from the trenches of those willing to work out the relationship between their own experiences and those of "Richard" and his neighbors. For Bimbo Rivas, "a free man in the ghetto" must "pray for work, and food and clothes" or "pick up the gun . . . hoping that dying will help the rest to get together." Supplication or revolution: the problem is being caught between Puerto Rico and America—"We do not belong over there nor over here. We are somewhere in the middle. But we are brand new in our thoughts, our emotions, in language, in custom, in color, allegiance, expression, and speed" (ibid., 174–75). An Other to any conceivable home, Rivas challenges his white listeners to construct a political analysis that undoes the segregation of art and tenement politics.

The economy turned mean as the number of blue-collar jobs in the city dropped while the working-class population rose (all this obscured by the increased jobs in "the business service sector or in financial industries"), and as the growth rate distracted attention from the tightening of eligibility and funding for human resources programs during the Reagan years. The *Time*/William Bennett lie about sixties' political and cultural life became official media dogma. But those heavily influenced by the sixties' partial recovery of activism, and of a vision within which the aesthetic and the political did not seem separate spheres, began inventing, gestating, experimenting toward alternative arts that would slice through the simulated economics of government statistics and the media's simulacral displacements of people and events. What both Delancey Street's "Richard" and PADD's Lippard call for is a structural analysis that goes beyond the storyboards of media narratology. And, not uncommonly, these artists turn for inspiration to someone used to telling it like it really is, Miguel Piñero, the Nuorican (a neologism for those caught in Rivas's "middle" between New York and Puerto Rico) poet whom Joel Rose describes as "one of the most brilliant writers I've ever seen":

> So here I am, look at me
> I stand proud as you can see
> pleased to be from the Lower East
> a street fighting man

a problem of this land
I am the Philosopher of the Criminal Mind
a dweller of prison time
a cancer of rockefeller's ghettocide
this concrete tomb is my home
to belong to survive you gotta be strong
you can't be shy less without request
someone will scatter your ashes thru
the Lower East Side.

When Piñero died in the summer of 1988, his ashes were indeed spread in the Lower East Side's Tompkins Square Park, right about the time, as it turns out, bloody protests broke out against the gentrifiers' efforts to close the park to its nightlife. Miguel Algarin, the noted Nuorican poet, and Josh Gosciak, of *East Informer* and *Contact/II*, together walked through the park carrying out Piñero's wish to be a permanent part of the ground on which "ghettocides" of whatever era might be contested.

### The Arts Scene

One good way to acquire the concrete sense of this milieu that can displace overly theoretical fictions about recent cultural history is to look back over the art community's activities in the last decade or so. This strategy is effective not only because so much has been written about these adjacent arts, hence giving us a rich body of dialogue to draw upon, but also because the last decade is one of those in which all the arts seem unusually closely connected in struggles to create new sets of possibilities for themselves. This communal quality is not just because so many individuals work in more than one art form. Nor it is just, as David Wojnarowicz—himself outstanding in more than one form—argues, a function of age ("a lot of the people working are young") rather than sensibility. More than a list of formal traits or a set of characteristic themes holds these arts together as a social environment, an aesthetic outbreak, and even these days a marketing concept.

At heart is a desire to use art in refabricating a basis of individuality in the face of our sharpened sense of the structural determination of our lives. That basis will not look like a Victorian self or a modernist master narrative. Far from being defeated by contradiction, these postmoderns take from it the cue for an alternative logic. Far from being rendered hopeless by the seemingly inevitable drift of (inter)national politics, they borrow from disinformation the ironic habitation of familiar forms for cross-purposes. Far from being paralyzed by the anxiety of past masters' influence, they appropriate them for commentary on classic motifs (such as mastery, originality, autonomy, representation) and art-world structures (such as publishing houses, galleries, museums, and criticism). Far from feeling compromised by the investment economics of art, they turn the art market into a microcosm of consumer capitalism and, as Carlo McCormick notes, reject modernism's "remote notion of living for art" in favor of a "pragmatic understanding, . . . to make art to live" (McCormick 1984, 1).

Jeffrey Deitch's essay in *Art in America* shows the diffidence typical of commentators talking about what seems at close range so heterogenous a group of creative talents. He is writing about the Times Square show in 1980, a month-long exhibition at Forty-first Street and Seventh Avenue, just off Times Square's drug and sex markets ("Nightly performances made it almost like a month-long party, coalescing the diverse new art energy, revealing it to a broad new public and to the artists themselves," as Moore and Miller describe it [1985, 5]). Deitch muses upon "that elusive process by which artists with a certain affinity somehow band together to form an unstructured but synergistic association which might almost be called a movement" (ibid., 12). We are already at sufficient distance to argue that there *is* a movement—even if diversity and self-difference are not only characteristics but also planks of the party platform and overall field tactics.

Much of the impetus for this movement stems from the experience those born in the late forties had in sixties' politics; those born somewhat later, in the seventies' art world: structures for the production and distribution of social and creative energies professed openness and practiced something quite different. As Gerald Marzorati wrote of the 1979 Real Estate show group, "they're being pushed out of loft space downtown to make room for their peers who pursued professional degrees. They're being turned away by galleries hedging in the face of ceaseless inflation" (ibid., 54). But although there is some truth that the movement may be "concocted of equal parts rampant careerism and internal esthetic necessity" (ibid., 42), the exact proportions in the formula are less interesting than the "esthetic necessity" that worked to align art with a more direct responsiveness to the effects of the art market upon the meaning and production of art and, in a larger sense, to the larger economic issues for which "loft space" is both instance and synecdoche. To separate these two questions is to miss the point.

One compelling statement about the Art Market is that of David Robbins, whose specialty seems to be avoiding anything like a style that could become the Robbins logo. William Olander quotes him speaking of his ilk in the lead essay to the New Museum of Contemporary Art's catalog *Fake* for an exhibition of that name: "Above all, we are reasonable, and consequently are suspicious of artistic practices that promote the neo-divinity of artists. The star search mechanism of the art world is unusable because if we've learned anything from a lifetime steeped in the public fictions of television, movies, magazines, and advertising, it's that people become stars so that their public image may better jump through the hoop of commerce. And for them to jump, someone else must be holding the hoop" (Olander 1987, 15). Those holding the hoop are the gallery owners and their patrons, the well-heeled collectors and art consultants who keep a steady stream of work going from downtown to uptown and points outward from city center. There is some analogy to the commercial presses only now beginning to sign up downtown writers, but the economics are at different orders of magnitude.

Michael Musto, in his zippily written guide to *Downtown* life, notes that Francesco Clemente's prices had, at a 1985 Castelli show, ranged from $35,000 to $90,000, a take few of our writers are likely to see anytime soon. Musto also summarizes Anthony Haden-Guest's description of Leo Castelli's pricing tactics in behalf of Julian Schnabel:

> Castelli selected five or six key collectors and gave them good deals. The collectors had excellent museum connections, which secured the possibility of the work being lent. Once the work was placed, the buzz went out with a vengeance. Then Castelli upped the prices, and that made other collectors feel they had to rush in before the prices went out of their reach. Schnabel had it made. Between 1979 and 1981, the price for one of his pieces jumped from $4500 to $15,000. By now [1985], he can command up to $75,000, maybe more. (Musto 1986, 111)

Schnabel has jumped galleries matching wits with the sellers jumping his prices, but the case is a useful benchmark for the reaction against the big-time art-market scene.

Some artists, such as Rodney Alan Greenblatt, seem still to be working with their galleries to keep prices down. Others, like Robbins, also aspire to deflate the whole mystique about the artist. Still others, such as Cookie Mueller (who has played in John Waters's films, written some very effective fiction for *Top Stories* and *Wild History*, and served as art critic for *Design*), pull back in disgust, complaining that "art's all about money now. People can't afford real estate anymore, and they don't like jewelry, so they invest in art" (ibid., 116). But perhaps the most interesting responses come from several groups of artists who have decided to follow the writers' example of starting their own presses and magazines and take matters into their own hands.

In their immensely valuable *ABC No Rio Dinero: The Story of a Lower East Side Art Gallery*, Alan Moore and Marc Miller talk about this gallery as a quintessential exception to the commercial rule. Members of COLAB, they describe their group as forty artists in the late seventies who found the art world closed and who wanted to create an alternative community: "The artists sought to forge their own outlets and audiences through cable television, low-cost multiple artworks, and different kinds of exhibitions" (Moore and Miller 1985, 3). To "forge" an audience one has to teach them the sort of alternative voice I find the crucial mark of the art and writing of this generation. Among those other kinds of exhibitions are events such as Jenny Holzer's 1977 Manifesto show. Richard Prince, controversial rephotographer and, as we shall see, a powerful writer, remembered the show well when we talked in his studio: "Artists were asked to write something down on a piece of paper. They were brought to the gallery in Xerox form and were distributed that way. People got to read what others were thinking." Xerography erases the uniqueness of art as a collectible, fosters confronting the straightforward technical problem of achieving one's effects with black ink on white paper (so it will reproduce well), and creates a community ready to be nourished by art that you can make yourself, that explores the chiaroscuro of social relations, and that is something for people rather than for rich people's stairwells.

ABC No Rio drew inspiration from Fashion/Moda, a South Bronx center run by Stefan Eins (who moved there to get away from his former location on Mercer Street in "the heart," as Lippard puts it, "of the art redlight district" [ibid., 127]) and Joe Lewis (of *Appearances* magazine). Moore and Miller conclude that "at their most idealistic, these arts groups sought to make ethnic culture, political analysis, and ideas about social justice fashionable components of the mainstream" (ibid., 7). They are corroded by big money on the Right, and challenged from the Left by more radical groups such as City Walls or PADD committed to broad public protests. But their Lawsonian strategy of polluting the "fashionable" with an understanding of the structural interrelations of art and society is the strand of downtown art activity most akin to the sort of writing we will shortly undertake to explore.

Hence when Fashion/Moda has an exhibition, its organizer is likely to say something along the lines that "this is an exhibition of 37 curators" (ibid., 18) in reaction to the galleries' commercial curating or even, for some, to the alternative spaces' museum-styled curating. This work emphasizes the collaborative—as ABC No Rio began operating, its members decreed that no money would be allotted to benefit an individual. Instead, they produced "non-curated, dense-packed shows on oddball themes, including art by children and the anonymous, all mingled to demonstrate a visual milieu" (ibid., 3) that presented the "gallery" more as what Joe Lewis called a "cultural concept" than an alternative exhibition space. ABC No Rio managers told *Bomb* in 1982 that it "is not specifically a place to exhibit. It's more like an art-making center" (ibid., 67), with emphasis upon community interaction. Some exhibitions involve contributions from the neighborhood. Other projects move outward from space to the community, such as John Ahearn's, out of Fashion/Moda, which involved plaster-casting local residents and mounting them not just in gallery spaces, but on the sides of the buildings where they live. Unaccustomed to being so visible, delighted to be participating in art-making, the residents find their torsos marking the landlords' buildings as their own instead. Their warm response to Ahearn and his friends belies the charge that galleries moving into the neighborhoods cannot produce models of presence other than gentrification.

Other shows operate like the 1983 Williamsburg Bridge show, which featured the work of eight sculptors on the promenade. Some works were stolen, others vandalized, some graffitied, some left alone. The point for the participants, however, was not the destruction of valuable commodities, but that all the works were *out there* for the response of area residents. On a WNYC broadcast, the discussants felt "that these people really made their own comments in what they took and what they destroyed," and Ann Messner said "it makes the whole thing integrated," especially when graffiti artist Fab Five Freddy left one of his own works to join theirs. This is no way to treat hot commodities. Adam Purple goes farther with his Garden of Eden, a large circular garden reclaimed from an abandoned city lot. At its center is a double yin-yang swirling cross that mixes its swastika's challenge to the city powers bent on destroying the garden with the multiple social contraries recalled by its oriental resonance.

The most sensational of the shows was the notorious Real Estate show, in which a group of artists, including many of the COLAB group, invaded a boarded-up city building, fixed it up, and opened an exhibition of art that was particularly responsive to the realty game played by city officials and developers. "A lot of people," organizer Alan Moore explained, "are tired of getting the short end of the stick in the real estate world because of forces they don't understand but that always amount to money" (ibid., 53). Those forces amount to the structural analysis of the interlocking directorate formed by government, big money, and media, and they illustrate why the real-estate issue is more than a matter of former suburbanites fretting about their rent. This statement of intent is the heart of the exhibition's manifesto: "The intention of this action is to show that artists are willing and able to place themselves and their work squarely in a context which shows solidarity with oppressed people, a recognition that mercantile and institutional structures oppress and distort artists' lives and works, and a recognition that artists, living and working in depressed communities, are compradors in the revaluation of property and the 'whitening' of neighbor-hoods" (ibid., 56). The show finds realty, the art market, and the largest of socioeconomic questions all implicated in one another and in the role and the audience that they need to forge as artists.

That show featured much immediately accessible work, such as Gregory Lehmann's "series of color photos of suburban homes, straight and unabashedly out of an estate agent's catalogue" with captions such as "3 BR, no rats, no unemployment" and "Etan Patz would not have been abducted if his parents lived in this lovely duplex" (ibid., 61). The later Times Square show, in which appeared work by Tanam Press's then more visually oriented Reese Williams, also emphasized accessibility and the immediacy of its images. John Morton, for example, painted on the ceiling, in blood-red letters, "I AM GOING TO KILL YOU!" Other work included Christy Rupp's posters of rats (originally put around town to remind daytime workers of what nighttime residents confront), Paulette Nenner's *Endangered* (a canvas with footsteps accompanied by photos of passers-by out front soiling it), a "Money, Love, and Death Room," feminist anti-pornography works, and graffiti by Samo (the tag of Jean-Michel Basquiat) (*EYE* [January 1987]: 24). Participant Peter Fend's way of summing up the more documentary content of the Real Estate show focused on exposing the city's plans for area residents: "Nobody around Delancey Street [where the Real Estate show took place] had even heard of these plans. Architecture was something that hap-pened to them. Artists . . . want the community as a group to be aware of what has happened to them and what has been planned by others for them. They want the community to see visions of their future, to have a say in what actually occurs, to help each other in realizing a future far better than what only certain bureaucracies have been able to build in recent years" (ibid., 59).

If we sift the large volume of downtown art activity a bit with an eye to the ethos out of which this vigorous work arises, we get a picture less dominated by commercial hustle and more given to exploring openings into a new relationship among art, its commu-nity, the powers that govern, and the media that process them all. It is this angle that helps most in thinking about the relationship between the fiction we shall look at and the activity in the adjacent arts. The sort of work that most irks Deutsche and Ryan, for exam-ple, is probably comparable to the kind of writing that sells with equal ease to the more glittering fiction magazines, where Heming-wayesque realism with eighties subject matter represents new writ-ing. Other art forms explored by the writers examined in this book are Richard Prince's rephotographs of media ads engaging the mass-imagery repertoire, Lynne Tillman's film *Committed* probing psy-chiatry's antifemale collusion with political and religious institu-tions in Frances Farmer's life, Peter Cherches's songs lacerating pop-song ideology, Anne Turyn's photo narratives staging in series her interventions into the network of normalizing attitudes and institutions, and so forth on through an impressive catalog of cross-over work.

It is worthwhile, then, to assemble a half-dozen emphases in the visual arts which will help prepare us for what we are to find in the fiction and that will make clear its place in a much broader, multitalented art movement. Lippard articulates the first principle: "A lot of artists have begun to take for granted that you can integrate your art and your politics without screwing up either one. And the more granted it becomes, the better the politics and the better the art becomes" (ibid., v). The best of the art and writing does indeed integrate politics and art, the former more than "a buzzword among middle-class artists playing at alienation, covering up their own fears with others' realities" (ibid.). Sue Coe (whose graphics are often accompanied by history and statistics and whose remarkable paintings appear on several Kathy Acker covers) goes so far as to distinguish between "political art," which seeks to advance a specific stand, and "Social Realist" art, such as her own, which tries to cut through hype and disinformation to show issues from the viewpoint of those being crushed. Coe's purpose is to counter "the idea of helplessness and despair" and to equip people with the sense of the power they have to change things in major ways (EYE [January 1987]: 33, 36).

The second principle is accessibility. One literal form of this is Ona Lindquist's Objets Vend'art, old ice-cream machines that sell art; an early purchase was 150 copies of the latest issue of Public Illumination (interestingly enough, the issue Secrets). The machines are placed around the city—at clubs (such as the Tunnel and the Lone Star Cafe), cinemas (such as the Quad), and museums. Another form is the work of painters such as Rick Prol, whose War (1984) shows a canine flamethrower climbing an impossibly suspended ladder over a burning city, or of David Wojnarowicz, whose images of maleness gone apocalyptic speak both immediately and after reflection (The Wild Boys Busting-Up Western Civilization [1982] is one of the more memorable). The street art of Richard Hambleton is quintessentially accessible, from his notorious chalked outlines of bodies (complete with blood-red paint smears) to his black shadows painted on alley walls and doorways or his self-portrait prints that fade, in time, to a white silhouette once the light of the urban day bleaches out the print's identity. On another front, the Talking Heads have moved out of the club scene into the middle of mass culture, the album cover of Fear of Music retaining the crisscross pattern of the steel loading ramps left around the downtown loft district, the song "Life during Wartime" telling of an intelligence operative at an unspecified vertex in the network of covert war:

> This ain't no party, this ain't no disco,
> This ain't no fooling around
> This ain't the Mudd Club, or C.B.G.B.,
> I ain't got time for that now.

The Mudd Club (home for music, performance, as well as a de facto casting room for independent filmmakers) and C.B.G.B. (which stands somewhat misleadingly, except as to its founder's first enthusiasms, for Country, Blue Grass, and Blues, and which was an early major showcase for Talking Heads, Blondie, and Television)—the social world downtown is not the reality during the wartime of American adventurism around the globe. Talking Heads' "Drugs" or the warning in "Air" that "air can hurt you too" keep material realities in front of a mass audience.

Another project of this sort is the remarkable magazine produced by Art Spiegelman and Françoise Mouly, *Raw*. A comic book for grownups, *Raw* has contents ranging from Spiegelman's famous *Maus* serial, which retells his family's experiences at Auschwitz, to Mark Beyer's chronicles of *Agony*. Most of the issues contain grim documentation, mixing text and cartoon graphics, of one media manipulation or another. *Raw* 8 quarries media images from the "Birth of the Bomb" showing how far cultural apparatuses went in conditioning Americans to embrace the Peacemaker with open arms. Pictured are labels from the pop record *Atom Bomb Baby*, atom bombers for kids to practice nuking their Kix cereal boxes, 1951 ads telling "the women" that "if you feel qualms about the possibilities of an atomic raid, remember that great-grandma faced and conquered critical situations" (16–17). There is even a *Popular Science* bit on a Monsanto Research Corporation atomic coffeepot. The text documents the network of pronuclear enthusiasm throughout the media that turned fear of the bomb into a crusade for nuclear superiority over the communist menace. Other comix, such as *Twist* and *World War 3*, represent the same interest in taking text and graphics onto significant ground.

Spiegelman thinks of *Raw* as an effort to fulfill the promise of the underground comix movement that had fizzled during the seventies—to produce "comics unselfconsciously redefining what comics could be, by smashing formal and stylistic, as well as cultural and political, taboos" (*Raw* 6). His comment cues us to the third principle: the takeover of popular forms for alternative ends. Implicitly, this subversion of media forms critiques Clement Greenberg's division between kitsch and high art. The subversion also provides a clearly politicized art that remains accessible to a young audience highly literate in such stylized forms as the evening news, MTV videos, sitcoms, and detective shows. Much of the New Museum of Contemporary Art's interesting exhibition Fake focuses upon this kind of appropriation.

William Olander states in the catalog's essay that "what Greenberg could not predict in 1939, and what he and his apologists have resisted ever since, is that certain forms assumed by kitsch would become, beginning in the 1950s, the most significant forms of almost any culture—high, low, official, sub-, or in-between: rock 'n' roll transformed into postminimalism, reggae, punk, and new wave; motion pictures turned into film; television made into video; and theater manifested as performance" (Olander 1987, 25). Hence for Olander the importance of postmodernity appropriating "the forms of popular culture, *without* necessarily appropriating its contents, so the artwork itself is no longer dependent exclusively on the totalizing site of high culture (the museum) and other audiences may be genuinely addressed (the same audiences that voraciously consume magazines, billboards, television, records, and films)" (ibid.).

Among writers, Kathy Acker appropriates all manner of texts to rewrite from the position of Woman, and Lynne Tillman appropriates realist fiction's techniques for a profound ethnology of the formation of female consciousness. Among visual artists, Jenny Holzer had a campaign placing slogans on the Times Square advertising marquee (PRIVATE PROPERTY CREATED CRIME, ABUSE OF POWER COMES AS NO SURPRISE) or posting her Truisms—aphorisms that, she says, are "what people believe" (Hagenberg 1986, 27) in all the contradictions of our operative maxims. (A MAN CAN'T KNOW WHAT IT'S LIKE TO BE A MOTHER, A SINGLE EVENT CAN HAVE INFINITELY MANY INTERPRETATIONS, ABSOLUTE SUBMISSION CAN BE A FORM OF FREEDOM, CLASS STRUCTURE IS AS ARTIFICIAL AS PLASTIC, CONFUSING YOURSELF IS A WAY TO STAY HONEST) (Wallis, *Blasted Allegories*, 103ff.). Olander dwells particularly on video, including Steve Van Zandt's anti-apartheid *Sun City* (an intervention for MTV), Branda Miller's rock-video parody *(That's It Forget It)*, MICA-TV's "commercials" for Laurie Simmons and R. M. Fischer. Such works either turn the form altogether toward different ends, as in *Sun City*, or create an ironic juxtaposition between the commercial context and, for example, Simmons's appropriation of the female imaginary as it is represented by the media. Such juxtapositions bring art into a dialogic relation with the commercial media to which their response would otherwise be a good deal more distant.

At its most pointedly political, such work showcases pieces of U.S. government disinformation with an appropriate documentation of the official deception. The exhibition Disinformation: The Manufacture of Consent was shown in 1985 at the Alternative Museum on White Street, its catalog featuring an essay by Chomsky documenting "the systematic expression of the way our institutions function" as a backdrop to the artists' appropriation and exposure (Chomsky 1984, 12). When Edward S. Herman, in the same catalog, analyzes media self-censorship "based on elite economic power and generally agreed upon principles" (Herman 1984, 34), he provides the sort of explicit political analysis called for by Lippard, an analysis largely in line with the vision informing many of these artists and writers.

The fourth principle grows out of the kind of response these works elicit, one that disrupts the otherwise voyeuristic role allotted a spectator audience. Barbara Kruger, for example, is widely known, as Sylvia Falcon says in her 1984 interview in the *East Village Eye*, for "her large-scale photomontages with confrontational slogans." But like many figures in this art world, Kruger crosses lines in works such as *Picture/Readings*, which, as the title suggests, puts text and photographs on facing pages. But for most people, Kruger is known as the artist whose guerrilla works show up on the boards mixed with posters for rock bands, performances at the Kitchen, readings, and used furniture. One work, showing a woman leaning over with tacks pinning her body into place, says: "We have received orders not to move" (*EYE* [January 1987]: 29). Kruger participates thoroughly in this socially reflexive expansion of the domain of art: "The problem is that the notion of art is such a restricted term. There are just *certain* things you can do that are art. What I'm interested in is generative work: the questions and notions of what is art. I'm more interested in how images work in society, that free-flowing ebb of image and of words and sound, and how they either reconstruct and perpetuate or displace certain conventions" (ibid).

Redefining the voice permitted art, so that it can speak to conventions that enable or repress, links Kruger to many of the figures discussed thus far. "I want to displace something," she continues. "I just want to change a stereotypical viewing and to make for a more active spectator in some way." Asked about her graphic with the legend "Your gaze hits the side of my face," she responds: "Being only the object in that subject/object relation, when I say that I want to construct a female subject, I want in some way to have women look at that work and say, 'That's the way it is,' knowing then that they can deny that address because they're hip to certain constructs."

Constructing female subjects means making them "hip to certain constructs," the sort of cultural analysis and critique we have seen recur. When Kruger, commenting on the hot art scene, says that "it's not whether you get publicity on a particular artist or a particular area which is phenomenal; it's the constructs that need phenomena which is the phenomenon" (*EYE* [January 1987]: 54), she adds the market structure of the art industry to her examinations of gender, subjects, and art itself, all in order to create an active spectator who *can* occupy a subject position that would otherwise "remain absent, unseen unheard and generally crippled. You have to make some movement," she concludes.

This disruption of the voyeuristic has a number of implications. It erases the distance between creator and consumer, allowing the absent and unheard in the culture to assume the subject slot in the syntax of art. That in itself is political, as is certainly the content we typically hear when "new" subjects begin speaking, whether you look to Hispanic writers, such as Rivas or Piñero; women writers, who at times seem almost to dominate new writing; or the subway system's spray-can "writers." Moreover, this disruption of the voyeuristic role characteristic of the gallery and museum setting of art and of film and video more generally aids the displacement of the rule of male neuroticism over "Visual Pleasure and Narrative Cinema," as Laura Mulvey analyzes it in her essential essay. "It is the place of the look," she tells us, "that defines cinema, the possibility of varying it and exposing it":

> Going far beyond highlighting a woman's to-be-looked-at-ness, cinema builds the way she is to be looked at into the spectacle itself. Playing on the tension between film as controlling the dimension of time (editing, narrative) and film as controlling the dimension of space (changes in distance, editing), cinematic codes create a gaze, a world, and an object, thereby producing an illusion cut to the measure of desire. (Mulvey 1984, 372)

Needless to say, the desire that is measured is patriarchal, and it is easy to see why Lynne Tillman, for example, speaks so respectfully of Mulvey's essay, considering her own effort in *Committed* to disrupt the gaze, as well as the world that created Frances Farmer's disaster. In describing the psychological mechanisms that lie behind the mix of fear and desire in cinematic looking, Mulvey opens the possibility for film viewers and filmmakers to create a wholly different film environment in which the subject position is a more open experience than it has been in traditional film.

Nam June Paik takes this mission in video quite literally, to the point that one enthusiast has dubbed him the George Washington of video for his role in liberating the medium from its commercially ruled colonial period. In the best overview of Paik's videos, David A. Ross collects the crucial assumptions behind this body of work to which Paik has increasingly turned since his Fluxus performance works of the late fifties. Ross's first principle is our fourth—a move from "the destructive nature of the one-way, passive delivery systems for electronic media . . . toward the activation of the TV audience," an effort to correct "the imbalance between information input and output with all its physiological, political, and social ramifications" (Ross 1985, 151). Vito Acconci, long-time performance and more recently video artist, puts it even more bluntly: "The television set 'shoots' images into the viewer: the viewer functions as the screen. With television, a person finally is enabled to become a 'model person'—but what the person is a model of is *non-self*" (Acconci 1988, 31). His videos are frequently allusive, elliptical, and call for considerable participation from viewers for their effect.

Paik was so interested in "opening the role of producer to whoever had the desire to activate their relationship to television" that he not only pioneered ways to play the television's tubes and wiring but also designed a "video synthesizer," a forerunner of today's special-effects gizmos, and staged public access to it for those who wanted to put their own spin on the range of broadcast material, taped interviews, and live transmissions—including the peculiar phenomenon of video feedback (when a live camera is pointed on its monitor, the viewer sees diving spirals). Ross argues that the synthesizer taught a generation of video artists that they "could take that next step into the core of television by reinventing the tools of production to fit their own needs," leading to fruitful and pointedly political manipulation of found images, as well as to the new realm of nonrepresentational television imagery. Paik manipulated tape speed and integrity, juggled circuitry and his "video compost" of old tapes, and produced a series of collage works that drive home the manipulative potential of the medium. One work is entitled *The Medium Is the Medium*, and by its end "it leaves the viewer with the question of who actually is in control: what is the basis of the decision to become a passive receiver of TV—or of art, for that matter?" (Ross 1985, 155).

Paik's insistence on making publicly available his equipment leads to the fifth principle of this "Neo York" art: community involvement. Examples are Adam Purple's Garden of Eden, John Ahearn's casts of residents mounted on buildings, and ABC No Rio's exhibitions, including work by area residents alongside the postmoderns, much the way that *Between C & D* includes Nuorican fiction along with work by Acker and Tillman, or the way that Kurt Hollander's *Portable Lower East Side* has published an *Eastern Europe* issue not only for the activist quality of the *samizdat* movement but also because of the local importance of Eastern European heritage in such still-visible Lower East Side communities as the Polish and Ukrainian. In Group Material's 1982 manifesto, "Caution! Alternative Space!" the collective vows "to tap and promote the lived esthetic of a largely 'non-art' public—this is our goal, our contradiction, our energy" (Moore and Miller 1985, 23).

Tapping that "lived esthetic" not only involves all the principles and strategies that we have seen—appropriating mass-media forms, using accessible imagery, activating the audience, analyzing with a political immediacy—it also involves the "contradiction" that necessarily pertains when those bred in a commodity culture set out to find a voice not so fully determined by that culture's values and (both material and conceptual) operational structures. To speak that voice is to speak in tongues, with both new and old accents befitting so multilingual an area. However, to try to speak that language with those whose experience of the commodity culture has been so radically different is yet a more vexing contradiction. It cannot be done, it must be done. Not to try is to leave oneself hopeless and dispirited, the powers that be untroubled and secure in their practices.

One such experiment that is as important as it is revealing is Hannah Gruenberg's work with schoolchildren both in the schools and in the more experimental galleries where their work has been included in the major shows. Her school studio, much the way that ABC No Rio has been described,

> is a place to make things, and the children of P.S. 20 have a vora-
> cious art appetite. Unlike children in more "well-to-do" neighbor-
> hoods these children have had almost no exposure to the making
> of art. They are not precocious, yet they bring an untainted rich-
> ness of purpose to the art room that almost becomes precocity as
> they acquire the skills they need to communicate. They bring
> their backgrounds with them to the studio. They bring a sense of
> color and order with them that is in their bodies. (Ibid., 119)

It is tempting to claim this as an epitome of the whole movement that has been described. There is a genuinely political specificity to Gruenberg's work with children: "For them to learn to control the materials is an act of power which is rare in their lives, an act of privacy they have hardly known" (ibid.). But to take power over the means of creation and production, and to fabricate a private voice not already determined by the chatter of media and the structures of power, is also what the movement has sought to achieve. The art that "is in their bodies" is like "Richard" 's direct knowledge of the monumental structures of economic and political power in the city, "a sense of color and order" opposed to the cellblock model of hous-ing for the elderly coming out of city planners' offices. Even the suburban "children" who have flooded downtown over the last dec-ade or two have had almost no exposure to the making of *this* kind of art, but they are learning.

What Gruenberg tells us of her students' work is a fitting epi-graph for this book: "The work that comes out of these children is fresh and intense and immediate. It goes right to the heart of the matter. It has soul and punch. Sometimes it hurts to look at it" (ibid.). Contradictions abound, to be sure, but our culture makes the position of the speaking subject necessarily contradictory for all who occupy it, even, finally, for the privileged white patriarchal bogeymen, whose appallingly comfortable and exploitative lives are also empty of what matters and thus unenviable. Ultimately, this work is about freeing the knowledge that is in our bodies, an effort to liberate a poetics of the multifarious voices of the Other(s) always already there in our discontents. To be contradictory, even compromised, is a condition of taking any action at all. What is interesting is how much has been done despite this fact of life.

### Ron Kolm and the Suburban Ambush

The trouble with classic narratives of cultural scenes is our expectation of centered structures and continuous plots. But the current arts scene is a postmodern, poststructural one, composed of many narrative strands that are interrelated, but also each with its own timing, unique influences, and effects. Intelligibility requires fiction and myth, it would seem, and hence my mythomorphic method shall, like Claude Lévi-Strauss's, take its narrative line to be a pathway through the ethnographic project at hand, a posited center from which we can begin to comprehend the cultural languages now being spoken. Because we are looking at fiction writers, my central character will be the protagonist of The Scene. Ron Kolm cannot be said to *be* the protagonist of this large story in any traditional sense of the term: he does not rule it as André Breton ruled the Surrealists; he does not stage it the way Tristan Tzara orchestrated Dadaist evenings in Zurich, or Raoul Hausmann and Richard Huelsenbeck did so in Berlin; and he is not the *critic's* center—the *Zeitgeist's* genius, the Pablo Picasso who lines the walls of the canonical museum that embodies twentieth-century art.

Kolm does *function* like a center for an era in which earlier kinds of protagonists are not thinkable—nothing so like a political party as the Surrealists exists, nothing so like a performing troupe as the Dadaists, nothing so like a hegemonic style or personality or univocal talent. Wherever we look along the networks that hold together the diverse creative talents who constitute this cultural revolution, we find Kolm. He has read his work at the important places—ABC No Rio (a crucial art-making and performance center), Hallwalls (Buffalo's outpost of new arts), the Kitchen (a leading performance club), Darinka (another key performance place), St. Mark's Poetry Project, the Ear Inn (the stalwart continuance of regular readings), Tin Pan Alley, Neither/Nor, Maxwell's and the Beaten Path in New Jersey, Dixon Place, the Alchemical Theater, 9th Precinct Gallery, Image Theatre, the World, the Medicine Show Theatre, and on through lists of benefits for Central America and the Poetry Project and galleries and colleges.

Kolm has published in virtually every significant downtown magazine. He is a regular contributor to *Public Illumination*, a credit-card-sized mix of text and graphics published by Jeffrey Issac. Kolm's work has appeared in *Between C & D*, a dot-matrix fanfold magazine encased in dope bags and published by Joel Rose and Catherine Texier, as well as in Michael Carter's *Redtape*, Robert Witz's *Appearances*, Allan Bealy's *Benzene*, Peter Cherches's (now defunct) *Zone*, Art Spiegelman's *Raw* comix magazine, and a host of others—*Twist, National Poetry Magazine of the Lower East Side, Big Time Review, Footwork, MC, New Leaves Review, Say!, Seditious Delicious, Semiotext(e), New Observations, Heat, 1,2,300 Sheep, International Poetry Review, A.T.W. (Around the World), Perpetual Motion, This Is Important, Gandhabba, LCD*.

Kolm's collaborations with graphic artists have been shown at places such as ABC No Rio and B.A.D. Museum (complete with an opening party at Limelight). The "Suburban Ambush" piece from which this book takes its title originated as a collaboration with Art Raveson for ABC No Rio's much-discussed Suburbia show. Moreover, Kolm is as involved in the publishing scene as he is in the writing and graphics scenes. He is a contributing editor for *Cover*, a monthly review of the downtown arts, and an associate editor of *Appearances*, an important arts magazine that has maintained its edge for quite a long run now. He contributes the muscle it takes to push alternative-press activities out into a marketing system dominated by commercial interests: a distributor for *Public Illumination*, a reviewer of little magazines, the sort of person called on to help stuff zip-lock bags with the new issue of *Between C & D* or to paste in the separately printed pages censored by the publisher of *Semiotext(e)*'s *USA* issue. He lost his own cash running Low-Tech Press, a now-inactive press that published softcover books in editions of five hundred, and typical of the sort of operation in which the editor, publisher, truck driver, distributor, and hawker are all the same person. Low-Tech Press published a range of writers, from Kolm himself to Tom Ahern, Richard Kostelanetz, Peter Cherches, and Thomas McGonigle, with graphics by the likes of Art Spiegelman, Ken Tisa, Drew Friedman, and Tuli Kupferberg.

When uptown editors decide to do a little piece on the downtown scene, Kolm is one of the people to disabuse them of the notion that *Bomb* is like Andy Warhol's *Interview*, that the community from which the new arts have been flowing is neither warmed-over Beat generation nor reinvigorated sixties' pop. Kolm knows these things from having been for more than fifteen years at one of the community's key institutions, the neighborhood alternative bookstore. In the golden era of Soho, for example, Kolm worked at the New Morning Bookstore (located where Spring Street Books now operates), where Laurie Anderson, David Byrne, Spalding Gray,

Kathy Acker, Reese Williams, and the rest of the avant-garde would
come in to shop in their precelebrity days and meet the self-de-
scribed "Fuller Brush Man of new writing." It was over Kolm's
phone, for example, that Acker negotiated her breakthrough contract with Grove Press. Later, when the Lower East Side was more
the center of writing, Kolm was to be found at St. Mark's Bookshop,
with a few of the slower stretches on the cultural scene served out
at the Strand and uptown at the Coliseum, where he now works.
Kolm is a human Rolodex of writers, performance artists, publish-
ers, editors, and hangers-on of indeterminate inclinations.

However diverse individual writers are, however much one
might want to argue for a distinction between Soho's visually cued
sensibility and the Lower East Side's street-inspired immediacy, the
boundaries and categories keep breaking down because the network
of connections spans the whole fertile crescent from Tribeca up
through Soho and over to the East River. One East Side writer might
tell you that "the split is pretty much along class lines—East Village
being populist (and therefore somewhat trashy/expressionist) and
Soho elitist ('coffee-table political'/minimalist)," whereas another
writer will say, "Soho versus East Side? I think that's funny!" Local
partisans exaggerate differences; crosstowners minimize gradations.

The resonances abound in a complex set of overlapping circles
which constitutes what has come to be a thriving community that
talks, creates, and socializes together despite the challenging economics of the Reagan era. This community lives on a combination
of dedication to the cause, state and federal grant money, and collective endeavors that include both group efforts or collaborations and
cross-media resonances. The bourgeois thematics that Philip Glass
purged from music Constance DeJong purged from fiction; the desublimation of ideological content in aesthetic forms which the
performance artists added to theater Kathy Acker added to the book;
the commodification of politics and subjectivity which Nam June
Paik exposed in video imagery Richard Prince and Reese Williams
explored in prose narrative; the socially engaged reflexivity of Anne
Turyn's photography or Hans Haacke's documentations is echoed
in the idiom of Lynne Tillman's Madame Realism; the range of war
conditions expressed in the painting of Rick Prol or David Wojnarowicz is documented in different ways through the fiction of Catherine Texier and Joel Rose.

All along the interstices of the community's network, people
such as Kolm are making connections and keeping the energy in
circulation. To hear Kolm talk about the early days before the *New
York Times Magazine* found The Scene fit to print is to appreciate
the importance of this network as a social or communal ground to
the work we are coming to terms with under the problematic banner
of postmodernism. Kolm recalls the days when Patti Smith was still

reading poetry on a Soho rooftop and Laurie Anderson had not bought $10,000 of digital sound processors or signed her contract with Warner Brothers records. Kolm tells the story of Glen Branca's *Art on the Beach* performance, "which was [at] the landfill—it's now the Battery Park. This is in the middle of the summer, and we're all sitting on this mound of garbage fill, and it was almost like watching covered wagons—they had these big amplifiers at the base of this hill and they were playing full volume and the sound just came rolling up the hill." A new frontier of a different sort, no doubt, one literally wild for the East Village émigrés at the end of the seventies before Operation Pressure Point swept a few truckloads of junkies and dealers off the streets and out of the boarded-up tailor shops and abandoned grills.

It is a frontier, however, in which the relationships among artists in different media is no less striking than the doubling of media within individuals. DeJong writes, performs, does video; Tillman makes films and novels and art reviews; Acker reviews the cultural imaginary in both her fiction and her own art-world essays; Cherches sings one night and reads the next; Prince is even better known as a photographer than as a writer or editor; Gary Indiana has been art critic for the *Village Voice* in addition to writing short stories and novels; Williams has created records, visual art, Tanam Press, and an important body of fiction; Wojnarowicz and Allen are both painters and writers; Gray is part actor, part contemporary folklorist, part fictioneer; Mueller is an actress, art critic, and writer; Turyn is an editor, photographer, and writer; Anderson and Smith are rock stars with trails of fiction and poetry behind them. This list could go on.

"Everyone was connected in some way," editor Richard Prince says of the contributors to *Wild History*, the important anthology he published with Reese Williams for Tanam Press. "Either musically, visually. . . . It's people who got connected in a way that I knew because I was *around*. That's what's so strange. And that's why I think there won't be another book like that. To have Wharton Tiers in the book, for example. He played in a band. And in that band there were artists." Williams talks in particular about the period between 1979 and 1982, when it may be possible to say that downtown energies were peaking:

> I remember there was much more of an interest back then in doing group projects rather than in getting a solo show or in getting a book published. The one I remember most strongly was the Times Square show. It was a very chaotic large group show where a number of us took an old building in the Times Square area and staged an exhibition for a month. There were all kinds of things in there

and performances every night, and it came together from a very
chaotic but centered group energy.

A "chaotic but centered" energy is one that somehow negotiates the tensions between political and aesthetic resistances that
bind a community and the "career-oriented" mood Williams laments in the current downtown scene, that keeps the variety of
visual and nonvisual media mixing well together, and that stages
itself without, as Kolm puts it, "sliding into fashion." He speaks of
the "exuberance, enthusiasm, and power" of a period in which one
could see how "these people support each other" through the parallels in their work in different media. As Williams notes, "another
way of saying it would be that you have a little ecology of ideas and
images and that they swim around together for a while and then
you're done. It's not such a strict classical development of things
but more that you have a pool of ideas for a while. I know that's the
way I was working in those days, and I feel that with Constance
[DeJong] and Spalding [Gray]. Laurie Anderson worked that way in
the beginning, too."

Williams at times sounds more elegiac than those for whom the
scene is not so much finished but shifted in its geographical center
to the Lower East Side, though even there many have the sense that
a certain first phase completes itself with the work this book dis-
cusses. It is hard, sometimes, to recover the sensation of that primary energy on streets now dominated by the logos of uptown art
dealers and upscale coffee shops. The magazine of Joel Rose, a great
advocate of alphabet city, established a link between the white postmoderns and Nuorican writers such as Miguel Piñero and Renaldo
Povod: "I thought theirs was such absolutely brilliant work. It's
amazing that a lot of downtown writers think that writing started
with them, or New York writing did, and didn't realize there was a
whole different segment of work out there that's just fabulous."

Patrick McGrath recalls the importance of the Life Cafe before
it became, as he puts it, "deeply yuppified," and had open mikes on
Tuesday evenings when unknowns would make contact. It was
through the Life Cafe, for example, that Rose, Texier, and McGrath
formed the friendship that led to their work together on Between C
& D. "I just opened up to something," Catherine Texier says, "I felt
it. There's this sense that people are reading what you're writing
and you're reading it aloud, and it creates an environment and gets
you feedback—that had an impact in terms of stimulating us, of
there being a ferment and you're a part of it."

Some of the sources of this ferment Texier recalls are John
Jesurun's Chang in a Void Moon, a serial performed over a two-year
period at the Pyramid and an example of what Fran Baskin calls

"celluloid theater" (*Say!* [June 1986]: 25), and plays such as *Deep Sleep* at Chez Mama, in which "fragmentation, the screen, and theatre" mix in ways that resonate with Texier's own fast-paced writing in *Love Me Tender*. "It's almost like tapping into some sort of energy," Texier explains, "rather than actually being influenced by one thing or another. Things can come just from a conversation in the street or from something that happens." Indeed, Jesurun says bluntly that his "idea is to engage people, and have them act upon what they see, arguing with themselves and with the television rather than just being a witness" (Baskin 1986, 25). No voyeuristic passivity, no innocence about the media's erosion of individual existence, no anachronistic notion of formal or generic purity in the arts—just engagement sparking energy throughout the audience of fellow artists.

Tillman stresses the importance of rock 'n' roll and the club life it sustained. "I was in college, disaffected, even from the idea of being in college, of being a 'college girl.' It was an underbelly, another side, this 'night'—my Manichean period. But I was raised on rock 'n' roll, and it was a very important form of protest in my life about various conditions." Cued to Velvet Underground rather than to flower children or hangers-on at Warhol's Factory, she recalls "the whole insane scene" of experiences such as the Exploding Plastic Inevitable:

> Velvet Underground offered this much more cynical view which paralleled my own feeling that life is very difficult. And there were also a lot of transvestites, a lot of gender-bending in this other world in which homosexuals and heterosexuals were mixed in a different sort of way—sexuality was up for grabs. It was like being part of this construction, something that was a real attack upon the middle-class American "good life" and that produced "the bad life" on the streets of Broadway at four A.M. It was a type of protest but not in some kind of ordered way. It wasn't about being "nice."

By the end of the seventies, the names of the bands had changed to Talking Heads, Blondie (in its precommercial incarnation), and Television, along with writers-turned-rockers such as Laurie Anderson and Patti Smith, and a host of bands ranging from the belligerently anticommercial efforts of John Lurie's Lounge Lizards to those whose names are lost in the changing configurations and rosters of club musicians. But the sense remains of a cultural night side that exposes the constructedness of social relations, gender, and identity, that attacks the suburban unconscious of America, and that honed its edge against the spectacles of flower children, fame-game players, and suburban sleepwalkers.

For Constance DeJong this edge was honed at crucial moments, such as the night she and Kathy Acker were the double feature at the

Kitchen, the first writers to be booked at this important performance space. It is this milieu, rather than the structure of academic
life, that helped DeJong be the kind of writer she is ("It was not
pleasant being a waitress, but I thought, better that than tenure"),
just as it is not academia's well-made story that opens creative possibilities to her but the assumption that "I don't think writing begins with a story. I think writing begins when you have some idea
about what language is." Edmund Cardoni's wonderfully concise
and pointed review of downtown writing in *American Book Review*
(8.6 [November/December 1986]: 18–19) makes clear its careful
balance between "describing the survival and mutation of individual consciousness in our times" and "a self-consciously critical
edge in relation to both its own praxis and the dominant culture,
which culture has nonetheless produced, as they well know, not
only their work but themselves" (18).

Kolm's work reveals both this double-edged quality and the
resistance to a commodity mentality about making art. Kolm labors
over every piece for months at a time, and his entire output, though
an important touchstone in the collective imagination of his peers
(as attested by his list of publications), would fill a single folder.
"Suburban Ambush," having already appeared in eighteen periodicals around the world in one of several graphic forms, may be taken
as one of those mythomorphic centers on which we must rely to
understand the "ecology of ideas" behind this writing. Some versions, such as David Ting Yih's for the Dusseldorf *A.T.W.*, are almost biomorphic abstractions suggesting the cell-level impact of
these antinormalization art strikes, but most are like Art Raveson's
version (see frontispiece) showing the jet hitting Suburbia (*New
Observations* 41 [1986]; see also Michael Randall's in *Big Cigars* or
Tom Zummer's in Bart Plantenga's *LCD* 3.1 [Winter/Spring 1988],
the WFMU avant-garde radio bulletin). These latter versions mark
the violence of the contest for "individual consciousness in our
times" between downtown art and "the dominant culture" against
which its art is mustered, to borrow Cardoni's terms.

In a sense, however, the most telling of these graphic collaborations is the one by Jörga Cardin which appeared, among other places,
in *Raw* 8 (1986). No suburbanite expects the family institution of
the dinner table to be firebombed, because this pleasantly regulated
regime takes place within the castle of bourgeois housing which is
supposed to keep out any awareness of contradictory twists in the
American ideological monologue, and which marks a sufficient
compliance with economic machinery to make its inhabitants immune from systematic violence. The "surprise" is being shown the
subtle violence done to all as commodity aesthetics penetrates the
inmost libidinal spaces of the individual—and its more literal exercise upon the many marginalized others of the culture. Suburbia is

SUBURBAN AMBUSH

THEY FIREBOMBED THE DINNER TABLE
TAKING US COMPLETELY BY SURPRISE.
WE EVACUATED OUR CASUALTIES FROM
THE PATIO — TRACERS SKITTERING
ACROSS THE SUMMER SKY. DAD IS A
MEMORY WE'RE TRYING TO KEEP ALIVE.

WORDS BY RON KOLM

both psychological and ideological anesthesia: it is the illusion of stable limits and safe space, the one emblematized in the walled neighborhoods of upscale Phoenix, the other in the patchwork of lawns and carports one sees from the air. To evacuate "our casualties from the patios" is to scurry for first aid in the social apocalypse going on behind the surface of Pepsi and Camaro ads.

With "tracers skittering across the summer sky" and marking the lines of violence in the cultural horizons, the suburbanite retreats to the inner sanctum of suburban enclosure: the fridge. Cardin's witty drawing places the committed suburbanite on a dark square of the linoleum chessboard, gaze fixed worshipfully upon the detached head of the Father in willful obliviousness to the ruin of the Dream surrounding the scene. The head is the point from which light emanates in an arch parody of American luminism, and "Dad is a memory we're trying to keep alive" despite the deterioration of the patriarchal body of Western culture. This brief piece is quintessential Kolm, quickly and succinctly distilling key attitudinal nodes in the ecological network of his community, and tracing the same structural stress lines in the cultural mechanisms that the art world pursues. The cultural language by which money and art, institutions and individuals, and social rituals and inner psyches are all produced becomes the central problem to be explored.

Kolm's poetry often takes the aggressively etched caption of "Suburban Ambush" as its style. "Swimming in the Shallow End of the Pool" (published in *National Poetry Magazine of the Lower East Side* 3.2 [1988]) is both the poem's title and its metaphor for its panicked protagonist's anxious wait for something to happen to her: "I sit by the telephone / watching the answering machine / for signs of life." The poem would offend any writers' workshop sense of the formal demands of poetry, but it is a poetry of intervention rather than monumentality, and as such draws the attention of artists such as Ken Tisa, whose drawing contorts the listener's anorexic body, turns furniture into Matissean tables suffering a menacing tilt, transforms the answering machine into a buzzed mechanistic death's head (complete with pinwheeling eyes, ritual-mask nostrils, and a skull's flat smile of teeth), and supplies dotted-line tracers across the floor to mark the impossibly contradictory pathways by which each table and chair leg reached its present position in the contemporary subject's posture, literally on the edge of an already uncomfortable seat.

Another Kolm poem that resulted in a graphic collaboration, this time with the much-exhibited David Sandlin, is "Self-Help": "Thinking of ways / To improve his life / He enters his wife / Absentmindedly." Sandlin's Blakean realization of the poem stresses the swirling nightmare in which "he" finds himself, the iconography of commodification whizzing around his head (a pool, a convertible, a

SWIMMING in the SHALLOW END OF the POOL

I sit by the telephone
watching the answering machine
For signs OF Life.

Words by Ron Kolm          Drawing by Ken Tisa

house, and so forth), his wife a pornographic object, his relation to her mediated by the toothy carbuncled monster from whom the spiked tentacles radiate and who bears the label "absentmindedly." Less subtle than direct and immediate, the work blends Blake and underground comix with its ideologically tinged reading of the degradation of desire, relations, and commodity-stricken subjects.

Other Kolm poems, most of which appear in *Welcome to the Barbecue* (Low-Tech Press, 1981, 1989) or the forthcoming "Suburban Ambush," run through a range of topics with the same quick punch. "Death in Köln" is a grim cultural memory: "After the air raid / I buried my friends / Under bouquets / I rescued from / A burning church." It is a sentimental turn, in a way, but the austere matter-of-factness with which it is rendered reminds the reader of the prose style of Lynne Tillman with its ability to state horror as normal. Decorating the corpses of a generation with the refuse of once-hegemonic institutions? Reminding a smug suburbia of the grim survival conditions its immigrant forebears left behind? Or a found remark at an East Side café puncturing the formalist protocols of academic verse? Clearly the lines are placed to mark that point at which we cope in an immediate way with the most devastating of experiences rather than following the model Kolm offers of "The Scholar": "standing in front / of the twisted body / of an automobile / he opens a book / and looks up the word / 'crash' and also / 'death.'" David Scher's drawing of "The Scholar" (published in *National Poetry Magazine of the Lower East Side* 1.8 [1986]) shows him buried up to his eyes in book definitions, community decorums, and encyclopedias of poetic terms and practices.

Kolm's poems often do not have the elaborate patternings that many of our recognized poets learned from their New Critical teachers. His poems have the direct force of graffiti and the immediacy of a street scene, and they are designed to function as social koans rather than as elaborate scripts for the Western ego's self-contemplation. Kolm does not shun the subjective experience, by any means. In *Welcome to the Barbecue*'s "Wars of the Heart," for example, he is as accessible as a pop song but as hip to strategies of distancing within the self as a confessional poet (if not nearly so prolix):

When you said you wanted
To be just friends
I put my fist
Through a window.

I seem to have lost
My sense of humor.

(45)

*Self-Help.* Image by David Sandlin. Words by Ron Kolm.

In "The Vision," the suburban ease ironically figured in the title of
*Welcome to the Barbecue* (and emphasized in Drew Friedman's
drawing of Henry Miller and James Joyce as the main guests) piles
up in the details of heat waves shimmering above the patio, the wife
going to mix up more margaritas, and the speaker adjusting a towel
as a lawn-chair pillow before the final stanza of the poem (and volume) lacerates normality with apocalypse: "I look up / And a wheel
of fire / Fills the sky" (48). Kolm is keenly aware of the ironies of
poetry as a medium for such issues—he has one poem, for example,
whose "Confession" is less the agonist's self-torture than the entre-
preneur's guilt over "turning my misery / Into money" (26).

Kolm is, however, also serious about the insurgent role of this
poetry in "Mercenary," whom we see "Swinging his jaunty weapon
/ In wide nervous sweeps / Bathed by the metallic aura / Of absolute
gravity / In a zero-cold zone" (*Low-Tech Manual*, 10). Absolute
gravity is a crushing force under which to try to move, clearly the
situation of the artist-insurgent interested in any sort of real change
in a "zero-cold zone," that state in which, the dictionaries tell us,
"substance has minimal energy." Kolm notices that for the bag lady
with her shopping cart scavenging in the ruins of buildings for scrap
iron, "Pipe Equals Life," as if high culture had lost hold of basic
economic equations in its privileged view of what constitutes survival (*Welcome to the Barbecue*, 24). And, unlike his tenured colleagues in the art of poesy, he is willing to abdicate his voice altogether to let the found lines from Chinese fortune cookies weave
platitudes together in encouraging "creative artistic study" toward
a self-made destiny: "Your greatness is in what you aspire" (31). The
poem seems to offer a real vocation in creative counterpoint to a
normal job. However, its succession of platitudes reads like Holzer's
Truisms and cancels the possibility of a real voice.

The poem "The Conceit" (*Public Illumination* 18 [November
1981]: 12) provides a transition from Kolm's poetry to his prose. The
first of two short stanzas tells us with the usual Kolm directness
that "I suffer from the illusion / that life is dangerous; / this makes
it so." What a series of switchbacks between street reality and suburban illusions! Life *is* dangerous, of course, especially in New York,
as Kolm will be among the first to tell you (ask him sometime about
the junkie with the penknife). Because it is already no illusion that
life is dangerous, the particular illusion of its danger from which he
suffers is no doubt the media's version of distant crime framed in
the hot pink and purple color scheme of "Miami Vice." The *real*
threat thus comes from substituting the media illusion for the real
dangers on the street. That mediated perception obviously removes
the possibility for confronting directly either the menace itself or its
causes. The "conceit" is not only egoism but also the media metaphors into which reality has passed. The poem's other stanza re-

ports on the material consequences of metaphoric illusion: "I douse the lights, / Paint my windows black / and dye my Keds a dark color." Anticipating Eric Bogosian's *FunHouse* character in "Night," Kolm's speaker retreats into the paranoia peculiar to our simulacral society: sealing himself in the refrigerator of "Suburban Ambush," he tries to make himself invisible, an unlikely target of the social outlaws masked by media illusions and cultural mythology.

Hence the importance of the connection Kolm draws between the Lower East Side and the fiction being written in so "blighted" and violent a neighborhood:

> Even in [Peter] Cherches's work, with all the humor, underneath the surface everything is absurd. And there is a sort of violence. Or in the things that happen to Lynne [Tillman]'s characters, or in Patrick [McGrath]'s work. In the end, in the time period where we have on the national scene various policies that are brutalism, and a brutalism in what we're doing to other countries, that neighborhood is a microcosm. Those things *do* relate. I think that's the reason why this work is germane. I also think that's why the work has a vitality.

That relation is what Kolm strives for in his fiction, notably *The Plastic Factory* (published originally in five parts and later as a 1989 Red Dust Pamphlet) and his classic *Duke and Jill* stories (in eight segments in a multitude of publications, most recently in *A Day in the Life: Tales from the Lower East*).

The former draws upon Kolm's own experiences working in a plastic factory during a "vacation" he took from coping in the city. "My conception," he told me, "was to write about something so horrible in the most mundane of terms, as if it were an instruction pamphlet on how to work this machine. But to write about people who were actually dying, and they were! And I was there." A bit of Kolm's own suburbanite shock at the sheer reality of the industrial deathscape comes through in his comment. To read the episodes is to see Kolm distilling his factory's process of making plastic lenses into his own process of writing more like plastic explosives than the merely representational lenses of the workshop fiction he dislikes. In the opening section, the manufacturing process displaces, in true tech-manual style, the people who must carry it out. "My name is Ron, I work in a plastics factory," the story begins (with a comma splice, appropriately enough). Even the setting is appropriate: "miles of flat sparse fields" dominate the foreground while, far in the distance, "a low range of blue mountains" stands for some more idyllic landscape than the asphalted industrial zone in which he works.

This section describes the "safety wall" that will blow the workers out into the fields rather than into the shipping room should the highly volatile plastic explode. The styrene is not only so flammable that portable radios are banned, it is also noxious: "It eats away the rubber soles of our shoes. It gobbles at bare skin. It devours eyeballs." Ron does not have to tell us that industry consumes its victims. Even the fumes are deadly, despite refrigerated storage: "Each time I enter the freezer to remove a drum, I gag on the stench, my head spins, I almost black out, but if I'm lucky, and fast enough, I know I'll probably emerge intact. It's happened before. I usually survive" (*Appearances* 9 [Spring 1983]: 18–19). A Nation at Risk? Perhaps a class, though to "usually survive" suggests many smaller deaths occurring constantly.

Part two shifts abruptly into what is almost more depressing than the factory: the domestic arrangements of Ron the worker. "My wife and I live in a decaying two-hundred-year-old stone farmhouse, which clings precariously to the side of a steep embankment" (*Appearances* 11 [Fall 1984]: 43–44). Beware, deep readers; but because the landlord refuses to get rid of the rats or the leaks, this bit of Americana seems well on the way to the sort of "Decay" and "Broken Promises" that John Fekner stencils in the war zones of the city. Precarious, inaccessible (one gets to the slope below by a "tilted flight of badly chipped steps"), only rented rather than owned (the American dream belongs, it seems, to others), the house is "wallpapered in a zig-zag pattern of random reds, oranges, and greens" designed by a "deranged sensibility." As Ron recounts his efforts to paste over the cracks and construct troughs to carry out the rainwater that comes in, we again see the process—this time of domesticity—displacing the people involved until the very end of the section, when, abruptly, we are told "My marriage isn't working out." He smells so badly of chemicals that he is allowed to use only one of the entrances to the house and is frequently exiled to the couch if too much styrene spills on him. His wife "has created a new lifestyle right before my eyes," filled with "strange electrical appliances" from the health-food store where she works, hotly pursued by the owner (of both the store and, it would seem, its workers).

Ron tells us he suffers not so much a nervous breakdown as one "of the imagination": "I have no conception of the future any more. . . . I can't seem to think my way out of the dilemmas I'm faced with," as if he were another version of "Richard" (the Delancey Street spokesman quoted earlier), with a "day-to-day" brain unable to cope with how the cultural structures just pile up on the individual. "If it was one problem, or two, I might have a chance, but the job, the house and my relationship are all tied together," and, as he waits in the oil-embargo gas lines, he realizes that his wife is right: "I seem to trap myself, plan my own destruction." It all happens, as "Richard" has already told us, before Ron has any idea of the consequences. Hence it is no wonder that part three of *The Plastic Factory* retreats to the manufacturing processes, even if that centers upon the ludicrous unworkability of the plant's safety measures to keep the exmer from exploding after equipment failure. The culture equips both zones of Ron's life with safety procedures that do not begin to address the reality behind the illusions. His wife's commodities and flirtations, his confusion and heavy drinking, the factory's Wells Fargo alarm system, and the spectacle of Ron "standing on the side of the hill like some kind of crazy person pitching little meat-trays [of exploding exmer] like baseballs, risking my life for three bucks an hour, while frightened drivers swerve about below, shocked by the orange puffs of smoke and concussion. Sure—I'm a sucker—I'd probably do it" (*Public Illumination* 27 [September 1983]: 6–7). Suburban ambush and the *mea culpa* of its accomplice and victim.

Part three concludes (in *Redtape* 4 [Fall/Winter 1983–84]) with the antistatic rod, a nuclear device Ron knows makes "my sperm die, . . . mutating my cells, opening the genetic door to cancer, that unwelcome though everpresent guest. In fact, this whole factory is a cancer machine of sorts, a microcosm of America; all unnatural, slow-decaying substances." He realizes that there is always a hidden trade-off behind every commodity, sometimes "merely psychological" and sometimes "spectacular; a hand, a lung, a life," sometimes even multinational in its calculus ("if America has kidney transplants, subways and TV dinners, then Africa has starvation and war").

With this grim analysis of industrial capitalism in place, part four (in *Appearances* 14 [1988]: 50) switches back to the private lives of Ron and his partner, Arnie. Ron knows his wife playacts sleeping and other forms of distance, and he sees his empty refrigerator, walks two miles to be picked up for work, finds himself frozen out of his own parody of suburban domesticity (he does not even get to drive the marital truck anymore). Arnie's life is no better, pinned to the wall by the forklift, falling off the pressure cookers into the life-threatening pools of chemicals on the concrete floor, reappearing moments later from the infirmary "looking no worse for the wear, an unlit cigarette dangling from the corner of his mouth." Part five (in *Appearances* 11 [Fall 1984]: 53), with all the dizziness of Ron staggering in the freezer, moves from more deadly details of the manufacturing process to nighttime illegal entries by Arnie's buddies, who bring booze and drugs to help things along. But part five ends with Ron's nightly ritual of a phone call to his wife, in which both realize "we're just repeating the same old endless, unresolvable argument." One or the other hangs up on this ritual "picking at a scab." Ron wanders back, sees that "everything in the [factory] room is normal," and ends the piece in an appropriate image of entrapment with a utopia too far receded to cross the threshold of awareness: "Peering through a heavy steel grate I can barely see the outline of the mountains in the distance, darker than the night."

*The Plastic Factory* as a microcosm of America makes clear that the forms of order we fabricate are deadly to those who make them and who live within their high-pressure moldings. Oppressive and unrelenting, the series represents the darkest, most barren, most apocalyptic dimension of Kolm's suburban ambush. The *Duke and Jill* stories, in contrast, blend an equally austere look at life in these times with a quite witty laceration of pretensions on all fronts, including the artistic: these stories read like fairy tales of life on this particular "edge." Scattered through a number of magazines, the seven stories that Kolm calls "canonical" appear in Josh Gosciak and Alan Moore's important anthology, *A Day in the Life: Tales from the Lower East* (1989). (The exiled eighth is "The Anarchist New Year's Eve Party," with Art Raveson's sketch, which appeared in the 17 December 1986 issue of *Downtown*.)

Art Raveson's drawing of Kolm's protagonists shows the importance of the underground comix tradition in the sort of engaged humor that plays through the series. The very details that are sensationalized in a Bret Ellis or a Jay McInerney turn wry here as the Quick Read School's Blank Generation gets filled in, its bony sexuality and predatory air immediately obvious, its comic pretenses in living on the urban edge shredding between economic rigors and existential drift. Raveson wittily notes the detritus of abandoned class status which Duke and Jill try to sell—the Mickey Mouse ears of a suburban childhood persisting this late in the economic slide (kept as sentimentally as the clumsy nostalgia of Ellis's characters for fifth-grade after-school soccer), the Wayne Newton album's suburban placebo beat, the old bowling ball and accompanying trophy to the more innocent athletic triumphs of adolescence, the toaster and coffee mug from breakfast-nook consumption rituals, the shirt they have lost since breaking faith with the corporate world's plans for their labor.

"Duke and Jill," the series begins, "do drugs." They have little in common except that they are Wisconsin immigrants hanging on. "Bad things keep happening to them" without, it seems, their ever finding any particularly effectual response. Duke buys a gun after their best friend cleans out their apartment. A friend, playing "Deer Hunter" with the supposedly unloaded gun, dies. "After the police leave, Jill calls all their friends to tell them the news. She has to shout to be heard above the sound of Duke vacuuming the dried blood off their shag carpet." The suburbs persist within the grid of chain-linked lots still segregating thoughts, feelings, words, and deeds. Duke and Jill throw a party at which booze and reefer make up for the fact that "there wasn't much to talk about," at which spouse-swapping precipitates group nudity, which turns "bummer"

DUKE & JILL

when the photographs, a high point, are "mailed to Jill's mother by mistake."

That calamity pulls an almost Dobie Gillis humor out of those sandblasted efforts to have a good time, though we do see consumer novelty organizing sexuality and the transformation of body into image and experience into represented event. And Mother, goddess of suburban order and restraint, knows, her offspring helplessly perpetuating their childhood through a ritual of exposure and humiliation. The series continues the play between slapstick and seriousness with "The Murgatroyds Leave Town" (from Gary Indiana's *Here Come the Murgatroyds* issue for *New Observations* 31 [1985]), in which Duke and Jill try to make their breakthrough with $20,000 worth of cocaine; they snort a few lines and turn paranoid about a bust, flush the cocaine down the toilet, and leave town. Sock-hop uncoolness mingles with stash anxiety, poverty pushing them into scenarios they cannot master, the shortfall between Duke and Dude making painfully obvious their outsider status, their imprisonment within the thermopane barrier dividing urban and suburban.

Jill finagles a credit card and gets her friends' cash for their purchases, and Duke takes eight different deposits for a sublet of their apartment, but their imagination for scams and the economic realities remain structures of entirely different magnitudes. Duke even "makes the art scene" in one number, trying to bolster his fortunes, and Kolm takes his swipes at yuppiedom and the art world when Duke, after almost getting arrested trying to do a Keith Haring in the subway, sells to a Collector a broken generator armature attached to a scrap of pegboard and signed with his leftover spray paint. Jill's turn is her make-over at the Astor Place Haircutters and at a cheap boutique—she metamorphoses from laid-off Novelty Company worker (itself a nice detail) to blue-mohawked leather punk with nose ring. "There was a gaggle of punks hanging out in front of the Pyramid Club. Jill joined them. Nobody said a word. She'd been accepted." Pyrrhic victories with the repertoire of available poses.

The series collapses in Kafkaesque inevitability in "A Bad Day" when Duke, hungry with a barren cupboard, is definitively downtrodden. He breaks his "borrowed" bike on a pothole and has that and his money robbed on the way to a coffee shop. By the time he gets back home, two guys are just leaving with the last of the salable goods. "It took him a couple of hours to panhandle enough money to buy a new lock for the door and a sandwich," but he is robbed on his way back up his building's stairwell. "Can I at least keep the *sandwich*, Duke asked. No, the voice answered." The "voice" is a bit of comic necessity, but it is also the voice of the faceless economic structure that cancels safety and security in urban spaces and that hunts renegades such as Duke and Jill as relentlessly as it does the outsiders (of race, class, and bad luck) who prey on them. Kolm

takes the disembodied laughter of prime-time sitcom and situates it
in urban realities that reconnect it to the meanness of the scene, the
"brutalism," as he calls it. It is that same brutalism that drives the
young into the American MGM costume shop version of punk culture, seeking what feels like a lifestyle of protest and alternativism
even though, deprived of the more class-oriented economic edge of
British punk, it is always already assimilated into media imagery.
To look back over the *Duke and Jill* series is to index a whole list of
manifestations of the frenetic forms that the "Blank" side of downtown life adopts, however comically and artificially, in a nonetheless real effort to counter the unrealities of the Mouseketeer World,
the voyeur's cage in a media society, the playactor's script in the
station-wagon itinerary of suburban maturation, the Feknerian
"Broken Treaties" of American ideology.

Even those of us who prose out these analyses are not spared. In
"Duke and Postmodernism and Jill," Kolm's collaborator Tom
Zummer (TZ) did his own Duke and Jill comic after the two had
imagined a host of unwritten Duke and Jills in a downtown bar.
Zummer, himself an accomplished semiotician, sets out to deflate
those for whom theory is a blood sport. Duke argues that "the primary defining characteristic of the post-modern subject is its inces-
sant deployment across the surface of multiple discourses," TZ's
drawing showing only the broom-handle mustache and megalenses
through which Duke's never-visible eyes strain. Jill, presumably a
late modernist, counters that "the very conditions constituting the
appearance of the post-modern subject are purely symptomatic demarcations of the fragmentation of the subject . . . at least, she
added, since the mid-seventeenth century." Zummer and Kolm
must attend Modern Language Association meetings, because this
piece captures not only the lingo but also the subtext of panel exchanges between the Left and the Right on the critical spectrum:
"That's stupid. You're stupid! You are! You're more!" and so forth
into the litany of "you's" from Izod kids astride their Western Auto
motorcross bicycles. Duke does not allow the "fundamental multiplicity" of the " 'I' and 'not-I' " to keep him from commanding
"Two more Molson's" in the heat of battle. Class ironies, intellectual pretense, idle chatter, and the central debate of the age are all
telegraphed in these lancing distillations.

As we turn from Kolm's work to that of the larger community,
we leaf through not only the important works of individual writers
but also the network of magazines and anthologies that best represent the collective endeavors of this generation of writers. Richard
Prince's *Wild History*, Barbara Ess's *Just Another Asshole*, Tom
Ahern's *Diana's Bimonthly*, Edmund Cardoni's *Blatant Artifice*
(from the Hallwalls reading series), Brian Wallis's *Blasted Allegories*
(artists' writings following up his vital critical anthology, also for

the New Museum of Contemporary Art, *Art after Modernism: Rethinking Representation*), the *Between C & D* anthology (from Penguin), and *A Day in the Life: Tales from the Lower East* carry the voice of our era most engaged with the actual conditions in which we find ourselves.

Cardoni states the case even more strongly, representing such anthologies as an ambush of the efforts of the "writing schools"—more than a pejorative term for him—to take American fiction out to lunch at McDonald's. In his introduction to *Blatant Artifice*—which contains some of the most energetic polemics since Richard Kostelanetz's epic blasts of the writing market in *The End of Intelligent Writing* or of the grant agencies in his journal *Precisely*—Cardoni argues his case against the "uptown neo-tweeds": "It isn't David Leavitt *per se* that makes the ink in my veins boil, merely everything his writing represents. (I've no doubt that, personally, David is a more than usually sensitive and polite young man.) But it's the critics trying to cram him down my throat who really piss me off, him and Jay McIrninny [Cardoni's pun] and the rest of those pale print counterparts of Hollywood tyke idols who are supposed to be the cream of my generation and somehow represent our Zeitgeist" (Cardoni 1986, 7). Cardoni looks for the heirs of Laurence Sterne and Gertrude Stein rather than writers in the "slicks" and prestigious reviews who "have returned to making 'well-crafted' (read 'drearily linear, slavishly realistic, stylistically vapid, and verbally lifeless') stories about recognizable contemporary experience, predominantly white, educated, middle-class family experience bloodlessly severed from any messy historical, political, or economic context" (ibid., 8–9).

Cardoni is exasperated by those who were born middle-class and rest content within its confines rather than hunting for the pockets of otherness resisting here and there in an otherwise reified commodity culture. "If this stuff is on the cutting edge of anything," he insists, "it's of a sterling silver butter spreader resting on the gilt edge of a white china bread plate on a thickly padded white linen tablecloth on the table in the family diningroom, with father at the head and the writers' napkins in their laps. And the butter had better be *real* soft" (ibid., 9–10). Tempers run high, no doubt, as the prize-and-publication circuit closes around those compliant with the sophisticated and demanding formulae of late modernist prose narrative. More representative, perhaps, is the respect Joel Rose maintains for anyone who writes daily: "To do any kind of work, it's really hard. I don't care if it's Jacqueline Susann, it's *hard* to do that. You go out and do that."

Cardoni is quite clear about what marks the fiction he really likes, and his markers serve us well as a general guide. He wants stories that "partake to one degree or another in a subversion of the structures of fiction and of language (which is, of course, profoundly political, if only in its renunciation of the accepted forms so dear to plot-summarizing reviewers and the young, neo-conservative, literal-revivalist writers so eager to oblige them), as well as in a vigorous critique of contemporary culture through the hardly 'new' but fundamentally anti-realist means of satire and ironic distancing" (ibid., 11). All good fiction, for Cardoni, is engaged in suburban ambush, and it is no coincidence that many of the writers discussed in this book have read in his Hallwalls series.

Catherine Texier's description of the writing scene for the French-language *City Magazine International* opens with a similarly political slant: "Ce n'est pas un mouvement, comme les Beats. Ce sont des voix disparates qui hurlent, chuchotent ou rianent dans l'ombre du ghetto artistique new-yorkais, en opposition à Reagan, à l'Amérique middle-class et aux cannons de la 'bonne littérature'" (Texier n.d., 59). Although quick to cite the Beats, Stein, and the avant-garde traditions as a background to the new writing, Texier mixes William S. Burroughs and Walter Abish, the Marquis de Sade and J. G. Ballard, Roland Barthes and Michel Foucault in the literary brew that the downtown writers tap.

Brian Wallis, who in addition to curating at the New Museum of Contemporary Art and editing some of the best anthologies of postmodern culture, offers his own subtle and insightful précis of new writing, a précis influenced particularly by his own background in the visual arts and his preference for "artists' writing." In one of the most important essays on this work, published in the European magazine *Parkett*, Wallis points up central assumptions of the four writers he singles out for specific analysis (Lynne Tillman, Kathy Acker, Gary Indiana, and Richard Prince); these assumptions serve well for the whole community:

> A principal characteristic is their consideration of language as a system of representations which constructs its subjects. These writings are less concerned with the explanatory (transparent) function of language, than with demonstrating its ideological function as a structuring discourse. To this end, these new artists' writings employ certain formal operations, shared with contemporary visual arts, such as appropriation or reinscription of existing images or texts; adoption of nonsequential structure, as in television or film; privileging a form of writing which is fragmentary, digressive and interpenetrated with other texts; attention to the role of the reader (viewer). The effect to these textual strategies is to call into question the otherwise seamless closure of conventional writing and of representation in general. (Wallis 1985a, 65)

As many have argued, "seamless closure" often proves on close examination to be less sutured, more open than polemics always encourage us to admit, and Wallis's summary is brilliant and to the point concerning the reflexive semiotic that carries this new writing's cultural critique. In his preface to *Blasted Allegories*, Wallis adds to these traits an insistence upon "a collectivity of voices and active participation of the reader" in place of the traditionally omnipotent author, as well as a disparagement of the cult of "newness" and "originality" in favor of acknowledging "language and stories as 'already written' and shaped by social and political conditions" (Wallis 1987, xiv).

In conversation, Wallis emphasizes the implications of allegory as a formal mode that allows a portrayal of relationships to serve as a critique of "male-female relationships, about male society in relation to women, and so forth. One could say that all good literature does this, but I think this fiction does it much more self-consciously in the area of representation." The critique goes beyond exposing the "represented" as "constructed" to exposing "what goes into that construction and into making or allowing us to accept those constructions as natural." Suburban ambush requires a politicized reflexivity whose anatomy ranges from technique to ideological content and the mechanics of inducing consent. If these strategies seem weak in the face of the magnitude and intricacy of the social machinery they challenge, Wallis grows eloquent arguing their potential:

> They afford a way of creating new models, new identities, and new options for movement. These writings demonstrate alternative capacities to generate ambiguous, complex, and experiential forms of knowledge which are collective and cultural but not equatable with bourgeois norms—this is stressed as a basis for broad political change. While often this political meaning is not explicit, it is encoded in the images of resistance and renewal which structure the secondary or allegorical level of meaning in these texts. The recovery here of "hidden" knowledges or resistances feeds our understanding of the nature and variety of cultural and social oppressions as well as the means for their reversals. (Ibid., xvii)

Clearly Wallis is one of the most important and useful commentators on our evolving cultural scene, because he articulates well this community's faith in a literary experimentation that all but sublates theory and practice and that achieves the objective Mikhail Bakhtin characterizes as "penetrating into the social laboratory where these ideologemes are shaped and formed" (Bakhtin 1985, 17). In opening that cultural laboratory, these writers enable their readers to join them in encountering precisely that knowledge, that otherness, and that potential of resistance repressed by the kind of fiction which so angers Cardoni and by the larger cultural structures that have thus far maintained its prominence in our literary topographies.

# KATHY ACKER

## *The Blood and Guts of Guerrilla Warfare*

"Reading Kathy Acker is like reading the subway walls." "If my mother saw what I was reading, *she'd die*." "I never thought I was a prude until I opened this book. I was reading it outside between classes and I found myself holding the book half-closed so the people sitting around me wouldn't see the illustrations." "My roommates couldn't believe I was reading this book for a course!" Well, there is some truth to these minority-opinion gasps from the fiction class to whom I assigned Acker's *Blood and Guts in High School*. Reading Acker *does* take you close to a voice not often heard from the sub-urbanized media of American culture, one that is full of pain, rage, and lacerating barbs of social commentary. Her work *does* offend mothers, particularly those who serve unreflectively the patriarchal establishment that determines mother-daughter relations as, shall we say, problematic. And we *do* discover in reading Acker's work internalized regiments of repressive and oppressive codes we may well not have been conscious of harboring as part of the heavily contradictory cultural chromosomes in our psychological DNA. And though my student's roommates were probably surprised at the language and drawings of this pivotal novel, they might well have wondered how a regularly offered college course came to feature a book that critiques so relentlessly the ideological functions of the educational establishment.

Unfortunately, much of the critical response to Acker's work has not gotten very far beyond these first comments of my more conservative students. As Acker commented to me, most accounts "have left some or many concerns out, usually the political, and most fetishize the sexual." She knows that the culture works on its members most subtly and most profoundly by colonizing the libidinal aesthetics, turning desire into the most productive means of channeling, normalization, and, even if by pure distraction, social control. Much of her work does confront directly the sexual material of the culture in order to carry out her most basic project. "[T]he center of my writing, if there is a center, is a search for value, or lack of value," she wrote me, and the play between "search" and "lack," between "center" and the iffiness of the very idea of a structure with center, is precisely what is finally at stake in Acker's fiction. Trying to understand a pathological culture and to locate some potential for freeing the body from the hold of that culture means confronting sexuality but also all the concerns that mainstream American writing typically prefers to omit.

Acker's own comments in a radio interview upon the critical tendency to "fetishize the sexual" are perhaps the most telling:

> When you write sexual material, I mean, you know, pornographic—I hate the word "pornographic" for this—but direct orgasmic material, it's almost like pure writing, it's really rhythm, you've got to get those rhythms exact. It's also a way that you know there's a direct connection between you and the reader. And if you mix that really *hot* kind of connection next to political material, you're doing a very violent number. And that's interesting. But sex is also a way—it's a little like Jean Genet's *The Slaves*—it's also a way of looking up from the bottom to see society in a different way. The sexual material of a society is very revealing. (Vitale n.d.)

Pure writing, the direct connection, the interaffiliation between the sexual and the political, and the desire to "see society in a different way"—these utopian impulses play constantly alongside the most devastating narrative critique of Western culture to appear in American literature. The resulting mix of the sacred and the profane, the utopian and the despairing, carries us far beyond the titters and thrills of the first-time reader to a profoundly moving, detailed, and instructive analytical critique of the cultural processes precisely at the point from which they are experienced by the Other of the culture—children, women, the poor, the trapped. Acker's work moves steadily toward an imaginative demolition of the oppressive dimension of our cultural machinery. Indeed, a former Village dweller who now writes in rural Virginia came to campus one day to meet me. "I knew it must be the end of the world," she said by way of opener, "when Kathy was being taught in southwest Virginia." No such luck, I think to myself. But now that Grove Press is giving Acker's work a wider distribution than was possible for the TVRT Press, which published her earliest work, perhaps we are moving at least a bit closer to the end of a certain kind of world for which genocide, a first-strike policy, poisoned ground water, and irradiated children are daily news.

Acker's career as a writer began in the early seventies. Disowned by her parents, she worked a number of different jobs supporting her involvement in the arts revolution brewing in Soho at the time. There were a number of reviews, readings, collaborative projects with various visual artists, and, beginning in 1973, the emergence of a series of hard-hitting novels which was fully steeped in the intellectual ferment of the period. Her own way of answering Tom Vitale's question, "What are you like?" directly puts the cultural intersection at which we find these works: "I think I'm basically a painter who uses words. And I'm pretty influenced by a lot of political semiotic theory. And I like rock and roll." Her work has the immediacy of the visual that Richard Prince likes in painters who write; it is indeed quite shrewd about the ideological implications of both social and artistic patterns, and it takes the dare to position itself in the outlawed voice of the cultural other, so much so that she is sometimes called a punk novelist. I wonder whether the real punch line there is that to be a *real* novelist now, one *must* risk the violence some experience as "punk."

Acker's work taken as a whole carries its central importance not only because she was among the first downtown writers and remains the most extreme one, but also because of what her work achieves. It is a postmodern narrative *Being and Time* with a streetwise poststructural footing. Her phenomenology is that of bodily experience rather than Germanic speculation; her *Alltäglichkeit* is not Heidegger's anesthesia but a predatory death cult; her dasein is confused by complexly interlocking forces of history, economics, politics, media, and gender, rather than by the business of life distracting her from her true Being; and her focus is less on Being-toward-death than on a Being-for-life. But however different her assumptions, she is as serious as Heidegger in understanding the worldness of the world, dispersing the active force of traditional thought, exploring "care as the being of dasein," and recognizing Understanding as the fullness of ways in which we live rather than as some kind of knowledge either apart from the world or compartmentalized within some particular discipline. Acker matches wits with the most brilliant of contemporary theorists and leads us through a career whose stages reprise the intellectual revolution that the last two decades have wrought in our thinking about Being and history.

After some survival time during the radical politics of the sixties, Acker produced a trilogy of novels pushing the limits of appropriation to document the plagiarized Being to which we are consigned. To look in detail at these novels is to identify the starting assumptions from which this entire revolution in narrative takes off. Indeed, the first of these, along with Constance DeJong's *Modern Love*, struck with tremendous impact a generation that had not yet begun to find its own narrative voice. Her books take, as she puts it in talking with Vitale, "the society as a series of texts. . . .

And using new additions, new renderings in the texts to attack the society. First of all to find out how it works and then attack it." Hence we must look closely at *The Childlike Life of the Black Tarantula by the Black Tarantula* (TVRT Press, 1975, but completed in 1973), the first volume of the trilogy, and at the also important *The Adult Life of Toulouse Lautrec by Henri Toulouse Lautrec* (TVRT Press, 1975). (The middle volume is *I Dreamt I Was a Nymphomaniac Imagining* [Traveler's Digest Editions, 1974] and is not now readily available.) In *Kathy Goes To Haiti* (Rumour Publications, 1978) and *Blood and Guts in High School* (Grove Press, 1984, but completed in 1978), Acker turns the language of the body against hegemonic forms and institutions of every description. Building upon the earlier works' appropriation tactics, these two books offer a bruised and bruising portrait of coming of age. In the early eighties a pair of works, *Great Expectations* (1982) and *My Death, My Life* (1983), both now also published by Grove Press, rethinks the problem of language as it affects Acker's enterprise to work beyond the theoretical impasse of the radical writer working within the culture's sign systems. Finally, in *Don Quixote* (Grove Press, 1986) and *Empire of the Senseless* (New York: Grove Press, 1988), Acker carries us to a profound vision of the contradictory nomadic life she prescribes for those who desire more than "the grey of yuppy life." At midlife, in other words, Acker has already achieved a career of major proportions, both in its ambitions and accomplishments, and it is no wonder that she is on most observers' list of figures most instrumental in the emergence of the narrative sensibility that this book addresses.

### The Black Tarantula's Art of Appropriation

Although pursuing it very far could obscure much of what Acker is about in *The Childlike Life of the Black Tarantula by the Black Tarantula*, the relation between that novel's citation of the sources it appropriates and appropriation in the visual arts is important to note. In fall 1985 Elizabeth Ferrer put together a show and catalog on *The Art of Appropriation* for the Alternative Museum. The show provided a useful occasion for considering the implications of appropriation, given its importance in the work of artists such as Sherrie Levine (whose *After Piet Mondrian* and *After Fernand Léger* replicate works by those painters).

The show itself included a variety of strategies: Russell Connor combines Rubens's rapists of the daughters of Leucippus with Picasso's demoiselles, Peter Nagy's *Eight Hour Day* is a wrist watch that marks the "hours" with appropriated images of hot sellers in the art market, Jim Jacobs turns the corners of the flat surfaces of Mondrian and Frank Stella, Alexander Kosolapov's *Mickey M.O.M.A.* depicts

Mickey Mouse in the styles of a half-dozen blockbuster shows. In other words, there are skirmishes with four of the forces that have determined thought and practice in mainstream art: periodization, the art market, extreme formalism, and the role of museums in the art world, not to mention a more general assault upon the cult of Originality. Both essayists (Ferrer and John T. Paoletti) cite Duchamp, Ferrer stressing that artist's effort "to produce a semblance of equality among all things that might qualify as art" and to provide us "with new ways of evaluating originality" (Ferrer 1985, 7), particularly against the backdrop of a commodity market in which the creator's fame and intentions, as well as the work's monetary worth, sometimes dominate responses to the work. Paoletti stresses the "issues of definition about art and creativity," but also the effort "to engage discussion of the social order" (ibid., 5).

Catalog essays allow little space, however, for more than a hint of the "more emotional, personal message" that emerges in the relation between the appropriator and the appropriated. *That* message is difficult indeed to trace in the twenty or twenty-five paintings (by eight artists) that the Alternative Museum can mount in a single show. But with such critical discussions a feature of the art world going on around Acker (and this catalog is representative, not exhaustive in either time or scope), we can see a strong relationship between the skirmishes noted above and Acker's own mixing of historical epochs in *Black Tarantula* (virtually every era from that of Moll Cutpurse on is represented), her comments on the difficulty for a writer in making a living, her disruption of the "original" and well-made novel for a collage of experiences, and her pursuit of alternative modes of publishing for the novel.

That *Black Tarantula* is an extended text rather than one or two paintings makes it easier for us to track the more "personal" dimension of its meaning in a way that reaffirms the rich blend of resonances in effective appropriation in all the arts. As always in Acker's work, that personal dimension is calibrated against a "discussion of the social order"—in this case by relating through the filter of appropriated materials the protagonist's coming to awareness. And, as is also the case in her work, Acker gives us plenty of help in seeing what she is about in a novel that, at the end of every chapter, cites the sources (from sensationalized histories to pornography, from W. B. Yeats to the Marquis de Sade) from which she takes her material: "I'm trying to get away from self-expression but not from personal life. I hate creativity. I'm simply exploring other ways of dealing with events than ways my lousy habits—mainly installed by parents and institutions—have forced me to act. At this point, I'm oversensitive and have a hard time talking to anyone. I can fuck more easily" (145).

Acker's hatred for "creativity" targets work that effuses from the autonomous, unquestioned structure of the self that, in this novel, becomes a problematic entity. The novel is very much involved in the issue of "personal life," but the "personal" qualities of life for a woman of this era are an endangered dimension of her Being. Normalization through various social institutions (parenting, marriage, schools, hospitals, and prisons are among the list of those treated here) have both co-opted any "personal" direction and wounded deeply the "I" that is left. Sex is easier than real communication because it seems that flesh rather than an "I" is all that is really requisite. Earlier, we read that "by the time anyone's 26 years old he/she's crazy unable any longer to communicate with more than 1% efficiency genitals meet but no info gets across" (85). Perhaps even more deliberately than the works in the Alternative Museum's show, this novel plays the institutional against the embattled "personal life" of its protagonist(s) with a thoroughness that almost makes Being itself an art of appropriation.

*"I become a murderess."* Acker's chapter titles and lists of appropriated works force readers to confront the larger intertextualities within which the novel works. The first two chapters, for example, derive from a stack of sensationalized accounts of crime (the titles from which she borrows include *Enter Murderers!*, *Murder for Profit*, *Blood in the Parlor*, *Rogues and Adventuresses*, *A Book of Scoundrels*). The titles connote a narrative style and perspective as important to Acker's appropriation as the tufts of history she transplants. These popular accounts feed off a fascination for antisocial excess apparently related to their readership's resentment of normalizing forces in their own lives. But this psychological dynamic in which "scoundrels" act out a rebellion long since surrendered by a suburban readership is not what Acker means when she precedes the text with this motto: "Intention: I become a murderess by repeating in words the lives of other murderesses" (1).

When Acker appropriates, it is less to escape "myself" (the other source she always cites at chapter's end) into someone else than to bring into a narrative of herself as the (predatory and repulsive female) "black tarantula" the social institutions, economic conditions, and cultural discourses that structure "scoundrels" as well as the heavily conflicted psyche she spins out in these pages. To "become a murderess," then, does not entail the compensatory pleasure of vicarious experience. Rather, it involves making explicit within one's consciousness both a murderous anger and the "exterior" conditions which arouse that anger. In 1973, when the novel was being written (Acker obligingly dates the chapters), this appropriative strategy gave Acker access to a kind of voice not readily available within the narrative grammar of the day. The emergence of that voice in the novel may help explain why it had such an impact in the circles within which it first circulated.

"I'm born poor St. Helen's, Isle of Wight. 1790" (16), the Sophie Dawes chapter begins. A child when she sees her parents "dragged to the local poorhouse," Sophie suffers molestation, blacklisting from employment for sleeping with a workman, and near-starvation until a wealthy army officer takes her in. Male protection has its costs and its temptations, however: "I make my first mistake: I become too calm I identify too much with this man who stops me from starving. I become confused, I forget my ambition and the ambition becomes misplaced: I have clothes so I want more clothes; I think I can do what I want without fear of starvation so I order my lover around. I'm learning about lies" (17). She lacks any real protection from starvation—wrong gender, wrong class—and the first wave of comfort induces the suburban illusion that commodity consumption, freedom, and power are natural rights.

When her lover dumps her, Sophie must complete the transformation of herself into a specular Being: "I look at myself in the mirror I don't understand whether I'm beautiful plain or ugly I have to use what I see as an object make it as attractive as possible to other people. Now I'm two people" (18). Woman's social schizophrenia, self and specular self, recurs throughout the novel, but that "self" is as socioeconomic and gendered as it is psychosexual and personal. "What does this wealth mean to me?" she asks herself once she is again well-established. It means, she realizes, that "I can no longer remember any of the events of my childhood" (22). The specular self that wears the "mask" of gender and the game-playing self that must "rely on my wits, like any man" (21) run the danger of forgetting childhood events that include class origins. The gender game, that is, cannot be played apart from the economic game in which she continues to have setbacks. She does not have "enough control" to force people to love her or to win a permanent position. She makes a "major mistake" when she stops "trying to gain more power"; whenever she pauses in the socioeconomic game to enjoy herself in suburban illusions and non-gender-bound sexuality she makes herself vulnerable to the effects of power.

During the "exile" such interludes impose, Sophie begins "to become monomaniacal and learn about the nature (nonnature) of reality" (24). The "nature of reality" is "nonnature": we live in culture's institutional life of economic and political power in which gender is no less immediate than the economic threat of starvation, the social threat of ostracism, and the political threat of royal displeasure. All three of these threats menace her until she finally (through murder) owns enough wealth and property in her own name to command security.

Keeping pace with the career of Sophie and several other appropriated lives is that of Kathy, a character whose "life" is slipped into parenthetical pockets of the others' narratives. Charlotte Wood's early-nineteenth-century imprisonment by parents and husband parallels Kathy's experience of relationships in which the man calls all the shots, in which parents are repressive and insensitive, and in which fathers (such as Charlotte's) are rapists. Charlotte says, "I don't want anyone to tell me what I should do. I don't want anyone following me around, secretly gossiping about me, because I'm not also a robot" (10). Not being a robot means not complying with the power of an uninteresting husband; Charlotte's fantasies tend toward a male lover who satisfies, and her sexual thoughts fade right through the parenthesis into Kathy's. Similarly, Charlotte's inability to hold her own against men ("one of the disgusting men insults me" [13]) in the "booze-parlor," even though she has "learned how to speak the correct language," parallels Kathy's dream of returning to New York but "miss[ing] an important meeting of radicals." Kathy stares out a window instead and wanders "into the church when it's empty night." That is, Kathy's invisibility in a gathering of radical males leaves her as speechless and thwarted as Charlotte in the booze-parlor.

Charlotte then poisons a pair who are stand-ins for her parents (after feeding them arsenic, she can "feel elated. I've succeeded forgetting my parents"). Kathy's course is less fatal, no more satisfying; she speaks "to almost no one because I find it difficult to find people who will accept my alternating hermitage and maniacal falling-in-love," a pattern of work and passion reserved for the male geniuses of the species. Neither Charlotte nor Kathy has a viable course open to her through society, and both must poison relations in order to continue at all. Like Sophie, both must play both a hyperaggressive version of the male game and contend with the satisfaction of desire within a highly compromised female game. Gender is a social arsenic, and they are both poisoned and poisoner.

Whereas Sophie tries to balance the pleasure of commodities with the struggle to dominate men, Kathy wears men's jeans and keeps working while balancing two men against each other and against masturbation. Both women share the same fear: "I want what I want if I let myself become involved with a man his socially-made power over me will make me merge with him. I'll lose myself, my ambition" (19). Sophie's conflicts are arrayed largely in the externals of her struggle to remain wealthy, accepted at court, and satisfied through her female friends; Kathy's in the internal sphere in which she struggles to keep her work going well and to cope with the psychological effects of having placed herself outside her assigned gender role: "When I decide I like someone I overreact I scare the person. I know I'm going to overreact, no one I like will like me, I try to hide my feelings by acting like a sex maniac, excuse me, would you like to sleep with me, I begin to think I'm only sexually interested in the person. I chase the person, I'm vulnerable, I act as tough as possible to cover my vulnerability" (25).

What Kathy describes is the male sex role, a sort of tough guy's predatory promiscuousness masking inner vulnerability, except that she pays dearly through self-doubt and self-deprecation for so unauthorized a role. It is the only role she can easily imagine as an Other to her "own" because it is the only other role in the lover's discourse of the culture. She can imagine, though not achieve, a different kind of relationship: "I don't know how to tell people I like I want to be friends, sit next to them so I can smell the salt on the skin, try to learn as much as possible about their memories, ways of perceiving different events. Because most people I like don't like me, I'm scared to show them I like them. I feel I'm weird" (25).

She *is* weird according to cultural norms, and that is precisely the vulnerability to which she exposes herself. She has trouble reading the nonverbal language of relationships because of the variant dialect she wants to speak: "I don't comprehend what signals a person I like gives indicate the person likes me, what signals indicate the person dislikes me" (25–26). Violence breaks out in the lives of Charlotte or Sophie or Laura Lane when the material conditions of survival or desire require action not permitted her subject-position in her culture's grammar. A psychological version of that violence goes on within Kathy when she attempts to occupy a subject-position even more difficult in 1973 than it is now—a female permitted libidinal and professional license, but also nonsexual relationships.

Laura Lane, the third major analog in this chapter, oscillates between going for money and power and coming, instead, to "descend into slavery, I let a man drive his fingers into my brains and reform my brains as he wants" (30). Kathy also is in the chapter's final pages, alternating between an effort to break free of enslaving roles and abuse by male lovers, between trying to meet more women and coping with a rejection that leaves her "sitting under the clothes in my closet; I don't see anyone; I wait for the hole to close" (33). The hole won't close until she finds a way to speak an alternative grammar in which the "subject" is not, for her, a gap.

Chapter two parallels Kathy's career with that of Moll Cutpurse, one who again goes outside the law in order to establish a domain of Being for herself. Moll challenges private property as well as gender (the latter most publicly when she wears men's clothing for her famous ride from Charing Cross to Shoreditch). The careers counterpoint well; both fathers wanted a boy and want to rape the daughter, both try to enslave her to an appropriate class-bound niche (at a saddler's for Moll, a rich husband for Kathy), both rebel, are imprisoned, and escape. Moll's ideal is baiting in the Bear Garden, Kathy's "to be a tough sex motorcycle hood silver leather on a

BMW." Both have to survive in a world that doesn't much permit this and to find a model of relations which will sustain them. Moll, as we know, turns to crime, finally organizing petty criminals into a counterkingdom over which she rules. "I'm trying," she says as she begins running her gang, "to figure out what reality is" (40).

Like the characters in chapter one, Moll finds she must "get rid of myself as a woman" in order to make her way in that "nonnature." "I'm constantly drunk, shouting roaring obscenities; no one can daunt my endless madness which echoes through the grey and wet streets of the laughing city" (41). Kathy's "roaring obscenities" are her rampant sexual fantasies as her inner life of desire diverges steadily from the outer life possible for her. She stops reading about "pornography and murders which was all I used to be interested in" and starts reading about schizophrenia, a subject that no doubt gives her some models for understanding the divided Being opened in her through her efforts to evade the suburban life. Unwilling to emulate Moll's celibacy (though Moll tells us "I like my sex with animals"), Kathy keeps struggling to have sex with something other than (male) animals and to earn a living "without becoming a robot and with my clothes on" (40).

*"And become the main person in each of them."* Crime narratives give way at this point in Kathy's story, for she has committed the crime of violating the class laws that ordained her to "marry money" and the gender laws that prescribed compliance with "femininity." What takes over for the next two chapters is pornography. Having followed desire into "illegal" territory, Kathy draws upon the apparent freedom of this outlaw genre to imagine forms of Being that will bring her the fluidity of pleasure and control which is pornography's chief attraction. Opposed to that fluidity are the key villains of the opening chapters—the mother who betrays her daughter (telling her to use the free clinics downtown), the father who represents patriarchal law (wanting to rape her), the class position (which would restrict even her friendships at boarding school).

More significant in these chapters is the realm of normalized behavior: "I'm forced to wait; I'm forced to enter the worst of my childhood nightmares, the world of lobotomy: the person or people I depend on will stick their fingers into my brain, take away my brain, my driving will-power, I'll have nothing left, I won't be able to manage for myself" (90). Sexual frustration renders Kathy dependent upon men who want to "reform my brain" to be compliant. But just as menacing as heterosexual relations is becoming a worker drone: "If I have to semi-prostitute again for money I will because getting a straight job would lobotomize me a wall breaks down I'm a single animal fending for myself I'm clever and relentless" (53). As gender constricts sexuality, so capitalism constricts "work," and

Kathy is determined to use a bit of Moll's wits at playing outside these prescriptions.

Kathy's vow is clear: "I despise people because they accept the shit they live in and get, limits limits no complete absorption into anyone/anything I can feel my fear" (73). It is indeed fearful "to make myself become/put down everything before they try to destroy an anomaly such as me. I hate the robot society I know" (78). Hence, at one point it is difficult to tell whether the walls around Kathy are those of a prison, an asylum, a hospital, or a school—all are institutions conditioning her to be "normal" and disciplined. Jobs negate whatever is really "her," whatever in the way of a genuine identity, or perhaps a genuine engagement with her own experiences. The world of lobotomy takes away the drive to write, which seems to her to be what she is. " 'Earn a living' as if I'm not yet living," she complains; "lobotomized and robotized from birth, they tell me I can't do anything I want to do in the subtlest and sneakiest ways possible" (97). Living is defined as earning in one of capitalism's fully funded positions, not as doing what "I want to do" in the face of the subtle and sneaky avenues of normalization.

If, earlier, wealth, and now survival threaten to assimilate Kathy to an economic definition of identity, so sexuality proves equally menacing because it is so strong a draw to enter those "childhood nightmares" of a predefined robot life. Her male lover is "a death person" she needs but must beware, and she can "see policemen in the streets waiting for us with guns" (79), ready to fire, presumably, if her deviations are noticed behind the "disguise" of compliance. "My revolt against the death society," she notes, "collides with my desire to be touched I have no identity I can feel the hand softly running up down my leg inside the leg" (82). When she allows her imagination to take the shapes of her desires, "she" is negated, a robot within a male pornography's form for passion.

This form of heterosexual desire and Kathy's work are almost inversely related, as she finds after a very intense passage: "I give myself entirely to each desire because there's nothing else to give myself to nothing else exists I have to hide my work am I scared?" (82). The strong self that would show her work is the same strong self that would like to find something "else to give myself to." That strong self knows that "my sex is myself my strength" (75), but chapters three and four, which are told through the filter of pornographic "sources," try but fail to link the sex that "is myself" with a form of desire that does not "entrap me."

One of the two major fantasy sequences features Kathy as "a young lesbian in a French boarding school who's growing up too quickly to have a childhood" (63). Reality quickly intrudes upon childhood innocence for the cluster of protagonists in this novel. Kathy enacts a lesbian fantasy sequence with Jean that is part eros and part rebellion ("I want to enter into her body rise up through the metal ceiling blow the select girls' school into tiny bits. Are they going to catch us?" [50]). Desire and fear, rebellion and discipline. Girls' school porn ("in every other bed a girl has her lover") alternates with giggling, defiance of norms, and a relationship less marked by the ingredients of power, domination, and pain, which occur with a male (as in a lesbian love scene in chapter four when suddenly Kathy's lover is male and slaps her before modulating back into a woman).

That modulation at the point of orgasm points to the failure of Jean's plan: "I want to do whatever I want to do fuck everyone I don't want to listen to anyone. I want to blow my identity outward, away, until I'm always running in a black ocean under a black sky and I can control my emotions" (55). Jean wants to expand her identity to a virtually infinite fluidity in which *she* controls her emotions rather than finding them already triggered by the porno cues that Acker occasionally makes explicit within parentheses, such as "(I begin to copy THERESE AND ISABELLE)."

What Kathy finds, however, and significantly enough at orgasm with a male lover (fantasized?), is something quite different: "I see a frame around me: my space. The rest is blackness, money-death-necessity coming to destroy my gropings toward, sex-money looming over me destroy my tentative beginning human sex, I rub my body against P. I become a parrot. O.K." (83). No simple either/or exists, just "a frame" that defines the space that Kathy can call hers, as well as pressures both cultural and otherwise compromising her into becoming a "parrot" of conventional sexual dynamics.

Indeed, the second major fantasy sequence in chapters three and four features Kathy captured by an Arab caravan in which she is exhibited and repeatedly taken by a series of men. More a series of sexual fantasies than a traditionally coherent narrative, its protagonist experiments freely with submission. She writes secretly, fearful that the boarding-school teachers, that is to say Arab white slavers, that is to say patriarchal critics, will catch her and "take away my writing; I'm still me, I'm still scared by my passion and sex. Reporting involves memories involves identity: I have my identity and I have my sex: I'm not new yet" (83).

This kind of writing, in which she expresses herself in familiar agonistic idioms tied to representation ("reporting") and metaphysics ("identity"), embodies a form of "personal life" which nonetheless cannot move outside the social frames she seeks to escape. Such writing is an existential pornography of specular Being in which she watches her reruns of narrative forms rather than "experiences" life directly. Hence writing is where a newer though nascent form of identity resides, passion is what threatens that identity (it occasions her submission to those who might take her writing), and she is "not new yet"—she has not found a form of Being in which writing and sexuality can work their way beyond these various forms of patriarchal order code-named "pornography."

At times Kathy seems willing to rely entirely on sexuality to take her to that "new life." She says at one point that "I use my writing to get rid of all feelings of identity that aren't my sexuality. I have to exist only when someone seeks to touch me or I touch myself" (84). This comment suggests that writing passes beyond the identity that the above passage finds sustained by "reporting," and its impulse links up with another passage in which she says, "I'm no longer interested in my memories, only in my continuing escalating feelings" (81), and another in which she notes that "my sexuality's impersonal. I'm rapidly losing my identity, the last part of my boredom" (86). Although leaving behind the "boredom" of static identity seems positive, to "have to exist" sounds almost reluctant, just as "escalating feelings" are a soothing escape from the hard contradictions with which she has been struggling.

Indeed, Kathy's ambivalence to this sexual avenue toward new Being cannot be suppressed even with the pornographic framework, and that framework's motifs of domination and surrender and its hieratic scenarios suggest much of the problem here. That is, "people are unused to love because they don't go far enough. As far as possible, and farther, into their intuited desires" (97–98). "All forms of love are drag," she notes, a pun on the masquerade that is gender (we are all cross-dressers?) and the disappointment of the ideal of "complete love" in the culturally devised "forms of love." The roles of lovers' discourse are determined by the institutions of gender and private property bound up in the social function of marriage. But at the same time, "I find my being dependent on love. Physical passion for others and thus myself" (98).

What's a girl to do? "I want to become as stupid and mindless as her and yield to the hard thighs of my next faceless lover. I want control over my environment. Like a fat spider I sit and wait" (96). Her body is "a web, solely a way of asking people to touch me." Yielding and control, solicitor and predator. Is passion a mode of evolution or a form of entrapment? Is writing out one's voice the discovery of identity or the repetition of appropriated Being? It is no wonder that, as for passion, she feels that "I'm two people and the two people are making love to each other" (49), and that, in writing, "in my head I'm telling someone about me the two voices become voices outside my head I almost hear, not quite, I feel I'm closest to people in loony bins" (56).

Trying to voice "personal life" in the era when the hyperreal includes individuality, trying to follow passion in a culture that stylizes its every nuance, trying to write in a culture that mass merchandises the conventional, Acker makes schizophrenia a formal principle that articulates the cultural contradictions at the heart of Being in the late twentieth century. "I can see anything in a set of shifting frameworks," she writes in the middle of a dizzying set of contradictory give-and-take sentences that leave her "not sure if I think of myself as a person" (97). Writing may be "my break to get rid of my damaged mind" (95), but it also situates her amidst the "shifting frameworks" inherent in the schizophrenic, heteroglossiac world of language. When she follows the pornographic line of drugged sex with the caravan's customers, she comes to feel its pleasure as a "masochism which occurs *only* when I give my consent" (102), but also as an access beyond identity and emotions to the pure energy of the "object world. I don't exist" (101).

At the end of chapter four, this use of pornographic appropriations to pursue the contradictions within passion and writing comes to an ending that does not resolve these complicated twists and turns, but simply stands after them as a persistent desire. "Human communion. There's nothing else I want" (103). The exercise has succeeded in a strategic schizophrenia announced just as Kathy juggles her thoughts between the Isabelle of her source and the Jean of experience: "I'm trying to make someone else's fantasy, fantasy caused by fears, my reality so I can deal with my fear. I can do it but I don't want to. Can I do it?" (65–66). Becoming "the main person" in her "favorite pornography books" (as chapter three's title puts it) means that she lives out their complications in those voices inside her head, in the reporting of memories she writes out, and in the continuing series of relationships she picks up and drops. The fears she both wants and does not want to confront are derived from the problematic position into which the individual is, as Althusser would put it, interpellated. However, to "deal with" them is not to resolve them, but rather to know their "subtle and sneaky" contradictions, as well as the "human communion" that remains the utopian ideal behind even this outlaw narrative genre. It is no wonder that "I've always feared most that someone will destroy my mind," because the play of that mind against cultural forms, through their contradictions, and with the persistence of desire is what keeps her eluding the schoolmasters and white slavers of the culture.

*From Yeats to de Sade.* The final two chapters (five and six) feature the unlikely pair of Yeats and de Sade, tracing their metaphysical and sensual absolutism against the deprivations and contradictions of their family lives and their historical contexts. That the latter give rise to the former's compensatory energies parallels earlier chapters of the novel in which the poverty and evanescence of relationships give rise to the pornographic motifs of "complete love" and domination, and in which the rigidities of social and economic order spur violent counterattacks upon the hierarchies of power and gender. Kathy's life is again merged or interfiled with the appropriated texts, and many elements recur: the (abused) power of the father, the distant mother, "the image of love and destruction of the self," and the motifs of murder, pornography's stylization of "human communion," and the robot world.

The novel's final push is a concerted ambush of readers' complacence in and complicity with existing orders. Kathy/de Sade takes an extreme position, for example, on the individual's position in the culture: "I had no money, no resources. I became sick with a dread sexual disease, mistreated by a doctor of the poor who called me a 'whore': I desperately needed everything I quickly learned that I was no favored son of the rich. Nor was anyone else" (147). We have seen before that characters without money or inherited position are vulnerable to the effects of power, but to say that *no one* is finally a "favored son of the rich" reminds us of Foucault's lectures on the nature of power. No one "holds" power; it circulates through networks on the institutional and discursive level.

"I'm trying to destroy all laws," she writes in the middle of an absurdist treatment of Murder (in the mode of an undergraduate philosophy class), to "tell you not to follow laws, restrictions" (150). But hers is not a "dopey question" (such as "Is murder objectively evil?"), but a position related to the use to which Law is put. "'Murder' is not a general act," she argues, then summarizes the Malthusian law as an example of "different customs about murder, killing children, enforcing public assassinations." This use of abstraction for depoliticizing issues with racial and economic determinants is the ultimate form of pushing "human communion" into a sort of ideological hyperreal, a mode in which policies of death go unrecognized as such until appropriated and exposed by the Black Tarantula: "It's not necessary for American soldiers to kill men and women who are poor and live in foreign countries except for a few rich white men who get lots of money when an American soldier needs a new weapon. Necessary according to the rich men" (150). "If," she concludes, "I'm constantly terrorized and starved by laws, I cannot come" (151–52). The Black Tarantula welcomes readers into her web of appropriations in the hope that the "paranoid schizo freak sex freak" she discovers in herself *as* a web of appropriations might unravel a bit, and that the "shifting frameworks" of a set which she has been tracing might jostle against one another enough to bare at least some of the often unacknowledged contradictions in which they entrap us all.

*The Painter with Words.* Acker's novel featuring her own Toulouse Lautrec undertakes to make those unacknowledged contradictions even clearer partly by taking to its greatest extreme Acker's emphasis upon the shifting frameworks. Indeed, the "I" of classic fiction, though not disappearing altogether, gives way to these frameworks just as effectively by modulating through a whole series of gender- and genre-related identity changes. This modulation strategically indexes a repertoire of cultural materials which constitutes identity, but it is a reflexive anthology that makes clear its political and economic implications. We find a M. Poirot mystery, art history, fables, adolescent exempla, porn, the movies, Hollywood tabloid, economics, and crime biography, to name the extended examples. The protagonist, Henri Toulouse Lautrec, is female (as Acker's narrator says in another novel, "I always get my sexual genders confused"), Vincent Van Gogh's daughter transforms into the nine-year-old Janis Joplin, Scott the architect is sometimes known as James Dean the movie star (having an affair with Janis), and the novel ends with the life of Johnny Rocco (who subsumes the novel's males, as the victimized "dame" does the females). The "he" and "she" of these shifting narrative situations thus represent the Imaginary of two genders emerging from the various popular genres included in the novel.

Even before the "novel proper" begins, Acker makes clear that this *adult* life will make explicit much of what the *childlike* life of her first novel holds on the edge of articulation. Specifically, the novel rejects "Fielding," whom we may take to be Henry Fielding:

> "Make sense," Fielding said. "Tell the real story of your life.
> You alone can tell the truth!"
> "I don't want to make any sense," I replied. (3)

Fielding's injunction indexes the classic assumptions of realistic narrative, assumptions that include the whole traditional structure of logic and metaphysics underwriting "sense" as he would have understood it, the belief that a "real story" is one that measures up to an ahistorical "truth," and the epistemological conviction that the direct observer-participant is a reliable, virtually unmediated source of that real story and can, moreover, record it in language that is transparent to the nonverbal reality it represents.

If this is "sense," then the "I" of the novel has little use for it, for her story is, as the verso of this page of front matter makes clear, monstrous by such standards: "I'm too ugly to go out into the world. I'm a hideous monster." Because the "world" is a construct determined by various patriarchal code systems, it is no wonder that this voice rejecting narrative's father would feel itself monstrous, a disfigurement of the prescribed mien it should be wearing in order to play by the rules. To have chosen the persona of Toulouse Lautrec is highly appropriate, then, for this troubled artist quite literally could not measure up to his father's example of masculinity, could not move easily and powerfully according to the male code, struggled in a painful existence in the Parisian demimonde, and found himself

attacked as an immoral influence, his work derided as shallow popular material, his pleasures all but restricted to the glass column of
brandy secreted in his cane.

Although perhaps an extreme emblem for either Woman or the
female writer, Toulouse Lautrec's career, caricaturing his world and
struggling for pleasure despite deformity, matches the experience of
Acker's narrator. "I used to think being crippled meant being in
constant pain," she says. "I can stand pain. Now I know no man
wants me. I can hardly bear to live" (6–7). "If," she says a bit later,
"I was living with a man, I would have someone who'd tell me if
I'm hideous. Now I have no way of knowing if I'm hideous or not"
(12). Life means being loved, just as beauty means being approved,
both actions the exclusive province of males. But self-esteem is only
half the issue, particularly for one who must buy sex:

> Fifty dollars an hour, honey.
> I shudder. How disgusting. How painful. Love's the only
> revolution, the only way I can escape this society's economic
> controls. I can't pay someone to really truly love me. (15)

The resonance between these quite specific economic roles and the
more general economic determinants of pairing off are part of the
issue, for this Toulouse, unlike her namesake, is poor and cannot
wield the sort of economic power that purchases a mystique sufficient to insure companionship. In a realm in which economic factors play a significant role, love *is* a revolution in which some part
of daily life attempts to evade the generally prevailing economic
forces, but, like the rest of daily life, it changes decisively once it
enters the economic sphere and is therein reorganized and recoded.

The novel closely follows its characters' doomed efforts to stage
this particular revolution without being simply reassimilated as sex
commodities or depoliticized hedonists. Acker repeatedly underscores economic realities to offset the incipient idealism inevitably
introduced with the sphere of subjectivity, just as she infuses the
narrative with the irreverence and profanity of punk culture to un-
settle the complacent innocence of ideology in mass culture, and the
frankness of "pornographic" elements to unmask the force of desire
in all the heavily conflicted spheres in which we make our lives.

Much of the first three chapters of the novel is taken up with
the (conscripted) efforts of Henri to aid Poirot, her "father," in the
solution of a murder. The master detective embodies ratiocination's
assumption of a coherent, logical, meaningful, and knowable "answer" to the confusing and mysterious surface appearance of experience. This particular detective tale is, however, a hopelessly incoherent sprawl of attempts to detect order amidst the chaos of the
underclass, the dispersed and significantly overdetermined desires
of the participants, and the incommensurability of its order of rea-

son with the (dis)order in which the people involved actually live. Like the logic of which he is an emblem, Poirot is better able to list and recount murders than to fathom explanations that lie beyond the simplistic causality of the whodunit (with its credo of unitary beings, intentionality, and linearity) to be found instead in the multiple determinations of the real socioeconomic world.

Henri's attention, for example, wanders constantly from Poirot's plodding discourse sorting out clues and hypotheses to recall moments of intense sexual frustration, run through a highly stylized Art History version of the life of Van Gogh (a "brother" to whom she is strongly attracted), and become aroused by and ultimately go to bed with the brother of a murdered witness whom Poirot interrogates. Thus there are numerous major strands of narrative in counterpoint: (1) Van Gogh's struggles for love, money, and recognition as a painter, (2) Henri's almost desperate desire to be loved, (3) Poirot's labors of detection, (4) the never quite discernible details of murder in the demimonde, and (5) the side excursions into the brutal suppression of the Paris Commune and of the Haymarket affair conducted by Berthe (one of Henri's fellow women, that is to say whores, for all the female characters in this part of the novel are culturally determined prostitutes).

All these strands constitute the same narrative we could chart in almost Proppian terms of a protagonist whose force is concentrated upon a fulfillment frustrated by socioeconomic structures obviously beyond the protagonist's power. At the risk of looking like an old-fashioned structuralist, I might show more quickly why Acker intertwines these strands by constructing such a table (see below). We ought to add other elements, such as the two prostitutes who may "want men!" and who are "not sure they want each other," but "their warmth and need for warmth drive them into each other"—another version of desire frustrated into displacements by socioeconomic structures. "Sure we're waitresses. We're part of the meat market. We're the meat. That's how we get loved. We get cooked"—commodified and marketed. Berthe goes on to hit the same utopian note sounded by the anarchists she has been discussing: " 'If we lived in a society without bosses,' Berthe says seriously, 'we'd be fucking all the time. We wouldn't have to be images. Cunt special' " (24–25). Berthe imagines a libidinal utopia apart from the spectral existence of manufactured images and sexual objects on sale. The tag "says seriously" indicates some distance between Berthe and the narrator, but the point is the political content of these characters' imaginations, a content there as well for the unidentified murderer (whom the women think could easily just be "a person who lives in the same hell we live in") or for Poirot's lists of criminals who were "only trying to survive" in a world controlled by lawyers and wealth.

We might ordinarily prefer to believe that the underworld works by a logic different from, say, that of the judge and jurists murdering the Haymarket leftists (or of the police, whose firing upon union organizers precipitated the Haymarket affair), and we may not ordinarily associate repressive police with reactionary art critics, fathers insisting upon a "good" marriage for their daughters, johns shopping for pleasure, or lovers seeking a beloved. However, what Acker gestures toward with such a narrative structure is precisely an economically determined master narrative that not only induces general conformity but also programs as utopian "escape" nothing more difficult to reassimilate than Berthe's idea of sexual possession. Certainly the common conflict between each of the protagonists and his or her respective frustraters in the table is an economic struggle over a thing (often something that "ought" not be reduced to an object this way) to be possessed and held, whether something material (such as wages or a beloved or the art marketplace) or something metaphoric (such as the understanding sought by detective, writer, and reader).

This set of intertwined plots stresses the master narrative that structures consciousness with the economy of possession and retention. Chapter four's set stresses power, mastery, and the hierarchical organization of relations of desire. The chapter's frame features Henri, like her namesake, drinking and talking long past the staying

### Plot Strands in Chapters 1–3

| Protagonist | Force | Object | Frustraters |
|---|---|---|---|
| Vincent Van Gogh | Ambition and desire | Fame, respect, marriage, etc. | Poverty, art establishment, class coding |
| Henri | Desire | Love and acceptance | Deformity and poverty as emblems of femaleness and thus powerlessness |
| Poirot | Mastery as a will to power | Knowledge and the Answer | Impossibly (absurdly) complex reality |
| Killers | Survival | Money | Lawyers and others who control State and economic mechanisms |
| Communards | Idealism and Survival | Equitable government | Repressive arm of the sociopolitical establishment |
| Anarchists | Protest | Just and fair society | Police and judicial forces |

power of her companions. The genres include a creation fable, a fifties-style teen-magazine exemplum, hard porn, and a soft-focus kiddie-porn segment. The content and context of the latter are indicative of the common theme running throughout the chapter: Henri sits telling these stories, resentful that men use her as an object simply because she likes sex and is powerless. So she imagines herself as Scott, the architect, encountering Marcia (the ten-year-old illegitimate daughter of Van Gogh) naked in the woods; Marcia allows looking and masturbating but not touching, and speaks with a quite precocious sense of erotic gratification.

In her fantasy, Henri assumes a male guise in order to achieve the position of mastery she lacks in her own relationships, and she reduces the love object to the ambiguous status of a child who is vulnerable, by size and age, and yet masterful in that she knows which shots to call and calls them (Marcia is, of course, also an empowered version of Henri). In the third segment, we find a hard-core fantasy in which Jackie Onassis can invoke her wealth and mystique to pick and choose among available men at the disco but, once in a room alone with her choice, is forced to submit to her black lover's commands to "beg" and to comply with his orchestration of grass, cocaine, class and racial fantasies, and sex.

This repetition of mingled power and vulnerability characterizes the other two segments as well. One is a sentimental tale of a young woman who has been raped by her Vietnam-veteran brother during his flashback (in which he dresses her as a Vietnamese in silk pajamas before forcing her), is almost raped by her boyfriend, who, after a blowup over being "teased" by her ambivalence, hears her tale and, paternally and patiently, nurses her back to sexual health as fiancée, future mother, and "a real woman" (83). Both the brother's fantasy of overpowering the Viet Cong and the sentimental fantasy of the determining role her boyfriend plays in her psychic recovery feature male mastery achieved over resisting elements that derive at least partially from various sexual, racial, and economic hierarchies.

The fable segment features an arrogant male baboon and a passionate female cat who secures all the food in the world in the effort to win his love. The baboon simply consumes everything the cat brings until there is nothing left in the world and she is too weak to love—*then* he wants her, and sings these three songs:

> Finally I've found you love
> I realize I have to open up
>
> I'm scared you'll hurt me
> I've never let myself love anyone
> I don't want you to hurt me and I
> don't want to stop being this open

I don't understand love
it's not rational

Acker is, as always, deadly accurate in her sampling of the self-indulgence, excessive rationality, and egocentrism of male talk, yet even this sardonic glimpse of modern mores features the conflict of fear and desire, vulnerability and mastery. The result of all this hierarchy, rigidity, and heavy socioeconomic content in relations of desire is that there are no fulfilling relations to be found—only Scott and Marcia standing close without touching, or the two prostitutes who make love in desperation only to have Giannina blast their intimacy away by saying, "If you were a man, I could love you" (28). If Berthe *had* been a man, Giannina would more likely be in the position she is in with Jim (who is beginning to enjoy his marriage and is cutting back on girlfriends) or Ron Silliman, the poet whom she loves, though he does not even know her ("He doesn't love me which means he'll be mean to me so I can look up to him even more").

Chapter seven, "The Life of Johnny Rocco," shows us the third feature of the cultural logic Henri struggles with, the final lawlessness of power, whether wielded by government or by the underworld. Johnny is a Mafia fruit shipper hired to run guns for the "Feds" to the Dominican Republic, but the deal is quashed after such policy setbacks as the Bay of Pigs fiasco, and the CIA shoots up Johnny's business when he talks a bit too much and corrupts a female agent. The CIA agents have decided that they are "going to do our own shipping [as they call it] instead of hiring people like you. Strong individualism is the American ideal" (199). Johnny has his own claim, also ironic, though for different reasons, to that ideal. He saw early on that "if I didn't go ahead and make it for myself, no one would make it for me. It was black, nothing, a hole. I just made some moves. I wasn't smarter than you guys, I just had more guts" (196). So he built up his own territory, held his own in the gang wars, was indeed a strong individual. It is only the most obvious example of the chapter's condensation of thuggery and the operations of the State, the beatings by one equivalent to the covert interventions and assassinations of the other. Like the State's forces, Johnny is "one of the people who makes the paths everyone in this society follows" (196), and, also like the State, "I can make any move I want cause I've got the know-how to create reality the way I want it so all the others accept it as reality" (187).

Johnny is proved wrong by the shoot-out, of course, and runs out of his warehouse. "I had no idea where to go. I kept on running" (199), a bit like Rabbit Angstrom, perhaps, except that Johnny has realized that, like power, ideology (such as "strong individualism") is one thing for individuals and quite another for institutions. Johnny runs because he has always understood a central fact about sociopolitical realities, as he reveals in this comment early in the chapter: "All I knew was I was legitimate because I was powerful and power causes legitimacy in this country" (175). As the female agent he has corrupted warns him, "we're up against people who are much stronger than us" (190) precisely because they employ the State apparatus. This section thus adds to the novel's broad analysis of the cultural formation of subjects a treatise on institutional power, including the asymmetry of individual and institution, the gap between ideology and the exercise of power, and the fundamental lawlessness of power in itself.

Perhaps the most pyrotechnic exploration of Henri's encounter with patriarchal logic is in the fifth and sixth chapters, when we follow Janis and Jimmy in Hollywood and Marcia and Scott in Paris. Janis's tale is intertwined with that of Henry Kissinger's career and theories of diplomacy. The key themes of the latter, aside from the "class" privilege of his base at Harvard, include the Metternich school of diplomacy (with its twin notions of limited war and areas of common interest) and the diplomat's commitment to a long-range historical perspective in solving problems. The nameless narrator's response is unambiguously negative: "But a policy and a man who speak not to concrete realities or to contemporary concerns, but merely to what the man sees as the vindication of history, are a policy and a man who harshly exclude those human beings who are not living with the historians of the future in mind, and who completely disregard whatever torment and anguish happen to be generated at this time" (131). The indictment parallels the novel's implicit commentary on all patriarchal thinking, including the features in the parodied genres.

More specifically, the indictment implies that maintaining this diplomatic economy of State interests excludes the possibility for individuals to achieve any comparable balance or satisfactions, unless by chance or special privilege. And, indeed, that is the experience of Jimmy in both his personal and in his screen roles. As the rebel without a cause, Jimmy has relationships with males that are structured by conflict and competition, ones with females by domestic scripting so complete that it becomes an object of parody, and ones with institutions (school, police, family) by the absolute disjunctions identified in the Kissinger commentary. As "himself," Jimmy can "understand what it is to be driven. My mother died when I was 9 years old. She just left me like that. Then my father sent me away. I knew I was bad and I knew I had to create my own world" (110). But the world is not his to create—it belongs to the interdiscursive cultural environment. *His* writing of his life is displaced by others: "Every word these two youngsters whispered to each other in public, every word of trust and affection, every gesture of trust and desire, was immediately reported in the gossip columns, the scandal sheets, the teenage heartthrob mags. Reported and distorted. Were Jimmy and Janis beginning to believe these distortions of their feelings and of themselves?" (133). Their very literal experience with these stylized formulations of "trust and desire" is a more obvious version of the unconscious stylizations of emotion experienced by anyone in the culture who has absorbed its lover's discourse.

Even worse, perhaps, than this invasion of textual variants is the conflict between the commodity culture's incentives to transform oneself into an image and the tug of human ties against that image: "Jimmy began to realize that his affair with Janis was forcing him to remain human. Remain stuck on the ground when he wanted to soar into the air, a myth. As he put it, 'Up here, I hate all earthlings' " (135). Jimmy lives the cultural contradiction between the ideology of "strong individualism" and the commodification of subjectivity as image or "myth," the same contradiction that, in another context, features Kissinger the man amidst "concrete realities" versus Kissinger the character in the future historians' texts he projects for himself.

To turn to Janis is to follow the issue of individual subjectivity onto the terrain of gender. Janis interrupts Jimmy's speech about creating his own world to note the hard facts of sexual difference: " 'You still don't understand.' Suddenly Janis didn't care anymore if she was impressing him. She was caught up in her own pain. 'Men can do what they want. Those who got visions can try to follow them.' " (111). Partly Janis notes how much easier it is for Jimmy to carry out his dream "to make myself be someone else, be JAMES DEAN," and partly she notes the disparity in the sexual game in which if women have "got kids, they give them up; any woman gives up a home life, an old man, probably, a home and friends," and in which a strong woman is "always going to be alone" because equally strong men want "ass-lickers" rather than "women they're constantly going to have to fight" (111).

Sure enough, it is Janis who is more viciously targeted in the tabloid articles near the chapter's end for her drugs, sex, and psychosis. Even in chapter six, when Janis and Jimmy have fled to Montmartre and become Marcia and Scott, matters are not much better. If in Hollywood they were trapped between the experience of desire and their assimilation to media imagery, in Montmartre, in which their story is juxtaposed to a treatise on capitalism, their relation is subsumed within the (sexually differentiated) economics of, on one level, Jimmy's effort to become successful in the architecture business, and, on another, love relationships reified by the larger order of capitalism which the chapter anatomizes.

The chapter begins with a three-way conflict that Marcia and Scott experience between very strong primal love, the intense ambivalence that each feels in both needing the other desperately and feeling something akin to invasion or self-destruction from the intensity of the other's emotion, and, finally, the desperate poverty of street-living, with only her earnings as a "street chanteuse" to support them. These themes are followed by the first part of the chapter's anatomy of capitalism, including a historical review of exploitation, relations of force, reorganized structures in colonies, imperialism, and so forth. That juxtaposition has the effect of chronicling the socioeconomic forces that invade even a "personal" or "individual" state so intense as to be experienced in terms this primary: "Being wet and dark with someone. Being touched and being able to know the person will touch you again. Being in a cave you don't want to leave and don't have to leave. Being in a place in which you're able to be open and stupid and boring" (137).

This utopian state of primary pleasure is quickly invaded. When the political treatise breaks off, the tensions between Marcia and Scott have intensified as he is increasingly drawn into his professional sphere. "Marcia woke up one morning and realized that Scott no longer loved her. I'm free" (149). That freedom is an opening toward venting desire that "his sexual uptightness" and "his scaredness" and "his egotism" seems not to have begun to satisfy. She fantasizes about arousing a bar full of men and about awakening the sexuality of bums. But Scott "wanted to get his own work known. . . . Scott wanted fame and fortune. I live totally by my emotions. That's who I am" (152–53), a gender, that is, which is *supposed* to live by emotions rather than by intellect or "serious" creative work.

"Scott wanted beautiful Parisian women to drool over him because he was the guy who was making the most powerful architecture in Paris." But Marcia is "always thinking about" him and has no other outlet for her emotion, a fight ensues, and she "realized she was a bum and didn't belong in this picture of Scott's success" (154). She is a bum mainly because she is not a productive worker— he produces massive buildings; she, street songs. He is a male with power, options, and a sexual draw; she is a female for whom power is achieved only by conforming to prescribed role models, for whom options are limited to choosing a male or no males, and for whom sexual draw means selling herself either literally or figuratively.

When the chapter then shifts back to the subject of capitalism, it is to emphasize the malignant necessity of military spending to sustain the economy, the class nature of the conflict between developing and undeveloped areas, and the "friendly fascism" of concentrated power in America. When the chapter returns to Marcia, she is torn apart between soft longing and defensive withdrawal, dreaming of her old home shrouded now in labyrinthine shrubbery—she finds herself the "undeveloped" beggar nation dependent upon, but exploited and marginalized by, the "developed" male status of Scott with its fully concentrated power. Capitalism and geopolitics move inside the body, as the chapter's final paragraph makes clear in portraying her unresolvable internal conflict: "Feeling like a thing rather than living. Knowing that wanting a lover, wanting Scott back, is wanting to be dead again, wanting one feeling so much that feeling becomes a thing, my possession. Knowing this but not feeling it all throughout my body" (165).

Marcia's experience of cultural contradiction is carried out on a far more visceral plane than that of Jimmy or Kissinger. Marcia experiences herself and her emotions both as *things*, virtual commodities in a culture within which exchange value and symbolic value efface any other sort. But she also experiences self and emotion as pain, a pain of impossible longing for that utopia of primary emotion which she can imagine and dream but not locate within the sphere of actuality. By the beginning of chapter seven, when Marcia and Jimmy have passed from the stage, the novel's "I" is a moll who makes three mistakes—making love with Johnny Rocco in the first place, thinking he might fall in love with her when he said "My love, . . ." and asking him if he does love her. She is a thing or possession that tries to behave as a human, an inferior who addresses her superior as an equal, an individual who steps out of sync with the institutions and, faced with the absolute groundlessness to which these contradictions expose her, walks out alone and, emblematically, into a snowstorm so bad "you couldn't see the hand you stuck out in front of your body." As the next sentence tells us, "She was being even more stupid when she threw herself in front of a moving car" (170). It is a desperate end for Woman, but then *Toulouse Lautrec* is perhaps the bleakest of Acker's novels in terms of the position of women in all of these configurations of the social and cultural.

The trilogy consisting of *Black Tarantula, Imagining,* and *Toulouse Lautrec* uses a most revealing narrative form in which to examine female identity. Appropriation as formal strategy allows Acker to keep subjectivity and ideology from effacing each other in the way that more conventional forms of writing often allow. The strategic shifts, sharp cuts, and deft mixes she achieves exhibit the found materials of consciousness in a way that makes unmistakable both anger and its sources, desire and its displacements, the utopian other and the powerful agents of co-optation. In her later works, Acker grows increasingly sophisticated in desublimating the content of social and educational forms, of the classic canonical texts of the culture, and of the violence and contradiction that register upon the body as pain and confusion.

*Kathy Goes to Haiti* was originally published in 1978 by Rumour Publications (the edition cited here) and was reissued in 1988 as part of Grove Press's *Literal Madness* collection, though without the Robert Kushner drawings from the earlier edition (Kushner also illustrated the *Persian Poems* from *Blood and Guts in High School*, a beautifully printed edition done in 1980). The novel takes place amid the phantasmagoria that is Haiti—the fantastic poverty that makes almost any American wealthy by comparison; the sinister *tontons macoute*, whose silent passage through a scene reminds the passionate how immediately disappearance and death can happen; the packs of boys begging to pet and kiss the white tourist; the racial split in which Creoles hold the money and blacks hold the power; the utterly bizarre economy in which nothing but guns, dust, sun, malfunctioning machinery, and decaying buildings are plentiful; and, most of all, the amazing heat, which makes daily existence all but hallucinogenic.

The novel ends with a visit to the père, and Kathy's trip to his voodoo den is almost emblematic:

> The city cab soon leaves the straight black tar streets. It winds basically upward and to the left, sometimes round in circles, sometimes in huge snake-arcs, sometimes it goes opposite to where it wants to go, there's no time in Haiti. It goes everywhere. Through driveways and around falling-apart single building single-room stores. On gray (broken) cement roads that go under while the old mansions alongside the road go up so it seems to go under mansions. Ahead up a narrow street hedged in by two-story wood houses into a narrow gray wood garage then straight back down the street in reverse. (137)

Winding and snaking, sinking and tunneling, hedged and garaged, this road and its equally distressed syntax carries us to an "everywhere" that does not exist within time as we know it. The closer Kathy and her guide get to the père, the more surreal the space becomes:

> A narrower pebbly unrideable road juts off of the dirt road the taxi's been riding on. The new road is covered with dust. Thick yellow dust. This dust hides women carrying huge parcels on their heads, walking in the ruts, and two-story stucco houses, painted all colors, yellow and black. They walk into the dust. The sun seems to get hotter and hotter. There's lots of noise and hot dust and heat. On one side the dust sharply descends through the air into a ditch crossed over by a modern trestle. They keep on trudging upward. (137)

Passing up into dust, sun, and a ritual that, as the novel's last line tells us, leaves Kathy "more dazed than before," they must leave behind the cab, a last reminder of western culture's effort to master through technology.

What they *do not* leave behind is misogyny and victimization, for Haiti preserves these patterns with appalling rigor. Just before Kathy reaches the père's hut, she meets Kung-Fu, who tells her: "I don't like violence. I don't go with women because they're tricky. They don't do things honestly. I only go with men" (138). Papa, "a 76-year-old American perhaps ex-CIA ex-sailor," tells her that "I always pay my girls as soon as I use them. That way there are no hard feelings" (101); "women," he adds apropos of Baby Doc's mother and sister, "can never be satisfied." The taxi driver who propositions Kathy tells her that no woman can be alone in Haiti, and the boys who follow her tell her that she is considered a prostitute because she talks to men. Even Roger, her lover, tells her that women "all lie and do everything behind your back" (128). Kathy's passage to Haiti goes beyond the complexly shifting frames of media imagery and romance plots down underneath the mansions of the patriarchy to its roots in violence, power, economic privilege, and the exploitative relationships between different levels of the hierarchies of class, race, and gender. It is no accident that this journey's "dust hides women carrying huge parcels on their heads, walking in the ruts" of traditions that place impossible burdens on women and the other victimized groups in the novel.

Betty, Roger's wife, who is considered "like a child" by him and is held under virtual house arrest, a prisoner, supposedly, of sun allergies and, the foreman supposes, of her desire to get Roger's money. She is ill-equipped to sustain herself, for she is isolated, thinks Irving Wallace may well be a great writer, and lacks the initiative to use what power she may have. Her sisters-in-law wield their economic privilege, buying goods and bossing servants. Native Haitians, they have struck their deal with the black magic of patriarchy, whereas Betty (who is from Kansas) and Kathy (the New Yorker) seem "dazed" by the way this society is absolutely explicit about the worst elements of patriarchal culture. Haiti desublimates in neo-expressionist frenzy what in America is best found through the Black Tarantula's analytical appropriations.

Haiti is hallucinogenic because it keeps out in the open both what patriarchy controls and the force and weapons with which it controls. What it controls, Kathy believes, is women's sexuality. Roger keeps her off-balance with tales of other dates, his unpredictable and at times mysterious comings and goings, and his complete control of their sexual encounters. The novel illustrates the "hot connection" and the "pure rhythm" of sexual material of which Acker has spoken, but amidst all its oohs and ahs is the physical pain, insecurity, and dependency that constitute the "political" content of its place in her fiction. Kathy glimpses in Haiti not just the most obvious forms of harassment, discipline, and control, but also possibilities for ideal gender relations, social responsibility, and communal living.

The desire for ideal gender relations is most clearly articulated (but, significantly, only to herself) as she lies with Roger.

> Someday there'll have to be a new world. A new kind of woman. Or a new world for women because the world we perceive, what we perceive, causes our characteristics. In that future time a woman will be a strong warrior: free, stern, proud, able to control her own destiny, able to kick anyone in the guts, able to punch out any goddamn son-of-a-bitch who tells her he loves her she's the most beautiful thing on earth she's the greatest artist going fucks her beats her up a little then refuses to talk to her, and able to fuck (love and get love) as much as she wants. In that future time the woman will be beautiful and be the hottest number whose eyes breathe fire, who works hard, who's honest and blunt, who demands total honesty. Greta Garbo in QUEEN CHRISTINA. (68)

Kathy knows what keeps her self-abusive ("Disgusting putrid horror-face no one wants to fuck you you make a fool of yourself you always make a fool of yourself everyone's always laughing at you everywhere you go you don't belong anywhere nowhere nowhere you're worse than a bum" [75]). It is the cultural world within which perception is schooled and enacted, and her escape from the dependency in which she finds herself means having the full list of enabling "male" character traits, the power to "punch out" anyone speaking the patriarchal patter of seduction and exploitation, a structure of desire in which sex is transformed from profane expletive to the ability to "love and get love," and an environment in which beauty, strength, work, and honesty look as good as the movies' Garbo illusions.

Unfortunately, the passage cannot stop there.

> Meanwhile things stink, Kathy thinks to herself. I have to be two different people if I want to be a woman. I'm me: I'm lonely I'm miserable I'm crazy I'm hard and tough I work so much I'm determined to see reality I don't compromise I use people especially men to get money to keep surviving I juggle reality (thoughts of reality) I feel sorry for myself I love to hurt myself and to get hurt etc. i.e., I'm a person like any goddamn man's a person. (68)

To live strongly at all, Kathy must be both object and subject, a position that leaves her not complete, but doubly estranged, neither pure mindless object or fully empowered subject, smart enough to understand the "thoughts of reality" she juggles to keep perspective, vulnerable enough to feel keenly her isolation and her guilt for transgressing cultural categories. Her experience in Haiti seems to have led her to a powerful desublimation of the contradictory status of gender and to reform media imagery towards the resolution of that conflict.

Our narrator's sense of social and communal values is equally bound in contradiction, an almost media-bound unreality, but a nonetheless sincere desire to reform the social scene she is "determined to see." Riding through the night past "a secret police shark chute [that] swings down to the sea," she tells Roger "you can't treat the poor people like animals" (85). Earlier, she makes her point more fully: "It's not just that they're poor. There are a lot of poor people in the world. These people don't have a chance to be anything else. Your father's business is going to come to you and you're going to have a chance to do something for these people. If nothing else, you're an example for these people" (78). Kathy knows that both economic and personal changes are essential, but she also knows that her "solution" does not wash well in the patriarchal scheme of things. Almost apologetically, she gets down to a basic social value that almost dissolves into Disney cartoon lingo: "If you have love in your heart and live for other people, these people will have love in their hearts. I know I'm sounding soppy, but it's what I believe."

She does sound, perhaps, a bit soppy, though few of us would really want to oppose it: it works well on the local scene. But it is not particularly potent against the institutional inertia of an entire society; Roger's response is to talk about retreating to a castle with "a few huge dogs who'll stay outside" and keep the people away, "the best stereo system money can buy plus all the records I can get" so that he can retreat into a self-indulgent cocoon, "tennis courts, swimming pools, and a golf course" so he can stay in shape, and "only older women." Kathy is taken aback and asks why older women. "They can't be younger than fifty. I like older women cause they act like nursemaids. They'll take care of me. They might all have to be dumb." Clearly the patriarchal side of the culture prefers a very posh Bleak House to a wish upon a star.

Kathy, however, keeps trying. She at least hopes to relate to women in a way not ordered by the motifs of violence and exploitation. She has been told by her first female friend in Haiti, Marguerite, that "a woman can't have girlfriends. Not the way things are in Haiti. . . . If I have a girlfriend, immediately she steals my husband or my boyfriend. I've never really had a girlfriend" (30). Kathy finds that "terrible," and one of her first questions to Betty when they are left alone looks for something better: "It must be hard for you. Do you have anyone you can talk to around here?" (60). There is Suzy the macramé artist, but, predictably enough, Betty's car has broken down and Roger does not get it fixed because "it's hard to get machine parts in Haiti"; Betty is not allowed to ride a scooter because "they're dangerous"; she is not allowed to ride a bicycle "because the natives might bother me because of who we are"; she will not walk because she is terrified of getting syphilis from the open sores of "the natives" from whom she is permanently estranged because of Roger's paranoid warnings.

None of Kathy's attempts to help Betty escape this prison is successful—too many social mores, economic and racial tensions, and political strikes and counterstrikes are crisscrossing for Betty to make it across the cultural no man's land that surrounds her. Kathy is explicit about wanting not a sexual but a sisterly relation to these women, but we are forced to see the irony of her conforming to Marguerite's fears—Kathy does compete with Betty by trying to steal Roger from her. *Kathy Goes to Haiti* clearly sketches the dilemma of the disfranchised subject who wishes to make fundamental alterations in the structure of gender, economics, and social relations. Coaxed by her desires into sexual scripts that pain as well as please her, Kathy is drawn by necessity into mortal competition in order to survive emotionally. Haiti is a locale that shows an unsubtle version of the double bind that such a subject faces, its local color and lush sexual undergrowth used as the Day-Glo accenting to Acker's nascent reading of American culture. That reading becomes increasingly complex and penetrating as Acker's career progresses, as we quickly discover by confronting her extraordinarily rich *Blood and Guts in High School*, completed the same year *Kathy Goes to Haiti* was published.

If in *Kathy Goes to Haiti* Acker turns travel narrative into cultural exposé, in *Blood and Guts in High School* it is the Bildungsroman that, in taking as its subject the consciousness of Woman-as-Other, becomes itself something Other. This novel takes the early novels' attentiveness to the experience of the body and complements it with the fully reflexive analysis of the later fiction, making it the real turning point in Acker's career. As she puts it well into rewriting Hawthorne's masterpiece, "at this point in *The Scarlet Letter* and in my life politics don't disappear but take place inside my body" (97). The stigmatized Hester and the contemporary writer both discover the extent to which they have internalized the complex sphere of contentions which composes the larger world around them. Acker analyzes that world with so much bite that now, in retrospect, she is almost a bit embarrassed. "I was more like a little nasty kid who was having lots of fun," she told Tom Vitale in an interview about the book. But she is hard on herself, I think; we hear less of a "nasty kid" than a superb mimic of the cultural lingo who is adept at revealing what that lingo typically represses.

The novel's opening line sets the agenda for a section entitled "Parents stink": "Never having known a mother, her mother had died when Janey was a year old, Janey depended on her father for everything and regarded her father as boyfriend, brother, sister, money, amusement, and father" (7). The novel begins where, it would seem, Woman must in this world begin, with the Father, but who is in this narrative conflated with the Lover, with the motifs of rape, unsatisfied female desire, unmet needs for love, and finally abandonment, all of which serve to desublimate the more violent and destructive lines along which the female psyche is often disciplined. An oddly comic air pervades this opening segment; it reads almost like a Woody Allen takeoff on the way that live-in couples finally get around to breaking up, complete with the fencing, the self-deception, the reluctance to deal openly with relationships, and the Other Woman (slim, attractive, and according to Janey, predatory), about whom the man is predictably incoherent and unsure. What is *not* comic is the emotional devastation to Janey, the powerlessness that this archetypal male figure imposes upon her, the scenarios (drawn partly from egoistic needs and partly from the film *Gilda*, which she holds in her mind) with which Janey and her father attempt to control each other.

The episode shows Acker's skill in mixing generic strands, her fine ear for the discourse of romance and power, and a good deal besides, particularly in this crucial dialogue and accompanying stage directions:

> Father: I'm just having an affair, Janey. I'm going to have this affair.
> Janey *(now the rational one):* But you might leave me.
> Father *(silent)*
> Janey: OK. *(Getting hold of herself in the midst of total disaster and clenching her teeth.)* I have to wait around until I see how things work out between you and Sally and then I'll know if I'm going to live with you or not. Is that how things stand?
> Father: I don't know.
> Janey: You don't know! How am I supposed to know?
> That night, for the first time in months, Janey and her father sleep together because Janey can't get to sleep otherwise. Her father's touch is cold, he doesn't want to touch her mostly 'cause he's confused. Janey fucks him even though it hurts her like hell 'cause of her Pelvic Inflammatory Disease. (9–10)

In case the reader is caught off balance by the passage, Acker illustrates these pages with the highly stylized poses of pornography in a spare line-art style that drains them of their usual photogravure allure. It is all quite literal, really. Why is Janey only ten years old in this sexual relationship? The sexualization of all her relations and behavior begins early for the unempowered object. Why is her lover her father? The Father is the role for every powerful male in patriarchy. Why is he so inarticulate? Because one need neither understand nor explain oneself to chattel. Extreme? Yes, but then Acker's object is to desublimate culturally conditioned patterns of relationships and to articulate through bodily pain (pelvic disease, sexual starvation, crippling anxiety) the cost of those patterns to the Other.

The rest of the dialogue between Janey and her father alternates with travel notes about the part of Mexico where they are staying and magazine articles about the "new era" with which she occupies herself, trying to cope with his rejection. She both wants him—he monopolizes her entire structure of desire—and wants not to be used by a man she knows is infatuated with Sally. Capitalized headlines specify the "LASHES" with which she punishes herself while trying unsuccessfully to avoid taboo subjects at farewell dinners and final nights together. Near the end of the section, however, is perhaps the ultimate gloss upon its primal scene, in a "break" in the dramatic form not at all uncharacteristic of Acker: "If the author here lends her 'culture' to the amorous subject, in exchange the amorous subject affords her the innocence of its image-repertoire, indifferent to the proprieties of knowledge. Indifferent to the proprieties of knowledge" (28).

To be an amorous subject means to be immersed in the Barthesian image-repertoire, "innocent" of its constitutive properties, "indifferent" to the customary use of "knowledge" to denaturalize myth, careless of the opportunities that owning such knowledge might afford. The author's "culture," however, frames and contextualizes the amorous subject, and allows to surface in the text not only the stage directions that punctuate the dialogue but also the unspoken that is not permitted by the lovers' discourse. For example: "MAKE MORE FIERCE AND MAKE SEXUALITY STRONGER. THIS IS THE TIME FOR ALL PRISONERS TO RUN WILD. YOU ARE THE BLACK ANNOUNCERS OF OUR DEATH. (BE SUCH TIME YOUNG HORSES OF ATTILA THE HUN. OH ANNOUNCERS WHO US SEND DEATH.)" (23).

Violence, strength, and wildness are antidotes to the prison created by the lovers' discourse and by all the other scripts and discourses by which consciousness is culturally generated. Janey notes as she begins "a book report" on *The Scarlet Letter* that "we all live in prison. Most of us don't know we live in prison" (65). Much of Acker's fiction is precisely about the struggle of the writer and of the individual to contend against imprisoning cultural forces of one kind or another. Janey, however, is about to be packed off to yet another institution that victimizes—boarding school. Having in her childhood come to the schismatic consciousness of the incest participant—"ME NO LONGER MYSELF"—she will hereafter experience herself, her sexuality, and her lovers within the double bind of desire and self-abasement.

In the novel's second section, "The Scorpions," we encounter Janey's adolescent gang. Its members constitute what she has of a family, given the absence of her father, who even stops sending support payments after a while. Less sentimentally, the Scorpions are collective violence against normalizing influences even though, in the end, they fall into the cliché of a rock band killed in a spectacular van crash: "We don't hate, understand, we have to get back. Fight the dullness of shit society. Alienated robotized images. Here's your cooky, ma'am. No to anything but madness" (35). In typical Acker fashion, the seriousness of protest is laced with Janey's compliance with the economic realities of earning a living (she works in a bakery, hence the cookie).

What also is typically Acker is the narrative structure of this important section. Unkind to the casual reader, the narrative neither follows one thread nor signals its transitions. Metaphors fail to describe fairly—it is not exactly layered, because no one thread is higher than another; it is not as continuous as a multistranded cable or rope, not as orchestrated as polyphony, not as staged as choral reading. Perhaps it is most like riding along a country road with someone who keeps changing the channels. We come to recognize the stations to be heard, and we feel that there are important relationships to be drawn from the juxtapositions that occur. We do not have the illusion that they add up to a whole that is coherent by the standards of the formalists. But the juxtapositions do seem to compose the collective but disparate babble that constitutes the consciousness of the contemporary subject.

Among the "stations" to be heard in this one section are life with the Scorpions, a long important dream, an abortion, a shoplifting incident, a treatise on visionary dreams, scenes inside an East Village bakery, sex with a pickup, a multiple-fatality crash, and assorted theoretical and historical bubbles floating by, presumably from Janey's reading. Taken together, these elements arraign the forces hemming in Janey and complicating her effort to establish her own zone of Being. The crash, if a bit melodramatic, serves well metaphorically to mark the tactical hopelessness of the punk rebellion of the Scorpions—chased by the police, blazing toward a red light, they have the ultimate encounter with the disciplinary side of the Law. Even before the police car kicks in after them, they live lives of unquiet desperation. Tommy, Janey's boyfriend, is a case in point:

Tommy was a SCORPION
He was an intellectual criminal.
He believed his plans worked and they did.
He couldn't see reality beyond his plans.
He was too smart to believe his plans.
Totally scared out of his mind in the blackness no ground SPLIT.
(42)

A smart player, Tommy can devise functional plans, but he is caught in that difficult space of being too smart to believe his own fictions but not smart enough to develop a saving analysis of the reality beyond them. Crime is both literal, as in the shoplifting incident, and a metaphor for trying to think or do for one's own ends against the social determinations of one's Being. An outsider, necessarily a predator (scorpion), Tommy encounters the "blackness no ground" of one who steps outside convention.

The abortion clinic to which Janey must go (because all her boyfriends "refused to use condoms") seems to be run by Nazi dentists, and the patients are harassed by guilt, pain, callousness, and pointless punishing lectures deflated by Janey's asides ("A female can use any of the many methods of birth control, all of which don't work or deform"). The bakery is full of snooty or all but psychotic customers and coworkers badgering Janey, who becomes in the dialogues the "Lousy Mindless Salesgirl": "Because I work I am nobody" (38).

The dream and the shoplifting incidents may be the most revealing evocations of Janey's impossible position. Carefully groomed for her trip to Bloomingdale's, she manages to walk out in a leopard coat, itself a nice symbol of the independent predator reduced to a commodity (reduced moreover to a layer, a covering, that is part of "the look" of that era). What makes this incident charged, however, is the way it trades the narrative line back and forth with an especially rich dream.

In her dream, Janey visits Daddy and his girlfriend at Richard Nixon's favorite Laguna Beach hotel, a stark ultramodern affair:

> Of course, daddy and Sally and the boys in his band are given their rooms first. My room is the room no one else in the world wants.
>
> My bedroom is the huge white hexagon in the front left corner of the hotel. It has no clear outside or inside or any architectural regularity. Long white pipes form part of its ceiling. Two of its sides, which two is always changing, are open.
>
> My bedroom's function is also unclear. Its only furniture is two barber's chairs and a toilet. It's a gathering place for men.
>
> Hotel men dressed in white and black come in and want to hurt me. They cut away parts of me. I call for the hotel head. He explains that my bedroom used to be the men's toilet. I understand.
>
> My cunt used to be a men's toilet.
>
> I walk out in a leopard coat. (36)

Janey's space is an unwanted, undifferentiated, barely finished, vulnerable, uncomfortable, and alien place in which she is always exposed as spectacle and subject to piecemeal possession by whichever males choose to hurt her. The hotel's black-and-white decor suggests the black-and-white logic of the empowered versus the Other, the binary opposition in mastery, management, and control, just as its austere geometry suggests the reductive effects of that logic. The narrative timing of her leopard coat suggests the peculiar mix of predator and sex object which she is forced to become by gender roles that assign her no easy route to pleasure, except by complying with the peremptory control of the boy who picks her up a bit later.

A final element in this section concerns dreams and visions, Janey's one point of access to the possibility of something different from the scenarios of gender, economics, and political subjection readied for her. Her dreams "are the only thing that matters"; they are her "hope" because they "are rawness and wildness, the colors, the scents, passion, events appearing"—they are access to a self that is not already disciplined and delimited. "Dreams cause the vision world to break loose our consciousness," even "destroy us," although "once we have gotten a glimpse of the vision world, we must be careful not to think the vision world is us. We must go farther and become crazier" (36–37). Janey is neither André Breton seeking Nadja nor Tommy content to live in "his plans." She is serious about Foucault's End of Man: "Every day a sharp tool, a powerful destroyer, is necessary to cut away dullness, lobotomy, buzzing, belief in human beings, stagnancy, images, and accumulation. As soon as we stop believing in human beings, rather know we are dogs and trees, we'll start to be happy" (37). The passage is obviously more hopeful than Foucault would care to be about getting outside the culturally determined "dullness" of human beings, of overcoming the "lobotomy" that prevents a being-of-the-body.

The van crash, however, cuts short this first of the novel's three major parts. At its conclusion, Janey is "Outside High School," and what she finds there is even worse than the proverbial cold cruel world. This second part sets four major zones against one another in a powerful mix: an early measure of her vision world; her imprisonment by a white-slave trader, who teaches her to be a prostitute (the section is called, acidly enough, "Janey becomes a woman"); her poetry (in both Persian and English); and her "book report," a rewriting of *The Scarlet Letter*. Janey moves beyond family and friends to the ever-larger institutions of myth, education, language, and literature.

The myth material is divided into six pages of dream/vision maps and the fable of the monster (female, of course) and the beaver (with whom she lives in domestic cliché), their little pet rat, and a hungry, lonely bear, who is the independent, nomadic counterpoint to the monster's domestic version of Woman. The power roles, neuroses, and the monster's fixation upon their treacherous pet rat make the domestic side of the fable fairly standard. Much less so is the role of the bear, who comes to the house in a midwinter hunger. Unable to get in out of the cold, the sad bear sits desiring the dream of happy comfort embodied in the house shared by the others. Seeing a Pegasus creature killed by people, the bear feels trapped: "He knew if he left this bondage, there'd be nothing else left in the world" (55). This unsubtle vision of Janey's predicament is followed by "The bear's vision of blackness," in which the whole universe turns black: "You, the thing you called 'you,' was a ball turning and turning in the blackness only the blackness wasn't something—like 'black'—and it wasn't nothingness 'cause nothingness was somethingness. . . . You don't know what to do cause there's nothing, 'cause there's not even nothing" (55). "Your self," we learn, "is a ball turning and turning as it's being thrown from one hand to the other hand," and the bear emerges from this with a wild Nietzschean joy of release from the prescripted "you" he has come to see as "ephemeral." He sings a song ("I don't have to do anything / everything lives") of release, sprouts wings and flies away out of the grasp, we assume, of the agents of culture, for whom even "nothing" serves as a place holder for the space of metaphysics.

The dream maps consist of three two-page spreads of drawn and hand-lettered fairy tales, visions, and dreams—three zones in which the mind labors to resolve, at least imaginatively, the contradictions of experience. We can locate the house where monster and beaver live in the fairy tale, we can see the dream's disguises of bodily sensations and threatening phalluses and liberating journeys and enclosing spaces, and we can follow the vision's play of Baba against the god of changes, the god of underwater, and Janey's desire for a permanent lover (expressed as "I want you to be my life" but also literally canceled in order to mark her entrapment in the bear's similar initially contradictory state of desire, the very trap that would preclude desire's satisfaction). We can spot these things, that is, but had better not try to do so linearly. The maps must be read relationally rather than linearly, as an Ambience of the Unconscious documenting the sedimentation of individual psychology; cultural motifs such as economics, politics, gender, philosophy, literature, mores, ritual, sacrament; and the whole list of structures organizing and disciplining experience.

Janey's mind still struggles to contain such experiences as her father's attempt to have sex with her. In one of the dreams responding to this incestuousness, Janey is on a street at night, terrified at a "huge jellyfish worm, translucent, almost like vomit. no eyes cause no brain. huge pink tongue and sharper than shark teeth, the most frightening being and gets more and more so. fills up the whole street to the blue sky." The menace of the patriarchal phallus becomes ambivalent when she *becomes* that "glob" in the second dream, having been caught and killed by the worm and then passing through "an area of almost opaque white, the same color as the worm." This dream of rebirth is ambivalent, because what has happened, apparently, is her assimilation to the stuff of the phallus—language, law, and textuality, if we take the white area as a page, the unitary consciousness she then enacts during the rest of the dream if we are a bit less adventuresome in our interpretation.

Janey is struck with a fear of dying, the consequence of taking on the monumental ego represented by the huge worm she becomes (it is almost as wide as the page), and her dream then erects a series of fences. The most important of these is labeled the "writing fence," and we see there Janey's decision to use writing as her primary weapon from her position of abject vulnerability. That she must protect the very ego that has engulfed whatever she had been before is the irony, for she must fight the phallogocentric battles in which she has been forcibly enlisted, as well as her own guerrilla campaign to fence off some zone not dominated by the fear, vulnerability, and stymied desire that constitute her enlistment bonus. This is a version, in other words, not only of the bear's internal division between wanting freedom and wanting domesticity but also Janey's internal division between wanting the Father and wanting to escape him across these dream map fields or into subsequent relationships when she is back in New York.

Those subsequent relationships tend to repeat the pattern set by the one she has with her father. This repetition should come as no surprise, but Acker works powerfully with the versions of this relationship as Janey shifts us through the other three zones of this important part of the novel. In "The Mysterious Mr. Linker," Janey has been kidnapped from her place in the East Village slums and sold to a white-slave trader who takes on the paternal role of training her to "become a woman." Mr. Linker, born an Iranian beggar boy, hustles his way into the University of Vienna to study psychology with Carl Jung, but his other lines include neurology, lobotomy, materialism, the summer-resort business, culture criticism, and white slavery. He links together a nice round of occupations which suggests the dimensions by which the Father functions as slaver: as psychologist, Mr. Linker both defines normality and counsels individuals toward it; as neurologist and lobotomist, he manipulates the physiological side of medicine as a Foucauldian discipline of power/knowledge; as materialist in the summer-resort business, he cancels religious or mystical antidotes to his capitalist order and turns leisure into a commodity structure; as culture critic and slaver, he polices the creation and reception of art and works to reproduce the relations of production (good Althusserian Ideological State Apparatus [ISA] that he is).

One sample of Mr. Linker's theories will make clear his embodiment of a cultural system that survives through violence and exploitation:

Where does culture come from? I will tell you. It comes from disease. All the great artists, Goethe, Schiller, and Jean-Paul Sartre—
you must read *Nausea* in the French, in English it is nothing—
have said this. They are aware how evil they are. They are aware
this life is truly evil; due to this awareness, they are able to go
beyond. You know that medically, I am a doctor, a body cannot
live without disease. (64–65)

Ever attentive to the forms of Polonian pedantry, Acker deflates Mr.
Linker with his aside, but the real point here is his performance of
the classic argument for the worst manifestations of power: the
threat from an evil empire, the total depravity of the soul, the naturalization of the profit motive in capitalism and constitutions—all
are versions of this self-justifying tactic of patriarchal rhetoric. In
case we miss the point, Janey goes on to tell both Mr. Linker's tale
of his dead wife (she insisted on weaving a wool tapestry despite its
lethal effect on her lungs) and Mrs. Linker's tale (she was driven
crazy and locked up). Perhaps the point is that both Penelope and
the Madwoman are equally pathological products of Mr. Linker's
brand of culture.

Janey's poetry, the third focus of this part, appears in two different forms. *The Persian Poems* are those she writes while held prisoner by Mr. Linker, with whom she falls in love. Partly, they show
her learning this root language of Western culture, a process in
which it seems that *women* are objects interchangeable with *peas-
ants* and *hairs* and similarly stigmatized nouns and that Janey in
particular is frequently the object of its verbs of violence. There are
moments of escape from the regimen of learning Persian ("Janey
hates prison"), and moments when an even larger escape is desired
("Language / to get rid of language"), but more typical are exercise
verses such as "a woman is a dirty / blackhead" and those that
feature her as the object of verbs such as *have, buy, want, beat up,
rob, kidnap,* and *kill.* She finally acquires the ability to write her
own story of pain, both the lesser pain of offering herself to someone
who does not want her and a greater pain: "The biggest pain in the
world is feeling but sharper is the pain of the self."

In these poems, Janey comes to an explicit sense of what being
a female in patriarchal society entails. Her own poetry, both in "A
book report" and in the next section, "Translating," extends this
understanding. In the latter section, redone exercises (Sextus Pro-
pertius, among others) from high-school courses wittily combine
the awkward syntax of inept translations with more work at desublimation. "On the desire for love," for example, is addressed to Slave
Trader: "Then my strong he threw down the drain individuality"
(101). By the time that Janey gets to "The diseased," she treats love
as the means by which she can be forced to drink poison, walk on

coals, stay in prison, do anything—all the motifs of pop songs become bitter complaints about love as the means of internalizing The Man. "He compulsions alone can fetter forces wildness," she writes, testifying both to discipline and the resulting wildness that it generates. As these poems continue, many break down syntactically into voicing sexual desires or into rituals of self-abuse in which Janey smears herself with excrement and proclaims the "end of me me me who is this?" Others are interrupted altogether by meditations such as the following, in which she lays out the cultural trap in which she is caught: "Mind slavery: I want more than just money. I live in a partially human world and I want people to think and feel certain ways about me. So I try to set up certain networks, mental-physical, in time and space to get what I want. (I also set up these networks to get money.) These networks become history and culture (if they work) and as such, turn against me and take away time and space. They tell me what to do" (111). Janey's condition of marginality is radically different in its specifics from, say, Mr. Linker's position, but hers is the one truly typical of the individual in society.

Perhaps the most extraordinary of Janey's poetic texts is a tour-de-force in which two different lines of thought alternate verses down the page. Both cue from the same insight: "Sex in America is S & M" (99), a conclusion reached because "materialistic society had succeeded in separating sex from every possible feeling," thus producing the "sexual revolution" of "robot" lovers. Against the strand that follows the theme of "slavery and prison" is one on "freedom." This second strand takes "the black night [as] an open space that goes on and on . . . a black that is extension and excitement and the possibilities of new consciousness." But if you "open her up," you "find her all gooky and bloody and screaming and angry hurt pain inside": the need for a new consciousness is acute indeed. The voice becomes a contemporary Hester Prynne asking, "How are the lobotomy children supposed to act?" and it ends "all alone in outer space," afraid to have sex with her Reverend Dimwit (as Dimmesdale is renamed).

The same polarities are in evidence in the other voice, which begins with a woman bound, beaten, and sadistically taken. She finally refuses the man she loves "desperately," because "more important than any desperate love [is the] desperate possibility of going out farther, / going out as far as possible in freedom." That last line repeats like a broken record as the other voice ends its track alone in space. A woman is either alone and lost, or with a lover but subjected to a world in which sadistic violence and masochistic self-loathing are built into gender relations. The two tracks cross, making an *X* over possibility.

After the dream myths, Linker's education of Janey, and Janey's poetic experiments with language, the fourth dimension of this part of the novel is Janey's dialogic relation with Hawthorne's masterpiece. We have already seen her poetry address *The Scarlet Letter*, and if the Persian slave trader's prison is a metaphor for the "prison-house" of Western culture, it is a doubly appropriate site for both her writing of poetry and her reading of Hawthorne's novel. Her "book report," as she calls it, pursues its subjects bluntly and without the disguises she thinks Hawthorne needed because "he was living in a society to which ideas and writing still mattered" (66). He had to be careful. Janey is in a different position:

> Right now I can speak as directly as I want 'cause no one gives a shit about writing and ideas, all anyone cares about is money.
> Even if one person in Boise, Idaho, gave half-a-shit, the only book Mr Idaho can get his hands on is a book the publishers, or rather the advertisers ('cause all businessmen are now advertisers) have decided will net half-a-million in movie and/or TV rights. A book that can be advertised. Define culture that way. (66)

As if she had read *Blockbuster* or Kostelanetz's salvos against multinational publishing houses, Janey points to capital as the culprit, as she did in her poem about the materialization of sexual relations.

She takes time out from Hester's tale to splice into her own experience with her father. If sex has been drained of feeling, and culture of value, even morality has been replaced by security:

> My father told me the day after he tried to rape me that security is the most important thing in the world. I told him sex is the most important thing in the world and asked him why he didn't fuck my mother. In Hawthorne's and our materialistic society the acquisition of money is the main goal 'cause money gives the power to make change stop, to make the universe die; so everything in the materialistic society is the opposite of what it really is. Good is bad. Crime is the only possible behavior. (67)

Shades of shoplifting leopard coats in Bloomingdale's. When Acker talks about the "death society," this is what she means: capital erects the monumental, versions of the phallus, in all the spheres in which it seeks "to make change stop" and to preserve its structure. Capital reifies the sensory, not to mention the sensual, and the beings who desire the more fluid existence unreckoned within the patriarchal logic. "Crime," intellectual or material, is the character of free action.

Indeed, when Janey contemplates the fate of women on these crucial pages she makes this point even clearer:

> It's possible to hate and despise and detest yourself 'cause you've been in prison so long. It's possible to get angrier and angrier. It's

possible to hate everything that isn't wild and free. A girl is wild
who likes sensual things: doesn't want to give up things being
alive: rolling in black fur on top of skin ice-cold water iron crinkly
leaves seeing three brown branches against branches full of leaves
against dark green leaves . . . one thing after another thing! . . .
you keep on going, there are really no rules . . . goddamnit make a
living grow up no you don't want to do that. (66–67)

Hating what is not "wild and free" becomes a tactic for opposing
the hegemonic forms of cultural discipline, a resource that enables
the individual to say no when the patriarchal voice invokes its economic ("make a living") and existential ("grow up") sanctions.

At the heart of Janey's thinking about the novel's issues is her
assault upon the culture's conceptual categories. Roger Chillings-
worth and the religious and legal establishment become for her
reminders of how institutions wage their interests against those of
individuals: "Hester's husband's a scholar. A scholar is a top cop
'cause he defines the roads by which people live so they won't get
in trouble and so society will survive. A scholar is a teacher. Teachers replace living dangerous creatings with dead ideas and teach
these ideas as the history and meaning of the world. Teachers torture kids. Teachers teach you intricate ways of saying one thing and
doing something else" (68). When "dead ideas" are naturalized as
"history and meaning," they displace students' privilege to create.
The classics become so strait-jacketed in scholarship that students
can learn to be political conservatives even from reading William
Blake.

When Janey/Hester tries to get out on the roads herself, she
finds that "all the land on both sides of the highway, cultivated and
wild, was private"—Acker links the academy with the reigning distribution of economic resources and privileges—and people, traveling only by technological marvels, can no longer get off the roads.
"Everyone's a slave" of an educational process that serves the pleasure of the power elite (Acker attaches an obscenity to the aims of
Hester's judges). The process works, as we have seen repeatedly,
partly by discipline, and partly by simulation, replacing experience
with drive-in services until reactions as extreme as punk are required: "The roads are getting so super-paved and big and light and
loaded with BIG MACS and HOWARD JOHNSONS that the only time people are forced into danger or reality is when they die. Death is the
only reality we've got left in our nicey-nicey-clean-ice-cream-TV
society so we'd better worship it. S & M sex. Punk rock" (94). The
bitter ironies cover the fact that her requirements are relatively simple. She wants something other than a friendship defined as Chil-
lingsworth's predatory relationship with Dimmesdale, or a married
couple defined as "one who loves plus one who lets love"; at the

very least, she wants love that would let her "write myself between your lips and between your thighs" (94–95).

She finds that she lacks the power to create this state of affairs or to write that sentence. Dimmesdale owns the language, and its deep kernel is simple: "You'd. Verb. Me." Still, the utopian impulses will not quite die: "People have and can change the world. In the beginning, on the desert island, the world was totally beautiful. Today in my room in New York City the world is horrible and disgusting. What the hell happened?" (69).

The novel is all about what happened, and the emotional close to this primary part of it is when Janey plants her utopian vision in a writer's time capsule: "I live in pain, but one day, Hawthorne said, I'm going to be happy I'm going to be so happy even if I'm not alive anymore. There's going to be a world where the imagination is created by joy not suffering, a man and a woman can love each other again they can kiss and fuck again (a woman's going to come along and make this world for me even though I'm not alive anymore)" (100). Dreamers, Janey concludes, "must be unhappy criminals," and, in the novel's final part, when she sets out on "A journey to the end of night," the unhappy criminal she accompanies is a godfather of the new writing, Jean Genet.

This third part of the novel ends with a long pictorial visionary narrative in which Janey mixes Mayan and Egyptian motifs, among others. She gambles with a figure who metamorphoses from Catullus to the devil in order to get a book about "human transformation" that allows her an ironic death and rebirth. Janey's mixture of pain and lust, victimization and aspiration, becomes prototypical for Woman. Janey can achieve an understanding of her existential dilemma, but the knowledge does not allow her to transcend its conditions, despite all the transformations between alligator and bird which are negotiated in this visionary material. The constraints of culture remain in force, for though "we create this world in our own image," the novel's persistent critiques place "image" securely in the context of patriarchal constructs.

Two passages express the social wisdom that Janey achieves while wandering across Egypt with Genet, wisdom that keeps her final utopian visions ironic rather than triumphant. One such vision occurs during a visit to a brothel:

> In Alexandria women are low and these are the lowest there are.
> For them there is no class struggle, no movements of the left, and no right-wing terror because all the men are fascists. All the men own all the money. A man is a walking mass of gold.
>
> The rooms are done in gold. . . . The scene is two whores talking professionally. It is clear that the whores regard what most people regard as (them)selves as images. Sex, that unblocked meeting of selves, is the most fake thing there is. (129)

Gender and socioeconomics are in complete alignment, and for the women, at least, selfhood is a class luxury, and the image—the created specular object—is the only form of Being. Interpersonal authenticity is therefore the ultimate fakery, and its (false) promise is a powerful means of inducing compliance with the voided politics Janey describes.

Later in her wanderings, Janey winds up working in a rich man's fields, an interesting metaphor in itself. She complains to Sahih, the foreman, that "for 2,000 years you've had the nerve to tell women who we are. We use your words; we eat your food. Every way we get money has to be a crime. We are plagiarists, liars, and criminals" (132). Her jailer's comment a bit later sums up the novel's desublimation of patriarchal energies: "I realize you when I tell you who you are. I realize you by judging you. I love you, Janey, when I beat you up" (134). His devastating triad matches point for point that of Janey: as a plagiarist of patriarchal sign systems, she articulates her Being within the values of those systems, as she did earlier in her work with dream maps. As one who can only therefore be a liar, neither "her own" woman nor a "real" man, she is caught in the primary cultural contradiction of that systemic master narrative. As one who thus exceeds its limits and categories, its social and economic roles, she is necessarily criminal in every step she takes. She is both beloved difference and beaten criminal.

"Having any sex in the world is having to have sex with capitalism" (135), because one can find no easy way beyond the grip of the powerful institutions, mores, and media forms that enforce capitalism's materializing, devaluing cultural logic. As a child under the starry skies, whirling around, Janey notices that "the whole universe is starting to revolve like a giant wheel. This wheel isn't a thing: it is everything. Everything is on the surface. That everything is me: I'm just surface: surface is surface" (97). Recognizing that her perspective is not cosmic or universal but perspectival, she also realizes the absence of traditional metaphysical depth in the "I" of subjectivity. Instead, she intensely feels the pagelike surface on which the cultural grammar spells out the sentence of her selfhood. Later, she is similarly demystifying when she observes that "you is just vibrations so there's no difference between self and music" (122): both are compositions of a cultural poetics whose worst features this novel focuses upon with a wise and bitter irony.

### "All I Want Is a Taste of Your Lips, Boy"

Acker ends *Blood and Guts in High School* by rhyming "hips" (as in, I like the way you move yours) with "lips," a bit of pop lyric which attests to her desire to link the organic and textual. When she returns to fiction after some other projects, notably her libretto,

*The Birth of the Poet* (a 1981 work included in *Wordplays 5* [New York: PAJ Publications, 1986], 305–34), it is with *Great Expectations* (1982). This novel joins a more militant practice of appropriation (or "Plagiarism," as she calls the first division) with the social analysis just discussed, and it also begins to develop the equally detailed study of language and textuality which climaxes in *My Death, My Life*. Very early in *Great Expectations*, she interrupts a steamy sex scene without warning to explain "that's why one text must subvert (the meaning of) another text until there's only background music like reggae: the inextricability of relation-textures the organic (not meaning) recovered" (15).

Reggae is specifically designed in the mixing room with sounds all up and down the sound spectrum and with an especially organic rhythm section; played in its early days mainly at outdoor sessions on huge sound systems, the tones hit the body head to toe with special impact from the bass and percussion right at hip level. Acker's appropriation subverts textuality that is canonical with one that recovers not meaning but that "organic" utopian dimension which Acker imagined in *Blood and Guts in High School* when she wanted to forget human beings and "know we are dogs and trees." Opposing the reggae beat to high culture's Meaning makes tangible not only the body rhythms of the music but also all the other "relation-textures" of the body politic.

Acker's aesthetic principles are more explicitly in evidence in this novel than in most of her fiction, and we begin with the existential rationale behind her art:

> If everything is living, it's not a name but moving. And without
> this living there is nothing; this living is the only matter matters.
> The thing itself. This isn't an expression of a real thing: this is the
> thing itself. Of course the thing itself the thing itself it is never the
> same. This is how aestheticism can be so much fun. The living
> thing the real thing is not what people tell you it is: it's what it is.
> This is the thing itself because I'm finding out about it it is me. It
> is a matter of letting (perceiving) happen what will. (63)

The obvious echoes of Stein are probably more attitudinal than filial in their relation to Stein's meditations on language and things, but the colloquial tone should not distract us from the seriousness with which Acker, like Stein, felt the connection between recovering the "thingness" of things from language and recovering the organic and the "me" of her Being from gender roles.

Also like Stein, Acker finds the work of Paul Cézanne and the cubists crucial in understanding the real potential of narrative in our century. As Acker explains after quite a discourse about the artist and desire, Cézanne allowed the question of there being simultaneous viewpoints, and thereby destroyed forever in art the possibility of a static representation or portrait. The Cubists went further. They found the means of making the forms of all objects similar. If everything was rendered in the same terms, it became possible to paint the interactions between them. These interactions became so much more interesting than that which was being portrayed that the concepts of portraiture and therefore of reality were undermined or transferred. (81–82)

This passage is vital to understanding the fictional practice of Acker, because her performance of "simultaneous viewpoints" is multiform and indispensable to her kind of analysis. Whether we are discussing imploding an appropriated text, voicing both the hegemonic and the marginalized, or hearing the multiplicity of voices within, we find Bakhtinian "heteroglossia" with a vengeance. The "same terms" in Acker's work are the generally poststructural social analyses by which she is able to recognize these voices, their institutional affiliations, and their internal conflicts. There *is* something of a sameness to Acker's novels, but as we move from book to book we continue to learn more about the "interactions" among all the ideologemes she identifies, as well as those among the various conveyances of that ideological content. The traditional senses of both "portrayal" and "reality" are undermined when Acker reveals them to be ideological closures, containments of the "living dangerous creatings" that Acker valorizes. She "transfers" our concern for identity in portraiture to an encounter with the multiplicity of identity and with the cultural contradictions that alienate the fragmented social and individual polity. The cubist planes in *her* portraiture cannot be intellectually resolved by the master viewer. Moreover, she transfers our concern for unity and wholeness in plot design to an encounter not with the totalizations of this or that ideological containment of difference, but rather with the "relation-textures" of the patterns of interaction among the genders, classes, desires, and disciplines experienced by her characters.

Acker makes these transfers plain a bit later in the novel when she splices sexuality, as it is formed in the culture, with writing:

We shall define sexuality as that which can't be satisfied and therefore as that which transforms the person.

(Stylistically: simultaneous contrasts, extravagancies, incoherences, half-formed misshapen thoughts, lousy spelling, what signifies what? What is the secret of this chaos?

(Since there's no possibility, there's play. Elegance and completely filthy sex fit together. Expectations that aren't satiated.)

Questioning is our mode. (107)

These stylistic markers could be derived from the sort of reviews that are insensitive to Acker's work or to the cultural paradigm within which it makes sense. But this argument is more than a defense of her tactics. To say that there is "no possibility" is to abandon the metaphysical nostalgia for the "transcendental signified," for a foundational or originary meaning that anchors the textual (and existential) flux. Her "play" is as deadly serious as Derrida's, because "questioning" as an intellectual "mode" is what keeps change, movement, fluidity, the whole experiential realm from reifying within a given ideological closure.

Neither sexual nor intellectual nor aesthetic expectations can be "satiated" when we have so filtered a sense of the complex "interactions" of the features of our collective life. Even the idea of satiation is of a piece with the motifs of completion and plenitude which Acker undermines—onto the body's experience of pleasure, culture grafts the image of absolute satisfaction as a performance standard. That is why "incoherences" are labor, are productive, are a form of questioning which pries loose the conceptual boundaries (between, say, "elegance and completely filthy sex") that we have so profoundly naturalized in our language, our institutions, our mores, and our formal conventions. Simultaneous but unresolved internal and social contrasts keep inescapable the contradictions that unreflective reviewers seem not to appreciate.

"Art," after all, "is the elaboratings of violence" (123), at least for those who use it analytically, as does Acker, to desublimate the violent conditioning of the organic in the individual. Her task is not easy. "I'm going to tell you something," the narrator pauses to explain. "The author of the work you are now reading is a scared little shit" (70). She is scared because she is compelled to rely upon "a language that I speak and can't dominate, a language that strives fails and falls silent can't be manipulated, language is always beyond me me me. Language is silence" (96). However skillful she becomes in elaborating the violent interactions of her disciplinary culture, however effective she becomes at teaching us to understand the "incoherences" to be heard only from the position of the Other, she is still dependent upon a medium that is beyond both her domination and, finally, *her*. Language is a "not-me" that stays that way, empty of *her* meaning, silent on *her* account.

Language can render the interactional matrices of the culture, but not some "me" apart from those matrices. The black hole of her narrator's fears is that this "me" is at best physiological, and that the only "me" she really encounters is the one always already implicated in the problems that she elucidates. Why fiction, then, instead of silence? Because it *is* both her medium and her.

There is just moving and there are different ways of moving. Or: there is moving all over at the same time and there is moving linearly. If everything is moving-all-over-the-place-no-time, anything is everything. If this is so, how can I differentiate? How can there be stories? Consciousness just is: no time. But any emotion presupposes differentiation. Differentiation presumes time, at least BEFORE and NOW. A narrative is an emotional moving.

It's a common belief that something exists when it's part of a narrative.

Self-reflective consciousness is narrational. (58)

She is "scared" because she knows that "anything *is* everything," that the notion of identity as a discrete entity is a story we tell to differentiate consciousness from the "just is" that lurks "beyond me," beyond culture.

For story to mean at all, for story to *be* at all, it must depend upon language and the sociohistorical layerings and texturing of "emotion"—that is, upon a system of interactions which assimilates organismic twitches to the codings of laws, hierarchies, and other cultural forms. From that system derives the differentiation that produces time, that produces emotion, that produces narrative form, that produces consciousness. Perhaps the only difference between the reflexive and nonreflexive consciousness is knowing precisely this gulf between the "just is" and the domain of culture where we have our origin. If marking this gap dashes the Great Expectations of a species that has always wanted to place its origins and its nature in the hands of a surer ground than that of fiction, it is, at least, not the first time such expectations have been dashed.

*My Death, My Life* (London: Pan Books, 1983) features Pier Paolo Pasolini's effort to solve the mystery of his own life and death, and is hence a book important to Acker's efforts to pursue the implications of dashing our metaphysical expectations about ourselves and of the need to continue quite on our own. As is the case with much of Acker's fiction, the body is an ultimate test of the complexities in which her narrator finds herself. Almost emblematic of Acker's fiction is the doubly parenthesized kernel sentence of many of her more sensational protests: "((the body, the body, that which is present, is the source of everything, and it has been made to disappear)" (278). But her more mature work sets next to this raw appeal an increasingly sophisticated analysis of what is at stake in the body's critique of culture. If *Great Expectations* becomes almost religious in pushing the dark envelope of identity and values, *My Death, My Life* aggressively pursues its own approach to the fundamentals of life and death fully informed by various patches of poststructural theory stitched into its narrative quilt.

Normal behavior is repression, so the paraphrase of one part of Acker's argument would run. One representative passage on this score occurs in an exchange of letters between Charlotte and Emily Brontë (though in our time), with Acker's narrator taking the more asocial Emily's part: "Whenever I talk to one of my friends I perceive my friend is even lonelier than I am because he's less willing than I am himself to see the loneliness horror and awkwardness: solitude: nothing: what I call 'the actual state of existence.' These people have to act normal to avoid seeing what really is, because if they did see like my father the day he was dying they wouldn't be able to bear it because it's not bearable" (333). But not bearing this unbearable burden is much of what this book is about. Acting normal is the last thing that any of Acker's narrators could tolerate in their efforts precisely *to* see. The narrator makes clear that her reading and writing necessarily emerge from the marginal status to which her tactics consign her. She even cites Theodor Adorno from her reading on these matters: "What is writing about; what is writing? If it is anything: Adorno 'Art expresses the individual, the unique, the utopian, the critical, the new, the innovative vision' and is the opposite of opposes media advertising commerciality or the market" (338). These lines are good cues to the list of more specific concerns which this novel addresses, but they also loosely link Acker's work to other theoretical programs on the Left. Art seeks to reverse a certain determination of the individual which reduces it to blind desires or to the charade of normality we have just seen:

> I no longer need to be told or given art in order to perceive what they want me to perceive.
>     This is my last thought before I disappear: I'm living without emotions because desire's the only thing that can save me.
>     That's it. I can no longer speak. I've been trained to be catatonic or a dog. I might as well tell you the same story again and again. (288)

Acutely conscious of herself as a cultural product ("By buying [eating] I'm bought [eaten]. *I* am the commodity"), the narrator sees the contestatory part of herself dwindle down to a desire therefore revolutionary in its potential but also painfully reductive for the evaporating "I" of the text. Hence, as in *Great Expectations*, Acker again and again retells the ideological master narrative whose many subplots are her stories.

*My Death, My Life* thus completes the more theoretical work begun in *Great Expectations* by gathering radical insights through a now-classic Acker tactic: rewriting the classics. She redoes *Macbeth* by placing the British in Ireland and changing Macbeth into The Porter, thereby occasioning some interesting class markers, much humor, and a good deal of theoretical profit. Mrs Porter, given to blunt declamations, reads imperialism's subtler mechanisms quite clearly: "In this century what we know as 'natural' our conquerors have invented as their identities and use as a tool to control us" (359). This pithy distillation of the ideological function of a whole range of naturalized assumptions, particularly stressing the hegemonic uses of Identity, is one way of concretizing writing's opposition to media mythmaking. Purely fictive assumptions can be rewritten, and a fluid sense of identity disrupts a powerful tool of normalization.

Shortly before this, amidst a bit of family history mixed with the 1956 student uprisings in Poland, the narrator turns to Jean Baudrillard for help in working out the implications of the widening "separations between signifiers and signifieds": "In the case of language and of economy the signified and the actual objects have no value don't exist or else have only whatever values those who control the signifiers assign to them. Language is making me sick. Unless I destroy the relations between language and their signifieds that is, their control" (340–41). Meaning has gone commercial and floats with the market. Moreover, language carries a social pathology into individual consciousness, and certainly into one whose position by class and gender does not privilege her. But this version of Baudrillard's notion of sign value has more hope than does Baudrillard because she is willing to contemplate disrupting the controlling relations between the medium and the particular ideological set that "they" maintain.

The narrator even goes so far as to test the classic humanistic resource of creative projects taken in good faith—intentions that would counter "their signifieds": "The value of this life is what I make or do. I live in absolute loneliness. What's the value of this life which is painful if it's not what I make or do in the world? Assumption of this question: I am the subject of the making and doing. I make (my) values or meanings. *I do* means *I mean*" (341). Her "absolute loneliness" is the writer's fate, as she notes at a number of points; the Cause absorbs her personal energies and makes her "a Puritan; I write; I don't love; *I*." But she cannot act normally on this faith; she also knows that the assumption she isolates here is suspect and that the conclusion of her reasoning is a grim reminder of the "scared" narrator of *Great Expectations*:

> But what if *I* isn't the subject, but the object? If the subject-object dichotomy is here an inappropriate model?
>
> (Note: the war is now, further than the body or sensible fact, on the language level.)
>
> I don't mean. I am meant. That's ridiculous. There's no meaning. Is meaning a post-capitalist invention?
>
> The shits have made me. The shits have determined the sick bad relations of these parts sexually to each other. What I'm trying

to say is that I can't just say, well human lives have always been miserable pain is just another event like shitting. Be above it (no meaning). (341)

The conceptual categories are themselves part of the problem and the narrator's war moves beyond the body to language itself in her attempts to disrupt what makes her its object. This war even moves to the very category of meaning itself as she recognizes how problematic it has become—it is part of the arsenal of the "post-capitalist" managerial types, but it is also what keeps her from the very state of abstraction and valuelessness which characterizes the era of market-economy sign values. *How* meaning has been used is the problem, and the narrator's hope is to turn it back from a semiotic category assimilated to ideological ends toward the organic, bodily, sensory domain of use value. "Meaning" and "no meaning" coincide in postindustrial semiotics, and Acker's strategy is to recover the difference by desublimating the repressed, agitating among the colonized, and melting down the reified through her "hot connection" to her readers.

One example of this strategy is when Juliet breaks down halfway through a rewritten *Romeo and Juliet*, unable to continue speaking English. She has just dipped again into James Joyce's *Ulysses* for one of the moments of home-rule anxiety, and she speaks bitterly about a home rule in gender relations: "Je suis à bout de mes forces. Les hommes sont des bébés. Ils doivent pronouncer la réalité, déclarer à moi qu'il est necessaire pour moi faire d'accord avec leurs grandes modèles de la réalité, et à la même temps mentir. Leurs mensonges ne sont pas intelligents. Par conséquent leurs mensonges nous insultent et nous rennent incapables de le langage parler" (268). This specifically feminist slant on the issue resists a regime of pain as normal and is willing to contest seriously at the level of language for a different cultural logic.

Midway through *Macbeth*, The Play's Writer offers a grisly metaphor for this new narrative logic: "What's AIDS? A virus. A virus' seemingly unknowable who gets identity by preying on an entity, a cell. Writers whose identities depend on written language're viruses. I'm trying to break down the social immune system. Even this sentence's false" (385).

If identity is that cultural construct within which the individual experiences both thought and the body, then writers are as dependent as anyone else on language. But this writer knows that she is a virus, and the entity on which she preys is the collection of "grandes modèles de la réalité" which we have seen Acker appropriate and infect, even those at so culturally subliminal a level as that of language itself and the kind of consciousness or identity it constitutes. Viruses are noteworthy, moreover, for not only dwelling like foreign bodies inside a host but also programming the very DNA of that host.

The rest of *My Life, My Death* examines a number of perennial Acker issues in which she works toward altering the ability of the cultural entity to suppress the radical virus that she introduces. If suburbia is a "social immune system" against change and difference, Acker's fiction functions as a very busy antilogic. The corruption of art by the commodity system, the necrophilic dimension of gender relations which "kills" one for the benefit of the other, the interactions among the various discourses and institutions with which we come in contact—these critiques are pursued in a remarkable quilt of perceptively recast appropriations, which are cut and sewn antithetically to any formalist preconceptions of order, coherence, or unity.

The novel repeatedly returns to one or another form of the basic dilemma that we face in trying to rethink and alter culture so fundamentally from the necessarily inland site of Acker's viral guerrilla campaign. Profoundly attentive to the double bind out of which she must work, she says quite directly: "Right now either a female dies of exhaustion cause she can't be a male and a female and live without love or else she's still in prison only now she knows she's in prison. Fighting against what's unchanging" (348–49). A woman either violates gender roles altogether and finds herself outside the only structure that culture provides for desire, or she complies knowingly with an impossible script in which that desire is bruised, deflected, and transformed. Either way, she loses—heterosexual love is too permeated with the motifs of power and violence to really satisfy, but the writer who chooses to fight finds the institutional resources seemingly boundless and their forms "unchanging." But the metaphor of the virus holds the promise of reprogramming those forms from within. Perhaps in that promise Acker has suggested how to connect the sensuousness of moving hips with the lips that engage in the heated battle of language, and in a way far more effective than that of a pop song whose political content remains unconscious and thus unspoken.

### Don Quixote's Insurgent Writing

This section might well have been called "Night, Knight," both as Acker's facetious sign-off from her London expatriation and, more importantly, as the pun she relentlessly works. The pun places her female Knight of La Mancha in the Night of the American soul, dreaming the female imaginary as it has been constituted and attempting to glimpse something about the resolution of its contradictions. The knight's "crazy" vision is that of finding love, "love" serving as the sign for the knight's utopian vision (or, perhaps, uto-

pian *glance*, because something less than a social blueprint emerges).
Her vision is crazy because it requires a radical revision of what
counts as "whole" or "sane." The book's mood is richly evoked at a
high point of the section "I dream my schooling," in which Acker
gives a desublimated version of one woman's cultural education. In
attendance are her teacher (the "old creep"), her nomadic associates
(the pirate dogs), and the corpse of Duranduran (who, dying, asked
the creep to cut out his heart, perhaps an indication of the self-evis-
ceration of the pop generation). The novel opens with a quote from
the teacher:

> "The political mirror of this individual simultaneity of freedom
> and imprisonment is a state of fascism and democracy: the United
> States of America.
> "What is your choice?"
> I was stunned. "I have a choice?" I asked, though I had no idea
> what I meant by what I was saying, for I was stunned.
> "Since you have no choice and you must choose," the old creep
> answered, "this is what being *enchanted* means—tell me: who are
> you?"
> "Who can I be?" I looked at the victimizer and his victim, who
> were tied to each other by friendship. I have started to cry and I
> cannot stop crying,
> for those who, having nothing, homeless,
> would flee,
> but there is nowhere to flee;
> so we travel like pirates
> on shifting mixtures of something and nothing.
> For those who in the face of this mixture
> act with total responsibility:
> I cried so much I bothered everyone around me.
> "She—"
> Upon hearing this, all the dogs barked.
> "*She* who can tell us who victimizers are, *She* who can see and
> tell us because *She*'s loony because *She* has become the ancient
> art of madness, or literature. *She* is in front of us right now." (187)

Having to choose when there is no real choice is Acker's analysis of her characters' existential double bind and what they struggle,
though stunned, to articulate. Having to flee when there is no utopian space to reach, driven to the cultural piracy of appropriation in
order to speak at all, proceeding not on the solid ground of authoritative truth but rather on the "shifting mixtures" of sensory and
historical somethings and the nothings of cultural fictions, the
knight becomes the one whose crying texts disturb everyone around
her. But she is also the one who can name the victimizers, the
enchanters by whose brutal logic she appears "loony" and against

whom all her outlaw techniques (appropriation, pornography, fragmentation, transforming narrators, mixed genres, and so forth) are the only resources. Avatar of "the ancient art of madness," Acker's Don Quixote is mad only by the lights of the logic she opposes and frequently transgresses.

In the section "Texts of Wars for Those Who Live in Silence," Acker defines the logic of the enchanters through an ideological reading of a film in which Megalon meets Godzilla, among other elements floating through (a somewhat fuller version, called "Scenes of World War III," is in Richard Prince's collection, *Wild History*). Before the rewrite of that film gets underway, Catherine reverses roles with Heathcliff and is the one in *Wuthering Heights* to go off adventuring for "life." A type of Acker's Don, Catherine is clear about what she wants: "The liberty for love, the liberty for instinctual roamings, the liberty for friendship, the liberty for hatred, the liberty for fantasy: all of these have faded" (69). She knows that "males dumber than nonhuman animals're running the economic and political world," and her own motto is that "civilization and culture are the rules of males' greeds."

In the middle of reading the film, the narrator imagines a dialogue between Megalon and Godzilla, who become types for Reason—"the monsters created from human beliefs and acts will no longer follow human orders," but instead become an all but invisible regime under which "those who live in silence" must labor unconscious of the regime within. Arguing that "all qualities have been and are reduced to quantitative equivalences," the monsters conclude that "this process inheres in the concept of reason" (72). Although reason "signifies the idea of a free, human, social life," at least in the intentions of its more benign champions, it also "adjusts the world" and "has no function other than the preparation of the object from mere sensory material in order to make it that material of subjugation."

The monsters then collapse the distinction between a beneficent reason and its more sinister form:

> Instrumental or ossified reason takes two forms: technological reason developed for purposes of dominating nature and social reason directed at the means of domination aimed at exercising social and political power.
>
> This tendency . . . now pervades all the spheres of human life: this exploitation or reduction of reality to self-preservation and the manipulable other has become the universal principle of a society which seeks to reduce all phenomena to this enlightenment, ideal of rationalism, or subjugation of the other. (72)

The Don is the voice of that subjugated other, and what she contests is precisely her reduction to a "manipulable" silence. The novel's cacophony is the disruption of that ideological silence and a voicing of the heteroglossiac multitudes within. "Who can I be?" we saw her asking a bit ago; the answer throughout *Don Quixote* is one who carries on despite the contradictions we found emerging from our look at *My Death, My Life*. She tilts with the windmills of an "unchanging" culture in which reason is so naturalized an invention that it is barely possible to budge it aside in order to let other human dimensions share the scene of consciousness.

The Don knows that "International finance (that is, American finance) is a war strategy" (73) fought not just in international trade but against and within the silenced ones. The Don, who opens the novel in another one of Acker's gruesome abortion scenes, uses the image of abortion several times to represent lives cut short both existentially and in terms of their levels of awareness. "The bloody outline of a head on every desk in the world. The bloody outline of alienated work. The bloody outline of foetuses" (122). We are all aborted foetuses. The Don's job is to discover the many forms of this state, hence she uses the image differently for herself. As the outlaw who *is* aware because she has voiced so much from her marginality, she passes the point at which the languages available to her allow her to say directly what she finds on her quixotic quest. Hence "I am a mass of dreams desires which, since I can no longer express them, are foetuses beyond their times, not even abortions" (194).

However restless some reviewers may have become with Acker's fiction of indirection, its strategy is essential if readers are to experience *in reading* the breaks, fissures, and contradictions within Western reason's ideological arrangement of reality. Appropriation leaps from *Wuthering Heights* to Megalon, from Shakespeare to Hawthorne, from Baudrillard to de Sade, precisely because crossing their textual margins performs in the reader the same quiltwork reassemblage of ideologemes which the Don attempts. Jamming mini-essays into the middle of a stream of narrative bubbles teaches "those who live in silence" how to speak for themselves. Assaulting reticence with steamy sex scenes is not a way to reclaim sexuality as a subject for realism (that was D. H. Lawrence's project in modernist days), but to awaken bodily readers' awareness of internal censors whose operation should be no more silent than the "subjugated other" of the culture, and no less examined, managed, and conditioned than alienated workers. If the multiplicity of voices streaming out of the Don's mouth is a disorienting evocation of the fragmentation of the self, Acker's technique is not designed to recover any nostalgic fiction of a premodernist unified subject. Given fragmentation, given the internal estrangement of those fragments from one another, given the lack even of much knowledge of their forms and trajectories, and given the organization of these fragments according to a Lyotardian socioeconomic "performativity," Acker's simultaneities, fragments, juxtapositions, and rewritings nested within appropriated pieces all function to reclaim this basic multiplicity for ends other than those that Lyotard so gloomily determines.

Although cultural conservatives might feel a bit uncomfortable with the assertion, there is nonetheless something to the claim that Acker is almost sacramental in her approach to individuality and to the world, that her ends are profoundly therapeutic, that her values are radically demystified forms of mythologized metaphors become Megalons, and that her practice of fiction is an attempt to regain for narrative a voice and form that are commensurate with our information age but capable of performing, against that age's colonization of its "processors," the novel's quite traditional function of renewing the possibility for fresh subjectivity. If fiction that still looks familiar is bound to reruns of the same symptoms we have learned to recognize in the etherized patient of modernism, Acker's work breaks up the surface of an increasingly mandarin cultural page and puts into motion what lies beneath. And if the most important fiction of each age demands that we retrain a bit as readers, certainly Acker is among those writers who impose the most drastic requirements upon us to think differently. That difference, not coincidentally, requires the suspension of precisely those categories of thought most implicated in the exercise of power and violence. And it encourages the development of skills and habits that lie at the heart of the feminist program of writers such as Hélène Cixous, Luce Irigaray, and Gayatri Spivak.

In her classic "This Sex Which Is Not One," Irigaray speaks of "the condition of underdevelopment arising from women's submission by and to a culture that oppresses them, uses them, makes of them a medium of exchange, with very little profit to them. Except in the quasi-monopolies of masochistic pleasure, the domestic labor force, and reproduction" (Irigaray 1985, 32). Acker says this about a dog's life: "The maintenance of a dog's life or of dog-like life depends on unequal (power) relations between the subjects or dogs. In this case, the relations are those of ownership and desire. . . . The condition of a dog is a condition of war, of everyone against everyone: so every dog has a right to everything, even to another dog's body. This is freedom" (114). Or at least "freedom" under the regime that Irigaray and Acker oppose.

Cixous, in her equally classic "The Laugh of the Medusa," calls for "the invention of a *new insurgent* writing" that "will return to the body," that "will tear her away from the superegoized structure in which she has always occupied the place reserved for the guilty," and that will enable the writer "to forge for herself the anti-logos weapon" (Cixous 1981, 250). Acker's is one version of that fiction of insurgency, shrewd and perhaps more engaged with its problematic aspects than most varieties. But exploding the logic of what Cixous calls "superegoization" is the aim of Acker's fiction, and developing the "anti-logos weapon" is the project of its transgressions of traditional form. Cixous and Acker resonate at far too many points to enumerate here, but Cixous's description of the "propriety of woman" comes strikingly close to the self-sacrificing quest on which the Don is engaged: "It is . . . her capacity to depropriate unselfishly, body without end, without appendage, without principal 'parts.' If she is a whole, it's a whole composed of parts that are wholes, not simple partial objects but a moving, limitlessly changing ensemble, a cosmos tirelessly traversed by Eros, an immense astral space not organized around any one sun that's any more of a star than the others" (Ibid., 259). My description of Acker's work with fragmentation and multiplicity recounted the fictional realization of this depropriation. It is precisely the abandonment of the logic of "*principal* 'parts'" which lies behind each formal tactic of Acker and which most offends the unsympathetic among her reviewers. To think of her fiction as "a moving, limitlessly changing ensemble" is to recognize its kinetic form and the ongoing productivity of the endless connections we can make among the textual bits that she provides.

Even at the literal level, the relationship between Cixous's "propriety" and the Don's career is striking. If, as we have seen, the Don's ideas are "foetuses beyond their times," then the abortion to which she submits at the opening of the novel is the means by which she forces her insights into a language and a formal medium that can never be fully her own. "I had the abortion," she explains, "because I refused normalcy which is the capitulation to social control" (17–18). The Don ends the silence of "normalcy" by aborting the overdue foetuses of her angry critique, thereby converting the "sickness" of her life experience into the "knightly tool" of fiction. "I want love," she continues. "The love I can only dream about or read in books. I'll make the world into this love." Body without end, she keeps writing, keeps encountering the disciplinary mechanisms of the culture in a long series of beatings, rejections, angry encounters, and episodes of the sort of "masochistic pleasure" of which Irigaray spoke. The novel's first part, "The Beginning of Night," consists of these violent encounters in the Don's quest. Its title refers to the cultural night of the female soul as the social pathology that the Don turns into her strongest weapon. A guerrilla fighter, she takes on the "partly male" role of knighthood in order to turn its discipline against the "dualistic reality which is a reality molded by power" and to make possible for human beings what the "bitch" already knows: "All being is timelessly wild and pathless, its own knight, free" (28, 29).

To succeed in her attempt to remake the world into love requires remaking the texts of which that world is composed, and in the second part of the novel, "Other Texts," the Don carries out this textual version of her strategy. Using strategies and insights consistent with those we have already seen, she refabricates four very different cultural texts, culminating with a version of Frank Wedekind's *Pandora's Box* in which Lulu escapes triumphant at the end, looking for "others who are, like me, pirates journeying from place to place, who knowing only change and the true responsibilities that come from such knowing sing to and with each other" (97). Drawing upon the therapeutic energy of Eros, as Cixous suggests, the Don generously goes on in the third part to pour herself into the effort to teach her dog friends how society works and to serve as an "anti-logos" to its logic. More problematic is the Don's attempt to open possibilities for a different kind of Being that, as Irigaray says of Woman, "is indefinitely other in herself," not in the alienated and estranged way that the Don finds to be characteristic of life in the Nixonian times that she anatomizes, but rather intimately "in touch," in Irigaray's rich sense of the phrase.

In the autobiography of the Don's dog friend, which takes up an important portion of "The End of the Night," the dog tells of her complex experience of love amidst gender roles that switch sometimes in the literal sense of transvestite experiences and sometimes in the more figurative sense of role-shifting. In one section, the dog recalls reading about Juliette, a student at a girls' school, who is led by her teacher Delbène into the graveyard one night, past the coffins of schoolgirls, and down into a room white, we suppose, to connote the absence of any cultural markers in this hidden space that lies literally under the sign of death. Delbène has blindfolded Juliette so that she must "trust" her teacher's guidance over the uneven pathway, a guidance that becomes more than a literal passage when Delbène begins to lecture: "What we do in this room is be happy. With our bodies. Our bodies teach us who've been poisoned" (165). "Since these [patriarchal] educators train the mind rather than the body, we can start with the physical body, the place of shitting, eating, etc., to break through our opinions or false education" (166).

What follows this descent is Juliette's initiation into both vaginal and anal orgasm. The episode is a female parallel, perhaps, to the reading that Bakhtin offers of Rabelais's use of "the plane of material sensual experience" as the means by which "official medieval culture" was labeled "false education," as Delbène puts it. Bakhtin argues that such an episode in Rabelais "destroyed and suspended all alienation; it drew the world closer to man, to his body, permitted him to touch and test every object, examine it from all sides, enter into it, turn it inside out, compare it to every phenomenon, however exalted and holy, analyze, weigh, measure, try it on" (Bakhtin 1984, 381). Characters in *Don Quixote* are engaged in a similar process of groping their way beyond an abstract and oppressive metaphysics. Acker's women have all found logic, morality, and social hierarchies to allot them a near-medieval "place reserved for the guilty," in Cixous's phrase. And their attempt is precisely to rediscover the world from a perspective less determined by a totalizing logic that, for them, has functioned with all the omnipresent oppression of the "official medieval culture."

In *Don Quixote*, sexual pleasure comes to involve Delbène, Juliette, and the other schoolgirls, and Juliette realizes that "watching these sexual actions which I couldn't actually feel made me feel my own physical sensations less. My decreasing sexual abandonment let me feel a more general spreading or less focused sexual interest" (170). Far more than a pornographic primer, the passage takes us back to Cixous's discussion:

> Though masculine sexuality gravitates around the penis, engendering that centralized body (in political anatomy) under the dictatorship of its parts, woman does not bring about the same regionalization which serves the couple head/genitals and which is inscribed only within boundaries. Her libido is cosmic, just as her unconscious is worldwide. Her writing can only keep going, without ever inscribing or discerning contours. (Cixous 1981, 259)

Cixous's language keeps sexuality, politics, and writing tightly paralleled in a way that Acker's fiction appears to understand quite tangibly. It is as if Juliette must learn what is *her* being first by unlearning the logic of "principal parts," as Cixous puts it, and then by learning through her body.

Hence her friends try to lead Juliette into a realization of what she has experienced against her best efforts to block them—"I'm too young to know," she responds, taking the defense of the ingénue. "I haven't any experience of this," she tries again, taking the defense of the overly sheltered. But one of her friends comes back aggressively: "I'm not asking you about your overlays of memories, like the overlays of culture in Europe, culminating in a decayed seaside hotel whose walls peel away from themselves into the literature they think is supporting them. I'm asking you what you know. What do you know, what do you perceive?" (171). Cultural memories, culminating in the psychological locales of sentimental romances in the Harlequin mode, peel away once we critique the patriarchal logic sustaining those overlays.

Juliette, who is confused over a mixture of pain and pleasure her mates find highly significant, finally opens up this experience to analysis:

> I'm too scared to talk to you because I'm too scared to talk to anyone, especially older people: I'm scared because I have or know

no self. There's no *one* who can talk. My physical sensations scare me because they confront me with a self when I have no self: sexual touching makes these physical sensations so fierce. I'm forced to find a self when I've been trained to be nothing. Therefore, I perceive that physical pain, if it doesn't scare me because it's happening without my expectation and consent, helps out and enlarges sexual excitation. (171)

The passage is both alarming and, in a sense, promising. It is a frighteningly blunt description of *why* Irigaray perceives "masochistic pleasure" as the "quasi-monopoly" of women. If identity is painfully etched, then pain recalls the moment of inscription and the *non*cultural memory of flesh before the cut of the pen. With no self that Juliette knows of as hers, with no *"one"* voice that is hers to use, she can only fear talking, especially with those whose age has, in her experience, allied them with the institutions of mastery. Like Bakhtin's Rabelaisian Man, like Cixous's insurgent writer, she encounters in her mixture of pain and pleasure, of focused and cosmic Eros, "a self when I have no self." Promising, but problematic, as the rest of the section suggests (its narrator makes love to Laure but is aghast at the pain she inflicts, the unnaturalness of her dildo, and the pleasure of her own orgasm—the mixture makes clear the ambiguities of trying to realize fully this episode's more utopian promises).

An equally agonizing venture is the Don's attempt to turn language to the ends of her quest. She explains her poetry fairly straightforwardly to the pirate dogs:

I write words to you whom I don't and can't know, to you who will always be other than and alien to me. These words sit on the edges of meanings and aren't properly grammatical. For when there is no country, no community, the speaker's unsure of which language to use, how to speak, if it's possible to speak. Language is community. Dogs, I'm now inventing a community for you and me. (191)

This audacious program attempts to place beside patriarchy an alternative community informed by the Don's "mad" vision, but it does not have the luxury of making this effort in a cultural vacuum. The dogs are creatures of their culture, however much they wish to escape its norms. The Don can define art as to "dream publicly" (202), but some of the dogs at least are mainly disappointed when the Don does not simply collapse and thus provide them "fresh (dead) meat" (195). She continues, instead, but the stress of her project shows in the near-paradoxical hopelessness with which she perseveres. She joins a voodoo service where "all ways were allowed: all cultures: aloud" and in which everyone sings "songs of desire" in communal warmth. But her response to the experience is mixed: "It is necessary to sing, that is to be mad, because otherwise you have to live with the straights, the compromisers, the mealy-mouths, the reality-deniers, the laughter-killers. It is necessary to be mad, that is to sing, because it's not possible for a knight, or for anyone, to foray successfully against the owners of this world" (193).

Mad singing of the sort we find in Acker's fiction is no doubt one way to respond to the "owners." Dispirited, the Don wishes an apocalypse of the "malevolent" upon the suburbanites and sadly concludes that "'I wanted to find a meaning or myth or language that was mine, rather than those which try to control me; but language is communal and here is no community.' Having concluded, Don Quixote turned around and started walking home, although she had no home" (194–95). What she does not realize is that whereas she has no home in the sense of a recognizable space in the culture surrounding her, she *has* achieved a different sort of textual place. That is, though she did not find language and meaning wholly her own, and though she forged no community on the order of the great nineteenth-century communes, she *did* weave a crazy quilt of songs, narratives, outbursts, and essays which inspired her listeners. The dogs realize their hunger; "this was the first sign of their having language" (196). Then they recognize that their homelessness is caused by landlords, and that only landlords call terrorism "useless." The dogs' own "mad" song weaves bits and pieces of bad family life, oppressive working conditions, and this recognition of the slave culture behind such pieces: "It is you, city. Market of the world, that is, of all representations. Since you're the only home I've ever known, without your representation or misrepresentation of me I don't exist. Because of you, since every child needs a home, every child is now a white slave" (197). There is no home, no freedom, no "I" without the "history and culture" that they label "the world of death" (198) near their song's conclusion. Such consciousness is apocalypse in the eyes of the landlords, but for the dogs "the work and the language of the living're about to begin" (198).

The dogs' journey off into the adventures of a pirate band does not include the Don, however, for she is a self-confessed "freak" still poised between the need for "a home" and a fear of "the bickerings and constraints of heterosexual marriage" (202). She still faces the conflict between loneliness, when "I don't touch anybody so I'm immersed in my own selfishness," and the knowledge that "as soon as I'm married, I'll be a prisoner; I'll be normal. I'll have to stop having the dreams by which I now act." The novel winds to its conclusion in a dream in which God confesses her imperfections: "Since I am no more, forget Me. Forget morality. Forget about saving the world. Make Me up" (207). It is, perhaps, the Don's farewell to the concept of Messianic quest that she has held throughout the book and an implicit recognition of the more diffuse effect that her work will have. Not God, but effective fictions; not morality, but values. "I thought about God for one more minute and forgot it. I closed my eyes, head drooping, like a person drunk for so long she no longer knows she's drunk, and then, drunk, awoke to the world which lay before me" (207). That world seems not to have been so available to her before, as if the intoxicating mission of taking on the "partly male" qualities of knighthood had, perhaps, enabled her to experience what Cixous calls the "vatic bisexuality which doesn't annul differences but stirs them up, pursues them, increases their number" (Cixous 1981, 254). The Don has conceived the sus-pension of such absolute limits as God, and she has provided the material for what Acker's dust jacket calls a "collage-novel" of stirred-up, increased textual and existential differences. If she is left feeling the full set of contradictions revealed by her analyses, it at least leaves her awake to the world's realities and to the problematic but hopeful possibility of "Make Me up." That is a great deal to hope for from the language community forged by the novel. "Eye/I" say the piratical dogs as they weigh anchor.

### Empire of the Senseless

Acker's recent novel (New York: Grove Press, 1988) is well-titled, because *Empire of the Senseless* documents life under the imperium of the multinational corporations, taking the quest of the Don forward under other names into the socially apocalyptic era of the eighties. The book's premise is that the much-prophesied apoc-alypse of Western culture has already happened, but Suburbia didn't notice. Those expecting bombs bursting in a thermonuclear glare are likely to be disappointed, for Armageddon is spiritual, not mili-tary, and is marked by the retreat from dreams to surfaces. Its sur-vivors encounter not full-metal platoons, but poverty and boredom. Those expecting real social change after a violent cleansing of social structures will also be disappointed, because the CIA steps in and takes over the revolution—nothing really changes except the in-creased human devastation wrought by the sociopolitical forms of multinational corporate mentality.

Much wit is involved in working out the nuances of this con-ceit. The book's three divisions measure the stages of the protago-nists' awareness of this event and their paths through and, to some extent, beyond it. "Elegy for the World of the Fathers" marks the passage of crisis from that of the Father as the nexus of power, op-pression, and meaning, to the rather different patriarchy of the mul-tinationals. The characters never fully free themselves from the Oedipal script of incest and sexual power, but they must also come to understand the extent to which that personal metaphor of the cultural father is displaced by a "they" as corporate and invisible as a board of directors. Attention to gender issues is assured by dividing the novel's narration between the female Abhor (abhorrent, but also a bore and a whore) and the male Thivai (he is a would-be thief of Abhor's "I," and as a competitive male he vies with her for control and superiority), but this pat separation is not always neatly maintained.

The first of five sections of "Elegy," "Rape by the Father," stages a recurrent scene (12) in Acker's fiction, but the fifth section's version contains a new element in her narrative. "I've always known that story," Abhor says, though in this recounting the Father does not carry through what he has initiated. "What I suddenly remembered or knew is that I sexually desired my adopted father" (67). To the simpler reading of incest as victimization, Abhor adds a reading that perceives more than the personal relation. In this institutional flavoring, a significant admixture of *wanting* violation is bred into those who learn early on the sexualization of identity and relationships.

How do we understand this scene of incest, a theme that appears in virtually every Acker novel and is a crucial part of her cultural analysis? In Acker's earlier scene, when the Father actually rapes Abhor, she is a victim who learns to slash her wrists because withdrawing from the system is the only option possible for its victims; however, her father attempts to regulate her comings and goings in a very literal colonization. The traditional "world of the fathers," one of colonization, violently imposes its will in order to control the natural chaos of "native" cultures, even if its officers frequently abuse their "stewardship." The female body becomes a valued object to be protected or stolen; it is nature itself and hence to be possessed.

Incest as a crime of patriarchal malfeasance might be rethought as a crime of cultural decadence if the scenario shifts from colonization to sadomasochism (one recurrent in Acker's fiction). The newer scenario locates "wild" desire less in committing theft than in enjoying this reified form of pleasure and identity. In Acker's second version, the father's overt dominance is less necessary because Abhor's libido is invested in the relatively covert disciplinary process of which he is the local agent. Some part of Abhor desires her father—wants, that is, the ritual of submission, degradation, and violence, which is also the quintessential pornographic script and which defines pleasure in contemporary society. Hence "pornography" is Acker's device for desublimating the content of all the media transformations of her pornographic kernel. Desire itself (and not merely woman's body) is spectralized and assimilated to a script in which the violence of power and the pleasure of sensuality fuse in the unconscious. The vehicles of power include pornography as well as social structures, just as, in a complementary way, pleasure has significant social effects when it becomes a stylized mass-media spectacle rather than the truly vital personal connection of our utopian fantasies.

The outlaws of the older scenario resort to rebellion (to repudiate rule) and suicide (to destroy property value). Outlaws of the newer scenario become most dangerous when they reattach the emptied imagery of the simulacral society to the effects of power obscured by the mesmerizing play of that imagery. In the relationships she portrays, Acker shows not only how an older form of power continues through violence and inequities but also how a new form arises in individuals for whom the only pleasure *is* playing the script. That both scenarios take place simultaneously in so transitional an era as ours is clear in "Romanticism," the fourth section of "Elegy." Thivai straps down a woman so that "she will never . . . be other than me, be not me, be against me" (62). She becomes his property, even an extension of his own body—colonized. But the real sexual kick involves watching her submit to his discipline. What the scene presents as literal and explicit usually takes the form of a pervasive cultural logic internalized by the individual, a logic of which Thivai is also a victim even if his relatively empowered role serves to mask this. Hence the forbidden sin shifts from uncolonized natural desire to uncolonized ideological awareness, more specifically to becoming aware of culture's primal scene in which Lacan's Law of the Father begets the social self upon the physiological organism. Ultimately, what we find is Acker rewriting her work from a shifted perspective. She has troped her own primary scenario, shifting from the dream of a predatory stepfather usurping her lost biological father to a drama of the Foucauldian model of power as internalized network displacing the classical model of identity as patriarchal sovereignty. The shift from the desire to possess to the desire to submit parallels the shift from the self as sovereign to the self as the internalized Other of the cultural *langue*.

In ideological terms, the scenario collapses pain and pleasure together as the masochism of good citizenship (we are all "women" submitting to the paternal state). The scenario also condenses the textual and institutional force of culture into the figure of the sadist, for whom pleasure becomes *seeing* pain and wielding a power he derives only from the more powerful institutional licensing of society. But these definitions of citizenship and power are perhaps less significant than the success with which even the role of the sadist, let alone that of the much larger audience, is that of the passive spectator. That is, his power is that of *watching*, and "action" becomes spectatorship as surely as "desirability" becomes the masochism represented by this spectacle of Woman finding pleasure in submission and pain. The sadomasochist of this scenario *is* the dialogic relationship of these specular genders of pleasure and identity, and hence also the type of individual identity constituted in this era.

A commodity culture transforms everyone into extras seeking roles in culture's porn flick. This equation—of desirability, masochism, and good citizenship—enlists considerable libidinal energy for the individual sacrifices required by high standards of performance. The equation has considerable economic value, then, but its equally important political value is that it makes monstrous and ugly—even obscene—any effort to disrupt this tight scripting of libidinal energies, and particularly any effort to turn them to less passive models. Economics, politics, and the body all become joined in this primary scenario, and the most illicit dimension is the very pleasure we take watching passively as it runs and reruns in all its minor daily variations.

Acker repeatedly connects rape by the Father to this definition of gender roles according to the sadomasochistic halves of the pornographic scene (and the reintegration of their specular sides as individuality). By revealing the paradoxical heart of the culture's primal scene, Acker seeks to disrupt what Althusser has characterized as the most basic function of ideology—the formation of "subjects" as simultaneously "subjects of" and "subject to" (Althusser 1984, 45, 56). Abhor is no doubt enabled to "suddenly" remember her desire precisely because her experiences have made explicit the ideological content of Acker's sadomasochistic reading of the culture. Because Abhor finds her own body responding to the masochistic role assigned her and experiences the most literal forms of her culture's pornographic imagination, she understands the interrelated dynamics of power, ideology, narrative, and desire. Perhaps pornography's stylized S&M exists in order to make ordinary human relations seem *not* sadomasochistic.

If we look closely at how Abhor responds to oppressive power, we find that her politics parallel her libidinal shifts. In "Rape by the Father," she breaks off the incest narrative for one of those Ackerian apparent *non sequiturs* that follow with deadly precision:

> The German Romantics had to destroy the same bastions as we
> do. Logocentrism and idealism, theology, all supports of the re-
> pressive society. Property's pillars. Reason which always homoge-
> nizes and reduces, represses and unifies phenomena or actuality
> into what can be perceived and so controlled. The subjects, us, are
> now stable and socializable. Reason is always in the service of the
> political and economic masters. It is here that literature strikes, at
> this base, where the concepts and actings of order impose them-
> selves. Literature is that which denounces and slashes apart the

repressing machine at the level of the signified. Well before Bataille, Kleist, Hoffman etc., made trial of Hegelian idealism, of the cloturing dialectic of recognition: the German Romantics sun brazenly brassily in brass of spending and waste. They cut through conservative narcissism with bloody razor blades. (12)

This passage stages the scenario of colonization and liberation, with its motifs of repression by the homogenizing regime. The passage also subliminally links the scenario to Abhor's father raping her, because, in the parallel narrative, she uses "bloody razor blades" on her wrists, and because "conservative narcissism" resonates with the Father's desire for his self-reproduction. Order is thrown off, so the natural can thrive in the form of brassy "spending and waste." In subsequently denouncing the sex show that fronts the brothel where father goes to live, Abhor counts on "most humans" to feel "totally disgusted" by the devaluing of sex from a natural pleasure to a "revolting phenomenon" (16).

Later we find a different form of denunciation once Abhor comes to the end of her elegy to this cultural moment. The section also called "Daddy," but in "Let the Algerians Take Over Paris," concludes with Abhor about to embark in a rowboat to escape revolutionary violence:

> "My father's no longer important cause interpersonal power in this world means corporate power. The multinationals along with their computers have changed and are changing reality. Viewed as organisms, they've attained immortality via bio-chips. Etc. Who needs slaves anymore? So killing someone, anyone, like Reagan or the top IBM executive board members, whoever they are, can't accomplish anything," I blabbed, and I wondered what would accomplish anything, and I wondered if there was only despair and nihilism, and then I remembered. . . .
> In the boat my father I had never known was dead. (83)

Interpersonal power is no longer contestable within the model of colonization because its neat binary oppositions between outside and inside, mercantile state and colony, patriarch and daughter, are as anachronistic as the too literal melodrama of masters and slaves. Therapy for a victim, like liberation for a colony, does not remove the ideological "bio-chip" of a cultural imaginary programmed within mass culture and social forms. An altogether different service is required, one that addresses the pornographic scenario's narratology and disrupts it midperformance. What Abhor "remembered" in this crucial moment is a postmodern form of rejecting nihilism and hopelessness. The real Father-Rapist is one she has never known, and his death occurs when the cultural daughters "blab" in the new narratology we traced in *Don Quixote*. That narratology's open questing involves not only the Acker protagonist's perennial search for pleasure but also parallel strategies on the planes of politics, gender, and writing.

Some of those parallel developments emerge even in the first division of *Empire of the Senseless*, at least in rudimentary form. Thivai, for example, is eloquent on the nihilistic impasse experienced by the subject-as-role: "When I was young frivolity and trivia had been my weapons; now I did whatever I was told because I was no longer me" (33). Frivolous consumer, trivial pursuer, he knows that "the I who desired and the eye who perceived had nothing to do with each other and at the same time existed in the same body— mine: I was not possible. I, in fact, was more than diseased." Thivai heads off "to be a construct" in the hopes that the unknown is better than the cultural contradiction his Being has become.

Abhor seems to benefit as a thinker from experiencing gender from its nether side. She knows she wants to be "mad," not as in "senseless" but as in "angry beyond memories and reason," key agencies of colonization which are assimilated to media imagery and smart shopping as we pass beyond "the world of the father." She also knows that people do not "lovingly relate to each other in equality, whatever that is or means, but out of needs for power and control. Humans relate to other humans by eating each other" (54), a mode of mutual consumption which preoccupies otherwise political energies. "Our code was *death*. I needed new instructions. We, humans, need new blood" (56), differing from that laced by the drugs of media hyping. Not only colonial "poverty" but also simulation's "boredom" may account for terrorism (58), as if spectators could tire of the same existential pornography repeatedly played in the ads and movies of prime-time reality.

Abhor comes closest in this division to outthinking her initial stance when she opens the last section with this reflection:

> I ran away. Not only from Thivai. I would have run somewhere if there had been anywhere to which to run. But there wasn't. I knew, I know there's no home anywhere. Nowhere:
>    Exile was a permanent condition. A permanent community, in terms of relationships and language.
>    In terms of identity. But from what was identity exiled? (63)

To have a program would mean conceiving of herself within the binary logic that preserves illusory havens such as nature, freedom, home, identity. Abhor must experience a fair portion of the novel's long central division, "Alone," before she is able even to begin answering that crucial final question with a community conceived in the diacritical terms of "relationships and language." To avoid nihilistic despair, she must either return to the nostalgia for authentic selfhood or natural being that she celebrated in the German Romantics, or find a postmodern answer that does not leave her as with-drawn and docile as Thivai.

"Elegy" ends with a section consigning Paris to the revolution-ary Algerians; Abhor's first section in "Alone" confesses that "the Algerian revolution had changed nothing. There is always a reason for nihilism" (110). But Abhor does not stay put in nihilism. This rebellion is not your standard coup d'état. Its energy derives from a lesson that Abhor's grandmother learns in the novel's opening. Her young boyfriend tries unsuccessfully to get revenge by taking out the vice squad that busts her for prostitution—"it was one of the final revolts of the non-existent against their economic controllers" (6). What Nana learns is "that society is a filthy trick," so she mar-ries a rich man. "The poor can reply to the crime of society, to their economic deprivation retardation primitivism lunacy boredom hopelessness, only by collective crime or war. One form collective crime takes is marriage" (7).

Another rebellion is "*urban* rather than *political*" in its form, as when the Algerian population ghettoizes a zone of Paris "until every Parisian deserted the zone altogether" (76). Mackandal, the revolutionary leader, spreads class- and race-oriented crime throughout the city until "it was unwise for whites to act," and he feels emboldened to go beyond "dreams of negation" to the paradise of "a land without whites" (77). Because "whites had industrialized polluted the city for purposes of their economic profit to such an extent that even clean water was scarce," the servant class can poi-son the bourgeoisie by dosing the bottled water that they fetch. Because the poisoning is accomplished with fugu, or puffer fish, we might think of this as a literalized version of letting the privileged class atrophy from the effects of luxury and delicacy. But violence and pollution are part of the larger cultural ecosystem, something the CIA knows when it steps in and begins administering chaos for the pleasure of watching drugged johns from behind see-through mirrors and of enacting upon the flesh of children the pornographic scenario of bondage, rape, and snuffing. This official practice of management through "construct" produces nihilism, in Abhor's eyes, and it explains why she runs away to be "Alone" for the novel's second division.

Mackandal's response to power is as "collective" as Nana's, and his marriage, if not to a rich man who owns a chunk of the garment district, is to the liberationist dream that utopia is literal rather than figural, that what ails the Algerians is white people rather than the much larger complex of institutions, discourses, and imagery for which they are the figure. The CIA manages that cultural machinery in the power vacuum left when the industrial masters become a social rustbelt. Basking in the new site of power—the sunbelt of service, information, and media industry—the CIA/IBM nexus re-

mains the invisible management of a culture to which Abhor can no
longer relate. She understands that both joining and opposing the
ruling class reinforces the class structure, just as both wanting and
hating the Father perpetuates his power. What she must learn is a
fluid model of society appropriate to her new mode of narrative and
to her need to contest the emptying of all cultural forms in an increasingly simulacral era.

This model emerges in Abhor's thinking in the metaphor of the
sailor. Sexual gags aside (many appear), Abhor herself becomes a
kind of sailor: "I say that a sailor is someone who came out of
poverty which was hateful. Because a sailor has spat on and shits on
poverty, the sailor knows that the worst poverty is that of the heart.
All good sailors espouse and live in the material simplicity which
denies the poverty of the heart. Reagan's heart is empty. A sailor is
a human who has traded poverty for the riches of imaginative reality" (114). Bred in poverty, the sailor does not marry its binary
opposite as Nana did, but rather suspends the dialectic of wealth
and privation with which the state of poverty encloses the individual's perception of social possibilities. To live in "material simplicity" means to displace commodities as the determining signifiers and to create the possibility for something other than "poverty
of the heart." But this strategy, the passage continues, is a form of
revolution:

> Such an act constitutes destruction of society thus is criminal.
> Criminal, continuously fleeing, homeless, despising property, un-
> stable like the weather, the sailor will wreck any earth bound
> life. . . .
>   Though the sailor longs for home, her or his real love is change.
> Stability in change, change in stability occurs only imaginarily.
> No roses grow on sailors' graves. (114)

If theft is stealing something of value, the sailor is a criminal
indeed, for she steals the whole system of value-making, empties it,
and adapts to the nomadic life to which she consigns herself. Stability is to be found neither in the status of intellectual or political
mastery—the colonial scenario—nor in the performance slot in the
pornographic culture. It is found in the constancy of change, fluidity, a very female voyaging in which no preestablished metaphysics,
demystified or not, rules. This state "occurs only imaginarily" because it is *not* a state but an ongoing voyaging that does not stop.
"No roses grow on sailors' graves" because they are lost at sea if
they are really sailors. If this ideal preserves a bit of German Romantic brass, its orchestration is distinctly postmodern.

"Sailors set out on perilous journeys just so that they can see in
actuality cities they have only imagined" (118), but, if they were to
settle in one of those cities, no doubt they would become like "those

whose only fortune was living death in a city where there was no future" (115)—no change, that is. Agone (agony?), a Cuban sailor whom Abhor follows around (she herself wears the uniform of a navy lieutenant for much of this subsection), comes to a similar understanding:

> He was amazed how indirect his human soul was: how there were goals of desire, objects of desire, resting places, beds, and he never sailed to these places directly. There were no straight routes, except by chance. Rather, the soul travelled in such turns and windings, snails, that a world was found, defined. The soul created out of its own desires. (136)

The direct and straight routes of logocentrism are long gone at this point, and the world to be found (and the soul that finds it) is not there until the journey is made.

Such fluidity is dangerous because "the world was reduced to evil, to just tactics, to how" (126). This sort of fluidity is the marketing department's sense that the need for a product can be created, the politician's sense that winning is everything. But the kind of self-knowledge which the sailor's way suggests is not really a knowledge at all, but something closer to dreaming. Abhor affirms this wisdom that is not knowledge several times, as when "I realized I had met change in myself. Since it was change, I had no way of being conscious of what was happening to me" (127). Not surprisingly in Acker's fiction, Being and sexuality are closely related. Abhor assumes, illogically enough for the culture in which she has been bred, that "physical pleasure can only be pleasurable if it is pleasurable, not the cause of suffering and fighting all the time. I'm beginning to believe that physical pleasure can be pleasurable now" (127).

However, this belief rests upon a new understanding of gender roles:

> A man's power resides in his prick. That's what they, whoever they is, say. How the fuck should I know?
> I ain't a man. Though I'm a good fake lieutenant, it's not good enough to have a fake dick. I don't have one. Does this mean I've got no strength? If it's true that a man's prick is his strength, what and where is my power? Since I don't have one thing, a dick, I've got no thing, so my pleasure isn't any one thing, it's just pleasure. Therefore, pleasure must be pleasurable. Well, maybe I've found out something, and maybe I haven't. (127)

Abhor probably has, though she may not be able to use it immediately to experience the pleasure that she can imagine. But what she finds out here is Irigaray's point that female "pleasure is denied by a civilization that privileges phallomorphism," that such a culture's "scoptophilic lens" fails to see the hidden genitals of woman, and that its "phallomorphic" tendency counts pleasure as "one thing," rather than "that contact of at least two (lips) which keeps woman in touch with herself" and generalizes her pleasure all over the body (Irigaray 1985, 26–27). Abhor breaks into coarse diction at this point precisely to profane the decorum that naturalizes a form of pleasure which excludes her. That damnation consigns to oblivion both the sacred scenario of theological prostration and the profane roles of pornography.

That Irigarayan pleasure complements the kind of Being developed in the metaphor of the sailor, because both escape any unitary or fixed, any visible and singular, form. When Agone encounters a most unusual tattooer, the encounter becomes sexual, even though it breaks the taboo against men touching men:

> His lips were waves which had parted to let the kid walk safely through the monstrous ocean. The father parted himself, all of His world, all of being, to let the child walk in safety.
> The as-yet-hairless child ran his hands through his father's hair as if the hairs were nets which had caught the fish of dreams.
> The dreams of criminals became alive. (137–38)

The older man's lips, which might be expected to speak the predictable lines of power and patriarchy, instead part those waves for "the child" to discover a mode of sexuality which will not threaten him with the castration of phallomorphism—a fetishizing of the penis, after all, that removes it from the body and sends it into the phallic imaginary of the culture. Acker is as sensitive to the plight of males as she is devastating to the rhetoric and roles with which they often rest complacent within that plight. In any case, this experience, this wisdom, is precisely the "fish of dreams" that this nonpatriarchal "father" has netted for Agone. "Agone pulled away from the tattooer before either of them came because he didn't want to reach any port. No roses grow on a sailor's grave" (140). Agone has passed into a sensuality that, if it is not literally Irigarayan, at least preserves a pleasure generalized through the body, a less orgasmic kind of sex antithetical to Thivai's addiction to "shooting up" (Thivai's grim pun marking phallomorphic addiction).

If the sailor's exile from home is the state of Being which Thivai and Abhor must come to terms with, the tattooer's art represents a kind of "writing of the body" related to the marginalized ethos that all three share. Acker adduces tattooing's social history, beginning with the Romans, who "used tattoos to mark and identify mercenaries, slaves, criminals, and heretics," and it is significant that the next sentence reveals that "for the first time, the sailor felt he had sailed home" (130). Agone stops short of reaching a "port," something temporary, given over to commerce, and lacking the sense of belonging offered by the sailor's home on the margin. Not coincidentally, the next paragraph relates tattoos and that sense of belonging: "Among the early Christians, tattoos, stigmata indicating exile, which at first had been forced on their flesh, finally actually served to enforce their group solidarity. The Christians began voluntarily to acquire these indications of tribal identity. Tattooing continued to have ambiguous social value; today a tattoo is considered both a defamatory brand and a symbol of a tribe or of a dream" (130).

Sailors on the margin live that ambiguity, just as they have constantly experienced a branding of the body—Abhor, in particular, as sexual object—but also Thivai, because living in the culture means bodily experiencing its disciplinary regime. But Acker adds one more piece to the puzzle: "In 1769, when Captain James Cook 'discovered' Tahiti, he thought he had sailed to paradise. In Tahitian, writing is 'ta-tau'; the Tahitians write directly on human flesh" (130). A paradisiacal writing of the body suggests the potential of writing to engage in more than the abstract registers of logocentrism, and to achieve that ambiguous mix of branding and communal bonding which highlights the "dream fish" that Acker's imagery connotes.

For Abhor, working with the marginalized connectives of pun— the sensory (sound) rather than purely the abstract (denotative) sign—the connection between tattoo and taboo becomes primary, just as, for Agone, the taboo against male homosexuality falls as his tattoo appears and, for Abhor, the incest taboo initiates her awareness of her own marginalized status. Privileging the unconscious as a zone at least relatively "free of control," Abhor writes a politicized prologue that charts a change of writing strategy and that parallels another kind of change we have already seen:

> Ten years ago it seemed possible to destroy language through language: to destroy language which normalizes and controls by cutting that language. Nonsense would attack the empire-making (empirical) empire of language, the prisons of meaning.
>
> But this nonsense, since it depended on sense, simply pointed back to the normalizing institutions. (134)

Abhor appears to have absorbed Fredric Jameson's critique of postmodernism. This critique of what earlier in the novel she *liked* about the German Romantics, the nonsense violations of the order of sense, rejects the closure of those violations within binary logic. The rejection parallels Abhor's awareness that the Algerian revolution replaced middle-class cops with Arab Revolutionary cops, that exile from a nonexistent home is a fundamental condition of Being, and that the oppositional relation to her father had been displaced by the kind of relation which a marginalized speaker has to a foreign language (she is allotted, that is, only a few lines in a scenario that makes no sense to her).

What follows this moment criticizing, in effect, the kind of "cutting" Acker has done throughout her career of appropriated texts and sudden shifts and splices, is a remarkable program that Abhor announces for the kind of writing which she would like to attempt:

> What is the language of the "unconscious"? (If this ideal unconscious or freedom doesn't exist: pretend it does, use fiction, for the sake of survival, all of our survival.) Its primary language must be taboo, all that is forbidden. Thus, an attack on the institutions of prison via language would demand the use of a language or languages which aren't acceptable, which are forbidden. Language, on one level, constitutes a set of codes and social and historical agreements. Nonsense doesn't per se break down the codes; speaking precisely that which the codes forbid breaks the codes. (134)

Even when fiction concerns politically vital stories, such as "unconscious" and "freedom," it has truth effects that enable us to survive the transverse journeys of the sailor's exile. Nonsense, whether as outbursts or as dreams, lacks the impact of dreams and outbursts that voice the forbidden knowledge which arises precisely in our experience at the margin. A tattoo is also a drum roll, and Abhor's parenthesis is a call to arms for an ambush that speaks what suburban teaching and writing do not know.

The new tattooing method of this practitioner "consisted of raising defined parts of the flesh up with a knife. The tattooer then draws a string through the raised points of flesh. Various coloration methods can be used on the living points." The "defined parts" are raised in response to the "codes and social and historical agreements" by the tattooer, whose own body is completely covered with this Foucauldian experience of the culture's disciplinary functions. The tattooer cuts not into language, which points "back to the normalizing institutions," but into the body, which shares as a nonverbal Other or "unconscious" a knowledge of the margin and of the impress of cultural machinery. These remain "living points" rather than the machine-tooled points of the phallogocentric apparatus. Abhor uses this knowledge when she critiques Thivai's chauvinism in the novel's final section: "'You shut up, fatherfuck,' I said to Thivai. 'You know what you are? You're nothing since you do nothing and you feel nothing and you have nothing that is no actions. But you're so scared you are the nothing you are, you keep pretending that you control this earth'" (211–12). Abhor assumes that writing on the body, knowing with the body, and speaking the forbidden knowledge of nonphallomorphism make "doing," "feeling," and "having" add up to something more positive and effective than Thivai's nihilist compliance with "The Rape of the Father," compliance that her epithet for him clearly marks.

Not that Abhor does not share, at times, Thivai's fear of being a "nothing." Earlier in the novel, as part of her shift from liberationist politics to her decision to speak the forbidden, Abhor understands that overcoming this fear means finding the kind of Being to which the sailor's life leads her: "Because I'm stupid, it's taken me half a lifetime—stealing from a government, an evil one, as governments go, killing a boss, as bosses go, a revolution, blood upon blood on every level of human existence, as blood flows—for me to learn that I have to say what I want to get what I want. Who. Perhaps if human desire is said out loud, the urban planes, the prisons, the architectural mirrors will take off, as airplanes do" (112).

Still wobbly enough at this point to abuse herself and to flip from "I" to "Who," Abhor nonetheless understands that a knowledge derived from the ways in which "blood flows" is the origin of discovering how to say "out loud" human desire. For urban real-estate terrorism, the media-made prisons of imagination, and corporate skyscrapers all to "take off" is more than a little utopianism, perhaps. But she does know that the abstract tendencies of Western thought estrange her from the more bodily awareness of human desires which she seeks: "The demand for an adequate mode of expression is senseless. Then why is there this searching for an adequate mode of expression? Was I searching for a social and political paradise? Since all acts, including expressive acts, are interdependent, paradise cannot be an absolute. Theory doesn't work" (113). But experience and even fictions do work, for they bypass the one-to-one criterion of a "phallomorphic" epistemology, they recognize the interdependent character of the cultural ecosphere, and they seek out a community of exiles, of sailors, whose wisdom keeps them at sea rather than in theoretical closure.

In "Pirate Night," the novel's third and final division, Acker plays a version of a classic off against its revoicing in the experience of the characters. Thivai and his gay friend Mark restage Tom Sawyer's rescue of the imprisoned-but-already-freed Jim, complete with the elaborate, absurd, and unworkable schemes and the uselessness of the whole project from the outset. Abhor, who has already achieved some freedom (but is enslaved by her continuing need for her friends), suffers the consequences far more than "the boys." Once free, she writes a devastating letter to them which ties together many of the elements we have found thus far: "Everytime I talk to one of you, I feel like I'm taking layers of my own epidermis, which are layers of still freshly bloody scar tissue, black brown and red, and tearing each one of them off so more and more of my blood shoots into your face. This is what writing is to me a woman" (210).

Abhor's body is a permanent scar tissue because her experiences of both writing and Being have subjected her to the wounding discipline of identity and sexuality. Writing is bleeding, not in the relatively benign menstrual sense but in the fully painful self-revelations of the sailor with nothing to hide. The passage continues:

> The whole world is men's bloody fantasies.
>
> For example: Thivai decided he was going to be a pirate. Therefore: we were going to be pirates. If I didn't want to be a pirate, I had to be a victim. Because, if I didn't want to be a pirate, I was rejecting all that he is. He, then, had to make me either repent my rejection or too helpless to reject him. Then, he decided that he loved me. By the time he decided that, I was in jail. (210)

This is not one of the outlaw pirate bands in *Don Quixote* but the play bands of Tom Sawyer's overly romantic imagination, with its nonsense dreams. Thivai clings to the anachronism of his patriarchal script; a predatory sailor, he takes commodity culture with him and tries to convert Abhor into the helpless object of that script, a bit like Freud reducing Dora to a choice between repenting her own notions of her experience and a helplessness before the master analyst.

Significantly, Thivai's love coincides with Abhor's imprisonment, because he is unable to realize she has eluded the closure of both colonial logic and performance scripts. The passage continues:

> You two collaborated in keeping me in jail by planning escapes so elaborate they had nothing to do with escape. That's western thought for you.
>
> This is what I'm saying: you're always fucking deciding what reality is and collaborating about these decisions.
>
> It's not that I agree with you that I'm a wet washcloth. It's that I don't know what reality is. I'm so unsure, tentative, tenuous, lonely, uncertain from loneliness, anguished, sad that I'm not certain enough to fight the decisions I should.
>
> I guess I'm going to get into more and more messes cause that's the way I am, but I hate all of you. (210)

Collaborators in a habit of Western thought that maintains closure rather than imagining escape, Thivai and Mark embody the Reality that remains the problem Abhor faces. Strained by the stress of this writing in blood (literally, in the narrative), Abhor has the strength not of the Hero but of the Sailor. Lacking the certainty for pitched battles at every street corner of history, Abhor nonetheless knows that her venture entails real historical costs, "messes," but also real gains once she is able to compose her own fiction of reality with enough truth effects to survive the sadomasochistic Western thought in which Mark and Thivai remain mired.

Abhor has known for a long time that, as "mercenaries" in colonial wars, she and Thivai had an "adversarial" partnership in which "at every moment we undermined, subverted, and feared one another." As partners, "we didn't attack each other directly," but, without other partners, their nuclear relationship allowed "no escape for either of us from the reality of each of our attacks" (112). But unlike Thivai, she thinks her way beyond the "adversarial" binary logic of one system as she ventures on into uncharted waters. It is in a section Thivai narrates that we read of Shahra'zad as a woman who "wanted to end patriarchy" and did so with her tales of "travelling, poverty, sensual pleasure, the unknown, wonder, disease, sex" (152–53). And it is in the same section that, imprisoned by the CIA in the "isolation of air," Thivai learns that only "an act of will kept the fiction of 'me' going" and could keep him from becoming one "who descended into nihilism, who descended deeper than nihilism into the grey of yuppy life (the worship of commodities, the belief that there is nothing left but commodities, who turn to the surfaces of class race money for reality, who despise taboo)" (147).

Thivai cannot make use of these insights, however. He can critique American life quite penetratingly: its liberty is one "to speak words to which no one listens" because both life and liberty are so economically determined (163–64), its "rich know nothing . . . strangers . . . strangers to the world they own" (165), and, "the USA is a dead nation. It's devoid of dreams. The USA has destroyed all that we call human life and substituted religion. This religion is worship of money and blind faith in stupidity. The USA has decimated its own soil and air. The USA has substituted learning how to be controlled and the rote memorization of facts for any education in living" (167–68). What Thivai lacks is the wisdom of the tattooer's art. True, at the end of the novel's first division, both he and Abhor are "carved into roses" (86) by a tattooer. But these roses are part of the "Elegy" for the older, patriarchal world. The tattoo marks their knowledge of this world's death, a knowledge they carry with them into their separate experiences during the novel's second division.

The tattoo that Agone later receives teaches a more complex lesson. That lesson's context in the relation that Agone has with his tattooer is an important feature. Agone is initially "caught between the rock of a false self-sufficiency," much like the illusory self that Thivai maintains, "and the rock of a need to go beyond his identity" (135), as Abhor succeeds in doing. But he and the tattooer share first an uncertainty about their relationship and then, through that uncertainty and "insufficiency," what is for Agone "the first time in his life he began to feel something sexual"; that is, something sexual beyond the phallomorphic (and sadomasochistic) sense. Agone is taken beyond his traditionally male identity, one so formulaic and prescriptive that even he is alienated from it.

As the tattoo begins to take shape, the "outlines of a sailing ship" evoke the "dream-time when humans were free" (138). However, this is not an exercise in escapism. "Historically, criminality is the only freedom humans have had." Liberty, as even Thivai understands, must be evaluated in economic terms rather than in public pronouncements of rights and freedoms. "Like the edges of a dream during the waking state, tattooing showed the sailor that dreams are made actual through pain. Humans make themselves and're made through pain plus dreams" (138). These dreams imagine, as Abhor attempts, glimpses of a radically different world but do not repress the pain of living within the history of this one. These are not, in other words, the ideologically pollarded dreams of sitcoms and Dirty Harry movies, and they do not manage popular culture's repression of its consumers' pain in the displaced and disguised forms of splatter flicks and space opera.

As the tattoo develops and Agone begins to feel, through the resultant pain, the "wrecked" status of his old self (one that brags of past sexual conquests as it fades away), we see a perfect rose as the ship's sail and the allusion to "paradises" in the far seas, where "people lived harmoniously with themselves and their environments." But the utopian impulse inscribed here is not so blind: the edges of the rose petals turn into the snakes of raw desire (which belong in the "void" of the more traditional "I" that can find desire but not "a heart" [160]). A Medusan tangle, these snakes are what reify Thivai within the sadist's role, finally, and what "writhed through the holes in the skulls of innocent humans and ate out their brains," leading them to applaud the ending of films such as *An Officer and a Gentleman*.

If desire makes one vulnerable to romance scripts, it is not the only menace to the sailor's life. Surrounding the ship and its rose border is a blue ocean out of which looms the blue dragon of *real* rather than romanticized nature: "It was inhuman. It was inimical to and separate from humans" (139). The scene calls to mind the human struggle to keep some measure of control over nature (we hear of a young warrior who kills herself rather than letting the dragon steal the jewel that controls the tides). It also keeps the reality principle at play here. If "the earth, home, nations are the sailor's enemy, end to his journey, his death," the sea of undomesticated experience and unrepressed history is equally dangerous. Hence the necessity of Agone's having "to pay attention to the pain" if he is to know the sailor's emblem as Abhor's quest rather than as Thivai's adventure story. "Tattoos," we read, "were originally icons of power and mystery designating realms beyond normal

land-dwellers' experience," and even today we find them "transfer-
ring to the bearer some sense of existing outside the conventions of
normal society" (140).

Tattoos, finally, are another of Acker's conceits for the altered
consciousness of those who, recognizing Armageddon has already
happened within the human soul, venture out beyond the known
categories and narratizations of experience to find out what postapocalyptic life is like. "The realm of the outlaw," Acker tells us,
"has become redefined: today, the wild places which excite the most
profound thinkers are conceptual. Flesh unto flesh" (140). In a most
important way, the new "conceptual" is that of the flesh: Acker's
tactile sense of individuality is one modeled on the body rather
than, as traditionally, upon conceptual abstraction. One "knows"
in the bodily strata's pains and pleasures all those contradictions
that characterize the programming in the cultural "biochip."
Abhor's final tatoo, appropriately, is of a dagger thrust down through
a (vaginal) rose dripping blood; its banner reads "DISCIPLINE AND AN-
ARCHY," and Abhor can gloss it well: "It doesn't matter who has
handled and shoved in this sword. Once this sword is in me, it's me.
I'm the piercer and the pierced. Then I thought about all that had
happened to me, my life, and all that was going to happen to me,
the future: chance and my endurance. Discipline creates endurance.
All is blood" (224). Abhor's comments clarify the key traits of her
postmodern subjectivity—its complete internalization of cultural
discipline within the body, its passage beyond metaphysical selfhood, and its enduring chance of something bloody but still possible.

That is, among the writers studied in this book and the theorists whose work is on their shelves and in their dinner conversations, the "conceptual" revolution of a postmodern, poststructural
era provides "wild places" far beyond the imagination of the mainstream's Tom Sawyers. What we find are many variations upon the
analyses and assumptions these writers for the most part share with
Acker. But nearly all of them also maintain this faith in a world that
will not likely be known according to the propositional standards of
the old culture, but one that nonetheless can arise out of the body's
wisdom about the disciplinary, perhaps pornographic, script in
which we are asked to take parts. Many of their characters might
well be standing alongside Abhor as she closes Acker's *Empire of the
Senseless:*

> I stood there, there in the sunlight, and thought that I didn't as yet
> know what I wanted. I now fully knew what I didn't want and
> what and whom I hated. That was something.
>
> And then I thought that, one day, maybe, there'ld be a human
> society in a world which is beautiful, a society which wasn't just
> disgust. (227)

# CONSTANCE DEJONG

*Eco-paleo-psycho-electro-cosmo Talk*

In her *Artforum* review of a television symposium, Constance De-
Jong gives us a rare glimpse back into her adolescence: "The music
was played by disc jockeys on WKYC-Cleveland, the TV was tuned
to 'My Three Sons.' My job: to simultaneously keep track of the Top
Ten in numerical order, follow the TV plot, write a grade-A book
report—basic training in the event that some of life might play polyphonically, not just in the ditch of familiar strains" (*Artforum* [Jan-
uary 1981]: 25). DeJong still lives and writes polyphonically, but she
now monitors language and media from a much more complex perspective, and her grade-A book reports have metamorphosed into
some of the most finely crafted, shrewdly—and implicitly—reflexive fiction now being written anywhere.

Many first encounter DeJong, however, in some form other than
the written page. For many, it is through the Philip Glass opera
*Satyagraha*, for which she wrote the libretto. For others, it is through
her performances of texts. Originally blending props, setting, Glass
scores, even other voices, she now more typically appears with only
a stool and her microphone and speaks from memory some ninety
minutes of written work to audiences all over the art world. Indeed,
the list of locations in which she has read is a good place to begin in
chronicling performance art, because it includes, in New York
alone, the Kitchen, Franklin Furnace, St. Mark's Poetry Project,
Artists' Space, and even the Whitney Museum; Hallwalls and the
Knox in Buffalo; A Space, Art Metropole, and the Ontario Gallery of
Art in Toronto; and other such venues in Paris, London, Montreal,
Hartford, Minneapolis, Seattle, San Francisco, Los Angeles, Houston, and on through a list pointless to exhaust.

Sometimes called the "Homer of modern times," DeJong opens
a performance of *The Lucy Amarillo Stories* this way:

this is the way it was a long time ago
before there was television
when people sitting together like this
would allow a stranger to come into their midst
and provide the social life
by spinning out one of those tales
from the thousand and one nights.
Those desert nights?
O, those desert nights.
My favorite is . . .

DeJong's voice establishes just the sort of vital social relation we shall see advocated by performance theorists, leading audiences through the polyphonic consciousness of her protagonists and away from "the ditch of familiar strains," which provides a spectacle of entertainment rather than, as DeJong makes explicit, concrete "social life." Even her video work insists upon this direct relation—I have seen a work in progress done with Joan Logue which shows DeJong close up, the visual pages turned from one corner up across the image, like those of a book, as she tells her story. Book and image, writer and performer, coalesce. But DeJong is a crucial figure in downtown writing not just because, along with Kathy Acker, she initiated the appearance of fiction writers in performance halls such as the Kitchen. We must add to this contextual element her willingness to take on the radical fluidities of form and Being in this poststructural age.

En route to her preeminence, DeJong passed through alternative spaces rather than through the established corridors of the literary world. The authors she likes to read, for example, certainly distinguishes hers as a downtown temperament, for she cites "people like Stein, Apollinaire, and Baudelaire, and people who weren't so strictly speaking 'literary,' 'philosophical.' They belonged, I belong, to a world in which there are correlations—Stein was a part of a very visual world," and DeJong still operates on the polyphonic track of such correlations. The other major reading influence to which she points, in addition to this avant-garde tradition, is the structuralism flooding into American intellectual circles during the period that she was becoming a writer. The avant-garde tradition's commitment to social change, reflexivity, and formal innovation, combined with structuralism's potential to correlate language, institutions, and social practices, supplies the key elements of the intellectual substrata on which DeJong's writing works its subtleties.

That combination requires a stance apart from the "familiar strains" of suburban homogenization, however, and no doubt DeJong's socioeconomic background has something to do with her resistance to the class structure in the academic and literary worlds. From the Ohio Rustbelt, the daughter of a steel worker and a department-store clerk, "a background in which there *isn't* such a thing as Art," DeJong would certainly have begun, at least, on the outside of the gentrified professions (though with a welcomed abundance of solitude, because her home life revolved around steel-mill swing shifts and the store's hours). But college already entailed something of a betrayal of the working-class background she left behind: "Nobody in my family has ever gone to school; I'm the first person to go, and it was a very defiant act to leave the vocational world of 'getting a job.' And it was in order to get an education, which is the worst reason of all. I couldn't say, 'I want to be a nurse.' " DeJong had thus, by the end of her teens, stranded herself between social strata among outsiders who were working to make their own kind of social reality.

DeJong tells the story better than I can:

> I belonged to a larger artistic community from the time I was
> seventeen or eighteen years old and I never disengaged from
> that. There's another world that's called "the literary world,"
> from which some writers emerge and are always attached. I've
> really never been closed off in the English department or the aca-
> demic world or, in the large cities, the closed writing circle. I've
> always been in that larger art-making world. Because of the time I
> was in school in the late sixties and early seventies, that meant
> people who made films, people who made music, people who
> made dance. It was my luck that just at that point certain people
> couldn't fit into the mainstream of dance, music, and filmmaking
> and provided *themselves* with a working existence. You know who
> I'm talking about—Yvonne Rainer, Philip Glass, Michael Snow,
> and these people. They were really my models as a writer, which I
> used when I came to New York, because it allowed me *not* to be a
> writer who wrote things and put them in her desk where no one
> could see them. And it allowed me to channel myself toward an
> audience without running interference with the established writ-
> ing and publishing world, which I *knew* would be a lot of trouble.

The activity connoted in the verbal structure of "art-making" versus the stasis of "literary," the self-sufficient existence apart from the mainstream, and the direct approach to audience are important constituents in DeJong's career and in the narratives that have emerged from it.

We can begin to track these broad attitudinal indicators toward an aesthetic practice by considering DeJong's work as a critic, a role that dominated her career at the beginning of the seventies until her transformation into a mainly narrative artist mid-decade. Indeed, to look closely at her essays is to assemble something approaching a

theory of art that helps greatly in considering her fiction. As basic     127
as her antipathy to class privilege and to the insularity of the "closed   **CONSTANCE**
literary circle" is her aversion to the model of literary meaning           **DEJONG**
implicit in new critical reading habits. We see this first perhaps in
her article on a work by Joan Jonas which mixed performance and
video (Jonas performs to camera and screen rather than to the audience, a camera moves from closeups of objects to her to a different
room, a monitor plays both the live camera and taped material):

> Her images and activity create a complexity of associations. The
> associations are electrical and visual, not psychological. They may
> be mysterious and obscure. But their mystery and obscurity isn't
> used to disguise or symbolize psychological meanings. The em-
> phasis is on creating a theatrical context, in which images and
> activities have their own power and make their own meaning. The
> making of a visual composition prevails. (*"Organic Honey's Vi-
> sual Telepathy:* Joan Jonas," *Drama Review* [April 1972])

DeJong circumvents the dimension of psychological resonance
which defines the central focus of modernism and late modernism,
and her interest in the interaction of conceptual and performance
art signals the reflexive issues so important in all her thinking.
Symbolism, stigmatized in these comments, suggests an ontological relationship between that which is apparent and a higher order
of truth and Being, of which the appearance functions almost as a
Platonic shadow.

For DeJong, however, the relation is almost *spectral*, without
any familiar sort of ground. Jonas "conjures herself," the audience
seeing performance, drawings being made of the performance props,
a video camera's selection from both, a pretaped film of the performer. No one of these suffices as authoritative—even the performance features objects difficult to see at times except in video closeups, an artist asuming the identity suggested by a mask, and other
disruptions of a "real" ground against which the figures of the image
world, the "distinct other" of artifice, might be thought to move.
The "complexity of associations" woven in this "electrical" world
of artifice emphasize not the Subject but "images and activities,"
and particularly their material power to fill the time and to structure
the audience's consciousness. That consciousness becomes not so
much a subject as an accumulation that is "a collective, not a sum":
complexity and multiplicity do not resolve themselves into identity
or singularity.

One key phrase is "the making of a visual composition prevails"—activity over stasis, multiplicity over identity, simultaneity
over resolution, the pervasiveness of material and spectral constituents over the sovereignty of the subject or its mastery of its sur-
roundings. Another important piece is DeJong's commentary on

Charles Ross's *Sunlight Convergence/Solar Burn*, a work in which Ross focused the sun through a lens onto boards changed daily, recording the solar year in burned streaks and photographing the results for a book. DeJong's piece (which appears in Ross's book of the same title) traces the interplay of the artist's intentionality and the inherent elusiveness of the natural phenomena whose performance is the piece's "content." Light is so pervasive and, scientifically, so "outside the measurable dimensions of space and time," that making it the *subject* of art challenges an artist's resources to conceive how to stage something whose precise nature and whose absence are unknown. Ross's solar narrative is a visual form connoting the pure energy of light without claiming to make statements about it: "Within the situation that was provided, light projected a picture beyond the frames of reasoning and imagining. It transcribed the interconnected motions of sun and earth into a series of energy hieroglyphs: each solar burn is drawn by a combination of celestial and terrestrial forces acting in different dimensions of time. The sun drew its own image, its own conclusions."

What seems to draw DeJong the writer is the way that Ross's work evades the sense of sufficiency presumed by any piece of monumentalized art (or, for that matter, any scientific text)—at the same time that, as a book of photos of these boards, his work becomes "images [that] mediate a context of human scale within the weave of cosmic placement" and thus launches us on what DeJong calls "the journey of relationships." Because "image" resonates with an epistemological tradition that defines knowing as making (literally or figuratively) a *picture* of a subject, that journey is a significant one. Ross's multiple counterpoint among images, the natural, and the conceptual artist's intention to set various scales of reference against one another raise some issues similar to those in Jonas's piece—in particular, the experiential character of scaling, the artifice of reference, and the "journey of relationships" into which such questions lead us. Quite far, in fact, from that ditch of familiar strains.

The implications of these "scales of reference" are of acute concern in the commissioned catalog essay that DeJong did of Nancy Graves's *The Near Side of the Moon*, a sort of pointillist or dot-matrix painting of topographical maps of the moon beamed to earth by satellite—more of the "electric order" that DeJong found in Jonas's work. DeJong writes about the "autonomy" of each dot, but also of the dots' resolution "at stages or levels," and especially of the kinetic nature of that resolution. "Appearance as experience; rather than an idea about it," is one way DeJong reads that kineticism in which conceptual art or the conceptual dimension of art leads to the experiential rather than to abstract qualities of art and Being. Another aphorism relevant here is that the painting "is more about being as seeing than being as object," the electric order of composing on site rather than a metaphysical ontology or some sort of behaviorist or animalistic physiological ontology. One thinks not only of DeJong transforming her own pages to events but also of hallucinatory passages such as her famous sunrise/sunset piece in India, in which the times of its content and of our reading intermingle, particularly when she brings her catalog essay to its end:

> Painting as occurrence. Surface phenomena generates and re-generates itself. Resolution is incomplete, always happening. It is also always there. And, there is the clear drift between the two. A journey from determinate to indeterminate: back and forth.
>
> There are no overlays of content or meaning. No private meanings or symbologies. The emotional content is contained in the formmaking.

Occurrence rather than only object, always happening rather than only complete, but most significantly a "drift" or "journey"— motion and indeterminacy rather than "symbologies." That the "formmaking" is not only Graves's, not only the satellite transmission's, but also the viewer's, speaks to the open nature and to the social qualities of the art DeJong admires. DeJong considers art neither a free-for-all licensed by the artist as epistemological anarchist nor a predestined term to which we are sentenced by a juridical artist enforcing the legitimated code of reality. Instead, art consists of forms that reawaken the scary, primal, performative quality of "being as seeing," but within an acutely reflexive context in which artifice and energy are necessarily coconstituents.

In a second essay on Jonas's work, DeJong makes explicit the implications of her understanding of artistic practice for traditional categories such as the subject:

> The TV was both a toy and an other, both means and ends. Play took the form of fixing on her monitored image, exploring its visual relationship to objects and materials . . . her accumulated special effects. As a means of constituting, the monitor supplied an opposite: oneself given back. An intrinsic quality of the media—feedback—was taken metaphorically. It suggested one who could become a multiple identity. ("Joan Jonas: *Organic Honey's Vertical Roll*," *Arts Magazine* 47.5 [March 1973]: 27–29)

That multiplicity functions both in simultaneity—the "double focus" created by both live and video performances—and when, as DeJong puts it, "the string of vignettes passing by becomes interconnected by memory serving you well." DeJong is by no means so austere a conceptualist that we lose the "humanness" of experience, but she does relocate our Being in an "electric" or "compositional" order of seeing and performing. The materiality, the tangibility, of artifice in the work she admires foregrounds constantly what, for lack of a better term, we might call the semiotic medium of Being. Not the semiotics of the separate subject encoding a message to be decoded by a separate receiving subject, but a more grammatological semiotics in which the sign has "its own power" and "makes its own meaning" around, beside, beneath, amidst the plural intentionalities lurking in subjects and their social relations.

It is no wonder, then, that DeJong is drawn to Tony Oursler's 1984 installation at the Kitchen, a "seeing at first sight" in which images are played on tin foil hanging midair, or on tinted water in "an eccentric video game/peep show," or on "the house of broken glass" resting on a black paper boulder, or on a monitor that replaces the field of stars in an upside-down American flag. (Her essay on Oursler appears in *The Luminous Image*, a catalog from the Stedelijk Museum in Amsterdam.) These dislocated video images break up the monologic of the television eye that burns in America's darkened living rooms, refracting images from network broadcasts, children at play with sci-fi war toys, a woman narrating the invasion of her house by extraterrestrials, clay figures in motion. All of this plays in a darkened exhibition space, an image perhaps of the unconscious experience of television's iconology and rigorously disciplined forms for plot and character and of its presumption to totalize the national psyche.

The images are there in Oursler's video, as they are in DeJong's fiction, but so is their ideological aura framed not in the neat forgetfulness of a television screen or cabinet, but in the fragmented and commodified heavens of current media mythology, the war games, the fractured "at-homeness," and the inverted national vision of our times. Oursler's show desublimates the performance in video's society of spectacle, reconnecting the viewer with the ideological frames that our imagery sets into place within our collective unconscious. Radically reflexive, this installation resonates with DeJong's own efforts to play fiction against the grid of plot and character within which its lines have been so tightly inscribed.

DeJong's review of a television symposium rounds out what we can learn from her critical writings. Circulating through three days of panel discussions and twenty-two speakers addressing "Television/Society/Art," DeJong began to feel some of her antiacademic feelings rise to the surface. An inveterate foe of oversimplification, she dismisses one speaker as "still too much like Television":

> And knowledge made to go down real easy makes you real sick. Thousands of kids who ate out of the hand of American universities know what it's like; how insufficient education leaves a deep burn the day you realize: nothing's that easy unless it's the ease with which you've been taken for a ride. In this business, some-

one's gaining publish or perish tenure at school, someone's rising to TV stardom at home, and the cost of these ventures is absorbed in the price paid for an easy ticket: everything at your expense. (25)

DeJong's animus against academics is partly due to the canon's censorship of certain key figures—"Gertrude Stein might as well never have picked up a pen," she told me. And it is partly due to the persistence of old forms and old ideas in writing programs. But the animus is primarily the separation in academic thought between theory and practice, though, to be fair, bad practice by academics and bad theory by artists draw equal fire.

DeJong supplements the conference with DeeDee Halleck's bibliography for "factual" areas—that is, examples of concrete and material practice—and Ron Clark's list of "general theoretical" readings, including works by Louis Althusser, Roland Barthes, Walter Benjamin, Jürgen Habermas, Fredric Jameson, Julia Kristeva, and the rest of the current pantheon. But most interesting for our purposes are some passages near the end of the essay in which DeJong builds upon a conversation with Stephen Heath (whom she appreciates as "someone who hadn't discoursed in refined, specialized terminology"). Heath takes the old "A + B" of form and content and adds "C," "in which one considers the work in relation to institutions, and by extension, one considers the immediate institution in relation to other institutions."

This explanation begins to take off into "terminology," but DeJong provides her own readings of "C," first isolated, then integrated. To isolate "C" is to achieve a critical awareness that she clearly feels essential to the making and experiencing of art: "We are affected by social, economic, political, many elements which, in a particular historical moment, act upon us and we in turn upon them; as products caught in the net, we are also producers in and of the moment, conceivably more evolved when we act with awareness of these relations. And so, the idea of production begins to shift a little, shedding some of its mechanical self-reflection" (28). DeJong has the performance artist's very material awareness of producing certain kinds of consciousness in her audience as a means of disrupting the programmed beings turned out by the society of spectacle. One is "more evolved" to act with awareness of the social relations traced out by the likes of Althusser, Jameson, and Foucault.

DeJong is no fan of fiction or theory that is solely about itself, hence the importance of "C integrated": "It comes in moments when there are signs of engaging-disengaging with the network, when forms appear which are infused with awareness. An infusion at least suggests that theory is a sustaining element that vitally enters the practice, without being too visibly didactic or drawing attention to itself" (28). So much of the energy of downtown writing comes from this infusion of critical awareness and this fencing with existing networks that DeJong's perceptions here should not surprise her readers. But this balancing of contraries—of engaging and disengaging, of theoretical sophistication and vital practice—is central to her work. We must, she notes, envision "our working processes as something more than events in isolation, devoid of the critical scrutiny so frequently shelved as a separate activity."

Indeed, the interplay of those supposedly contrary activities is much like the interplay of various other contraries which attracts her to the range of performance and conceptual pieces she examines. It would be a mistake to think that these contraries are either in simple opposition or heading toward some Hegelian sublation or pseudo-biological synergy. These contraries function in a relation more like sun and lens in Ross's work, only more militantly conceptual in their "art effects." Mutually displacing, each member of a pair undermines the hegemonic tendencies of its counterpart. This rhythmic interplay affects the reader as a process of dishabituation and rehabituation, as if DeJong were updating the *ostraneniye* of the Formalists with a sociocultural vengeance. She defamiliarizes in a profoundly reflexive way that reconnects process and product, figure and ground, art and its context, within an *experience* of texts which is strongly cognitive, vitally emotional, finely aesthetic in a sense much larger than the woefully diminished notions of our own more rigid formalists. As those contraries reach out and include nature and artifice, tradition and innovation, simultaneity and memory, consciousness and multiplicity, reference and performance, object and activity, DeJong's work takes us straight to the heart of the most difficult issues grappled with in contemporary culture.

### "O, Those Desert Nights"

DeJong closes a performance by suggesting that "every day is the occasion for confirming *real* social life. And if that becomes *this* situation, then I can be done now." She tells stories in order to change our social relations as well as our relation to narrative, her interest focusing upon an audience coming together to hear her recount her narratives, or upon what happens to readers as they progress through a book, dishabituating to familiar modes of reading and rehabituating to the alternatives she offers. Her work can trip up readers trained in the psychological symbology of new critical reading habits. Perhaps we must understand her protagonists as alienated members of a media culture, but we must also remain mindful of DeJong's sense of her objective:

I'm *not* the kind of writer who thinks, what is my story? And I'm not a character developer. I always thought my first question was, what are these forms? What *is* a novel, a short story? It's just the way my mind works. . . . It was my inclination to try and address language as an institution that's evolving and as the workplace where literature comes from, a concentration on what language can do in narration and its forms.

"It's not," DeJong points out in distinguishing herself from writers such as Michel Butor, "that I don't want to bring substantial material to the form," as indeed she does. But her stories *are* less rich as a guide to modernist character development than as a series of performances, conceptual art staged amidst an audience that may not immediately recognize either its role as participants or the narrative voice as that of a conceptual artist.

Chronology, character development, the sense of an ending—these kinds of elements are part of a narrative world that DeJong disrupts in order to pull her readers out of a role as spectators of a novel or a life. To consider "language as an institution" is to begin working out how "C" operates in the daily web of narratives composing our lives, but in that "integrated" way we found her stressing earlier. Language and narration bring with them significant ideological frames that DeJong makes us experience in her fiction much the way that Oursler's installation does with video. DeJong does this in part by stressing artifice, which she defines as "conscious structuring and the structuring of consciousness." Language and form are powerful dimensions of the "net" of relations in which we are both producers and produced, and she seeks a "more evolved" form of fiction which keeps its readers "seeing at first sight," mindful of it as a "made thing" that structures a reader reading.

"I'm a member of a species," DeJong tells her audience, "endangered by the many stories that get told." She is quite intent upon disrupting the audience's intellectual passivity and many of the stories of which we are made, and she offers these "two working thoughts for the living":

(1) that many people find their way to the general through the personal, the individual;

(2) the individual *is* the social being. One's individual and species life are *not* different. In one's consciousness of species a person confirms their real social life, just as, conversely, the being of the species confirms itself in species consciousness and is therefore itself as a thinking being.

The first "working thought" reminds us that DeJong also works by means of what she calls "the residual tease of the Himalayan breeze"—with characters doing things that we follow with great interest as we read or listen. But these story elements are designed to carry us "to the general," rather than holding us chiefly in the modernist preoccupation with inner life. Her second "working thought" is more sweeping in its implications, because it assumes a Marxist or semiotic understanding of the individual consciousness as a function of the "stories that get told" in the social being of the species. We tend to be so habituated to our stories and forms of narration that we do not see the kinds of frames which Oursler attaches to his videos.

We assume, that is, that we are reading or hearing an individual's speech, an individual's point of view; our critical terminology reflects this clearly enough. As we read the fiction of DeJong, we persist in trying to resolve its narration into these conventional habits, despite her manipulations of the "source of language." As she said to me concerning *Modern Love,* "one thing was denying the reader the singularity of the first person, so I gave the first person singular to many people. I knew I wanted to deny 'authorship' this identity or singularity. That was really something important in all my work and it has stayed important to me. I could hardly get from end to end in some books because of the singularity of The Author. It's like Chinese water torture dripping on my head, this one voice, one identity, one author given in some books." The fiction of singularity in voice or identity blocks access to the general and pretends a distinction between individual and social being. The master tactic of DeJong is to make her narrative voice that social being, the repertoire of stories that are told. Reading her texts is a recurrent process of being picked up by the "tease" of a story and set back down again once we realize that to follow a life or a character is to discover its derivation from the culture's narratives about economics, politics, and sentiment.

A ready example appears in "Twice Told Tale" from *Top Stories* 23–24 (1986). It concerns a character who buys not a house, but an experience, from the dream merchants of real estate. The agents are "part of the technostructure" of our multinational economic scale rather than simply entrepreneurs, and their malign force stems not from the simple corruption characteristic "of an earlier era and methodology," but from the fact that "the dream merchants are busy spinning the sale of Buzzy's house into an international epic" (12). "A fast talker converts a roof over Buzzy's head into peace in his mind which clinches the sale that initiates the complicated passage of Buzzy's money back to the mother company, whose real estate holdings are but one of its many offspring." The money is multiplied through computerized investments, the company's "deep concern for the economic stability of the country" becomes "most visible in the area of defense procurement," and DeJong extends the economic narrative to its starkest endpoint: "Buzzy's money is now resting peacefully down in South Africa as a couple molecules of nitrogen in an atom bomb. If it goes off some people will stand around applauding money making as the highest social achievement" (13).

In performance, DeJong calls this a "fairy tale," and its "moral" about moneymaking is the malignancy of the economic narrative in which we all play bit parts. Corrupt government officials or lobbyists are the kind of *individual* villains our social narratology conditions us to perceive: "Their public destruction is a purification rite. Minor sin is washed away in an orgiastic burst of indignation" (12). Meanwhile, the social being of the multinational corporation is invisible, or nearly so, because *its* narrative is of a collective nature alien to our apolitical reading habits. Our "consciousness of species," structured as a plethora of individual narratives, does not facilitate our seeing that *corporate* determination of "species life" necessarily makes power and money our highest values. We persist in thinking that morality is an individual matter and that immoral effects are produced by bad individuals rather than determined by institutional structures.

This example is a relatively simple and straightforward illustration of the way that DeJong's fiction draws us toward the collective agency of narrative in culture. As it leaves behind the individual mythos, however, the fiction becomes more complex and deceptive. We find something akin to Stanley Fish's "self-consuming artifacts" as narratives that appear at first to be about what a person is doing shift on us. For to think of the individual *as* social being introduces a double movement in the process of subjectivity. An individual both is and is not itself—is self-differing in theoretical terms—because it is both its ongoing individual experiences and the Other of the social narratology from which those experiences are derived (not to mention the Other of language, within which those experiences are rehearsed, or of memory, within which they are narratized).

The process is further complicated by the multiplicity of simultaneous narratives and the multiple selves that each narrative inscribes within the subject. In DeJong's stories, several characters repeat the same action or speech or bear the same name, and, because the narrative voice is social, collective, that voice may issue from any character's mouth and, often, may shift without warning. The reader wants to ask at such times whether those are really different characters, or just different manifestations of the speaker. But that question depends on maintaining the distinction between individual and social being which DeJong undermines. Hence the reader oscillates between individual and social scales of reference, learning almost experientially what DeJong means by the "working thoughts" quoted above. That learning leads the reader almost into a different ontology within which capitalism, nationalism, and warfare are no longer thinkable, and to a sense of narrative that opens far beyond the reader's usual boundaries, as defined by the tradition of the novel.

In a letter to me, DeJong puts the case for these diversities with the full force of artistic gusto:

> As a writer in the late 20th Century, my narrative concerns have not been confined to the novel and, in fact, I resent the publishing-literary institution that still insists on elevating the novel as the ultimate measure of a person of letters. I resent the culture's attitude toward singular production, toward confining a person to a singular endeavor and form—as if a person were not serious and accomplished if she doesn't grind away at one convention. For me, narrative concerns are one consistent thread winding through a variety of forms. I think this diversity (or multiplicity) defines me as a writer as much as the multiplicity of individual writing moments.

The diversity to which she refers is impressive indeed, because, in addition to her radio tapes of the late seventies and her remarkable performances, DeJong is now engaged in a whole series of projects simultaneous with her work on the novel "At Night." She has accepted the invitation of the Seattle Arts Commission to serve as one of two artists carrying out projects connected with the renovation of the Woodland Park Zoo (the larger effort involves releasing the animals into natural habitats and designing bioclimatic zones for them). "My idea," she writes, "is to create audio/lingual/musical narratives to be heard on headphones (or maybe in the round) at certain animal sites in the zoo." Always engaged in undoing the worst effects of our narrative "consciousness of species," she will focus on "the low end of the hierarchy where certain beings have been given a bum rap and are seen through the myths we've imposed on them."

The zoo is a remarkably public and popular point of engagement between an artist and her audience, but DeJong does not stop there. She is also working with composer David Behrman on some "spoken word/musical narratives" for radio and, perhaps even more beyond the pale of the "publishing-literary institution," is engaged in a number of video projects besides the Logue narrative tape already mentioned. A mini-opera with Logue and Michael Nyman is nearing release, and November 1988 saw the opening of *Relatives*, a video done with Oursler in which images and words combine, at the Boston Bi-national exhibition (for which, interestingly enough, Lynne Tillman also did a piece). By way of suggesting just how important to our sense of DeJong's work these videos are, we should consider the two most recently released works.

*Joyride*, a video collaboration with Oursler and available

through Electronic Arts Intermix (1988), addresses American culture's manic appetite for packaged stimulation by taking us to the strangest of theme parks. We find ourselves waiting for the show, the "other" patrons (with only stylized bodies) tossing coins into the pool while a voice urges us to read the warning screen (the show may cause "back pain, flash back, night terror, after images"). The show itself packages utility companies, plastic leisure activities, and the administered society in a sort of world's fair self-congratulation by commodity capitalism: "Think of the dollar as the energy, the current. You, the dreamers, are the conductive medium, and the main event is the transformer, responsible for the safety of the lifelines that feed it. And so it goes, returning to the starting point."

*Joyride* knows that no artful sublimation is required in celebrating the transformation of doers to dreamers, of individuals to conductive mediums, of moral or ethical or artistic or even ideological energy to raw capital. The video's second part shows corporate planners whose credo is that "crowd control depends upon good design, and good design depends upon statistics." Explaining procedures over a scale model of the theme park, the managerial type functions as a windup Baudrillard toy, explaining the statistical model behind the toy model of the theme-park model of the social model that replaced reality when no one was thinking. "Invisible control is the best control," and a form of control which the media manages best, however unintentionally.

The very artifice of it all is stressed in the video's third part when the camera takes us on a fun-house ride over impossibly expressionist tracks. We see a green-faced average joe locked in the stocks (which take the form of a dollar bill with cutouts for head and extremities) and pelted with fruit and vegetables as we ride by. The manager's voice explains that through souvenirs (a nice metaphor for consumer goods sold for their image appeal) "public experience becomes private property," a good summary of how reality passes into the commodity realm of the simulacral society. We pass one point at which four channels mix economic news (boiled down to "some make more money than others"), someone's aching eyes and breathing difficulties, a voice urging us to "watch closely" (nothing shown on this ride will really threaten the ambience), and another voice proud that "we've created the most extensive network this country has ever seen." The key signifiers of that network appear when we pass the zone of corporate logos on into the smoking eye of the future, with its pulsing light and electronic Morse code sounds. The last voice we hear links the constant interchange of matter and energy with the metaphor of music's attack and decay in order to clarify the apocalyptic vision this video shares with theorists such as Jean Baudrillard and Arthur Kroker.

It is difficult to say that *In Shadow City*, a 1988 video that

DeJong did with Ken Feingold, is that much more hopeful. But if *Joyride* stresses DeJong's critical reading of mainstream culture, *In Shadow City* stresses her interest in how narrative weaves our culture and identity. Its warp and woof include the political ("Once upon a time there was a president who imagined things rather a lot. He saw himself as a hawk, his country as good, or, as a big *X* maneuvering in a worst-case scenario"), but also DeJong's distinctive focus upon the narrativity of Being:

> According to certain theories a living entity dies and transmigrates into another body. Thus the dynamic character of the world is acknowledged. That there are no unchangeable and no separate individualities. Neither things in themselves nor souls in themselves. Positively expressed, that there is an infinite relatedness among all that lives.

Note that "acknowledged" does not leave the "dynamic character of the world" as open to debate as theories of transmigration. DeJong's theories are cultural and narrative rather than spiritual, as we can tell when she jettisons "souls" and preserves the narrative pun in "relatedness." That narrative line has very real effects: we see images of a street market with exotic birds in small cages being bought and sold (according to an economic narrative of owning and profiting from nature), we have the ideological line lampooned with the presidential imagination, we have the video's opening sequence from a street fair with all the animal metaphors that chatterers are using to put down one another, we have a tale of a wordless encounter with a lynx alternating with images of villagers killing a pig.

The real tour de force of *In Shadow City* is the long concluding narrative that ties all these elements together as dream-transformations of one another, a masterful weaving that serves as a microcosm of culture. We encounter at least ten levels of nested narrative (each narrator, animal or human, dreams itself into the next level until the innermost begins to bounce back through the waking hours of its predecessors). The narrative ends with an almost dub-style echoing of the question, "Where am I?" The question would be hard for the dreamers to answer with authority or truth, because they take their places in a narrative chain (even a food chain) linked by the transformations of the video's narrative "eye/I." These intense fifteen minutes are easier to experience than recount, but the viewer comes away from *In Shadow City* realizing that it is a powerful encounter with the heterogeneous narrative strands of which the social fabric is woven. This video leaves politicians self-inflated, animal merchants quintessentially antilife capitalists, conventional narrators fumbling before the mute difference of the lynx, folk narratives slinky in their transformation of daily experience into myth. Like the video narrative in which all these pieces appear, each of them derives its power from narrative transformation and its ability to obscure that each of its figures is precisely that, metaphor, "just made of thought."

*Joyride* reduces the grand metaphysical journey of the theme park's history-writers and transcendental railroad to the obviously plastic, fake artifice of an uninspiring, even apocalyptic eye-behind-a-toy-wagon-wheel, ominously smoking and pulsing like a thoughtless countdown. *In Shadow City* suggests that we dwell in narrative caves, doing artful (and often destructive) finger plays by firelight, still convinced that we are souls conveying truth. Theme park, museum, and media package are finally the instruments by which the city of culture becomes a shadow of itself, and DeJong and her collaborators are doing much to change the attitudes of those who have lamented her fascination with working beyond the page of traditionally esteemed forms. Both videos convincingly illustrate the success with which DeJong moves in the essentially unlegislated worlds of narrative beyond the novel.

In an interview in the *Daily Magazine* of the *Philadelphia Inquirer* (11 March 1988), DeJong helps us understand her zest for the more open forms that she practices: "Rather than arm-wrestling with a long history of convention, a vocabulary that's like a forest all around me and I'm finding my way through it, I'd prefer to stand on the empty horizon and look out at nothing. Just nothing." That "nothing" has much in common with the "desert nights" that we as a species fill with stories. If we are, as she has said, "endangered by the many stories that get told," at least hers can still function to undo the worst effects of the worst stories. Certainly she takes her art into places where many of our late modernists have not thought to go, perhaps because *their* poetics are still allied with a patriarchal logic that precludes the openings DeJong's work makes for us. "My writing is nonrepresentational," she told her interviewer, though that term has more to do with jettisoning conventions than abstracting from reality. "It's very much involved with artifice and stylization, and the space and coloration of video is very appropriate to artifice, to a world that is nonrepresentational." The key term shifts: the world we live in does not represent itself, but is stylized with all the artifice and coloration of statistical modeling and invisible control, and with the transforming energy of capital flowing through our experiential circuitry in more ways than we are likely to know. Unless, of course, we take up an invitation to "allow a stranger to come into [our] midst" and show us precisely what narratives have done and what, with enough attentiveness on our part, they can do.

DeJong's practice of alternative narrative began with *Modern Love*, a work serialized for three hundred to five hundred subscribers between September 1975 and July 1976 (and published in book form by Standard Editions in 1977). "Mail art, conceptual art, was in the air," she recalls, and, while not wanting "to provide five hundred people with junk mail," she did want to reach her public without tangling with the established literary world. She draws an analogy with Philip Glass's early performances "in truly awful rooms, but two hundred people would come. And we were 'real'—we were a reality as well as Lincoln Center." That real audience also came to the Kitchen in fall 1975 to hear Kathy Acker and DeJong read in a hall that usually featured video, dance, the visual arts, and music. The novel became, along with Acker's *Black Tarantula*, something of a founding text for the new downtown writing. Although *Modern Love* is technically out of print in its Standard Editions incarnation, small batches of copies still surface from time to time at places such as Printed Matter and St. Mark's Bookshop, and *Top Stories* began distributing it early in 1989.

The characters of *Modern Love* include Monsieur Le Prince (an odd sort of wise man), Roderigo (matinee idol to the female voices), Fifi Corday (alias Rita, a performance artist), Charlotte (a writer who in other stories has DeJong's titles to *her* credit). Any of these characters may take over the "I." The novel begins with a voice that "saw the historical bogey man coming around the corner hustling for a place to crash" (4) and thus rushes around "making up stories as fast as I could go." What she finds, however, are losers in streets full of men—"It's always night and all strangers are men" (3):

> I hear talk of a new world. Everywhere I go: eco-paleo-psycho-
> electro-cosmo talk. Of course men do all the talking. I don't get
> the message, my ears ache; my eyes are falling out. I don't see
> these street talkers as the makers of a new world. Anyway, they're
> not real losers. And the new world's an old dream. (4)

Males monopolizing theoretical discourse just confuse the speaker, who is "tired of dreams" repackaged in new lingo and who keenly feels her isolation ("I wonder if I'll always be alone") and powerlessness. The men are not even real losers ("They all have bank accounts: can afford to be losers") because they are talkers rather than makers—nothing is at stake. Something *is* at stake for her: "I'm broke," and she risks an aspiring writer's nightmare end: "Here today, not there tomorrow, gone leaving no incriminating evidence of my unpopular half-baked world view. That's a good girl" (5). She repeatedly quotes mentally the culture's voice of discipline for her gender while fighting against "these crowded narrow passages" through which she is channeled. "I live 2, 3, 4 multiple lives," as we learn when her voice begins to animate a variety of characters, at least some of them stock parts. She picks up a man: "I call him Roderigo, my favorite romantic name. All strangers are men with romantic names. And romantic pasts" (6). And so Roderigo enters the picture as a man she spends time with and as the way that she sees him through the cultural filters of romance.

Roderigo is one of the "stories that get told" but which endanger the female of the species. " 'I can see right through you, baby. I could write your diary,' says Roderigo" (7), sizing up her room, in which everything "fits together," and a life whose script he already knows. "I don't want to be a metaphor," she complains, but she really means *his* metaphor, because she sets about scripting him into her own drama: "We're in my room. I can do anything I want. I want Roderigo. I want him to do everything to me. I want him to feel easy with me and my possessions and my burning desires. I have to turn my self and my place inside-out so he'll enter into the deep, dark, hidden, secretive, mysterious, fabulous magic inner meanings of my life. So he'll disappear. With me" (8). The "inner meanings" are placed in her life through the cultural determination of female desires, a process of which gothic and sentimental romances are manifestations. The point is for Roderigo to "disappear," as she has, into the role.

He does and he doesn't. " 'I gotta go now,' says Roderigo. 'Maybe I'll see you around.' That's modern love: short, hot and sweet" (9). The "he" playing Roderigo leaves. "I want to tell you my life story," the narrator says, and she begins to do so. But the Roderigo love scene recurs, this time more flowery, this time only in the telling, this time more responsive to her desire, this time a lover "condensed into a single, mythical moment" she can hold as the construct that, for the rest of the novel, serves as the model of desire for all the female characters. Roderigo is doubled by Monsieur Le Prince, who "stands for love, truth, wisdom, honesty, etc." (15) and thus collects the manly virtues of the gender type.

This opening shows how the narrative "I" mediates her experiences of both self and other. Ultimately, all the character types are also dimensions of herself, means of distinguishing elements within her, of personifying them and mythologizing their interaction as the culturally determined voices that speak in her consciousness: "People used to tell me, if you keep on writing maybe you'll make a name for yourself. They were right: My name's Constance DeJong. My name's Fifi Corday. My name's Lady Mirabelle, Monsieur Le Prince and Roderigo, Roderigo's my favorite name. First I had my father's name, then my husband's, then another's" (10). The book is full of gags of this sort but is also an extended treatment of making names for oneself both in composing oneself according to stock fantasy material (such as the pornography that she is reading the first time she meets Le Prince) and in comporting oneself according to the patriarchal law of power and possession. Individual and social, personal and general, narrative and socioeconomics, each always also the other.

Part four of the novel, which contains, among other things, Fifi Corday's story, illustrates the point. A performance artist, Fifi trains under Marcel Marceau but breaks with him because "men had all the good parts" (30). Her routine evolves into part tease (she changes costumes on stage), part review (she intersperses character types, such as hipster or cowboy or starlet, with famous people, such as Charlie Chaplin and Marilyn Monroe), even lip-syncing "Pennies from Heaven" while passing the hat. Fifi is a quite thinkable role for the narrator to give voice to: as a woman, she plays sexual and other stereotypical roles; as an artist, she teases an audience into watching narratives that articulate the sublimated social content of the cultural pantheon.

Fifi has a long affair with Jacques during the period in which, finding "Fifi" too tame, she takes "Rita" as her stage name. Jacques is the very type of the Male Scholar, and Fifi/Rita passes through him like a phase. A long phase, however, because their affair runs some ten years until its bitter demise. Jacques "had an amazing memory" but also "had notes": "Hundreds and thousands of references and quotes on scraps of paper, clippings, copies of letters, letters sorted and stored in envelopes. Filed by subject and name always at hand, added to, used, replaced, brought out again. Fifteen years worth of exact information" (33).

Jacques has books and journals, "an elaborate system centered on centuries of poetry, journalism, private papers, fiction, drama, philosophy, history." He is a contemporary Casaubon "writing on every manner of human delight fear hope disbelief fantasy." Instead of the Romantic desire, however, to demystify the key to all mythology, his is the dream of the information age, "one of those complete encyclopedic chronicles of the western world." Jacques's mode is not so much to raise human experience to Casaubon's philosophical sublation but to reduce it to (literally) material bits he can possess like commodities, as per the socioeconomic reality of which he is a part.

Rita, of course, is one of those commodities, and Jacques becomes increasingly restive as her fame grows and her act becomes more sensational: "I want to have you all to myself. I don't want to share you with anyone. I want to talk to you about our future, a future to last forever and plans to make the world anew—a world to hold only the pair of us. You understand, don't you?" (53). She does understand, but she does not want to pass into a private commodity system, with its motifs of monopoly, self-absorption, and the fetish of permanence and domestic insularity—suburbia, in other words. She understands her place in this male fantasy world and tries to communicate this to Jacques through one of her dances.

Rita is disappointed about Jacques's anger as she begins to slip away from him, because *her* fantasy script calls for smooth flowing from one scenario to another. In her performance, she enters in "primly wrapped" white silk, passes through a Gay Nineties gown to a Renaissance gown, "then magically a pants and tunic. She was Joan of Arc circling in a magic trance. She twirled into a Nordic girl, wild and spinning. When she stopped, Rita was a frieze. She danced on the Parthenon. Her white robe fell into fluttering folds as she glided towards the fireplace. Slowly, almost invisibly she lowered herself and began pushing the yards of silk into the fire" (56–57).

Rita twirls back through time, impersonating female iconology until the last stitch of gendered garb is burnt. The script she recites, "solemn and even," is of "the great female who sits there guarding the Island." A sort of antipatriarchal earth goddess, she is "the last of all," and her red hair gilding the clouds is "all there is left of the sun." The myth recounts the futility of her efforts, "throughout eternity," to make herself a cup of tea, with a ship's hull as her teapot, over the ashes of two forests. She will never succeed because of a fog "which has become much too thick and all-pervading," like a patriarchal culture, perhaps. But "there's no life left in the world for anybody, except just a little for her and it is all very nearly over now" (58); the very idea of an alternative gender ideal and the life it might afford are scarcely thinkable.

The responses of the audience are instructive: "All the women thought Rita had embodied the spirit of all women for all times. And they were happy. All the men thought she'd outclassed every stripper they'd ever had the pleasure of knowing. And they were happy. Jacques thought she'd finally revealed her true self. He'd always known that deep down inside she was lewd crude, a contemptible woman. Now even Jacques was happy" (58–59).

The women seem happy to find the combination of eros and mythos which marks the absence of *their* power in the cultural forms in any disguise other than sexual tease and lush costume, movement, and "Island" locale. The men mistake Rita's ironic habitation of striptease for compliance with their erotic fantasy, whereas Jacques is immersed in a super-Calvinist degradation of Rita which justifies his attempt to reduce her to an object in his own libidinal economy. He can be happy because a certain justice prevails in which no one receives pure pleasure because no one deserves it—we are all bits in an information grid or objects in a matrix of money and power.

Fifi/Rita is not the only protagonist. The narrator also mixes in her own story, and the intertwining of the two becomes "literal" at the end of part four, when Fifi attends the party of the narrator, hears about her trip to India, and shocks her by carrying on with Roderigo. But the narrator's story parallels Fifi's thoroughly, though often on the analogical level of art. Whereas Fifi is obsessed with the past roles accumulated in the cultural grammar, the narrator focuses upon *her* past and the relationship between art forms and her own desires. A trip to India yields "better energy" than she gets "trusting only artists" (23), but also a five-page incantatory passage in which the recurrent solar cycles described rather minimally and the reading of those descriptions become synchronized. As DeJong explained to me, there is a gag here about the sort of "pure description" in writing which many people like to skip. But there is also something central going on.

That is, textuality and experience appear to intertwine present (reading) and past (experience) in a way that is an obverse of the narrator's arousal from reading pornography at Monsieur Le Prince's. In both cases, as in Fifi's dance, the female artist dreams of fusing what functions separately in the culture at large—theory and practice, past and present, textuality and experience, identity and multiplicity of roles, to name just a few that cross the narrator's mind. The narrator moves from reading at Le Prince's to coming back to have tea with him. Like Roderigo, a prince of romance, he gives her good counsel about her "obsession with the past": "You think too much," he tells her. "Come back when you have more experience Apple Face. Make use of your disguise" (42).

The narrator's disguise is what she sees in the mirror that he hands her. The mirror, she knows, is "a typical show biz tactic" of the stage seer (and romance prince?)—but it is also a perennial metaphor for writing, just as disguises are one way we talk about the multiple identities we can create for ourselves. What she sees is a remarkable series of images which loosely parallels, in her terms of writing and language, what Rita's more erotic iconology establishes as *her* psychological lineage. The narrator sees her own "baby blues" and "whispy blond hair," then an older woman writing (herself later writing this down? a character who is a writer?), a maid rushing to serve at one of Jacques's salons, and, finally, a regression episode, which moves from "melting goo goo eyeballs" to a failed Cartesian epiphany of a Being on the verge of conventional identity:

> I see more confusion. I have to think. Can I? I feel I'd better; I realize I must; I decide I will: won't I taste smell feel better when I can think realize decide? Won't I? Shouldn't I? Mustn't I? Well, I feel I should therefore I think I am. I mean I think I can. I
> My thoughts have gone astray. (45)

Shifting through the modal auxiliaries of the Western subject, she tries juggling the Cartesian *cogito* before fumbling it all away.

The "insight" she comes to is not Descartes's but a very contemporary sense that "more and more I see I know less and less"—perhaps a recognition that the modes of identity racing by are no more containable within the Cartesian subject than Fifi's desires are within the patriarchal striptease that she undermines and, simultaneously, performs. "I" begins, as above, an unending sentence, going "astray" from the fixed identity of the self as object of ratiocination (or possession, or desire, or power).

Writing, at least partly a function of that objective economy, becomes something of an enemy to the narrator's effort to conceive a writer's equivalent of the dance in which Rita burns her gender's silky confining wrappings: "To go on and on, spreading and changing and growing to become something beautiful, strong, clear, enduring . . . something tells me if I continue turning my insights into adjectives I'll turn into a criminal. I'll steal the splendor of this moment and commit it to a long, sorry sentence. I'll murder people and bury them in gorgeous metaphors. I'll mutilate events and objects, cut and arrange everything into pretty patterns. Into spectacular but empty images" (46). What follows is a scary session in a "house of mirrors" in which the narrator finds "these mirrors, these images, these empty signs, this diffusion, these words" to be "my problem," the very consideration of which means "I'm insane" (i.e., not a Cartesian whole or a social norm). Adjectives, sentences, metaphors, patterns—the specular culture of Image can absorb writer and writing into its galleries. The narrator desires a strategy of evading that absorption.

DeJong achieves just such a strategy by constantly disrupting "singularity" in Being, and by juggling names and their roles as energetically as these characters display for us their modalities or mirror images or costumed twirls. Just as pigeons defecating on the tombstones of dead writers (50) undo the myth of Paris in the twenties which the narrator constructs for herself, so the ease with which the sentences that held together Jacques and Fifi, as well as the narrator and Roderigo, begins to shuffle the four names into other couplings. What semioticians call the "combinatory" logic of syntax is played out here as a grammar of desire which structures not only libidinal and experiential energies but also identity, writing, and memory.

Parts five and six of *Modern Love* work out this social syntax, respectively, in the suburban existence dissected in five and the almost racial memory that the narrator, now named Charlotte, composes to frame her Roderigo's identity in six. Part five begins with the narrator ambushing the reader's desire to be "dazed and speechless" and "totally overwhelmed" by the feelings derived from reading. "For once," we read, "you're not making distinctions about where you stop and where anything else begins. Where you're heading or what you're going to call it." Described here is a state of wordlessness in which something of the fluidity of Being can be experienced, feelings that can "tell you you're alive" because pure singularity in consciousness has fallen away. Without these feelings "you're just like the chair. Cold, hard, waiting to be used" (72).

DeJong wants the reader to be more than the chair in a philosopher's lecture, and part of that fluidity requires shedding the naïve corona of suburban ideology. She creates a character who feels "28, good for nothing":

> Like a lot of other people who wanted to live a life that would have some dignity and meaning.
> Who thought it would be easy to get what they wanted.
> Who now realize that not only is it not easy, it isn't even a possibility. (73–74)

Escaping from the suburbs means you have to push on many fronts at once: "to keep from shriveling up and dying in this forsaken barrenness," "to have a separate identity from the ghost people," "to become someone special, someone worthy," to escape, in other words, "the totally vacant unreality you're facing here in subsville" (75–76). New York is both the source of "pure energy that races through the city" and "a city lost and beaten and full of emptiness," not necessarily more a guarantee of authenticity and validity than is the suburban dream.

Characters face a culture that both generates an extraordinary set of existential demands and deploys all manner of economic, social, and conceptual barriers to block the fulfilling of those demands. For Charlotte and Roderigo, matters are worse because they have no special edge acquired from a family perch on the social extremes: "They knew neither the idealized childhood of a privileged minority; a secure, affluent, unclouded beginning spent in homes of inherited wealth and culture, full of affection and play. Nor the dark caves of the majority, full of hunger, violence and misery. Theirs were the colorless childhoods of middle class families, spent in obscure corners, where only the days are wide and manners, views, interests are pinched and narrow" (88–89). DeJong's eloquence on the midriff bulge of American culture points to the peculiarly postmodern situation of these postsuburbanites privileged enough to see existential possibilities beyond the nine-to-five world, but lacking either the gentry's wealth or the "majority's" desperation as the means of achieving these possibilities.

What Charlotte and Roderigo have are fictions—fictions of identity, fictions of art. Charlotte "gathered together little bits of information and constructed a picture of the [Roderigo] Cortez family," having only "to look at Roderigo to verify her picture" (90–91). Her "picture" is a romantic and adventurous narrative that consumes part six of the novel with the tale of Elizabeth I and Ruiz Cortez, a Spanish Jew whose espionage in Elizabeth's behalf is central in the case against her royal rival Mary and the war against Philip. The narrative constructs the context within which Roderigo can supply what Charlotte has missed—a "real" role on history's main stage, full of the widest implications and (between the Spanish nationality and the Jewish subculture) complex resonances. Her construction is far from homogenization, but also far from factuality, at least as far as Roderigo knows.

Her narrative is powerful enough to sustain a relationship, however, and a level of energy which allows them to contend with New York in their twenties. Charlotte issues a quarterly, *The House Organ*, and Roderigo begins to make his way as keyboardist. They hope to sift through the culture, to "pick and choose and put together some kind of life that isn't totally pre-planned" (161), a life on the economic margins of the seventies' surplus. Roderigo's strategy is pure intensity: "When he sat down, he became part of the instrument. He slammed at the keys, he coaxed them gently, he got them to speak a language you'd never heard before, but you understood every word" (100). Roderigo's compositions create a language whose power and individuality are clearly postsuburban.

Charlotte's periodical is not so much a "type" as a series of subjects which "came out as part of her life, almost a product of it." It no doubt looks like some of the downtown magazines, such as *Paranoids Anonymous Newsletter*, printed like a newspaper and very close to the experiences of a generation inventing its own art world. As she puts it:

> Going someplace and staying there and getting deep into the subject, practically becoming it. Or at least assuming it as much as one can do that while you're there. Do you know what I mean? I actually live through my subjects, the things that interest me, and as a result it's almost like living many lives instead of just one. It's not totally fantasy. And the result, that's just residue, a leftover. It's a newspaper for Christ sakes. People wrap their garbage in it. (162–63)

Charlotte manages both an intensity of near-identification with "exotic" lives and an existential fluidity in which "she" is no one of them. It would be overreading to suggest that she is both self and other, but the highly disposable textuality of her "many lives," which are also "her life," carries out an antipathy to a singularity of Being which she shares with her author (this perhaps, is what Roderigo means when he senses a sustaining "constancy" in her).

The novel is not, however, as simple as all this may seem to make it. Escaping suburbia for the racing energy of New York, carving out authentic space on the commodity market's margins, burning with an aesthetically authentic, hard gemlike flame, immersing oneself in the tangibility of experience itself—if all this sounds like a very romantic aestheticism rather than a postmodern confrontation of harsh realities, it is only because DeJong's postmodernity consists of the *interplay* of the two. Against the energies of its suburban exiles, the novel sets the facts of life. The power of gender remains, for example: "All the things you've been trying to get that have always been and still are in the hands of all those goddamn motherfucking men. No matter what you've done and accomplished in your own personal life, you still live in a world that's owned, ruled and controlled by men" (86).

Moreover, the "spirit and good energy floating around" turn out to have more to do with the "years of growing," a sort of hormonally induced mode of perception, than with the state of reality itself: "Nowadays, you can't feel it anymore. The promises're crumbly. You can't make a dime and all your time's eaten up with surviving . . . work, work, work, until you're stupid with tiredness" (167). Even love gets old; though "complicated," some version of the same tale of a breakup occurs "and then, suddenly, it's not. . . . It's always late at night and someone's walking home alone" (169). Roderigo's monologue charts politics, economics, and love in a single rush toward "holes" filled with cognac: "Hello. I'm a politician. This isn't really a depression we're having and anyway it'll all be over soon. Good luck. Hello. I'm the record man. We're cancelling your album contract. See you next year. Hello. I'm your best friend for five years. Go to hell. She slams the door and that's that. Charlotte . . ." (170).

Roderigo even experiences a sort of psychic transport to another realm that is "an unimaginable distance from the world we know as earth," another life he goes to live in part seven's Oregon sequence. But the wisdom he carries with him marks the unraveling of any suburbanite's version of artistic success in the big city: "But you're no longer having your say. Because this is no longer our little step-by-step world. Once you've stepped in here, into the realm of darkness there are forces moving on a course of their own. Courses that pass through the walls of this and many worlds until they reach their unknown destination" (175). Roderigo has experienced something quite different from any American dream of the sovereign subject constructing his or her own realm, suburban or otherwise. What he *has* found is closer to a Foucauldian network of power relations in which forces move across "worlds" beyond our control or even knowledge, and in which the individual is more side effect than center.

This, at least, is the wisdom that Monsieur Le Prince offers Charlotte: "Theories put man in the center of everything; everything exists for him, the sun, the stars, the moon, the earth. Theories assert that if people want to they can change their whole lives, organize it on rational principles" (165). *Modern Love* does not achieve the sort of novelistic closure which would reiterate these traditional cultural assumptions about identity and rationality. Instead, it winds down into narratives of Roderigo on the Oregon coast, detective Dan Wolf on the trail of Fifi Corday's former lover, gangster episodes, James Bond dialogue, and, finally, the parable of the New York water commissioner, who, for a time during the city's most acute water crisis, was the name "on everyone's lips" until, with the rains, the reservoirs filled. "One day he was quietly dropped. No one noticed" (219). Individuality—even the multiple selves that Charlotte cultivates for *The House Organ* or "Constance DeJong" spins out in this narrative—twirls like Fifi back into the repository of cultural scripts, the economy of history, and the blankness of the page after THE END.

*Modern Love* develops every bit as complex a practice as DeJong's criticism might lead us to expect. The novel develops its materials with all the potency of Roderigo's music, new language we nonetheless understand, a performance that displays the means by which we draw and are drawn into narratives of identity, gender, economic roles, romance, and power. *Modern Love* celebrates this performative Being without tolerating the illusion of its centricity in any but the cultural scheme of things. Its play with the "personal" shifts us toward the "general," toward awareness of the "stories that get told" in the formation of "social being," and toward a readiness to play the "seriocomic," as another generation once termed it, game of postmodern narrative.

### The Lucy Amarillo Stories

DeJong's other work continues the exploration of postmodern fiction with some elements from *Modern Love* and others that supplement what we learned from that novel. *The Lucy Amarillo Stories* (Standard Editions, 1978), published a year later than *Modern Love* but often mingled with it during DeJong's performances, includes five parts, each of which features, at least part of the time, the title character, who takes her name from the aunt who wills her money and a house out in the nowhere beyond Amarillo. Exasperated by the legal range war opened by the crusty patriarch who resents Lucy's inheritance of "his" land, Lucy finally takes off and drives across the country. As she meets fellow travelers here and there, "she got in the habit of making the most of those conversations. Yes, she too thought the country was pretty. Especially from a director's point of view—or an anthropologist's, a journalist's, an architect's, a foreigner's. These were her stories" (46).

Lucy responds to the predictably scripted chitchat with her own

scenarios, which structure her relationships as narratives characterized by many of the elements that DeJong eschews (and that the
larger form of the book undoes)—including chronological development and integrity, identity, and preestablished meaning. What the
narrative performs is more the stage directions of the script than its
speaking roles. Watching Lucy is like watching a personification of
social and libidinal grammars as they frame the life moments of us
all, grammars that repress, for the moment, what might otherwise
disrupt the more pleasant suburban surfaces woven of such lines as
"she too thought the country was pretty." Undermined by DeJong's
irony, those surfaces tilt in a variety of angles worth noting.

The part entitled "The Desert" contains the "story" of Lucy
and Joel on a trip to Rome and Morocco. The trip is a miserable one
because of Joel's preoccupation with Elaina, a business associate's
secretary, whose assets include a good supply of Colombian cocaine
and a large, hospitable bed. When Lucy dares to question his re-
moteness, asking what is wrong, his words feel like blows: " 'Why
don't you tell me?' he shouted. 'We're going to the desert. We're in
the same bed. What more do you want?' " (9). His male condescension hits its peak after she finally realizes what *is* wrong: "he patted
her on the head and called her Lulu and said, 'There, there, don't
feel sorry for yourself' " (15). Her response is depression, despairing
over choosing which dress to wear, staying "in bed with the TV on
one side and the radio on the other, drifting around in bits of movies
and half-heard melodies" (16), eating and sleeping erratically, staring at the "blank glow" after the television signs off.

It is quite possible to read "The Desert" "simply" as a story
about a woman depressed over a bad love affair and the patriarchal
order that abetted it. But this part also ends with the same sentence
that begins it and sidewinds its way through chronology—good
starts toward destabilizing the uniqueness or individuality of experience, as well as the tyranny of narrative time. Most disconcerting
to the traditional reader, however, is that "The Desert" features
Fabou of many shapes, who transports Lucy to the desert, brings her
back to her bed, and dwells within her, waiting "for her heart to beat
evenly and her belly to go gently in and out" (17). The stubborn
traditionalist can, I suppose, decide that Fabou is Lucy's own dream
merchant, a principle of escape from the turbulence of her relationship with Joel and also a potential source of peace.

Indeed, it is useful to think of Fabou as precisely that dimension
of cultural mythology which, in *Modern Love*, appears in the form
of the name, bogus family history, and romance of "Roderigo." Fabou is one of the most devastating "stories that get told" for women.
He embodies the male principle that, seeing Lucy, is smitten precisely by the powerlessness of "a tiny thing in the middle of the
desert" (12); that possesses the mysterious malevolence to live in

dangerous places ("ruined houses, water cisterns, rivers, crossroads, and markets"), causing mischief, disappearing and condensing in ways incomprehensible to her; that can become a real animal ("a jackal, a wolf, a lion, a scorpion, a snake") and "kick up a storm," finally metamorphosing into a fire bird whose peck at the desert floor flames with life (11); that is drawn by the wish to "prolong the effect" of her calmness.

What is more damaging than resigning all these kinds of potency to the male jinni is that it is Lucy, Woman, who voices, has learned to voice, his tale. In "I.T.I.L.O.E.," a *Top Stories* pamphlet (15 [1983]) that features the same character, we hear Fabou feel himself "fading to a soft whisper, a wisp of breath passing through her lips":

> For it seemed that he was back at the beginning, that with the sound of her voice he had arrived at the source of his long, untold existence. It was spellbinding, really—that voice of hers that made words that were him, the Night always unfolding into other nights, beings, entities, shapes that piled up, a dizzying and dumbfounding edifice which spilled over into an intricate system of spaces, a world within a turning world of hours, eons, time fanning out around him, the One-Upright among the horizontals, the Visitor, the Man of Women's Dreams as she called him. (4)

Phallic obelisk in Lucy's sacrament of the horizontal, Fabou the jinni has an "untold existence"; it is untold precisely because it is an opening into the fantasy that draws Lucy into her traditional gender role like a sleepwalker oblivious to the punishing realities of her relationship with Joel. The "dumbfounding edifice" with its "intricate system of spaces" is the social grammar with its intricate system of syntactic spaces, filled when organisms become that grammar's figures of speech.

Because Fabou *is* that spacing, he occupies a curious ontological niche in DeJong's cosmology:

> It called itself Fabou and told her many interesting things: Angels are formed of light. Men of the dust and earth. Fabou of the subtler substances in between.
>
> He was caught in the absolute: moving from place to place but never coming to rest; assuming many forms but never becoming one; carrying out endless actions that retreated into a once that never was. He belonged to a vast astronomical cycle in which the world repeats itself in all its details under the repeated influence of the same planets. (10)

Perhaps those "subtler substances" between physiology and phenomena are semiotic and hence as close to "the absolute" as anything we experience—a generative syntax of consciousness which enables "many forms" without "becoming [only] one." Astrology and mythology are only two manifestations of the cultural narratology by which the human world repeats the dynamic interplay of individual and social being.

The narrator of "I.T.I.L.O.E." takes drastic action once she recognizes this "astronomical cycle" which has carried her along with it: "over and over it's been said until in an instant it rhymes with drop dead. I've had it. I'm done with you in a word. Actually two of them: THE END" (4). The rest of this story, which draws upon *Modern Love, The Lucy Amarillo Stories*, and the forthcoming "At Night," sounds out various configurations of coping with experience without Fabou's "help," the title's initials spelling out a basic question: Is there intelligent life on earth? For the narrator, the calm she achieves is "the breath-taking quiet when a long monotonous sound suddenly breaks off" (23). In *The Lucy Amarillo Stories*, however, the break is less clean. Like the protagonist of another era, Lucy lights out for the territories, but she takes suburbia with her both mentally (Fabou "enters" her in the form of the many casual lovers she takes along the road) and materially (she rents an air-conditioned Oldsmobile for her travels).

Those travels take the form partly of an aleatory route to Los Angeles ("she couldn't help but notice a whole network of secondary roads going every which way and not at all related to the direct route. And what was the direct route anyway? Eventually she would get to L.A." [41]). Lucy does not, reaching San Francisco instead, just as her self-narratizing, following a similar "network of secondary" selves, reaches not the "L.A." of an identity (even one fictionalized like the name itself) but the nonsingular experiential Being(s) we have seen before in DeJong. Hence the anthology of selves which she displays for interlocutors along the road, and the anthology of narrative genres moving through the book.

In addition to the oriental tale of Fabou and what she calls the "fairy tale" of the real-estate multinationals, which we encountered earlier, there are the southern gothic (Dona Maria, her magic, and her golden eagle, defending the old abandoned house from hippies and teenyboppers), the Western (old man Jordan battling the eastern lawyers to keep the family land together), even an almost forties' tough-guy story about a state trooper who wants to see more than Lucy's driver's license. These formal worlds, however effective they are narratively, do not suffice to manage the limits against which she strains. There are still the times of loneliness, made worse by cute cyclists in little shorts; "the land," which exceeds the narratological control conjured by the protagonists of gothic or Western scripts; the commercial interests that script so much of our social being; and the Men who are anything but the "nice guys who'll take her seriously and not fuck her for the hell of it" (68).

Lucy finds herself "yelling about how there's not going to be any more disasters," but the book's third part, "Trouble," ends with the script for a disaster film taking over the pages and fixing Lucy on her knees in a corner of her San Francisco "dream" house, a bit the way Baudrillard argues that "it is the social itself which, in contemporary discourse, is organised according to a script for a disaster film" (Baudrillard 1983, 76). Although Lucy knows this, she does not have the power to manage matters otherwise, and thus DeJong discards her in the book's final part, "More Trouble Afterword," for although Lucy has been "everywhere I went," one of the "shadows" playing on the narrative wall, she is an exhausted heuristic who can tell C.DeJ., who signs the last part, nothing more. "Like her dirty underpants shoved in the back of a drawer, her uneaten avocado rotting in the bottom of a refrigerator," the relation between them is exhausted. When DeJong says that "the individual *is* social being," then, she is speaking literally about the way that cultural forms continue themselves by inhabiting individuals the way Fabou inhabits Lucy. When Lucy sees through at least *his* form of normalization, he, no longer held in credibility, "slipped away" as surely as C.DeJ. slips away from Lucy once the narrator has exhausted the metamorphoses and vicissitudes of Lucy's daily life.

"For us," begins a passage near the end of the book, "all is everything and nothing, which more or less describes what it means to be caught in the absolute" (65). This is the language that Fabou used to explain himself, and it underscores the extent to which DeJong locates individual Being in the narrative medium itself and why, therefore, she is intent upon disrupting the repressive or limiting agencies of narrative form. We can make our mark—a grammatological one that traces the mixture of condensations, displacements, and stylized "narratemes" which is "shaken loose from the fabric of the night" (66). But that mark must be made in a "calm spell" in which we evade the conventional definitions of Being as identity ("it's something like death only you stay alive") and of libidinal pleasure as couple-bonding ("it's like being alone always only you never get lonely"). "It's a place," C.DeJ. tells us, "where if you don't have the normal dreams of building empires, acquiring fortunes, accomplishing great deeds—you're still okay" (76).

That place is found "At Night," when one is, like Lucy or C.DeJ., "having trouble with sleep" in its figurative sense (unable to dream with the merchants and their scenarios). DeJong's novel by that name, one in which we see a good deal more sifting through the cultural dream work of displacements, condensations, repression, and "disguise," has been published thus far only in a few excerpts, the longest of which appears in Richard Prince's remarkable anthology, *Wild History* (Tanam Press, 1985). Against the rationalist dream of Lincos, an intergalactic language of simplicity and utter transparency, is the heteroglossia of cultural night talk. One quotation from this work helps sum up what we have discovered in De-Jong's fiction: "No one said: that what one really is, is knowing oneself as a product of a historical process to date which has deposited in you an infinity of traces without leaving an inventory; the job of producing an inventory is the first necessity" (34). DeJong's work is an extended effort to achieve that inventory for her generation. These virtually Derridean "traces" of the culture's semiotics of Being are the "marks" that DeJong makes in her own moments of calm. These "traces" are also the sort of fusion of (critical) theory and material practice which is central in her critical work and which dominates the whole spirit of her libretto for *Satyagraha*.

Satyagraha depicts visually the success of Gandhi in organizing Indians in South Africa. His efforts are presided over by Leo Tolstoy (an early mentor to Gandhi), Tagore (the Indian poet who was Gandhi's lifelong friend and "moral authority"), and Martin Luther King, Jr. (whose own civil rights campaign carried on Gandhi's work). Gandhi's "satyagraha" expresses the concomitance of a sense of truth with firmness, the first yielding love and the second yielding force, so that "passive resistance" was discarded as an impoverished and misleading description of a movement in which theory and practice were one. The libretto, however, follows not the stage action but the *Bhagavad-Gita*'s teachings about *action* in order to escape the paralysis of doubt, the distractions of desire, and the preoccupation with various binary pendula within which life is sometimes thought to be defined (the text includes pleasure/pain, profit/loss, victory/defeat).

DeJong's own practice, then, carries something of this austere and antiestablishment moral force as its animating energy—a force that, like *Satyagraha*, asks us to watch history keenly and to act within it, but also to hear as commentary upon it the stories of Krishna and Fabou, Lucy and C.DeJ. Those stories counter powerfully the reigning plots of ideology and mass culture, economics and ontology. Against these plots' totalizing and univocal hold upon our imagination, DeJong opposes her sense of culture as a multitude of different stories, some of which may well serve logocentrism, but some of which disrupt its credibility and open to us new models of social being. The meaning of Gandhi is a harmony composed of Tolstoy, Tagore, and King playing against historical events and ancient scripture. The meaning of our own lives is an even more complex composition, consisting of the rich juxtaposition of oral immediacy and narrative conventions, of fantasy and realism, of representations and their artificiality, of self and the most multifarious of self-differences, of imaginative evocation and devastating critique of media culture's most profound Other.

At an early point in her career, when she considered the implications that "life might play polyphonically," DeJong discovered how to avoid the cultural norm of "confining a person to a singular endeavor and form," whether in consciousness or in art. In her criticism and her performances, in her fiction and her comments about it, DeJong gives ample evidence as to why she was one of the first writers mentioned by every downtown figure I interviewed about this well-populated cultural scene. When her characters speak their "eco-paleo-psycho-electro-cosmo talk," they permit us a wholly new understanding of how culture's discursive strands weave the complex fabric of our lives.

# LYNNE TILLMAN

## *Madame Realism's Feminist Ethnology*

"That was an idea I had had since I was eight, to be a writer."
However, Lynne Tillman came perilously close to becoming a
painter, having encountered in Hunter College's English Department a professor who found it necessary to look out at his freshmen
and tell them, "By the time Joyce was your age he'd already written
*Dubliners*." Tillman took her electives in art, thinking that a good
response to terrorist teaching. But Madame Realism was already
nascent, dooming her efforts to be a dutiful school painter:

> I did a lot of watercolors and a lot of oils, and I was encouraged
> because I was an oddball in the Art Department. I mean, I was not
> not going to be an artist and I think some of the teachers found me
> kind of hilarious because I could never get the whole body on the
> page in life drawing. Somehow the head was gone, or the arms or
> the legs would be off the page. I could never figure how you put a
> person on the page.

I have no evidence that she ever did literally draw the whole person,
but after a stint at London's Arts Lab scheduling poetry readings and
lecture series, and then a period running an experimental-film cinema in Amsterdam, Tillman returned to America to put her many
talents to work as writer, cultural critic, and filmmaker.

Tillman's writing shows the effects of this varied career, the
paragraphs shifting like cuts in a film, the visual details as telling as
any Northern Renaissance painter's, the theoretical sophistication
reflecting her reading of key figures such as Freud ("as a writer I like
the idea that 'you' are made up of words") and Bakhtin ("the idea of
there being a dialogic imagination, that a novel can be shot through
with many different voices"). Her friends among writers are not
those who went from undergraduate to M.F.A. writing programs to
teaching jobs, but those who, like herself, learned by doing, drawing

a critical edge from urban living: "Where we [she and her writing friends] are geographically indicates where we are socially. All of these things are ultimately, deeply, political. If the writing is different, then this is part of it. If you're teaching writing in a small town, the experience around you is going to be very different from living on East Tenth Street. Sometimes I open a novel and I can't read it because it seems so complacent." Her own parents, first-generation Americans of families from Austria and Russia, keep her close to the immigrant experience that is so much a part of the Lower East Side, where she lives and works. Her mother was raised on Ludlow Street, and Tillman is mindful of her family's tri-generational epitome of the American saga.

Tillman is, however, also mindful of the ideological inconsistencies in the American dream, as readers of her May 1988 *Art in America* piece (76.5: 176–81) know: it features her remarkable narrator, Madame Realism, "On the Road" to such emblems of cultural contradiction as Monticello, Malcolm Forbes's Moroccan museum (which features his seventy thousand toy soldiers), and other wry venues where the simultaneity of mythos and bathos catches her quill. She likes her fiction to reveal "different kinds of states of reality going on all at the same time," matching those Bakhtinian heteroglossiac voices. We escape the naïveté of lineal causation and simplistic characters only by responding to the multidimensional complexities of the age:

> I'm writing in an age when film and television are around. Virginia Woolf said that "all books continue each other," but now all television, books, all *media* continue each other. If you separate them too much you create false categories. If you're living in this moment, being of it, you will make different kinds of things [than modernist narrative]. When I see people making the same kinds of things, it's not that they're not doing it well, it's just that I wonder *why* they're doing it. As if this other kind of consciousness were not available to them.

Tillman's commitment throughout her writing is to capture the difficult planar surfaces of contemporary consciousness, planes shaken together in the semiotic sack until the reflections become the multifaceted ironies of a Madame Realism.

Capturing those surfaces requires an acute sense not only of the implications of electronic consciousness but also of the semiotic medium in which our thinking and writing take place. As she explains:

> Writing is different from walking around. When I sit down to write something I have to deal with the problems of writing as well as the problems of living. Problems of living seem to me to be

different from the problems of writing about the problems of living. If you're not reflecting on the fact that you're writing with sign systems, if you write as if what you're writing is totally transparent, a given, then I think you're in a lot of trouble. I'm not dealing with writing as if it's an activity which is not constructed.

Part of Tillman's suburban ambush is precisely of that fiction which has not reflected upon the constitutive poetics invoked by the narrative act.

But her richest assault on unreflective living and writing is the intensity with which she reads the minute details of daily life. In one of her most revealing comments, Tillmam told me that

> when you write you are doing a bit of ethnology. How you choose to represent the characters—the cultural objects with which they come in contact and what they do in their day—all this is *not* transparent but has social meaning. Truly contemporary writers are very conscious of the social conditions of their characters and understand that if you use a detail, you must use it critically, not just to set a scene, but to say something about the social conditions of that person's life. It's not just local color.

Tillman's critical interest in the formation of women's consciousness requires her attentiveness to cultural contradiction, her sensitivity to the implications of a media-saturated culture, and her deft ethnological touch in identifying the "social meaning" of what too often passes by as "local color" in the more suburban reaches of the fiction world.

A great deal of her strength as an artist stems from, in effect, pursuing three parallel careers, each of which achieves these complex goals. As filmmaker, she wrote the script and, with Sheila McLaughlin, codirected and coproduced the uncompromising *Committed* (1984), a time-delayed counterattack in Frances Farmer's behalf against the studio, political, and psychiatric systems that entrapped, broke, and disposed of a typical Tillman heroine—one who attempts to create a full life to replace the somewhat android function designed for her. As Madame Realism, Tillman has become one of our most incisive reflexive essayists about the larger cultural poetics out of which our art, our fiction, and our lives are composed. As a narrative artist, she has published in the honor role of downtown magazines—*Top Stories, Bomb, Portable Lower East Side, Between C & D, Wedge,* and *New Observations.* Her novel, *Haunted Houses* (Poseidon Press, 1987), stands as one of the most important single volumes of downtown writing. To examine these parallel careers is to appreciate how telling a postmodern narrative feminist ethnology can be.

Although *Committed* was generally well received and is responsible for the reputation of Tillman among those determined to rescue American film from E.T. and Conan, the difficulty some reviewers have had in discussing her film is a good point at which to begin considering the challenges and rewards of her art. Anticipating another Jessica Lange film, apparently, some viewers missed the point of *Committed*'s play with the conventions of documentary film, its neo-expressionist use of tableau and camera angle, and its use of monologues to break up popular film's tendency to gloss over the social, political, and psychological contradictions of real life. One critic called it "a real theatre emptier," another spoke of "ineptitude" and "embarrassment," a third apparently left the film and concluded that "the less said about those involved in this film, the better for their careers."

Without a simple message to proclaim, without a single relentless story line, and without either final triumph or simple empathy to carry its audience, *Committed* is as deceptive in its relation to mainstream film as Tillman's fiction is to the *New York Times* bestseller list. Even McLaughlin, who in addition to sharing production and direction with Tillman also starred in the film, found Farmer a difficult subject, as she explains in an interview: "There were times when I didn't like her; she couldn't play the hero. I don't know if I've seen the presentation of an ambivalent female as the central character in a film before. Either one is the complete victim, totally abused, or else a hero who is wonderful and right" (Prina and Williams 1985, 140). Tillman is blunt about the effects of this history of women's portrayals in film: "Why something seems either conventional or unconventional—why something 'works' or 'doesn't work' for someone—has already been 'programmed' in that person's mind." Like much of Tillman's art, *Committed* contends with that kind of programming in order to open up the range of responses we can have and to get beyond the sort of taboos to which McLaughlin refers.

Hence the film's value to readers of Tillman's fiction is obvious in several ways—in its general rhetorical stance, its commitment to certain key motifs in contemporary thought, and its handling of narrative. In some conference remarks reprinted in "A Film *with* History," in the *Independent* 10.1 (January/February 1987: 12–13), Tillman calls the film an "intervention into the mainstream," trying to locate "a person's life within a particular social, political, and historical framework" (12), and hence breaking with the classic film rhetoric of identification. Within the first eight minutes of *Committed*, the viewer is exposed to anticommunist ranting, the first hint of problematic family dynamics, and radio reports fusing mental hygiene with "good" citizenship and other forms of normalization.

In a particularly incisive comment that prefaces the rest of her work as well, Tillman writes about her strategy:

> One of the things *Committed* does is construct a voice, a fictionalized voice, for someone called Frances Farmer. And it places that voice against at least five others—law, psychiatry, politics, Hollywood, the family. By having these "voices" in juxtaposition with each other, we arrive at a way to see an individual operating within the institutions; we allow for an interpenetration of ideas, voices, institutions. We allow for ambiguity and contradiction. In this way *Committed* problematizes what makes an individual and what an individual might be rather than simplifying that process. (13)

Her intervention is partly our contemporary quest to rediscover a viable voice for the individual, partly an exposure of the collusion of various institutions in defrauding us of our individuality, partly an effort to capture the complex cultural contradictions within the multiple "voices" that speak our Being, and finally a rejection of the suburban flattening of all these issues to the two-dimensionality of a slick film still. *Fiction* becomes the mode of choice for imagining the voice capable of opposing the forces that destroyed Farmer.

If this description of her rhetorical stance places Tillman on the critical edge that typifies downtown writing, her more specific targets suggest that she is one who has honed the poststructural or postmodern point of that edge. One of the first things we hear in *Committed*, for example, is a contemptuous dismissal by a judge of that "talking cure nonsense." The 1930 Congress on Mental Hygiene, featured in the opening minutes, was about better living through chemistry, not self-knowledge—psychiatry, not psychoanalysis. Again, Tillman's comments are to the point when she argues that "through speaking you can undo things," a radical act, because "you" is "something that is made of language" (Prina and Williams 1985, 44). Speaking is an especially charged act when one is not compliant with the institutionally empowered discourses of one's culture. More specifically, as Tillman observed during our conversation, a "drug-oriented" psychiatry implies that "individuals are really much less complex, and perhaps even dismisses the unconscious as a problem."

The problem is more acute when the words of which one is made are someone else's—as is preeminently the case for women. To the extent that *Committed* is about more than Farmer's dilemma, it is about "how a woman can get pleasure and not succumb to all that which allows this pleasure." Love, Tillman explains, is conditioned by "Hollywood's representations of the life you're leading." What contemporary women share with Farmer is the difficulty of escaping that "extraordinary grammar": "we as women are rejecting that [Hollywood] notion and yet still are not outside the thrall of it." "That which allows" enables and disables simultaneously, and Tillman thus situates herself squarely among poststructural thinkers theorizing the "prison-house" of language and culture.

In her most radical moments, Tillman disposes of anything resembling our traditional notions of "truth" and "self." "History," she observes in her piece about the film, "is working with and constructing meaning(s), and power depends on the ability to define and impose meaning" (13). All history is "a series of interpretations or constructions," hence the film's objective of representing Farmer "through a clash of fictional interpretations" which anthologizes dominant voices of her social era. "We did not hope to arrive at who Frances Farmer really was," she notes, disposing of the traditional narrative desire to know, to possess. Tillman's film instead raises our awareness of what Bakhtin called *heteroglossia*, the many voices that constitute the self. "We wanted to present a set of possibilities, a complicated matrix that could represent the fact that the self is not an absolute, divinely set entity."

Tillman summarizes the complex balancing act achieved by the film in ways that clarify why major commercial distributors thought it too demanding for the mass market:

> We were interested in trying to show how the construction of a subject is produced by internal and external forces. There is not simply a psychology to that person but there is also a sociology; it's not only that the mother committed Frances, it's that the mother is complicit with the law and with psychiatry, and that the political structure is repressive. These elements work together, they intersect. One way to show that is by using, as you call it, a montage within dialogue. (Prina and Williams 1985, 41)

The montage effect of heteroglossiac dialogue complements the film's visual strategy, which repeatedly defeats our well-trained desires for cinematic satisfaction. The film almost feels like a documentary at the beginning, with its radio replays of Lillian Farmer's anticommunist broadcasts and its news reports of the Congress on Mental Hygiene. But that interpretive frame drops away almost immediately, as if the convention were unable to deliver the stable truths that its paraphernalia promises. The viewer knows at this point that the film's chief players are the institutional voices that speak through the characters, broadcasts, quotations, and background details. If this is not enough, the camera pans slowly and almost interminably across the asylum grounds. The space of psychological and sociological imprisonment is the film's focal plane.

The often harshly lit black-and-white frames become neo-expressionist tableaus. When Frances appears before a judge (for drunk driving), we hear his period rant conflating religion, politics, and know-nothing psychological prejudices, but we cannot hear *her* responses. Toward the film's end, when she makes a careful appeal for relief from drugs and shock treatments, we *can* hear her—it is the doctors who apparently cannot, discounting her as woman, patient, and proscribed political voice. Sometimes it is the viewing angle that distinguishes a scene, as when the camera orbits almost dizzily around the table of psychiatrists assembling the official language that they can use to commit Farmer. That movement emphasizes the closed circle of their language of power; when it is oddly fixed, as it is on the ceiling of the asylum at one point, it emphasizes the painful stasis of inmates warehoused as "abnormal," the center of the frame an empty space with obvious symbolic significance. *Their* circulation is clearly arrested.

It is difficult to speak of "narrative structure" in the film because of the recurrent displacement of familiar attitudes toward narrative itself. The unwary critics already mentioned no doubt chafed at the apparently irrelevant scene with a psychiatrist's family, but it shows his daughter (who wants to be an anthropologist rather than a housewife) and wife (who, though silenced, covertly affirms her daughter's aspiration) chafing against the monolithic (male) order he tries to maintain at home as well as at work. The stormy scenes between Farmer and Clifford Odets, her lover, "fail" by traditional terms to advance a story plot or take us toward some resolution or single key insight into her "condition." But these scenes do make clear the lines of power running through their lovers' discourse, constantly working to orchestrate his ascendancy and her abasement, his monopoly over the text(ure) of pleasure and her complicity in its abusive ritual (he forces her to say "I am a monster" before giving her love).

We cannot, then, make much headway by considering this film as the story of Frances Farmer—it is a talking cure, a speaking through of what the other voices that she internalized inflict upon her, an effort to undo the silent tyranny by which the voices appear, as in the Hollywood film with Jessica Lange, to be simply *Farmer's* failures, conflicts, or pathology. The film almost asks to be misread as the familiar psychological scenario—the materials for a simplistic diagnosis of Farmer as the victim of a bad mother are all here. But, as Tillman points out, Lillian Farmer is *both* a psychological cripple—she is herself isolated from and fearful of the larger world—and a repertoire of social attitudes cribbed from the media of her era.

We have to take Tillman's psychoanalytic inclinations seriously to see how to construe the film's jagged cuts, juxtapositions, nonsequential scenes, and dramatic monologues. It is as if Tillman allowed the political unconscious of an era to speak to us in cinematic form, thereby inviting us to play the psychoanalyst's role by means of our film conventions and our interpretive protocols. That era's own voices transact with our film conventions in ways that make evident that era's will to power, its naïveté, its vulnerability, its pain, and its violence, and with all the immediacy and contradiction that characterize the gritty reality of history in process. If we fail to approach history as this kind of analyst, we will never succeed in tracing the "extraordinary grammar" of an era's traumas and repressive mechanisms. The judge who dismisses "that talking cure nonsense" would no doubt be even angrier were he to discover Tillman applying it to his historical era.

Tillman's narrative art uses film to intervene in the process by which the same material our media calls *Frances*, Tillman terms *Committed*. She supplements the popular logic of the purely personal with a problematic view of the individual saturated with social history. Activist art, poststructural assumptions about "truth" and "selfhood," and a tough quest for formal techniques that belong to such narrative objectives mark her other work as well, and they provide the framework in which we need to conceive both her "reflexive" and her more clearly "representational" prose.

### Madame Realism

Tillman's reflexive voice most clearly dominates when Madame Realism comes back to town to write another piece, as she does in "Madame Realism's Imitation of Life" in the catalog *Fake* (New Museum of Contemporary Art, 1987), for the museum's exhibition of that title: "Never wanting to outlive her welcome, Madame Realism every once and a while disappeared, without telling anyone, and returned some months later, reassured. For as much as she needed to leave, she needed to return. One produced the other, in a sense" (46). Leaving only to return, Madame Realism can neither rest content with simulation and *méconnaissance* in the art world nor stay too long at the extremes of ironic distance. When she finds herself at an opening at which "conspiracy is merely breathing together," then she becomes Tillman's means of pointing out the ironies of our dilemma as a culture that does not quite know whether it should be coming or going.

If *Committed* works by loosening an era's tongue about itself within our own media, Madame Realism operates by so saturating her writing with irony that one feels at times like a provincial at a sophisticates' repartee rally. Exhibitions are closely commented on in the *Art in America* pieces, making them relatively easy fare. In

"Dynasty Reruns" (74.6 [June 1986]: 35–37), a review of the Treasure Houses of Great Britain, for example, Madame Realism does not exactly gut the exhibition, but she does muse on the disjunction between the official history sanctioned by "Charles and Di" and funded by Ford Motor Company, and the "other" history "of those without access to power." She finds in the family-album room one small plain book showing the house servants—and it is metaphorically closed: "the return of the repressed," she calls it, but its photos of unofficial history are "barely open" to view (that is, visitors can see only a single page). The extra twist is that the pictures were taken by the mistress of the house: the "repressed" do not have their own voice, their own faculty for imaging. It remains for Madame Realism to give voice to the culture's Other.

This theme of class is worked two ways. Describing the simulated gallery based on a painting, Madame Realism notes she "would never have been invited, in that day, to stroll down the Countess's picture gallery. (The British don't fool themselves about all being one happy classless family.)" (36). They don't, we do. After seeing the painting, *The Tichbourne Dole*, she notes Prime Minister Thatcher's attack on social welfare and concludes that "at least the poor are shown to exist . . . which is more than can be said for Reagan's picture of America." Perhaps such shots are easy to take, but taking them in the context of an arts magazine works against the absence of social meaning in some art criticism and makes one telling point about the exhibition's apparently unabashed enthusiasm for life under the Reagan regime and its class politics.

A second point is made, not untypically, at Madame Realism's expense. It involves her love for "Dynasty" reruns. "Again Madame Realism thought about *Dynasty*, and imagined that Elizabeth I might have been like paranoid Alexis and Bess of Hardwick like trusting Krystle. Guiltily she looked around her and wondered if anyone else was making such plebeian comparisons" (35). Such irony is nearly universal in its effect. The exhibition is as glitterstruck as the schmaltzy television show; Madame Realism, like most tourists in blockbuster exhibitions, has a hopelessly middleclass consciousness structured within a gallery of reductive portraits and ideologically unexamined plots; "Dynasty" and similar shows perpetuate the cobra-charming play of the media and its capacity to absorb a populace into a (dis)simulation of the very condition at which it should strike.

Madame Realism considers with equal irony several other pertinent questions. She bridles, for example, at a slide show with a taped English voice trying to persuade her that the English country house was both the epicenter of civilization and as "natural" as the landscape: "Houses natural like the scenery? Was this the divine right of houses? She doubted that something could be both natural

and civilized at the same time" (35). The ideological function of the
House is to claim precisely that. Madame Realism's observation is
a poststructural bit of criticism undoing the ideological naïveté implicit in identifying "civilized" form and "natural" truth. Formalists may repress history and politics in their enthusiasm for technique and form, but Tillman's work never allows such a distance to
open.

In an earlier piece about a Renoir exhibition in Boston, "Madame Realism Asks: What's Natural about Painting?" (74.3 [March
1986]: 123–24), Madame Realism pursues the problem of the "natural" in artspeak. She ironically records both highbrow and lowbrow
responses to the paintings (Renoir's rise as a tailor's son is a bit like
Frank Sinatra's fame, "cream to the top," an observation triggered
by wandering tourists' chatter). And, as in the piece on the Treasure
Houses of Great Britain, she plays a bit with her own responses,
particularly after the exhibition when she slips home to beer and
cheese, television and cat. This mix juxtaposes daily life to the
museum's monumental setting, again unsettling the unreflective
elitism that can pervade the world of high culture. She is explicit
about the economic and ethnic divisions in the city surrounding the
museum but excluded by elitists. "[I]n an institution such as a great
museum, where lines of people form democratically to look at art,
such problems are the background upon which that art is hung."
Part of Madame Realism's sensibility is to keep that background
before us. Hence at the mention of "genius" by a highbrow, Madame
Realism walks out because he makes Van Gogh sound like "an animal holding a paintbrush" and thereby reduces a complex human
being to an object in the hands of a patronizing consumer. In these
cases, art lovers seem enclosed in artspeak and oblivious to its reflection of class interests. As she looks at the paintings, she also
recoils from the "vacancy" in the faces and from the almost grotesque fleshiness of the women, as if Renoir were "so uncomfortable
that what he painted reflected his discomfort by a kind of ugliness."
Responding partly because she feels that her own body is as out of
style as those of Renoir's nudes, she seems also uneasy with the
sheer anonymity of these female others, bristling over the ethos of
possession in *"his* nudes" or *"his* peaches." She is similarly both-
ered in the Treasure Houses of Great Britain exhibit when portraits
of family groups seem to show the same face on everyone, "as if
stamped rather than painted. But then dynasty isn't concerned with
individuals but with continuity, and so it can be faceless."

Madame Realism's most philosophical piece is in *Fake*. As is
appropriate for the exhibition, she turns loose the exchange between
the real and the simulated. Her notebook reads, "DON'T FORGET TO
WRITE ABOUT THE TIME I WENT INTO A BATHROOM AND IT TURNED OUT
TO BE SOMEONE'S ARTWORK. ARTIST CAME RUNNING WHEN I FLUSHED TOI-

LET" (45). When asked if she is indeed Madame Realism, she responds, "Not really. . . . Why, do I look like her?" (46). She is relieved to hear that the image she sees of herself, which she dislikes, is *not* from a "perfect mirror," an idea that is "terrifying anyway" in its assumption of absolute representation.

The crux, though, is the pervasiveness of simulation everywhere from conversation to the deepest reaches of the self. Madame Realism breaks off recalling a conversation to reflect: "From art imitating life, to life imitating art, and here they were at art imitating art and life imitating life" (47). The principle of infinite regress quickly makes all work and all talk Fake, but even Being is not above the fray:

> Still, she thought, if there is no inner life or self, and I'm not being conduited, this physical presence, this facade, might be all one really did have. This raised the image stakes immeasurably, making the peculiarity of her image to herself even more burdensome. On the other hand, it could be consoling to know that that empty feeling is not just a feeling. After Madame Realism left the room, one woman said, "I think that is Madame Realism, but do you think a fictional statement can ever be true?" (46)

If there is no "inner light" to redeem a bad image, then one is all the more an outcast from social circulation, but at least "emptiness" is less a personal failing than an existential precondition. In a typically arch abrupt transition, "Madame Realism" as an artifice, as a fictive trope, is batted about in the context of the Fake (she recalls cross-dressing for a costume party as the kind of man she could not stand, then as a thirties' governess, and moves more generally into the unsettling implications of representation, imitation, and hoax).

The piece ends by bringing the whole issue of the image up against the real. Madame Realism considers the difference between the "homeless" (a word "naming, categorizing, and dismissing in one blow") and herself, able to both return and leave voluntarily her own home. Personal authenticity is a function of whether one's image can circulate in a verbal economy. "IS THE UNREPRESENTED LIFE WORTH LIVING?" she asks, aware that those who have no place in media narratology are like the underclass in the almost-closed photograph album. "NO TAXATION WITHOUT REPRESENTATION" in this context shifts us from liberal humanism's democracy to a postmodern simulation culture's airplay. Our social integration is no longer thinkable in terms of political institutions, but only in the narrative forms of the collective electronic repertory.

Perhaps the relationship between Fake and Representation is best clarified by a passage from the Renoir piece: "Women are home to him, she thought, big comfortable houses. And if representation has to do with re-presenting something, what is it we repeat over and over but our sense of home, which may become a very abstract thing indeed. She imagined another sign. It read: Representation— A Home Away from Home" (124). For a semiotic Being without a metaphysical home to fix its identity, "home" becomes that simulation which, as long as it can sustain our suspension of disbelief, appears to satisfy what it describes to us as our desires. For Renoir, fleshy big women; for us, "Dynasty" reruns?

This same narrator appears in an excellent artist's book, *Madame Realism* (1984, with drawings by Kiki Smith), turning her attention upon more "personal" material, but maintaining her typical reflexive focus upon the code system from which our thinking and Being derive. Tillman keeps us mindful that "all ideas are married," presupposing their opposites and thus necessarily a part of that code system. Moreover, Madame Realism knows that "my boundaries shift . . . like ones do after a war when countries lose or gain depending upon having won or lost." That is, just as "power has always determined right," so Will determines the "boundaries," if not the "limits," of self.

If the self is thus constructed, and if its relations are with the images and emptiness of others, then "we are like current events to each other" in evanescent encounters that are a bit like miniature media events featuring conflicting types. However, many such contests are internal, and on a page facing a drawing of a stairway (it is ambiguous whether it is up or down) is this vignette from a dinner party: "A young man, full of the literature that romanticizes his compulsion, drinks himself into stupid liberation. He has not yet discovered that the source of supposed fictions is the desire never to feel guilty." Having not yet penetrated the ideology that romanticizes subjectivity, the young man has not seen its ethos as a compulsion to build oneself into the cultural marriage of ideas and to participate in its approved rituals. His drunkenness is less a release of an otherwise inhibited wit and genius than a "stupid liberation" of the ambivalences internalized from the larger cultural contradictions of which he is composed. The "desire never to feel guilty" is thus that desire to escape the primary contradiction in American culture between the absolutism of its various founding ideologies and the limits and contradictions of its history. From such desire stems fiction, that medium of resolving imaginatively what will not in history go away.

One such fiction is that of the subject. In this passage Tillman links our culture of the image with the problematic subject:

> Talk shows especially encapsulated America, puritan America.
> One has to be seen to be doing good. One has to be seen to be
> good. . . . A face is like a screen, when you think about projection.

A mirror is a screen and each time she looked into it, there was another screen test. How did she look today? What did she think today? Isn't it funny how something can have meaning and no meaning at the same time.

Material success is the only signifier of authenticity in the Puritan's binary and absolutist ontology, hence one *is* only insofar as one is an image to be seen (that is, projected, constituted by one subject or another) and consumed. The materialist and "loose" eighties thus plays a variation on the Puritan themes of three centuries ago, which are less different than we might have thought. But because we lack the Puritans' transcendental beliefs, our projected image has the meaning we give it, but perhaps no ultimate meaning of its own.

"Clever people plot their lives with strategies not unlike those used by governments. We all do business." Lives as narratives, subjects as willed constructs, acts as strategies on contested terrain, selves as businesspeople trying to keep the existential account books in the black. It is no wonder that when the story comes around to explaining Madame Realism herself, her Being is located not on what we might once have called a "natural" plane, but rather on a semiotic one: "When the sun was out, it made patterns on the floor, caused by the bars on her windows. She liked the bars. She had designed them. Madame Realism sometimes liked things of her own design. Nature was not important to her; the sun made shadows that could be looked at and about which she could write. After all, doesn't she exist, like a shadow, in the interstices of argument."

Madame Realism designs the bars of her own prison but experiences that prison as a site of pleasure, comfort, and writing, just as our culture's mimetic epistemology designs its own "prison-house" of language and finds that enclosure ample incitement to productivity of every kind. Because she exists in the gaps between the many positions argued in that language, it is appropriate that she projects her own Being not in Nature, the thing itself, but rather in the openings of language. But the cost is that one becomes subject to the anxieties of the cultural contradictions inherent in that language, to its reduction of self to image, and to the guilt imposed on one for *not* being Nature instead. Projected image, linguistic figure—Tillman's subject all but disappears "in the interstices of argument."

Even argument itself does not escape Madame Realism's eye. A nosebleed trips her into an unconsidered metaphor: "I must get this fixed, she thought, as if her nostrils had brakes. There is no way to compare anything. We must analyze our lies. There isn't even an absolute zero. What would be a perfect sentence?" This typically elliptic passage opens to include a wide range of implication. When the metaphor explodes, it brings her to the insight of the deconstructionists—all language is, finally, catachresis, lies. Ultimately, even our scientific theories presuppose fictions like "absolute zero" to complement our formalist idylls of a "perfect" sentence. Madame Realism remarks on this fictive, narrative dimension to thought and language, even going so far as to conclude that "it's only a story really should read, it's a way to think." That is, making up stories and altering their status from embedded narrative fiction to Truth or Nature is how thinking takes place. It is no wonder that, in talking about *Committed*, Tillman has this to say about her project: "In this I believe I'm participating, both as a filmmaker and a novelist, in the recent turn to and interest in narrative as a way to tell 'the truth.' Or to complicate it—to represent our lives in fiction through narrative or as fictions" ("A Film *with* History," 13). Madame Realism's comment might well be, What alternative is there?

### Living with Contradictions

The strongly social and ideological aura of the film work of Tillman and the richly reflexive insights of Madame Realism are essential to a full appreciation of Tillman's novel and stories. A look backward from *Haunted Houses* demonstrates how pervasive these dimensions are in her earlier work. One of her earliest publications, for example, was in a 1976 issue of *Wallpaper*, a British art and literary magazine whose cover explains the title (my copy is a floral number that my grandmother might have liked). "Myself as a Menu" benefits from its layout (the narrative is cut and pasted onto a menu) and its "natural" breakup of a self-portrait into the courses of a meal, as if the self were something to consume in writing, just as the writer is herself something that readers consume.

These narrative cuts replace recognizable autobiographical narrative and provide a structural if not a linear sense of the narrator, also giving us many of the perennial themes of Tillman's work. The writer-filmmaker as voyeur watches a man who then takes on the male role of watching her in the bath (she is both guilty for "poisoning" him into becoming himself a voyeur and fearful of being caught filming or worse). This pattern of the watcher and the watched takes place both internally in Tillman's protagonists and with those characters who find themselves shadowed by the culture's normalizing voices. A psychiatrist terrorizes a patient with pat explanations designed more to control than to help. A woman and a schizophrenic man are in a mental institution, and the female narrator is part victim, part voyeur, part sympathizer with the sick and the wounded. That wavering distance, itself a denial of any absolute basis from which to judge or narrate, also anticipates later narrative stances.

*Paranoids Anonymous Newsletter* (1976–79) was a tabloid-size newspaper of eight to sixteen pages which Tillman edited with Carla Liss. Its mix of popular culture, high art, and severe postmodern narrative made it an early champion of the new writing. Published in runs of five hundred to a thousand copies, this seemingly low-profile venue gave its anonymous authors a quite marginal pathological status and presented the spectacle of a consciousness acutely aware of itself as object of the (male?) culture's forces and energies. For Tillman, there were the multiple ironies of being a "new" writer in New York who lived on John Street (i.e., in the financial district), and her narrators reflect the capitalist reduction of individuality to a repertoire of phobias and idiosyncrasies.

A hyperaggressive Dutch boyfriend is thrown out of a screening of *The Way We Were* and eventually hauled off by the police for denting cars at the crosswalk. A woman mixes the pleasure of an evening escort to the subway with thoughts of death, ultimately losing the thread of "reality" between fact and interpretation. Pretending to be a lover, a whisperer calls women and extracts intimate revelations in the process of making them guess his identity. A casual comment at a film showing triggers an old woman's memories, racial craziness, and fixation upon the public library. The "P.A.N. Meeting Notes" records the conversations of a group of paranoids from behind their masks, their appearance on a midnight talk show (identified only by initials and masked even for radio), and vintage Tillman themes of fiction and truth, identity and anxiety. "P.A.N. Meeting Notes," incidentally, was the first of Tillman's pieces to be read aloud—by Harry Mathews, as it turned out, who had been a contributor to the first issue.

These characters' urban environment irritates into a psychic rash what for most people is simply an undercurrent of anxiety. That anxiety pits the body of desire against the antibodies of cultural and economic roles. In "The Way We Are," Tillman records as paranoia the anxiety that individuals feel over the shortfall between their own display and the image of perfection held before them on the slick surfaces of *The Way We [Never] Were*. The masked conversants, the rambling older woman who tells the narrator (of "Not Dreams, NYC") that Gaelic and Hebrew are the same language, the woman on the phone forced to guess her place in the male caller's world, the woman who feels futile anxiety while her boyfriend strikes out at theater ushers and traffic cops enforcing the rules—all of these are "finds" in Tillman's ethnology of the experience of being marginalized by mainstream culture.

The writer is the other type in this gallery. The woman (in "The Interpretation of Facts") alternating thoughts of pleasure and death, as she tries to sort out interpretation and fact, shows us clearly enough the physical vulnerability that law and order are supposed to guard. But she also shows us such vulnerability's psychological analog, an undercurrent of anxiety about death, danger, and meaning which is both pleasurable and worrisome. Even at this early point in her career, then, Tillman's work displays the characteristics that mark her mature work: a steady focus upon characters—most but not all of them women—who suffer from, and are even destroyed by, the prevailing forms of order; a narrative form that relies upon segments like cinematic cuts which trace, in short scenes and in the found objects of the consumer culture, the fracture lines of both individual and society; and, perhaps most contemporary, an increasingly sophisticated counterpoint between the psychological and the semiotic, the internal dynamics of personal history and the internalized dynamics of cultural discourses, rituals, and other social forms.

Two very fine longer works show these traits as they explore the problematic nature of relationships in the postmodern era. The characters seem at times to be holographs of themselves, projections of laser-age snapshots from the pop-culture repertoire. Ultimately that emptied-out, artificial three-dimensionality stems perhaps from the loss of the adventure of authenticity that seemed such a central ethos in the formative decade of the sixties. The casual, near random sexual encounters in many of Tillman's stories grow out of what is traced in these lines about a Fourth of July party from *Weird Fucks* (a novella published in *Bikini Girl* 6 [1980]): "Firecrackers keep popping off and everything feels slightly evil. For the urban dweller whose adventures are limited to sexual ones the Fourth of July has nothing to do with America's independence. One's own independence being severely circumscribed anyway, we play out the hunt we can in limited ways." Partly the age lacks the historical resonance that would make Independence Day signify, and partly "independence" as an infinite ideal has been "circumscribed" by political and economic institutions to the point that freedom amounts to little more than sexual license. If in the idealism of the sixties one felt that the realm of the authentic was everywhere but in the system, it seems that the eighties radiate a "slightly evil" feeling that nothing is likely to be better than the long shot of intimacy.

That almost carnivorous sexuality is a symptom of circumscription closing in on both the existential and material realms. Because spiritual or existential paranoia displaces a special charge of energy onto materialism, and because the conflict between the ideology of opportunity and the reality of class privilege deflects that energy back from materialism to existential matters, characters seem caught in an anxious cycle of ontological consumerism. Their product is experience; their mode of production is image-making; their chief raw materials are art and sexuality. Primal and historical motifs such as "the hunt" are thus attenuated to a sexual topography of Greek island retreats, London flats, Amsterdam rooms, New York parties—all mildly anesthetized with drugs and alcohol and frequently punctuated by moments of uneasiness at the weirdness of intimacy between shadow selves in the age of imagery.

In *Weird Fucks*, for example, a woman finds herself shuttling from country to country and bed to bed, her lovers seeming always already to be living with another woman or to have a girlfriend or wife who suddenly returns from one coast or another. No male is the promised land, but then the promised land is not really one either. In a distinct tone of matter-of-fact resignation, she comes to feel like an immigrant whose expectations of a new world strike against an old and closed one instead. When she calls herself "a greenhorn who has the wrong expectations about America," we should be able to see more clearly the metaphoric implications of her sexual circuit, her coast-to-coast lifespan, and her part bohemian, part jet-set, part exile's European episodes. The drama of desire and the entropy of culture are each figures to the other's ground, and she is a carrier/victim of what amounts to a pathology of American culture.

This pathology is a condition in which "the last ritual [is] attending parties." As the narrator observes when a girlfriend gives her blessing to her (just barely) ex picking up the narrator, "there's something bloodless in the modern age." That something is not really "fatal" until she meets a man who is nice but impotent and *therefore* she falls for him: "Here is Puritanism, liking someone because the sex is bad," the corollary of which is that "uninspired sex can win a masochist." Here, too, is the apparently utopian and illusory desire for something with more depth and resonance than the holographic entities of the ritual partiers.

Tillman explores the consequences of long-term relationships in "Living with Contradictions," her *Top Stories* pamphlet of 1982. Part of the story's appeal is the wry humor over how the couple, Julie and Joe, are to speak of themselves, for "they had been living together for three years and still didn't have a way to refer to each other that didn't sound stupid, false, or antiquated." But the issue really is more than that "language follows change and there wasn't any language to use": it also concerns the popular pastime of comparing "new cars, new lovers," a "consumerism in love" that Julie must look on "from the outside," because she "didn't have anyone new to talk about." "One friend told her that talking about the person you lived with was like airing your clean laundry in public."

In the age of consumerism, under the regime of the image, "being in love is a fiction that lasts an hour and a half, featurelength, and then you're hungry again" for another ephemeral image to tip into the album. The alternative is "unromantic old love," which "comforted her, like a room to read in"; that is, like a space in which the linearity of reading supplies a comfort and "familiarity" missing in the simultaneity of seeing and feeling. Perhaps the readerly is the teleology of tradition and the cinematic is the present era of simulations. The two options represent a double bind for Julie not only because she is shut out of the gossip circle or because she feels a bit old-fashioned, but also because she realizes that neither is quite right. Part of what is (or at least can be) wrong about that old-fashioned closure in both the arts and relations is that Julie and Joe "were just part of the great hetero-sexual capitalist family thrall, possessing each other." They have become objects under capitalist ownership rather than being, like many of their friends, the subjects of consumerist experience. Or perhaps the difference is only apparent, because "intimacy is something people used to talk about before commercials. . . . What could be more intimate than an advertisement for Ivory soap?"

Tillman accentuates our sense of these perplexities and contradictions by alternating her text with Jane Dickson's drawings—by juxtaposing visual and textual kinds of experiences and their mutual commentaries. The ideas that make this aesthetic strategy so successful for Tillman make Julie's life almost unlivable, and she struggles with the implications of her realization that contradictions are a fact of life in the "capitalist . . . thrall": "Contradictions make life finer. Ambivalence is just another word for love, becoming romantic about the unconscious." Innocuous at first glance, this page of text is an incisive analysis of the penetration of cultural contradiction into both the unconscious and our codings of it. Contradictions break life up into internally opposed desires, forces, factors, making it "finer" in the sense of fragments—of interest in an aesthetics of arrangement but costly existentially. An all-consuming force in popular mythology, love is a necessarily ambiguous phenomenon that reproduces the internalized contradictions (in general terms, between desire and limits) of the unconscious. To call the feeling either love or ambivalence is romantic because both names preserve a nostalgic desire for the pure "love" of romance, a text in which "ambivalence" is a temporary aberration to be overcome in the denouement.

We are, that is, like "infant[s] outside of reason, speaking reasonably about the unreasonable," as if the naming and hierarchies and taxonomies of a system (whether patriarchy, logocentrism, capitalism, romance, or whatever) could control or resolve the primal ambivalences that mark the subject. Sometimes this dilemma leads to comedy, as in "Hung Up," one of Tillman's *Between C & D* stories (1.2 [Summer 1984]). The narrator, anxious about the (in New York, at least) major step of "signing a lease together, moving together, a form of recommitment, a modern marriage of sorts," phones her lover from a pay phone. He hangs up, repeatedly. It is not until after several hours of angry internal wrangling with him that she sees him and discovers that the pay phone was out of order and that he heard no one when he picked up the receiver.

Perhaps the story is emblematic of our problematic system of communication, one that sometimes gives the impression that there is "no one there" when there is, that blocks or disrupts contact even between lovers, and that can by means of its semiotic (and electronic) interpositions menace any relationship. But the story also toys a bit with the narrator's relation to the larger systems of gender and even of psychiatry.

> He looked at me over his coffee cup. Didn't you ever consider that the phone might be broken? No, I said, I thought a lot of things but I never thought of that. He lit a cigarette. Why would I hang up on you? he asked. He said this in a kindly way, much the way that the psychiatrist examining Paul Bowles as to his fitness for the Army spoke. No one's going to hurt you he reassured Bowles, having already moved a pair of scissors out of Bowles' reach. Why, indeed, I thought. Why does anyone do anything?

The comic comedown is nicely timed, but so is the linkage between the reassuring lover and the crisp psychiatrist. Is removing what "triggers" a mild paranoid like removing scissors from a suspicious patient? Does the comparison suggest that being in a relationship is like being in the army? Does one need to be screened and counseled as carefully to love as to kill? Does the male monopolize the same role of classifying and normalizing in relationships as that played by the army psychiatrist for *his* institution?

To the extent that the lover and the psychiatrist flow together at some level in the narrator's sense of the episode, there is some parallel to the crisis in *Committed* in which the lover, the psychiatrists, the studio chiefs, the ideologues, and even the mother of Frances all operate *upon* her, as if she were the emblem of that point at which institutions impinge upon the individual body. A series of stories adds to this confrontation between the institutional and the individual an exploration of the internal violence set off within the female gender. These stories play what is internalized, as in the paranoia of the narrator of "Hung Up," against what operates outside the work of consciousness. There is an agency even prior to internalized ideology and discipline upon which such directly institutional processes build. Foucault speaks of "a network or circuit of bio-power, or somato-power, which acts as the formative matrix of sexuality itself as the historical and cultural phenomenon within which we seem at once to recognise and lose ourselves" (Foucault 1980b, 186).

In the haunting story "Absence Makes the Heart" (*Portable Lower East Side* 1.2 [Winter 1984]: 30–33, and more recently in *Blatant Artifice* 2/3 [1988]: 63–65), written shortly after her own father died, Tillman employs an almost gothic mode in depicting a woman at a ball receiving news of her father's death, pursued to the hospital by a man who has fallen in love with the image of beauty which she projects. Most of the words, appropriately enough, are his, but a few paragraphs are hers. One describes seeing her father's body: "His head was turned from her and frozen. Couldn't she give him life, she who loved him more than any man? His hand was ice. . . . This must be death. And as nothing is attached to you anymore, no tubes dripping colorless liquids, I must also become detached from your body. Now, what man will love me, and who will I be able to love" (32). It is as if *he* is her "formative matrix of sexuality," the essential point of flow of a "somato-power" now interrupted like the hospital's tubes.

It is as if she has no specific being of her own. Later she attempts to demystify the would-be lover who pursues her—"love is an invention, but death is not." Without her father, only death seems at all real, because he has taken with him the "somato-power" more culturally constituted than we usually suppose. "I was not able to give my father life, though I am unchanging and eternal. And you too will die and blame me." Males live and die, males blame and give, but she is "unchanging and eternal," not her own self so much as a function within a male matrix. Earlier in the story, for example, is this picture of her poised to enter the proverbial ball as the (male) image of femininity: "I am the one who waits. I am the one who will be waited upon. I have the kiss that can change men's lives. I can awaken the dead. I can never die. I am empty. I am perfect. I am full. I am all things to all men. She shook her head violently" (31).

She is aware of herself as men's empty signifier waiting to be filled. His voice, at least, operates on that assumption. The passage continues: "He watched everything. The shake of the head, a sign to him. A fire lit. Something was burning. He felt ill, he felt wonderful. She was sublime, and he wondered how words like that existed before her." Every image and every movement is already coded as "a sign to him" of *his* experience, but one so intense that it is difficult to believe that it is another utterance in an existing grammar. Even her physical beauty strains credibility as he gazes upon her: "But she was flesh, and he was careful to conceive of her—her breasts, for instance—as possible. He thought, Unimaginable is not the state, not-yet-realized is better. He was drawn to her, as if drawn by her, her creation. She was a painting, a study in purple, she was a dangerous flower, she was a fountain bringing youth to those who drank her. He felt stupid, like a story that doesn't work" (30).

It is the male who negotiates the passage from the unimaginable through the possible to the realized. He is drawn to her, but only "as if" by her; *he* composes the painting that she becomes. He watches her, invents narratives to explain what he sees, and the resulting artifice of color, breasts, and gesture is the sexual/maternal matrix that sustains him—the way her father served her. He is indeed "a story that doesn't work" until, at the end, he has succeeded in inducing her to walk into the ballroom. That entrance is to a dance of "somato-power" she performs for him, a power that derives not from her but from the texture of the culturally inscribed story that precedes and exceeds them both.

"Absence Makes the Heart" because each is absent to the other at the point of relating—each relates, that is, not to a person, but to that "formative matrix" for which each is a sign to the other. The "heart" is the matrix that impels one's energies along the lines we are accustomed to considering "instinctive." One step closer to the surface are the more familiar psychodynamics explored in "Diary of a Masochist" (*Paranoids Anonymous Newsletter* 2), which represents the female gender at its self-victimizing extreme. If one of Tillman's attractions to Frances Farmer as a subject for *Committed* was her participation in her own destruction, "Diary of a Maso-chist" pursues further the motif of the self-destruction coded into women's experience. The opening sets the tone: "Remember when you pissed on me in San Francisco?" The narrator refers to a literal event, but that event is certainly a metaphor of her relationship with her lover.

The narrator is a filmmaker touring America with a Dutch boy-friend skilled at both physical and psychological cruelty. Theirs is a relationship almost designed to be torture, as if sex were his means to reduce her to pain and to a renewed lesson in her worthlessness. He makes sex physically painful, "biting me so hard my skin turns blue and red," leaving her to look at her "shoulders after one of our sessions and think, the stain of you lasts so long." He regulates her pleasure ruthlessly—"you start me, you stop me." He injures her self-image: "You say you don't like my body. . . . You say you're not turned on by me." He is on again, off again, with her: "You tell me you love me, I'm a fascist and you hate me." He even makes a pass at her sister, explaining he is "not attracted" to the narrator but finds the sister his "type."

Although, finally, the narrator sends him back to Amsterdam and breaks off the relationship, for a long time she is capable of defending him to this or that host in front of whom his cruelty has been displayed. And she remains clear throughout about what she is doing to herself: "I feel I am voluntarily committing myself to a concentration camp." As the narrator of "Hung Up" asks, "Why does anyone do anything?" "Masochism" is often a diagnosis suffi-cient to terminate the inquiry, a pathological state in which one deviates from the obviously more pleasurable states of being open to the individual. The peculiar thing about this diary, however, is that no classic psychological explanation is provided—no dirt on the father, no innuendoes about a crippling mother, no uncle or brother as simple cause. "Why, indeed"?

The pronouns are, finally, the clue. The narrator is capable of complying with his desires or terminating the relationship, but not of recoding the terms of this relationship. The degree of direct address in these pages' second-person narration is possible only in the simulated context of the diary—a text he tries at one point to "insist I stop writing." Private writing allows her a voice that social roles do not, and "masochism" becomes a code word for women's compliance with relationships spoken according to a male grammar of power and determination over women's lives. "Sadism" is the corresponding trope for relationships that, with all the unconsciousness of desire itself, are managed by men according to an abusive structure. Hence the relationship chronicled in this story exaggerates a general undercurrent in sexual relationships.

As we have seen before in Tillman's work, purely psychological explanations displace into the realm of individual "failure" problems that are situated in more basic social matrices. Achieving an awareness of this deep a layer of social formations is difficult precisely because, as Foucault suggests, it is within such formations that "we seem at once to recognise and lose ourselves." This layer both determines the form of our conscious and unconscious desires and releases us into their blind pursuit.

Perhaps the most poignant of this group of stories about gender is "Dead Talk" (in the Between C & D anthology), Tillman's Marilyn Monroe story. "I was going to write her autobiography," Tillman told me, "but it ended up being an eight-page story because I just couldn't live with the material. I got so depressed I decided I would just make it her last day on earth." Giving voice to Monroe, supplying the final narrative explanation of self she *might* have written, is akin to providing Farmer's counterattack on the systems that victimized her. The most explicit of these notes shows Monroe thinking back to her beginnings: "And the photographs, the first photographs, showed I could get that soft look on my face. That softness was right inside me and I could call it up. Everything in me went up to the surface, to my skin, and the glow that the camera loved, that was me. I was burning up inside" (127).

A sex star is someone whose insides are replaced by the social matrix of sexuality which has been featured in the last several stories. Once the coded "softness" is drawn up to the surface, a "burning" remains which suggests the disastrous results of becoming so assimilated to this cultural formation. "Me" becomes the image, and what is left is a void Monroe tries to fill, in Tillman's piece,

with fantasies of her son, Johnny, playing at the lake. The conflu-
ence of father, lover, and son, all essentially absent in Monroe's life,
produces a murky sexuality that connotes the extent to which compliance replaces her own right to conceive and initiate pleasure—
the males she can imagine being in her life both monopolize sources
of pleasure and fail to provide for her: "I told Johnny that more than
anything I had wanted a father, a real father. I felt so much love for
this boy. I put my arm around him and pulled him close. I would let
him have me, my breasts, anything. He looked repulsed, as if he
didn't understand me. He had never done this before. He had always
adored me" (129). It is not surprising that "to Marilyn love and
adoration were the same" (128), because compliance, rather than a
less mediated form of desire, is her cultural lot. But this leaves her
without either the license or structure within which to pursue anything like fulfillment. Tillman includes another ineffectual psychiatrist whose glib line fails to address the social dimension of Monroe's crisis.

In these pieces about gender, Tillman's feminist ethnology
searches out the margins of issues we have classically considered in
purely psychological terms and approaches a striking embodiment
of the hazy goal that Foucault set for himself in *The History of
Sexuality*. Tillman's protagonist's find themselves "Living with
Contradictions" internalized from the social formations that thus
become their most primary mode of Being. Hence the epigraph to
her novel—"We are all haunted houses," beings haunted by cultural
coding so prior to any consciousness that we never quite know if the
apparition we see is ourselves or an Other of some indeterminate
description.

### The Interstices of Argument

*Haunted Houses* comes as close to determining a description of
late-twentieth-century ontology as we are likely to get, one of a
Being that transpires, as Madame Realism says, in the "interstices
of argument." Given the quality and amount of work which preceded this novel, it would be ridiculous to call it a "first novel." It is
more like the consummation of the strands we have been following
through the various forms of narrative Tillman has pursued in her
career. *Committed* brings to "biography" a narrative mode for understanding the institutional determinations of individuality, *Madame Realism* interfiles narrative with the implications of doing
things with words, and the short stories carry the reader back
through social, semiotic, and psychological dimensions to a Foucauldian core prior to its meltdown into more familiar and recognizable individual forces.

*Haunted Houses* can be deceptive, because Tillman's eye for ideological detail and for the trace elements of trauma give the novel immediate emotional impact. One senses here and there among the reviews a reader who has felt that impact and filed the novel on the shelves beside "traditional" fiction, not sensing the full implications of what Andrei Codrescu's sensitive review calls "the unobtrusive nature of Ms. Tillman's innovations" (*Exquisite Corpse* 5.1– 5 [January-May 1982]: 13). To talk with Tillman about the book is to hear her present her aims in ways that are satisfying from a traditional perspective. She describes the novel partly as another example of her "ethnology," and partly as filling a significant gap: "One of the things I was thinking about when I first started writing *Haunted Houses* was that there was no *Catcher in the Rye* for women, not that I think *Haunted Houses* is like *Catcher in the Rye*. But there was nothing that took early female experience and allowed readers to go through it in a more or less unadulterated way."

Tillman's feminist ethnology uncovers an experience of social realities from a position distinctly marginal to any point of power. Her protagonists metamorphose from girls to women; by age, sex, and class, they encounter from a "weak" position the institutions of power and the media which serve to normalize us. Much of the novel's success is because of Tillman's concern to focus upon the "writing *as* writing" in ways that keep this content from sliding back into some all-too-familiar tale of adolescence. *Writing* makes evident the crucial formative social and literary languages that might otherwise remain naturalized or transparent and hence cancel much of the value of the analysis.

Traditional problems remain: Grace struggles with the internalized voice of her mother crippling her at every turn; Jane remains arrested in a complex relationship with a King Lear of a father, for whom she plays all the daughters' roles at once; and Emily, the writer, has as much trouble rescuing a desirable gender role from the cultural repertoire as she does a female voice from the dual "prison-houses" of language and of American history.

"Real" individuals and "old" problems are understood in new ways. Tillman disrupts the American fetish of private inner life by mixing up these three narratives. Rather than reading each character's narrative all the way through (as, for example in Gertrude Stein's *Three Lives*), we encounter five triads mixing up the narratives. At times we confuse the three narratives, but this is part of Tillman's design. To the extent that the three remain separate in our mind, we have encountered the details of personal and psychological history that individuate us. But to the extent that the three run together, we have engaged with the larger cultural mechanisms underlying individuality.

These mechanisms are anything but simple, and the inadequacy of any linear model of their operation within the psyche accounts for the book's distinctive formal traits. *Haunted Houses* creates a cultural structure within which the lives of these women take place more than it reduces their "personal" Being to traditional cause and effect or developmental models of explanation. Hence the novel respects the temporality of experience (it does not shuffle events), but, by bringing the three women together into the same social space (but without the Dickensian interfiliations) and omitting classic plot structures (there is plenty of crisis here, but not resolution), Tillman leaves us with a novel that resists assimilating its material to familiar formulae and their underlying assumptions.

Tillman's prose style is startlingly direct and "unliterary." It is unmannered and undercoded, resisting any totalizing illusions that would weave an organic whole out of disparate and contending elements, evading any stylistic "system" that might claim normative status in this narrative world. At times a hasty reader might find the style abrupt or even puzzling, sensing the movement of more forces and nuances than are neatly laid out upon its formal surface. But Tillman's love of understatement and of nodal passages that open communication lines to all manner of thematic elements, but without the heavy advertisement of literary foregrounding, is her means of remaining open to the multiplicity of voicings within each protagonist rather than homogenizing experience to a perspectival monotone. Stylistically, by resisting literary systems with all the vigor of a contemporary Stein, she preserves the dynamism of the contending social forces that her "ethnology" seeks to describe.

The key to the novel is that this contention takes place, most importantly, *within* rather than between characters. There are conflicts of the latter kind, naturally, but what distinguishes the novel is the complexity of internal strife within Emily, Jane, and Grace. Tom Jones fought out the conflict between appetites or temptation and his true inner nature; Pip fought out the collision between socially and economically defined status and moral and personal authenticity. But Tillman's characters have multiple internal voices speaking all sides of the larger cultural contradictions afflicting Western society.

To look closely at these characters is to appreciate how richly Tillman intertwines psychological, semiotic, social, ideological, and philosophical strands, which our intellectual disciplines have conditioned us to maintain separately. The novel is a prime example of Foucault's comments about fiction's truth effects, and those effects are most obvious in Emily's case—perhaps because, though each of the three women has her literary side, Emily is the Writer.

Emily is sufficiently nonconformist to wear army fatigues rather than "outfits," but also finds herself spending long periods depressed, alone in her room, and unable to circulate comfortably in society. She struggles with available gender roles, setting her reading of Simone de Beauvoir against her compliant role near the novel's end in an affair with an older (and married) Dutchman. Her intimacy is with men, but it is a lesbian piano teacher whose face and voice echo in her memory. Although her mother (a failed writer) and father are no doubt important, we hear only of her relationships with substitutes for parental figures (especially for the mother—like Edith, the woman with whom Emily boards, or her Dutch landlady and her landlady's mother).

Tropes circulate in the language of Emily's unconscious, and their diacritical relations with one another make the reader's job challenging. One system of tropes to which Emily has recourse is that of American history: "Revolution or evolution, her young male history teacher had asked. The question plagued Emily, who could find no easy answer for it, yes or no, and it seemed to be both. But was that an answer?" (46). She decides later that the real answer is a "rotation" and thus "combined both aspects that she so desperately wanted to mesh" (46–47), because part of her difficulty is reconciling the contradictions of experience with the rigidities and single-mindedness of "young male" rhetoric. She knows her words may not be recognized as "an answer" within its juridical system.

The meshing of aspects is further complicated by Emily's divided attention: while she reads her history text, she watches *Duel in the Sun*. The passage above continues: "Gregory Peck, who she thought looked a little like her father, and Jennifer Jones, madly in love, dying, crawling toward each other for one last embrace, after they'd shot each other. They loved each other but they had to destroy each other. That was as big a problem as the American Revolution and exciting, in a different way, from thinking, for instance, that it's impossible to know anything for sure."

Parental, libidinal, and epistemological overlays sift down onto what is already a site of historiography, pedagogy, and rhetoric to create the sort of complex palimpsest of consciousness which is typical in *Haunted Houses*. Each system is a trope for the others, and their shared traits include the indeterminate, the agonistic, the exciting, the destructive—and the interrelated. Tillman's characters subdivide many times, and each "entity" within plays out its roles in multiple overlays of scripts until self-knowledge becomes as uncertain as romance and history.

Emily's historical speculations fall with even greater intensity upon the Puritans, perhaps because their own contradictions offer Emily a site to give voice to her own internal contests. Intellectually, her goal seems an evasion of discursive constraints: "It's when you get told things over and over that you hold opinions about them. Emily wrote: If you have principles, you don't have to think" (111). She questions principles and discourse systems in order to feel their contradictions. For example, her history paper states: "Because of

the schizophrenic quality of their tenets, the Puritans worked fever-
ishly without hope. (Or should that be double-edged quality? and
worked fervently?)" (152).

Was their problem a chemical imbalance in the ideological
brain or a self-destructive tool? Both, no doubt, because that formulation is not an entirely unsatisfactory definition of ideology
itself. Fever and fervor have, more than once in our history, been
difficult to distinguish. But equally important is that this activity
goes on "without hope," indeed because there cannot be hope—just
as language goes on because there cannot be determinate meaning;
love, because no consummation is really final; philosophy, because
no truth is obtainable; diplomacy, because no peace is final; and so
forth on through every overlay we find in sifting through the discursive systems in these characters' consciousness. But Emily
continues:

> Hopelessness was at the bottom of everything. Sin was inevitable.
> No one ever knew if they were of the elect. In a new world, one
> without tradition or order, the Puritan work ethic could be the
> driving force for the new settlers, throwing them into a frenzy.
> How to show their goodness, their saintliness? It follows that para-
> noia and materialism walk hand in hand (does that really follow?).
> And fame will become the visible proof of God's love or approval.

All of these characters live "in a new world" in which any kind of
"tradition or order" has lapsed in the cultural memory and there
remains the quandary of how to summon forth the "frenzy" to
settle an existential wilderness. One can easily be paranoid about
one's authenticity in the absence of transcendental assurances, because materialism has proved itself no guarantor of anything but the
fruits of ruthless exploitation, class privilege, or both.

Anxiety over a state of grace manifests itself in various degrees
of obsessive-compulsive frenzies over (im)perfection. Aptly named,
Grace has her most decisive confrontation with this mind-set not
with teachers and historical subjects, but with her mother. We learn
early on that Ruth "liked animals better than people" and accepts
others' praise of Grace only "with reservations" (24). When Grace,
as a child, buys her mother a pin for a birthday, Ruth "said it was
ugly and that she'd never wear it. . . . she told Grace that it was
important to tell the truth" (26). "Every time Grace hurt herself
Ruth said that God was punishing her" (30), and for the rest of her
life Grace finds Ruth's voice within her distrusting others, discounting others' supportiveness, criticizing her efforts, devaluing her
sense of self-worth.

Grace ultimately discovers that Ruth has thrown away all of
Grace's childhood memorabilia as just so much "clutter," as if she

had all along blacked it out as a state of Calvinist depravity. With so much negative energy in her experience of normalizing institutions such as the family, it is no wonder that Grace becomes something of a pirate commandeering the bodies of almost-random males. Or that she remains independent of the claims and constraints that a real "relationship" would place upon her. As she struggles to explain to Mark, her gay friend, why she broke off with an impotent boyfriend, we begin to see just how she and Emily are affected by their experiences with cultural forms: "Grace had cut off from Bill the way her mother used to cut away material when sewing from a pattern. The big scissors bearing down, her mother's hand steady, discarding without a second look. The revulsion had turned into disinterest. She couldn't explain to Mark how Bill's impotence caused her to feel. Trapped with him in a kind of void, and then maybe they'd disappear together. It was as if she were that soft penis" (92).

Grace has "a pattern" of domination in mind whereby *she* controls her sexuality and her pleasure by picking up men rather than allowing herself to be courted. Bill's failure is a threat to her ability to maintain the boundaries of that pattern, and she cannot risk being trapped in the void outside patterns—that is, in the free forms of "spontaneous" or "authentic" creation. Although she can only think of herself "in opposition" to Ruth (204), Grace has acquired simply a more contemporary version of Ruth's reliance upon the sort of principles that Emily seeks to dismantle.

Ruth's Puritan obsession with imperfection renders her daughter's existence specular, unreal except as the embodiment of an image pattern—like that of the sexual rebel she adopts. "Sitting at the bar, images running rampant, one abandoning another, she looked at a woman who was looking at a woman who was looking at a man. That's the way love is" (97), a chain of imaging and being imaged in which no one is herself, himself. "There's a rock & roll dream in your heart. . . . You're Mick Jagger and everybody wants you. You can get anybody" (98). And she does get anybody she wants—except herself.

It is difficult to say that Jane is any better off; in many ways, her situation is the saddest. At least Emily deflects her quandaries through her writing and Grace deflects hers through her sexual episodes. But for Jane, for whom the chief crippling agent is her father, there is mainly an arrest of life itself, a state of near non-being preyed upon by the sense of all that is missing. The novel is full of characters such as Uncle Larry, who slept in the same bed with his mother until he was thirteen, or Jimmy, who still seems to peak in his excitement when his mother—"the most beautiful woman he'd ever seen" (105)—walks in. But as the type of the female relation to the patriarchal figure, Jane's with her father is central to the novel's investigation of the agonistic relation between the individual and the culture's social forms.

Indeed, *Haunted Houses* opens with this passage: "Her father liked to scare her. He knew she adored him. He'd creep into her room early in the morning or late at night and jump on her and she'd cry. He'd console her with kisses and hugs. Years later Jane would say, It's a hard habit to break. Loving madmen" (9). Jane's libidinal investment in the primary social form of order secures for her a peculiar ritual in which an unpredictable figure monopolizing power first frightens and then loves her. It is no wonder that her libido is like an amputee's stump and that cultural expectations are the prosthesis by which she attempts to finesse her way through a sexuality that can yield her no pleasure. Her long-time "boyfriend," Jimmy, finds her always ready with an excuse, and, when she finally does lose her virginity, it is a heavily deliberate, perfunctory, unsatisfying coupling with a toy-department salesman who passes uneventfully out of her life soon after.

The angry tirades of Jane's father (he throws her out of the house on one occasion for her make-up) condition her to expect violent tyranny from men, and she experiences his bedtime reading of Lord Chesterfield's letters as "giving advice in order to repress her" (106). He so dominates her psyche that "she hardly ever thought about her mother" (176), and, when she is attacked one night in a borrowed apartment, she knows she cannot risk telling her father about her brush with death and violation: "Never Daddy. Daddy loves me so much he wants to cook me in the oven and eat me. Daddy throws me up in the air and always catches me. He pushes my swing and I don't get scared. He goes into a rage and screams and his face turns red. He takes me shopping and tells me I'm good. He buys me whatever I want and my mother doesn't" (176). Because of her father, Jane is a permanent child, forever dependent upon a maleness that renders her according to its own recipe, that wants to consume her, that arrogates to itself the privileges of protection, emotional violence, approval, and providing—hence multiplying the forms of dependence. That maleness is above all what keeps her "up in the air" in a role that lacks its own script, and what "always catches" her—but more in the sense of snaring than saving.

Perhaps the most poignant passage comes a bit earlier in the novel, when Jane thinks of her father as "the only man for all of us, all of us women, wife, girls, daughters" (131). But she stops herself:

> Why had she written the only man for all of us. He is ugly with madness, he is beautiful with his own smell, he is different from us and he comes and goes. He eats breakfast with us. His smile is worth a million bucks. He thinks nothing of himself. Things de-

pend upon his coming and going. He wanted sons. He contents himself with attention. He has ambition and he has no ambition. He hates himself. He hates all of us. He loves himself sometimes, he loves us sometimes. Oh, Daddy. (131)

He is the very type of the patriarchal male (there are other kinds in Tillman's world). But his is an intermittent force—just enough to keep the female psyche off-balance and oscillating between "women" and "girls" or between beloved and hated, feeling repulsed by and attracted to the father, finding itself less valued than his sons but acceptable as his attendant, yet always "different" and dependent upon the father's "coming and going."

Jane never quite works all this out. Something keeps her blinded, something that makes one of Jimmy's friends call her "suburban." She does understand her father; she knows about his difficulties as a child who was overly close to a mother so unaware of social forms that she often looked half-crazy. But Jane is too middle-class to get much further than the libidinal economy that keeps her in thrall. Maria, her Hispanic friend, must supply Jane with the sociopolitical dimension from Maria's own working-class background. Jane is able to raise her hand in class and say that "Lear wanted Cordelia sexually" (169), but she has trouble connecting with Maria's reading of the play. Maria defends Regan and Goneril—not that they "were heroes, just that they had gotten a raw deal" (172), that they "were scared of" Lear (169–70) because of his power. Maria is contemptuous of Cordelia because "she believed him," and Maria has not experienced any power structures worthy of belief.

"Maria's idea was that King Lear was about power and who gets it and why. You can lie to get it, kill for it, or be born to it. Whenever Maria mentioned power Jane felt sleepy" (173). Maria is not surprised that the powerless, particularly women, suffer in power struggles and that sentiment is a dangerous form of blindness. Jane feels sleepy because power is the great repressed horror to the suburbanite in that precarious position between the poor, who have nothing much to lose, and the rich, who have enough power to keep what they have. Maria continues her interpretation: " 'Cordelia's like a sacrifice. She may have been born into power, but she's not smart enough. She thinks that love's enough. And Shakespeare shows that it isn't.' Love isn't enough, Jane repeated to herself" (175). It is not coincidental that Maria's interpretation alternates with the account of the intruder who tries to rape Jane, then cries and leaves. Jane is left, perhaps by both episodes, muttering Maria's demystification of sentimental romances—uncomprehendingly, we surmise.

"Where does fear go when you don't feel anything?" Jane asks herself, "possessed" with finding reasons for the things that have happened to her ever since her adolescent friend Lois died—and even before that, as we, at least, know. Jane is "possessed," but by a network of repressions which insures that her questions do not get beyond the boundaries laid out for her. Her talking cure is the least effective of those in the novel because all the "right" materials are there—but are left for the reader to perform. Part of what blocks Jane's efforts is that she has no one around her who can read those materials as problematically as she does. Jimmy is typical of the kind of help available to her. "His response to the attack [upon her] is to see as many movies as possible. Old ones. Like *Johnny Guitar*. It's so obvious, he said, loving it" (176). Jimmy wants familiar and obvious narrative frames to which to assimilate experience, and, if something happens too far outside their margins, he puts up a Do Not Disturb sign for the duration of his efforts to repress that event. He lives an almost anesthetized life on steady doses of financial support from his parents (when his antique store fails, they set him up in a cinema).

Jane, however, though perhaps not as reflective about such matters as Grace or Emily, runs several times into the heart of the issue. When Jane recalls family stories about her grandmother, a beautiful Russian Jew in whom the landowner's son took a potentially dangerous interest, she "tried to imagine her grandmother, who later covered newspapers with towels and bits of cloth to keep the people in the pictures warm, extending a gloved hand to the lord's son. The two images could be placed side by side, but could not be superimposed to make a whole, and looking from one to the other was like reading two different languages in the same sentence when you don't know one of them" (123). Jane cannot conceive the "two" grandmothers in the same frame precisely because they *do* involve at least two different languages.

Jane's expectation is that the two images *should* superimpose, for so the culture's logic of identity runs. She has a reasonable sense of the epistemological difficulties in resolving those images, for though she struggles hard to gather family memories and to retain memories of her own life, she is sharp enough to argue that "there was just as much invention in versions of the past as in what's written about the future" (100).

That argument takes Jane fairly close to a reflexive sense that all "knowledge" is fiction. And she is almost able to use this insight to invent a new definition of selfhood: "She wrote in her diary: Something remembered is invisible. What did I think about BEFORE, when I was young? I'm part of what I was thinking about then but it's not there anymore. The sum of my parts is invisible. Jane liked that line, 'sum of my parts,' a person could be added to or subtracted from, or a person could add up to anything. Or not. 'She didn't amount to much.' 'It didn't amount to much'" (82).

The diary, writing, becomes the line at which she tries to defend the erosion of "I" into the "not there," the point at which she can

intervene with "invention" to simulate some control over her own
history. She likes the idea of adding and subtracting—that one is an
aggregate rather than a unity or identity. That frees her to continue
her near-fetishistic attitude toward her past, because it is malleable
in her editorial hand. But it is also a threatening insight, because in
addition to the potential to be "anything" is the evaporative metaphysics of "or not"—of nothing, of having no Being apart from the
(cultural) ledger sheets in which one compiles transactions, as in a
diary, trying to record entries before the assets are lost in repression
or simple dispersion. Jane can make little use of this level of speculation; indeed, she seems to repress it. She is, like many people of
her era, between two ages (the modern and the postmodern?) and as
a result paralyzed. But the other two protagonists venture much
closer to the edge marked here between traditional formulations of
the self and the radical speculations implicit in *Haunted Houses* and
Tillman's other fiction.

Grace sometimes operates as if the self were *hers*, a thing she
possessed: "Her private life was her business. She owned it like a
coat or a record" (93), she tells herself. She is talking about fantasy
at this point, but the illusion of mastery and unity is there nonetheless. More typically, however, Grace is acutely aware of the peculiar
form of Being she inhabits. If Jane indulges in "invention" with her
memories, Grace applies it to the present as a sort of survival strategy left over from coping with parents and quite useful in dealing
with men:

> Whenever Grace lied, she did it so well, she believed it. Maybe
> that's why Bill's letter hadn't bothered her. She believed every-
> thing she had said to him and forgot it just as fast. Lying was a way
> to get out of the house, away from the fights, and it came so natu-
> rally, it didn't feel like lying. So if lies weren't lies, what was the
> truth. It was all right Mark saying there wasn't one truth, that's
> easy to accept, but she was talking about her insides, knowing
> what she felt from what she didn't feel. (96)

Lying is a form of ongoing repression, but it takes us beyond epistemological to existential questions. As the fictive identities needed
to cope with life crises proliferate, both our mastery and our unity
give way to a multiplicity of selves.

As her linguistic texture grows more complex, Grace feels increasing pressure from the dissonance among its strands and from
the conflict between that dissonance and the consistency of performance required by the culture. Told by a friend with a very contemporary sense of narratology that she "shouldn't expect anything
to lead to anything," Grace "reviewed the conversation along with
her split ends," a nice metaphor for the proliferation of narrative

leads in a subject become multiple: "Grace told Mark that she hadn't slept at all and that she felt she was filling up, and one day she might spill over. She was a story. There was hers, Mark's, Lisa's, the play, the people at the bar, hundreds of stories. Mark asked her to concentrate on her role, forget everything but it for just a few days, until D day, then he said he could talk to her about how she was in a story and so was he. Not in one, she said, we are them" (146).

Raised in a culture of identities, Grace feels deep anxiety over the proliferation of narrative lines that compose her. Mark, a late modernist *par excellence*, is perfectly capable of acquiescing in the *metaphor* of life stories as he coerces her to be more consistent in her role for his play. First produce, then we will indulge in a bit of easy talk about pronouns—which stand, of course, for classic identities, *in* stories going on around "us." But this encounter is one of those moments in which Grace experiences her postmodernity. The "we" in our syntax could apply to "Grace" as easily as to "Mark and Grace," and the copula evaporates both unified identity and preexisting entity from her sense of selfhood.

Perhaps Grace's most profound meditation comes after realizing that her "guilty pleasures were usually enacted in the dark. Sex, movies, bars, dark pleasure and places where she was inescapably alone" (63). The touch of another person, she realizes, is not finally "touching this singularity." Having separated from "friends, home, neighborhood"—from the networks that reinforce traditional conventions about the self—she comes to a radical sense "that her thoughts, like the physical site, could be shifted, thrown about or thrown out. Why she thought one thing rather than another. Why she liked anyone at all. Why she was heterosexual. Why here rather than there. Europe. Mexico. Colorado. Changing the landscape might change more than the view, her views being, she realized, predicated upon what she had or had not been given, a set of facts, conditions over which she had no control" (63). Grace realizes the extent to which "she" is a condensation of givens that could be recoded, but that otherwise determine everything from attitudes to sexuality itself. She realizes that she is "carrying qualities she had learned like a disease she didn't yet have" but would have when the right environmental episode triggered the semiotic organism.

Emily, the writer, formalizes this sense of things in terms that a critic can love. She takes advantage of the fact that "not being known is a big playground for any identity" by going to Amsterdam, achieving there what Grace finds by leaving home. But Emily's most important meditation on subjectivity comes before she leaves America, and it is cued by her crucial reading of de Beauvoir. Snippets from that reading are entered into the text as if it were a commonplace book; one of the most important snippets touches upon identity: "It is a strange experience for whoever regards himself as the One to be revealed to himself as otherness, alterity" (150). This insight lies behind the postmodern experience with Being that all three women have.

For Emily, the experience takes place as much in writing as in life: "What Emily read she became, identifying with the hero or heroine, the protagonist or the ideas, much as she did when she watched movies and cried. To this becoming her dictionary was a map, and learning new words was like leaving home" (150). This process of identification is more than sentimentalism, however, because it is mapped out through language that takes her away from the "home" of monosyllabic Being to a diacritical experience of self as a multiplicity of possible relations, each carried within the cultural languages that she is asked as a college student to master. That otherness encountered through language is wittily arrayed in the passage as it continues: "A map picked at indiscriminately. 'Pastiche . . . hodgepodge.' 'Passionate . . . easily aroused to anger; capable of intense feeling; *see* ardent, fervid, fervent.' 'Imperialism . . . the policy, practice, or advocacy of extending power and dominion of a nation. . .' Looking up words she knew or thought she knew reassured her. Finding out that she was wrong scared her. Any sort of discovery, especially of contradiction, satisfied her." "Pastiche" is what these characters experience themselves to be. "Passionate" is what Emily simply is not until she leaves for Amsterdam and tries out that role on an older Dutchman. "Imperialism" is what she encounters with language itself, comforted like a "fervent" patriot when she conforms to its denotational dogmatism, frightened when she finds herself outside its prescriptions, satisfied when "contradiction," speaking against imperialism, occurs.

The passage radiates out immediately, because Emily browses in her dictionary through *violence, virago,* and *virtuoso* to sample her own rebellious, nonconformist, and creative tendencies, because while she reads she "bandages" the thigh of her fatigues to cover a "hole" with obvious symbolic significance, because she wrangles a bit with Christine over the latter's wearing make-up even to bed with men ("The man's desire"), and because she recalls de Beauvoir on "alterity" and narcissism. Emily is caught in the middle of an increasing awareness of the many contradictions within her own Being, as well as those between hers and the socially prescribed Being that Christine more fully approximates. No doubt their names suggest their basic attitudes—Emily's linking her to Brontë and Dickinson, both nonconforming women in their eras; Christine's, to the norms of "Christian society" (at least from Emily's relatively withdrawn perspective). Emily is both mindful of the disciplining force of language and ready to use it to travel outward from identity along the fine lines on the map of alterity. She is puzzled by and longs for the words associated with *passion*, and sews a patch that both covers and, because it is contrasting and fragile material (from an old T-shirt), flags her "hole."

Somewhat later in the novel, Emily comes to an even richer sense of the diacriticity of it all. Finding herself "despairing of losing her English and never learning Dutch," she is delighted to receive a thesaurus: "The thesaurus provided associations. One word could replace another but not fix it with meaning. There were shades of meaning. Things in the vicinity but not exactly the same" (183). For someone whose life moves with and by language, this understanding of difference and of the "alterity" within meaning is an important moment. Emily writes Christine "that the more she thought, the more she thought things weren't one thing or the other but both" (185). Or even more, perhaps, if one really wants to work out the implications of Emily's diacritical metaphor for Being.

Perhaps that metaphor fixes most problematically, and perhaps most painfully, upon the issue of gender. That construct has lingered in the background of every question that arises in *Haunted Houses*, and its difficulty for the protagonists and for many of their friends is acute. The themes of alterity, difference, and fluidity are much in evidence, and the argument about gender in the novel is in many ways a logical extension of its theories of meaning, Being, and social forms. Tillman's "ethnology" of female experience extends to unsettling the poetics of gender dominant in our culture.

The dreams of the characters are good evidence of their considerable anxiety on this score. As a child, Grace sees a sack full of kittens dropped into the water, and the farm boy's "different attitude toward animals" becomes government policy when, in a sort of waking dream, "fifty or more stray cats moved toward her in a group. They were skinny and sick" (36). She feeds them, then learns that the government wants to get rid of them. From then on she has a series of dreams in which cats and kittens, obvious female symbols, experience types of the ebbs and flows of her own psychic contest against cultural limits.

Burdened by Bill's impotence and devotion, speculating about the extent of coding that she has internalized, Grace "dreamt she was in a swimming pool that was a room. It kept filling and she realized she couldn't get out. Just then she saw a cat and a door appeared" (63–64). Her way out of the amniotic prison, her way to escape the claustrophobic room of her body, is to use the door signaled by the cat. In another dream, "a mother cat has five kittens, very fast, in a big, messy house" in which the toilet has been pulled out at the wrong moment and "a child is sleeping or dead under piles of wet clothes" (133). Water again menaces, and, if the standard dream equation of house and body pertains, again the victimized cat-self multiplies within Grace while her human self is lost under old clothes. Her body's enlarged and messy status suggests the conflicted nature of her own feelings about the gender being bred within her.

Because Emily is the narrative artist, it is no accident that *her* gender dreams take on the trappings of melodrama. Her dream, which appears a number of times in only slightly different forms, is of violation:

> Someone like her is enticed into a room whose walls are deep red. Like shame, she thinks later. She is given a seat by a man smoking a cigar. Then there are many men. All of them want her, whoever she is. Want her very much. They're willing to give her anything. Anything at all. She says she's not interested in money, that she wants to be respected. One man spits into a silver spittoon. Her hands are bound behind her. She's not going to get anything. She's made a mistake of some sort and can't correct it. One by one the men lift her dress, although she thought she was wearing pants, they lift her dress and fuck her. She is taken over and over again. She does not resist. The dream disgusts her although she thinks she has had an orgasm in her sleep. (149)

At her most serious, Tillman is also at her wittiest, and the collection of stock dream symbols here pokes fun at glib analysts while making clear how Emily experiences the form of gender. Disdaining money but sorry that she is "not going to get anything," disgusted but orgasmic, Emily is well-trained despite herself but obviously divided over the role allotted her. She wears pants in both dream and daylight, but her gender retains the wide opening of the dress anyway. Her sense of herself is of having made a mistake she cannot correct—the mistake of being female in a culture coded "male."

Grace tests gender limits by experimenting with her lesbian feelings: "These thoughts she had about women. When she looked at their breasts like a man. Were they her thoughts. She couldn't tell. It was like lying and telling the truth. Where does a thought come from?" (97). She can think of movie scenes and the like, but no more sophisticated answer comes to her. She is aware that the thoughts she has are not necessarily hers and that her savoring of the female body is strongly influenced by the way men look at women. But she is not able to sift out the inner and outer, what arises within her and what has been planted.

When Grace *does* take a female lover, her response is both anxious and giddy: "It was different, and Grace was at a loss. She worried that she wasn't doing it right. Later it induced in her a state of psychic weightlessness that made her giddy with possibility" (142). She even worries "about the etiquette with women," because public sexual coding (in movies and popular fiction) is heterosexual, closer to Emily's dreams than to some utopian meeting of equals. But

Grace's weightless state as she floats above the messy house of traditional gender is at least a joy in the possibility of a sexuality outside all the coding.

Unfortunately, Grace finds even homosexuality a tightly coded world, and her gay friends exert considerable pressure on her to "make up her mind" and conform to one coding or the other. Her response is complex:

> Make up her mind, her face. Dress it up, rearrange the pieces, move the furniture, change the décor. The design. I'd like a few more angles on that part of my mind. Remove the frills. She felt she was up for grabs, even to herself. It was as difficult to know what to fill her days with as her body, or mind. It wasn't like learning the alphabet; it was more like unlearning it, not taking it in and not spitting it out. (143)

Emily's argument with Christine about make-up and Grace's dreams about her house-body feed into this passage's resentment over being sculpted by the cultural conditioning that floods in at every pore. To be "up for grabs" is suspense, not weightlessness, a form of vulnerability that drives Grace to a movie that she knows by heart and can respond to consistently, the way culture tells her to (she realizes that she learned *this* bit "in the movies, or at her mother's breast"). Gender is an alphabet, a phonetics of existential speech that catches her between two languages, unsure how to articulate her days. No "option" available to her is an escape from restrictive coding into some utopic freedom.

If sexuality within gender is necessarily problematic, so also is the flow of discipline and normalization into a mother-daughter relationship in which the mother seems always at least halfway coopted by the cultural regime. Ellen, a girl Grace meets while working at a mental institution, chants a revealing passage: " 'My mother is the Rose of Sharon, my mother is lily white, my mother is the whore of Babylon. My mother is better than your mother.' Then Ellen stuck her tongue out and wiggled her fingers at Grace, the way kids do" (198). Ellen clearly swings between the poles of devotion and abuse and is both a mature woman and a tiny child. She is something of an extreme case of woman carrying within her both herself-as-her-mother and herself-as-child.

Grace feels this most acutely after her mother's death. "Dead is dead, as Ruth would say, and homilies rushed into Grace's mind and out her mouth, so that after saying one she wanted to slap her hand over that mouth, but even that gesture may have been borrowed or stolen from her mother" (199). At such moments, when she cannot escape awareness of this internal relation, Grace cannot still the maternal to which she gives voice, cannot escape being the child in need of firm discipline. She cannot think through a winter funeral without humming "the worms crawl in the worms crawl out," and she knows she is now in for a struggle:

> People told Grace, now you only have your memories, but she wasn't sure she wanted to remember or, if she did, what would she choose to remember. She'd have to pick and choose carefully, to construct something that hadn't existed anyway. She could almost hear Ruth saying life wasn't a pretty picture with only happy endings. . . . She felt peculiarly free, because she was really alone. Although when saying that to herself, she caught herself and restated it as if giving a lecture to someone else. There's no difference now. (200)

Ambivalent about remembering, Grace is ready to fictionalize—perhaps to protect herself against the voice that rises within her (later we find her in silent internal dialogue with Ruth, "playing both daughter and mother with an accuracy only she knew" [207]). Grace thinks of herself as alone, but also feels herself in a dialogue—clearly the mother-self and the child-self carrying on the troubled relationship in which, with Ruth dead and buried within Grace, there is indeed "no difference now."

Emily's strategy is to attempt something close to Grace's "unlearning" the alphabet. It is as if Emily wants to "unwrite" herself, to keep her distance from the official writings crowding her internally. Hilda, her lesbian piano teacher, is more than once a reference point in her mental fight against her parents, whose "united front" poses the basic question: "Why can't you be more normal?" "The one thing Emily wanted less and less," we learn, "was to be more normal" (47). It is not that she makes an effort to find Hilda, but that the teacher represents an option to the gender script beginning to close around Emily's adolescent Being: "It was more like a novel that was living in her head and at the end of it there Hilda would be and everything would be all right again" (47).

When Emily finally does fall in love with a man, she is almost embarrassed, "stuck at words like feel and fell being so much the same" (179). She is highly suspicious of the Barthesian lovers' discourse she finds herself acting out: "Her feelings humiliated her, they were meant to embarrass her, and ever since she'd met him she couldn't shake the sense of its being fated, as in a fairy tale, fated and doomed. It was more than being in love, she considered that childish. It was written somewhere and she was inscribed in it. It didn't matter what she did, it couldn't be helped or stopped, and it wouldn't be" (179). More than love, "it" is the gender script as tightly and conventionally plotted as the fairy tale in which princes always act and princesses wait for them to do so.

Emily finally decides upon a crucial metaphor: "Love is . . . like an occupation, being occupied by. He swept over me, she wrote, his body larger than mine, and I am helpless against him. I let myself be taken. Her own words unsettled her, marching in as they did from what, if she spoke it, might seem enemy territory. She couldn't tell anymore, she didn't speak it" (179–80). It is one thing to contend against partly internalized cultural structures, but quite another to find one's own words and desires growing out of the primary Foucauldian matrix that is embodied in Tillman's fiction. At this point, very late in the novel, Emily seems to have found herself unable to tell where *she* is amidst these unsettling words, and hence also unable to speak a language that cuts against the gendered discourse of her own unconscious.

Earlier in *Haunted Houses*, Emily had written a poem of adolescent defiance, though only after "having buried her mother's phone call into ground that is not conscious":

> Leo strides in a field of men
> like a motorcycle passing cars.
> She is too different to be used yet.
> The cat wears its coat
> mindless of any beauty
> because beauty is only a word.
>
> (75)

No longer "too different to be used," Emily still wants to avoid the cultural word on beauty, but she has taken a decisive step toward the normality urged by her mother from the unconscious. If at one point Emily knows that, as a student historian, "if I ever graduate . . . it's because I'll have agreed to this language" (159), she has at novel's end come quite close to graduating to a "womanhood" predefined in language equally alien to her. Such a division within herself, such a conflicted alterity within which to struggle, is no peaceful state.

Grace's version of this estrangement in gender shows most clearly when she goes to a transvestite club with her gay friend Mark. He recalls going to a nightclub that featured a riveting dancer who turned out to be transvestite: "You should have seen the looks on the men's faces, men like my father. So disappointed. All this buildup and nothing." Mark enjoys the joke, of course, but Grace becomes uneasy: "Grace looked around the club and thought she might be the only woman in it, although that was hard to tell, or could she say born woman, or was it natural woman or real woman. It didn't matter. She told Mark she felt like a transvestite" (197). "Born," "natural," and "real" all collapse in meaninglessness as the club's spectacle drives home how ritualized and how *supplemental* "woman" is to the culture's male foundation.

Even worse, to play this "female" role is finally unsatisfying, as Grace realizes in watching and thinking about Marilyn Monroe, the quintessential "woman": "You look at Marilyn and she looks like she could make you so happy. So soft. She looks like you could make her happy. But no one could make her happy. Everyone tried. She looks like she can give you everything, that you'd forget with her. But she can't forget, and she can't be satisfied" (205). Grace recalls that Monroe once played Cordelia, an appropriate sacrifice to the male dominion that Maria had analyzed for Jane. And, echoing Grace's words (or rather Ruth's words) over Ruth's body, Grace mutters, "Dead is dead," a tying together of maternity, gender, and hopelessness into a Gordian knot of conflicted Being.

Emily's narrative ends by recalling the story of Margaret Fuller drowning with her husband and baby off the coast of Fire Island. She had returned from Italy after two years of revolutionary activity with Giuseppe Garibaldi: "Now she was returning home to face everyone who had laughed at her, and she never got there. Never got home. There was something sad, even tragic, Emily thought, about how Margaret Fuller's happiness was not allowed into her mother country" (193). There is *no* real home, perhaps, for a revolutionary woman, any more than there is a form of happiness attainable in what might more honestly be called the fatherland.

If Being is so heavily conflicted, if subjectivity is at best diacritical, if gender is the terrain of the "enemy" and includes the contested ground within, then consciousness is forever skittering between a terrifying sense of inner void and the play of wit and verve above it. Perhaps the ultimate image of this state is a children's book that Jane "loved and hated because it confused her": "There was a little girl who had a blanket. The blanket got a hole in it. She wanted to get rid of the hole so she decided to cut it out. She cut it out and the hole got bigger. She cut that out, too, and the hole got bigger. Eventually the hole disappeared but so did the blanket. The little girl cried and Jane was genuinely puzzled" (10).

The story resonates on so many levels that it is appropriate as a key to all of Tillman's work. Inadequately loved, her characters all try to repress that gap and wind up virtually without the capacity to feel love themselves. Given secondary and dependent gender roles, they cut out the givens and find themselves not liberated into utopic freedom but empty, listless, occasionally even nostalgic. Given cultural coding rather than Nature or Truth, they undermine verity and find mainly irony or silence. Given institutions that discipline and normalize rather than nurture and sustain, they live in one kind of exile or another—counterculture, foreign culture—and find only other customs, other norms, other laws. Given language rather than knowledge, they find not presence but absence. Given roles rather than identity, they find otherness within.

The little girl with her blanket is a fitting emblem for the contemporary individual trying to make something out of the void as defined by the metaphysical tradition that has elapsed. One wonders if the void would have been experienced as such without logocentrism's desire to fill the world with presence. Tillman's works articulate an analysis of our network of relations over which such a nonlogocentric character might have played like a radiance of energy. But no such utopian Being is at hand, and Tillman's characters have come instead already expecting unitary identity of themselves and legitimate sovereignty out of their social institutions.

Recognizing this difference is precisely what the ultimate talking cure leads to. If we talk out into narrative form that primary social matrix within which our Being is woven, we allow the fluidity of narrative itself to accelerate the recoding of cultural forms. Tillman's characters, however, live on the postmodern cusp between ages—late modernism is a living anachronism around and within them; postmodernism is a reactive if energetic dance in midair, like a cartoon character who races over the precipice into space. Some of her characters seem to look down and take the long fall. A few, however, seem to have the vision and energy to keep the legs pumping onto some new, changed ground. Do they patch the blanket's hole, the way Emily does her fatigues, or do they reweave its fabric in the pages of their diaries and stories?

# TANAM PRESS

*Fire over Water*

When Reese Williams's success with Tanam Press reached the point that "it wasn't really big enough to capitalize it or hire a staff, and yet it wasn't small enough to be a part-time thing," he found that "the texture of my days was ninety percent business and ten percent creation." In order to return to his own work, he closed down one of the most important of America's multitude of small presses (though McPherson and Company still distributes the literary and media titles, and the artists' books are available at Printed Matter in New York). After all, if business had been what Williams had wanted, he might have stayed an architect. He recalls his days as an undergraduate at Washington University:

> We started off with a good Bauhaus education where they trained us how to think visually. Then, at that point in the junior year where they start trying to get you to design shopping centers and office buildings, I transferred over to the Art Department and finished my undergraduate work in art. And I was doing a little bit of everything, but the most serious things were performance events that involved sound.

Williams's interest in making spaces was neither hypothetical nor particularly commercial: after graduation, he built and remodeled houses in California. But there is an important continuity among making dwelling spaces that people experience as "home" in the Heideggerian sense, weaving sound into a performance generating communal rather than consumer events, and creating Tanam Press as a distinctive venture in American small-press history.

Putting aside for the moment the sheer beauty of the books that Williams designed, we notice something important about the way he talks about his editorial practice in the preface to the last book he produced before ending Tanam Press, *Fire over Water* (1986): "I remembered my first impulse to publish which took form as *Hotel* (Tanam Press, 1980). This book, a collection with seven contributors, was not 'edited' in the usual sense of the word. Instead of selecting work that I felt merited greater attention, I invited seven people to create new work for *Hotel*. It was understood that we would go with whatever they came up with, and that their 'being together' would be the book" (1). Rather than creating a monument to completed works, or a bastion for an editor's particular theory of writing, Williams stimulated creation by bringing together energies that more typically disperse into the "wild history" of urban life. For this last book he also asked for new work, but without the generic restriction to fiction that guided *Hotel*, and published it, Williams writes, knowing that "bringing this group of people into the space of one book would articulate the synthesis that I had been attempting with Tanam Press more clearly than ever before" (2).

Williams explains that synthesis as "a sign representing the sense of place that is created whenever diverse forces come together inspired by the desire to (re)establish connection" (2). Tanam Press brings together very diverse forces indeed, including artists' books (Richard Nonas's *Boiling Coffee* and the collaboration of Jenny Holzer and Peter Nadin, *Eating through Living*), writing by Werner Herzog and Cecilia Vicuña, critical essays on television *(Transmission: Theory and Practice for a New Television Aesthetics)* and film *(Apparatus)*, artists' responses to mass media (Douglas Kahn's *John Heartfield: Art and Mass Media* and Peter D'Agostino's *The Un/ Necessary Image*), and works of fiction (Richard Prince's *Why I Go to the Movies Alone* and Theresa Hak Kyung Cha's *Dictee*). Whether critical or creative, these books have in common establishing connection, creating cultural space, and healing a culture in which, as Williams told me, "the market economy gets into a very fierce managing and incrementing of time," and in which "advertising brings entertainment to soothe the pain caused by the market."

The community that Williams sought to forge with Tanam Press believed "that the system we have in place for exchanging art, and that's very accentuated when you come to New York, doesn't really work. The gallery/museum structure doesn't serve us very well." As the social, so the individual, and he sums up his unconventional view of being an "artist" this way: "What one does as an artist is that one labors to receive a gift which comes and passes through you on to the next person. But that laboring for the gift is a very different process than what's encouraged by the culture right now in terms of pursuing an arts or literary career. There are a lot of people who are off that track, who've been knocked off-balance. It makes them ill." As editor, publisher, and writer, Williams directs his efforts toward reestablishing a track of cultural health through the pathological wildlands of the eighties.

We learn more of that track by considering the title of Tanam Press's last publication. "Fire over Water" is more than the title of Williams's third anthology of writings from Tanam Press. It is, as Williams explains in his preface, "the image of the 64th hexagram of the *I Ching*, before Completion":

> Fire over water:
> The image of the condition before transition.
> Thus the superior man is careful
> In the differentiation of things,
> So that each finds its place.
>
> (1)

"Its place" almost suggests the sort of systematic incrementing which Williams complains about in the market economy, but "place" is more Heideggerian than digital, more experienced than contrived, and results from what, as a Tanam Press catalog would suggest, is a thorough critique of the market economy and its media culture. The "differentiation of things" is less a classificatory than an analytical procedure, and one that, as the explanation of the press's name makes clear, involves a dismantling and reordering designed to allow a renewed and renewing address of the Reader, a "thou" recovered from its alienated state of consumer:

> The word *tanam* is related to the Sanskrit *Anantam twam* mean-
> ing "endless, thou." The "endlessness" reflects in a way of recit-
> ing chant which involves the breaking up of a text into syllables
> and the continuous reordering of them in all combinations, both
> as a means of obtaining mastery over the sound system of the
> chant and of acquiring insight into the truth within the text.
> There is a point where movement ceases, where sound returns to
> Silence, where the active individual melts into the great tradition.
> (229)

This is not T. S. Eliot's "great tradition" but rather a tradition of seekers and healers who provide a powerful antiphony to the flickering transmissions of the media culture. As Williams says in his introduction to *Unwinding the Vietnam War: From War into Peace* (Real Comet Press, 1987), he places a view of the world "in which biological, psychological, economic, environmental, and spiritual phenomena are all interconnected and interdependent" against the reigning "concepts of an outdated world view: the think-ing of Cartesian-Newtonian science which sees the universe as a mechanical system; the view of life as a competitive struggle for existence; and the belief in unlimited material expansion through economic growth" (5). *Tanam* involves recovering the "sound sys-tem" of the nonlinear chant *as well as* understanding "the truth within the text" of the culture, and it is this dual process of analysis and alternative, critique and healing, that marks Williams's work in particular and, in various ways, most of the work published by his press.

A quick sampling of those books makes the point. *Transmission: Theory and Practice for a New Television Aesthetics* (1985) is intended by its editor, Peter D'Agostino, to "create an 'interference pattern' within the seemingly continuous flow of television's pre-packaged ideology" (5). Its essays range from the theoretical to the critical, from documentation to history. Theresa Cha's anthology on film, *Apparatus*, is designed as "a 'plural text' making active the participating viewer/reader, making visible his/her position in the apparatus," and clarifying Jean-Luc Godard's reminder that the viewer's relation is one of production. D'Agostino's *The Un/Necessary Image* (1982) is an anthology of artists' works that one would likely call "conceptual art" for the vigor with which they desublimate "the content and meaning of public information" (5). Essays, appropriated advertisements, and montage are among the means by which its contributors connect their readers with the ideological content of contemporary imagery. Readers are drawn from "it" to "thou" under the spell of these works, just as Douglas Kahn's *John Heartfield: Art and Mass Media* (1985) studies the inventor of political photomontage with an eye toward an "expanded oppositional politics of artifice" (142) to counter the simulacral realm of the image.

The artists' books that Tanam Press has published also seek ways of escaping economically conditioned roles for their readers. Williams has argued, in a piece for the 1986 Printed Matter catalog, that artists' books are necessary both to our full sense of an artist's work and to the very possibilities of expression itself. His reading of the hold of galleries over the production of art takes us back to comments we encountered in my opening chapter: "The art world of the 1980s is virtually overrun by a hyped-up market economy, and much of what you see in galleries has passed through the control room of marketing strategy" (24). Tanam Press's artists' books are among many one finds at a place such as Printed Matter; some of them are all drawing or all photography, some all text, some an intriguing mix of the visual and the written, some even less conventionally describable than this.

Richard Nonas's *Boiling Coffee* (1980) is in some ways an expanded version of "Montezuma's Last Dead Breakfast in Mexico," a photo-and-text work appearing in Williams's *Hotel*. *Boiling Coffee* lacks the first version's strong ethnic punch, its pictures of Chicano workers with their fiddles interleaved with a text in which Montezuma becomes for Nonas the type of culture's victim. Montezuma's last writing feels bodily "the scratching of pens . . . the scraping of words . . . their slow weight pushing down as they thicken into

slabs." The narrator's shadow is cast over Montezuma's shoulder,
fixing him the way he is also fixed by the water diviner's stick from
the photographs and the push of the fiddles, until the narrator comes
to know that Montezuma has stopped writing and "is waiting for
me" to join the dead king's last breakfast. Not anything like a Last
Supper, Montezuma's meal marks a cultural "fellowship" that
means the subjection of one race by another.

*Boiling Coffee* is not a "pretty" book. Its photo cuts and blow-
ups are complemented by black ink splatters and Franz Kline
strokes and masses, and its text is crayoned in a sort of graffiti
scrawl. Its narrator, a sculptor in the very urban medium of steel, is
equally urban in his paranoid responses to the "who," "what,"
"where," and "how" questions that an unidentified "she" asks. He
withdraws to "home," where his attempt to sculpt alternates with
an empathic passage into the photographs of Chicano workers who
are boiling coffee and cooking a breakfast, perhaps before a day picking crops. Boiling coffee is the narrator's way to "keep me warm,"
"keep me here," and "keep me him," so the reader feels uneasy
about the contradictions in nature and allegiance for an artist whose
roots and sympathies reach back into the subjections documented
photographically alongside the shaky, almost white-knuckled text.

*Eating through Living* (1981) is a joint work by Jenny Holzer,
known for her Times Square slogans and her Truisms—street-situ-
ated texts appropriating the "wisdom" by which people live—and
Peter Nadin, better known for his art but also represented in the
*Wild History* collection. The visual part of *Eating through Living*, a
slickly produced book (the paper is high finish, the typography is
ultra-Helvetic in its plainness), consists of precisely drawn heads of
female and male speakers alternating with bits of information, news
items, adages, observations—bits reminiscent of the pages of Truisms that Holzer posted around New York. The exception appears in
the book's middle, where a different sort of text is accompanied by
rough crayonings of a couple making love. Stylized and almost smug
faces opine conventional wisdoms and cocktail-party "did-you-
knows" as a frame for the "central" text, a meditation about a
never-specified it(s) whose antecedent seems to shift. The meditation defeats readers' expectations that its sentences follow one another, that its rhetoric leads toward insight or conclusion, and that
its speaker understands an answer to a question of significance. We
come away with a sense of the *non sequitur* as the essential figure
of Western logic, of contradiction as the characteristic relation
among its specific practical enunciations, and of a fundamental estrangement between the thinking or speaking self and the body (the
sign for which is in the sex acts drawn amidst this most abstract of
discourses).

The "endless, thou" evoked by the name of Tanam Press is

richly evocative of its authors' desire to address readers as subjects, rather than objects of any cultural process of normalization. The obviously ideological works on figures such as Heartfield, the analyses of media, Holzer and Nadin's desublimation of the version of cultural logic we carry in our heads, Nonas's exploration of the conflict-ridden voice of the artist in a racist and exploitative culture—all these strategies seek more an interlocutor than a consumer, a subject capable of escaping administered time long enough to encounter the endlessness of what Williams, in his story in *Wild History*, calls "gift waves." Those waves are moments of healing not entirely reified when meditation becomes religion, art becomes commodity, organisms become citizens.

### Reese Williams: Writing as Gift Waves

From his education at Berkeley in the mid-seventies to his participation in a number of important exhibitions on into the eighties, Williams has worked at the center of a generation thinking out in contemporary terms the relation of text and image, culture and the individual, consciousness and the unconscious dimensions of the subject. To superimpose, for example, the alphabet's family tree on a Vietnam War–era photograph of chained prisoners driven along by their captor is to evoke something of the "prison-house" of language with all its sociopolitical ramifications. To use the same photograph at the end of a book, this time bearing "a sequence of seven universal symbols," is to disturb the distinctions that we sometimes maintain between "kinds" of sign systems and between forms of cultural order. To superimpose a fragmentary arch from a Leonardo drawing on a still of a woman with scissors from a Godard film is to draw together differing temporal and formal zones within which we assemble the collage of derived elements constituting culture. And to mark with an ink drawing (a fish's backbone?) images as diverse as an extreme closeup of Ray Charles or a reverse of a Pudovkin still (in which a white, human outline swims up the stream of a road in an apocalyptic landscape) is to menace the stylish surface of cultural imagery with the animality and primary consciousness it organizes and in part represses. And to follow images of the media commodification of war (and ABC's self-congratulations for an "entertainment event" such as "Winds of War" or CNN's pride in exposing cameramen to live ammo in Beirut so that its "viewers could see, and almost feel, what it was like to be there") with the Aztec Quetzalcoatl (whose front is the face of Life, whose back is that of Death) is to begin a line of thought about culture's transformation of Death into unreality and commodity, primal anxiety converted into the bait we consume within our economic and religious institutions, culture as a narrative explaining away into the unconscious the ultimate Other to its collective life.

Throughout Williams's work there is an especially acute focus on the dilemma confronting the contemporary thinker attempting to evade longstanding philosophical prejudices about the nature and structure of consciousness and to reach that zone where our essential Being rises in all its obscurity, complexity, and problematic character. This effort to spiral down through the sedimentary layers of cultural codings accounts for Williams's habit of writing in short stretches of textual imagery, and of returning to these pieces (he calls them "texts" in his notes to himself) repeatedly over the years to rework, recombine, and recontextualize them.

This method is in part following the way that cultural materials in general are constantly reworked and reset in new places and at new angles, and partly Williams's own spiraling evolution as he tracks the visual and verbal materials of consciousness back to their still point. To glance across the sequence of his writings is to recognize the special intensity with which he has pursued the ever-elusive point at which the internal and external meet. What begins as a sharp recoiling from the social determination of individual Being moves steadily toward Eastern meditations that are a bit Zenlike in character. Williams has his own model of our internal apparatus, one that shares enough features of this or that contemporary theory to place him amongst those probing the margins between a largely verbal consciousness and its nonverbal Other, and between these "internal" planes and the "external" cultural elements that are, as in much current fiction, inextricably mixed with them.

Williams's contribution to *Hotel* (1980), "A Study of Leonardo," works both senses of the title's preposition (Leonardo's "study" of the behavior of animals is one of Williams's devices for circling the junction between cultural conditioning and that which is conditioned). There is a circus barker too short to "pass" as a real man in the culture and too tall to become a commodity object with "an upwardly spiraling career in the circus of movies." A "shaman as well as a charlatan" and "a brilliant transmigrational strategist," he warns all listeners of the danger "that *they* are going to devour us, that we are at the mercy of a vast officialdom." He teaches his disciples Leonardo's notebook entries on animal behavior as one way of "carrying that knowledge from one transmigration into the next," but more important as a preface to Williams's work is the barker's "Art of Suspension": "One should work to a position just below the surface and hover there for eternity; this is a position of power, *they* can not harm you here. He warns that *they* will always be encouraging you to surface. *They* will use many disguises and will never give up" (61).

Suspending oneself in a socially stigmatized zone between surface consciousness and a depth Williams elsewhere calls Silence is
a way of resisting the "disguises" culture takes to draw one, like a
fish on a line, to the surface. This *"they"* recurs throughout Williams's work, though not always so explicitly glossed, and is the
collective voice of culture calling: *"They* is a giant summa, a mosaic
of power and authority that he has constructed over the years; it is
all encompassing, spanning from the ancient Chinese yin/yang to
the current bureaucracy of this circus. *They* is always regenerating
into new forms to *get* you" (61).

Totalizing "summa," artistic "mosaic" representing the sociopolitical force of culture, index of religious totalities of the Orient
and institutional structures of the "circus" of modern civilization,
the "they" of culture is a fluid network of codings, forms, discourses, and institutions designed to encourage individuals to surface on its ideological plane and attenuate to that plane's two-
dimensional grid of Being: "If you do surface, they will love you and
everything will seem favorable. But after a short period of grace,
they will begin to eat you. And after they have picked your bones
clean, they will throw your corpse on the heap and turn their attention to the next one" (61). Williams returns often to this sense of a
culture that consumes its members, pulling them out of the depths
of their own consciousness, picking clean their bodies, so neither
dimension of the traditional dualistic self is "free" or "individual,"
but reified, collective, coded.

In *Figure-Eight* (Tanam Press, 1981), Williams features this
"they" in the sounds of the city: "Each new sound is a fact-bearer
instantly re-referencing me to one of the huge tracts of information
that comprise the day." He lists examples and knows that "the hook
has caught hold in the roof of my mouth." The subject who swims
in the dreams of the unconscious is "hooked" and netted by a predatory culture that blocks free access to the Silence within. Most
episodes in the book feature a "born-again" industrialist who leads
convoys into northern Laos (he made his first fortune supplying
opium to the French syndicate in the days before the French defeat
at Dien Bien Phu). He passes out Polaroid cameras, postcards, tennis balls, pantyhose, felt-tip pens, and the rest of the paraphernalia
of consumerism in order to lure "primitive" societies into the anticommunist camp, and his rhetoric of "the millennium" of "peace
and material wealth" climaxes in a mass "rapture," which is a cross
between Superbowl halftime show and Nazi spectacle. If it is
through luring and hooking that individuals are assimilated to cultural norms, those norms are presented through the all-but-ritual
discourses of what Althusser calls Ideological State Apparatuses.
Hence the mass rapture in which, as in the industrialist's campaign,
we find a mixture of religion, politics, economics, and media (video

cameras seem to be everywhere) functioning overtly to determine the form of Being.

"A Study of Leonardo" evokes this mix in terms of a tent preacher whose sermon probably reveals more than he intended. He begins by telling his audience that their lives are busy but hopeless. He grows almost Heideggerian when he argues that common objects are an unsuspected menace because they "carry with them endless generations of the dead" (69–70). Their weight of history and custom determines our lives in many subtle ways and hence leads men to "deal bitter blows to that which is the very source of their life." The preacher's myth of the dead transformed into man-eating winged creatures is an eerie evocation of the force of past thought to consume us through such minutia of daily life as "chairs, tables, books, cups, etc." These objects "are openings which allow dead things to come up from the underground," and thus they function to set deadening social forms against the vital signs of an underground much healthier than the political unconscious he seems to be describing.

So unhealthy are the cultural contradictions thereby internalized that "it will become soothing to have others derive profit from your suffering or from the loss of your only wealth, which is health," because that physical cycle of suffering and therapy simulates the more difficult cure of a diseased ontology. The cycle of environmentally induced illness and artificially high health-care costs is one metaphor of the cultural vise; religion is another—the preacher offers a theological bargain, "only two dollars for a love that lasts forever" (70–71).

"Common Origin" (1986; most easily available in Brian Wallis's *Blasted Allegories* [New Museum of Contemporary Art, 1987]) offers an apocalyptic script in which individuals try to create a vivid life after American culture simply disintegrates. The villain in this piece is that zone of "public information" pursued by Tanam Press's media analysts: "It appeared as though the nation was hit with an epidemic of lying, as if the lying that we commonly accepted in advertising and politics spread suddenly into all other sectors of the culture. There was an irresistible pull, something maniacal about it. Within just a few weeks, everyone was lying to each other. It was a thrill, like revenge. People took their pleasure in spreading the lie into new regions" (198). Food is poisoned, forged letters clog the mails, clerks type "incorrect data" into banks' computers, the credit-card network is pillaged, and the domino theory finally has a real theater as a collective and maniacal pleasure trip of revenge topples the Bauhaus boxes of modern institutionalized life.

The collapse, however, is "an opening up of time," a "great leveling" of opportunity—"and most people walked in," almost "as if the nation had unconsciously forced a catharsis to free itself into this new time." The utopic dimension of all this emerges in the final image of a man who survived the dark days by hunting with a hawk. He *almost* merges his consciousness with that of the hawk calling out to his man self to "wake up . . . those who are with me, fly with me." He hears without, of course, flying, for though Williams circles constantly this or that utopian opening in his grim analysis of the media culture, he does not succumb to any of the three most common failings of such utopian longing—the naïve simplifications of our era's nostalgic returns to tradition, sentimental neo-romantic assurances about unmediated Being, or unreflective and hence unwittingly stylized views of culture's Other.

Part of this utopian impulse is as cathartic as the apocalyptic purging of American institutions in "Common Origins." In *Figure-Eight* the "I" experiences a more literal form of an apocalyptic vision: "Without warning, my sight gives out—it's not that I am blinded, but I can no longer make any sense of the light images that are constantly entering me. Why are they occurring? What does one do with them? It is as if my brain has abandoned the sets of memory routines that it normally uses to make vision. It is no longer synthesizing. . . . Finally it is gone—into the biological past—like a wound that has healed" (103). The mechanization of consciousness into "memory routines" falls away, suddenly, and the culturally prescribed "synthesizing" breaks down until this wounded (and wounding) way of seeing disappears into the evolutionary past. This is the "art of suspension" (as "Leonardo" calls it) with a sociohistorical vengeance.

One thinks also of the ending of *Heat from the Tree* (Benzene Editions, 1984), in which language rather than vision is the focal medium:

> The first word.
> Millions of words later, I have remembered the feeling of its sound. I can't voice it yet, or send it to my hand, but that will be my goal.
> Like light searching for an opening.
> A constant longing to give something of my origin. (49)

*This* first word is semiotic rather than theological, but, like the preceding passage's desire to get past preconditioned vision, its status as the originary event of the self draws the writer's interest. He hopes it will provide him an "opening" into "new ways of thinking about ourselves" that are less determined by (if not free of) the many cultural languages criss-crossing our consciousness.

In the revised version of this work published in *Fire over Water*, there is a sketch of a man who "climbs the mountain of terror," leaps off, and finds that "energy long saved for this moment ignites his spinal column, flushing out every cell in his body," and plunging him into a primal ocean: "And in the water, millions of silver jets—each of his cells now a salmon. They are returning, each with the same desire, into the mouth of the river. Leaping and thrusting in the white water, free within instinct, relentless toward union" (173).

A few pages later, accepting the pine's invitation to listen, "My ears become fish in the trance of water, white changes to blue-green and I am drenched with the sound of her voice rising to the high note" (181). In both passages it is important to realize that what appears at first glance to be a simplistic return to animality "free within instinct" or an unmediated originary state in "the mouth of the river" is not as simple as the opposition of psychological depth to cultural surface. The prose makes clear the meditative site of this "return" by anchoring the figures of movement not only to emotion (mountain of terror) and physiology (spinal columns and cells) but also to the linguistic "mouth" of the river of individual Being that begins with the first word. This movement is not a Western sort of progress or development. As in "Common Origins," time can be experienced other than as the plot line of traditional narrative culture, as instead an opening (just as in *Fire over Water* the "I" learns to experience things not as "objects" but as "openings"). That opening leads not to a free zone "before" or "next to" but rather *within* cultural form.

Perhaps the best image of this notion is the turf-maze design on the back cover of *A Pair of Eyes*. It is a labyrinth with a single path crossing and recrossing any imaginary straight line into its center. There are no dead ends, but also no *place* in the center—just the space inscribed by the path's boundaries. It is a path that ends (or begins, depending upon one's perspective) with the "hook" of cultural forms that not only enable but also channel one's course. To follow that course is not to escape the "river" except into the oceanic ecosphere of organic life.

That sort of escape counterbalances—but does not, until death, dissolve or even fundamentally alter—the cultural codings in consciousness. At most it denaturalizes those codings to sharpen our sense that an Other that is us abounds in its difference all across the same ground mapped by visual and linguistic semiotic systems. This maze is best glossed in a passage near the beginning of the book that follows it chronologically, *Heat from the Tree:*

> A recurring moment in the life spiral when a man can see the specific pattern of his survival. Why he acts as he does, what he must visualize to continue into what has already happened. In this spark a thread appears, weaving through every breath in a ringed web.
>
> Everything alive has a direct line to the center. To become "un-

strung" is to die. To live is to "be woven," to be dependent, to be in a constant state of communication. (7)

One delights in Williams's complication of any simple line through this subject. The sinister image of the "web" in which he is caught, but which is also the "pattern of his survival," the connecting thread "weaving through every breath" as something both extrinsic to him but what connects and directs, the ensnarement and dependency of the web as what constitutes life—all compose the "constant state of communication." That last word puns on the linkage between the semiosis that *is* the problematic form of consciousness and the media-age connectedness by which it catches us up into the taxing economy of collective survival. The "spark" of insight into this decidedly post-Husserlian phenomenology is one important thing that Williams's work has to offer us.

This ultimately ambivalent awareness of the rites and rights of the passages we make in our various forms of consciousness is what distinguishes Williams's work and places him at the heart of the polyglot world of postmodern culture. To do him full justice, however, we must take a sustained look at a single work published at the turning point of his career, one of what he calls "transition pieces, as I moved from visual concerns to writing."

*A Pair of Eyes* (Tanam Press, 1984) is an engaging work alternating two-page spreads of images—some of them advertisements, some photographs, some drawings—with two pages of text. Some of the images have already been commented upon, but their alternation with text means that both the verbal and nonverbal eye/I is called for in a work that looks into the phenomenology "of our common memory, past and still to come" to see what might lie "behind the mask" of semiotic systems flashing by at full hypermedia pace. Without what at times these days becomes either naïve neo-romanticism or pop mysticism, Williams sifts through the aftermath of Marshall McLuhan and poststructural semiotics, looking for what we are when we are not being culture's creatures. Williams elaborates along the way a phenomenology of the image which is quite useful in approaching contemporary culture.

Near the end of *A Pair of Eyes* we get a sense of the effect Williams hopes for: "Pound the drum, left hand right hand. Take the images faster, let the words become a body. These signs began as physical things, they can still work on our senses. This is not a transmission of information." The recurrent drumming signals the incantatory phase of the book's rhetoric when it seeks to conjure beyond words and beyond media images into the material experience from which both ultimately derive. The drumming taps the tradition of meditation exercises without surrendering allegiance to any one institutional guru or sacred text. Beyond the fine mesh of information networks and the code webs of discourse are the bodily sensors that Williams wants to reach. To "let the words become a body" is to make words objects again, linguistic things with etymological roots in the sensory perception of reality. To increase that sensory and historical depth is to become aware of the cultural typology in the word's fossilized record of experience. The strategy escapes naïveté through the double movement of deconstruction which both foregrounds the cultural artifice and conserves the complex figurative process by which experience is assimilated to cultural form. The first movement denaturalizes discursive blinders; the second restores to the subject a license to perceive, to engage in the process with his or her own experience.

The next paragraph characterizes what the whole book is, in part, an attempt to accomplish: "Pound the drum, hold still in the form of extreme mobility. . . . This Sunrise is different from all the others on our journey. Today we are entering into the opening of an image, whirling back in a counter-clockwise motion into the symbol of the cross." Williams might have chosen another symbol—he scatters through his text many with potent traditions—but this one does allow him to gauge a number of sedimentary layers in the cultural imagination, including fertility cults, Christianity, fire worship, "life energy persisting in Time" (like a vertical blip on the horizontal line of a heart monitor), a generic transcendental cosmology ("union of heaven and earth") and ontology ("spirit descending into matter"), gender ("creative and male" intersecting "receptive and female"), and a vaguely Hegelian sort of phenomenology (time is "the means of making actual what is potential"). By spinning the dial of the semiotic clock, Williams turns it into a wheel of fortune on which the reader's finger may fall almost anywhere among the sign's resonances. We want to turn the cross on its side, make it the $X$ of the culture's signature, and relate it to a number of other $X$ patterns marked by Williams. This deeply carved image is typical of those Williams opens in order to show us how thoroughly saturated with history any sign or image is and to connect us to the living process of semiosis by which signs can be (re)made rather than unreflectively received. Williams is ready to trace these symbols all the way back to an almost precultural flow of physiological energies underlying our theological impulses.

*A Pair of Eyes* is more than a basic primer in semiotics, then. Signs and images have a constitutive function in forming consciousness, and Williams takes us to the edge of what we can think about that formative process. On the first numbered page (Williams numbers only pages 1, 7, 14, 21, and 28—for the numerologically inclined), he introduces Screen and Mind, two key characters in the inner drama:

Screen comes of her own will, from her own tradition, rising in a swirling heat up through the body to the dome of the skull. Opening from seen to unseen. Memory of homeless wandering, of things hidden, of feelings to be regained. Mind responds automatically, filling the moment with the beginning of an image. Wind turning, mother tree welling into the sky. On the ground, a drove of people and animals hovering on the verge of sleep, heads slowly falling forward.

Female Screen, rising from its own countertradition in a bodily heat to the male Mind's domain in the dome (one to be echoed later in architectural and meteorological forms) of the skull, brings something of the unseen to the consciousness. That unseen is anything but simple, compounded as it is of nomadic subsistence, repressions ("things hidden") that could be positive or negative, and feelings worth recovering from their loss in, presumably, the rational age of Mind. The drove image, named as such elsewhere and reinforced by a photograph of Vietnamese War–era prisoners chained and marched, is that "grand illusion" of "truths learned collectively," the everyday drone reality one fuses with in "going down into the street." To see the alphabet's genealogy superimposed on prisoners reminds us how system-building—theological or economic, political or linguistic—colonizes basic points of human energy as subjects of its regime.

The relation of Mind and Screen is fully problematic. In this first passage it is almost cooperative, Mind generating images that presumably catch something of the unseen opened by Screen. But *screen* is an ambiguous term: it is a barrier, but also possibly a gauze screen that in the right lighting reveals what lies on its other side; a screen that Mind "fills" with *its* images (rather than awaiting that Other side's Unseen?); and also a screen that carries all the media images that alternate with the book's text, "invading" and constituting this "inner" world.

A few pages later, a dense passage pursues this drama. "Screen, the receptive, comes up from Silence, a spinning rebus of the perfected cries of monkeys and dogs." Gender stereotypes again lay out the roles as Screen, something like a primal mental faculty, emerges from the Silence (rather than from the cultural Word), showing as it emerges on *this* (textual) side of the consciousness a puzzling mixture of words and images. That the puzzle is the "perfected cries" of animals suggests that one of the "things hidden" is the pained animality that, rather than transcendental spirit, is the ground of Being. Screen "looms unknowable, a space vast enough for the words, *mother, father, soul, home,* and *world* to continue branching forever." Again "female" in its spacious receptiveness, Screen serves as the womb in which language divides and multiplies.

Is Screen a membrane between visual unconscious (or precon-
scious) and verbal consciousness, or is it a three-dimensional spati-
ality of consciousness generated in some primary movement of *différance*? One could perhaps argue that the metaphors are fatally
mixed, but the point is rather the ultimate ambiguousness of any
effort to beat out images and words fast enough to shoot the gap into
materiality, most of all when that gap is consciousness itself. More
subtly, this oscillation is between the two-dimensionality of the
representation and the three-dimensional invagination of that representation by the diacritical cultural matrix within which the image transpires and "makes sense." Williams works close to the phenomenological side of Derrida's interest in the spatio-temporal axes
(another *X* shape) of *différance*.

As if the drama were not vexed enough as it is, Williams adds
sound to image, word, space, and screen as Mind responds: "Mind
probes the feeling of the sound with his I-ness, projects his newest
model of the psyche into it, then falls back to wait for the echo, for
the change." Mind projects obviously arbitrary models of the psyche
upon the sound and entertains himself waiting to see the results of
his seminal act in Screen. Because the drum beat is a meditation
device for calling images and words forth into consciousness, a passage such as this one becomes a reflexive meditation on both the
phenomenology and the fictionality of thought and writing. Representation is an "echo" of the model by which it is projected, and the
"change" it produces is our experience of consciousness as if its
world *were* that representation.

Williams develops the latter dimension more pointedly a few
pages later in a passage that begins in the physiological and ends,
perhaps, in the grammatological:

> Nerve exposed to light. When to cross, when to stay? To arrive
> once again at this point in the cycle, the seventh position, the
> moment of self-reference before change. An animal searches in a
> figure-eight pattern, always crossing back across his path. Why
> am I writing at all? Am I just emptying out what others have put
> in? Or am I recovering what is mine noweover?
>
> An image is turning over and over in my mind on its journey
> back to Silence. I see only a small part of it, but I can feel the
> power. It is a living spirit, bearing gifts. I am making marks in
> honor of its passage.

Like a metronome, the first few lines tick back and forth between
body and mind, or perhaps between "animal" and "human," and
the elaborate mandalas of the mystical tradition flow into the figure
eight (which contains another of those vital *X* patterns in the narrative). The "moment of self-reference before change" is the intersection of the eight's loops when the animal then shifts its course

to cover new territory. It is a figure for writers' discovery that their work is always crossing (Xing?) "what others have put" into the cultural repositories of language and convention.

The complication is the final query in the first paragraph: Could writing be conceived as recovering a "mine" from the well of Silence whence Screen arises and whither image in the next paragraph goes? "Emptying out" suggests a part-behavioristic, part-semiotic answer (befitting the "animal" half of the opposition here), whereas "recovering" points to the traditional subject's unique and securely grounded identity. The "solution" is not the kind we find to a problem, but rather the kind in which we find ourselves immersed in a "mine" of deposits which has accrued interest of an indeterminate rate and payer. The moment of self-reference is that earlier "spark" by which one's "I" is a primally conditioned perceptual faculty. Hence the "I" in the passage can "see only a small part" of this nonverbal phenomenon, which is an "image" and at the same time "a living spirit," another version of the bifurcation with which Williams repeatedly plays. What *is* certain is that, like a good grammatologist, he is "making marks in honor of its passage," words that mark its absence, its having already gone. The image's "gifts" are enabling, but require honoring with (infinitely) more passages of writing. In light of that reading, the "I" would appear, borrowing a metaphor from Hélène Cixous, to swim the stream of consciousness rather than cross on the stones of any Mind's "newest model of the psyche." In the process of that swim, the "I" encounters the vanishing point at which Mind and Screen, word and image, "put in" and "mine nowever," "male" and "female," "human" and "animal," "I" and Other shimmer at the point of dissolve into each other.

These sets of "contraries" are ultimately the arms of the cross, X, or figure eight that marks the spot (even if it is a constantly shifting spot) of culture. The narrator "can feel the power" of this figure and also can mark its degenerate forms in the two "most pervasive symbol[s] of the industrial era"—the dollar sign (in which one of the straightaways is machined into parallel tracks, rotated to break the shape, and used to railroad us all into the commodity/consumer culture) and the swastika, an even more sinister sign of the nexus of military, economic, and political power whose trailing scythes cut a swath through the cultural imagination wider than neo-Nazi cults, Hitleriana, and assorted more literal emanations. The swastika is also a dramatic illustration of culture's power to transform a symbol with uplifting sources in mysticism into a sign facilitating the most brutal exercise of modern institutional power.

More typically, Williams pounds his meditation drum "to follow the lines of forces as they pulse through things. . . . What is behind the mask?" His ellipses mark a fundamental gap. On one side is what the writer *can* do by way of seeing, if not the forces themselves, then their lines insofar as they can be noticed pulsing in things. On the other side of this gap is what the writer can *not* do—answer that primal question of what lies behind the mask of the culture's manifold semiotic networks. Three of the book's "plots," which look at pulsing "things," are knotted together at this point in four one-sentence paragraphs using semicolons to apportion equal time to each of the three (numerologists will note the persistence of *three* and *four* in Williams's structures). Partly this technique simulates the image "turning" in his mind, partly the crowded screen of consciousness, and partly the inextricable relations of the kinds of strands composing the ultimately alienated texture of that consciousness.

The first plot features jeeploads of journalists shuttling from Angkor Wat ("to feel the light-giving energy of the temple") to the site of a Khmer Rouge massacre ("to feel the terror emanating from the mounds of skulls"). "They" are opposed to an "I" and later a "you" "begging for food or money," all combined in the last paragraph's maxim for this plot—"We feed on the past, the future hunting us down." We consume the past as the commodified images of the stock photo agency and the wire services, processing the silent place of the temple into the driving pace of the contemporary mindset (the way that the Silence behind Screen is filled by Mind's projections?), and containing the movement to ideological slaughter as a still from another place. The "you" of consumers is deep in complicity with the merchandisers from whom they beg sustenance and profit, of one kind or another, and thus keep the wheels of culture turning. The "future hunting us down" is not, then, some malevolent predestination descending upon us, but the culture we are weaving out of the commodification and hence the evacuation of the world around us.

This dark reading of culture shows clearly in the second plot. The fish-self of the "Night" segments, in which the "eyes" (or "I's") become dolphins coursing through dream waters, is caught on the baited hook "they" cast out. This strand's maxim, "We eat plants and animals, information devouring us," makes clear that our unconscious is caught and reeled in like every other consumer of cultural discourse (another version of Althusser's "interpellated subjects"). There is a whole series of blunt anatomies of this constitutive dimension of culture. Some anatomies are playfully serious; some are grim. A group of glitzy producers discuss an idea for a television show that epitomizes Williams's reading of the culture: "Can one consciously act to forget and lose all knowledge? Do you think we could get an entire country to do this en masse? I think it would make for a great episode, don't you? And at the end we could send a microwave pulse that will explode all the picture tubes."

It is not difficult to see that media empties the mind in order to make room for advertising to generate consumption. The producer muses on "all those jobs making more televisions," and then decides to project a three-thousand-mile-high Walter Cronkite packaging the Ernest Becker book *The Denial of Death*, "tracing our fear back to its source so we can get on to the next america." Presumably this "special report" on the primal source of our fear enables the conclusion we see later in *A Pair of Eyes* when the producers fly by, along with the signers of the Declaration of Independence and an airborne flotilla composed of the nation's television sets following (ideologically?) the lead plane. The "next america" seems one in which projections of a commentator reading a report on a book's packaging of primal fear interposes many levels of mediating imagery between consumer and experience—a "great episode" for the national maxi-series.

There are more explicit socioeconomic analyses of the media, as in the reflections on the dollar sign and swastika in "the latest avant garde styles" transmitted "all over the world to generate more dollars." There is also a discussion of "the culture of the rich" busily "trying to sell the idea of war" to the "culture of the poor," with its "Peacemaker" bombs, "Patriot" missiles, and the like. "War is now a commodity. It makes good TV," a point that Williams underscores by including ABC's self-congratulatory ad on the success of its "Winds of War" and other entertainment packages. In another segment he notes that "the grid of commerce" might just be absurd humor if its "filaments" did not also "lead off elsewhere": ".The way we promote accumulation of material wealth in advertising and entertainment leads directly to shortages, poverty and death in other parts of the world; and the way we position women in advertising and entertainment leads directly to acts of violence against women." Starkly explicit analysis contrasts to media soft-sell episodes. Entertainment is used "to soothe the pain caused by the market," but this sort of cultural "painkiller" is "chemical warfare," and the difficulty is to wage "what triggers *seeing* the filaments" against "what numbs *seeing*."

That effort is writing, the third plot. Elsewhere in the book Williams talks about falling "toward a point" in Silence (conspicuously "toward" rather than "to" in a book that does not suppose one reaches the pure zone of untouched and authentic self-identity). "And then up for a moment to *Book*, the space between your thumb and forefinger. *How do people connect?*" They connect, if at all, in writing, whether the space between the "thumb and forefinger" is the authorial pen or the reader's tome.

In the trifold passage that was traced, "I" is "one word after another on this page," as if Williams were reminding us that an "author" is that interpretive construct we make as we read, and that Williams makes as he writes. In the second paragraph, "they" comes "into one book after another," as we all do in passing through the tutelage of culture, consuming one text after another and, in a more sinister sense, as the collective body of conventions and their latent ideologies do in invading book after book through its language, images, and conceptual frames for experience. In the third paragraph, the grammatical person shifts to the "you," writing "page after page, breaking apart to re-build again." Reading is a form of writing, as the theorists now tell us, and to read is to break apart (to deconstruct?), and, then, to repeat ("re-") a building process that was already a repetition ("again" emphasizes this clearly enough).

This rebuilding is a version of the figure eight, so central in Williams's imagination, of tracing back around the reflexive circuit of language and textuality, as on the next page when he decides that "Tonight I know that this book is leading nowhere, except perhaps in on itself." Hence in the fourth paragraph the trifold meditation culminates by observing that "we dance this strange ritual of reading and writing, *other* to *other*." It *is* a ritual because it is a formalized process—that is, it is one that necessarily and inevitably conforms to semiotic systems as its preconditioning. Hence the "other to other" is a multifaceted alienation or estrangement. One shift "to other" is between writing and reading, and this in turn further complicates the prior internal shifts that the writer experiences in himself and in his own meanings. Finally, the estranged otherness of reader and writer is yet another antecedent in this maxim. It is no accident, then, that this potent page ends where it began, asking, "What is behind the mask?" The passage has its potency not in finding the solution to the question, but in swimming through the complex interrelations of media, consumption, politics, and language—in "making marks in honor of its passage," the "its" here standing for the almost Lacanian subject that is "always a fading thing that runs under the chain of signifiers" (Lacan 1970, 194).

The "bottom line" in Williams is not itself seen except as it "pulses through things" as an absence to which poststructural theory has begun to make us accustomed. But this pulsing requires us to see and write in a way contrary to what is sanctioned. "Images connect together in momentary resonances" once we begin the sensuous coursing of the dolphin "I's" lurking beside the daylight verbal world of Mind. These resonances offer us many different "openings" (or gaps), each of which "is a life and a death, a stolen moment in another cosmology, or any projection you desire." To live in the images that we screen in our cinematic consciousness is to die to the normalizing "grand collective illusion" and those who dwell there; to stir these deliberately and "take off" into them is, indeed, to steal a trajectory of desire from our culturally repressed repertoire and to pass into an Other "cosmology" of Being. The trick is to "get past the guard at the door": "Sometimes he takes the form of *fear*, other times *routine*. There is no end to his inventory of disguises, you will invent them faster than you can uncover them."

The guard is that compound within us of cultural censor and cautious animal sniffing the air distrustfully, and it resides as much in language and its attendant conventional forms as anywhere else. As fast as we can "uncover" one form of delusion or error, we can unwittingly "invent" another, as we might well gather from Paul de Man's comments on irony or on the relationship between blindness and insight.

The passage continues: "So at this point we turn to the monkeys and dogs for they are the masters of this type of play . . . they play both ends of the paradox simultaneously—*nothing matters* and *everything depends on this one moment*." "Nothing matters" if, finally, we do not make it across the Gap to Self, to Reader, to Truth, to Reality, or to what John Fowles calls "all those other capitalized ghosts in the night that are rattling their chains behind the scenes in this book." If one expects to find what Plato liked to think was out there, then nothing in *A Pair of Eyes* will matter. But if that aspiration is put on sufficiently deep hold, then everything indeed depends on the moment-by-moment experience that we share with the other animals on the globe. In a quite real sense, this perspective makes all the more important such issues as the penetration and reification of consciousness by media images, plots, and commodity values, and this is no doubt part of the earnestness behind the book's more direct moments. But this perspective also takes the "self" to the very edge of any line of thinking we can manage, but without breaking through to any free zone. As with the nineteenth-century turf-maze design on the book's back cover, there is one line in, leading to a center that is the point of the one line out. This line is language.

Williams makes the argument more explicit in the last segment, in which the infant's first "Da" is also its last. This "Da" is a post-Eliot "little thunderclap" in which "de-making" and "de-learning" are the comedowns needed before entering "the pool of continuous-tone babble" which we speak in the "grand collective illusion" of our daily rounds or before entering the ultimate pool of death. In the last book Williams produced as the "line of force" in Tanam Press, he explains the source of the press's name, concluding that "there is a point where movement ceases, where sound returns to Silence, where the active individual melts into the great tradition" (229).

It is and is not Eliot's "Tradition and the Individual Talent." When Eliot notes that "art never improves, but that the material of art is never quite the same," in the same way that "the mind of Europe" changes but does not "superannuate" the past (Eliot 1975, 39); or when he stresses the catalytic quality of the poetic mind as a "medium in which special, or very varied, feelings are at liberty to enter into new combinations" (ibid., 41); or when he adds that it is a medium "in which impressions and experiences combine in peculiar and unexpected ways" (ibid., 42); then Eliot goes as far as Eliot could (and still be Eliot) toward the radical demystification of consciousness in Williams's work. Williams's tradition is not Eliot's "existing monuments form[ing] an ideal order among themselves" (ibid., 38) but rather, as he says in opening *A Pair of Eyes*, a cultural memory that is history's "gift to the life instinct"—not an ideal order, but a repository and a signing system that both enables the individual consciousness and assimilates that consciousness to itself. Eliot's catalyst does not "melt"; he abstracts or formalizes until he resonates with the tradition. Williams's writer swims through a stream of images and words projected by Mind and junk-mailed to Screen by mass culture, experiencing bodily (rather than simply being inscribed in the collective address), as much as possible. He drives through the night on "Speedway Boulevard" with faces and images stringing together inside, and outside, "the pull toward Silence" as death in its many forms.

*A Pair of Eyes* deals with death on the scale of mass apocalypse: Oppenheimer is a character, and we learn of the current bomb project "to blow up the sun." But mostly the forms of death here concern "a people using their resources to die," "a society of people who make money to live by doing things they don't want to do." Despite the validities of these political, economic, and social analyses, however, the more subtle deaths are those growing out of culturally induced perceptual habits. An unidentified "she" warns a narrator anxious about the flow of images racing by (in history, in present experience): "What are you looking to see? It is in the darkness of their own eyes that men get lost." Men see images and signs, but understand them according to institutionally sanctioned distortions rather than with the immediacy of living truth.

When I asked Williams about the pervasiveness of various sacred and mystical symbols in his works, he made it clear that his interest in the cross or the Yin and Yang was as "a sign that connects you with a certain group of people." Personal connection rather than denominational allegiance, this relation to sacred sign stands behind a passage such as the following: "My dream this morning was that the world is a dream, dreamed by many different powers. These dreamers war among themselves to gain control of enough energy and matter to realize their latest episodes, but there is never enough to go around so the world is always in turmoil." Those who build systems and serve institutions are dreamers, powers who contend for a hegemony that Williams so distances and so abstracts as to make clear its secondary importance to healing those in turmoil.

Williams shares his narrator's desire to understand what the images arising during meditation will discover "searching for their carriers in this era." Such an image is less a content, a primary concept, than a resonance, a vibration of energy that recovers something otherwise lost in a culture for which a rich word such as "image" has come to mean a manufactured lie about products and candidates. He becomes almost mystical talking about Tantric and Pythagorean scales, five-element theory, and other such ancient wisdoms about the body predating the Western alienation of body and soul, synapses, and identity. In "Gift Waves," a story in *Wild History*, the grandfather disposes of the merely rational prescriptions of the Administered Society: "Better to settle on an answer, even if you have to make believe that you have one. That was the grandfather's advice. The answer will change again and again. In long view, it has no meaning. Think of it more as a shape, see it as a channel. The important thing is to never be without one" (12–13).

A particular answer, in other words, is a "carrier" rather than the foundation of true theory, true state, or true church. The father is one who has been wounded by war, and he listens rapt as the grandfather relates the point at which asking "if he was at home" triggered the healing moment for which Williams's fiction strives. After watching a nighthawk drink from a pond without breaking its flight, the grandfather tells the members of two younger generations: "I reach my hands down into the silver and into the fine red mud below. One hand finds sadness, an echo from World War II, the pain of millions of interwoven deaths. The other hand finds an animal pleasure, the touch of earth to body to sky" (14).

The sociohistorical shrewdness of the former architect, Pacific Film Archive devotee, publisher, media analyst, editor, and writer balances with the polarity therapist's skill at tuning primary body energies. Both are essential to Williams's cure of the culture's battered spirits. When the grandfather sees a dog come over, smiling, sliding over to touch, he receives the dog as "a gift" that takes him back to childhood, healing not just his own fear of homelessness but also the "separation" afflicting his son:

> *The separation began with your first exposure to a lie.*
> The next step was to learn to lie to himself, then to refine this process until it became invisible. And the last step had been to join the national lie. (10)

These systemic lies—identity, ideology—disrupted what the father had felt as a child, his ability to live "with a continuous outflowing of desire." By thinking back upon the memory of the trip with the grandfather and son, the father builds a memory of being "connected to everything" and recovers that virtually prelinguistic self's vitality and Heideggerian "at-homeness" achieved by the grandfather. The memory is like a pyramid, "and from the apex, gift waves

will ripple out from one generation into another." This character
seeks in his life what Williams seeks in his art, the healing "gift
which comes and passes through you on to the next person." The
"endless, thou" that Williams set out to encourage with Tanam
Press is therapy without psychiatry, wisdom without theology, writing without literariness.

### Richard Prince and Prior Availability

Richard Prince is undoubtedly better known as a visual artist
than as a writer. In 1977 he began rephotographing media images, a
practice that has by now included among its subjects Marlboro men,
entertainers, rock bands, travel shots, bikers' girlfriends, and advertising models of several descriptions. "This action," Kate Linker
explains, "slightly in advance of similar practices by other artists,"
"repeated, in picture form, a procedure that had been applied to
writings the previous year, when Prince published texts 'lifted' from
Elvis Presley bubble gum cards" (Linker 1983, 2). Prince "ganged"
his appropriations so that viewers would see a number of similar
shots at once. In a conversation with *Art in America* interviewer
Jeffrey Rian, Prince explains the "cumulative density" of these image series: "The recognition of cultural patterns, of 'the same
within the different,' is a big part of all my work. These patterns—
for example, the generic quality of rock star photographs—are initially disbelieved and then sometime later, perhaps very much believed. What's strange or disorienting is that a lot of us are not used
to believing media, advertising or editorial images" (Rian 1987, 91).
At some point the "prior availability" of these images kicks in and
structures perception, experience, even identity itself, and the initial disbelief is eroded under the constant flow of media repetition.

Prince's most telling analyst, indeed perhaps the most astute
commentator on artists' writings in general, is Brian Wallis, whose
introductions to Prince's work in *Parkett* remain the place to begin
studying it. Wallis brings into play Prince's subversion of the classic
mirror epistemology of the culture:

> For Richard Prince, reality is literally a mirror, except with reality
> and the image inverted. What used to be termed "reality" has
> been replaced (as the primary referent) by simulations, models of
> reality. The glossy images of television, video, and commercial
> advertising established the "reality" for identity formation. Iden-
> tity becomes equivalent on the level of the image or pure surface.
> This is the end of the original and the beginning of the fiction of
> identity. (Wallis 1985a, 71)

However, Prince goes beyond simply recoiling from this scenario of
Foucault's End of Man, for, as Wallis says in this essay, Prince "ap-

proach[es] this environment with a mixture of fascination, risk, ecstasy, and voyeuristic pleasure." Prince understands both the hook and the bait in the simulacral society.

What startles Prince about that society is the absence of anything resembling an author, a history, an imperfection—those traces of the real which are airbrushed away in the iconology of the era, and without which the unsuspecting are lost in the land of Day Glo sunsets. He told Rian about the effect of re-presenting these images:

> The authority behind the image, or the believability of the original image, is put into question. And I think I'm able to do this, at least to some degree, by making the image look as *realistic* as any other media or art image. Like everything else that happens, it's hard to locate what's figurative and what's literal, what's fictive and what's nonfictive—whether it's an image in a magazine or a gallery, or an event out in the street or up in your room. . . . Most of the audience receives what looks to be authoritative information, that is to say, it receives media reality as fact. They still don't see media representations as a *version* of what's real. (Rian 1987, 88)

Prince is intensely interested in the production of versions, and it is difficult to say whether his visual or his textual art offers the more subtle analysis of that production's workings. Linker reminds us that Prince's "practice has been not only to re-present these images of commercial persuasion, but also to reproduce the very processes by which they are produced" (Linker 1983, 4). His is "a reality in which the roles of both creator and copyist have been replaced by the more complex one of the arranger who, working with the sophisticated technology now almost universally available, 'manages' the production of imagery." Her verb is crucial, because Prince's fictions are about the "management" of identity as if one were so many more bits of information racing along the cables to be screened.

Prince uses this computerized layout imagery himself in one of the segments of *Pamphlet* (a 1983 catalog from Le Nouveau Musée) as he dissects his characters' self-assurance:

> The ways of the world are set in type like maybe someone composed them on a copy terminal and then flashed the whole thing on a screen to see if everything would fit and justify in neat little rows, and anything that didn't fit got edited out or hyphenated so the look of it was just like the look that goes down straight on the right side of a page . . . that magic side in a book, where a gully of even space is. (18)

Prince turns the bit on them, however.

Survival of the fittest they would laugh and say was another way of saying it. They would say this . . . would say the survival thing right after the copy process rap . . . and say, I guess that's another way of saying it, but putting it in a way that I didn't think they were meaning or talking about survival.

They care more about becoming "mainstream" and of making "the next condition *even*."

They are atypical of Prince's characters, because most of the time his players know *that* they are playing and *what* they are playing. They are like the narrator in *War Pictures* (a 1980 Artists Space pamphlet), who says "our motive is to taste power and abdicate," to play without being caught. "We do not make art. . . . We modify fabrication into a temporary refuge that gives the appearance of order." To make art is to risk enclosing oneself in the market economy that governs artists. After all, as Prince told me, he began writing partly from "the need to make work that you couldn't really speculate on" the way three-figure early visual works become five- and six-figure commissions later on.

The very idea of art begins to interpose precisely those unexamined layers of technical mediation and economic motivation which Prince's rephotography was designed to foreground and, as he says, "dereferentialize." Prince is quite frank about saying that "it's hard for me to read a regular writer. The way they talk on the page seems to me really stilted." They seem, he thinks, "to be screwed up with the structure of how to present," and they lack the "zip" and immediacy of writers with backgrounds in the visual arts. The only thing worse than "literary" is "commercial" writing when "someone comes along and pretties it up, takes that rawness and forms it in a way that it can be digested. I think they're looking for more stories about downtown life—that's what's really coming out now. The *After Hours* effect."

When you pass what Prince calls the essential "rite of passage" of "seeing all that everybody else writes as fiction," you are prepared to write something quite different from what comes from the "*After Hours* effect," a fiction with "the barb or the edge" that comes from "trying to sit down and say, precisely, what exactly is going on." From his earliest pieces, short pamphlets done to accompany exhibitions at CEPA gallery, Artists Space, and Printed Matter, Prince has pursued in his writing the cluster of issues found in his visual work. In *Menthol Pictures* (CEPA, 1980), for example, a narrator shares notes about war, horror, and sex films. "Picture" notes the clichés stocked in our "collective unconscious" during "hours of late-night cinema viewing." When we find ourselves in a moment like one of these cinematic "tight spots," "we sometimes refer to it not as an observable reality, but a situation that was once previously experienced in a cinema movie. This prior availability can suddenly become factual reactional behavior in a day to day routine."

Prince's style here seeks out the tone of our information age, "as if," he tells Rian, "in this culture information touches a chord in us the same way a hit song makes you impulsively keep a beat with everybody else." The tone makes us receive "the information as a genuine experience," the way his characters often perceive the image-draped space around them as their own experiential authenticity. In *Menthol Wars* (Printed Matter, 1980) Prince gives us vignettes of a whole cast of characters in the process of moving from "carrying on a menthol war with [their] enemies" to realizing "how easy it is to get rid of [their] choices" (22). Some characters like slick media packages precisely because such widely available material is not only immediate in its impact but also has the extra kick of having already been looked at by others: that "in effect defines a lot its desires and threats" (12), a prior availability that puts a twist on keeping "a beat with everybody else."

In *Pamphlet*, which features both text and photographs, Prince reuses some of the earlier pamphlets as well as some material from his Tanam Press book of the same year, but this booklet remains an important opportunity for seeing his drawings and photographs together. One section defines his characters' use of "Very Really" as "a sign of a self-imposed sentence, signaling the inability (but the desire) to 'connect.'" Drawn from the "prior availability" of Paula Prentiss films, the phrase contains the means of coping with a man in the Diamond District "with a numbered tattoo on his forearm" who is *not* wearing "the make-up of a character actor." The narrator quotes the characters' own explanation: "'From out of nowhere,' they say (as if to re-affirm their own un-authorship), 'usually due to an accelerated exchange where our relationship between ourselves and an apparent impossibility becomes switched from the almost familiar to an unquestionable, spirited, "fact"'" (26).

It is worth noting that it is their *relation* to the "apparent impossibility" rather than the impossibility itself that becomes "fact," because their expression ("Very Really") has to do not with the real but with the management of the realistic according to the margins of their layout program. They sense themselves as living "something like a post-mondo menthol generated, (extended) adolescence . . . trying, if nothing else, to deal with the things that go on and on and on and on." What we recoil from is clearly a strategy for containing the contradictions they experience daily while living at media pace.

*Pamphlet* ends with a passage saturated with ironic self-reference: "They say, 'Whether he's stolen or produced . . . copied or pointed to, isn't the controlling share anymore. It's more about has to be than how. . . . And as long as the exchange at least simulates the effect of what should be . . . then we're prepared to see it, support it, buy it.'" This is one of those passages in Prince's work over which we could fret indefinitely trying to limit the irony to something "local" or "finite," as theorists of irony would have it. Taken straight, the passage points out that Prince's work jettisons any fetishizing of craft in favor of the patterns of determination built into the production of imagery and identities in this age—what "has to be [rather] than how." Prince's work "at least simulates the effect of what [art] should be," justifying its support by those whose lives bear the cost of what, instead, takes art's place. But it takes genuine determination to maintain such a reading once the irony of "they say" or "controlling share" begins resonating. Understood ironically, the work (Prince's or anyone else's) is seen assimilated into the market economy as another simulation doomed by necessity to its realist (rather than real) status. (After all, *Pamphlet* is a limited edition that may someday redeem my research expenses once the collectors carry out the very speculation that artists' writings were intended in part to circumvent.)

Before we turn to Prince's most important work of fiction, it is worth a moment to note his 1988 artist's book, published under the auspices of the Barbara Gladstone Gallery, which contains both text and a helpful range of his photographs (including examples of many of his subjects or genres, a number of his "gangs," and even a shot inside his studio). The narrator, a New Yorker staying briefly in California, savors the pleasures of suburbia (enough room to display his collection of car hoods, regular delivery of newspapers and pickup of trash, and appliances galore) while adding cars to his garage and famous engines to the living-room decor. The skew of the humor opens out from a deadpan style in typical Prince fashion and makes the book an excellent sort of traveling exhibition of Prince's analyses and sensibility.

Prince's *Why I Go to the Movies Alone* (1983) collects many of his best pieces and adds some new ones. It features his usual very sophisticated narrator capable of both very slippery irony and dangerously oblique syntax, which will confound the hasty reader. "When people ask me about that book," Prince told me, "I say the book is my autobiography. And you can be really truthful that way. It has to do with the fact that I might have been talking about only one person and that idea about a double. That's all throughout the book, the idea that your image is over here and you're over there and your image has nothing to do with you. It's just like the media: when are you going to come to terms with it?" These sketches are all about the contemporary subject coming to terms with the displacement of self by image, with the proliferation of pronouns whose references—internal? external?—have grown indeterminate. Prince emerges with something akin to an ontology of Being in the era of simulation. Like his publisher Williams, Prince works with the relationship between the individual consciousness and the media images out of which it is constituted.

Wallis suggests that "there are no characters, only pronouns," a reminder not to restrict these figures to modernist character types (Wallis 1985a, 73). Even more telling is his description of *Why I Go to the Movies Alone* in another essay: "The characters in his stories are an attempt to make true the fiction of the advertising photograph by supplying a narrative and a coherence to the images of the models" (Wallis 1985b, 61). To read the book is to discover the energy we expend trying to "make true" the images instilled in us as our own psychological repertoire. We are connected, in other words, to Prince's objectives in his visual work.

The book's part titles, "Cowboys," "Mountains," and "Sunsets," make obvious the concern with the stylization of perception and of Being, and they bear out Prince's autobiographical claims for the book, because Marlboro men, travel shots, and ad cutouts reshot against fake sunsets are among his important series. The "I" who goes to the movies alone, at least in one segment, is almost anesthetized by the uncertainty that takes place in the overstimulated urban environment when people see too much, read too many popularized versions of contemporary theory, encounter too much of the inescapable alienation of the culture: "He's not sure who he is when he's there, or if in fact, he's comfortable and wants to be there at all. He says one's identity is easily changed when what's in front of you is reversed and transparent, directed and produced" (54–55). It is disquieting for a number of reasons to be there. He becomes aware of a queasy fluidity of identity, as if some not-self or unknown part of himself were responsible for his being there, for being comfortable, for responding to the film's direction.

Moreover, the genre of film foregrounds the culture's capacity to make its audience want forms of desire which preclude "gratification" except within this image-world's script (or, perhaps, preclude it altogether?). Finally, because this is a porno house, there is an element of danger, seaminess, and a delicate territorial balance among the "audience 'peppered' throughout the theater" (54). That territoriality is perhaps a metaphor for the violation of the self's inner space in a media-saturated age. In any case, the narrator chooses the most violent option in slang for what appears on the screen, and the emphasis upon size in "huge details of someone getting banged" only underscores the violence and victimization characterizing the age. This image is central because the narrative's main business is to probe the cinematic stylization of consciousness and the mutual victimization of individuals subordinating each other to the current reels of their own identities. Their own consciousness and anything around them become the "easily changed" stuff of Being on the transfiguring screen.

This whole process is also complicated by the force of desire—it is not simply for a grimy atmosphere appropriate to the subtext of culturally inscribed subjectivity that this "I" chooses pornographic movies. During the film "there's lots of talking and shouting back to the screen" as spectators vent their anger over there being "no good sex movies made for a paying public" and, by extension, problematic sex roles engendered by those one does find. The narrator observes that "sex movies in a public theater are not what's censored or private." They are, instead, the very public stylizations that exclude the possibility of any "private" or "personal" interaction (the spectators may shout, but the screen's response is the subliminal stylization of their libidinal forms and "plots"). As Wallis argues in a more general context, "what is private is public, and what is public is the only reality" (Wallis 1985a, 73). Above all, these films certainly do not show in any direct way "what's censored" by the culture's determinations of gender and sexuality—the reader must go to Acker's fiction for that feature.

What we do find, then, is a state of desperate ambiguity in which individuals are driven at a frenetic pace through a succession of images that are fearfully fixed definitions of Being but seductively smooth and stable refuges from the temporal and configurative fluidities of existence. Prince traces this conflict through his characters' bloodstream with the skill of a surgeon of consciousness. "He," for example, works for a magazine; "he rips up magazines and tears out pages so if anybody wants a particular page they can call down for a couple of copies" (55). The job is an apt trope for the constant recycling of media images and banalities, and there is a measure of ambivalence in "his" attitude: "He tears them quickly, with one tear at the bind. He likes to do this. It makes him feel good" (56). If he *really* "likes to do this," we wonder why he leaves his job to watch porno films during working hours or why he leaves much of the work to "someone a bit more on the job," or even, finally, why ripping the magazines in half is such a pleasure of vengeful hostility.

Prince's anatomy of alienation here is finely detailed. Even the images in the ads "he was just beginning to see" are alienated: "The scenes had suns going down in the background. It looked like they used a photo-projection of a sunset and the projection made the principal parts of the picture look flat and cut out" (55). The projection of a photograph (of a sunset) makes the only once-removed photograph of "principal parts" look unreal, like collage elements, and even the time of day selected, dusk, seems special to him because the mix of fading natural light and the artificial lights of the city "set[s] up a kind of pseudo-reality that seemed to suggest something less than true." Again, this figure suggests well an almost erogenous liminal state between reality and image which, though "less than true," is also "nice" and pleasurable in its mediation of the rough edges and threatening planes of experience.

The sinister aspect of these photographs is not to be overlooked, however. "Just in the past few weeks he's seen a lot of these pictures, Saab, Volkswagen, Ford, Pontiac. They all have them out" (56). This "they" resonates sharply with that of Williams, and points to the steady beat of stylized definitions of "life" which this character is in an ideal position to see as such. But the end effect, as in going to the movies, is to make the subject desire that which estranges him from himself. "There's nothing there that seems to be him, and no matter how he calls them his, it's not like he's the author of whatever their design is supposed to be." The consumer authors neither the imagery of the culture nor, finally, much of the self that unfolds on its set. But he *likes* it: "He likes the fact that it's not just one company putting them out. The way they show up gives the images a curious, almost believable fiction. Their symbols make him feel reassured. And the way they're put together and their over-emphasis, dares to be believed. It's almost as if the presumptuousness of these pictures have no shame" (56).

There is no sure way to know how much of the narrator's analysis is shared by the character. But the outrageous presumption of the culture to determine for the subject its view of experience is as much (perhaps perversely so) a pleasure as the reassurance of its recurrent symbols. The "pseudo-reality" need not pass by unrecognized as such; it is part of the kick. The free artifice of "the way they're put together" is a controlled and safe sublimation of the threatening fluidity of self, just as the glitter selves that the characters in this narrative can assume are safe forms in which to assuage the itch to change into something closer to the perfected fun and beauty that the imagery promises.

Nonetheless, alienation persists: these characters are displaced from any real authorship, homogenized by the replicated quality of the imagery, and anxious amid a series of conflicts—between the comforting stasis of the image and the vague hope that change might alleviate dissatisfaction and unfulfillment, or between the glossy allure of the image and its two-dimensionality, or between the fear of losing oneself into the collective pool and the equal fear of risking real rather than simulated change. We see such conflicts emerging in the character who likes to go after work to Howard Johnson's (itself a suitable subject for the reader of images). The attraction is partly that "there's as much open, predictable action there as any place in Times Square," and partly because "the scene and all the movement and hustle" are framed and screened by the window between his table and the street realities: "He especially likes it because of the silence that goes along with his location. The silence he thinks makes the obnoxiousness smart and stylish, and whatever the outrage, the inability to hear it makes it reasonable" (56). He sounds like a fan of "Miami Vice," the window of the restaurant functioning like television, realist fiction, bourgeois ideology, radical chic, or any other cultural frame to style reality to its "smart" location in the cultural matrices and to make "reasonable" the incomprehensible outrages of real experience.

The effect, finally, is to evacuate the innerness. The character himself speaks of this experience: "It's like my looking in that particular place has become customary because the looking there is no longer accompanied by what I have always like[d] to think as me. Sometimes I feel when I'm sitting there that my own desires have nothing to do with what comes from me personally because what I'll eventually put out, will in a sense, have already been out" (57). The perceiving self has become spectral, its desires are the already circulating conventions of subjectivity broadcast in media format, and, finally, this self-become-image is itself a desirable end to what "I have always like[d] to think as me."

Another way to think about it, he tells us, is "that what I see there is somewhat fragmented and additionalized onto something more real, and this, in effect, makes my focus ordained and weigh significantly more than the spiritual displacement the view sometimes suggests" (57). The very action of consciousness is the process of sifting through the relationship between the "fragmented and additionalized" in what this heavily programmed "I" sees, the "smart and stylish" street theater, and the "something more real" that menaces the integrity of the frame itself. This process is "ordained" in the simulacral society and hence a "weighty" phenomenon to understand. Presumably, the understanding compensates for the emptying of self which the experience produces as the ambiguous side effect of "spiritual displacement."

There is one more element, however, in this analysis: "After all, artificial intelligence, like fiction, whether displaced or fabricated, makes reference to the particular, to the sensory detail . . . and it is these 'details' that are terrifyingly beautiful" (57). However sinister these processes are from one perspective, they nonetheless *enable* an encounter with "sensory detail," even in the "displaced or fabricated" image realms of our cultural fictions and of that simulation of ourselves we tend to become. These details are beautiful both in the sense that we prettify them within our framing and because, simulated as they may be, they still *look* like points of direct and unmediated experience. But although they are refreshing exceptions to such "pseudo-realities" as photo-projected sunsets, these "terrifyingly" raw experiences are also unsettling as pinpricks in the screened images through which reality may leak. These tense relations between simulated and real, framed and unframed, mediated and direct, run throughout the narrative and challenge characters, narrators, and readers with the difficulties of maintaining an awareness that does not simplify complex interrelations.

Prince calls this character's section "The Counterfeit Memory," and, in the one that follows it, "The Velvet Well," we move from the self of stylized imagery displacing spirit to the tension between the velveteen packaging of simulated experiences and the tendency of "real" velvet to spot in the rain and tear in actual wear. One segment focuses upon a couple who see an ad for the zoo, and the prose takes place very much on the other side of the time line between a traditional and an advertising culture: "They were used to seeing things cropped, with the scene or the image up close and filling up the whole frame . . . making whatever was there, 'larger than life' . . . making it a lot more than what it was supposed to be" (70).

Cropping, focus, and magnification are some of the more obvious forms of styling reality (and, again, three of Prince's primary manipulations of media images in his rephotography). But, as the passage goes on to say, "this particular way of looking at what was *inside* was nothing new and the effect of its experience was only questioned by those few who still couldn't quite come to terms with the idea of substitute or surrogate relationships" (70). "Those few" include the traditionally minded thinking with high seriousness, because their "terms" strive for the mimetic, the "real" without quotation marks, the originary and authentic relationship between sign and referent rather than the semiotic or simulated relations to which this couple are accustomed.

The trouble comes when this couple "found themselves 'falling for'" the image in a traditional interpretive fashion—taking the image to represent the thing—rather than maintaining a sense of the play of style across a surface fragment of "something more real." In this basic interpretive error they "thought maybe what was outside was as good or even better than how it had been previously presented inside the crop." And, under the influence of "the 'go for it' pitch of an entire industry," they actually go to the zoo, a comically disastrous "fall" from the simulated zoo made by the ad. "They should have known better, but after they had seen the commercial for the Bronx Zoo they said, 'let's go, it looks incredible!'" "Incredible" is an almost familiar pun at this point in cultural history, because the literal and evacuated senses of the word exist simultaneously with perfect appropriateness. Their "absence of mind" has been to seek the experience depicted in the ad rather than enjoying a "substitute or surrogate" relationship with its piece of "the real thing."

Sophisticated creatures, they attempt to swim with the stream

of images rather than trying to cross it to the solid ground of reality
or, as in their "trip-up" over the zoo, trying to walk on it. His
personal theory removes the Universal from a concept of "Man."
Instead, he thinks that "magazines, movies, t.v., and records" are
more convincingly "everybody's condition" than any kind of Being
apart from the media: "It was going to be hard for him to connect
with someone who passed themselves off as an example or a version
of a life put together from reasonable matter" (63). Even his attempt
to imagine an alternative to a media-based consciousness is full of
such terms as "example" or "version," suggesting that even those
who *do* try to ground themselves on "reasonable matter" are probably basing themselves on a media special about that reasonable
matter. They are, in other words, simulations of tradition-become-
commodity.

He has "already accepted all these conditions and built out of
their givens" the perfect image-self he appears to be in the book's
opening section, "The Perfect Tense." Already "physically perfect,"
his embodiment of the magazine man means that his "condition"
is his "surface," that "the literal could be as true, perhaps truer than
the symbol," and that "his literalness was what was real." But this
is an ironic case of when "the tables had turned," because the liter-
ality of surface is a minimalist reduction of traditional "deep" reality: "What was left of his life came to be lived as a version of one,"
his effect on others "like confronting his peers as a set of exposures"
(4–5). When "he transported these givens to a reality more real than
the condition he first accepted," we find him stylizing his behavior
according to his external resemblance to the magazine men who
appear in several of Prince's "gangs." He is a semiotic manager
rather than ontological originator, and "his way to make it new was
*make it again*, and making it again was enough for him and certainly, personally speaking, *almost* him" (63).

That "almost" is Prince's vital indeterminacy, because to make
the image real in one's own beautiful flesh is still not to have
achieved the perfected state promised by the allure of that image,
its evocation of the contemporary utopias of the glossies. Later in
"The Velvet Well," we read that the character "liked to think of
himself as an audience and located himself on the other side of what
he and others did" as a spectator of their "remakes." *Consuming*,
that is, works better than *Being*. The "emotion that was once experienced only as an author" is "exchange[d]," and he can in all existential honesty merge with Smokey Robinson and "second that
emotion"—third and fourth it, for that matter. The logic is explained carefully enough in the next paragraph:

> Being the audience, or part of one, was for him, a way to identify
> himself physically and a way to perceive rather than affect . . . a

way to share with others in what might be described as a kind of impossible or promissory non-fiction. A way to see or realize what essentially was a surface with public image, a surface that was once speculative and ambitious, as something now referential and ordinary. Referential because the image's authority existed outside his own touch and ordinary because their frequency of appearance could be corroborated by persons other than himself. (75)

Escaping the activity of "affecting" is a refuge from the "terrifyingly" real choices that action might entail. Even his "physical" identification is easiest as consumer of his own life. An "impossible or promissory non-fiction" is how one would describe simulated existence; it is "impossible" in the sense that its realm of possibility is located between that of image and actuality, and "promissory" in its deferral, until this narrative's great unspoken word (death), of any direct payoff from (or in) actuality. But it is at least comfortingly widespread in a culture with mass-produced subjectivity.

Whatever the Futurists may have thought of the potential of modern technology and the then dimly glimpsed, if at all, information age, by this point its "speculative" ability is co-opted as "ordinary" routine, and the whole concept of referentiality shifts from its classic sense to a post-Kuhnian paradigmatic currency. The "out there" against which frameworks, images, concepts, styles, behavior, and models of consciousness might be tested is not even a picture of Dr. Johnson's stone, let alone the actual kick, but rather the *idea* of kicking a stone—a stone that, as the "counterfeit memory" of a photo-projection, is an image of an idea of a "fabricated" and "displaced" fiction.

This infinite regression leads to the vanishing point marked in contemporary theory by such notions as *différance:* one no longer hopes to reach a zone of pure referentiality or pure authenticity. Prince is especially telling on the latter, as we have seen, and explicitly victimized is the sovereign subject choosing his or her identity and course of action, choosing between the authenticity of radical confrontation with death and temporality and the inauthenticity of *Alltäglichkeit*. The individual's radical confrontation with more postmodern realities takes place within an everydayness formed by media stylization, the consumer culture underlying it, and the postindustrial economic structures determining the whole. All of these elements are seen in Prince's play with the character's enjoyment of the pseudo-"diversity" or pseudo-"variety" of "this place" in history (73), in which "the continued availability of these ingredients" (consumable goods, images, and lives) would "make things less conflictive and more even." If it is reassuring that every car ad looks like a pleasure montage, there is a still more "even" feeling about life if we can all order the same glossy experiences from

Sharper Image and Banana Republic, two aptly named catalog out-fits for commodity imperialism's constantly honed existential im-agery. Part buyoff of dissonant energies, part topping the highs and filling the troughs with the dissociative effects of the tranquilizing spectator existence we have seen analyzed, "this place" can offer "a kind of density" that is, in a certain frame of mind, attractive.

It is not a frame of mind, however, in which the concept of the traditional self makes much sense. The "possibility of choice . . . was mostly a promise," one that "looked good on paper" and serves to promote the cult of upwardly mobile tastefulness. Its existence as "mostly . . . a notion" is the vital safeguard that avoids the "disaster" of its "availability in reality." Real political and eco-nomic choice might implode the whole structure of things, as hap-pens in Williams's "Common Origins." Here, however, the main danger seems to be that the technological revolution produces not only the "fallout" of consumer goods but also the "techy" and "the stranger with the thick glasses" who might "slip away and turn outlaw." For the outlaw hacker to become the only available image of someone choosing outside the current behavioral models suggests the extent to which the computer program is our current cultural model for the determination of "user" options.

Those who play such options well find that "the game was ghost. And whoever became the least recognizable without totally disappearing, got to go home" (66). One's public appearances are, in the publicist's sense of the term, "performances," in which "he was almost there" and "one step away from [an] autonomy" quite different from the intentional self of traditional thinking: "He was the look generation and the effect of his appearance was so unreal that his real reality began to resemble a kind of virtuoso real . . . a very real Real capable of instamatic ambience" (66). Comparative degrees of "Real" collapse the difference between the attenuation of "disappearing" and the accumulation of "began." In place of the merely present or merely absent traits of that sort of entity antici-pated by formal logic is the spectral logic of simulation. In simula-tion, the objective is the two-dimensional "instamatic ambience," the sign that one has learned to "discipline the gestures into pos-ture" (68). In the interplay of Real, real, and unreal, one passes into the "counterfeit memory" of the cultural repertoire and hence *is* on a different plane of ontology from anything imagined in traditional theories of the self. To *be* is to be atmospheric, like "ambience," rather than substantial, like the "self" we used to know.

It is no wonder, then, that the couple hope to see Rod Serling included among "the names of the great '50s artists," especially "before the official fiction . . . what usually came to be called *his-tory*, would be written" (69). Nor is it a surprise to find them more interested in a celebrity photograph of Jackson Pollock than in his paintings ("since painting was something they associated with a way to put things together that seemed to them, pretty much taken care of"). Nor, finally, is it a surprise to find how carefully she packages herself as Connie A.: "She had become successful fronting a no-wave band and had just signed a recording contract and got a nice advance" (23). Her manufactured identity and her distance from any conceivably real self are ways "to push a personality that had to do with what she thought was expected of her." Her strategy was "about how things worked and was as calculated as it was fictive" (24).

The trouble is that "the fiction was always about five seconds away from coming apart," and Connie A.'s great fear is being found out as "a basically serious funny woman with about as much chance for a 'rep' as a spayed puppy." Dwelling between fictive image and spayed self, she frets: "quiet and semi-alcoholic. Credible and polite notices. I'm winding up an uninvolved woman" (20). "Uninvolved" may mean cut off from the media merry-go-round, it may connote sexual isolation, and it may also point toward "uninvolved" in a more etymological sense of the uncomplicated two-dimensionality that is her own self-image. Her not-too-surprising tactic with him is to videotape their love-making so that the framed spectacle of their "love" might be a package that he also buys (and might replace the movies that he sees when he should be working). Like a good member of the Me generation, though, she had the camera pointed at herself and "only half of us were in it" (26). One problem, then, is that the tape is too revealing of the egoistic stance that each takes in the relationship.

Another problem is that the tape is too literal. Because "he doesn't like the real thing . . . just something close to it," she writes a narrative of the tape rather than showing it. Writing it, she reasons, "would make my voice and thoughts seem a lot more memorized," more stylized than the dangerously extemporaneous taping could be. She could also become her own "dummy on my knee," a simulated self whose voice "could sound like it was coming out from over there instead of here," a distance that would enable her to add in the writing process another layer of stylization of any real "I." "And this," she concludes, "was the closest thing I could think of that could come anywhere close to the unreal real of the real thing." Writing, as Derrida might agree, is certainly one way to guarantee that no effort to get to the "real thing" would get further than "close," would get to the "unreal real" of a certain simulation of the thing rather than to the "real real of the real thing," if this is even imaginable. The couple's erotic investment in these interacting layers of artifice, simulation, and sensory reality is the capital that keeps this cultural economy expanding.

The relationship between these two denizens of the simulation era is, predictably, anything but easy. His initiative comes less from seeing her than from consuming her photograph; to have her "on paper" was to have "her resemblance all in one place" rather than walking, talking, and generating her own ambience. A photograph is "a place that had the chances of looking real, but a place that didn't have any specific chances of being real," the *real* having become a horrific term to someone whose "fantasies, and right now, the one of her, needed satisfaction" (11). His needs are hardly for real experience, but rather for the right "substitute or surrogate relationship." The text spells this out:

> And satisfaction, at least in part, seemed to come about by ingesting perhaps "perceiving," the fiction her photograph imagined.
> She had to be condensed and inscribed in a way that his expectations of what he wanted her to be, (and what he wanted to be too) could at least be possibly, even remotely, realized. (11)

Relating, as well as Being, in this era means consuming, and that entails "cropping" each other until the images can be "inscribed" in a theatrical form to be, however imperfectly, realized.

The couple competes: he says she situates herself "at the back of my head, projecting herself in front of me, keeping me from closing my eyes, deluding my ego" (41). To be, as he calls himself, "the originator of the unoriginal" is an "acknowledgement of an inability" to care "to plot in a direction towards a center or an axis." Hence his dispersed and highly stylized self is vulnerable to a strong self-stager such as Connie A. Desire is that gaping hole through which all his self-encapsulation in glitzy images drains out and what is left is the body. Sex for him is an almost incongruous moment of escape from these dilemmas, because it "was mostly about reversing himself, both physically and mentally. A kind of regression, where inoperative parts of the mind became colonized, set upon unexpectedly, with the body becoming the directive, becoming the starting point from which the thinking originated" (38).

If the body is indeed the "directive" or "starting point" for colonizing "inoperative parts of the mind," then sexuality is a regression from image to part of what image organizes and flattens. The psychological dimension is striking: "He would receive and give simultaneously, in what could be best described as unprotective sensations . . . as if what was inside his outer shell disappeared or spilled, and what was left behind was skin and bone" (38). The passage is an almost startling contradiction to all of his interest in perfecting a performance self, an outer shell that is the absolute empty image. Although some readers might find the passage a disturbance to the flow of character, it is part of Prince's persistent though not often so explicit reminder of a counternorm to the ontology of simulation overtaking these characters.

In some ways, as we turn to the other aspects of the couple's relationship, she is ideal for someone who wants to be the spectator at his own life but who can at times be unnerved by focusing upon his own almost too-perfect reflection: "When he looked at her the only thing he never saw, was his own body. Everything was there but his own reflection, and because it wasn't, she made him feel, at last, absent" (41). The pure otherness of *her* imagery allows him to be utterly out of his own, a state he seeks before their relationship begins, when "he thought that if he kept himself behind the camera, determining the direction of how and where he looked, and sharpening his attention on only those areas specifically set aside by his own absence, then perhaps he wouldn't have to live it, in order to have any memory of it" (10). The energy of his projections seems, at first, the ideal: " 'You can sit,' he muses, 'and watch her and never care if you'll show up. . . . She helps you to turn yourself in . . . to pawn yourself so to speak. She helps you to sell yourself down the river and you love it' " (41).

Before long, however, he experiences her presence as a "pressure" that disrupts his own ability to "act gracefully." That disruption threatens the "description" others have of him, and "he felt the distance between him and the threat should become unforwardable, like a dead letter" (42). His specific complaints are these:

> She seems to be able to overlay everything, receive it all, as if everything is real and non-real at the same time. She walks around like this, like she's involved in a weird kind of configuration. Like she's wearing mirrors and so's everything else. She becomes so goddamn possible. It's just not fair. She mixes it all up. She takes herself for the things she's already seen. She can imitate anything because as far as she's concerned, she already looks like it. (42)

Canceling the difference between the "real and non-real" is a function of what he calls "a pseudo belief," because her "weird kind of configuration" is conviction that she is fluid enough to stage any of the "things she's already seen." She lives in a mirror cult in which the differences among things do not signify use value or surplus value, but a Baudrillardian sign value one can (ex)change by setting oneself in the right context and overlaying the desired sign, the way she becomes Connie A., the saleable fiction.

His fear of a "tell-tale seam" or "skip," a "visibility" in his own image, is the cost to him of admitting his spectator role into the circle of her energetically staged "affective" role. He comes to fear that "he would always be out of the frame, off to the side of the picture, (off to the side of her) and anybody who wanted to see him, would have to see her, looking towards him, first" (43). If she is trapped in the activist's dilemma of staging a role that she could blow at any moment, he is in the passivist's dilemma of finding his fine patina a merely reflective rather than radiant surface.

She is left with "what her friends referred to as her weakness for cowboys, mountains, and sunsets" (43) after a succession of short relationships "imparted a feeling of compression." The hyper-romanticism noticed by her friends shows partly in her ignoring "any sense of saving or thrift," partly a desire "that each exchange be classical" and that each kiss be carved "in stone," partly a desire toward an "emotional bullying" in which she releases a barrage of "subconscious images" at inopportune moments as part of her pre-occupation in her work, and, finally, partly a weakness for the kind of image—blanked-out, evacuated, a bit too impossible in its perfection of passivity—which he projects.

Something happens to the couple, however, during what appears to be the midsection of their relationship—neither the segments in Prince's six sections nor the sequence of those sections in the book are chronological, and the reader does shuffle a bit, testing out different orderings. (As Prince explains: "But it's like my uncle asked, 'Where's the beginning, middle, and end?' And I said, 'Well, you can start it on any page. It's not designed to be read that way.'") This event, which is about the worst thing that could happen to media creatures, is detailed in the book's final section, "An Undesired Fidelity":

> There was a psychological orientation of the selves. A mental mechanism where both of them became gratified, supported . . . almost relieved by consciously attributing themselves to the characteristics of each other. And as long as they were together, participating collectively, there was no confusion or need to adjust. No pressure or personal anomie. (82)

Note how different this relationship is from traditional romance ("there was none of the usual flirtation that accompanied a courtship"). They achieve a collective image, and they do so not by attributing their characteristics to each other, as in classic sentimental projections, but in attributing *themselves* to the other's characteristics. Does that mean each is literally the result of the other's image traits ("attribute" in the sense of tracing causation)? Or does it suggest that each is constantly projecting into the other's "characteristics" to develop yet another line of vicarious character? In either case, "self" is reduced to plot function in their dramas.

As we have seen, however, the implicit narrative of one's image does not always mesh well with another's, and so they experience a "back and forth bounce between independence and compromise" (85). They are drawn off into feeling happy but are fretful about "the formation of an addiction, a fixation, where the dependence on each other's mental make-up continually increased the regularity of a performance rather than [the] relaxation" (83) of reproducing a "typical and usual" picture. They have "the attitude like, sure . . . I want to be happy but not now" (85), lest the movements of a romance script disrupt their perfected images. He, for example, "had seen all the movies and the scenes already played out," and what he wants in his softer moments is *not* "to believe there couldn't be any new twists to make the endings different." "He just didn't want to believe what he knew." Time and stasis do not reconcile. What he wants is "a deal like in the advertisements, where things looked truer than they really were. Where the conditions were even. Where all the conflicts were made fun of" (89).

What happens instead is that the cultural contradictions between these media modes and the virtually unspoken "real real" do not go away as easily as in the ads. The couple finds "the chances of a political tide becoming subject to menstruation and the movements of the moon, improbable" (87), because life in the electronic age is fast-forward. "Things" in the daily course of the relationship are no "truer than they really were," and, to feel fully sophisticated, they must become "customers" of the commodified relationship and the "stand-in" self. Once they buy it, it comes with its own scenarios and with the inevitable gap between the promise and the product. If the couple could escape the consciousness of that gap—regressing into some primal sensory being or becoming completely unreflective media creatures—they could be happier, no doubt. When we talked about *Why I Go the Movies Alone*, Prince mused on just this dilemma:

> The media set up a guideline for who is to be in front and who behind. They set down a style the characters are always fighting against or fighting in. They're constantly asking, should I conform? Should I nonconform? Do I actually know what the difference is between what's real and what's realistic? And the fact that they know the difference is their problem. Consciousness. The idea of being conscious is scary. Like late-twentieth-century life: we all feel like sometimes we're dreaming even though we're awake. And you can say that's a new kind of surrealism.

The dreaming consists of our instant replay of the culture's "prior availability," and this surrealism takes us not inward to a more real authenticity but outward to what our inmost dream elements are quoting.

Prince also recalled an early line in *Menthol Wars* when Susan takes a dislike to a group of young artists who "weren't even smart enough yet to stop paying attention to how intelligent they were" (18). That kind of intelligence is more like a skill at Connie A.'s game of wearing mirrors. One becomes so smart at managing the technology of self that experience itself has more regularity than relaxation, more production than sensation, in the constant deferral

of "not now." Consciousness and intelligence, central values in
modernist narrative, become treacherous allies, the very processing capacity that facilitates the colonization of the subject by culture.

Perhaps we should add one last complication to this reading of how "he" and "she" cope with these dilemmas. My students have wondered at times whether the same "he" and "she" appear all through *Why I Go to the Movies Alone*. Indeed, if a new edition is published, Prince would like to add a graphic device to divide further its segments. But we must also remember that he called the book autobiographical: "The he, she, it, is whatever. It has more to do with the first person even though there's all those pronouns. Those pronouns are just first person. It's why *I* went to the movies alone. The word 'I' is only in the title, and I thought that set up the whole thing."

The "whole thing" is his process of "stepping into those pronouns' shoes and looking back from a point of view in which I wonder what sort of horrors or comedies *they're* involved in." That existential theater certainly involves identity and consciousness. But it also involves gender, and Prince's ability to limn just how the media shapes gender elements is more resonant here than in the Marlboro men and perfume women of his photo images. The couple comes close to representing the extreme alternatives in an ontology of simulation. His option is self-evacuation, an emptying of the self in order to hold rigidly to a single image—a very "male" strategy for coping. Her option is self-commodification, a fluidity of self which allows her to become the ever-new, ever-changing object of desire—an equally "female" coping strategy. Their loss of the real and of actuality has the "payoff" of enabling them to circulate in the economy of signs—to acquire a hot-property sign value that provides both currency (the latest seasonal color from the mags) and formal coherence in an otherwise ungrounded, purely fluid existential crisis.

Their relationship anatomizes a media-arranged marriage in which each seeks and wants what the other has, the missing dimension in their reduction from three to two dimensions. Change means disaster for the photo-perfect man; stability means unfashionableness for the compliant projection of others' desire. Each desires the missing dimension, is drawn to the other for it, keeps exchanging places mentally with the other to try out *its* comedies and horrors. But each fears the devastation the other would wreak in their economic and existential survival strategies, the loosing of the contradictions otherwise contained within their respective lines of repression. It would be a mistake to point to this novel as a comprehensive study of gendering, but it does nonetheless offer these useful ways of thinking about the lines of reduction involved in our production of subjectivity. We all go to the movies alone every time

we dip into the public surrealism of our common dream repertoire
in order to cope with life's surprises—whether those surprises are
the gap between reality and the image, the surprise when reality
seems almost to become the image, or the daily grind of the social
and economic forces beneath the flicker of the films going on around
us.

### Dictee

Those who struggled with high-school French classes know the
word *dictée* very well, because dictation has been a time-honored
means of instructing students in foreign languages. Theresa Hak
Kyung Cha's remarkable book *Dictee* tells us a good deal about
having to learn foreign languages of many kinds, including the bul-
lets with which the Japanese responded to schoolboy demonstrations in her native Korea, the French she herself learned at one
point, the English she perfected after immigrating to Honolulu and
then to San Francisco, the Catholicism of her parochial education,
the literary and mythological idioms of cultural memories, and the
crosshatching dialects of gender and race. One feels helpless before
the wash of cliché in adding that she also learned the violence of
American cities when, just after finishing this book, she was murdered. *Dictee* is a brave testament struggling with memory, language, and culture, in the hopes of winning out some measure of
individual identity and even, perhaps, peace, against the odds that,
in life at least, claimed her.

Donald Richie's moving review in the *Japan Times*, reprinted
by Williams in the final Tanam Press catalog, calls *Dictee* "a multifaceted narrative which reflects history, mirrors past lives, touches
mythology, transcends time and casts a multi-linear present, *pli
selon pli*, into infinity." *Dictee* is organized into eleven sections, the
central nine of which are linked to the Muses; its pages remind one
that the title's other principal meaning is a posthypnotic sugges-
tion, as if thought and writing were themselves efforts to contend
with the residues of history and ideology carried by our mesmerizing language and texts. The introductory section retrieves from
memory the documents of elementary school, including dictation
passages, translation exercises, bits of catechism, and a teacher's
voice ("the words are in the blue books, in case you have forgotten
them"), all woven with the experience of discipline (how many
students per pew, who gets to crown the Virgin Mary, what does
*novena* mean). Its title, "Diseuse," is the feminine form for *speaker*
or *reciter*, and appropriately so, because the novel features a woman
attempting to achieve more *speaking* on her own and less *reciting* of
what she has been taught. The other meaning of "diseuse," *fortuneteller*, is also appropriate because the section works well to foretell

the effects of the narrator's schooling as a threatening encounter with a powerful educational establishment determined to regularize students' thinking and writing.

"She mimics the speaking," the section begins, after a bit of dictation about the opening day of school. The narrative becomes quickly a parable of her struggle to win the possibility of speech: "That might resemble speech. (Anything at all.) Bared noise, groan, bits torn from words. Since she hesitates to measure the accuracy, she resorts to mimicking gestures with the mouth. The entire lower lip would lift upwards then sink back to its original place. She would then gather both lips and protrude them in a pout taking in the breath that might utter some thing. (One thing. Just one.) But the breath falls away" (3).

The narrator *knows* she always speaks an alien tongue, and she physically experiences the contradiction of desiring the rights of a native speaker. An allegory of gender, race, and adolescence all at the same time, the book echoes feminist motifs in tracing her determination to turn the foreign idiom to her own ends. The next paragraph is equally important: "*It murmurs inside. It murmurs. Inside is the pain of speech the pain to say. Larger still. Greater than is the pain not to say. To not say. Says nothing against the pain to speak. It festers inside. The wound, liquid, dust. Must break. Must void.*" This imagery of abscess connotes the pathology of discursive discipline for her, and the swelled sac of pus, blood, or menstrual fluid recurrent in the novel links her desire for a writing more real than official discourse with the *l'écriture feminine* of recent theoretical manifestoes.

The struggle is not easily won. At first, she "allows others. In place of her. Admits others to make full. Make swarm. All barren cavities to make swollen. The others each occupying her" (3). Education becomes akin to rape or to the Japanese occupation of her homeland, but to be "caught in their threading, anonymously in their thick motion in the weight of their utterance" is worse than compliance. "*She would take on their punctuation. She waits to service this. Theirs. Punctuation. She would become, herself, demarcations. Absorb it. Spill it*" (4). The word "*Theirs*" becomes the rhythm track to this surrender to cultural "*demarcations*," but the movement from "*Absorb it*" to "*Spill*" is one that leads through the sensation of air rising from her lungs to "the delivery." "Delivery" connotes the paradoxical act whereby she surrenders to the alien sign system but also delivers herself from the bondage of silence and objectification. "Uttering. Hers now. Hers bare. The utter" (5).

There are some nice touches of ideological critique in the rest of the section, particularly the attitudinal pruning carried out by translation exercises. But the real outgrowth from this opening parable is her effort to move beyond experiencing the Virgin Mary as a mode of patriarchal discipline and to take for her own uses the power accessible in historical and mythological women. Hence Sappho, Joan of Arc, Saint Thérèse of Lisieux, Persephone, and Demeter join the nine Muses as resources from the past, while the narrator's mother and Hyung Soon Huo (through her journals) become important resources from the present. The narrator's voice becomes progressively richer and more independent during *Dictee*'s course, but even the first of the Muses, Clio (History), is a powerful example of the narrator's determination to reclaim the repressed through the very language and genre complicit in that repression.

The section "Clio" recounts the Japanese involvement in Korea in 1919. The documents by which the Koreans appeal to world leaders for help against the Japanese fail because the outside world "cannot know"; the language and images are lost in the larger narrative of official history, "not physical enough. Not to the very flesh and bone, to the core, to the mark" (32). Asking herself why she resurrects it now, the narrator answers: "To name it now so as not to repeat history in oblivion. To extract each fragment by each fragment from the word from the image another word another image the reply that will not repeat history in oblivion" (33).

The official historian neutralizes "flesh and bone" with the genre's automatic word choice, prefabricated syntax, and conventionalized rhetoric. To write and think this way is to repeat the genre rather than rendering experience itself. It is to leave faces and lives in oblivion: "Their image, the memory of them is not given to deterioration, unlike the captured image that extracts from the soul precisely by reproducing, multiplying itself. Their countenance evokes not the hallowed beauty, beauty from seasonal decay, evokes not the inevitable, not death, but the dy-ing" (37). Those whom the narrator can recover escape being "captured" by culture's mass production of interchangeable images of banalities; they are individual human beings actually dying in front of her rather than simply signs of the abstraction with which culture displaces the realities of death, oppression, and violence.

The narrator realizes that "the present form face to face reveals the missing, the absent. Would-be-said remnant, memory. But the remnant is the whole" (38). That is, Cha's narrator manages an experiential rather than merely textual encounter with these lost ones. What enables such an encounter is that the narrator is not apart from memory's content, from the "flesh and bone" of history. The till-now-unsaid "remnant" *is* her flesh and bone—physically, imaginatively, and culturally—and recovering the "remnant" is "the whole" of her project to escape the effects of translation, immigration, and assimilation. "The longing in the face of the lost. Maintains the missing." The section ends appropriately enough with a page of much-revised manuscript in which Cha's *écriture* is plainly visible in its effort to overcome the "pain to say."

"Calliope" (Epic Poetry) deals with a mother's exile in China during the Japanese occupation. "Urania" (Astronomy) takes the opening section's liquid imagery, renews it ("Contents housed in membranes. Stain from within dispel in drops in spills. Contents of other recesses seep outward."), then extends it to "near-black liquid ink" as the book breaks into poetry for the first time in a meditation upon writing, memory, and the body struggling for speech. "Urania," which spirals back over content similar to the opening section, parallels English and French versions of its poetry as if working for a higher (more astronomical?) version of delivery:

> Images only. Alone. Images.
> The signs in the rain I listened
> the speaking no more than rain having become snow.
> True or not
> true
> no longer possible to say.
>
> (71)

Signs and images, rain and snow, memories and texts—the "having become" the narrator encounters involves complex transformations that remain problematic by any traditional categories of analysis, such as the simplicities of true and false. "Urania" ends with medical-school posters of the physiology of speech and a lyric about "broken speech" which concludes by saying "no more" to the requirement of "Stop start. / Where proper pauses were expected" (75). The fluidity of the verse is, perhaps, a victory over her conventional training and a realization of the writing of the body, for which Cha seems to have great sympathy.

"Melpomene" (Tragedy) retells the shooting of the narrator's brother in a 1962 street demonstration by soldiers for whom "the execution of their role their given identity [is] further than their own line of blood" (84), a grim testimony to the skill with which the State has hidden soldiers behind guns, camouflage uniforms, and the ideology of absolute loyalty. Because of this experience, she insists upon a revolution: "SHE opposes Her. SHE against her. More than that. Refuses to become discard decomposed oblivion" (87). Refuses, that is, to be erased as an active, living subject and remain quietly the object of State power, of cultural gendering, of international racism, of economic co-optation. "Erato" (Love Poetry) layers a whole series of marriages (including a nun's to Jesus) and pierces it with this analysis of the (generic) husband's touch: "He touches her with his rank. By his knowledge of his own rank. By the claim of his rank. Gratuity is her body her spirit. Her non-body her non-entity. His privilege possession his claim. Infallible is his ownership. Imbues with mockery at her refusal of him, but her very being that dares to name herself as if she possesses a will. Her own" (112).

The section ends with the recurrent imagery of language as snow covering everything, silencing memory, creating a weightless "snow self": "In the whiteness no distinction her body invariable no dissonance synonymous her body all the time de composes eclipses to be come yours" (118). The space in "de composes" requires us to face the fact that the wife's compliance is both a *destructive* and a compositional act, that it is an eclipse of her internal difference ("her body invariable"), her difference from her husband ("no dissonance"), and of her own bodily particularity. Being, that is, means coming to him—we are back to the opening section's submissions—and disappearing as a subject into a possessive pronoun.

The last sections of *Dictee* become increasingly sacred or mythic with the motifs of the journey, of memory as a hole that swallows all into formlessness, and of the desire to transcend the limits of language and real time. The final section, "Polymnia" (Sacred Poetry), tells the story of a small girl who obtains herbs for her ill mother from a woman (a healer? a goddess? someone who only appears mystical in the eyes of the girl?) at a well. Myth lives, because in order to heal her (m)other tongue, Cha resorts to the wisdom of a long history of female seekers in the process of achieving the voice embodied in *Dictee*. Indeed, on the last page a little girl asks her mother to lift her high enough to see out a window, and the words that repeat all but incoherently refer to stone weights attached to ropes scraping on wood. The passage is about opening the window to hear the peal of bells, just as *Dictee* as a whole records its narrator's effort to open a cultural window in order to ring out the full resonance of the voice of her personal, family, national, racial, and gender histories.

### The Wild History of Tanam Press

Reese Williams brought together at Tanam Press the best of the downtown sensibility, a group of people who moved into Soho when it was still a district where by day you looked through doorways into plastic factories and by night you found yourself alone, where lofts were still cheap and the boutiques and Castellis were still mostly uptown. Tanam Press's print runs were never very large—a thousand copies for *A Pair of Eyes*, up to five thousand for *Apparatus*—but the people who are making and thinking about art know about Tanam Press. Many of them appear in one book or another. The temperament of this Soho community is arch, media-conscious, art-hip, and at moments in some figures almost mystical (such as Williams in his polarity theories, Cha in her invocation to past bright points of energy, Vicuña in her mythic impulses, DeJong in her study with a Tibetan Master). An intensive study of the district's creative energies would require one to read closely less personally related work, such as Jennifer Bartlett's *Creation of the Universe*, and to probe in far more detail the artists' books, photography books, humor, broadsides, pamphlets, catalogs, bands, performance evenings, and readings that are documented in places such as Printed Matter.

Even a single anthology such as Richard Prince's *Wild History* (1985) can demonstrate the point about the community of talents that Williams involved in Tanam Press. Many of its writers have produced so much important work that they are discussed in more detail in other chapters of *Suburban Ambush;* others are best seen in the selections in *Wild History*. So well-chosen are these pieces that if the anthology were also to have included the more resolutely East Village types—Texier, Rose, McGrath, Cherches—it would be the ideal sampler of downtown writing. Like Wallis's also superb *Blasted Allegories*, it does emphasize those with denser relations to the visual arts world. But "chosen" is not the best word, at least for the pieces. As Prince pointed out to me, he had a more basic criterion in mind in framing the anthology: "There are a couple of other people who should be in that book. That's how I approached that anthology—it was more like *people*. I don't know if those people [in *Wild History*] are writers. I didn't approach it that way. I didn't know what they were. That's why the portrait is at the beginning of each story. I figured *that's* what they were. And they got to choose their own portrait: that was part of the book."

Prince describes the book as an "orange object," just as he called Barbara Ess's important early anthology, *Just Another Asshole* 6, "a souvenir." *Wild History* captures a community in the process of making objects that force a rethinking of our assumptions about texts, images, and fiction, rather than offering itself as a memorial to a literary formula or as an archive of masterworks. However, Prince chose his "people" aptly enough that their work measures quite well against the yardsticks of "pure" merit. Their often-comic photographs may mock the seriousness of the monumental literary object, but the quality of most of the writing speaks well for the communal energies of Prince's friends and acquaintances.

Among those pieces discussed elsewhere in *Suburban Ambush* are Gary Indiana's "American Express" catching a couple for whom Being means consuming and striving for imagehood, Reese Williams's "Gift Waves" developing strategies for reversing the negative energy one carries as a cultural product, a handful of pieces from Roberta Allen's *Traveling Woman* anatomizing the cultural processing of desire, Spalding Gray's witty piece about becoming a cultural object (in this case, of pornography) in order to afford lighting out for the territories, Richard Prince's "The Bela Lugosi Law" continuing his dissection of media-determined relations, Anne Turyn's subtle connections among language, consciousness, and feminist issues in "Idioglossia," a particularly intense section from Lynne Tillman's *Haunted Houses*, and a typically rich piece from Constance DeJong's "At Night" looking beyond the daylight world of social engineering into a whole series of displaced languages (alphabet talk, tapping by skylight, CIA gumshoe files, comet-claiming, the correspondence of a collective identity constructed to secure health insurance for several people, and midnight paranoia on the psych ward).

A character in DeJong's piece asks the anthology's central questions: "What is this civilization in which we find ourselves? What are the ceremonies and why should we take part in them? What are these professions and why should we make money out of them? Where in short is it leading, the processions of the sons of educated men?" (37–38). This last is an arch question, with its emphasis upon the *sons* of education and the mock-irony of "processions," but the piece is also quite serious about the suspension of any naturalness to civilization's ceremonies, professions, and economic determination of day-to-day living. Kathy Acker's "Scenes of World War III" makes equally explicit some of the central assumptions of the anthology. We find a sociopolitical reading of *Megalon Meets Godzilla* cuing off the opening premise that "males dumber than nonhuman animals're running the economic and political world," and the following blunt write-off of a large chunk of the Western tradition: "This exploitation or reduction of reality to self-preservation and the manipulatable other has become the universal principle of a society which seeks to reduce all phenomena to this enlightenment, ideal of rationalism, or subjugation of the other" (110). The anthology is full of characters who view themselves primarily as a "manipulatable other" to some at-times-unimaginable privileged subject and who stop suddenly and start popping DeJong's questions either outright or through the peculiar subterranean twists and turns of a socially embattled psyche.

Tina Lhotsky's piece, "The Tunnel of Fire," narrates a stunt man's run through fire for prime-time television; he emerges raising high a triumphant stump where his hand had been: "that's entertainment," Lhotsky concludes, a piecemeal destruction of the objects of its consumption. Robin Winters gathers dream segments, Wharton Tiers contributes a species of science fiction agonizing over the loss of the "Absolute Forms" its crazed narrator briefly glimpses, and Paul McMahon contributes a number of his performance pieces dissecting the "So-Ho-Ho Art Giant" and, in "Saving My Heart for the Magazines," one about "spend[ing] my *Times* on the pages of these rags. Any other kind of *Life* would be a drag" (200).

More powerfully sustained are the contributions of Peter Nadin, Sylvia Reed, and Cookie Mueller. Mueller, first known for her roles in such John Waters films as *Pink Flamingos*, is "unliterary" enough to call her contribution "Six Stories." She seems uninterested in them as "Art," as a class of activity, as species responsible to a literary decorum. There is a hip sensibility that plays through all six stories, a constantly satiric attitude toward the culture at large, and a loopy sort of double-edged humor that resonates with her director's irreverence and her friend Divine's genius for staging the many contradictions of the contemporary self. The first three stories ("Baltimore," "Provincetown," and "British Columbia") resemble travel pieces only in their titles. What they really show is the nomadic character of the unattached. Their narrative "I" roams these places with no visible ties, no imaginal boundaries, no conditions to be met.

In the first story, the narrator looks back upon her two teen-aged lovers, hepatitis Jack (who ends up shooting speed and writing a novel) and Gloria, "born of a light bulb it seems," whose breast injections spread all over her body until she "died of a silicone heart" (155). Speed writers and silicone hearts populate the world this nomad leaves behind as she goes on to Provincetown, where Divine presides over a house full of similarly unattached nomads through a hilarious if insolvent winter, and then to British Columbia, where she and her friends burn down a cabin while snorting coke and guzzling rye whiskey. Straight margins lie on every side of them—the couple for whom she keeps house (well, they are *relatively* straight), the shopkeepers from whom they lift the food and booze for their Christmas party, the neighbor whose lawn holds the "perfectly symmetrical blue spruce" that becomes their Christmas tree, the antique collector whose treasures burn with the cabin. Absolutely deadpan in their style, the stories stop rather than ending (she and her son Max hitchhike to San Francisco "to see Divine and that trip is a story in itself").

"Andrew the Skinny" is another genre altogether. The story is about a boy so thin that his parents clothe him in multiple layers even in summer just to fill him out. His secret pleasure is undressing and blowing around over into the neighbor's yard, occasionally at the expense of the décor (the "blue reflector ball that sat on its pedestal like an archaic pagan shrine" is one casualty of his crash landings). Andrew is so light that he can become airborne, but he is not equipped to control his flight. No one can quite deal with his desire to escape his heavy clothing, revel in his boniness, and escape on the airwaves; his parents cover him obsessively, his neighbors bag him with the brown-paper logo of the A&P, and, later in life, after he achieves phenomenal but unexplained, unspecific fame, necessity covers him with bodyguards to guard him against packs of wild journalists. His libido smothered under the wraps of parental image-makers and economic role-playing, Andrew exchanges this object-position for that of the primary form of subjectivity open in the culture: consumption. Specifically, of food, and lots of it. He becomes so fat that he loses all fame, all bodyguards, and all outside interest, and he floats in his indoor salt-water pool. Consuming as ultimately an amniotic fantasy? More unsettling than this possibility is the ending: "His huge contented cheerful flesh was now his only burden, but it was his, a wrapping to belong to" (165). The alternative for someone who wants to escape the scratchy wrapping of an alienating culture is not flight to some free, utopian space. More likely is Andrew's withdrawal into an infantile self-absorption in which his identity is still founded on a "wrapping" rather than any essentialist core, but a wrapping that grotesquely parodies the libidinal release to be found if one were really to live out that classic sensual dream of flight.

"Randy Eros" is a similar evacuation of the cultural subject, featuring an image-perfect young man who is "attractive, not conventionally, but in that extremely suggestive way" (166) that makes him the perfect sex object for both genders. Mueller has a good deal of fun with those who fly Randy here and there for their liaisons (Hoover Dam is right there along with Borobudur and Shwe Dagon), but the story's kicker comes when this sexually anesthetized character finally falls in love—with a retarded dairy worker. Randy, whose mother is a prostitute and whose father is a pornography star, has followed their example—like his mother, he is an object to be used; like his father, he conforms to the image repertoire of others. Randy's eunuch, however, "turned out to be like an old fashioned doll, the kind that have no genitals to speak of," and he places no demands at all upon Randy. Neither mentally nor physically all there, the eunuch screens Randy from even the possibility of conceiving or desiring a real self, libido, or relationship.

"The Story of Frank the Dog and Frieda Ann the Third" is the literary version of "Randy Eros," there being no story about Frank (the narrator leaves him with Divine, who promptly dumps him at the pound) or the *Frieda Ann the Third*, the boat on which the fateful journey of identity is to be conducted in high literary fashion, but which runs aground and is abandoned in the backwaters of the Chesapeake Bay. Rather than our coming to some great revelation at the story's conclusion, some informing insight that orders and culminates the trials and changes wrought by this classic metaphor of experience and maturation, we have instead Cookie hitchhiking to Baltimore, "where my mother exchanged tales of sea-faring life. She was raised on a ship with her father the captain" (174). But the tales do not happen onstage; no mother-daughter wisdom is given; the totemic males are essentially worthless (both women's fathers are entirely absent, and even Cookie's captain is most memorable for crying in his bunk over the loss of the cookstove that Cookie threw overboard when it caught fire). Frank is rescued from the pound the day before he was to have been gassed, and Cookie buys him "a new collar and a triple scoop chocolate ice cream cone" (175). The end. Absolute nomads, Cookie and Frank do not seem to be permanently marked by their Significant Experiences.

Mueller's wry send-up of existential and literary matters contrasts sharply with Sylvia Reed's haunting tale, "The Murder of Lady Tashat." A feminist fable of embattled identity, it splits its time zones between the story of the narrator, whom we know only as "T.," and that of Lady Tashat, an ancient Egyptian, whose story T. tells as she contends with her lover, Mark. He is no prize; a married psychoanalyst who tells her about his troubles with his wife, Mark seems to like T. for her sexual availability and her willingness to be bullied by him (her interest in Tashat is a fantasy not "age-appropriate" for her, "it annoys him to see my work" on Tashat's story, and his reach for T. can only be described as "half guilty, half indifferent"). T.'s own insecurity is tangible, her existence as a librarian under an oppressive supervisor precarious, her fascination with Tashat obsessive but, finally, productive. Tashat is a mummy discovered to have a man's skull between her legs. What the scientists found "has disturbed them, confused them" (130), but T. has "tried to forget what they said about her, because I do not trust them, I will never trust them with their measurements and fingers smelling of chemicals" (131). T. understands that "in my own life which has never been easy for me to solve, her mystery seems a companion to my own," and she realizes bit by bit as she rejects Mark that "I have her true story."

The story of Tashat which T. invents for us is that of an oppressive polygamy in which women are starved of pleasure and turned against one another—Tashat and her lover were murdered by her vengeful husband—he was tipped off by another of his wives, jealous of Tashat for unwittingly taking over the lover. As Tashat consummates her passion, T. vomits over a phone message from Mark. As Tashat feels the thrill of talking to her lover in a way she has never before talked with a man, T. throws a bouquet that Mark has sent her into the bathtub. As Tashat lies in an afterglow with her love, T. feels that "the dependency on Mark is finished." And as T. relates how the now-remorseful wife spends all her money to have the priests place the lover's head with Tashat's body, affirming a kind of recovered sisterhood in conspiracy against the husband—and granting Tashat, within the Egyptian belief system, the eternal service of her lover—T. shakes her head to a fellow librarian who holds Mark's phone call to T.

Reed's parable takes seriously T.'s observation early on that "we have nothing better to believe than a true story" (131), a kind of truth which belongs not to the patriarchal world of scientists, psychiatrists, and husband-lords, but to the poststructural world that Foucault talks about in terms of the truth effects of fictional discourse. If "The Murder of Lady Tashat" is a moving and enabling use of fiction, Peter Nadin's "The Live Pool" is a much more disturbing approach to the relationship between Being and fiction. Nadin, whom we saw earlier in his collaboration with Jenny Holzer, is British-born and, as Williams describes him, "likes to read T. S. Eliot and Pound and things like that." That measure of literary density is in evidence in a complex tale that weaves lyric verse with the scary prose of Chester, a mad, misogynist narrator who loves, kills, and waits for the reappearance of his lover Julie (Juliet?). Roman-type prose plays the relatively uncensored voice of the psychotic individual off against the italicized verse outlining a manifesto of the cultural logic which sustains his logic of "removal" as the Final Solution.

The opening lyric establishes both context and problem:

*So, here we are tethered to time and place*
*One room, one body, one thought, one face,*
*Alive in political system, work and race.*

. . . . . . . . . . . . . . . . . . . . . . . . . . .

*For here or there, all time*
*And chance and circumstance*
*Make face and place our choice,*
*The one choice, you over some other*
*A singularity, one night, one lover.*

*For every window conceals a life*
*A place, a refuge, for husband and wife.*

(51)

Chester intensely feels the cultural bondage to homogenized and normalized identity in all spheres of life—ideological, economic, ethnic, domestic. Our lives determined by our placement, our one choice is that with which the advertising and mass cultures are obsessed—the spouse with whom we retreat to the mass-produced domestic refuge of suburbia.

To listen closely to Chester's voice is to hear the psychosis into which this conditioning drives him. What "makes me Chester" is the judgment he is privileged to pass on Julie, who, together with his "experience of her," is the material of the matter at hand: the act of murder which constitutes his identity. Chester gave love a real try, yet he found not existential fulfillment but reprocessed bits of culture: "When you're lost in love you act abnormal, you act like a sap. You write letters and all you can turn out is sap shit. Hours are spent trying to regain yourself through words, hours are spent trying to express love's devotion and all that happens is that the same old sap comes oozing out" (56).

Driven back from "political system, work and race" as viable arenas for the discovery and exercise of individual identity, Chester finds painfully that love, the "one choice," is no different. The lovers' discourse is structured according to the same motifs as other discourse systems, and Chester's comments give constant testimony to his experience of power, competition, and possession as the forces at play in his relationship with Julie. It is no accident that he "realized the pleasure was in the possibility not the reality" (56), because the reality consists of "what she always made me feel about myself" (59), of his need to lie for self-protection, and of her recourse to what she knows about psychology to whittle him down to a malleable size, as if, by "always telling me I was an asshole and I was fucked up because of my relationship to my mother" (63), she understood clearly the nexus of power/knowledge of which Foucault has so much to say. Chester has even lost the gender wars with her: "Julie was always crying and I would always give in to her demands, but if I was to start crying she would tell me to pull myself together" (67); she also tells him her dream about his fetal sobbing when some street toughs approach them.

The verse doubles the narrative's characterization of the "surrender" of Julie and Chester as more to the cultural system under the sign of love than to each other, and it supplies bits of motivational effluvia about his mother, his weak sense of identity, and other echoes of emotional stress. But if "The Live Pool" is not as finely crafted as Reed's story, or as full-blown in its sociopolitical analysis as Acker's, or as stylistically exquisite as Tillman's, it shares with all the anthology pieces an attitude toward life, culture, and art. Tanam Press's writers have far more in common than not. The very range of technique, material, form, and performance suggests the strength of the community's attitudinal edge in cutting through the suburban integuments to the social tissue beneath. Prince produced an "orange object," but it is part of a larger body of work engaged in the endless task of recouping a "thou" from the inhospitable physiology of the body politic. As "Fire over Water" is the "image of the condition before transition," Tanam Press's writers may be said to have defined powerful perspectives on a culture that is itself transitional. Their wisdom about media, ideology, and the shards of selfhood may well be vital if we are to avoid their worst images of alienation, displacement, violation, and a history too wild even for the most resolute of nomads.

# CONDENSED BOOK

## *Performance Art and Fiction*

Are the pieces that make up a performance a *Condensed Book*, as Peter Cherches's title might suggest, or are works of fiction really transcripts of extended performances, as is literally the case with Spalding Gray's *Sex and Death to the Age Fourteen*? Any of the pieces in Cherches's book performs well, certainly with Cherches on stage, though it is also true that Gray found that his effort to *write* his book produced "derivative and imitative" prose rather than the "original breath and rhythm of [his] voice," which he and his editor, Melanie Fleishman, preserved by working from perform-ance transcripts instead.

Obviously the answer to my question is finally less important than what it points to—the complementarity of performance art and downtown fiction. We might well observe, at the most superficial level, that the quick cuts of Lynne Tillman's *Haunted Houses* share as much with performance routines as with her work in film, or that the equally fast pacing and sharp jabs of Kathy Acker's work have their counterpart in the biting desublimations in Eric Bogosian's material. Is there direct influence, one form shifting the course of another? Probably closer to the truth is a shared commitment to "fast" displays that allow writers and performers alike to keep a step ahead of the electronic pace of life in the media age.

In an article in the first issue of the *Act*, a journal dedicated to performance art, Bruce Barber quotes from Christopher Gray's ac-count of the Situationniste Internationale a useful definition of the "society of the spectacle," spectacle meaning a "one way transmis-sion of experience; a form of 'communication' to which one side, the audience, can never reply; a culture based on the reduction of almost everyone to a state of abject non-creativity; of receptivity, passivity, and isolation" (Barber 1986, 14). Assuming Guy Debord's thesis that "spectacle is not a collection of images, but a social

relation between people mediated through images," one characterized most basically as "nonintervention," Barber argues for an "interventionist" theory and practice of performance art.

That radical edge seems already there in most performance and
performance-inspired texts. It appears not only in the content of the
sketches themselves but also in the "social relation" it seeks with
its audience and for its performers (at times including the collapse
of a distinction between the two). What makes developing this sug-
gestion a bit complex is that performance art ranges as widely in
emphasis as does postmodern fiction, the extremes of a Soho conceptualist inclination on one hand, and a Lower East Side insistence
upon gritty immediacy on the other. Henry Sayre's reflections upon
Eleanor Antin's *El Desdichado* represent well the more reflexive
bent of the former, and his borrowings from Fredric Jameson are
instructive. Sayre says that Antin's strategy

> draws attention to the *rhetoric* of her work as opposed to its *style*.
> Jameson sees rhetoric as addressed to a "relatively homogeneous
> public or class" ([Richard] Schechner's integral audience, for in-
> stance), while style represents "the sapping of the collective vital-
> ity of language itself" and "emerges, not from the social life of the
> group, but from the silence of the isolated individual: hence its
> rigorously personal, quasi-physical or physiological content, the
> very materiality of its verbal components. . . . What was hitherto
> a cultural institution—the story telling situation itself, with its
> narrator and class public—now fades into the silence and solitude
> of the individual writer." (Sayre 1986, 45)

Hence in Antin's piece, which relies partly on flat puppets in its
staging, "a seemingly stylized language emerges as, or reveals itself
to be, a rhetoric."

We must not overly simplify this distinction, for the "sapping
of the collective vitality" is no worse, perhaps, than the menace of
the totalitarian potential of homogenizing rhetoric, and style, if not
fetishized, can enrich the collective life. The appeal of performance
work is its ability to play style and rhetoric against each other in
order to recover a spontaneity and directness, either experiential or
conceptual, which in turn recovers (perhaps only temporarily) the
"storytelling situation" from its more reified forms in the culture.
In what some feel is more a Soho style, the conceptual may dominate, but these sorts of labels can cloud our ability to see that both
are necessary elements in the strategies by which this kind of work
ambushes the suburban norms of theater and fiction.

Allan Kaprow, for example, looks back a decade later on his
*Useful Fictions* (1975), a performance piece in which the participants are the audience, as a way of thinking about what emerged
from the "experimental arts of those days." Marking a basic break

from reified art forms, "activities, events, body art, land art, noise music, *ordinary*-movement dance, found-poetry, conceptualism and the like, all were unconcerned with high or low art and their internal, historical dialogue" (Kaprow 1986, 11). "It was," he argues, "the real, changeable world, the people in it, the ideas we used in making sense of that world, and the ways we behaved in it, that formed the nub of the quasi-art of those days."

At first glance, this antagonism to conventionalized art does not seem to have led directly into "the real, changeable world." *Useful Fictions* asks pairs of people to walk up and down steps or a mountain, one member mimicking the other's movements while the other watches in a mirror one carries, then both telling stories of the experience to each other and later alone. The tapes of those stories may or may not be shared, but the "oddness" of the piece by ordinary standards may obscure the very contemporary insights Kaprow wanted to arise in his participants as a result of the experience. He hoped that the "special conditions of a piece" would strike the participants as "reframed" and "italicized" versions of the more subtle constraints that determine the form of relationships in "real" life: "Society's learned rules are in principle no different than those of an Activity, just more complex and more internalized over a lifetime." The "useful fictions" of the title include art, psychotherapy, and "not-so-plain life," and are stories that "could be useful for understanding ourselves and our relationships."

### Spalding Gray and the Colorful Quilt of Culture

The work of Kaprow is relatively conceptual, though his emphasis upon movement, interaction, and "normal" settings beyond the boundaries of theaters and performance halls points his participants the way back into life from art (or vice versa?). His relevance here to more recently emerging downtown performance artists is only one of several ways in which the conceptual art movement has informed recent writing. We see it in the sophistication of performers such as Ann Magnuson, Ethyl Eichelberger, and Karen Finlay, each of whom takes the role of club performer and expands it in variously subversive conceptual directions without losing the stand-up socko. The suburban boundaries to live performance are more than a little exceeded in Magnuson's musical about the Charles Manson family, Eichelberger's drag-queen rewrites of the classics, and Finlay's willingness to make Acker's most graphic passages seem like only starting points. But the conceptualists' influence is more richly registered in Gray and Bogosian, perhaps our most celebrated performance artists from theatrical backgrounds. They are relatively *less* conceptual than Kaprow, but their explanations of what they are doing are close in important ways to what Barber,

Sayre, and Kaprow have to say about less recognizably "narrative" forms of the art. Gray, for example, might well be talking about *Useful Fictions* when he notes in the preface to *Sex and Death to the Age Fourteen* (Vintage Books, 1986) that "we exist in a fabric of personal stories. All culture, all civilization, is an artful web, a human puzzle, a colorful quilt patched together to lay over raw indifferent nature. So I never wonder whether, if a tree falls in the forest, will anyone hear it. Rather, who will tell about it?" (ix). Who will draw it into the quilt of useful fictions we use to understand the relations that society's "learned rules" lay out for us?

Gray has also endeavored all during his career—first with Richard Schechner's Performing Group, later with his own Wooster Group, and finally in his solo career—to work in ways that are not fully assimilated to the prevailing norms of theater and performance. For example, Gray's work with Elizabeth LeCompte in the Wooster Group collected a number of highly talented people (perhaps Willem Dafoe is the other most visible member of their group). Works such as the trilogy *Three Places in Rhode Island* layered different forms of experience to disrupt the traditional relationship between a passive audience and method actors preserving the illusion of reality on a raised stage (Gray still prefers working in a banked theater with only a table for a prop).

We can get some sense of what this experience would be like by examining *Point Judith*, an epilogue to *Three Places in Rhode Island* which was deftly edited by Cherches for his important early magazine *Zone* (7 [Spring/Summer 1981]—a tabloid-style magazine not to be confused with the more recent journal of art and politics). *Point Judith* has the same feel as the earlier pieces, such as *Rumstick Road*, a play about his mother's 1967 suicide, about which Gray taped relevant phone conversations with his relatives and her psychiatrist. Using the tapes mixed with live performers created a mini-scandal when the *Village Voice* withdrew the play from the Obie nominations; as Gray tells it in an interview with *Bomb* (Fall 1986), "it was a political thing that the artistic section of the *Voice* decided to ride police on." But Gray and his colleagues at the Performing Garage were creating what he calls in that same interview "a surreal docu-drama," Gray wanting particularly to disrupt "that New England shuffling it under the rug and smile and let's not speak the truth" (31).

*Point Judith* works at a greater remove from such intensely personal material as Gray's unresolved grief over his mother's death (he was out of reach in Mexico when she died). If anything, it is more complex an experience than the works to which it is called an "epilogue." As Cherches describes it, "the work is in three overlapping sections: 'Rig,' the play by Jim Strahs, 'Stew's Party Piece'—a condensed version of *Long Day's Journey Into Night* accompanied by Berlioz' 'Roman Carnival Overture,' and Ken Kobland's film 'By the Sea'" (15). What is especially valuable about Cherches's editorial job is that his pages "represent an attempt to document, simultaneously, the performance of *Point Judith* and the process of composition. This documentation includes various materials: texts and transcripts from the performance, photos, descriptions, choreographic notes, memoirs, and excerpts from Elizabeth LeCompte's notebooks" (15). Itself a docu-drama, this material is important to those of us not involved in the performance environment because it shows how very different both process and product are from the standard pattern of choosing and staging a play.

Part of that difference is the work's evolution. As LeCompte, the director, says in a journal excerpt, "the performers construct their performing personas in the presence of all of us—they don't come in with an idea of who they are beforehand. Their final character is a combination of my physical actions and their performance of those actions. The interstice between those two realities is what makes the performance" (18). Even the writing of the play segment of the performance is more communal and spontaneous than private and "literary": "Jim Strahs would come in and watch a rehearsal. The rehearsal might be a structured improvisation that I set up for the performers, or it might be work on other material that didn't necessarily have to do directly with the part of the piece he was writing. Then he would go away. He would write and he'd come back and we would perform for him what he had written. It wasn't as if we ever made up the words. We made up ourselves in front of him, and he made up the words" (20).

LeCompte's description of this process parallels the paragraph-length memoirs that Cherches had the participants write for *Zone*, their comments clearly indicating the spontaneity, communal improvisation, and sheer fun of working this way. As Gray recalls in his *Bomb* interview, it was Schechner's direction in the Performing Group that first opened these possibilities to him: "'Look,' he told his workshop. 'I want to see who you are before I see any character.' See we were doing a lot of . . . this was popular in the sixties—confrontational workshops in which we were asked to be ourselves. No director had ever done that before. First, be yourself, and *then*, the role will be an overlay over that. This was a really radical idea" (20).

From this history of working "the interstice between those two realities," to recall LeCompte's phrase, came the form of drama found in the Performance Garage. "The Rig" is about male (un)bonding among a rowdy group aboard an oil rig; it is full of cards, sex talk, the arrested adolescence of violence, bravado, and bluffing, and even includes The Kid, who of course does not understand much of the sex slang and is wide-eyed at the violence. But LeCompte was in quest of "some substitute for plot. Non-linear" (23), she wanted

"a confrontation with storytelling" (22), and she wanted to break up theatrical illusion by placing "mediated voice against the realities of being heard in 'the theater.'" Hence tapes of the actors whispering are played loudly in competition with their live speech, outtakes from the film (the piece's third part) play across the set all but indecipherably while the actors are still at work, the film proper (16mm) is shown alongside 8mm retellings with the actors half out of character and clowning, and the O'Neill play is cut almost randomly from four hours to thirteen minutes and performed with dance, fog machines, and actions only partly synched to tape, megaphones to help the actors be heard over the tapes, and Tyrone gunning down the cast to allow "The Rig" to finish before Gray guns *its* cast down to make way for the film.

The simultaneity of live and taped realities, the often obscene maleness of "The Rig" versus the nuns' lives in "By the Sea," the political and economic overtones of the absent Mr. Grim's control over his workers, the burlesqued play within a play, and the boundary-breaking of Gray's direct addresses to the audience are all elements that are part of the Wooster Group's efforts to perform the interaction of lives and the media and to cope with the issues of gender, politics, economics, and representation which arise once these issues are broached. But this unconventional performance theater was also the origin of Gray's career as a monologist. His character as the Wooster Group's narrator evolved over the five or so years he had warmed up the group by telling stories about his experiences or performing as its narrator. Gray told *Bomb*'s interviewer that "I realized I was giving pleasure to them in telling these stories and it was the first time I ever had the sense of giving something totally from myself. Up until then I'd always *been* through a role. I'd been interpreting someone else's work. But the excitement of being the *auteur* and the performer[—]I knew there was nothing else I wanted to do at that moment and I decided to go solo" (30).

The group work gradually diminished and the form of the monologue emerged in Gray's work as a means to accomplish ends that are partly formal, partly social, and partly personal. As if he were the group working out persona and scenario through improvisation, "none" of the monologues, Gray recalls in the preface of *Sex and Death to the Age Fourteen*, "had been written down prior to performance; they always came together in front of the audience" (xiii). This strategy enabled a formal recovery of the social setting of storyteller and audience and a valorizing of oral spontaneity over written stylization.

This formal shift complements both social and personal changes for Gray. Having done the Rhode Island trilogy, he felt he "had come to the end of a way of working." Looking for new directions, he found himself at the University of California at Santa Cruz in Amelie Rorty's class "The Philosophy of Emotions":

> Because my work had stopped I had a feeling that the world was also coming to an end. I told her I thought we had come to the end of the white middle-class world as we knew it. She took me at my word and said, "Well, Spalding, during the collapse of Rome, the last artists were the chroniclers." And all the bells went off inside me. Of course, I thought. I'll chronicle my life, but I'll do it orally, because to write it down would be in bad faith, it would mean I believed in a future. Also, it would be just another product cluttering up the world, not to mention destroying all the trees needed to make paper for the books. Each performance was to be a personal epitaph. Each night my personal history would disappear on a breath. (xii)

Suffused with Gray's typical irony, self-deprecating and otherwise, the passage nonetheless represents his own version of the hopelessness of the "white middle-class world," the dubious credibility of a self with either a future or ultimate substance, and even a touch of anticonsumerism. It would be a mistake, perhaps, to see Gray as among the more radical of our contemporaries, but the stance he takes here is an alienated one in which the performance medium, because of its evanescence, spontaneity, and immediacy, seems the only viable form in which to chronicle even a playful eschatology.

It may well be something in the social relations this form created between Gray and his audiences, some restoration of a Jamesonian collective life, and some redemption of storytelling itself that led to a more personal redemption of the storyteller. At least Gray is able to say that "the whole process of writing these stories down has been very healing, to the extent that it has projected me into a future" (xiv). The impulse to launch periodicals such as the *Act*, to document performance art, to compose histories and theories of its practice, and to translate what seemed like performance into what looks like prose narrative is one of the profounder evidences of a sense of future all this work seeks to affect with its "healing" criticism.

Gray's *Swimming to Cambodia* (Theatre Communications Group, 1985) is a masterful performance, though perhaps for reasons somewhat different from those of the enthusiasts quoted on the back cover of the less problematic *Sex and Death to the Age Fourteen*. The blurbs speak of a "WASP Shelley Berman," of "everyman's perspective," of "quirks" and "affection." But Gray's book "about" his role in the film *The Killing Fields* is most notable for the slyness with which, in the same mild voice of the earlier book (written, though not published, earlier), it identifies so many trace elements of media culture in the psyche of this age. It is a

much richer demonstration of what Gray means when he says that
"all human culture is art. It is all a conscious contrivance for the
purpose of survival" (xvi).

Typical of his irony is this reflection: "What is America? Every-time I try to think of America as a unit I get anxious. I think that's part of the reason I moved to Manhattan; I wanted to live on 'an island off the coast of America.' I wanted to live somewhere between America and Europe, a piece of land with very defined boundaries and only eight million people" (27). This passage reads like one of Stanley Fish's "self-consuming artifacts," baiting the listener with the promise of Definition, barbing the hook with the anxiety of the would-be totalizer, reeling in the rhetorical victim of this preten-tious and "literary" question with the absurdity of Manhattan as an Other that is "off" in "defined boundaries."

When Gray suggests that "all meaning is to be found only in reflection" (xvii), we can be sure that it is not the Cartesian ego sorting out rational truths, but the sort of reflection James Leverett has in mind in his introduction to *Swimming to Cambodia:* "It has gradually become Gray's chosen lot simultaneously to live his life and to play the role of Spalding Gray living his life, *and* to observe said Gray living his life in order to report on it in the next mono-logue. Perhaps this hall of mirrors, this endless playoff between performance and reality, has always been the situation of the artist. . . . But has it ever been more plainly the predicament of everyone else in this media-ridden age of instant replay?" (xii). As in his "reflection" of America, Gray often undoes the rhetoric of both the play-by-play historian and the color artist, leaving the spectator without so safely framed a spectacle—perhaps rather with the anxi-ety that both culture and the self, "as a unit," are effects of the hall of discursive mirrors. Emulating Gray—daily talking oneself into Being (if only to "disappear on a breath")—is perhaps how one keeps the image in play.

A variation on the theme is played by those for whom validation is saturated by (or perhaps insulated within) media imagery, such as the Marine who asks Gray to autograph the Polaroid of the guard's participation in a scene: "Would you please sign this picture for me? I want to send it to my folks in North Carolina. Because if I never do anything else in my life, at least I can say I have done this" (48). Gray does not let this stand as a piece of condescension, however; he deflates it first with a passage about the Cambodian prince who dies rather than fleeing, his mistake his having trusted the Ameri-cans' ideological imagery. Gray deflates it again as two reporters, Sidney Schanberg and Elizabeth Becker, both tell him of having had that stereotypical feeling that "I'd never felt more alive in my life than when I was right on the edge of death" (53). The reporters, that is, are immersed in the hyperreality of the media as much as the

Marine guard, and their one moment of feeling back in reality is that much-filmed, much-narrated moment of near-death.

Not even death is sufficient to shatter the suburban media simulation. Becker's anecdote is related to an inattentive Gray watching ants crawling after some dropped pâté: "And into my frame of vision came Elizabeth's hand, holding a white linen napkin. She just reached down and wiped out the entire trail of ants with one sweep of her hand. I appeared to be listening to her but inside I was weeping, *oh my God, all those ants, all those innocent ants dead for no reason at all*" (54). Liver pâté, linen napkins, and cocktails have little to do with the dream of raw immediacy lurking behind the scenario of flirting with death, and the casual extinction of a chain of ants suggests both a certain callousness in the murderer and a delightful deflation of Gray's response. No moral quilt over an "indifferent nature" really makes sense of experience or carries us beyond the range of the puzzles and stories by which we weave one day and then another. From within the web, for a day, something may cohere, but much distance on the matter deflates all the pretensions of media creatures to something ultimate.

To the commentator and the adventurer on the razor's edge, Gray adds the transcendentalist. His narrator tries magic mushrooms and Thai prostitutes, but it is really the film world that takes us the closest to the all-important "Perfect Moment." In one inspired passage, the narrator realizes that the "holy people in the West," the counterparts of Sri Rama Krishna "who can say they don't know who they are and not be put away in an insane asylum for it," are actors and actresses, with Hollywood their Mecca. "And where does their immortality have its being? On film. The image set forever in celluloid. And who is God? The camera. The ever-present, omniscient third eye. And what is the Holy Eucharist? Money!" (115). That Peter Sellers, for example, "made himself up and acted as a conduit through which he allowed many voices to pass" equates him with the Indian holy man. In our "materialistic, utilitarian" world, the perfect Being has no identity but the series of perfectly played roles set in film by the camera, which can be omniscient primarily because there is nothing sacred to know in a culture of simulation.

The narrator pulls himself up short in his search for "Cosmic Consciousness," taking himself severely if ironically to task:

> After all, what is this film about? Survival! Whose survival? My survival. Go! Get an agent! Go do five Hollywood films you don't really like. Do them! Get a house out in the Hamptons where you can have your *own* Perfect Moments in your *own* backyard. Have your friends come over for an afternoon of Perfect Moments. Return to your own ocean. Go! Go! Go to Hollywood and get an agent! (92)

Saturated in irony, this evocation of suburban paradise plays off all the traditional moral and spiritual norms absent from its shrill imperatives. More ironic is that "Cosmic Consciousness" as conceivable within the book's terms is no better.

The book's final episode is perhaps the most telling. It is a dream of a straw boy who runs in and out of a fire, alternately burning and reconstituting himself. Finally he is burnt to gray ashes despite the narrator's efforts. So the narrator takes the ash, blows it on an effigy of the straw boy, and sees it come to life just long enough for him to realize the straw boy "hadn't wanted to come back" (126). Trying to tell the dream, the narrator wanders in Hollywood, comes upon friends from the Wooster Group, and tells them instead he has seen himself in a movie (Sam Peckinpah's of Chekhov's *Seagull*!) he does not remember making, "an image with no memory attached." Perhaps we are all the straw boy, getting burned and coming back until we lose the will to persist in so phoenixlike a cycle. But we are also the narrator trying to find some way to intervene, but failing and, even worse, finding ourselves with no memory of having become whatever image we suddenly, upon reflection, realize we have become.

Making ourselves into an image, even if we must forget the process in order to pull it off properly ("play along and make myself up as I go," the narrator puts it at one point), is like reconstituting ourselves. But telling ourselves about the artifice of that repressed process, of straw rather than spirit as the substance of its product, is like jumping into the fire to be consumed: "And I knew all the time I was telling this story that it was a cover for the real story, the Straw Boy Story, which, for some reason, I found impossible to tell" (127).

Impossible because it is too scary a future to contemplate, weaving ourselves out of the breath of narrative day by day. Gray's engaging candor throughout *Sex and Death to the Age Fourteen* and almost as fully throughout *Swimming to Cambodia* is "a cover for the real story" he tells in this parable. It is a postmodern story of Being in the era definitely after semiotic innocence has been lost. It is just possible that the "voice" Gray labored so long to achieve is just that spark of style he sets against the rhetoric of suburbanized Being in the effort to keep playing his mirror game.

### Eric Bogosian in the American FunHouse

Known most widely for writing and starring in Oliver Stone's film *Talk Radio*, Eric Bogosian is more direct and probably more acerbic in his responses than Gray, as his comments in the introduction to *Drinking in America* (Vintage Books, 1987) indicate. Bogosian remembers how, "numb with boredom, I would walk out of a half-baked theatrical production of *Hedda Gabler* and find all the drama I could stomach on the street" (4–5). Although he wanted to be an actor, he did not want a role in a soap opera or "in a play that the New York critics would eat for breakfast. I wanted to have fun *now* and make work that excited me *now*." For a while, the Kitchen, a mecca for performance art in the seventies, works such as *Einstein on the Beach*, and the semiotic and minimalist activities inspired by Susan Sontag and Barthes all served to rescue him from the dullness of straight traditional theater and show him some directions for his work.

Partly because of neglect (he chafed, it seems, to be reviewed only in the *Soho Weekly News*) and partly because the energy and immediacy of the street were still somehow missing from his work on stage, Bogosian was ready for something else. He wanted an art that was "about the way we of the mass-media generation react and act on what we see" (14). He found it in the art of Michael Zwack, Cindy Sherman, and Robert Longo:

> What was their stuff like? Ironic in the extreme and dependent on letting the pictures—which had a superficial quality that gave them instant impact—tell the story. These artists shared the belief that in our age of mass media we are saturated by imagery, and this familiar imagery, if framed, set off, edited or piled up, can reveal deeper currents flowing within us. In other words, they were slam dancing with pictures. (14)

What emerged in Bogosian's own practice was an aggressive gallery of characters "each going 'all the way' into his world" (16). He uses adjectives such as "repulsive, unnerving, pathetic, or melodramatic" to describe the individuals, the noun "collage" to suggest the total impression we get of our social reality, and a distinctly postmodern theory to underwrite his theory of acting:

> Even more interesting is how you figure out how to act like a cowboy. I've never met one in my life. I must have learned how to act like a cowboy from John Wayne, an actor.
> Everybody does this, not just actors. Truck drivers act out the stereotypical truck driver. We've all seen them do it. Doctors play-act at being doctors. Yuppies play at being Yuppies. Punks, punks. Lovers, lovers. And so on. (109)

Bogosian wishes to explode the "rhetoric" of Being in the age of consumerism and the media, to set the "styles" of class and profession interacting with the rhetoric of economic roles until "society's learned rules" could be exposed, put up for grabs. He wears one costume on stage, switching characters "like you were turning channels: first this guy, then that guy. Fragments. Chunks of personality" (17). Those chunks are the learned roles, the actor's models, internalized along with the rules. He draws on the way rock stars "played to the audience," but in order to make them "laugh at violence and prejudice, then feel embarrassed for the laughter" (17).

Bogosian's dialogues are collected in *Drinking in America*, a volume that includes the title show as well as earlier material, such as *FunHouse* (much of which is included in the *Alive from Off Center!* film), *Men Inside*, and *Voices of America*, some material going back to 1981. Perhaps the best way to think of how these pieces work is to pursue Bogosian's comment on the 1981 *Men Inside* as "an attempt to sort out all these people inside me" (110). Whereas Gray emphasizes the narrative or fictive basis of identity, Bogosian stresses the multiple (and incompatible) identities lurking in our internal galleries. Bogosian is almost belligerent about canceling the distance between the privileged member of the audience and the characters he assembles—they are inside everyman.

Perhaps the archetypal Bogosian sketch, then, is "Honey, I'm Home!" as bitter an inversion of American dreaming as we are likely to find. A drunk in the gutter accosts Mr. Commuter without getting a response—each represents what the other most needs to repress to preserve equanimity, for they are psychological opposites in the class warfare between those who can and do comply and those who do not. So it is no wonder that only one can speak at a time on Bogosian's stage. In the sketch "Fried-Egg Deal," another casualty in the same situation explains the state of things: "You know what I mean, fried-egg deal? *(flips his hand)* They flip you this way, they flip you that way . . . just like a fried egg, you never know which side you're ending up on" (71). One of the powerless, he salutes with mixed irony and genuineness the commuter who "beat 'em," but he also reminds his successful Other that "if I wasn't where I was . . . you couldn't be where you was . . . 'cause, you know, 'cause *(illustrating with his hands flipping)* you can't have a top without a bottom" (71). This is a fast take on the exploitation necessary in a wealthy consumer society.

In "Honey, I'm Home!" the speaker begins with a drunken rendering of "God Bless America" that degenerates to "blah, blah, blah" and coughing right after the "guide her," as if the most apparent quality of his American reality was the lack of divine guidance. What he asks the commuter first is for a hand up off the street, a transparently symbolic request. But the speaker feels the need to justify his claim on a community, citing his Korean service record and Kennedy's "ask not" address. Without conviction, however: "Remember that one? JFK said that. . . . They blew *his* brains out!" (99). Bogosian's bite is like that, direct and undisguised. "Hey buddy, what do you say? Am I invisible or something? What, am I talking to the fire hydrant here? You! Mister! The guy with the *New York Times* under his arm, how about it?" Of course, he is invisible to his yuppie Other, whom he imagines needing to rush home and "skim the pool" or drive his wife to an Amnesty International meeting. The "you" is also the *"hypocrite lecteur,"* who, like the silent commuter, goes home to "asparagus tips" and the suburban salutation of the sketch's title.

Bogosian's sketches are full of characters such as these, or the speaker in "The Pacer" who know he's not "gettin' it" and wonders who does:

> You're either winnin' or you're losin', you're either sinkin' or you're swimmin' . . . and I'm sinkin', see! I'm in a little lifeboat with no oars and I'm sinkin' in the ocean . . . *(indicates with posture)* I'm on a little piece of ice, just gettin' smaller and smaller and smaller day by day by day, goin' into the water . . . and that water's polluted, it's dirty, it's disgusting . . . and I can't swim! I can't swim! (102–3)

In performance Bogosian convinces, his body shrinking as his character loses the very ground from under him, knowing he lacks what it takes to swim the Reaganomic seas. To the extent the speaker knows that "it's just gettin' harder and harder, every day, day in, day out," and that those who get it are those who make it harder, he understands the radical subtext of Bogosian's work, which makes up in impact what it lacks in subtle analysis. Even the burned-out yuppie passed over for promotion can feel "Held Down" at work and, by his lover, held up to the impossible ideal of "a superman and a superstud, . . . a real cowboy" (123), as if the system's demands create casualties at every niche of the class ladder.

Hence the procession of emptied beings on Bogosian's stage, characters whose impact upon us comes partly from the kindred part within us and partly from their clattering registration of capitalist radiation. The tile salesman talks a mad streak and hires a hooker to battle loneliness on the road (38); the junkie feels "life is a monkey on my back" and is content to leave his Other to "ride aroun' in your car, swim in your warm swimming pool. Watch the fire" as long as he can have his "taste" (62); the speaker "In the Dark" dresses in a "black cocoon" doubled by his darkened apartment, "where no one can find me, no one can hurt me, no one can touch me . . . I don't have to think, I don't have to feel . . . and the best part is . . . I don't have to see" (75–76), an obvious cultural dropout who blacks out all interaction to escape the costs of any real interchange.

The central importance of that withdrawal from interaction explains why the monologue works so well for Bogosian's writing: he can assault his audience as the "Mister!" responsible for the unimaginableness of dialogue in a world pushed so close to the edge of endurance. In Bogosian's world, class divisions are absolute and

economic relations are the only interactions. This class of characters can not only speak what the privileged class does not often hear,
but, isolated in monologue, it can also make clear how "invisible,"
as one of them expresses it, they are to the suburban psyche. Moreover, casualties declaring themselves bring to the monologue a voice
that undoes the kind of social relation (the passive nonintervention
of entertainment) typical of the form. As Bogosian says in a *People*
(!) magazine blurb, "I'm not going to get up in front of 2,000 people
and talk about my doodoo and my weewee and my psychiatrist and
what it's like to take LSD" (17 August 1987, 99–100).

Monologue also lends itself to Bogosian's equally adept desublimations of the class his victims envy, hate, and disdain. In addition
to his victims, a number of characters are pushers. The insurance
salesman narrates enough disaster scenarios during his suppertime
call to push his victim into a purchase, knowing life is enough of a
"fried-egg deal" that insecurity will reward him. The M.C. at a rock
concert can push his audience into a self-destructive frenzy—"Are
you ready to be FREE tonight? Break all the boundaries tonight? Are
you wasted? Are you wrecked? Are you . . . FUCKED UP! Ya! I know I
am" (68–69). No wonder the "band that wants to get inside your
head" is Cerebral Hemorrhage, for this commodity serves as a social
insurance that adolescent energy with nowhere creative to go vents
itself in a moneymaking way.

These more privileged members of Bogosian's gallery play social apocalypse for profit. Others of this class display the mechanisms of normalization that can maintain so disastrous an order.
The Hispanic deejay pushing the "College of Cashier Education,"
the success merchant "Looking Out for Number One," the preacher
in "Starving Children" asking for "just eighteen bucks" so that his
listeners do not have to feel guilty ignoring the next beggar, "The
Specialist" who in corporate workshop style tutors tomorrow's tor-
turers, and the evangelist who reads "The Law" of God as burning
abortion clinics, shooting "black urban barbarians," and nuking
"some country filled with nothing but bearded, terrorist heathen"
(66) are all characters who open up the hood on the engine that
motors "Mister!" home each evening.

It may be safe to say that Gray's warmth and humanity coax a
sense of the collective from his audiences, restoring the quality of
"social transaction" Jameson wants from storytelling, and that Bogosian's character sketches slam into an audience's passivity, disrupting its expectation of Debordian "spectacle" and imposing upon
it an awareness that corrodes the suburban roles and surfaces of
what the Situationniste Internationale calls "our alienated social
life." To place alongside Gray's and Bogosian's work that of Peter
Cherches is to define three contemporary versions of performances
as texts. Performance work closer to dance, or to theater, or to music

is still of course to be found, but for our purposes it will suffice to see a bit of what these three do with the performance dimension of writing and its tendency to reinforce the social and the collective force of storytelling.

### The Bagatelles of Peter Cherches

As committed as Gray or Bogosian to reaching a wider audience, Cherches underscores his effort to maintain accessibility, something he finds lacking in much postmodern work. He distinguishes himself from those who "are writing to an elite and are happy to do that." However, Cherches told me that "what turned me around and got me serious [about writing] was Pinter, his use of language and logic. It was the first time I'd come across a writer who really seemed to be thinking the way I was thinking." And, later, Gertrude Stein. Playing off his desire for accessibility is more a "conceptual approach" than a thematic or formalist impulse. Songs, information formats, classic story material, and even classic writers open a space of humor where cultural assumptions are caught in plain view.

Another way of thinking about Cherches's work is through his own preferences in art and music. His favorite painters are Piet Mondrian and Hans Arp; Cherches seems drawn to the clean minimalist lines of the former and what he calls the "visual linguistics" of the latter's recurring icons. In minimalist narratives such as *Bagatelles* (included in *Condensed Book*) and in some of his more visual work with Purgatory Pie Press, the direct influences can be seen, but pervasive in Cherches's work is this play between the spare conceptual thought that triggers his texts and the distinctly personal humor that has led to a "performance linguistics" followed avidly by audiences at Darinka, the Poetry Project, and La Mama La Galleria. This interplay recurs in his preferences in jazz—almost always playing when he reads, sometimes while he writes. He talks particularly of an appropriative jazz in which a recognizably individual style takes over a standard as a "constriction" within which the player is "making something new from the given and familiar."

We read Cherches, then, knowing that entertainment will occur and that humor will happen; however, as he says, "that's not why I do it." Some of the conceptual directions can be picked up by listening to him talk about the difficulties of making a living as a writer. "In '82," he told me, "I started working as a legal proofreader on Wall Street, and, as a result of correcting the grammar of capitalism, both consciously and unconsciously my work took a more political turn without ever becoming, I hope, really dogmatic and boring—like a lot of political writing." Although Cherches's political turn is often subtle and manifested through the wider cultural manifestations of the ideological, this interest is an important one to follow.

By 1984, Cherches learned computer-programming skills in order to escape the series of free-lance and short-term jobs because, he says, of "the treatment one gets from lawyers, the uncertainty of money and schedule when you're working free-lance, and the utterly depressing prospect of doing it fulltime." The political and economic issues lurking here are complemented by the conceptualist's interest in "playing with logic. Of course, in programming you have to stick with the logic instead of subverting it if you want your programs to work—as opposed to my writing where subversion is the thing." We shall indeed miss the point of these performances if we do not look for the subversion of all manner of cultural logics, because Cherches is supremely reflexive in the broadest sense of the term.

Eleven choice performances by Cherches with his band, Sonorexia, are available on a cassette tape *(It's Uncle!)* from Zoar; some of them were specifically written for performance, and others began life as texts and were later altered for a live context. For example, "It's Uncle!" something of a trademark song, was published with "Kennedy's Brain" in the first issue of Allan Bealy's excellent magazine, *Benzene* (Autumn 1980). There are steady losses in translation as we move from performance to tape to text to critical response, but the point if not the force can be conveyed.

At his simplest, Cherches simply appropriates a song such as "Cherish" and desublimates its subtext, wrenching his voice into the violence and domination implicit in lines such as "I don't know how many times I've wished that I could mold you into someone who would cherish me as much as I cherish you." Sentimental pop has more to do with coercing the beloved into the roles prescribed in a lovers' discourse, and particularly with subordinating woman to male desires, than with our more customary but innocent responses to the genre. Cherches's vocal style undoes the passivity by which we allow that discourse to program our desires, the social relations of domination and exchange it assumes, and the sugary surface by which all this subliminal chanting slips by us.

"Everything Reminds Me of You" represents one of Cherches's favorite genres, the list song, a sort of epic catalog in which all spheres of life are rhymed into place within the absolute egocentrism of love:

> The atom bomb, the senior prom, a swollen gland, a polka band,
> Everything reminds me of you.
> A telephone, an icecream cone, a canceled check, a broken neck,
> Everything reminds me of you.

The list goes on and on as all of life, including its political, medical, and economic realities, becomes sublimated within the "you" of the beloved, as if Cherches had decided to make Barthes accessible to the Walkman crowd.

The most extreme of these "analyses" is "Will You Be Mine," a sweet ballad that begins with the absurdity that we try not to hear in Top 40 lyrics:

> A chair has four legs most of the time,
> Will you be mine;
> A nosebleed isn't worth a dime,
> Will you be mine.
> When the crows begin to glow,
> And the dwarfs begin to grow,
> Then I'll want to know,
> Will you be mine.
>
> An omelet's better than a life of crime
> Will you be mine;
> I hope I'm not getting out of line,
> Will you be mine?
> A window frame frames your window
> Your molding's quite rococo
> All I want to know
> Is will you be mine.

Cherches does not stop with a theater of the absurd, however, but opens matters with a curious refrain:

> We were too poor to dine at eight o'clock
> Your shoelaces were just swell
> Your questions rang like insulin shock
> And into your sleep I fell.

Incongruity spreads into the zones of economics, "dress to impress" drops to a minimal level, and dialogue resembles a pathological condition before he invades her sleep. Such Cole Porter–style crooners customarily resolve everything into the neat package of romance, but Cherches's version instead leaves all the channels set at right angles to one another. The last verse, however, raises the ante:

> The capitalist system is covered with slime
> Will you be mine
> The bankers and brokers are filthy swine
> Will you be mine
> When the pigs we overthrow

And the people run the show 267
You'll give me a little sign CONDENSED
And I'll know that you're mine. BOOK

The detonation here seems omnidirectional, social apocalypse and
the romance motif butting together without really mixing, as if even
the most extreme political resentments and upheavals could make
no impact upon the absolute resilience of our social determinations
of desire's forms and conventions.

Most of Cherches's songs are, however, lighter in their satiric
effects, such as the wild metaphorist of "Love Me Like a Bitter Pill,"
who seems quite unwitting about the extent to which his imagery
crosses love with distastefulness and violence ("don't wrap me in
foil, don't boil me in oil, just love me like a bitter pill"). "It's
Uncle!" is a similarly light parody of the "glad to see all of you"
rhetoric when Uncle comes to visit even though Father "ain't in the
least bit glad to see" him. The punk vocalist of "These Things"
cannot "put into words these things that you do to me," a tribute,
perhaps, to the inarticulateness of some pop genres.

"Kennedy's Brain" is chanted through a distortion circuit
against an astonishingly discordant guitar track provided by Cherches's collaborator, Elliott Sharp. Its narrator spends his time, "in
the absence of anything else to do," staring at his $3.95 Kennedy's
Brain in a jar (he knows that it is not really Kennedy's—"I'm not
stupid"), to the sound of the Mulligatawnys fighting next door, by
the "bluish grey light" of his soundless television ("the best kind of
light to watch Kennedy's brain by"). A nightmarish version of the
culture of spectacle, the piece "was inspired," Cherches told me,
"by being in a loud club one night, and that sort of nihilism that
characterized the punk scene."

The narrator of "Kennedy's Brain" is absolutely arrested in the
passive social relation that the Situationnistes Internationale was
intent upon disrupting, not even caring what is on the television as
long as it is on, the soundtrack of domestic conflict fully appropriate
for the play of media imagery across the convolutions of that social
and political riddle. Why watch only a "reasonable facsimile" of an
assassinated president's brain? Because the assassination activated
the cycle of violence which undid America's innocence? Because
from somewhere in that mind everyone had expected answers to
emerge, as well as a kind of leadership that subsequent history has
shown we need even more than we knew? Is it simply that Kennedy
represented a vigor and independence that few people find credible
now amidst social realities we understand more complexly than we
did amidst the idealism of a quarter century ago? Or even that his
assassination is one of the hardest things for Americans to face, and
that Cherches's play with punk nihilism simply takes him to this

inner sanctum of national hagiography and commodifies it as a K-Mart blue-light special?

To talk with Cherches is to come away suspecting that all or most of these nuances are racing around at one level or another of this disturbing piece. What is clear is that, as in "Prehistoric Man," who "ain't here no more," Modern Man ain't either (he is the second verse of this postmortem round). Cherches's recent musical pieces take over the sublime melodies of Thelonious Monk; for example, in "Blue Monk" the narrator rhymes "anxiety" with "variety" in front of the abundance of the frozen-food counter, trapped because "indecision's got me blue / I just don't know what to do." It is the lack of any very momentous crisis behind this paralysis which marks Cherches's distinctive evacuation of psychological depth as he traces lives no deeper or more permanent than newsprint. To examine Cherches's remarkable *Condensed Book* (Benzene Editions, 1986) is to find him making good use of the greater expanse its pages offer him to define some of the ways in which that modernist, humanist self has changed.

In "Unfamiliar Tales," for example, the semiotic threatens to displace the semantic structuring of texts. The titles of these fifteen short sketches all rhyme and begin with "An Unfamiliar." They display the generative logic of the linguistic category of rhyme against the semantic backdrop cued by "unfamiliar," as if the sketches were a competition between the generative logic of language and the systematizing, normalizing, rule-building energies of cultural semantics. Almost inert in these sketches are traditional structuring forces such as plot—each section is a discovery of disjunction between the textual store of knowledge and the unsuspected anomalies of experience. And of character as well—Cherches calls the He and She of this piece (and of *Bagatelles*) "ostensible" characters. They have a pronoun but not a Bildungsroman to sustain them, and part of what makes these tales *unfamiliar* is that they pursue an arbitrary, if not fully aleatory, course.

Here, for example, is "An Unfamiliar Phrase":

> We were having a conversation, when all of a sudden I uttered an unfamiliar phrase. I became flustered, began to apologize. "I don't know where that phrase came from," I told her. "I assure you, it's an unfamiliar phrase."
>
> "It's nothing to be ashamed of," she told me. "According to Chomsky, it's perfectly normal to utter an unfamiliar phrase every once in a while." (111)

Surprised by language's generative possibilities, the "I" seems caught between social mores that normalize discourse and a radical linguistics that is receptive to the unpredictable thoughts and experiences to which the unfamiliar might lead.

That paralyzed "I" is, however, best played by the reader or critic trying to read these segments as I have this one. They do not necessarily lead down into a core of insight, but out across the unexpected and not necessarily meaningful connections made by the rhymes and slant rhymes among their title words (lace, case, maize, ace, face, grace, and so forth). Most readers are conditioned to want language to accrue in meaningful—that is, familiar—ways. "Unfamiliar Tales" is a moment of conceptual performance art deconstructing how thoroughly our textual pleasure is disciplined, and playing with the possibilities of quite different combinations than those unified by causation, personality, equivalence, or other such conventional forms.

Internally, some segments cohere in traditional ways: "Phrase" is reflexive; "Maize" is comic ("'I do not know this maize.' 'Oh, cut the corn,' she replied."); "Lack" is almost melodrama (to what male does the shoelace belong? "'I don't know,' she said, 'but I hope he gets home all right.'"); "Case" is hermeneutic ("First find the case, *then* solve it"); and so forth. But what holds "Unfamiliar Tales" together is the unfamiliar accretion of unrelated bits that may well have more to do with the real state of affairs than the ordered, harmonious, coherent, and meaningful metaphysical whole that we once assumed language approximated. "Doodads," which features a lot of phrase-variation games, shares much of the same linguistic focus as "Unfamiliar Tales"; perhaps the two together suggest that all tales are far more unfamiliar than our conventions allow us to see and that they are all doodads we accumulate as a result of our experiences with cultural forms. "Reading Comprehension" and "Problems" pursue more specific versions of those cultural forms. They take testing, that great disciplinary specter haunting the beneficiaries of education, and explain what Cherches means when he calls tests "implements of propaganda." The first reading passage, for example, is about happy Americans and unhappy Russians; another, on fast food's nutritional value, features this question:

1. A Good title for this passage would be:
a) America, Land of the Free
b) Foods of the World
c) The Truth About Pizza
d) Eating Sensibly

(70)

Part spoof on the test form, the question also makes its obvious plays off false marketing claims and the Republican equation between corporate and national interests. Throughout these two pieces are similar shots at corporate greed, foreign policy, consumerism, and their none-too-subtle inculcation through all manner of supposedly innocuous means.

*Bagatelles*, originally published as a chapbook, is Cherches's minimalist novel, a dialogue of power and confusion between I and She. Fear of loneliness surfaces, but "I had nothing to be afraid of: There was only one of her, but there were two of us" (22). The combative undercurrents between the individual and the relation surface also in this segment:

> You take a lot out of me, she said to me.
> I know, I told her in her own voice. (9)

*Bagatelles* is light verse, as its title suggests, but not entirely trifling, as its other meaning would indicate, if things so important as voice and Being are at stake. When he takes her voice, does she still have it herself? And what of his own presumably displaced voice? Voice is highly significant in the sequence as the power to determine the (narrative) reality in which they take place, even if Being seems almost beside the point. For example: "Her voice. It ruled me. Not she, not by any measure. But her voice, when it chose to speak to me" (4). She seems powerless, but her voice can, with sufficient will, rule his margins. But if voice rather than Being is her strength, we cannot discount the power of his recourse to voice either. He manages her in one sequence by alternating daily between calling her "beautiful" and "ugly," a narrative ambivalence that is its own form of rule.

Perhaps the most interesting contest between them is the last segment:

> I created you out of nothingness, and I can annihilate you any time I feel like it, I told her.
> I'd like to see you try, she said. (27)

Does the fact that *Bagatelles* ends with this segment mean that he did try and succeeded—that when his voice stops narrating, they stop existing? Or does the piece end in a standoff because his stopping would be her starting, thus yielding the full power of narrative creation to her? Like his portrait of her, a blank page he calls "an idealization" and hence can think but not write, the ending raises a question that writing cannot trace out—the answer, that is, to the relationship between writing and Being, grammatology and ontology. Cherches's minimalist novel ends with this unanswerable question perhaps because to strip down narrative to its most basic issue is, finally, to ask the same scary question about narrative and Being which Gray's work raises.

"Dirty Windows," Cherches's piece in the *Between C & D* anthology, continues this same sort of cultural skewing. He uses for his answering machine a tape that answers, "You have reached a nonworking number," as if we all had nonworking numbers on the cultural switchboard (63). When they go to a Halloween party "as each other," they find that "the costumes were so good that nobody knew who they were," a peculiar effacement of identity in coupledom (64). Another segment is vintage Cherches at his most metaphysical: "She had changed. She looked different to him. Odd, but she looked like him. It finally dawned on him what had happened— she had replaced herself with a mirror. So he did the same thing. Replaced himself with a mirror. Then he stood back and watched" (65).

If ours is an age of reflecting upon representation, Cherches here lets ontology slip into the Quaker Oats box game (the Quaker holds a box picturing a Quaker holding a box picturing . . . ) and disappear along with referentiality. The latter surfaces again when they both reject a famous painter's portrait of them. Each likes the other's likeness, but thinks "it doesn't look anything like me." The painter collects his commission when he has the presence of mind to respond, "I painted you as you see each other" (66). When *we* do not at first recognize the portrait Cherches's performances offer us of our ways and means, it is no doubt because he has the gift of seeing us in all manner of ways other than the one in which we see ourselves.

Cherches's pamphlet *Between a Dream and a Cup of Coffee* (Red Dust, 1987) branches into the slightly different terrain of dreamlike narratives which confound daylight order, both narrative and otherwise. A missing squid head in a salad at a Japanese restaurant sets off a mad encounter between an irate narrator and a crazed waiter, who wants to even out the salads rather than find the missing squid. The narrator works a few hours with Frank Perdue loading turkeys for Thanksgiving, dines in front of the detached head of a truffle pig, frets over a friend at *Sportsweek* who is kidnapped by a washed-up soccer player. The tales are stranger than that; Perdue looks nothing like the video fiction of his advertisements, the pig's head looks more like a baby's, his friend's hijacked plane lands in the Bowery. What the book's blurb calls "a New York as seen between rapid eye movements, where all subways lead to the bowels of the unconscious" is indeed apt to these strange tales. In their pages, connections are crossed and the grammar of events has become nonsensical—odd conjunctions like misfired social synapses leave the narrator always off-balance, always, as in dreams, at the mercy of uncontrollable forces we cannot identify amidst the mechanisms of displacement and condensation by which ideology, economics, history, and accident tumble together in his urban reality. His (only) apparent expectation that things make sense, function purposefully, and follow logically is the real comedy of the pamphlet and Cherches's ultimate target. Experience does not conform to the cultural orderings that are the bedtime stories on which we are raised. All of Cherches's work performs a dreamscape in which lines of order metamorphose into unpredictable mechanisms that chug away within a far more diverse and strange cosmos than any programmers or users had quite imagined.

Each of these three writing performers, then, works with his own emphasis to undo the seamless functioning and smooth predictability of the spectacle. Gray's work takes us to the edge of a semiotic ontology in which the voice of self emerges—and fades— in the telling. Bogosian's work locates an embattled individuality straining at the convergence of economic and social forces that seem to preclude a genuine collective life or a satisfying individual life. Cherches's work takes the assault so far as to emerge almost on the other side of the rhetorics of spectacle, whether that specular form be music, monologue, or fiction, arriving at something akin to the "unlogic" of culture's Other.

Dismantling the web of assumptions surrounding more familiar logics requires us to rise out of the lethargy of aesthetic consumers, to become even more active than Wolfgang Iser's readers "merely" filling textual gaps. We must become almost the inventors of some weirdly shifted modalities in thought and perception which would create not only new styles of recognizing and responding to gaps but also new rhetorics for maintaining enough of the right kind of gaps to preclude the tyranny of form and convention. Rather than succumbing to such a tyranny, these three writers engage in an activist, perhaps an anarchist, but certainly a pleasurable play off, against, and with the social, political, economic, and aesthetic rule systems we have inherited.

# BETWEEN C & D

The words *Between C & D* name America's most interesting fiction magazine, but also a particular point in a complicated nexus of history, architecture, class, race, and national origin. Between Avenues C & D is where Joel Rose and Catherine Texier have lived and published their magazine during the eighties—Rose after a California exile from New York, Texier coming from Paris via Montreal. But it is also the meeting of America's mythology and street history—the dreams of immigrants, the utopia of melting pots set on coals of gold, and the beat of bohemian culture colliding with the mayhem of gang life, drug wars of both the headline shoot-out and the mainline shoot-up varieties, and the economic warfare of food and water, housing and heat. The area has also drawn Patrick McGrath from his shoreline cabin off the coast of western Canada to seek his literary friendships and outlets here and to make his editorial skills part both of the Soho *Bomb* and the East Village *Between C & D*. McGrath, Texier, Rose, and the multifarious talents they have published in their magazine provide us with an important reading of life and fiction in this postapocalyptic Empire of the Senseless.

### Joel Rose: A Red Haze

Joel Rose is above all an interesting man to talk to, a mix of fairly volatile materials which has come out to be very appealing and productive. He took his time as a writer, detouring to the Pacific Northwest for a time with a group very into the Beats before doing an M.F.A. under the somewhat hostile auspices of Columbia University. Although he might have liked to stay in New York, waiting tables to pay the bills, it was too close to the scene of his father's hard work sending the first Rose to college. So, after a year in South

America, Rose spent three years in California working on scripts for "Kojak," "MacMillan and Wife," and the like. "I hated Hollywood," he said, "but I learned a lot about finishing work and structure which has helped me in my work." He has kept his hand in these other writing projects, working with Miguel Piñero on some "Miami Vice" scripts and doing a little journalism and the occasional film script. With the success of *Between C & D*, grants and publishing contacts have only grown easier. It is a long way from the years of living on $2,000 a year, "but we really caught some breaks." Made them, really. As he told me,

> *Kill the Poor* is actually my third or fourth novel, but it's the first one I ever showed to anyone else. It was *my* voice—the first time I actually fell into it, it worked for me, I heard that book more than wrote it—it just played out for me. I really believe what those people [his earlier teachers] said to me as a fiction writer: Have faith in the process of it and your voice will come to you with time. I feel like a tennis player who doesn't have to think about his strokes anymore. I work hard—I rewrite a lot. But just that first burst comes more naturally to me.

"Coming naturally" takes, it is clear, a lot of preparation.

Rose's voice is enriched not only by the diversity of his writing projects but also by his perspective on class in America, which differs from that of many contemporary writers with easier routes to professional notice. "I feel that it gave me an edge to come from the lower middle class," he told me. "For my vision, it's an edge." And he goes on to specify that edge with great clarity:

> It seems that there's a lot of Writing-School Writing that's incredibly well-crafted—and I know how hard that is to do—and I sit in admiration of it. But I'm not interested in it, frankly. I've seen how it's progressed and how it's made, but I feel that there are breakthrough areas that people are shying away from as far as their work goes. What I'm interested in is the voice that I hear out in the street, the "voice of contemporary America," whatever it is. There are underlying currents out there that are more far-reaching and more imperative to me. And sometimes, this well-crafted fine little world—I can't believe that that's contemporary life and contemporary work for some people. To me it's like putting on blinders or something, not seeing what's happening out there.

"Survival" means different things depending upon your class, your experience, and, especially, your affiliations. Rose and Tillman, who are friends, emphasize the importance of this matter of personal, professional, and institutional affiliations: both avoided the writing establishment until they had won the right to negotiate on their own terms. His brush with that establishment during his

Columbia days still has him telling stories that appall, renewed as they are from time to time when, as a magazine editor, he sees the before and after effects of the more aggressive writing programs. Rose's *real* affiliation grew out of friendships begun at the Life Cafe and through the contacts that *Between C & D* opened for him.

Survival, class positioning, and affiliation outside the establishment have all given Rose an eye for an America few readers have ever seen. He put the matter well at a key moment in our conversation: "I feel scared and angry and confused and very emotional. I have a red haze in my head so much not knowing where it's coming from. That's what I see out there—people turning around and shooting each other. Just this blind violence and desperation. I feel like *that's* the times we live in, and that's what I'm trying to work out in whatever way is possible." Rose places his work at an opposite extreme from certain kinds of "postmodern" fiction which, at their worst, can be "aluminized," taking their origins "from the idea first." His work takes its start from the streets of the Lower East Side where he now lives, having returned to the very block from which his grandmother led the family exodus. In the refurbished top floors of a century-old immigrants' tenement, he savors the ironies and the contradictions of writing on his computer across the street from the shell of the temple in which his grandmother was married, up the street from his grandfather's shop (now a neighborhood "drugstore"), down some blocks from the restaurant where his father worked as a waiter, amidst kids repeating his own childhood on the streets (a childhood he finds reasonably close to Jim Carroll's in *Basketball Diaries*). The motivating force behind our best fiction magazine and with a novel, *Kill the Poor*, published in Gary Fisketjon's Atlantic Monthly Press Fiction series (1988), he also carries the "red haze" of a complex set of cultural contradictions which his fiction explores not only with all the gritty reality of a Kathy Acker but also with the narrative "gotcha" of the "Miami Vice" episodes that he writes with Piñero.

*Kill the Poor* is so engaged with cultural contradictions that its protagonist, JoJo (or "Zho Zho," as his French wife calls him), has something in common with Walter Scott's Waverley protagonists. JoJo is caught on the middle ground between worlds that are themselves more or less coherent—worlds formed by class, race, law, even gender and drugs—and he is affiliated somehow with more than one side at a time. But unlike Scott's characters, JoJo also has more than two alternatives, he finds their intersections and overlappings complex and contested, and he experiences mainly conflicts rather than a "right" and historically determined resolution. There is no narrator to set it all into perspective, either, for there *is* no perspective to reconcile the social forces clashing in the novel. There is, instead, just JoJo, who is partly aware of the contradictions within him and partly a blind function of them. JoJo wants both understanding and resolution, and so he reveals a great deal, but he also rises through the ranks in a war of class, race, and history and is thus more interested in survival—and so he represses much. Readers must construe the relationship between what is said and what appears in other forms during the narrative if they are, on one level, to figure out this mystery novel of arson and murder, and, on another, to appreciate the social factors at work in JoJo's character.

The novel shares with Scott's works an engagement with social forces—"people turning around and shooting each other"—rather than the tendency of Anglo-American fiction during the Victorian and modernist eras to play one variation or another on the form of the Bildungsroman. Like Edward Waverley, JoJo does, says, and feels things, but he also seems at times curiously arrested at the point of contention in a series of cultural contradictions which grow out of the Lower East Side environment of both author and protagonist. The violence of those contradictions and the culture's desire to repress them account for the novel's title, taken from a Dead Kennedys song that is one of the novel's two epigraphs. *Kill the Poor* includes tales of a delivery boy murdered for spareribs, of a baby tossed out a window, of shots exchanged and flailing baseball bats, of a junkie shooting his needle-mate. The other epigraph is a line of desublimation from Michael Daly of the *New York Daily News:* "What they're saying is: 'Don't kill white people.'" The punk and the columnist highlight the lines of race and class which compose two of the novel's flash points, and Rose's writing draws strength both from the journalist's eye for street detail and the punk's irreverence for the "aluminized" surface that sometimes paves over layer after layer of street life.

Race and class lead a pack of realities which breaks through the suburban repression of America's unsolved problems, but it is important to note that JoJo shares with his family a measure of suburban flight. Their repression of conflict has its emblem in the name of his grandfather—when he fled Hungary for America, he rechristened himself "Greenfield" to mark the green fields he had crossed to freedom. The flight continues as first one then another utopia fails, JoJo's grandmother moving to Brooklyn in 1937, his mother to Long Island in 1951. But their fascination with what they have left is so strong that all of them visit, as if tourists, when JoJo moves into his place on Avenue E. His mother can smell the boiling eels of her childhood, his grandmother feels old life in the present shells of buildings, his father finds the Nuorican touches those of simply another immigrant group like all the preceding waves. But they remain uneasy, his mother sealing herself in the car at one point, his uncle dismissive: "Boool shit! Beautiful? How can that be? I grew up there, remember? Don't bullshit a bullshitter, Joey. There ain't nothing happening down there in that neighborhood. Never was. Not even when we lived down there. It's always been a hellhole and it's a hellhole today. Mark my words. Your grandmother worked her whole life get the family off that block" (14).

Nobody has found what Grandfather Greenfield was looking for—the uncle barely pulls his own weight at the family newsstand, and JoJo's parents have worked hard for a small portion of ease—and this contradiction between the immigrant dream of utopia and the sociopolitical realities of New York is at the heart of the novel. JoJo knows that "New York's a lock, and we locked out" (11). The parable of this realization concerns an immigrant family who, on their first night in America, are feasted by distant American relations but who die in their sleep after blowing out the lights: "They didn't understand America. The technology. How things vurked here. They didn't have such things in Europe. The gas from the vall lamp killed them. They didn't know any better, they didn't know from gas jets" (206).

A more militant demystification arises in the thoughts of JoJo as he recounts the suicide of Meyer, his mother's cousin, and tries *not* to recount his own sister's death in Vietnam, a traumatic event that cues his adolescent breakdown (I have retained within brackets here and elsewhere some material cut during the editing process but which Rose told me he will restore in a subsequent edition):

> Another one who grew up on Avenue E, fucked by the promised land. The place was cursed. America. Maybe no one knew it yet, but they were going to find out. Maybe not in my lifetime, maybe not in yours, but in the lifetime of our kids—Constance, poor Constance. I hate to say it, but maybe that's why she's always weeping, always crying—because she knows. America could have been beautiful for her, for me, but it's cursed and my kid knows it, can smell it, taste it, sense it. How many from my family, those I know, struck down before their time? Meyer, my sister[, my grandfather. Me]. (205–6)

"Me," indeed, because JoJo's life twists and turns through the effects of trying to live the "promised" life in the "cursed" land. For one thing, JoJo is not free of drugs and their physiological fiction of utopia. Imagining a later encounter with a dealer, JoJo evokes both promise and curse: "Maybe this other time he tells me, he's back in the arms of God. Maybe he tells me he's happy now. Maybe he is" (62). Everywhere he walks in the neighborhood, dealers are selling. "Oh, you hear them, and sometimes you just want to say, need to say, okay, all right, do me up, sell me a bag or two of that there 'Executive'" (13). JoJo calls the neighborhood "an outdoor drug supermarket. People marvel at it, they're actually mesmerized, fascinated. [I love it man.] How else do you account for all those writers and artists running off at the mouth about it, and how does it get into all the literature and magazine articles and movies?" (198). He hides his drug use from Annabelle, his wife, cooking up in the bathroom or another apartment, only occasionally getting caught by her. Rose, meanwhile, has his sardonic aside about those from uptown culture for whom these markers are local color rather than living history.

Heroin insulates him from the deaths of family and friends and of a part of himself lost amid the crossfire of family tensions. His grandmother tells him that "I pray to God you are a better father than you are a son" (65). His father thinks JoJo got "the only bad blood on my old lady's side of the family" (14) and bluntly tells him, "You're a fuckup, son" (102). Annabelle's (French) family calls him "le sauvage Commanche" (268), appalled he quit school at fourteen, recoiling from the taint of defeat they sense in a son-in-law who feels he "just lost it. The fates were against me" (218). Whatever disadvantage he started with by not growing up amidst money and education is magnified by how deeply his family seems to resent his caving in to grief over his sister's death and to the temptations around him. As far as the psychological strata go, JoJo harbors an overload of disabling emotions: "I sit up in bed shaking violently or I lie, my mind a blank, a shield like a sheet of three-quarter inch plywood protecting my mind from any thought, any emotion, any intrusion" (152). "Not now. Not ever. No response" (152). Internal flight is chemical, psychological. It is a flight that numerous characters in the novel make, including Ike the Woodrobber, a successful lawyer until his fiancée's death in a tenement fire, or John Plastic Hat, the street person who wears a garbage-bag turban and who refused the personal invitation of the mayor to ride in his limousine to a shelter.

The external situation is more complex, because JoJo and Annabelle have bought the apartment with the cash settlement she received after a bar owner (for whom she worked), high on something, had cut her cheek. The payment saves his liquor license, and it enables them to move out of the building that contains the home for blind Ukrainians and into the two-floor apartment on Avenue E. Their marriage is already a curiosity to JoJo. The relationship begins with her proposal—she is an illegal immigrant, and JoJo is her protection against deportation. Annabelle, who dances in a strip joint, is his sexual ideal: "Me, just a regular guy, the star of no novel or motion picture, I got her, a sexy beautiful girl, French like I say" (22). Rose's fine ear for the lingo makes ludicrous Hollywood's idea of working-class dialogue.

Purchasing the apartment, however, changes JoJo's life even more significantly. Instead of being the oppressed, JoJo is now a member, later the president, of the group that takes possession of the building, starts collecting rent regularly from the tenants, and works to gentrify the neighborhood. He assumes the position, but not the wealth or security, of a different class. This assumption of power brings him a long way back from the sense of defeat he feels in his life. Taking this power is "taking responsibility for where I live, how I handle my life," though it is also a futile effort to compensate for not having "two dimes to rub together," for being dependent, that is, on Annabelle's money for a place to live and on her sexiness as validation of his masculinity (140).

That personal contradiction is congruent with one on the level of principle: "The party line is: Everybody should get what they deserve. The haves and the have nots. Let's redistribute the wealth. The only problem is I want to be sure to at least keep what I got. It's not so much. No way I want to be throwing everything I got over for the revolution. Just put me right there in the middle, half the people above me, half the people below me. Fucked and fucking" (215). As is his family life, his marriage, and his role as president of the association, JoJo's social "theory" is undermined by the residue of his encounters with the dreams and the realities of economic life. "Fucked and fucking," he is on a contemporary version of Scott's middle ground, a "middle" that fails to escape the network of oppression and economic power hoped for in the personal and social utopian dreams that he shares with his family.

JoJo's part in those dreams shows not only in his desire to keep what he has or in his efforts to fix up the apartment, clear out the junkies, and make a "decent home" for his wife and daughter, but also in a kernel of nostalgia for another, perhaps mythical, era we can see underneath his crustiness: "Things are changing in this country. Used to be, you know, you could trust everybody, everybody's normal, everybody's like us, you and me, your neighbor and your pal. Nowadays who's gonna argue about convention, it's all up for debate, ain't that right?" (25). The homogenized populace of the suburban dream does not exist in the "red haze" of the Lower East Side. JoJo repeatedly tries to occupy a middle ground between conflicting forces only to discover that the pure reason of the golden mean is, in reality, the warring of cohabiting contraries. He is and is not the gentry; his family's class origins do not excuse or justify his role in the larger class warfare of gentrification.

Butch, a grad student in sociology, is one force who reminds JoJo and the other apartment owners of the persistence of difference. He leads a rent strike against the gentrifiers with the slogan "This land is our land." That, however, is also the unspoken battle cry of the gentrifiers themselves, "the cry on both sides," as JoJo says. The operative parable here concerns the parks, "off-limits, home to only hoodlums and thieves" until "everyone of the absence-of-color persuasion and the fat-wallet contingent wanted to be in top shape." A crowd abandons a mugged cyclist and chases down the mugger, breathing a "collective sigh of relief" when he gets "fifteen to twenty-five at Elmira even though he's only sixteen." The individual victim is less important than retaliation at the class level: "One down, a few hundred thousand more to go" (199–200). "[This is war,]" the block association speech states, and "[the poor in this neighborhood are not comrades in arms]."

Another metaphor for the neighborhood is the Wild West "a hundred years ago. Cowboys and Indians, treacherous, murdering savages, life in hand, homesteading in hostile environments" (38). And one of the homesteaders places it in an even more "primitive" context: "It's the way of the world. The scavenger and the scavenged. [We living at the end of the food chain here on the Lower East Side, bro]" (228). Butch, then, is one of several characters in the novel who forces JoJo to face his complicity in an oppressive economic order to which, intellectually, he would not subscribe and from which his family has always suffered in major ways.

Despite his family history and his own marginal status, JoJo cannot really feel part of the underclass around him in the neighborhood any more than he can feel at ease with yuppie gentrifiers, such as the couple who look down on him for smooching Annabelle on the stoop one day. This pattern of both and neither applies equally to his feeling "at home" in the neighborhood. He can "remember it from when I was a kid, when we came to the temple, came to the doctor, came to the nurse, came to see the lady with the alligator purse. To visit my mama's friend, still there, ensconced, long after my mama and her family got out" (23). It is a multigenerational at-homeness, but one that is also curiously expired; immediately following these memories we read JoJo's other side: "[No matter what you say, you ain't from here, b. You an outsider,] and now I see the little skinny soldiers of chaos and anarchy, creeping about in those low riders and beat autos, you see them in the street, they look you right in the eye, sitting on the stoop, and their gaze is cold, b, their gaze is fucking freezing" (23). Listening to himself is a lot like eavesdropping on the building's inhabitants—"one of the trickiest things was to identity the voices, who was talking, what were they thinking?" (166).

JoJo has within him both the voice that belongs and the one that does not, but what really aggravates the dilemma is that he cannot escape these voices rising in the psychic window well. He knows he is in *this* world, but that "there's another world, a world outside our world, for tv and movie personalities, politicians and sports heroes"—those who have the mobility to move out of realities into the dream worlds of mass imagery. JoJo is no more free than the man who threw his baby out a window; "in today's climate they blame it on drugs," JoJo muses, "but who knows. . . . Maybe his handcuffs didn't fit" (235). JoJo is a bit like that man, handcuffed to this neighborhood, at liberty without being free.

The poor, of course, are not only poor but nonwhite. Blacks, Puerto Ricans, and Native Americans live on either end of the street, their "[iron eyes, all bearing down on the last outpost, the fresh blood green horns sliced up like little scraps of meat. And, I wonder,] those boys, bro, they don't never smile at me" (104). But the key figure here is a wonderfully conceived character, Carl DeJesus, a Puerto Rican who is, under mysterious circumstances, burned out of his apartment. The only Hispanic in the building, he "looks like Che" Guevara "and knows it," uses it in his battle to keep dealers and junkies out of his building and his gym and, during the novel's main action, in his bitterness at the white gentrifiers who start trying to collect rent from him and, he thinks, eventually burn him out. "It was," we learn, "a Puerto Rican building when the corporation took over," and, when it assumed the landlord's debts as part of the purchase, "no one realized the better part of that was DeJesus, not money" (97). He is a debt because he recognizes neither a landlord nor legal documents, but only his own rights as someone living there, protecting the building, raising his family. Outside of the exploitative order, he is a black hole in its inequitable system of exchange. It is his resistance to the gentrifiers of his building—he sabotages many of their efforts—that leads to arson and murder.

The racial current is steady in the novel. DeJesus's cousin says in the first chapter, "You don't want nobody but white people" (3). Certainly JoJo can with appropriate irony read through his own relief at finding Velma's Play School for his daughter: "Otherwise, where were we going to send Constance? Into the projects with all those disadvantaged kids? All those poor kids? All those black kids? All those Puerto Ricans?" (5). And he complains, when DeJesus shows no sign of respecting the settlement agreement he has signed with the corporation (he has been paid to give up his claim to his apartment), that "the guy's an animal! Why can't he subscribe to the same standards of civilization that we do?" (9). There may be some irony in these comments, but if so it is playing off racism as the ground rules of the street game. Brown must yield to white, a principle the police first tacitly then materially support when they enter the neighborhood in force to clean it up for its new white gentry.

There is indeed room for irony in JoJo's implication in racism, because his own family has experienced anti-Semitism. Grandfather Greenfield is supposed to have fled Hungary because the army did not serve kosher food, and JoJo's father masked his Jewishness while in the army to protect himself from those who "hated jews" even though they had never seen one. But economics guarantees JoJo's response as surely as it does that of Benny, son of the Hispanics from whom JoJo buys the apartment, who picks up his educated parents' sense of class superiority to the blue-collar DeJesus. Benny returns after deserting from a South American army, having become a self-styled commando, the "modern warrior" with "no conscience" (191), and seems to befriend DeJesus's son, Segundo. When Benny lived in the building, he had feuded with Segundo; they even shot at each other. But Benny courts the younger boy, only to lead him across building tops to one jump too many.

If "white is might, right?" (213) serves as one of the battle slogans in what is also an economic war, gender becomes another factor confusing the picture. Macho homophobia collides with gays and lesbians and, again, JoJo is in the middle insofar as he harbors some anxieties about his maleness. He protests too much, perhaps, when Annabelle buys him one of the first dresses made for men, wants at one point to feel as pregnant as Annabelle, and, as he takes over more and more of the parental role after the birth of his daughter, realizes he has come to recognize himself not in *Sports Illustrated* or *Gentlemen's Quarterly*, but in the women's magazines at the doctor's office and the supermarket. These moments of vicarious mild transsexuality are juxtaposed to his obvious enjoyment of Annabelle, his (at least mental) strutting in street-tough style, and his own ambivalence to the gays in his building and to the lesbians across the street.

JoJo's ambivalence, not a very strongly developed theme, perhaps has more to do with the general vitiation of his belief in himself than with any serious exploration of fluid gender definitions. The point is how very *un*suburban we find his experiences, with all the conventions that normalize suburban life "up for debate" or for violent enforcement rather than functioning quietly, under the surface, homogenizing experiences. JoJo lives in what suburbia is designed to repress, as if he experienced the unconscious of that suburban mind-set in which the desire for green fields contends with the raw forces of sexuality, race, money, power, and the other blind impulses of the "red haze." The neighborhood is what JoJo calls a "pre-melting pot where people start maybe to get used to each other, but mostly what they do is just boil over" (213), their differences too great to disappear, the economics too unrelenting. As we have seen in a passage already quoted, that boiling over—a social apocalypse in which dreams collapse into violent realities—is what JoJo seems to think is coming in our children's lifetime.

The threat of that apocalypse increases as a middle ground becomes more obviously untenable, and JoJo's inability to connect between the differences within himself is an internal version of the city's isolation of this neighborhood: "The M14 bus runs up Avenue D, the toughest street in America, according to the *New York Times*. At Fourteenth Street the bus makes a left and goes cross town. One day there will be a link between the rich section of town and the poor. My grandmother said they were saying the same thing when she first moved here more than seventy-five years ago. But she doesn't live here now" (9). You cannot solve the contradictions in the American experience, but you can try to repress them by leaving them behind. But only if you are lucky somehow. JoJo has left them behind as he writes this book, but not happily. Indeed, he seems to have compiled the novel "sitting in the penitentiary," sentenced, it appears, at least for arson in burning out DeJesus, perhaps also for drugs, and perhaps also as an accomplice with Benny in Segundo's murder. We are not told directly because the precise nature of the crime is less relevant than the juridical decision that JoJo deviates in too many ways from the suburban norm and that he bears in himself too many of the contradictions he is supposed to repress. JoJo is symbolically and then materially incarcerated behind the various socially determined bars to free movement in the novel, including race, class, gender, and politics (his sister's death yet another emblem of pointless martyrdom in an ambiguous cause).

JoJo lives, in other words, in that immigrant quarter, that frontier town, that is the point of national origin, a psychological zone neither here nor there, past nor present, native nor alien. Its inhabitants are richer than before but poorer than the privileged suburban world, struggling to take responsibility under conditions that do not allow the connection between intentions or aspirations and consequences. They live in the gap between the hyperreality that Steven Spielberg's crew builds when it comes into the neighborhood to film *Batteries Not Included* and the realities that cannot be resolved in ninety minutes of careful plotting.

It is no wonder that *Kill the Poor* is both continuous as it follows JoJo's experiences and the mystery of arson and murder and, at the same time, an anthology of tales about the other world in the Lower East Side. "Reality" happens all over the place at once, its jagged edges in this particular world cutting through the mental blocks we try to erect, the personal narratives we try to inscribe, the tissue of beliefs, desires, and principles we substitute for the food chain on which these characters occupy a decidedly vulnerable position. Similarly, Rose's chapters mix slices of time in often very rapid cuts racing back and forth over the limited span of the main story, as well as over the timeless recycling of the immigrant and frontier experiences. The effect is to capture well the contradictory, dislocating collisions among spots of time that do *not* reveal stable entities in either the individual or the collective psyche. It is a novel that tells us stories to undo the smooth suburban feature-length resolution of contradictions that do not, for Rose, go away so easily.

When JoJo comes into his cell, he is asked the standard question:

"What you in for, bro?" the Avenue E boy ask me.

I say it don't matter. "Don't ask. I'm innocent."

"Ain't we all, blood," he says. "Ain't we motherfuckin' all."
(296)

Rose takes many other potshots in the novel—at the poseurs in the art world, at the nearly criminal negligence of Spielberg's social readings in a movie he films in the neighborhood, at slumlords and police policies and politicians and yuppies, and at the lawyers and do-gooders living off the poor. And Rose has whole galleries of characters whose fates epitomize the novel's themes, such as the punk Scarlet, who tells JoJo, "I was once straight, Joe. I really was. Looking for something—just, calm" (166), but who is anything but that now, or Annabelle, who, as an immigrant herself, feels the gap between her expectations and American reality—"nothing is as I thought it would be" (143).

Perhaps Annabelle's response epitomizes the ultimate suburban ambush, the reminder that we share more with JoJo than we know how to remember, more of the final confusion of innocence and guilt, victimization and violence, dreaming and failure, memory and repression, than our usual ways of thinking equip us to understand. When we talked together, Rose spoke of his love for American writers, particularly James Fenimore Cooper and Herman Melville. "At one point I definitely wanted to write novels of that kind," he said. I am not at all sure that he hasn't, that JoJo's memories of his time on Avenue E don't constitute the work of one important member in the family history of American romancers who mix fact and fancy only to discover the final ambiguity of the national experience.

JoJo's real problem is not that he is both white and Jewish, or gentrifier and underclass, or male and maternal, or antidrug and drug user; it is that he can be neither the socially privileged term nor its oppressed contrary. The repetition in his own life of the national originary experience of immigration and the frontier makes him a function of that primary movement of social *différance*. Scott's middle ground is replaced by a rather postmodern middle groundlessness in which JoJo finds himself living the existential deferral and the ideological spacing implicit in that *différance*. What Rose succeeds in doing is to let us all back in on that "nonoriginary origin" which is eschatologically real, existentially devastating, and deeply repressed in the national political unconscious.

The introductory background chapter of Rose's second novel, tentatively entitled "The Sunshine of Paradise Alley," appears in the *Between C & D* anthology Jerry Howard brought out for Penguin. The novel follows the twists and turns of some sensational nineteenth-century murders involving literary figures, and it takes place against the backdrop of the gangs that roamed the streets with set fees for "Punching," "Ear Chawed Off," and, for the deadly serious, "Doing the big job." It is a book to look forward to, because we have every reason to suppose that, again, Rose will himself be "doing the big job" on the suburban repression of the ambiguities in our national experience. The materials are a promising blend of the worlds of literature, wealth, and street history, for Rose follows the trail of the murdered darling of the literati, Samuel Colt's wealthy brother, who is jailed for murdering his printer, and the tangle of high and low life that mixed on those streets more than a century ago.

Right as we ended our conversation, Rose leaned back in his chair, reflecting on the luxury of the National Endowment for the Arts grant that gave him the time off to write *Kill the Poor:*

> I just tried to fit everything in between whatever else I was doing, then got an NEA a few years ago for the book, and I was able to take off some time and actually do it. And I sat down and had a manuscript. I could not believe it. It had been in my filing cabinet for four years and I'd been adding pages, and I sat down and said I was going to work and I had a really big stack, four hundred pages, and I began to shuffle them. And so I had a book. I was really happy when I finished it. I had done all these other books, and they all had sections that appealed to me. But I had forced so much onto them to make them into "a novel." And this book seemed to become a novel of its own volition, and it's much purer to me. It tasted much sweeter. I was really happy. I cried when I finished it and it was in front of me and I was a Writer. A dream.

### Catherine Texier: Touching a Nerve

Catherine Texier was born in Brittany but raised just outside Paris. She studied English and American culture at the University of Paris, and first came to New York in the late sixties. After a year in South America and stint in Paris, she finished out the seventies in Montreal, where she wrote for feminist presses and produced a study of prostitution and her first novel, *Chloé l'Atlantique*. She describes the latter as "a very straightforward novel about growing up in the sixties." She likes the discipline afforded by writing in a second language; she likes living in New York, where the fiction scene seems much more lively than that in Paris; and she likes approaching fiction through the discipline and close observation of her journalism. It is unlikely, then, that she would have been very happy in an M.F.A. program. Not that she is among those who vilify the workshop system; the contrary is true. When we talked in her apartment, she was quick to note that "American writers have the reputation of having very good craft—they are really *good* writers in that sense." Nor is the obstacle simply that her experiences have immersed her in a different set of cultural codings than she would have encountered among her M.F.A. classmates.

The reason is implicit in how Texier answered my question about what she wanted to *do* as a writer. "I want to touch a nerve," she told me. "I feel the plot and narration seem to cover up something. Something rawer, something underneath, something that makes people react or scream, something to do with death, or sex— you know, it seems so grand to say these things." And so she eludes the interviewer again, disavowing any "theoretical" inclination and preferring, she says, writing that comes out "abrupt" or even "aggressive" to her Parisian editor's ears as she works on the translation of *Love Me Tender* (Penguin, 1987) into French. The "grand" talk about things is replaced in her writing by experience as grittily immediate as the Lower East Side streets on which she lives.

At one point in *Love Me Tender,* Texier articulates a narratology of the void evident everywhere around you when you walk around the old immigrant tenements from the river west toward St. Marks Place and the increasingly gentrified district around Astor Place. In the middle of the night, a woman sits cross-legged on her bed, clutching her body, "pouring rain like a tidal wave crashing against the windows" (185). There is character, then, and character responsive to emblematic events, such as a storm. But "there is no story. Only cycles repeating themselves ad infinitum. No beginning no end just voices clashing. Too many voices too many voices. The soft one the violent one. A knife through the liver it takes and then you gasp. The little girl in the street with her Mickey Mouse from Disney World. When you said we met in Paris at *Les Deux Magots* in 1933, I thought, for a brief moment, that I remembered it. I ache for all these other lives" (185–86).

Violence, vulnerability, and the ache for remembered and adjacent lives all crowd into consciousness. They are the "voices clashing" from the selves within and from the many outer worlds colliding in urban energy. No metaphysical story holds these worlds together, nothing adds them up into a well-made cosmos that makes sense, has a theme, lays out experience on a line leading somewhere. "Only cycles" repeat an almost physiological fate for characters and wear away cultural illusions that, as Texier says of narration, are meant to "cover up something" difficult for us to put into words.

Such cycles abound in *Love Me Tender*—Salvine's immigration from France is retraced by Lulu; Mystique's career in erotic dance begins to repeat itself in Lulu's life; Mystique fears that she will, like her mother, develop cancer; Julian is perhaps the most difficult, but still one in a series, of young lovers for Salvine; Julian is also a younger, more sinister version of Henry; Myra Schneider links in

Lulu's mind with Isadora Duncan and Tillie the bag lady and perhaps also herself; such social occasions as costume parties recycle periodically; and numerous life and weather cycles from nature turn through the events of the novel. But the characters feel that all of these cycles turn around a center of gravity, and Texier tells us much about just what comprises that center.

Toward the end of our interview, Texier gazed past the weathered brick walls through the window overlooking a street of buildings, some of which were entirely rubble, some collapsed façades, some abandoned by landlords and held by squatters, some trying to make it back to the land of the living with varying degrees of energy and wealth. The question had something to do with getting "energy" from these very nonsuburban streets:

> I think it's New York that does something to me. I really had an
> incredible shock when I came here in 1969, and somehow those
> two years I lived here were extremely important in my life.
> There's something there; whatever chemical thing that happened
> in coming here from Paris *exploded*. I keep digging in there. So
> when I walk down the street it triggers something. It made a hole
> in me when I first came here.

That "hole" is the cavern over which suburbia is built, and Texier's remarkable novel devotes itself to "digging in there" and quarrying out what we have repressed. But this is as "grand" as Texier will get in character; you must read the fiction to see what she means here.

One of *Love Me Tender*'s central lines concludes a dream sequence triggered in a woman by a younger version of herself who has visited her. Life in the dream is "the game of the last chance," played by wandering through buses parked at the curb and looking for a sex partner—"As if sensuality becomes stronger as despair gets closer" (112). It is not quite clear how "As if" functions in the sentence; its conditionality compromises any universal claims of what follows. But that formula describes very well the rising tempo of emotion in all the characters as they plunge toward an ending that articulates this structural principle rather than a linear resolution of complication or contradiction.

If Texier is not describing the universal human condition, she is indeed marking its contemporary urban form. "Sensuality" in the equation includes the full range of libidinal investments from sexuality to the various dreamselves that characters struggle to embody. "Despair" means experiencing the effects of time in several ways. As *history*, these characters move in difficult social, political, and economic settings. As *memory*, individuals struggle to compose a self in retrospect against the persistence of unsettling past failures. As the *body* lapses from any conscious ideal into the involuntary states of disease, pregnancy, or aging, characters experience the physiological limits of time for which their media ideals have poorly suited them. And finally, as *failure*, these characters fall short of expectations, dream images, or simply that fine competitive edge. Each of these forms of despair punctures the surface of illusion created by décor, ambiance, gesture, and attitude—a surface designed, like narrative, to "cover up" the void we encounter in contesting time for our Being.

The two zones clash or, for much of *Love Me Tender*, run on parallel tracks that the characters struggle to keep separate:

> Beautiful Lulu, rose-bud-rose-nanan, rose-bud-bonbon-candy-acidule-de-vache. Peppermint-candy-a-la-menthe-poivree poivrot wino lying on the Bowery, unshaven, in front a cheap whiskey.
> Worlds/words slipping against each other. (67)

"Realities" and language, French and English, childhood and maturity, innocence and sensuality, beauty and Bowery. The novel is about the disruption of the well-made surface of American life when zones collide and, worse, when each turns up inside the other.

In the opening section, for example, Lulu and Julian have a steamy encounter while through the window drifts a loud and profane argument that ends with a shot, a body on the sidewalk, and sirens. But the violence outside is also inside; Julian calls her "slut," requires her to "dress up" for him in the stereotypical spike-heeled outfit of sex gaming, wants "to tie you up and give it to you real good," makes "his nails run quick lines of pain down her shoulder blades," slaps her. Julian's response is to ignore what is outside, a repression he achieves by drowning her questions about it and finally pulling her back down to the bed.

Sex seems to function much of the time as a means of submersion, a way of sinking below the level of any wider consciousness. Salvine, an experienced player, withdraws periodically into solitude, "emptying herself" of social residues and arguing that "the New York merry-go-round is more of an escape" than is her ritual of purification. We see ample evidence of the sexual carousel in such sections as "Halloween Night in Hell," in which sex serves as an at best problematic medium for interpersonal relations. For one thing, costuming is an important mask to the mundane identities of the participants, whether at Halloween balls or transvestite bars or simply in the ritualized garbs of spiked heels, leather, décolletage, or *Vogue* elegance (depending upon one's game).

For another thing, the personal identity of one's partners is less important than their distinctive contribution to sensory pleasure. Henry tapes orgasms to use with other lovers later the same day and is always searching for new playmates. Lulu juggles Mario, Julian, and Henry according to her needs for the ethnic, the sinister, or the power spicings each adds. Mystique rotates lovers biweekly, it seems, and Salvine appears to have purchased a series of young Julians for entertainment value.

The economic factors are not insignificant either. When Julian bridles a bit at Salvine's exertion of control over him, she undermines him with deadly accuracy, making reference first to her own marriage to a millionaire: "Keeping men so happy they will cover you with presents and leave you their fortune when they die is an art that is almost lost. She hands him a cup of frothy coffee and pulls out warm croissants from the microwave oven. Men are getting better at it than women, she adds, giving Julian a sharp look" (41). When Salvine points out that "you need me more than I need you," she also makes clear that what he hears as "a threat" is actually "a fact" (134). But Julian is as much the "dangerous type" (127) as Mystique takes him to be, and, when he makes bitter cracks about severance pay, Salvine hits him (142).

Salvine's force does not fully pervade and turn this relationship, however, until she takes full advantage of Julian's flirtation with bondage and with her as a maternal figure (he likes to bury his head in her breasts, and thinks of her penthouse apartment as "being inside a womb" [40]). She whips him until "drops of blood pearl on the surface of the skin," reducing him to perfect compliance with her will as the economically and, it seems, politically (or militarily?) superior force. In an effort to stop the beating, his promises progress from her favorite sexual practices to worship, love, and, finally, to the winner, respect. The scene is a brutal reversal of sexual violence perpetrated upon women; for example, Lulu is raped when barely an adult, is forced to submit to painful anal intercourse, and complies with Henry's compulsion for "asserting his power over women in public spaces."

The sequence of scenes between Salvine and Julian suggests the failure of their effort to make sexuality serve them as "an escape" from poverty and boredom back home in Poitiers and from murder and earning a livelihood in New York. They are both sufficiently bored to keep striving for something dangerous in sex (Julian himself for Salvine, sadomasochism for Julian). The economic constraints both have escaped from in a literal sense still shape their relationships. And the violence that reigns on the streets outside is quoted in their coital poetics.

For Henry, sexuality becomes the focal stylization of Being. He shares a fatal attraction to the stylized image with Lulu's earlier lover Raphael, who becomes a filmmaker, validates himself by making it to the glossy-photo pages, but then finally fails by repeating his own image. Lulu exults in a review that lambastes his new film as "a shallow and pretentious, self-referential and self-congratulatory exercise which is all style and no content" (210). The review could apply equally, however, to Henry's sexual performances.

Henry paints stylized female bodies, "obsessed with the poses of sex," a phrase anything but innocent. That is, he himself poses as the master playboy, using his perfection of that pose and his wealth to coerce women into playing out his almost trite scenarios—"no panties allowed," frequent sex in public places, and a dizzying pace both in terms of frequency and of sheer numbers of partners.

Henry even has "a new project, suggested to him by a publisher friend, a kind of erotic daybook, an artist's book, printed in a limited edition, on expensive creamy parchment and sold at a high price to selected collectors" (29). Texier is having a bit of fun with the genre, no doubt, but at the same time suggesting how thoroughly sexuality can pass into an elaborate and exhausting ritual of egoism. Even the insatiable Lulu removes his hand when he announces the marriage he plans, but more devastating is what she does *not* tell him when she leaves to be alone. "Why not the truth. That his age showed. And his prick not so glorious anymore wrinkled under his potbelly" (31). Henry has succeeded so well at assimilating himself to the commodified image of sexuality that, once consumed, he is simply a middle-aged organism with no further utility.

The dances that Mystique, Lulu, and their friends perform at the Blue Night are just as stylized and have the same effect of commodifying them—though this is less exceptional for women than for men. When a lesbian couple makes the mistake of being expressive to each other in front of the audience, they are almost fired as items unfit for (heterosexual) consumption. Mystique and Lulu have carefully orchestrated stances, costumes, and movements, which cue all the stereotyped signifiers of sexuality to be found in the erotic media; Mystique's historical numbers, for example, are more "pastiche" than reproduction, more X-rated Disneyland than ideological critique.

Even at its most positive in *Love Me Tender*, sexuality is closer to the coke and dope on the streets than to any form of "higher" relation. For Lulu, certain men have something she needs like a fix: "What makes her horny in men is . . . life running through them and flickering in odd shapes and moods" (80). "She doesn't know what love is," but she knows that Mario has "fire running in his veins. She can smell it on his breath" (91). Lulu shoots up with that fire: "When they make love, it's all smells and juices and textures subtly changing, skin arousing skin, the constant shifting of tastes and flavors" (152). However, this relatively positive evocation of sex is shaded by how soon afterward Lulu tires of her "spicy" exotic lover. Apparently the "fire" of his "hot curry" sweat wears off once the food value is extracted and she resurfaces from so full an immersion in the sensory.

The trouble with sensuality as an antidote to despair is that the body eventually rubs out the glossy surface of all these scenarios of

barely sublimated power, and what remains are the vulnerable bodies that take a beating in a variety of literal and metaphorical ways.
For example, Lulu becomes pregnant and is fully alarmed that her
body "doesn't belong to her" anymore, that "Nature is borrowing it
from her as a receptacle to process its young, as she pleases" (191).
Her body "is out of control, does its little personal gig without
asking for her permission" (187). What frightens Lulu is not really
the child so much as the disruption of her erotic scenarios with her
lovers. Starring in her own film, touring exotic sets south of the
border with her fiery Latin lover, she is yanked back to the physiological facts of life. Pregnancy erases the margins of the frame by
which her scenarios manage and control experience by repressing
what lies beyond them. She is exposed.

The more fearful exposure is disease, something Mystique and
her mother must face when the latter is diagnosed as having cancer:
"You don't see them. They just go. Their bodies removed. Their
memories hushed" (159). Disease is another radical demystification
of the youth cult's effacement of the physical—that is to say, its
replacement of real bodies with the media image of bodies in Sola-
flex and Diet Pepsi ads, perfect machines that are crafted objects
honed in weight rooms and aerobics halls. Texier's passage figures
the diseased as *desaparecidos* in the image culture.

For women, especially, aging is the inexorable demystifier of
sensuality, and all the women in this novel are haunted by the spread
of the lines of fate across their faces. For beings who are commodity
objects, aging shifts them quickly, as in Lulu's dream of Myra
Schneider, from Isadora Duncan dancing with perfect grace (140) to
Tillie the bag lady poking the refuse heaps (189, 211). As Lulu is
only twenty-five, it is significant that she anticipates Salvine's obsession with circles under her eyes or Mystique's "near-panic at
time closing door after door every day" (20).

If sensuality is perhaps the first resource upon which these
characters draw, the artifice of self-dramatizing, of performance, is
another. We have seen such artifice pervade sexuality. But even as
these characters struggle to get into words the anxiety they feel in
sustaining themselves amidst urban pressures, they strike repeatedly into the crisis of illusionary or simulated Being. The performance is not working, or barely working, or clearly about to fail.

The great horror is the normal. Even at her most depressed,
Mystique is clear about her flight from her native "O-hi-o": "But
now she doesn't remember why she fought so hard against a straight
life. Everything seems to have blurred, the acceptable and the disgusting not so clearly defined any more, except maybe her early
nightmare: ending up married to a doctor, with three kids in a suburban split-level" (15). She may feel her public image slipping from
Mystique to mistake, but she feels the biggest nightmare lies be-

hind; the trouble is, a bigger one could lie ahead the moment her energy gives out.

The passage continues: "She's come to see her life as fate rather than a struggle and yet she keeps struggling. And she still dreams of bursting out on the scene one day and she still wheels and deals and contacts and talks her way into potential deals, smokey projects, half-promises, without them she would be a middle-aged cabaret dancer stuck in-between, betraying her own axiom, you've got to go all the way, not stop in the middle, it's the most dangerous place: that's where you really get crushed" (15). Life as "fate" means that all the historical realities riding the novel's parallel track finally determine individual reality despite the struggle, and the main effect of that struggle is to carry a few lines further the fiction she puts over on herself. There is no place *but* the middle.

The sense of being in the middle between unrelenting reality and personal fiction shows up repeatedly in *Love Me Tender*. At a light-hearted moment, Lulu grabs Mystique and says in a rush: "But you were a product of your imagination. And you still are right now, Lulu says, turning the tv on to MTV with the sound down. Let's go through your clothes. Let's get dressed tonight. Come on, let's make ourselves into sixties bad girls" (98). Lulu is mastering the image repertoire through MTV and carries Mystique along in her youthful enthusiasm.

Other characters are far more serious about evading despair through the costumed life. Even Lulu can talk a tough streak about this process:

> In New York you create your own reality. You make yourself a set
> and costumes and you launch your life. If it doesn't work, you
> start all over with a different plot, a different set of characters. It's
> totally artificial. A man-made product. Sometimes beautiful. But
> unreal. It doesn't take certain things into account: like being
> born, death, aging, the process of living. It's a crazed merry-go-
> round, with bodies flying off the side when they can't hold onto
> the horses anymore. (95)

Lulu sounds as if she is fresh from a Bogart film, but her sense of the danger, fluidity, artifice, theatricality, and utter despair in New York life capture the novel's central interplay of the libidinal and despair.

Almost every character lives a version of this double life. Salvine, recalling her youth for Lulu, says: "For me New York was the world. It was the center. . . . It was the stuff of my dreams" (109). Henry relies less on forties' films and more on adventure novels for his version: "To want to make your own life and become your own hero. I supposed that's what I wanted when I came here. Build the life of my dream" (130). Salvine is sad, Henry speaks in the past tense, and Lulu, in another rush of rich prose, sees "Manhattan like an ocean liner adrift in the middle of the Atlantic, never reaching its port. . . . We're all thrown together on this phantom ship, hallucinating, without connection to the other world. It's a trip from which we'll never come back" (130).

All three characters share something with Mystique's sense that this whole self-dramatizing venture is a "cold-blooded, rational choice" in favor of a "red-hot optimism like a lid on white wan despair" (166). Lulu shows both heat and despair when she finds living in New York "like being on coke twenty-four hours a day" (183) and tells Mystique that "I don't think I can live up to my own expectations," her own plot. "You come here to measure yourself" as performer on an unforgiving stage. Mystique blames the rush to perform on the whole culture; we struggle, she says, "where we were told we were supposed to get to. Success. Money. Beauty. Men. Women" (25). But these destinations keep shifting; as Lulu says later, "you have to know how to play with signs . . . but instead of offering well-established codes, New York demands that you be ahead of constantly changing ones" (182). Constantly changing with the pace of consumption, the codes measure the steady approach of despair that eats out the imagery the way that cancer consumes Mystique's mother.

The headlong rush to escape the suburban may well be futile; as Mystique says, we are all "more homebodies than we'd like to admit" (76). More insidious is to "hold yourself responsible for your own fate," to believe that "you precipitated [failure] with your negative moods" (132). That is the barb on the ideological hook of the American dream, and to convince a failed dreamer that internal causes are to blame masks the more systemic reasons for that failure. If our only space is Mystique's middle at which we are to be crushed, and if those with wealth (such as Salvine) or power (such as Henry) are the ones who can hold on the longest to pleasing illusions, then the American dream is only part of what is a myth. Lulu says to Henry: "It's weird. There's still a sense that things are up for grabs here, that nobody really has a birthright to own this place. But it's not up for grabs, really, right? It mean it's a myth. We're all like flies blinded by the lamp hanging on the porch" (131). Someone else already owns the porch, and the ideology of individual rights and freedoms has shaded over into a faulty metaphysics gone decadent in media-hyped plots and porno desires.

The parallel track of history is inescapable, because it runs down both sides of the libidinal ties along which these characters are skipping, hedging them in and keeping them precisely in the vulnerable middle that Mystique dreads. Lulu knows the story of the fly who swam in the milk so long it was sitting on a pile of butter, but she also knows "the milk never seems to turn into butter" in New York. What *does* happen is the long series of crimes in the clippings Lulu collects, perhaps to keep herself from believing too much, and the crimes that appear periodically through the novel—murders, rapes, stabbings, and worse. Bums smell like "fermented flesh" (26), a bag lady is exterminated along with the cockroaches in her squatter apartment, characters are paid to marry so that someone can get a green card, Lulu's racism and classism suffuse her relationship with Mario, people take sexual and verbal abuse to hang onto their jobs, Lulu has another collection of clippings about nuclear war (she dreams of the rockets' red glare and tacks on her walls beautified color pictures of mushroom clouds). History does not go away, despite the characters' efforts to repress it or contain it as decoration for the walls.

Personal history does not go away either. Some characters wish it would; Salvine "is a rich woman with a past that she keeps to herself, because in the days when she was young there were certain things that a woman didn't do" (47). Others wish they could pin down a version that would satisfy. *Love Me Tender*'s most powerful image for the misbegotten self is that every woman in it experiences an either tragic or, worse, absent mother. Each woman is driven compulsively to replace the failed mother-daughter relation, as if redoing so primary a relation might generate a missing core. Hence Salvine hires Lulu to be a communicative daughter, Mystique and Lulu seek each other out, and Lulu has reveries about older mother surrogates such as Myra Schneider (whose child is institutionalized) and Tillie. Most tenuous is Lulu's case, because she seems unsure whether her mother died in childbirth or was committed to an asylum. Lulu's repressive aunt "kept rewriting history to suit her needs," and Lulu, without memory of her mother, "keep[s] inventing her" (71), and even in her childhood "kept looking for my mother" (122), dressing in her clothes, and imagining scenarios at the birthing clinic, the asylum, and so forth. Lulu keeps trying to weave a vicarious experience of her family's past which will make her feel right.

Mystique wishes she could edit convincingly her own life history: "There is no happy end. I wind back the film, reread the book, from the middle up. Erase and start all over again" (162). Mystique wants to recapture what *was*, at one moment, an apparent reality, to take memory and use it to "fix" the present. She wants photographs because "memory distorts," but Lulu reminds her that "so do photos" and that it is an "as if" that "life was more intense then, when you were younger" (97). She cannot fix the fluidity or hold off despair by finding an "old you" in a "box of memorabilia" or a retrospective narrative—only in performance (Lulu gets Mystique to stop looking at sixties' photographs and to start dressing herself in costumes of, and thus being, the sixties).

"There is no nostalgia in New York. The past dies everyday. Murdered, demolished, burned, abandoned" (186). Despite characters' efforts to make use of memory as they make use of performance, Salvine's memories of her adolescent lover recycle constantly, Lulu can never reach the absent mother to displace her disciplinarian aunt, and Mystique can neither edit out her mother's death nor substitute the stable form of a photograph for the cinematic existence in which she is always necessarily in the middle.

If the picture-perfect forms of sensuality and of memory fail to keep despair at bay, what do these characters learn when the games stop, the performance is in intermission, the lover leaves and they sit alone in the night? Youth is experienced as pure possibility. For the young Salvine, for example, her older lover "opened a door for" her which led to a fully indeterminate space, but one that feels better than being "held" or "owned." "I've felt the void when you're not here" (44), she tells him, and the youthful Salvine supposes that the void is simply the free zone of experience ready to fill her emptiness with meaning.

After a bit of experience, however, the women of *Love Me Tender* are haunted by a sense that the void persisting within is at least in part culturally induced. Lulu writes in her diary: "I am a hole. I am completely hollow inside with limbs quivering at the periphery of myself. Each man who makes me wet shoots a hole through my guts and then I leak words of love and all my insides spill out. Us girls are hollowed out when we grow up so that we always crave for a man" (86). Woman is trained to be a sexual orifice, leaking the (male) lovers' discourse, inevitably left the next morning "a big gaping wound." Mystique also wonders, of a man she is about to pick up, if "his lips would close her wounds," as if, despite everything she has seen, there were still the hope that the romance idyll's hero might appear. Woman is also vulnerable to becoming merely commodity, as Lulu feels she is for Salvine when she hires Lulu to bring "bits of herself she just gave away to be consumed by her," playing back her memories for Salvine (to help her relive her own or to help her replace hers?).

Lulu takes this image of the hole beyond the level of gender to the virtually ontological when she writes: "It was dark. There was a sense of perpetual darkness. Life wasn't radiant and spitfiring, it was deep muddy waters slowly flowing under concrete slabs, often eddying around entangled masses of weeds, obsessions swirling like twigs sucked in a vortex. . . . I was a hole at the center of the vortex" (126). At such a moment, Lulu is close to dropping her zeal to perform, to wing it around the porch light, and to face the flow of the repressed deep beneath the concrete slabs of her internalized version of the city. It is a vortex whose center is not some core of meaning, but a hole, a capacity to see from a perspective made finally not by the "I" doing the seeing, but by the cultural forces swirling around it: "It was distorted faces as if photographed through a wide-angle lens coming at you with thick lips and stretched-out eyes. The faces closed in on you threateningly, their stares pinning you like a dead butterfly in a natural history museum case." The "thick lips" belong, perhaps, to the aunts and rapists who have revealed the rawest, most insistent forms of cultural conditioning, their eyes stretched out to span her history of lapses and failures, still threatening her from the unconscious with the norms, injunctions, roles, and constraints of her particular vortex in the cultural waters.

It is no wonder that Lulu "happens to exist in different modes quasi-simultaneously. As far back as she can remember she has perceived herself in fragments at sharp angles with one another, like the facets on the crystal Corinne gave her years ago" (106). The "hole" of her self is bounded by the infinity of narrative and normative lines by which the culture crystallizes individual subjects.

Indeed, the only way to experience this ontological void is when all the mechanisms of repression pause, all the designs against despair freeze midweave, and all the insistence of sensuality abates long enough for us to focus bravely on that "inappreciable moment of time in which we step over the threshold of the invisible." From Joseph Conrad's *Heart of Darkness*, the book's epigraph is echoed in Lulu's words in her unsent letter to Raphael, a domineering former boyfriend:

> I topple into the abyss, but . . . it's a void, no gravity, the heart
> spins, the void is inside of me, spiraling out at high speed, the
> blackness spreads, it's a feeling of having been torn apart, of only
> existing in the fall, the only moment when the self actually expe-
> riences power (the puppet having had its strings cut off), but it's a
> power of chaos, or a chaotic power. (60)

The passage recounts the inability to recall the "long lost elusive dream . . . the short-lived ecstasy of harmony" before "mind/body/ soul [were] disjointed." Lulu may not be able to make full use of this insight, but she brushes with the knowledge of the self "only existing in the fall," cut loose from the cultural strings to swirl in the final formlessness of anything beyond the physiological. A "power of chaos" is an austere discipline to master when the individual has already borne multiple wounds and when the whole cultural apparatus keeps renewing its promise of a center, a fulfilled self just over the rainbow.

With so rich a sense of the meaning of despair, or at least of what is "despair" in the context of a culture that holds out a whole catalog of existential snake oils, it is no wonder that Texier's characters find the resources of sensuality so great a relief from the stark blackness of the vortex. Perhaps the ultimate extremes that are closing in on Mystique and the rest of the characters are the classic ones of physiology and metaphysics. But Texier's unsentimental, uncompromising, and utterly tactile rendering of these "grand" matters separates her work decisively from the host of late modernist raconteurs who still play around such terms, but without the courage to "keep digging" in the hole that our history, both social and personal, makes in the heart of suburbia.

### Patrick McGrath and the Postmodern Gothic

Patrick McGrath tells very cheerfully the tale of his three early novels, "written quickly and exuberantly, fairly thin and very playful," but so difficult to pigeonhole that his first agent "went lukewarm on me" when editors failed to recognize what they had. He is cheerful in part, no doubt, because times had already begun changing for him as we talked: his well-placed short stories, quite popular readings, and *Blood and Water and Other Tales* (Poseidon Press, 1988) were in the process of securing his reputation and, as it has turned out in the year since then, his economics as well. But even in these tales, which fairly zipped from McGrath to his agent to his editor, we can see some of the reasons why less astute agents and editors might at first be thrown a bit. McGrath's work disorients our expectations for the gothic with its lush blend of fabulist invention and elegant stylistic finesse. We see all the markers of someone who has sidestepped the brightly lit mainstream to work in the shadows of a marginal genre he further estranges through the witty and ironic turn he gives his beloved gothic tradition.

We could make the predictable observations about a writer raised in England by Irish parents, or about the five-year-old moved to the environs of Broadmoor mental hospital when his father became its superintendent. No doubt the Anglo-Irish ambiguities and the "Victorian gothic structure with fine red brick walls" exerted their respective pulls away from the England of the "middle-class lady writers of the thirties and forties" whom he nonetheless loves to read in the Virago Press reprints. Tales of England's most notorious psychotics must have mixed in interesting ways with the suburban social functions. Or we could nod with a smile at his own wry note that "I was educated by the Jesuits and I think once they've had their hand on you, you never quite forget it," a way of accounting for the wry skewing he gives the moralistic dimension of the gothic. That Jesuit hand is, one hopes, less lethal than "The Black Hand of the Raj," a piece of Indian conjuring that, as McGrath's story has it, grows from the head of a proper British imperialist and eventually strangles him. But *both* these hands have their grip upon McGrath's imagination, focusing his attention not only upon the culture's ruling metaphors for nature, the self, and the forms of language, but also upon the gothic mode's capacity for revenge against the hegemonic raj.

McGrath's career has become the project of turning the resources of this protean genre against society's evolution into what he calls "a hideously materialistic commercial culture." He shares with his fellow downtowners the sense "that the place is crumbling and falling apart and that the streets are full of desperately poor people." As if he were writing in the postapocalyptic era of Acker's *Empire of the Senseless*, McGrath turns the gothic into not only a renewed source of pleasure but also a means of documenting the decay and internal collapse that mark the culture's spiritual Armageddon. He also shares with the other writers in *Suburban Ambush* a mistrust "for received imagery" and for "the forms of middle-class or uptown fiction." The former shows in his work as systemic blinders to his characters' self-understanding; the latter as a suburban repression of the darker side of the social self.

What is distinctive, even unique, in McGrath's work is the specific strategy he adopts in turning fiction to the ends of ambuscade. We had been talking about his sense of the gothic tradition, and, when I pressed McGrath about his relationship to other writers working on the Lower East Side, he came back to their effort to escape the uptown mold in order to differentiate his own strategy:

> In Joel [Rose]'s writing or in Lynne Tillman's writing that impulse works out as a very careful, rather low-key style that does aim for clarity and accessibility. The same impulse in me pushes me toward an inflation of language to say that I can't trust language or standard fictive forms to do what I want to do. I've learned such things as that language is always rhetorical, it's always figurative, it carries meanings that are not clear on the surface but are thoroughly ideological, always deconstructible. And so my impulse is, rather than try to strip it down and get at a cleaner language, to take as the essence of language its essential trickiness, its essential unreliability for depicting the real. I exaggerate it, inflate it, until it all sort of implodes under its own weight and thereby creates a pastiche that becomes humorous because it is an exaggeration.

Like his peers, McGrath works in a poststructural age that some still think is "just theory." McGrath abandons the idyll of a clean or adequate language and—through his irony, his pastiches of gothic conventions, and his remarkable ear for style—develops a humorous version of the gothic which is deadly serious in its confrontation of the "essential trickiness" of both language and the culture that stands behind it.

Reviewers who miss this serious edge (one could, unkindly, adduce the examples) also miss the humor, especially when they complain that the genre of gothic is turning to camp. However, when the decorum of a generic rule system holds, what sustains it is a cultural consensus over its definitions of the light and the dark in that genre's pattern of illumination and shadow. This principle becomes especially important in the gothic genre because of its perennial linkages of the social and the hidden, the spoken and the repressed, patterns of light and shadow that go to the very roots of human subjectivity. When generic decorum breaks into pastiche, it is a sign that the world is changing indeed and that the trickiness and unreliability of cultural myths have become evolutionary liabilities. McGrath has only a guarded optimism about him. "I can't escape falling into metaphor," he observes, "so the best thing to do is not even to make the attempt, but instead to exaggerate the metaphor and make it ridiculous and somehow therefore to open it up."

The effort to open up linguistic and fictive systems is everywhere apparent in McGrath's work, from the hilariously effloresc- ing style (Ronald Firbank and Max Beerbohm are among his saints) to his transformation of the gothic from its originary spite for the church and the aristocracy into a reflexive critique of the medium and an amusing but uncompromised suspension of belief in the way we do business in the world. McGrath explores "reality-distorting states of mind" such as imagination, fever, dream, art, intoxication, and madness—perennial provinces of the gothic in its opposition to the reigning daylight logic of the culture. If, as McGrath argues (citing Rosemary Jackson and Tzvetan Todorov), "the gothic has two themes, transgression and decay," we can begin to see that transgression, for McGrath, involves crossing the boundaries of literary decorum, and decay involves the crumbling credibility of suburban attitudes toward social and individual life.

In his succinct oral treatise on the genre, McGrath said:

> Culture is organized along bipolar oppositions, and the gothic will always be moving toward the dark side, undercutting clarity, light, and reason in whatever form. And so the gothic will prefer to be dealing with a ruin rather than a sound structure, prefer to deal with a state of madness or addiction rather than with a state of sanity, prefer to deal with disease rather than health, with decadence rather than with morality, with death rather than with life, with some of the in-between as in the vampire or the ghost or the ghoul. So there's always this pushing over to the dark side.

McGrath offered a reading of George Romero's film *The Day of the Dead* as both standard Romero fare and a commentary on "the mindlessness of consumers homing in with some deep instinct toward the shopping mall" where the heroes are holed up against the zombie onslaught. The gothic "does enable you to go to the dark side," he concluded. "In any text there is something hidden that can be opened up, that which has been repressed, and it is the return of the repressed that the gothic is very good at." McGrath's version of suburban ambush is precisely this return of the socially and textually repressed in the life and fiction of the comfort culture.

If we divide the stories in *Blood and Water* under the two headings of transgression and decay, the former group will be seen "undercutting clarity, light, and reason" in the very models, mores, and artistic modes erected in order to manage darkness "in whatever form." McGrath has particular fun with Freudian materials not only because Freud's model remains the dominant one through which we understand psychological processes, but also because McGrath considers him a gothic writer: "He is always interested in that which is hidden, that which comes out in dreams, the archaeology of his whole project of digging down into the murky and grotesque things that have been submerged." Much as he loves Freud's writing, however, McGrath does not go easy on the master, especially in his debased forms as cocktail-party cliché or as an institutionalized professional toolkit.

"Ambrose Syme," for example, is a story about a Jesuit teacher, who, when his libido can no longer sublimate its energy in Latin poetry, murders and rapes a young boy. Caught between the fertility "masks and totems the old man [his rector, Father Mungo] had collected in Africa" and the ascetic "gaze of a large hanging Christ," Syme attempts to carry on indefinitely his record as "a textbook case of compulsory sublimation in the literary mode" (72, 71). The victim's body is discovered, however, and Syme is killed when he falls off the roof of an appropriately gothic tower while trying to retrieve the guiltily discarded trophy of the boy's underpants before the gutter cleaner gets them first. McGrath's twist on this relatively straightforward tale is twofold. The underpants are never noticed, even after the rain flushes them out; "the community, suspecting no evil, found none" (79). And the two deaths are never connected. The potential for high melodrama exists with Syme's classical erudition failing him as a mechanism of sublimation, and with his passionate transgression publishing itself in his white cotton "fetish." Both elements prove oddly irrelevant because the community cannot see what it does not expect to find. It is as if sublimation and fetishes could exist only elsewhere, as in Africa's exotica of masks and potent ritual. The twist is really to *our* expectations, though. We expect either the catastrophe of discovery or the off chance of eluding it; the catastrophic nondiscovery empties the moralism of the genre and makes the gap between passion and frames of thought the real site of the tale. It is we who hold the white spot of underwear at story's end, perhaps, having expected the daylight logic of evidence to lead the authorities directly to the culprit.

Also emptied, however, is the Freudian model McGrath described to me as that of "a hydraulic engineer of the mind." In "Ambrose Syme," he draws an analogy between Syme's libido and "the common refrigerator"—with rising fluids, compressors, and the libido-cooling discipline of the Latin poetry that Syme compulsively composes from adolescence on. McGrath makes unavoidable the metaphoricalness of the Freudian hydraulics but also, by splicing disparate pieces of the narrative together, the magician's misdirection that metaphor achieves. What both the Freudian model and the murder genre fail to explain is the connection between Father Mungo returning from the Zambezi basin with his fertility-cult deities, Syme returning from the bog with little Tommy Blackburn's underpants (Syme has, significantly enough, snuffed not a schoolboy but a farmer's son), and the pervasive force of authority and discipline (the rector took European Catholicism so aggressively into the Congo that he is still remembered with "awe and affection"; he orders Syme about quite imperiously; Syme calls out the prefects on a truant; Syme himself suffers from the austere discipline of the body called for by his order).

Hierarchy, imperialism, official morality, and psychoanalytic scripture, in their attempts to conquer, domesticate, and colonize the living energy of difference, cross in ambiguous ways the wild places of the bog, the Congo, the body, the unconscious. The building that houses the school, after all, was built by "an eccentric Liverpool merchant with a fortune made in the slave trade" (70), and Syme's father has "extensive holdings in Malayan rubber"; the weight of all this multinational exploitation and ethnocentric class consciousness is apparent but, within the story's generic ground rules, inert. Ownership and dominion seem to be motifs difficult to account for with the models at hand: we are ready enough to read the morality tale of Syme's moral fall as justifying his literal fall, but we are like the school community. Expecting to see no social evil in this framework, we pass quietly by the persistent reminders McGrath leaves dotting the narrative "proper."

In "The Skewer," a mad narrator undertakes to avenge the suicide of Neville Pilkington, his uncle, upon Dr. Nordau, the psychoanalyst who the narrator believes drove his uncle to his death. If "Ambrose Syme" plays with the hydraulic metaphor of the Freudian model, this story complicates the relation between analyst and analysand. That is to say, both the hydraulics and Nordau's diagnosis produce knowledge of a sort, but they obscure other insights, with disastrous results. Once Neville has begun to see Nordau, his visions of "sharp-edged instruments [that] loomed out of a black mist and attempted to amputate parts of his body" (119) shift to encounters with fifteen-inch-tall versions of Sigmund Freud, Otto Rank, Ernest Jones, and, eventually, the entire Weimar Congress perched in his study and buzzing through the air on brown little wings. We see Nordau testifying very smugly in court about "retributive delusions" for unspecified sexual experiences. Apparently a classic castration dreamer, Pilkington flees Nordau rather than admitting to himself or to others his youthful sins under Kenya's relatively lax colonial mores. Caught in McGrath's narrative machinations, we find ourselves assuming the lunacy of the narrator (who, after all, vows revenge with The Skewer that he is holding when summoned to his uncle's home) and accepting the accuracy of Nordau's analysis. It fits.

What we do not know until virtually the end of the story is that Neville is actually Evelyn, who assumed her dead brother's identity after their plane crash in Kenya, "for only thus could she transcend the most debilitating disfigurement of all, her womanhood, and make something of the suddenly narrowed range of possibilities that life offered her" (132). Her reclusive lifestyle stems not only from the burn tissue on her face and hands, as nearly everyone assumes, but from her transsexual passage from spinster condemned to crossstitch to noted art critic specializing in, of course, the Brussels of the 1890s. What she likely experiences is not so much Nordau's guilt-based "retributive delusions" but rather a more socially based anxiety about the multiple shearings to which she has been exposed, first as a woman (of the freedoms a Kenyan colonial loses when she returns to London) and then *of* her womanhood.

The textbook explanation, again, fails to explain. Too much is unknown for reductive generalizations to serve adequately in containing the case at hand. But McGrath also marks the gendered relations between analyst and analysand. In the summary of Nordau's testimony, we read that "Neville's psyche was well defended, and staunchly resisted the attempted penetrations of Nordau's insights" (120). The language of therapy and that of seduction veer dangerously close together here, the ghost of Foucault's analysis of power/knowledge hovering nearby. Clearly, the mark of gender is a decisive determinant in Pilkington's entire relation to the psychoanalytic establishment, which is part of the reason why life offered a "narrowed range of possibilities" to her and no viable therapy in a medical regime for whom Dora was the type of the female patient.

The position of the expert is also complicated by class and professional markers that make his judgments and conduct vulnerable to the blindness of his conceptual and role models. Nordau's "Old School" accent is just the kind to "always intimidate the lower middle classes" of the inquest panel, an intimidation he reinforces with "academic" paraphernalia, including the right spectacles, scholarly notes, and tweedy suits (120). Types of the professional expert, Nordau and the coroner represent official society appropriating and publishing the private. It is significant that the nephew is unable to stop the coroner from publishing Pilkington's true gender and thereby exposing to ridicule her scholarly career, we are told, and confirming Evelyn/Neville's worst apprehensions of a patriarchal society. The scientists' positions authorize violations that grate against the gentler ethics of restraint and reticence and serve to police the gender lines of the culture. As institutions of knowledge become ever more tangled up in the exercise of power, the darker play of personal and social identities compromises any claims to the pure daylight of truth.

We read McGrath's fiction in an eerie middle zone between the bipolar opposites of truth and error, right and wrong. Much of what Nordau says is right; none of it is to the point. The nephew's animus against Nordau is apropos in some ways; his defense of his uncle's actions is as nutty as those actions themselves. What we as readers are allowed to see is precisely the way in which the starting point from which these characters come to understand what is going on is precisely what keeps them from doing so, even if without such starting points they would remain utterly nonverbal. McGrath makes clear this theme of necessary error, a bit reminiscent of Paul de Man's comments about blindness and insight, by allowing us to read the uncle's diary:

> He had eyes like a hawk, Ernest Jones, and they drilled into my brain like a corkscrew or a sharp-tipped spiral bore. He began immediately to speak, in a low, hypnotic voice, a honeyed voice to which I listened with an increasingly numbed passivity, such that it began to seem that the voice was issuing not from the tiny apparition before me but from somewhere inside my own brain. How long this discourse lasted I cannot say, save that his words, spiked though they were with familiar analytic terms, yet flowed with such a potent and seamless logic that the arguments seemed not framed or constructed by any interested cognitive agent but instead snipped whole and intact from the very fabric of language itself. (127)

Much is evident in this passage, including the phallic imagery of the analyst penetrating the analysand, the honeyed voice of authority pacifying the object of discourse and displacing its will, the internalization of authority as an inner voice, and the naturalization of what is "framed and constructed" as "the very fabric of language itself." Clearly the encounter with the intellectual establishment of psychoanalysis subjects Pilkington to a "discourse" so oppressive that we are not surprised when the instrument of its textual incarnation, a pen, is taken up "by Jones" and employed "as a lance to put out one of my uncle's eyes" (127). McGrath is having great fun making literal the phallic invasion and intellectual blinding carried out by psychoanalytic (or perhaps any institutionally sanctioned) discourse, at the same time preserving Neville's characterization of

Jones as "apparition" against the nephew's apparent credulity in the literalness of the experiences. No one owns the day or is immune to the night.

McGrath manages to gather quite a cultural kabob on his skewer, the very heterogeneity of which makes any of his ideas "open up" rather than authoritative as the message of language, genre, or fiction. The hydraulic imagery of "Ambrose Syme" recurs in "Blood and Water" when the aging boiler of Sir Norman Percy's country house explodes again, sending him into "deep psychotic territory." What has left Sir Norman on edge is not so much his weak financial condition or his bratty, dissolute children, though these worries are made clear enough, or even his wife's increasing depression, but rather her "clitoral tumefaction." Lady Percy changes from the most elegant of aristocratic ladies to one from whose "hairless pubis at the base of her flat belly sprouts a small, soft penis, plump and pinkly wrinkled, lying upon a delicate betesticled sac which hangs against her closed thighs like a raindrop" (190).

Despite McGrath's wonderfully elegant prose, we still realize that, gendered female, now sexed male, she is the living transgression of the culture's most basic bipolarity. The instability she introduces affects not only the mind of Sir Norman but also all the categories, forms, and conventions of his culture. The "binding agent" of his supper table, the very figure of the patriarch, he is as lost as Ambrose Syme when Latin poetry loses its generic force to contain the mighty contraries of the Jesuit's life. Sir Norman does not know how to place her. She modulates from the stereotypically immobile queen of the aristocratic dinner table to scientific curiosity; from a classic type of the Virgin Mary (her favorite flowers are blue columbines, the symbol of the Virgin Mary for Dutch Renaissance painters) to the neo-Petronian hermaphroditic deity ordered to bare herself before her husband; and from, most spectacularly, in a burst of psychotic mythologizing, in the sky out the west window, "framed by the rainbow, a vast shimmering figure of light who slowly opens her arms and fills the sky with her radiance" (191), to finally and less grandly a suicide with slashed wrists.

There is no easy way to contain the contradictory markers that Lady Percy bears, despite her husband's ransacking of the repertoire of cultural frames. Turning to the consulting physician down from Harley Street, he resorts to a much simpler action of bludgeoning and beheading Dr. Cadwallader to prevent the scientist's plans to publish Lady Percy's hermaphroditic condition in the medical journals and to perform a clitoridectomy upon her newly transformed organ. Sir Norman, we are told at story's end, "spent the rest of his mortal span, in Broadmoor, in a state of happy and imperious insanity" (192), the calm avenging knight of the zone of contradiction having struck against the forces of rational understanding and (surgical) normalization. One of the curious elements in this little tale is the oddness of Sir Norman's sense of resolution. Dispatching the physician with a spanner and then sawing his head off is his triumphant solution of rather fundamental anxieties. It seems inadequate to assume Dr. Cadwallader's offense simply that of the bearer of bad tidings. More plausible, then, is that *publishing* this ambiguation of patriarchal assumptions and, even worse, butchering its central symbol are the key affronts that set off the mythologizing frenzy and the ghastly Greek revenge of presenting a bleeding head to Lady Percy. For Sir Norman's profoundest anxieties to be this sociocultural is an interesting update to a form that began by consigning aristocrats to the devil, unless patriarchy has become for our age the incarnation of Satan, himself after all a deposed aristocrat of sorts.    What Sir Norman ultimately protects is the gothic itself: to explain contradictions rationally and to remove the physical marker of rationality's other is to banish the possibility of the gothic.

Of the tales in this category of transgression, perhaps the most strangely mixed in its tonalities is "Blood Disease," in which a group of pernicious anemics acquires both the blood lust which that condition can foster and a phobia of doctors after the death of the first of the anemics. Vampires for the age of science, they in proper gothic fashion feast off the blood of three aristocrats who stay the night at the vampires' inn and who do what aristocrats should do: display their moral unfitness by philandering. The Freudian gags are rife: in one example, a boy hides fetally in a dark passageway until a girl with an orthopedic shoe clunks by and stops before him, an amusing celebration of foot fetishes enlarging their focal appendage. But the Freudian content is played for laughs rather than taken seriously for insights. Although she leads him down dark passageways to underground spaces and to her room with its enormous bedstead, nothing happens between them. He sees the dashing Ronald Dexter enter his mother's room, but this twist on the primal scene has no particular effect upon him.

The narrative of "Blood Disease" defeats us when every prefabricated plot structure that kicks in kicks out again without satisfying us. Clutch, the trusty manservant, recognizes the medical condition of the ghouls and heads off to the nearest hospital for help; ambulances and police cars arrive with sirens at full blast but are a cavalry too late to avert the massacre. The villains get their just desserts in the end, but the course is not punishment but red corpuscles. The adulterous couple, brought together by boredom and a touch of consanguinity, meets the fate of poetic justice, but so absurd is the overkill—they are stripped, hung upside down, and bled into large oaken kegs—that any model of moral closure becomes simply quaint. Even the psychologically resonant monkey, which the malaria-crazed Congo Bill gives his son, does not die, as it seems to do (its apparent corpse is the bond between the young pair), but is carried across the fields by the clunking girl to an utterly inconsequential end.

When I asked McGrath about this murder story, he told me of reading "a nice Freudian discussion of how the murder always happens at night, and there are always stains on the sheets, strange noises in the night; the murder story revises our memory of the primal scene. The clues that a small child can't make head or tail of are exorcised in our delight in mystery stories." The first draft suffered from the "schematic" quality of this interpretation, however; I suspect that in revision McGrath began unsettling the neat logic by which things were tied up by "nice Freudian discussion." In the process, he also unsettled the way narrative so easily dispatches some primal scenes—both social and individual—that ought to be left open to further inspection. The story's reflexive meditation on modes of closure suggests that, in the daylight world of ready theories and stable categories, the real monkey we seek so rationally to sublimate has, in the end, really escaped in the company of that which, like the girl's orthopedic boot, goes clunk in the night.

The utter insufficiency of our ordinary literary frames is a recurrent element in McGrath's fiction. "The Black Hand of the Raj," a wonderful parable of revenge on the British wrought by "a little old man with a bald head and a loincloth" (46), is a case in point. His "blessing" to British officers is a hand that grows out of their brainstem and through the top of their head, eventually strangling them despite their efforts to inject it with sedatives. In the situation of Cecil and his bride-to-be, Lucy, we find the extra oomph of an innocent English girl who finds her fiancé dead, lies beside him in prostrate grief appropriate for a British heroine, and finds herself succumbing to the seductive advances of the hand. The tale is a very funny version of sexual, racial, and imperial transgression. It also begins, however, with Lenin's diagnosis of imperialism, as well as the queasy recoiling of mainstream narrative from its explicit account of the master class in violent decay: "What this rather gloomy analysis tends to ignore, however, is Imperialism's other face, which is indeed more properly the preserve of fiction. This is the soft face of Imperialism, and it concerns itself with human relationships, and individual psychology—and not least with the education of the senses. For it was in the torrid climates of the various far-flung corners of the Empire that many Europeans first confronted the nature of passion" (42).

The proper "preserve of fiction" is to shun the sociopolitical content of its materials and to stay within the comfortably defined margins of subjectivity. What "The Black Hand of the Raj" does is to find that "occasionally, the encounter of East and West, of the sensual and the rational, did not resolve so satisfactorily" and that the traveler emerges as something other than the "richer, wiser, and more fully rounded human being" predicted as the fate of the politically and economically privileged member of the encounter. "Occasionally," the narrator observes, "darker forces seemed to be at work, forces committed to discord and antipathy between the races" (42–43). McGrath works entirely through his exaggeratedly ornate style and the ideological charges that go off in his uncomprehending narrator's unconscious. McGrath enjoys the artifice of the medium, but he also turns the tables on the gothic and rouses up *its* ghosts, its repressed.

The title "The Arnold Crombeck Story" reminds us that the tale is not simply about Crombeck, an infamous poisoner awaiting execution in Wandsworth prison who plants his (female) victims in his garden after living around their corpses a few days; one might say that his *modus operandi* carries to an extreme the patriarchal control of women. The tale is also about obtaining his story, and the narrator is a journalist, Miss Kennedy, looking back on her younger days, when, "fresh from Vassar," she escaped covering fashion and tennis to get a human-interest angle on the murderer. As she passes through "an interminable journey, broken every few yards by locked doors," past unfriendly guards resenting her entry down their dark, gloomy passageways and stairwells, she clearly is entering forbidden territory where "they hadn't seen a woman in ten years" (81, 85). She very much feels the pressure to prove her competence in a man's business.

It is, finally, the simultaneity of tennis lawns and subterranean dungeons which Miss Kennedy needs to learn. Crombeck has his utterly grisly side in his fascination with his corpses and his appreciation for well-done murders and hangings, but also his extraordinarily genteel side in his gracious manners, his exquisite pleasure and practice in English country gardens (his own is fine, perhaps from all the fertilizer), and his dapper dress (he is quite concerned that the hanging not spoil his pants). His is an obvious demystification of our illusions about well-mannered gentility and all that of which it is capable when its practice of mastery extends from gardening and civility to killing and domination. In the face of this ambiguous mixture, Miss Kennedy feels both during and after their conversations a dizziness and disorientation extending finally to nausea. But it is difficult to say whether the symptoms she feels derive more from the shock to her Vassar illusions or from the arsenic with which he laces the cigarettes he so kindly shares with her. Both her cheerful Vassar experience and our "received imagery" of the perfect suburban garden suggest stable and sufficient concepts of order with whole world views attached. But Arnold Crombeck enacts such concepts' utter unreliability as languages adequate for representing human experience. But perhaps she experiences more than she conceptualizes, because she interrupts his letter explaining the poisoning, and congratulating her if she is alive to read it, with the bracketed note of her own textual exclusion: "There followed several paragraphs that concern only Arnold and me." This gothic tale retains its own repressed.

McGrath's stories of transgressed genres and theoretical models loosen the hold of received imagery upon us and allow the exposure of what such tools of repression shade out of view both on the personal level of sublimation and on the cultural level of ideological and social normalization. His stories of decay mark the loss from the suburban consciousness of values, belief, and perhaps even so old-fashioned a notion as authenticity. "The Angel" is perhaps the most audacious metaphysically. Bernard Finnegan is a New York writer with relatively unpromising projects, which he seems more to toy with than to pursue. One is "an historical novel about heretics," prompted by a Gnostic tale in which a spirit's only consolation for being immured within a human body is its cohabitation with another spirit promising it release—Death. Another of Finnegan's projects is *An Old Man Remembers the Jazz Age*, based on his acquaintance with an overly sweet-smelling older man in his building. Harry Talboys turns out to be a gothic version of the titular being—a grotesquely decomposing body that his spirit will not leave. The story is rooted in McGrath's Catholic upbringing, he explained to me: "The human being is a unit composed of the body and the soul, and the gothic loves to play with that unity. To have either the body without the soul, which is the ghoul or the vampire, or the soul without the body, which is the ghost."

Or a soul that for whatever reason has failed to depart the body when it should have. McGrath said that "The Angel" "was prompted by an idea of Baudelaire, whose distress in the 1850s had to do with our souls in a materialistic age that won't accept the existence of souls. You can just imagine a highly sensitized poetic type in the first onrush of major industrialism. What are we going to do with our souls when nobody believes that we've got them?" Finnegan's writing seems a process of filling in the blanks of prefabricated genres, as if industrial production were indeed his mode. Thus it is no surprise that he holds up poorly under the weight of this revelation, for "writing seems futile now. Everything seems futile, for some reason I don't fully understand, and I keep wondering why any of us cling to the raft. The one consolation I can find is the presence of that other spirit traveling with us in the body" (26). He takes a sharp turn on Harry Talboys's slower curve from the hedonistic twenties, in which the body was "a shrine, to be adorned for the ritual of love," to the thirties, in which "my friends all seemed to be dead, or married, or alcoholic" (14, 15). Finnegan's earlier impulse is to contain Harry's melancholy in "an expressive personal document of modern America in the innocent exuberance of its golden youth," but the perfected banality of his prose is not proof against the spiritual depth Harry's revelation opens under Finnegan's two-dimensional surfaces. Finnegan does not "fully understand" because his spiritual decay is all too evident a counterpart to Harry's physical decomposition.

Other tales of decaying perception include "Lost Explorer," about a young girl who sees a malarial Congo Bill in her overgrown garden until she decides to follow her in father's footsteps and become a medical scientist. The pickled thumb in a jar he gives her early on is a totem of the phallogocentrism that, once she is committed to it, ends the capacity of her imagination to see the jungle explorer she herself will not finally become. "Lush Triumphant" is a very fine and witty tale about a Soho neo-expressionist. His aesthetic creed is to be with your work "until you saw it clear and straight, without illusion" (64), but he lives in complete blindness to the wreck of his life (we see his brief and almost nonverbal encounter with his estranged wife), his own inclinations (he is drawn to a street boy who becomes the focal turning point of his current painting, but he never quite realizes the content of the attraction), or the ludicrousness of his art (beginning as apocalyptic timbers, his shapes ingest the cheeseburgers and steaks he eats until the painting becomes *Beef on the Hoof*). Like many of the tales, these two suggest the decay of wider perceptivity as narrower cultural frames take over the faculty of vision and focus it within their flashlight beam through the larger darkness of experience.

"Marmilion" is a deft tale that carries McGrath's inquest over dead and dying frames of reference into the individual's capacity to maintain any real knowledge of herself. It features a woman famous for her photographs of monkeys. She has a "sympathetic understanding" that enables her to locate them, but her self-confidence proves unwarranted when she stumbles across a ruined mansion and the Faulknerian family narrative that explains its past. She digs out letters, journals, and a great deal of conjecture in reconstructing a tale that has much to do with her own ambivalence over men in general and her son in particular. Although the details of the latter relationship are never specified, that her husband was Cajun opens her to the bayou's spooky ambience of memory. She makes it clear that her suppositions ("no doubt the relationship of mother and son began to deteriorate at an early stage") are founded on the feelings left over from her own life ("I should know; I've had a son of my own" [139]). She hears scratching in a pillar of the mansion she camps in overnight and is convinced that one of the principals is trying to communicate with her, though the inexplicable catastrophe that scattered the inhabitants happened some eighty years before her arrival. Running out of documentary evidence, she tells us that "what follows is the construction of a sympathetic imagination" (148), and the narrative picks up speed in its melodrama of rivalries, violence, and sexual trauma. Even after these moments, however, we are surprised that it is a spider monkey she disinters from the pillar, so ready are we to trust a narrator and to assume that her reconstructive skills and her historical evidence have their relation in the daylight of facts rather than the deep night of self-delusions. The real decay in "Marmilion" is of her ability to have a genuine "sympathetic understanding," for, when the monkeys she *thinks* she seeks turn up dead, she experiences the skeleton of repressed memories scratching frantically by her ear all during the dark and stormy night.

McGrath's reopening of genres rescues the repressed, as well as the very process of repression (the repression of which is perhaps the ultimate sign of suburban existential decay). His comic touches and stylistic decadence mark the artifice by which we not only drop experience into the well but also forget we have done so. Occasionally a story seems designed to show the defeat of just this monstrous effort to will away a part of ourselves. In "Hand of a Wanker," for example, we find wonderfully witty satire of club life (we meet Lily, the lily [?] of Club Babylonia, and a number of half-spaced, half-blasé denizens of Manhattan nightlife) and the humor of a compulsive masturbator who severs his hand in an effort to quit his habit. The hand, hairy-palm jokes and all, keeps at its appointed rounds, but on the club's unsuspecting patrons, who prefer to choose their partners more deliberately. Compelled by guilt to return for his hand, its owner explains his affliction and appeals for help and understanding from the club folk. When the hand is hacked into a great many pieces by Gunther of the lederhosen, the story is over, but not what has happened to the stranger's "human desire": "Everywhere I look I see lips, breasts, bottoms, legs—and I've had enough! I can't stand it anymore—this—constant itch—this *compulsion!* I'm a sick man!" (159). He and the Babylonians live out a magazine dream of utterly sexualized human relations in which others are always already dismembered into the favorite body parts of the considerably degenerated Barthesian Amorous Subject. McGrath's moral touch is so light that one feels like a boor explaining jokes to make the point.

In "The E(rot)ic Potato," a different context is set—the postnuclear world in which mammals die but insects feed and mate lustily. Moved, he told me, by the German neo-expressionist vogue a few years back, McGrath wrote several literally apocalyptic tales in which the narrators are boots, beer cans, and—in this story—a fly. "All of which arose," he explained, "from the question I put to

myself: Come the bomb, all human discourse ceases; what happens
if the stories went on even though there weren't any humans left to
tell them?" Drawing inspiration from *The Sorrows of Young*
*Werther* and a rather nice book on insect parts and habits, McGrath
lets these discourses collide with nuclear anxieties in a stylistic tour
de force of pastiche, appropriation, and deflation. What emerges is
a wonderful send-up of the genre of sexual awakening. A venerable
literary type is reduced from metaphysics to an ovipositor; sexuality
is restored from its service as literary figure for the cosmic ego to its
eminently naturalistic plane of pheromones and the survival of the
species.

"The Boot's Tale," another postnuclear exercise, is narrated by
a boot, which recoils in distaste at the business-as-usual way in
which Gertie, the dead mother, is carved into rashers the morning
after her demise. That it takes a boot to protest the extent to which
pragmatism rules American life is pratfall satire. McGrath finds
himself amazed "at the doings of our leaders and the enormous
acquiescence in their doings by the population . . . it doesn't have to
be controlled by any particular obstruction of political procedures
or ethical concerns—one just goes straight for it." Worse is the family's refusal to let anyone share their food and warmth. When they
finally emerge, they are so much fatter than the wraiths huddled
around a fire that they are massacred in an obvious parable of First
and Third World relations. "To these starving and irradiated half-
humans the plump and robust good health of the Murgatroids must
have seemed monstrous, truly monstrous," muses the boot. "Good
health and a well-fed belly would of course seem monstrous in a
world of chronic and terminal hunger, a world where deprivation
was the norm" (174). This story is perhaps suburban ambush with
a blunt instrument, bludgeoning us to awareness of our multiple
acquiescences as sated banqueters at Caesar's table. "The Boot's
Tale" comes close to a terminal reading of well-fed suburban fiction
in a country where ideological deprivation is the norm. If the streets
outside McGrath's East Village walk-up are indeed in decay, then
what better genre than the gothic, raised from the dead, to deal with
the resulting megadeath of social apocalypse?

McGrath's gothic is a postmodern one, then, and not just for its
very witty surface and hip references. The very obvious markers of
postmodernism include its pastiche of styles and allusions, its abut-
ments of contending semiotic frames, its play of humor and seriousness, its political edge, and, perhaps more profoundly, its rejection
of the modernist and late modernist preoccupation with an individual's interior consciousness as a sufficient site of fiction. McGrath
possesses a vital reflexive awareness of the problematic nature of his
medium, one that makes his work a literary coroner's inquest into
what Congo Bill's pygmies might call a dead, but not absolutely

dead, narrative form. McGrath's patient comes back to life, perhaps with some poststructural malarial dream images haunting it, and interacts productively with his analysis of a postindustrial commodity society. That society's blend of imperialism and materialism is one in which pernicious anemics feasting on strung-up corpses may come close to being a metaphor for a deeper cultural anemia driving the population to consume rather than nurture the specimens of difference that come our way through whatever means. Perhaps, in the final analysis, McGrath's gothic pumps into the literary bloodstream a healthy dose of red corpuscles fresh from the bank of the unconscious.

### *"Not Writing-School Writing"*

"This is not writing-school writing," editors Rose and Texier tell us in the introduction to the Penguin anthology based on their now almost-legendary magazine. Featuring writers "closer to urban archaeologists than to landscape artists or campus sociologists," *Between C & D* evades the economics of magazine publishing by being printed on the editors' home computer; it evades becoming a full-time job by being printed in small runs—initially of seventy-five copies when the editors hand-delivered them to the Life Cafe, later of six hundred; it evades the loss of control entailed in the big-time magazine business by resisting any temptation to become an American *Granta*; and it evades gentrification by keeping its fanfold snug in the same plastic zip-lock bags relied upon by drug pushers. In their introduction to the Penguin volume, Rose and Texier explain the relations among their contributors by noting their geographical connection in the Lower East Side (Rose and Texier make a point of publishing both its postmodern and its Nuorican writers), their common inheritance (the editors cite William S. Burroughs, Henry Miller, Jean Genet, Louis-Ferdinand Céline, Roland Barthes, Michel Foucault, and J. G. Ballard), and the classic aggressiveness of the avant-garde tradition. As they say, the stories reject "middle-class family dramas or cute college tales" or "coy, slickly portrayed vignettes of modern life," the stereotypical fare of the writing workshops.

I like a story that Rose tells of how he and Texier came to launch a magazine on fanfold paper:

> I had a background in literary magazines. I started one called the *Seneca Review* at Hobart and William Smith College—it's still around. I really had no intention of doing a literary magazine. What really happened was that my agent was giving me a hard time about using a dot-matrix printer with the computer. He hated the printout. I loved it! And we used to get all these reams of

paper that would come out of the computer, and Céline [Rose and Texier's daughter] loved to draw and that was one of my main interactions with her—I sat down with her when she came home from day care and we used to draw. So we began to see that what was happening with the computer paper and the print and the drawings was sort of working.

Rose goes on to add his sense of a need for a strictly fiction magazine that could tap the diverse energies of the neighborhood in which he and Texier worked and lived. And they are both quite sensitive to the tradition into which their magazine falls. Rose told Carlo Mc-Cormick in an interview:

> I never felt that we suddenly arrived and this was literature. I always felt we were part of a process, especially because I've had ties here for all my life. I knew that Jack Kerouac lived right down the block. I knew that this magazine followed in the footsteps of *Fuck you*, that we were one of a long line of magazines a little bit more alternative and on the edge. (McCormick 1988, 55)

And so Rose and Texier sought out good writing where they found it, including the Nuorican writers, despite "such a backlash" Rose described to me: "It's amusing that a lot of downtown writers think that writing started with them, or New York writing did, and didn't realize there was a whole different segment of work out there that's just fabulous. I hungered for work like Piñero's, because I feel my writing is much closer to that than to some of the things you see."

There is something very appropriate in the combination of a literary type's dislike for dot-matrix and a child's delight in the possibilities for playing with paper, graphics, and the collectibles one can add to them. And collectibles there were—a free postcard and stamps (1.2), family photos (1.3), a David Wojnarowicz poster (1.4), a flexi-disk record (2.1), Salvadorian cocktail napkins (2.2). Work appearing on the cover or as inserts is also of note, including that of Art Spiegelman (4.2), Orshi Drozdik (3.3), Kiki Smith (2.4), Barbara Kruger (2.2), and David Wojnarowicz (1.4). *Between C & D* cuts against the literary and ideological stuffiness of high culture, keeping even in its success a willingness to play with the materials at hand, physical and otherwise. Fortunately, the Museum of Modern Art and the Whitney Museum collect these issues, along with more predictable repositories, such as the New Museum, for the title pages are the best index I know to the writers whose work makes talk of downtown renaissance more than hype.

Of the twenty-five tales in the Penguin anthology, ten are by writers of such power that they are covered in separate chapters of the present book and many though by no means all of the strongest pieces are by this group. Lynne Tillman's eerie "Dead Talk," Marilyn Monroe's suicide note, is here, as is one of Kathy Acker's child-rape shockers (slightly different from its version in *Empire of the Senseless*). Very strong pieces from Texier, Rose, and Associate Editor McGrath showcase the editors' fiction talents, while quintessential stories by Roberta Allen, Peter Cherches, Susan Daitch, Gary Indiana, and Ron Kolm explain why the anthology has few equals as a sampler of the new writing. Also noteworthy, however, are the many fine stories by writers who for one reason or another were not included in the Penguin anthology but whose work validates issue after issue of the magazine. These writers include Edmund Cardoni, Kurt Hollander (*Portable Lower East Side*'s editor), Michael Kaspar, Richard Kostelanetz, Mark Leyner, Ursule Molinaro, Miguel Piñero, and Mike Topp.

There are too many good stories to discuss, however, even if we restrict our focus primarily to those in the Penguin anthology. But perhaps we can achieve some feel for the fiction by suggesting a few of the larger categories into which the stories fall. The smallest category includes those that have not stood up well over time. But among those stories that have, the first category we might distinguish consists of tightly managed emblematic tales that evoke the particular stresses, internal and external, marking recent urban life. Stories by Allen, Daitch, Kolm, McGrath, Rose, and Texier compose the bulk of this category. But **Tama Janowitz**'s "Case History # 179: Tina" also belongs here. Akin to the stories in Janowitz's very successful *Slaves of New York* (Crown, 1986), this story features a protagonist quite effective in unconsciously triggering a series of accidents that punish her rich art-dealing boyfriend. About to be moved out of "his luxurious apartment on Madison Avenue," she manages while cleaning up cigarette butts to burn him out instead. Her inability to win—she spends a year in a hospital nursing her nervous breakdown before turning into a bag lady—links her to the characters in **Don Skiles**'s "The Loft." The narrator, who makes his living filling temporary jobs, resents the yuppies who "make large, significant decisions in their glassed-in offices" so much that he considers taping their downtime in the toilet: "An audio tape alone of this would change corporate image" (122). Random violence (women pulled out of cars on the street and beaten), the sense that others have it better (he wants earplugs to save him from the sounds of sex through the walls), curiosity whether others are also walking around with their heads full of nostalgic "remembrances of boyhood," fads, door locks, increasingly acerbic graffiti, and the jaded wit of the art magazines all wind through his loneliness to compose a very dead-toned portrait of urban alienation.

We get a rich sense of the state of the urban soul if we link these stories to Kolm's *Duke and Jill* sketches, to Rose's desperate gang histories, or to Texier's harrowing portrait of a woman haunted by a walker in a black fedora. The line between these stories and a second category is probably dubious to draw and marks perhaps a difference more of degree than kind. I think of these monologues as "shockers," because they include stories that rock the suburban reader with their sheer grittiness and unexpected violence, as if they were pieces of terrorist fiction targeting victims who had almost forgotten the offense. Certainly Acker's piece, with its evocation of bondage, rape, and coercions of every tonality (called "Male," it is the passage culminating in an Ackerian axiom, "War, you mirror of our sexuality"), would fit into this category. Tillman's "Dead Talk," with its disturbing evocation of Monroe's final pit of lovelessness, also belongs here.

**Bruce Benderson**'s "A Visit from Mom" keeps two voices within the narrator absolutely separate. One voice records Mom's apple-pie concern for her son's lack of a successful "career," and the other recounts his paralyzed drift through the menacing arms of an ex-convict hustler into the night of victimization. His *The United Nations of Times Square* (Red Dust, 1987) gives much fuller reign to the device of multivoiced narrative; its female executive sifts through reports about military forces and financial cartels, and its Hispanic male breaks in to add his episodes of passion and of class boundaries. **Emily Carter**'s "All the Men Are Called McCabe" follows a terrorized soul through her brutalizing encounters with men who have in common not only a last name but also the darkest side of the Father. She feels no safety until she learns a bit of survival wisdom from another victim in the hospital: "'It's easy to kill someone with a knife,' she told me. 'Stick it in and turn it like a key. They'll bleed to death'" (169).

**Renaldo Povod**'s fiction has appeared numerous times in the magazine. In "Things to Do Today" the thirteen-year-old narrator is teased sexually by a ten-year-old boy whom his grandmother babysits. He is drawn into just enough contact with the younger boy to realize that "I never ever gotten that close to someone 'cept my father & when my mother comes around t' see me I kiss 'er" (114). "La Puta Vida" (1.4) features a rooftop perspective on the block's violence. Down below, a fight takes place on a manhole cover that seems an altar to the god of wrath in the middle of this temple of a street. The combatants are egged on by instigators and gossips gathered at tenement windows like worshipers in temple galleries. A man "knowing he had no money, an' not knowing where to get a hold of some" turns and "eyeballs the area, the plastic covered furniture / the t.v. / set that only plays channel 45 / the BLADE / the Blade laying on the window sill / the Blade / tempting like a neighbor's daughter." He notices "THAT not even outside is there room for the street lamp to shine / OR / for the cars to park / the kids to stand / the BUMS to sleep" (10), and his decision to leave results in his

angry wife stabbing him. The tale ends a bit melodramatically, perhaps, in their brawling sequel on the subway platform, both hit by
an express train trying to bypass, no doubt, the "whore's life" of the
story's title.

Two of the better-known writers in the anthology also contribute "shockers." **Dennis Cooper** brings his well-earned reputation
from his novel *Safe* (Sea Horse Press, 1984) to an excerpt from *Closer*
(Grove Press, 1989). George is a beautiful adolescent whose feelings
about his dying mother and his classmates' treatment of his homosexuality keep him on acid trips and in the arms of older lovers, one
of whom almost kills him in an astonishing ritual of disembowel-
ment. In *Safe*, a character "says his sentences are like bars on a cage
that holds dangerous animals" (20). The only thing wrong with
applying the line to Cooper's sentences is that his are more like the
hinges on cage doors. The sentences swing open on readers who
have come as tourists to watch Cooper's Blank Generation characters be exotic zoo creatures. But Cooper is neither Bret Easton Ellis
nor the Jay McInerney of *Bright Lights, Big City*. Cooper's characters are not privileged dabblers who score a few hits of nightlife to
chase the boredom of having too much consumer electronics to keep
up with.

George knows "I'm walking around but I'm not really there,"
and that "if I don't sleep with people they hate me. But when I do
they think they know me or something. I hope not" (33). "I'm going
through things I guess I shouldn't because it seems fun, but it isn't"
(32), partly because his father is remotely out of sync with his son's
life, his mother dies before his eyes, his teacher hassles him for sex,
and his beloved Phillipe introduces him to a man who explains
paintings this way: "My friend believes corpses dream. . . . Try to
imagine each work is the dream of a murdered child" (38). Cooper,
who left Los Angeles for New York by 1984, has written on the
visual arts, film, and music for magazines such as *Art in America*,
the Los Angeles Institute of Contemporary Art's *Journal*, and *High
Performance*, and brings to his fiction an analytical acumen that
understands culture's death logic in a far more complex way than
some writers who treat alternative night worlds.

At the end of *Safe*, Doug and Skip make love: "They're in different worlds, but with each slap realize they're not alone, no matter
how far away their dream boys may ride bikes or lie dead. Doug
knows whom he wishes were here. He wonders who Skip is fantasiz-
ing about. He whispers, 'Skip,' to see what happens. 'Skip,' the boy's
voice echoes back. Later he laughs when Doug tells him about it"
(104). Too much fiction is a dreaming corpse like Skip, an inchoate
soul so estranged that only rhythmic slapping reminds him that he
is not wholly in fantasies, and even then the message seems not to
get through. Perhaps Doug, and certainly George, would understand

Skip's response, that the ultimate fantasy of culture's "murdered child" is himself. As this fine stylist's books emerge (a story collection, *Wrong*, is in the works), he will secure his place in the forefront of our narrative renaissance.

**David Wojnarowicz,** whose paintings have been among the most powerful of the Lower East Side art scene, has published in *Bomb, Redtape,* and the *East Village Eye,* as well as in *Between C & D*. His pieces are unrivaled in their immediacy, their impact, and their evocation of the terrible lacerations to which the soul is subject. His "Self-Portrait in Twenty-three Rounds" opens the Penguin anthology and, as is often the case when a piece of his turns up in a magazine or collection, it threatens to upstage the rest. In so strong a group as this, however, it is a keynote address with an impact akin to throwing the passengers of suburban sedans through their windshields and out onto the unkind streets. Its adolescent narrator wakes with double vision after being brained by a marble slab. Wojnarowicz does not frame his narrator's story so much as let it seethe before us with "large rats the size of shoeboxes," meat cleavers stolen from Macy's, friends locked in the attic for six weeks, and his memories of hanging seven stories up by his fingers, "testing testing how do I control this how much control do I have how much strength do I have." All of Wojnarowicz's characters test controlled strength against an omnipresent death that we usually think of only in connection with the Third World. These characters survive by hustling fetishists—such as the rubber-sneaker fancier of this sketch, whose turnon is to relive his drill sergeant's abuse with the unnamed narrator in the starring role. Survival requires street smarts, such as knowing where to sleep in winter. He tells us that "good times for me was just one fucking night of solid sleep which was impossible I mean the boiler room of some highrise the pipes would start clanking and hissing like machine pistons" (3).

In a poster that Wojnarowicz did with Marion S., the speaker of the monologue, reading about legalized homophobia, feels his entire body become "weapons":

> I feel prepared for the rest of my life; in my dreams I crawl across
> freshly clipped front lawns, past statues and dogs and cars contain-
> ing your guardians; I enter your houses through the smallest
> cracks in the bricks that keep you occupied with a feeling of com-
> fort and safety; I cross your living rooms and go up your staircases
> and into your bedrooms where you lie sleeping. I will wake you up
> and tell you a story. . . .

This particular story, another one of violence, is about a ten-year-old boy whose hands, too small to reach around the neck of his homophobic pickup, are unable to strangle him when he tries to beat up the boy. Wojnarowicz's narrators all have this same belief in the strength of the body and of writing to become weaponry in a battle for the survival of body and soul. Having been marked by blows rather than blades of grass, the violated body hardens for physical survival, as violent in its countermeasures as need be. Their narratives register the knowledge of their bodies and penetrate the defenses of suburbia in order to disrupt the "comfort and safety" of its cultural fortifications. That which is considered the exception or the marginal is revealed as the hidden norm in a population "so afraid of the impulses of heat stirring in [its] belly." As the narrator says at the end of this piece, "I will wake you up and welcome you to your bad dream," one that we share at some level, even if we have not yet tumbled through its violence and heat.

The third category of stories owes something to the pithy nature of the generally short narratives that comprise the anthology and something to the social commitments of its writers. We lack an ideal term for stories that may be as lean as a minimalist's or as lush as a fabulist's, but for these fictions that liberalize the laws of realism, perhaps *parable* will serve in a provisional way if we understand the term's rhetorical ambience in a poststructural sort of way. Most shocking to late modernist tastes is probably **Darius James**'s "Negrophobia," two episodes in screenplay format which take us into the fabulist grotesque of racism. Less overtly violent is **Lisa Blauschild**'s "Witness," an anthology of what is said by people who prefer not to report, or intervene in, the violence that they view. It recounts its narrator's recurrent evasions, culminating in one emblematic of the suburban response to history in general: "I cut him short. Officer, I say, I'm one of those lucky people who can sleep through anything" (9). Regular readers of the magazine may also remember "The Fetus" (1.4), in which Planned Parenthood's ashtray yields a pet fetus that the narrator keeps in a mayonnaise jar for a companion and paperweight, or "The Couple" (1.3) for whom a sexy evening is watching each other masturbate to fantasies of that day's sex object before rolling over or doing the dishes.

**Joan Harvey**'s "Plagiarism" shows how roles and hierarchies survive replacement of the individual who occupies them. Its narrator cleans house for the Fat Man until he overdoses. Because "existing is plagiarism"—their discipline is to play a game of recognizing quotations—she takes over the position of dealer and question master with a lover chosen from a portfolio (the image-repertoire of the empowered amorous subject?). Empowered, she sits in the Fat Man's bedroom and follows the world on video remote; unempowered, she joins a group in a rocky place where they build a fire and play a "Jack be nimble" game. "The moments when I hang in the air over the fire are the moments when I am most who I am" (118), when, no doubt, she burns both ends of the existential candle in the nighttowner's weightlessness. Spectator and spectacle are the unpromising options for this inmate of the coldly tiled house to which her father committed her.

Parables of the strangeness of life in the world of twenty-four-hour bank machines abound. Peter Cherches's wonderfully funny "Dirty Windows" is such a parable, as is Gary Indiana's narrative double cross, "I Am Candy Jones." **Craig Gholson,** at least as well known for his plays as for his fiction, calls the bank machine a "Temple to the Economics of Love." Johnny either is broke and has a lover or is rich and celibate, and, to get money from his overextended account, he must finally insert a card still dripping from a literalization of suburbia's love affair with after-hours conveniences. **Lee Eiferman,** best known perhaps for her narrative videotapes, tells in "Summer Flying" of a yuppie exec who parachutes into the twilight zone just before her plane fireballs. She already experienced some enforced leisure by hitchhiking to the airport after her car had broken down, complete with a Mosaic bush burning with monarch butterflies and a bit of skinny-dipping. But after her free fall, she does not even call the waiting board of directors to let them know that she has survived. She is ready to become a "northerner settling down in Texas" selling real estate instead of the unnamed product that involved the now-forgotten executive board. But it's less Texas than the hyperreal of her advertising world: what attracts her are the "firm and tanned" cast gathered around the focal commodities, the woman herself and a bottle of beer "posed high in the air," the sun catching "the glint of wetness" with the precision of a studio spotlight. Her "summer flying" is neither utopian escape nor catastrophic end, but rather a transmigration from individual to image. **John Farris,** longtime manager of the fabled reading series at the Life Cafe, provides a comic revue of fashionable Lower East Side topics in "You Can Keep Your Razors & Guns." Violence, sex, noise bands, and the pretentiousness of much "new art" all come in for satiric reduction to the experiences of a street-smart tomcat.

**Barry Yourgrau**'s gag pastoral, "Oak," portrays the violent encounter between the narrator and a "pastoral sociopath" of a storybook shepherdess who very nearly opens his skull with a mean swing of her crook. Yourgrau is well known for collections of witty pieces, such as *A Man Jumps Out of an Airplane* (Sun, 1984) and *Wearing Dad's Head* (Peregrine Smith Books, 1987), for reviews and essays in the *Village Voice, Art in America,* and *Arts Magazine,* and for stories and sketches throughout the network of literary magazines. Susan Seidelman's jacket blurb on *Wearing Dad's Hat* summarizes aptly his stories' effect: "They have the uninhibited honesty of a dream being recounted by someone who's not yet awake." A girl materializes out of a meteor shower to tell the narrator about her life in the stars before, clad only in her blue pajamas, she joined his life. He buries his mother in sand only to have it turn to "Cement" and all but kill her; he also has "The Vision" of her wintry ride behind him in the bed of his pick-up truck. His dead father returns as a gray-haired baby riding in a giant soap bubble and, in a different sketch, as a squat cavalier in a bottle agonizing over his memoirs and "his imprisonment as a homunculus in a knick-knack" until he is calmed down by a ride in the bathtub. In "Dante" he finds himself dead and conducted from his father's destiny in a rocky gray purgatory to his own in a jungle paradise, for "it seems every single little thing has been forgiven" (92). In "Flood" high water at the dinner table sends his father up the spongy stairs because, as his mother explains, "this flood is what happens eventually to all families, and your father knows this, and it makes him very sad that there is nothing he can do about it" (76). In "Climatology" he meets the worker whose summer job is making weather; she is not too good at tossing the clouds once she has puffed them, and he has to step in and shake a particularly nasty hailstorm out of the limbs of his birch tree. The previous year, as it turns out, her summer job had been "distributing the effects of entropy through this part of the solar system," and therefore "everyone went insane losing things" (41). Yourgrau's deft transformations and juxtapositions of ordinary moments and metaphysics make his stories a distinctive form in the world of postmodern fiction. They serve to keep us gently mindful of the fantastic strangeness with which desire and anxiety tangle with perceptual and conceptual habits to form what we at times too easily and simply call experience.

Rose was quite on the mark when he told Carlo McCormick that the *Between C & D* anthology included "more than one necessary style, certainly we're not hard lined about what we are looking for. In fact, we like to see a wide variety of styles" (McCormick 1988, 55). But those styles speak to one another across their differences. Texier told me they "did the magazine as a sort of network and got to know the other writers. We put our own writing next to theirs and saw what was going on." What goes on is a rich and diverse address of contemporary realities not enclosed within the suburban property lines that afflict some of our writing programs. As Texier explained, "there's a sense of something urban, ironic, something experimental with form . . . but really having something to say and stretching the boundaries of writing." Such writing leaves us with the same feeling that Texier's character in "The Fedora" must have when she stands by her winter window "as dusk comes down and the faint sound of a trumpet rises from the vacant lot" (60). That feeling is a wistful sense of being moved, both by the sheer sensory qualities of the blues and by the image of the "skinny black kid, perched on a stack of wooden crates" in a junk lot barehanding his trumpet in the bitter cold, the music cascading "down the string of empty lots, echoing through the gutted buildings behind him" (51). These writers do not suppose that any of these gaps becomes filled in a burst of liberal good feeling, but they know that art can be made to feel out the "gutted buildings" of these psychic landscapes and to place them with experiential, if not always theoretical, precision.

# VILLAGE VOICES

As we talked about the political edge to the arts in New York since his 1976 arrival there, Allan Bealy, the editor of *Benzene*, was quick to give Reese Williams credit for "starting that kind of critical investigation. I don't think anybody else was really doing that before." Bealy singled out the Tanam Press anthologies as beginning a ricochet effect of "people talking to people in a community—Reese publishes an anthology, then somebody else publishes one." We do indeed need to give great credit to the landmark anthologies, especially since our focus is upon fiction. Williams's *Hotel* (1980) was the first anthology to present downtown writing in all its difference, and its contributors were the core of a group from which many of the early currents flowed. Barbara Ess's *Just Another Asshole 6* (1983), edited with Glenn Branca, is what Richard Prince calls a "souvenir" of the sensibility that had been emerging ever more clearly as the eighties took shape. From his base in Providence, Tom Ahern edited *Diana's Third Almanac* (1983), which offered well-chosen writing, including work by Kathy Acker, Peter Cherches, and a particularly powerful piece by David Wojnarowicz.

These three books were often on the minds of people I talked with as they tried to field my less focused questions about the new writing, because these anthologies served the important function of naming names and exhibiting samples. Another round of anthologies sums up something akin to a second phase of the new writing as its practitioners grew more confident in their voices and took the second and third phases of their often multiple careers in stride. Tanam Press published Prince's *Wild History* in 1985 and Williams's *Fire over Water* in 1986, the same year that saw Ahern's *Diana's Fourth Almanac* and a pair of anthologies spawned by the Hallwalls Contemporary Arts Center's Fiction Diction series of readings in Buffalo (*Angle of Repose* and *Blatant Artifice*; Edmund

Cardoni has made this a series by publishing *Blatant Artifice* 2/3 in 1988). Although several of these anthologies include writers from other places than New York, most of the writers understand very well the literary map etched in *Suburban Ambush*. Finally, two additional anthologies quite nicely sum up the sensibilities north and south of Houston Street—respectively, the *Between C & D* anthology (1988) and Brian Wallis's splendid *Blasted Allegories* (1987). Differing greatly from the retrospective anthologies published in the mid-eighties by the more sedate literary periodicals, these anthologies come out of a community engaged quite actively in reconstructing the American imagination.

Wallis says in his introduction that the selections "demonstrate alternative capacities to generate ambiguous, complex, and experiential forms of knowledge which are collective and cultural but not equatable with bourgeois norms—this is stressed as a basis for broad political change" (Wallis 1987, xvii). However, these "collective" forms do not simply wait for Anthology Time to break forth over the heads of accountants on the morning train. Although these books are convenient for those of us on the outside in our efforts to catch up, for the participants of this community the crosstalk of the magazines has been even more important. There are at least three dozen magazine titles worth attention—some now defunct, some originating in Toronto or Michigan or San Francisco but still important reads for New Yorkers, many of them making the periodical shelves of St. Mark's Bookshop and Spring Street Books look, as a good friend put it, like a Hickory Farms of the literary Left. We have looked at *Between C & D*, so closely allied to the sensibility of its editors, Joel Rose and Catherine Texier. But our sense of downtown writing remains incomplete until we have looked more carefully at the monthlies, quarterlies, and outright irregulars that paced alongside this writing scene as it was unfolding. That done, we can turn to a group of writers whose work owes much to this opportunity to read and publish in these outlets.

### On the Rack: Downtown Magazines

Sometimes a magazine almost flies itself, but more typically we hear stories of six-member collectives (born of economic necessity) getting into ridiculously prolonged differences of opinion, of issues stashed in warehouses until the editor raises the cash to redeem and distribute another few boxes, of juggling benefit performances and small grants and sales to keep going from issue to issue, of renting U-Hauls to get from printer to binder, of setting type all night at co-ops in order to get discount night rates, of car-trunk warehouses, and of going bust right into the Kraft macaroni budget. The editors give you different reasons for this exercise in masochism, but, finally, what changes the kitchen-table decor from sugar bowl and teaspoon to glue pot and Exacto knife is a desire to keep a community still talking in accents not homogenized by the uptown slicks.

Because my focus has been largely upon fiction, I will merely mention those magazines in the adjacent arts that are important to the writing scene. We might look to *Act* for performance art, to *High Performance* for a more general focus (including video), to *Art in America* and *ArtForum* for those moments when they turn their attention to downtown artists and writers, to *ZG*, particularly for projects such as its companion to the Altered States exhibition, and to a host of film journals for their responses to a medium important to these writers. The truly archival reader might also keep in mind some out-of-town magazines that surface frequently with work on or by these figures, among them the Los Angeles Institute of Contemporary Art's *Journal: A Contemporary Arts Magazine*; *Impulse*, out of Toronto; and *Lightworks*, out of Michigan. Useful for sensing the resonance of fashion, painting, writing, film, video, performance, and politics are the arts tabloids that surface as giveaways, such as *Downtown*; compendiums of ads and reviews, such as the *Soho Arts Weekly*; and rather important titles, such as Leonard Abrams's *East Village Eye* and Jeff Wright's *Cover*. These last two publish useful interviews, reviews, and notices, as well as stories and poems, and their pages are fitting evocations of the community's multi-media mentality. *Cover* is not only informative but also quite revealing of an irreverence for received opinion, an impatience with the many forms of naïveté, and a zest for the innovative and even for the merely energetic. Finally, the particularly political aura of *East Informer* helps cue the reader to political and historical issues in the area.

*Contact/II*, *Gandhabba*, and *National Poetry Magazine of the Lower East Side* are among the magazines keeping poetry diverse, even chaotic, as it develops alongside this generation's fiction. *Contact/II*, which is edited by Maurice Kenny and Josh Gosciak, is helpfully attentive to the avant-garde of the sixties and seventies and, despite its main focus upon current poetry, also publishes other kinds of writing by, say, Richard Kostelanetz and Dick Higgins. Its book reviews alone serve to keep current readers posted to what they had missed in their canonical college courses. *Gandhabba* is produced by Tom Savage with help from a mimeograph machine, and *National Poetry Magazine of the Lower East Side* pushes the limits of xerography with its mix of text and graphics, particularly in its *Urban Gardens* issue (Summer 1988), replete with offerings by Jörga Cardin, Ron Kolm, Bart Plantenga, Mike Topp, and many others. Its editors, Stephen Paul Miller and Jim Feast, clearly know many poets of the multitude now working downtown. Steve Cee's

*Avenue E* also mixes interesting graphics and text on the xerox machine, though Cee's interests range into the art scene (issue 4 contains an interview with Dean Savard, founder of an early Lower East Side gallery, Civilian Warfare), comics, and fiction (Gary Indiana, Ron Kolm, and Cookie Mueller are among the best-known contributors here).

The most upscale version of these mixed-media magazines is *Appearances*. Edited by Robert Witz and Joe Lewis, with Ron Kolm among its contributing editors, *Appearances* has heavy, glossy paper with excellent black-and-white reproductions for its extensive art coverage and a good range of writers represented among its fiction and poetry. The rosters provided by the table of contents from issue to issue are one of the better indexes to the visual and literary arts, particularly because *Appearances* remains interested in performance work, film, and photography, in addition to the painting and sculpture one would expect to find in such an arts magazine. The editors keep the ads quarantined fore and aft, draw a well-deserved string of grants from the New York State Council of the Arts (NYSCA) and National Endowment for the Arts (NEA), and manage somehow to keep the cost per issue down. *Shiny*, a relative newcomer put together by Michael Friedman, has grown steadily and includes visual art, interviews, poetry, and fiction by a range of figures including Peter Cherches, Dennis Cooper, Allen Ginsberg, Brad Gooch, Rodney Alan Greenblat, Judy Lopatin, and Harry Mathews. Friedman is willing to cover everything from rock 'n' roll to Steve Poleskie's skywriting art (yes, with a plane), emphasizes shorter pieces that make for quicker reads, and, judging from the rapid increase in advertising, seems to be managing effectively *Shiny*'s emergence as a noteworthy downtown magazine.

Since 1984, Kurt Hollander has been issuing *Portable Lower East Side*, one of the area's more solid journals. Hollander divides his space among several kinds of material which develop his title's theme. There is important documentation of history and politics in the area, including historical articles about immigrant groups, an evocative log of quotations concerning the Lower East Side going back to 1900, and a study of current real-estate development in the area. The magazine also contains songs, poetry, and fiction. Different generations are represented—we find Lynne Tillman and Tama Janowitz, but also Jerome Charyn, Allen Ginsberg, and Grace Paley—as are different languages, for Hollander is attentive to the mix of heritages that makes his part of town distinctive. For example, volume 3's double issue is entitled *Eastern Europe*, and, in a letter accompanying it, Hollander writes: "Although Eastern European literature is enjoying its greatest popularity at the moment, only one or two (male) authors, no longer living in Eastern Europe, are widely known. PLES [*Portable Lower East Side*] attempts to counteract this cultural containment by publishing work from Eastern European writers who continue to live and struggle in their homeland, from women writers, and from less recognized Eastern European writers and artists currently living in NYC."

Hollander includes poetry, fiction, film stories, plays, and essays that "connect this work to the larger socio-political struggle" pursued by these writers. In a letter to me, Hollander underscores his aims "to highlight a commonality of experience shared by these two different worlds" and to explore other ethnic groups, as in the more recent *Latin Americans in NYC*. Hollander is emphatic on two counts in particular: his conception of the Lower East Side "as a community with a rich history of resistance to the homogenization, gentrification, of culture," and his commitment "to presenting the social conditions within which art and literature are produced, instead of just promoting artistic talent." It is no fluke, then, that the study of art and gentrification so often cited in my opening chapter is to be found in *Portable Lower East Side*. Hollander is paradigmatic of the area's writing not only for his own fiction—which is sharply observed and written with less a "literary" than a storyteller's style—but also for his editorial sense of diversity and resistance, of the sociopolitical ramifications of the area's writing, and of his magazine as a *mission* "dedicated to publishing and promoting writers whose works are not published by the official organs of literary culture in America," as he says in his more public letter.

Although "self-produced, printed and distributed," *Portable Lower East Side* somehow seems too substantial, too well done, to be the *samizdat* its editor dubs it. It has in common with many downtown magazines, however, a sense of freedom from the look and feel of the "official organs of literary culture." *Tellus*, for example, is a magazine published on audio cassette. Issue 7 is fairly typical of the diversity of its contents, with readings by Richard Kostelanetz, Patrick McGrath, and Lynne Tillman, mixed with performance art, music, and other less classifiable cuts. *New Observations*, which has different editors for each number, is a serious version of Steve Katz's one-issue hoax, *Guest Editor*. For example, Tillman put together the *Critical Love* issue (*New Observations* 26 [1984]), which included pieces by Kathy Acker, Kurt Hollander, and Gary Indiana. Indiana's *Here Come the Murgatroyds* (*New Observations* 31 [1985]) features Ron Kolm, Patrick McGrath, Joel Rose, Catherine Texier, Lynne Tillman, and Peter Wollen. Editors from the art world naturally enough turn toward the visual arts for writers, including Peter Halley, Jenny Holzer, Barbara Kruger, Sherrie Levine, and William Olander.

Jeffrey Issac's *Public Illumination* is noteworthy for several reasons. The reputation of a number of those contributing graphics and text are noteworthy—among them Keith Haring, Ron Kolm,

Thomas McGonigle, and Mike Topp—but the items are all pseudonymous. One has to be *very* inside, I take it, to find out who's who (my guesses are not too daring, considering the distinctiveness of Haring's style and the others' use of pieces published elsewhere under their own names). The magazine is also noteworthy for its credit-card size, easily the smallest of the downtown magazines. Its approach is often whimsical, though hard shots are taken with fair regularity. It is always labeled "International Edition," truer now that Issac lives in Italy. This label mocks arts-magazine pretense as effectively as its size deflates the glossies; its pseudonyms, the reputation builders; its wit, the pieties of the large themes *(Civilization, Pain and Sorrow, Races)* taken as each issue's title. Among *Public Illumination*'s features are a centerfold "Wormens Wear Daily" with a night crawler modeling "the very latest underground fashions," the menu for the Salvador Deli (perhaps you would like the Georgia O'Kiche Lorraine, a Clement Greenburger, or just a Braquewurst and, for dessert, a Tart Forum), a set of variations on UPC graphics guaranteed to confuse any bar-code reader, and a number of absurdist drawings and photographs documenting city violence. It has the distinction, perhaps, of enabling its distributor to use a shoe box for storage. Issac's visual work is frequently in the magazine, and his *Twelve Picturesque Passions* is an amusing take-off on the genre of saints' lives, complete with red leatherette cover, accordion-style pages, and neatly printed (if archly matter-of-fact) tales of martyrdom backing illustrations in a style that Donna Kolm aptly calls "Edward Hopper with a sense of humor."

Michael Carter's *Redtape* has long been one of the best of the irregulars—both its timing and its format seem to change from issue to issue. It began life in 1982, with a Michael Roman cover, as well as with comics, poetry, fiction, drawings, and photos detailing urban death, callousness, and economic distress. The second issue celebrates assemblage, its pages prepared by individual contributors, photocopied, and stapled together, a tribute no doubt to Richard Kostelanetz's important earlier efforts in this form. By the third issue the list of contributors was expanding through the downtown community, with poets Ron Kolm and Richard Armijo, among others, coming aboard. The fourth issue sports a cover with silkscreened skulls, and the fifth is *White Lies*, whose stenciled title labels the ethnocentric misrepresentation signified by the appropriated *National Geographic* covers. These issues show a magazine coming of age, with contributors Peter Cherches, Constance De-Jong, John Farris, Richard Hambleton, Greer Lankton, Patrick McGrath, Miguel Piñero, and David Wojnarowicz representative of the major names appearing in *Redtape* as it graduated onto glossy paper capable of high-quality graphic reproductions.

The issue *The Cracked Mirror* shifts to tabloid size and is a veritable index to downtown writers, artists, and photographers. With Kathy Acker and many others added to the writers' roster, painters from Gretchen Bender to Christof Kohlhofer joining the regular visual artists, and photographers such as Barbara Ess contributing, Carter has clearly built *Redtape* into a centrally located venue for new work. From the moment we see Greer Lankton's eerie black cover photograph of papier-mâché dolls, we are in for an experience of the city at its most apocalyptic. The graphics portray skeletons, grotesque heads eating fish bones, cartoon violence, and decadence. The photographs are no cheerier; some are staged (like a high heel in an ice block), but most are images of city life, urban decay, or performances full of violence and amok sensuality. Carter's prose piece "Cityscape" collects details from 4:30 A.M., when junkies scurry for a fix; a woman runs down the street, bleeding through her chains, to escape a bondage scenario gone over the edge; and the narrator sifts among "so many competing histories and individual semantics ever enriching and everclashing the metaphors of one usurping the vocabulary of another sometimes leading to poetry but just as often to violent death." Richard Armijo's "Arrangements" deftly mixes bits of song lyrics cut, dried, and rearranged to throw off the pop rhythms just enough to separate discourse from an absent subject. There are touches of humor from Peter Cherches and Allan Pearlman, as well as a bit of Cecilia Vicuña's fabulist verse, but the mood is primarily grim. Carter neither paginates nor provides a table of contents for his magazine; he leaves its pages there before us to surprise and oversaturate, like the city that *Redtape* chronicles.

Skimming the surface of so many fine magazines gives us some idea, perhaps, of the diversity of moods and forms which characterizes this zone of activity. To look more closely behind the scenes of these magazines is to realize the energy and forethought required to put them before us. *Benzene, Bomb, Wedge,* and *Top Stories* are four quite different periodicals whose pages contain some of the best writing to be found. In talking with their editors, I learned a great deal about the relationship between individual initiative, group support and vision, and the economic facts of life that make most magazines relatively short-lived. In examining *Between C & D*, we have seen some of this, but these four and their editors offer us a lot of help in coming to terms with the community in which the new writing has emerged.

Allan Bealy sounds a bit ambivalent about the difficulty of starting *Benzene*, but not about the effect he wanted to achieve. After coming to New York he continued his Montreal magazine, *Da Vinci*, for several issues, and might have been glad for a rest from the rigors of publishing had he not felt something was missing from the downtown bookstores. "My main concern for even starting the magazine," he explained, "was from a graphic standpoint, trying to do something that was a little more visible—interested in the writing, but doing it in a format that would shine a little more than the normal small-press magazine, 5 × 8 or whatever." Appearing approximately twice a year until ceasing in 1985, *Benzene* first appeared in fall 1980 in tabloid format, and to Bealy it "was an object I was creating, a work of art," rather than a collection of individual pieces. "What I was striving for was the feeling that it isn't just a magazine, it's more of a big concrete poem in itself."

Bealy was fortunate both in the magazine's reception—"we sold out about every issue we published"—and in the stream of small grants he received, but, even with his efforts to keep costs down, he always had to wait for one issue to pay for itself before publishing another. Although there may be another issue in the pipeline, Bealy is more interested in continuing his book publications under his Benzene Editions imprint. These are major undertakings for him, with typical print runs of a thousand copies and with the cost per title ranging around the $1,500 mark (as little as $1,000 in the early days, up to $2,000 for the more recent Michael Kaspar book *Plans for the Night*). Although one book failed to sell, for the most part *Benzene* is a success story both financially and artistically though, as is often the case with small-press activity, a burden to its founder. Using *Benzene*'s visibility to help make available longer works than the magazine's pages could accommodate, Bealy has published a string of important books, including Spalding Gray's first book, *Seven Scenes from a Family Album* (1981), Peter Cherches's *Bagatelles* (1981) and *Condensed Book* (1986), and Reese Williams's *Heat from the Tree* (1984).

Were there no books, however, *Benzene* would still remain an important repository of works in progress. Even the first issue, which contains writing by Peter Cherches, Dick Higgins, and Richard Kostelanetz, is impressive. By way of suggesting the range and quality of *Benzene*'s issues, we need only sample arbitrarily the different activities of the downtown arts Bealy and Coeditor Sheila Keenan mixed together with work by contributors from beyond the city borders. For example, there are interviews with William S. Burroughs and Richard Foreman (the latter, which explores the rigors of production and also the contradictions inherent in a successful avant-gardist, is appended to Foreman's *Penguin Touquet*). There are also screenplay synopses (Douglas Huebler's *Crocodile Tears*), dance features (on Molissa Fenley), and essays (Gerald Janecek's on the Russian visual poet A. N. Chicherin, and Wayne Ashley's on Antonin Artaud's theories of ritual metaphor). In fiction, there is the minimalism of Tom Ahern and Roberta Allen, the grim parables of Bruce Benderson, the wit of Harrison Fisher and Spalding Gray, the urban touches of Gary Indiana and Judy Lopatin, the remarkably acute cuts of Ursule Molinaro, and the arresting opening of Reese Williams's *A Pair of Eyes*.

Bealy's abiding interest in performance art makes *Benzene* an important source for those reconstructing the history of this influential form. There are representative selections from performance art's heyday at the turn of the eighties, including material from Miriam DeJong, Gary Indiana, Les Levine, Carla Liss, Carolee Schneeman, and the Wooster Group. (*Zone*, a near-companion magazine to *Benzene*—editor Peter Cherches is a close friend of Bealy's and they shared some of the same writers and even a joint issue in 1985—contains a similar mix.) Invaluable to fiction readers outside the city, such documentation gives the liberating influence of performance art on downtown figures; its multiple media, simultaneous events, and often sharp cuts or bits all have fictional analogs. There is a similarly rich diversity of poetry in *Benzene*, with work by Richard Armijo, Charles Bernstein, and John Giorno only the first round to catch the eye. The art and photography document the visual arts with sensitivity to developing currents, including neo-geo, underground comix style, action painting, kinetic sculpture, photo collage, installations of numerous kinds. One issue documents the event David Wojnarowicz and Mike Bidlo organized at the Pier, an old warehouse astride a tunnel, in which artists contended with police to stage an ongoing putting up (and sometimes taking down or painting over) in the crumbling shell of a warehouse painted, sculpted, arranged, planted with grass and flowers—all in order to move outside the gallery syndrome of ownership and commodity. Taken as a whole, *Benzene*'s issues provide an extraordinarily rich record of the creative energies that shaped the early eighties. The issues also attest to the editorial skills that shaped the magazine as an important early presence for the benefit of the creators themselves and that soon drew contributions from across the country from those who felt in sympathy with the renaissance it captured.

*Bomb*, which first appeared in spring 1981 with Betsy Sussler as its editor, drew on funding from Artists Space and COLAB and on a pool of energy flowing in from the underground film community. When I asked Sussler how she came to edit *Bomb*, she responded very quickly: "Naïveté. You don't start a magazine like that with no money if you know what you're doing." But there were other reasons as well. Whether from economic restraints or the critical preoccupation with language and textuality, everybody downtown seemed to be either writing or making films (or making music, considering the numerous artists' bands, such as David Wojnarowicz's Three Teens Kill Four). They knew one another, they were interested in working out the change in sensibility that had taken place, and they were passing into the most productive phases of their careers. Sussler explained:

> At the time, I was in theater, I knew people who had been doing underground films, and through that scene you meet a lot of writers, you meet a lot of painters who volunteer to do the sets—I'd met a lot of painters anyway because I'd gone to school with them—and so, I thought, I'll start a cultural magazine about conversation. I didn't like the way everything was separate—the painters and sculptors were in *Artforum* and then the theater people had their theater magazine—and it didn't seem like much fun. So *Bomb* was really started as a conversation piece among a small group of people who were working in the late seventies in underground film. And then it caught on like wildfire and I couldn't stop.

*Bomb* was a collaborative effort from the beginning, with Glenn O'Brien (bringing his expertise from *Interview* and his own "TV Party" cable show), Liza Bear (from *Avalanche*), Sarah Charlesworth (photographer and writer), Michael McClard (painter), Mark Magill (the magazine's graphic designer), and Craig Gholson (playwright and fiction and screenplay writer) all playing key roles. With Eric Mitchell and Michael McClard, Sussler had been producing a small but influential "rag," as she described it, called *X Motion Picture* and full of work by artists and writers and filmmakers. But she and O'Brien had also been talking about historical precedents to *Bomb*, such as Wyndham Lewis's *Blast* and Charles Henri Ford's *View*, which championed Marcel Duchamp, Max Ernst, and Yves Tanguy in the forties (Ford always mixed media as freely as *Bomb*'s editorial group). The more that Sussler and O'Brien talked, the more the time seemed right, and Sussler said that in spring 1981 "we borrowed $1,000, we had $1,000 of ads, and we printed 1,000 magazines."

The first issue carried fiction by a number of writers whose names now have sufficient star quality to more than vindicate *Bomb*'s literary taste, among them Kathy Acker, Craig Gholson, Gary Indiana, Tina L'Hotsky, and Lynne Tillman. Since then, virtually every downtown writer of significance has published in its pages and *Bomb* has grown considerably. Juggling NEA and NYSCA grants and cuts, drawing upon a vital group of patrons and the fund-raising efforts of a board of directors, *Bomb* has increased ads, sales, and subscriptions to the point of increasing its print run of a thousand to three thousand, five thousand, then (in spring 1987) to eight thousand, with plans to hit ten thousand soon after. Not counting typesetting, photography, halftones, artists' fees, staff salaries, and office expenses (including the staff's now-transatlantic phone bills), it still costs $1.22 to publish a copy of the magazine. *Bomb* is something of an industry, as befits its position at the center of the downtown cultural scene. The magazine is still expanding its program of commissioning works from artists and photographers, its use of color, and its series of poetry in translation.

If you ask its editor to consider what makes *Bomb* distinctive, Sussler shows the energy that has carried *Bomb* to its current prominence. "The first thing we decided," she said emphatically, "was that it was going to be a magazine of artists and writers. No criticism, no reviews. Practicing artists and theater people would do the interviews. We would publish artwork and fiction so that the viewers could see the work for themselves instead of having it mediated through another eye." *Bomb* was made both by and for artists—this shows, for example, in Mark Magill's interview of Kathy Acker in issue 6 (1983); his questions are sometimes irreverent and intrusive, always arch; her responses are equally those of someone engaged in conversation rather than in an interview. Sussler is particularly pleased with the Joan Mitchell interview in issue 17 (1986), because it typifies the difference in having artists do the work: "The interviews become about making conversation in a way that is more intimate, that makes it really accessible. The Joan Mitchell interview is the most successful, and it's because of the language—it's really the language used in studios among painters. Cora [Cohen] was great."

If keeping the journalists and critics out of the picture is one principle, using multiple media is definitely another. Sussler tells a story that illustrates well how "natural" it was for *Bomb*'s editors to keep so many aesthetic forms integral to the magazine's identity:

> I was doing theater and film. I knew a lot of artists, and I couldn't imagine amusing myself with theater without recognizing the writers, or being involved in film without seeing what the artists were painting. The last theater piece I did was Gary Indiana's *Phantoms of Louisiana*, and Ross Bleckner did the sets for it. We were walking around these big, big beautiful paintings on the brown paper you pack meat in. He'd hung them up, and when we wanted to change the set we'd literally grab the painting and walk across the set with it. It was a physical part of my being—I couldn't separate it.

Sussler speaks of a "transference" among the arts and of "using a potpourri of activity rather than simply the blank page." Indeed, looking through an issue of *Bomb*, one almost feels like Sussler on that stage as one turns its huge pages filled with work by downtown's most interesting artists. But her other metaphor for the magazine is that "putting these slices together is like making a movie. . . . You have a couple of different tracks going when you're taking texts and taking images and taking people's ideas and putting them down." The relationship is not the dependent one of illustration, but "like a flip-book," she says, one that films the interrelations of painting, sculpture, fiction, underground cinema, theater, poetry, and the ideas their makers have about them.

When I asked Sussler what she looked for in choosing the literary pieces, a third principle emerged: "I'm looking for people who love language, love the words, the act of writing. They don't sit down and say, 'I'm going to write a story about *X.*' That's not the first thing. I love words, and the way they put them together shows—it's almost sexual." Lest this seem a hermetic reflexivity, Sussler connects language to two key ideas she finds important to the writing. "Taking spoken language and making it into a text," she explains, is part of an "appreciation of the American experience rather than the English, it's how to build your own culture out of the people you live with." A perennial American project since at least the days of Walt Whitman, this reach into the streets rather than into strictly "literary" sources for style is an element present in numerous downtown artists and writers and that comes with political implications spelled out clearly by Sussler: "Language comes from the people, and our editors have a much more liberal, even radical, notion of what language should be used and how it should be used." As we leaf through the magazine's issues, we find excerpts from Kathy Acker's *Great Expectations* or *Don Quixote* or *Empire of the Senseless*, or from Gary Indiana's *Burma*, and it becomes difficult not to follow the thread of language which is outside the suburban enclosure of high cultural decorum.

The political edge accounts for a fourth principle in the character of *Bomb*, a dialogic relation between the downtown and the global communities *Bomb* nurtures. On the one hand, there is the local community of artists and writers to which the magazine holds itself close and accountable and from which it draws its contributors. Embracing contraries, Sussler at one point calls this "a provincial attitude" (in the better sense of the term) and, at another, "our grass-roots" support. On the other hand, there is the international focus of *Bomb*, with special reports on Los Angeles (a different country in one sense!) and Köln but, much more significantly, an impressive series of poetry in translation, notably from the Caribbean and Central America, but also from places such as India, the Soviet Union, and Japan. Many of the poets linked to *Bomb* do translations, so the magazine has a natural route to printing this work. More fundamental, however, are two attractions: first, the political content of writers struggling personally with issues that too often remain on American coffee tables; second, the inspiration of other local traditions, such as Nicaraguan oral poetry—campfire extemporizing—understandably appealing to a community that maintains its own less informal communal settings. The dialogue between the local and the international strengthens the downtown community while keeping it open to currents of difference around the world.

It would be ludicrous to turn the pages of all the past issues of *Bomb* and try to analyze individual pieces in depth. The sheer quantity of first-rate work is overwhelming; the quality of those pieces that one would for practical reasons have to exclude would impugn any logic of selection; a catalog of names would duplicate the who's who of downtown art; and the essence of the magazine is well summarized by its editor. Much of the fiction is discussed by the author elsewhere in this book, for Sussler has managed consistently to present *Bomb*'s readers with a very good sample of downtown fiction. Sussler set out to present "a cultural magazine about conversation," but what perhaps she did not foresee is that this conversation hardly stops with the interviews and juxtapositions that her cinematic layouts stage for us. The pages of *Bomb* are now and will continue to be perhaps the best place to begin for those who want to engage with the sensibility that has emerged into cultural prominence during *Bomb*'s years of publication.

*Wedge*, a joint creation of Brian Wallis and Phil Mariani, had an objective different from that of *Bomb*, one in keeping with their positions as curators for varying stints with the New Museum of Contemporary Art. When we talked at a sandwich shop around the corner from the museum, Wallis said:

> One thing we tried to do with *Wedge* was to adopt an understated, even conservative design in order to get into the libraries—which it did. We just didn't get into the bookstores. It looked fairly respectable, and it had all these people in it who eventually became familiar names. We wanted to reach students who just couldn't get hold of this kind of material. If you're in New York, there's a certain amount of this going on all the time. You can go into St. Mark's and something by Kathy [Acker] is in every other magazine. But those magazines don't make it very far. It was important to us to get those kinds of literary and theoretical ideas out to a wider audience.

Theirs was a self-sacrificial mission not only in terms of time and work ("editing, typesetting, proofreading, composition, everything except for the actual printing and binding") but also in terms of money. "We've gotten very few grants to do it; it's been mostly our own money and all our own time," Wallis told me. "But it's gotten really expensive: we did the first issue for $1,200, and the last for $7,000 or $8,000."

As curators-without-support to the nation at large, Wallis and Mariani have been committed in ways that are material enough for anyone's standards of dedication. What prompted the creation of

*Wedge* was that critical discussion was not keeping pace with the arts. Wallis notes that

> *Wedge* started with an article in the first issue on Robert Longo. I was interested in a lot of the younger artists who weren't getting a lot of coverage elsewhere but who were, for me as a young critic, already *major* figures. I couldn't understand it. All my friends thought these people were geniuses. Nobody was writing about them. It was perfectly clear to me at that point that Barbara Kruger was a *major* person as a writer, as a visual artist, as a person. But she didn't even have a gallery at that time, and the same thing held with a lot of people. And Longo was not the sort of demigod he is now. Phil [Mariani] was very excited about doing this as well. Her big concern was that nobody was looking at the broader political implications of this work.

The policy of Wallis and Mariani has been to mix these critical explorations with "interviews, artists' writings, fiction, and pages just given over to an artist," and the result was an important journal that was alone in trying to connect new creative work with the theoretical concerns of poststructuralism.

*Wedge* began in the summer of 1982 with the issue *An Aesthetic Inquiry*—Wallis is a bit disappointed nobody got its pun anesthetizing a certain kind of inquiry—which opened with a parodic interview between "Art Papier" and Joseph Beuys. The first two issues preserved the sedate academic appearance Wallis and Mariani wanted in aiming at the nation's research libraries. Fiction by Kathy Acker and Richard Prince, art by Jenny Holzer, Barbara Kruger, and Louise Lawler and Sherrie Levine, performance work by Robert Longo, Paul McMahon and Nancy Chunn, and Tim Miller, interviews with Robert Ashley, Rainer Werner Fassbinder, and collaborators Jean-Marie Straub and Daniele Huillet—these mix with essays by both critics and artists which explicitly develop the postmodern aesthetics of these figures.

*Wedge*'s next three issues had a change of format; they appeared together as a single box of fourteen pamphlets, including fiction by Kathy Acker, Roberta Allen, Theresa Hak Kyung Cha, Gary Indiana, and Reese Williams; there was a range of artists' books, including Silvia Kolbowski on the representation of woman, Nan Becker on involuntary sterilization of the poor, Matthew Geller on the selling of television, Richard Milazzo on "semblance and meditation," John Fekner's ideologically charged labels stenciled around the downtown area, and Sarah Charlesworth's "Lover's Tale," composed of stills appropriated from films. The blend of the formats of fiction (Acker's and Williams's particularly visual) and variously deployed strategies of imagery and text in the artists' books helps blur the dividing line between them, a line further questioned in the final pamphlet by Phil Mariani. "The difference between appearance and reality" runs these four tracks across the page: across its top are five lines of type mixing different apologias for U.S. policy in Central America; selected quotations from the Left and the Right are across the bottom; through the middle is a series of images appropriated from television sitcoms; and, finally, superimposed on the images are bits of Habermas's analysis of the State's need "to secure the loyalty of one class while systematically acting to the advantage of another." The editorial for the boxed set argues a balance between "recent literary theory" and "specific social and political circumstances" in the way these artists have developed "a newly structured text appropriate to its subject and capable of overcoming the crippling contradictions inherent in writing as it now exists." Appropriation, heterogeneity, openness to readers' participation, and the "transformation of the forms of writing and codes of communication" are the aims not only of the pamphlets in this powerful collection but also of *Wedge* as a periodical.

Indeed, to look at the more recent issues of *Wedge* is to see its dedication to what the editors call "a politically engaged form of writing." The 1984 issue (6) approaches *Sexuality: Re/Positions* (Lynne Tillman is the key fiction writer, and Alice Jardine and Jean François Lyotard are among the essayists), and the 1985 issue (7/8) considers *The Imperialism of Representation/The Representation of Imperialism* (with Gary Indiana's fiction and with Edward Said and Gayatri Spivak among the critics). Those who might suppose the downtown scene is somehow apolitical or only coffee-table-ish in its commitments should be convinced otherwise by the kind of conversation *Wedge* puts to the forefront. Its representation of the larger implications of this work has made unmistakably explicit the political content of postmodern art and of poststructural theory.

### Anne Turyn's Top Stories

It would be difficult to decide whether Anne Turyn figures most prominently as editor, photographer, or writer, because she is, as is typical of the downtown set, a person of multiple talents. To look at each of these three pursuits is to see again the distinctive dynamism of this community in which individuals and forms so productively mingle. Since 1979 *Top Stories* has appeared with heartening regularity, publishing fiction by many of the best contemporary writers. Not surprisingly, the venture comes not from any desire to publish a literary magazine for the sake of the project itself, but more out of Turyn's sense that too few people were having the opportunity to experience the quality and commonality of a community's work. When she was an M.F.A. student in the photography program of the State University of New York at Buffalo, she set about to transform

the Hallwalls arts center's reading program from a standard sequence of visiting writers into a fiction program with vision. "When
I asked them [the center's administrators] for the money to start
Fiction Diction," the series she coordinated, "they said if I wrote a
grant to have a reading program, then I could have the money to start
*Top Stories*." When the grant came through, Turyn began inviting
the likes of Kathy Acker, Laurie Anderson, Constance DeJong, and
Pati Hill, and *Top Stories* began as a series of pamphlets in which
writers had up to forty pages for their work.

The key literary figures appeared early in the Fiction Diction
series and in *Top Stories*; Kathy Acker, Constance DeJong, and
Lynne Tillman are among the best known. But the series also reminds us of how freely members of this community pass back and
forth between writing and the adjacent arts. We find Laurie Anderson from the music and performance scene, Pati Hill and Cookie
Mueller from film acting, Gail Vachon from filmmaking, Jenny Holzer from the visual arts, Judith Doyle from performance, Anne
Turyn and Richard Prince from photography. We find Janet Stein's
pointed update of fifties' True Romance comic books, as well as a
superb pair of stories by Ursule Molinaro, who is not only a painter
and an exquisite writer but also a significant inspiration to a younger
generation's efforts to open fiction to new possibilities. And one
finds, from upstate New York, strong pieces from Asher/Straus,
Suzanne Jackson, and Linda Neamon. But for the most part *Top
Stories* has grown out of the progress of Turyn from a Buffalo fol-
lower of downtown developments who was influenced by teachers
such as Walter Abish and Raymond Federman, to a participant in
that scene since her move to New York in 1980.

Turyn is clear about what a "top story" needs to be: "It's looking at language as a plastic medium—you can do things with it. Of
course, I called my magazine *Top Stories* because I didn't want to
lose track of the story—I wanted both." Discussions of Acker, De-
Jong, and Tillman have shown how that narrative hook is splintered
by the first, sublated by the second, and appropriated for a feminist
ethnology by the third. But to thumb through these pamphlets is to
see how variously the plasticity of language can be explored. Laurie
Anderson's pamphlet, for example, reminds one of her contribution
to Reese Williams's *Hotel*, only without the accompanying photographs. Both are texts from her performance pieces. "Words in Reverse" (*Top Stories* 2 [1979]) would be performed with a tape bow
violin, an instrument whose bow holds a strip of recorded audiotape
and whose bridge holds the playback head. The text is in short
segments that build a vision rather than the causal chain of traditional narrative. That vision consists of the nonnormative responses
within a neurotic culture, whether we are reading a vignette of the
notably peculiar (the shoeless Bowery bum with bright new white

socks who moves two small pieces of plywood step by step down the sidewalk), the merely odd (the man whose daily lunch is a carrot he eats into the shape of a spoon, with which he eats chocolate pudding before finishing the carrot), the socially inscribed (the seventy Jane Fondas who emerge with "brand new memories" from one of her films), or are encountering her one-liner psychosocial analyses ("I am in my body the way most people drive in their cars") and socio-critical capsules (she argues that both the detective novel and science fiction relieve us from having "to deal with human nature at all" because the former accumulates data about an already dead hero and the latter does not need to explain its hero's superpowers).

Language in Anderson becomes a point of arrest at which we see rather than cover the cultural stress lines. Not surprisingly, a number of the pamphlets work in this same quick-cut fashion, including Lynne Tillman's "Living with Contradictions" (*Top Stories* 10); Cookie Mueller's "How to Get Rid of Pimples" (19–20 [1984]) and Lee Eiferman's "95 Essential Facts" (14 [1982]) also work this way. Gail Vachon's pamphlet "This Is My Mother. This Is My Father" (6 [1980]) breaks down the narrative structure of chronology and continuity even further than Anderson's pamphlet does, because Vachon's bits replace those structural traits with something closer to the simultaneities of a scene, some segments crisscrossing different mental zones of a character (pieces of song mixing with daydreams, a shirt melted while being ironed, and the "exterior" event taking place), other segments running along like song lyrics, mixing quick takes of workmen on the girders with children's names and the disco beat as "the pulse of the nation." The pamphlet ends with a paragraph that evokes the feel of language on the edge between narrative, film, poetry, and list:

> I've worked hard all day. I've addressed serious questions. The Mother of Me says to the Baby of Me, "You've worked hard all day. What would you like for dinner?" I stroll into the supermarket, gleeful. I glide up and down the aisles humming with the Muzak. I had heard that a new tense had been invented. The apples were bruised, the lettuce wilted, the carrots rubbery. I suspected that it might describe the memories of what would be. (25)

Vachon's segments sound at times like memories of Abish's "future perfect," gathering four- to eight-line stills from possible lives paced by old Beatles songs, haunted by monsters snarling from the corner of her eye, buzzed by the supermarket's narcotic allure, and anxious over retirement benefits, someone falling "like a domino," and "heinous crimes in the dead of night."

Pamphlets by Jenny Holzer and Linda Neaman explore consumption (in Holzer's "Eating Friends") and the fetishized body of women (in Neaman's "Foot Facts") by mixing texts and expressionist drawings in the former and appropriated pieces and photographs in the latter. Janet Stein's "Shattered Romance" takes the style of comic books and all but abandons narrative in favor of quick takes on gender oppression. More recent issues, including *Five* (22 [1986]) and *Tourist Attractions* (25–26 [1987]), look more like a fiction magazine in that they feature shorter pieces by a number of writers. These issues suggest that Turyn has reached the point of wondering what *Top Stories* will become in the changed circumstances she sees in the downtown scene. She explains that

> *Top Stories* may have served its function. There's something going on now with the marketing of the East Village. I published Lynne [Tillman] and Kathy Acker six or seven years ago, and they're getting published now. But I published Susan Daitch, and her book is coming out the end of this year. And I published Tam [Janowitz] and didn't know the book was coming out the next week! Maybe *Top Stories* isn't necessary because all these people can get published. Maybe it should be artists' books now, or a forum for more established writers that is different: I mean, where else can you publish forty pages? I just don't want *Top Stories* to turn into what happened to alternative spaces. They started out showing conceptual stuff that couldn't be shown anywhere else. Now they're a bush league for the gallery system and actually serve that system.

With grants now received regularly enough to make *Top Stories* an easier venture financially—despite printing costs of $3,000 an issue for editions that have risen from the initial 500 to as high as 2,500—the magazine's greatest perils are probably its consumption of a tremendous amount of Turyn's time and the changed circumstances of its writers' improved access to a readership.

If *Top Stories* has been an important showcase for the midlength works of downtown writers, Turyn's photographic work has become a quintessential case of how narrative and other media interact in ways important to our understanding of media resonances among downtown figures. Her photographs have been both widely exhibited and performed (as slides during readings) alongside her texts—her *Top Stories* pamphlet, "Real Family Stories" (13 [1982]), is a good example of how photographs, fiction, and performance can meet. Typically consisting of a number of photographs placed as a series, and often including text as part of (or most of) the image, her photographic work is collected in *Missives* (Alfred Van Der Marck Editions, 1986). She describes *Dear Pen Pal* as "ironic, undermining," its target the monstrosities we have naturalized ("We don't just grow food. We manufacture it" is the legend for a photograph of a line of orange suckers), our mania for consumption ("We are a nation of consumers" is the legend for a photograph of dancing plastic cartoon creatures) and technology ("Our bodies keep up with technology" by updating the metaphors through which we understand ourselves), and the specularity of existence ("Life is a spectator sport, here in America").

*Dear John* plays with this most recognizable of epistolary genres, juxtaposing letters against scenes that tease our need to compose explanatory narratives. The pieces are humorous ("You're like a record I've listened to over and over, but the scratches have driven me crazy"), witty (the note about a relationship "lacking fiber" is shot against a sandwich made of white bread), and a bit mysterious (are the men the johns or their replacements?). *Lessons and Notes* is a more serious series, she told me: "I wanted to talk about lessons, about what they don't teach in the schools," at least explicitly. Some of the photographs reflect Turyn's longstanding interest in developmental psychology ("And when you think / to whom are you talking?"). But others probe the process of education rather sharply, such as the ones with two children out of focus ("This is not what I expected"), with toy babies crawling across a dictionary page ("Babies—place of origin"), or with a boy holding an out-of-focus frame in front a globe ("Where does history happen?"). The blackboard reads "Who Are You?" above a boy with both a book and a mirror propped in front of him, suggesting a sort of textual mirror stage institutionalized in education. Another photograph meditates on the problematic nature of language itself by showing the illustrated flash cards and texts of a reading class against the legend "If thoughts are yo-yos, words are tangled strings."

Turyn's suspicion of the tangled strings of words is revealed not only in *Missives* with their juxtapositions of image and text (we must move into a space between the two in order to fabricate our response), but also in her fiction. "If Only," a piece she did with Robert Fiengo for the Remembrance of Things Past exhibition at the Long Beach Museum of Art, is more readily available in Brian Wallis's *Blasted Allegories* and, like her *Dear John* series, works within stylized form, in this case of wishing upon a star, writing to Santa, breaking a wishbone. We might think of these wishes as written in the cultural subjunctive, for they wish their way out of a 1930 "hellhole," or wish for shoes in 1910 Kentucky or for a video game in 1980 Florida or for a larger dowry in 1830 Britain. Working without images against which to bounce her words, Turyn depends upon the context her datelines evoke and that of the reader in the eighties to achieve the tangle of the strings by which we try to tie down thoughts, memories, and desires.

Turyn's piece in Barbara Ess's *Just Another Asshole* 6, "Keep Talking," is told from the point of view of Sadie's dog. The dog overhears Sadie's phone conversations, her reveries in bed with a lover, her musings aloud. Skewed a bit by the dog's perspective and marked by the ellipsis left by what cannot be seen or heard, the story requires an active imagination on the part of a reader to keep up with Sadie's mix of banalities and wistfulness: "Dreams might just be memories . . . and who can trust memories?" (159). These alternative spaces in consciousness offer Sadie no haven from what is, for the narrator, the quotidian of a dog's life. "Real Family Stories" retains 27 of the 180 slides Turyn used for its performance version, its images quintessential family photos, complete with little black lick-and-stick corner mounts. Against these photos, Turyn sets stories from the point of view of various members of a family, the sort one might hear around the holiday dinner table. The sexual tangles, deaths, and, as the story calls it, weirdness of family members mix and shift as one voice corrects or rejects another's version of things. We do not get a story of the family, a recognizable chronology, or even a gallery of individuals—no voice is sufficiently fleshed out for that—but rather a system of relations which somehow holds up under all the changes and upheavals in marriages and individuals, and despite the variables of health, fortune, and age.

What makes this narrative "real" is partly its openness and partly its foregoing the naming of social and economic pressures in favor of specifying the displacements of desire and of self wrought by those pressures in the daily texture of family lives. In "Idioglossia," an extraordinary story in *Wild History*, Turyn takes on virtually the whole set of issues which has concerned her during her career. Her avocational interest in developmental psychology, her M.A. in linguistics, her photographer's anthropological eye, her political concerns about First and Third World relations, and her feminist commitment all enter into this story, which appears to mix the journal entries of a university anthropologist with the responses of his "primitive" female subject. When we talked, Turyn recalled a phonology class in which she read her way through glossolalia (speaking in tongues), xenoglossia (suddenly speaking a foreign language), and idioglossia (the private language some twins develop to communicate apart from the rest of the world), as well as the impact of writing systems on cultures that develop them.

These interests lead to the density of the inquiry into the relations among language, writing, culture, and gender in "Idioglossia," for its "he" and "she" occupy different sides of each key term. The Studier is stereotypically male and ethnocentric. He hopes for fame and fortune from his studies, which appear to be carried out (17) under the pressure to publish or perish (19), and his metaphors are full of economic markers, such as "invested." She is inventing a form of writing that is both a blessing (she can record her daily stories) and a curse ("my ideas about talking have set me apart from the people"). He likes to play Scrabble, a game in which one reproduces words from the existing pool, but her people's game is Deeper Meaning, in which new words are invented: "The coveted sounds are those we discover right before tomorrow, in the crevice between this night and that day, when everything but our thoughts are suspended" (18). His version of her explanation calls it "a game in which they invent new words to express thought and feelings which are without names or words," but when he watches it he finds that "the sounds they emit are not for use in a system producing language. The sounds cannot combine and are inevitably outside sense and language" (26, 27).

Deeper Meaning satisfies a community's need to extend language beyond the confines of what he considers "sense," for his grasp of language is of a piece with all of the technological paraphernalia he has carried into this remote region. The sophisticated rationalist looking down the medulla oblongata into language acquisition, he does not like what he finds, because his epistemology of correspondence is unsuited to one of evocation and of the unnamable that works in the gray areas between his categorical divisions. He finds a system marked by the consensual rather than the rational, the emotive rather than the intellectual, the fluid rather than the systematic, the inchoate rather than the preformulated. Her syllabary remains close to a spoken system, as opposed to his thoroughly grammatological system, her people's diglot practice (each individual has a public and a private language) resists his imperial homogenizing language, and the binary oppositions keep piling up— male and female, First World and Third World, subject and object, studier and studied.

We do not have an easy time sorting out these matters. We lose confidence in the anthropologist's narration not only because of his obvious inabilities to understand her but also because of the strikeovers in his journal entries, which reinforce the last page of newspaper headlines suggesting hoax and duping. But we also lack confidence in her entries, because we are asked to believe that she possesses not only the people's language (which we never see) but also English as her private language. Is she like the woman Turyn told me about in Ferdinand de Saussure's case history who woke up speaking "Martian" (finally dismissed as an assemblage from Geneva's polyglot environment) and Hindi (a harder competence to rationalize)? Is she a saboteur of his scholarship? Is she an invention of his fevered brain? Are the headlines at story's end authoritative? We seek the answers to these questions because we want this story line to "work out." But Turyn does not comply. "The funny thing about the human mind," she told me apropos of her work with texts and photographs, "is the way juxtaposition and narrative work. You put two things next to each other and the human brain just wants to make connections. If you put two sentences together, they start to become a story."

The ultimate point of "Idioglossia" is just this desire to forge connections between juxtaposed elements and to string them into a story resolving difference into meaning. The story is primarily concerned with the problematic relationship that all of us experience between the public language of narratological connections and the private experience of this desire, that feeling, and the intimation of some unnamable beyond. The former is cultural and the latter is organismic, and this internal division is yet another version of how to narratize what the two characters supposedly represent. The dialogue in this story is finally between metaphorical rather than the literal twins to which it refers several times. The internal siblings created by language, and especially by writing, set up binary poles within us corresponding to the sets of oppositions we have been tabulating. They also establish the sort of confusion and mangled communication that take place between the principals. She begins to realize the implications of this internalized community when she contrasts her writing to her people's oral tradition: "Perhaps my marking device will be to me the way the stories are to all of us . . . the stories exist in more than one place at a time, so these thoughts can exist in these marks as well" (21).

In her people's oral tradition, community members sit around the fire receiving wisdom through their toes. In writing, however, what is unique to her finally exists apart from her, taking a part from her and placing it elsewhere, as an object open to appropriation by others. My pun signifies the undecidability that writing marks in our ideas of difference and identity, of spacing and mastery, of otherness and colonization. That is, the tension between difference and identity is, for the individual, that between the social and the unique and, internally, between unity and multiplicity; writing opens the possibility for confronting these different selves and ages in a way not easily thinkable in a purely oral culture. Moreover, the spacing between these two characters, partly the result of their conflicting systems of writing, creates a battle of wits between his scrabbling of her into the abstractions of anthropological data (he interrogates her concerning language patterns, myth systems, kinships) and her desire to involve him in the spontaneous and unmediated articulation of Deeper Meaning. And, finally, their mutual otherness triggers efforts to colonize difference, he according to his hierarchical and she to her communal models of associating with the not-self.

If, finally, Turyn's interest is in "language as a plastic medium," we can see that such plasticity is an eminently social domain within and without the individual consciousness, as well as one in which the external divisions of gender, economics, politics, rhetoric, and myth resonate with analogous divisions that are wrought internally as language disciplines consciousness. By leaving the story line confused and confusing, Turyn manages to have us think about these characters in terms of both external and internal conflicts. Turyn's is, in a way, the inverse of Acker's strategy. There, language is turned inside out so that its repressed content of violence and mayhem is desublimated. Here, language is turned outside in so that violent self-difference is seen to be inherent in the very systematics of language itself. "If Only" is a series of unfulfilled wishes, "Keep Talking" is a dog's perspective on the strange discontinuities in human relations, "Real Family Stories" eavesdrops on contradictory and open-ended experience, and "Idioglossia" leaves us unsure of what actually has happened. But if the four stories sound utterly disparate, they share a fundamental commitment to the unclosable quality of narrative and to the absurdity of trying to overcome the internally fissured nature of language and consciousness so well revealed in "Idioglossia." Her fiction rejects the master narrative of the anthropologist and takes us much closer to the spontaneity and vitality of a postmodern version of Deeper Meaning. In Turyn's game our process of making up top stories wins out over the closure we might desire.

### Gary Indiana and the Burma Road

After a decade of plays, stories, and art and film reviews, Gary Indiana is as well known to readers of *ArtForum*, *Art in America*, or the *Village Voice* as he is to those who have followed his stories in *New Observations*, *Between C & D*, and *Wedge* or the serialization of his novel, "Burma," in *Bomb* (a final version of which Grove Press is publishing as *Horse Crazy* [1989]). When *Scar Tissue And Other Stories* (Calamus Books, 1987) was published, it became even easier for a wider audience to come into contact with his varied interests, his long-term observations of the downtown arts scene, and his determination to continue a very real search for wisdom in the arch and complex narrative voices through which he works.

In *Scar Tissue* Indiana's persona toys with us, posing in this piece, pouting in that, in most of them coming on to us through the protective fog of a very urbane, highly ironic, deeply hip wit that leaves nothing and nobody with an edge on him. That persona has not only seen it all, he has seen it so many times that it is an effort to get out and mug our pretensions and self-satisfactions. As cold and merciless as a serial killer, he is so used to surviving that his skills and tasteful touches in doing so have all gone slightly sour with an irony laced with ennui. But there is also "Burma," and its Gregory recognizes two Bretts, one of them *Scar Tissue*'s—who gets angry at Gregory's coyness and fights for the upper hand. The other is the "real you" of "Burma," also a veteran survivor, but one who risks all of that narrative's plot turns in order to keep open to the possibility of real connection. He maintains his eye for telling detail, his ear for prose rhythms, and his taste for a guarded love affair despite the improbabilities of life as an urban gay writer in the epoch of commodification and immune deficiency syndrome.

Some of the stories are expanded versions of the perfect party story, well-mixed Mickeys that dose the victim and let the rest of us recall them the next morning with a mixture of admiration and relief (admiration at the performance, relief we were not its object). "American Express," for example, which originally appeared in the *Wild History* anthology, devastates the perhaps-too-wealthy would-be writer, Amelia, "a type that invested more in appearances than anything else, if things looked fine, why, things were fine" (81–82). The "thinly fictionalized heroine" of her novel is likely to wait for her next "unpleasant situation" (76) until Amelia runs out of the quarterly dividends that pile up $5,000 in cash bundles under her mattress. "Pillow Talk" sets the infantilism of pet names against Claude's empty good looks and Melissa's faked orgasms. Its peripheral shots at the power of money and at her health anxieties evoke but do not explore the realities of economics and mortality alongside the main story line's sketch of empty relationships. "I Am Candy Jones" is a witty send-up of radio-show confessionals. Its protagonist is a schizophrenic Barbie doll with an indeterminate mix of CIA paranoia and hypnotic brainwashing; whether her husband or the CIA's Bea Lin is the real villain remains lost in the irreconcilable narrations by Candy, her alter ego, and her husband.

Other stories push their dislike for the commodity culture more aggressively. "Cl'Amour" quotes a series of notebooks which mixes a writer's problems with those of someone trying to understand his family, efforts that drown in the clamor of the television that infiltrates and then takes over the story by its end (fans of Doris Lessing's *Golden Notebook* will be interested in considering the relationships here). "Old Art, No Money" sketches a washed-up sensation whose ruthlessness on the way up costs him on the way back down and allows Indiana to let out some black bile over the art scene as a fashion market. "The Hidden Anguish of the Mouseketeers" takes up the shallow moments of American and even international Marxism and crosses them with the world of cartoon critters, former Mousketeers, Muppets, and the like. A Lillian Hellman character represents the high-rolling coffee-table Marxist, and "Dash" is public hero, private stoolie. The movement's ideological debates are reduced to the struggle between Mickeyites and Duckites for control of the Disney empire, the ultimate terrorist act being to blow up the cryogenically preserved father, Walt Disney. As if this were not already a sufficient deflation of radical chic, "The Role of My Family in the World Revolution" translates ideological factions into family squabbles. The family pretends Republicanism while expecting revolution but, to tide them over until the redistribution of wealth, diverts its town's interstate exits to Aunt Mildred's old farm and makes millions in the ensuing real-estate boom.

At yet a deeper level, Indiana works with the embattled world of gay relationships, at times maintaining the humorous tone and satiric pitch of the lighter stories, at times moving into what a seriocomic character describes as "deep down where the icky fish of your mind really swim" (46). "Shanghai" tricks us by moving from one extreme to another. It is a split narrative, its italicized segments presented as bits from a cheap paperback novel featuring a tough-guy imperialist in the Orient, but using a set of names which explodes the form (An War Sedan, Tu Dor Sedan, Le Duck Toe, Colonel Surrogate, and Lester Hardware the zircon king). Its other half begins with the Bangkok experiences of a witty narrator who is anxious about his boyfriend back home, a "blond Californian type, vain, the type that's always mentally on a surfboard" (61). But the tone has shifted to dangerous territory by the end. Under the influence of absolute excess bred by the scenario of white imperialists in the world of color, one ironically doubled from the parodied novel, the actress is snuffed and dismembered, and one perpetrator goes insane and the other is made a vegetable by a car wreck.

Comedy is also interrupted in its smug progress in "One Size Fits All." A rich art dealer's burial scene fractures into several possible endings that mix and may match with the other story lines that a very reflexive narrator toys with before our eyes. The broader satire lampoons the art world—the dealer signed a gay pair of artists without understanding their sexual or aesthetic practices—and the decadence of the rich—there is slapstick comedy when the dealer's mistress tumbles into the grave and her other lover falls in after her. Yet another story line features the revenge that blacks and Hispanics take on rich whities. The story turns a bit eerie at the end when the gay artists hear the dealer tapping and let the burial proceed. In one segment, the dealer then has a fatal heart attack, is dug up, and is found dead; in another, he rises from the casket, relishing the joke. But the casual reader gets pushed right off the comic edge by the reflexive narrator, who has been jovially distressed over his pronouns and is helpful in telling us "this is fiction" at the outset and "now for another fiction" as he starts Cooverizing his plot. This narrator takes over the last line to ice the gags: "The voice saying that there was another time, stranger still, is telling you the truth" (121). Just as in "Shanghai"—in which the narrator does not discover what happened to the actress until he finally develops a roll of snapshots—the urbane narrative frames turn out to have very narrow dimensions in "One Size Fits All." What lies beyond these frames is "stranger still" than the effort expended to make them appear sufficient.

When the humor is absent in *Scar Tissue*, there is only a grim

accounting of the real humorlessness of surviving outside the par-
tygoer's frames. The narrator of "Only You" confesses, a decade
later, real love to someone who has forgotten him altogether and
who has lived by the advice to "just leave without a word. The other
way is shabby." This narrator, who has more in common with the
one in "Burma" than with those discussed thus far, prefers "the
other way" of risking words, of trying to get past the impasse of
desire represented in "Sodomy." In this story the narrator, Philip, is
caught between two men, Jack and Dean, neither of whom can
really connect with him. Jack's one-sided and alcoholic sexuality
can culminate only in the bloody scene of masochistic lovemaking
which ends his relationship with Philip. Dean resides behind masks
so formulaic that Philip can label them, avoids sex altogether, and
tries to see "how far he could go without becoming involved in his
own actions" (27). Philip calls his own desire for Dean a "metaphysical principle" that goes beyond mere lovemaking to the wish "to
disappear inside him" (29), as if Philip's identity were too scarred
and ugly to maintain on its own.

The three characters in "Sodomy" feel at different moments
and in different ways their entrapment in contradiction. "Someday,"
Jack tells Philip, "we'll figure out that we really needed each other,"
a line Philip later realizes is "the most upsetting thing anyone ever
said to me" (30). It is upsetting because it implies that their identities have become so complicated as they crisscross back and forth
on the cultural margins that recognitions and opportunities never
quite match up. The book's title story holds grimly to the writer's
need to hold experiences until he understands them rather than
letting them, as Jack seems to do, sink into memory's mix of repression and delayed recall even as they happen. This short piece consists of fragments turning in the writer's mind and ranging over
many of the volume's themes. A lush Venetian sunset, a sense of
lost identity, the incipient yuppiedom of financial well-being, the
fear of AIDS, the buried workers in Imelda Marcos's film-festival
hall, and bad scenes during foreign travel are among the bits that
float along until the last page turns on an unnamed beloved: "You
were like a sliver of glass embedded in my flesh, a pain that stabbed
when I moved in a certain way. . . . When the sliver began working
its way out through the skin, you came back to push it in deeper.
You wanted to be sure to leave a scar. You did. But the scar doesn't
have your name on it, and I can always attribute it to someone much
more interesting" (41).

The narrator can recall more than one glass-sliver relationship
whose daggers are honed on economics, careerism, disease, and the
need to create. He knows that beyond the personal relationship is a
whole set of social and cultural determinants whose names it is his
business to recall rather than repressing them under the name of

one melodrama villain. He ends the story cataloging the experiences he has had since this wound, including finishing the page we are reading, telling the beloved that this is all "not what you're thinking . . . if it had all been to forget you, you'd have been forgotten long ago" (41). Repression is much easier than naming.

Naming in this very complex sense is what "Burma" is all about, and it is no accident that one of the most striking stories in *Scar Tissue* involves the same material in the same voice that we find in "Burma." Very much a New York story, "The Death of Maria Manchester" has a narrator who looks over the morning scene, where "below, in the street, everything is frantically sold, since flesh and sedation are perishable goods" (149). He tosses off parenthetically a sense of jaded disappointment in experience, "because all relationships are poisoned, and life doesn't live" (152). The mood invades his description: "Now the lurid Turner colors bleach out at the river end of 10th Street, dissolve in a jaw of rotting teeth. The sky turns slate, soiled, cottony, baby blue. I haven't slept; I haven't slept in a year." Both the tone and the sleeplessness derive from his frustrated efforts to love Gregory, another character who lives behind masks: "His wardrobe consists entirely of costumes. Nothing he has, nothing he keeps, is anything he thinks about as 'him'" (151). Worst of all, Gregory is "unmoved by the exasperation and grief his fecklessness causes," notably to the narrator (152).

Near the end of the story, we finally begin to understand why it is called "The Death of Maria Manchester." The title involves more than the narrator's longtime wish to make a film starring her. Although we are not directly told so, he seems to identify with her: "She was and always had been alone, had conceived obsessive attachments to people who were not attracted to her, squandered her emotions on unrequited loves. . . . She was formidable and subtly snobbish, but almost completely vulnerable. Each time she threw herself into love for another person, it ended in humiliation and embarrassment" (154).

Meeting her, he realizes that her "formality emanated from her shyness," one bred out of the recurrent pattern that seems so well to describe his own love life, and that her beauty was "strongly aligned with her intelligence" in a way that led her love objects to fear her, for "they knew Maria could never entirely lose herself" (154). Manchester embodies the combination of beauty and distance which is also in Indiana's fiction, and her mix of contraries is shaped by the bitter wisdom that the narrator articulates as his own version of Barthes's *A Lover's Discourse:* "Even decent people who are loved without loving back transform the affection of others into a personal weapon; and when he is young, the loved one looks for something more exalted than what he can have, despising what he is offered" (154). Gregory chooses heroin and the certain death it entails: "This is not exactly what Gregory wants, but it's what he can have with the least amount of effort" (153). Heroin's mix of energy and death is "more exalted" than the human relationship the narrator offers Gregory, and much of "Burma" is devoted to a struggle to understand why such a choice seems so inevitable for him.

When Brett visits Paul, a former lover dying of AIDS, he makes clear many things Brett would probably prefer not to face. Paul understands what is going on between Brett and Gregory:

> He's a shit, I tell him . . . an absolute and total shit. You always go right for the shits, Paul says, waving a fresh cigarette at the window. City with nine million gorgeous, well-adjusted guys, you'll ferret out the one shit like your life depended on it.
>
> I protest: Well, you weren't a shit.
>
> And look where it got me, Paul says. Right *in the shit*, can you feature that?
>
> It's all shit, I say bitterly, grabbing his hand and instantly letting it go, remembering the lesions. I'm sorry, did I hurt you, I ask him.
>
> They don't actually hurt, he says. They just suppurate.
>
> We listen to the hum and throb of the hospital, and watch the soundless river shatter light into thousands of white drops. We used to say: how can we live like this? And now the question really is, how can we die like this? (Fall 1987, 64)

The river is a silent witness to the craziness of urban conditions, to the ironies and bitterness of life's betrayal of hopes and idylls, to the toll of AIDS upon a community already under stress and upon the very concept of the body. It is only in the context of these larger issues that we can begin to follow Brett's efforts to understand *why* he always goes "right for the shits."

As in the passage above, Brett's descriptions of the city seem to emphasize verbs (such as "shatter") that mark the fragmentation of urban life, at times adding a pathological touch (such as "rotting teeth"): "Three in the morning. An iodine breeze off the river, the streetlamp rakes flecks of mica in the sidewalk. The middle-aged homeboys who usually occupy all the stoops on the block have crawled back into their flats like tuckered-out cockroaches" (Winter 1988, 71). Often, too, Brett describes apartments as cagelike. When he first enters Gregory's apartment, he is struck by this quality: "So, I thought, this dinky place contains his life. No wonder we all lose our minds in this city. Like kids playing at adulthood, living in these rabbit warrens with ugly floors and chipped ceilings. And areas instead of rooms" (Summer 1987, 48). He is always nervous about his own place, which is too small to allow him to contend with its disorder of books and papers: "Whatever measures I took were neutralized and overtaken by the action of time. This building is falling apart, year by year. The wooden floors are decayed. The brick walls leak plaster dust over every surface. Everything crumbles. It's impossible to move anywhere, since even a smaller place would now be twice as expensive" (Summer 1986, 34).

The implications of such living conditions and the work patterns required to sustain them are not difficult to see: "We live in large and small boxes in buildings on regularly shaped streets. We see each other seldom because we are busy. Nothing happens to us except dinner parties and visits to the dentist and work, our lives have the generic flavor of deferred pleasure and sublimation until we fall in love or die" (Spring 1987, 53). Boxed and regularized, the characters' lives turn generic with workaholism until falling in love or dying breaks the pattern. Even the work gets cannibalized, the boxes romanticized:

A few years earlier I had had more friends like Victor, marginals, who had and continue to have a great illusion of bohemianism, all the while the city changed around them, suburban kids had trickled into the neighborhood and used its fabled bohemianism as a media cachet, marketing the things they did as products of this exciting urban mix, a load of horseshit from beginning to end. And suddenly the slum housing turned choice and pricey, the blacks were driven out first, then the Puerto Ricans, now it's all white and gleaming and cold as cash. (Winter 1988, 72)

In my opening chapter we saw gentrification as an issue, and one that returns in such fiction as Joel Rose's *Kill the Poor*; here we see Indiana annexing its distinctively suburban qualities as an important dimension to the characters' "great illusion." Artists who began by living dangerously and cheaply in order to make art find themselves struggling to make enough art to afford increasingly upscaled rents. What at some moments is a locale Gregory likes to haunt to whet his edge is also a laboratory of how real-estate fortunes are made.

If the physical conditions of life connect with varying degrees of subtlety to the economic determination of lives and illusions, certainly the living patterns that grow out of this embattled state are equally important to the characters' psyches. The costs can be relatively subtle, as Brett realizes when he and a friend take the ferry out to Staten Island. Going out is full of giggles at tourists and "the military look of New York Harbor." But to return is to reenter the life that "military look" defends: "It was fine going out, barely tolerable coming back. This problem of attrition has been creeping into my experiences lately. Things commence in reckless hope and die away in stifled longing, not that we had hoped for much from the Staten Island Ferry" (Fall 1986, 48). Although Brett wisely did *not* hope for much from the ferry, the experience illustrates how even a local site is invaded and affected by the forces of attrition.

Much goes to make up those forces, but chief among them is the city's power of demystifying whatever illusions one has brought to its streets. For the gay culture in which Brett moves, that demystification has been cruel. He recalls an era quite different from the present one:

> A period of pickups and bizarre micro-affairs with boys whose points of reference belonged to another planet altogether, disturbed youths and borderline schizos harvested off Second Avenue in the wee hours, lean bodies and adorable faces that evaporated in daylight or loitered for days in carnal stupor, living out of the refrigerator, sometimes helping themselves upon departure to small, electronic objects or pathetic amounts of cash. Lots of inevitable bonfires. This all tapered off, wound down, whittled itself into chastity, a long time before disease made sexual loneliness fashionable. I lost the energy, the zeal for seduction. The script became too familiar. The real sex of our time is fame and money, and all sex is negotiated through the porthole of these ambitions. (Winter 1988, 71)

Brett, smarter and more analytical than some of his acquaintances, figures out why the sexual mythology of gay liberation turned out to be yet another exercise in capitalist recolonization. The script is the cyclic one of commodity consumption, and the real kick to life in the city has an economic base and a media superstructure.

Even at the level of "micro-affairs," even those less intense than the sexual, relationships become economic in their form and structure. Brett recognizes that Victor, whom he taps to clean Brett's apartment for Gregory's first visit, will cash in the debt for gossip and favors. But he also understands the underlying logic:

> That, I thought, is really how human beings are. Unless they perceive themselves as equal to each other, there is always some form of deranged accounting going on in one or the other's head, and we live in a system where no one is equal to anyone else, all are exploited by everyone, no one gives anybody anything and everyone owes everybody everything, the only equality available is equality in misery, and even the miserable argue about who is more miserable than whom. (Winter 1988, 72)

The passage does not hold its initial essentialism for long, but moves into how thoroughly the structure of hierarchy and the form of economics determine personal relationships down to the very ("deranged") functioning of consciousness itself.

However pertinent these factors may be, the impact of AIDS upon Brett and his friends cannot be underestimated, for AIDS not only turns gothic the relation between sexuality and death but also undermines the media mythology of health, youth, and the perfect body. The friends of one victim, Perkins, raise money for a color television; Brett pledges but does not contribute. "It showed" Perkins, Brett muses, "funny pictures that weren't really funny and brought him news of catastrophes that were somehow beside the point. The TV made his death feel vicarious and filled his bedroom with another world he could enter when this one had run its course" (Spring 1987, 52–53). However much Brett may feel that his pursuit of Gregory has distracted him from realizing that AIDS is a plague, he realizes that there is a gap between suffering the body's collapse and understanding it. The media versions of experience do not address experience, but replace it with a death of mind second only to the death into which Perkins fades. When Brett visits Paul, a death much closer to home, the impact registers with a starkness whose eloquence does not detract from its terrible reality:

> Lying down becomes a complex negotiation. Even if your body feels normal, you know the slightest unconsidered movement will shake something vital loose or shift something around, this big elastic bag of flesh you've carried around in total confidence for years and years falls in love with its own demolition and starts courting randy microbes, loose virus particles, plaques and embolisms and alien cells, it offers bits and pieces of itself for any invader to nibble on, you watch as your body entertains your enemies at dinner, its loyalties divided between you and them, and after a while, you become hypnotized by the disappearance of you. (Fall 1987, 63)

Caught up in myths of youth, beauty, and immortality, Brett and his friends discover the ghastliest of demystifications. To become "hypnotized" by one's own disappearance is to be drawn into a black hole of hopeless fixation on the vanished confidence in the countercultural utopia.

We will have even more trouble than Brett in understanding the maddening mix of desire and distance in Gregory if we do not perceive him in the light of these much larger myths and antimyths. Brett, a fiction writer himself, does understand Gregory in the process of narrating these experiences—Brett plans to build *his* "Burma" as a "book-within-the-book, the never-quite-remembered story, and my plan, as far as I could recall, had been to connect the climax of the book with the climax of the book-within-the-book" (Summer 1986, 36). In the infinite regress with which Indiana surrounds these nested books with his own, we are pressed to consider the issue of framing, the pervasively fictive quality of our lives, and the whole set of reflexive issues with which we have become increasingly familiar in recent years. Brett realizes that Gregory is one of those "people who've deliberately obscured the text of their own personalities, who can't be read without incredible difficulty" (Fall 1986, 50). But perhaps Brett's best one-liner about Gregory comes much later in their relationship: "I watch his face glide acrobatically through its lexicon of winning postures, a face seasoned and marinated in the shapes of other people's longings" (Summer 1988, 64).

As in "The Death of Maria Manchester," Gregory costumes himself according to the desires of others, and his peculiar suspension between loving Brett and not sleeping with him is a void in his own Being. But that void is a protective one, because it keeps Gregory free of the mad pursuit that afflicts Brett. In that freedom, Gregory plays the economized relationship for keeps. In a tiff during which he accuses Brett of wanting too much too quickly, Brett shoots back: "What about you?" "I want everything," Gregory answers (Winter 1988, 73). Refusing sex, Gregory offers to come over for a hug anytime, until Brett says: "I'm in a bad state right now, in fact. I can't come right now, he said. I'm doing paste-ups" (Summer 1988, 63). And what Gregory really enjoys is catching Brett off balance by arriving late at the coffee shop, early for dinner at Brett's.

Gregory's art conveys a similarly sullen counterattack against the kinds of larger determinations we have seen in the novel. Gregory—who was once not only a pretty boy, fresh out of high school, picked up by a rich man, but also a junkie hooked by a predator who wanted mainly to have his way with him—harbors much resentment against image commodification alongside his skill at playing it for his own ends. His gimmick sounds like a naïve version of Richard Prince's rephotography, but Brett lances Gregory's assurance by reminding him that his anxieties over how a show would be received are a bit premature for someone who has produced only four pictures. Brett also marks Gregory's pretentiousness in explaining his work:

> Gregory's artistic aims, he elucidated, were impossible to achieve through half-measures. It was, he emphasized, integral to his work that it resemble the most technologically crisp sort of advertising images. He was, he said, de-constructing the media in his work. The satirical qualities of Gregory's art could only be perceived, he said, in mental contrast to contemporary advertising, and therefore the technical level needed to be as high. (Winter 1987, 51)

Perhaps resentful of Gregory's self-absorption, Brett turns Gregory into a pedant of photo processing.

A bit later in the narrative is a description of what one of Gregory's pieces entails:

It was an arrangement of six snapshots, reproduced on a single large sheet of white paper, six different male types, all handsome, some clean-shaven, some bearded or semi-bearded, with various hairstyles, various types of clothing: college preppie, Kennedy type young lawyer, bohemian, blue-collar worker, and so forth, in age ranging from about 25 somewhere close to 40. The significant peculiarity was that these faces all belonged to the same person and all had been taken within four years, a so-called serial killer who had raped and murdered his way across the United States a few years earlier. A man who had impressed everyone who met him as extremely well-favored, sexy, intelligent, possibly brilliant, definitely middle-class, an exemplary neighbor and concerned friend, buckets of fun on a date. (Summer 1987, 49)

Gregory, who voices his resentment of Brett for "fetishizing" his looks, wants to disrupt the cultural equation between image and character which immediately makes a pretty boy everyone's object. Brett adds the ideological resonance that Gregory is still a bit young, perhaps, to articulate: "Such is the ambiance of American society, that a person who runs out of control in this manner can effortlessly impress those he meets as a paragon of desirable national qualities."

Another of Gregory's "gangs" shows a variation of sorts on the theme: "His collages had begun featuring porno models, spliced into settings that heightened the absurdity of their smiles, their foregrounded erections, and their brazenly offered buttocks to a pitch of supreme ugliness" (Fall 1987, 63). Gregory undoes the "fetishizing" of a porno pose by placing it in settings for which it offers no answers, supplies no meaning other than its own insufficiency as a sense of "male sexuality." Indeed, it is at this point that Brett becomes particularly acid in pointing out to Gregory how few such works he had completed and how unlikely it would be for the porn industry to police "obscure East Village galleries" looking for copyright infringements. Gregory's point hits too close to home with Brett, a highly intelligent writer who cannot be fully unaware of his own participation in porn's frenzy to turn people into exploited objects. Because Gregory in his junkie days had to do his share of hustling to pay for his habit, he intensely resents the economic forms to which identities and relationships are assimilated. It is no accident that one impediment to this relationship is the asymmetry that Brett's reputation and financial success create.

If we try to answer, then, why Brett is so hopelessly drawn to Gregory, we can begin with the image repertoire within which Brett sees the younger man. This perception holds despite Gregory's deficiencies. His excruciating innocence is almost cruelly displayed: "Bruno hates all this poverty and ethnic clutter, but I'm really moved by it. I like checking out all these tiny shops, listening to ordinary people talk. Bruno's so out of touch with real people, he just stays in that constricted world of art and artists and never comes in contact with anything real. When you watch and listen to the people down here, Gregory says, you realize each one of them has a life, full of particular things" (Summer 1987, 48). It is no wonder that Brett compares Gregory's social program to that of "a keenly deluded junior architect unveiling his plans for demolishing the red light district" (Fall 1987, 63). Gregory knows sexual commodification by having been its object, but he lacks the ideological resonances that Brett establishes for us. That lack of social wisdom cripples Gregory, leaving him permanently vulnerable to the siren song of heroin.

What most piques Brett's interest is Gregory's embodiment of a younger, naïve self still full of an energy; sitting with Paul in the AIDS ward, Brett understands that he himself has lost that self. When Gregory calls Brett to ask for sixty dollars for some prints, Gregory goes on too long about "how miserable and hopeless things are" (Fall 1987, 64). It takes Brett back: "As Gregory dilates on this theme, I remember myself as an adolescent, the incurable discontent I lobbed at my mother whenever she tried to improve anything." Gregory remains the egoistic adolescent at twenty-eight, brooding over the gap between the impediments he faces and the success he anticipates for himself. Brett feeds a bit on that negative energy, especially its more reformist elements. Brett attempts to see Gregory's "fixation with the inessential, the passing moment"

> through his eyes, and begin to learn what something will look like to Gregory. Magazine images start falling apart when I look at them, breaking themselves down into sex messages, sales points, prescriptions of what people are supposed to be, in this time, this place. He has more energy, more appetite than I do, as if the world were still offering him unlimited possibilities, endless options. As if he were born yesterday and still had a whole lifetime to make choices. (Spring 1987, 54)

Brett's ulterior motive in his "book-within-the-book" is to cannibalize Gregory's energy and drive and to nest them within the text of his own personality, to paraphrase Brett's remark about Gregory's self-editing. Brett shows an awareness of the world's ways which Gregory will not achieve for himself, but Brett also shows how that awareness has eaten out the heart of his own will. He is, after all, stuck on his "Burma" for weeks, months, even years at a time, unable to keep it going under the pressures of reviewing art for the thinly fictionalized *Village Voice*.

Brett wants both resonances of this novel's title. In "Shanghai," the narrator is encouraged by some "demoralized Australians in the publishing business" to look into Burma, "a country frozen in time" (60). A secure Brett, stuck in his same apartment, complains of how his job imprisons him in the art critic's role as "generic functionary" (Fall 1987, 64) and is engaged in an arrested novel his will is not strong enough to make coincide with his own desire. His is an identity "frozen in time" and in a world-weary sense of the futility of options and choices. At the same time, there is another Brett with whom he has all but lost contact. He shares with his friend Victor some notes about his uncompleted novel, events from his own travels when he was Gregory's age or younger: "This all happened, I tell Victor, though it's fictitious as far as I'm concerned. These things that go on between people who don't know each other and never see each other again might as well be fantasies. The big problem, I say, is getting him [his protagonist] from one place to another" (Winter 1988, 71). Brett is mired in one place. The passage echoes his memories of "micro-affairs," now "fantasies" of constant searching, relating, and connecting. History, told now, seems as "inessential" to Brett as Gregory's advertising culture. But his narrative of old affairs *does* draw Brett nonetheless, and for the same reasons Gregory does. Musing over the cold trail of his novel, Brett tells us very early on that "these streets with their low buildings, tenements and store fronts had once contained the mystery of *Burma:* I lived in them, but thought of someone on another continent who wandered rootless through the world, sometimes intercepting me in my travels. I met him not long after leaving East Hampton" (Summer 1986, 36).

The mystery of Brett's book is of that younger self driven by utopian longings to wander rootless rather than staying put. The Other he meets goes under many names; Alexis and Gregory are the two most recent embodiments of an edge and an energy that Brett is a bit too jaded to consider anything but a trifle "jejeune," a word he seems to like. Brett wants the story of a Burma frozen in time to coincide with that of wandering rootless; he wants Brett, the successful sophisticate, to coincide (in the "metaphysical" way of the story "Sodomy") with a Gregory who finally says what Brett is waiting to hear instead of what he only half-listens to (Winter 1988, 73). But neither society nor history, particularly as Brett carries them within, will let such a utopian nesting of life narratives occur. In that noncoincidence, Indiana marks the crucial existential gap that amuses, confounds, agonizes, and even kills his characters. It is the very personal and private version of "the ambiance of American society" in which looks can be killing indeed.

### Susan Daitch and the Colorist of History

Even if the sensory details of her fiction, including her novel of nineteenth-century Parisian revolution, did not include views of the

East Village cityscape, Susan Daitch would still be very much at home among the writers in this book because of her feminist and political themes. She is, perhaps, the most traditional in her narration, and her style shows little of downtown writing's distinctive variation from the mainstream voice. But her social and intellectual associations place her very much on the barricades of the suburban ambush. Many of her readers first encountered her Top Stories pamphlet, "The Colorist" (22 [1985]). Its protagonist, Julie Greene, colors the frames of *Electra*, a comic book about to be terminated by the front office. Our focus is initially upon the insecurity of her working conditions, the conflict between her rich tints and the blander tones of the final product, and the more significant conflict with the sexist writer of the serial, who, like most of the male writers in Daitch's fiction, is uninterested in women's ideas. The comic, after all, features Electra, a heroine who never quite manages to overcome the romance fixation in which her author locks her, and it is always the male cowboys of the space opera who insure she does not lose her last shred of a shirt.

Once the serial is finally phased out (the front office marries Electra off to the master male, Orion), Julie rewrites *Electra* as a fable of her own economic fall to unemployment and to dependence upon her rather unpleasant Irish boyfriend. Electra abandons the star lanes to return to her native planet, takes a heavy shot from Orion's deadly amnesia ray, and crashes in Central Park with only her incomprehensible Kandinsky volume as a guide to New York. She becomes a bag lady, her remnant of superpowers dwindling to a sensational effectiveness at fending off would-be rapists, her confusion exacerbated by New Yorkers' "combination of idioms, slangs, and the local habit of aposiopesis and metonymy" (30), her anxieties focused on the possibility that, without a serial to sustain them, her powers may disappear altogether. This is a tale, then, in which executives, writers, and boyfriends possess wealth, power, and stability, whereas women either navigate on their own, pursued as Electra is by Orion's dreaded (and no doubt psychosexual) amnesia ray, or comply with the demands of a position both tenuous and subservient. Julie portrays her fate in that of Electra, who, though bred in a secret laboratory by a woman who tries to create a feminist superhero, winds up as co-opted in the published version (the male writers marry her off to Orion in the last issue), enervated in Julie's: "Her carefully engineered genetic code goes haywire because her special talents are of no use to the disenfranchised and in the last frame her nostalgia for the test tube is impossible to draw" (34).

The alternative to Julie's grim independence in a sort of existential quarantine is her old classmate's submission to domesticity. The wealth of the classmate is signified in a photograph of her house like "a prison built by Louis Quatorze"; her life consists of waiting for her husband, the empowered male upon whom she is utterly dependent, "until early in the morning." Although longish by *Top Stories* standards, "The Colorist" only begins to develop this allegory of cultural contradiction in which women face the nonchoice between an empty dependence or a disabled independence and in which wealth seems the key to power.

*L.C.* (Harcourt Brace Jovanovich, 1987) is Daitch's effort to pursue at length this issue of women's place in modern historical conflicts. Daitch develops the view that wealth is impervious to any but the most violent historical upheaval and that movements for social change have failed not only by repeating the oppressive power of the old regime but also by leaving unchanged its treatment of women. The individual woman's options degenerate into the bland sellout of domesticity or the bitter isolation of the revolutionary whose politically correct estrangement from the suburban leaves her doubly vulnerable to her marginalization as Woman. What enables Daitch to achieve this modeling of women and social change is a tricky narrative structure—tricky enough to trigger an interesting series of reading errors in her reviewers. The diary of an 1848 revolutionary (the Lucienne Crozier of the title) passes down through the family of her friend to Wilma Rehnfield, a wealthy older scholar, in 1968; her translation in turn comes to Jane Amme, a young Berkeley revolutionary who redoes the final section (only part of the original diary survives). Daitch is interested in the obvious issues of perspectivism occasioned by using these three narrators, but almost entirely within the context of the issues I have suggested.

Rehnfield is co-opted entirely by her wealth and privilege, particularly if we believe the younger narrator (Rehnfield's "was the resistance of a passionate voyeur" [170]). Rehnfield lives in a building full of "major contributors" (218), surrounded by a personal art gallery (in the nineteenth-century style—no track lights, just individual brass fixtures) and a private library of choice collectibles. Her interest is partly in the artists Lucienne knew, partly the voyeur's thrill in the danger and violence in which she embroiled herself. Rehnfield has so little ability to conceive taking a vigorous part in history—she herself has never even taken a job, let alone acted on political beliefs—that, in the part of the diary for which we have two versions, hers is notable for killing Lucienne off with consumption. She is aware, as her introduction makes clear, of the political, feminist, and narratological implications of the document, but it all comes to her from the distance of one who has lived only in the comfort and abstraction of a nonparticipant. She even portrays Lucienne's last and most important meditation as a total rejection of revolution: "I'm the fugitive in Algiers. February [the Paris revolution] is a secret here, and all women are the mad woman locked in the attic, real or theoretical. The truth is I don't really care anymore,

but I don't know what it is I do care about in the place of an unat-
tainable revolution, social changes whose architecture I can no
longer implement, criticize or even desire" (198). Daitch's nod to
Gilbert and Gubar aside, one wonders if Rehnfield isn't performing
a fatalistic apologia for her own withdrawal from contemporary issues into the pathology of the "passionate voyeur." She is passionate
enough about them to feel the relevance of the feminist context but
is still the apolitical voyeur.

The other translator lives under the false name "Jane Amme"
to elude FBI arrest for her involvement in a 1968 bombing. It would
be tedious to cite all the parallels between her case and that of the
diarist, but so many, both major and minor, exist that we almost
wonder whether Rehnfield and Lucienne ever existed—whether the
diary is an effort by Amme to justify her own career as a radical by
projecting backward the sobering case of one who came only to the
brink of direct action. In any case, she uses the metaphor of eleva-
tors in thinking about the difference between Lucienne's case and
her own as its continuation:

> Lucienne's story and mine run in tandem, then mine keeps going
> where hers leaves off. Imagine stories arranged like a bank of ele-
> vators, one set stops at the first floor through twentieth, the paral-
> lel set makes stops twenty through forty. If the reader believes
> Lucienne Crozier was more of a witness than a participant (and
> this is probably what made her attractive to Dr. R.), then Book II
> might belong to someone like Communard Louise Michéle. For
> Lucienne, the confrontation with revolution caused affairs behind
> her to appear trivial and childish, but she is paralysed into the life
> of a fugitive rather than galvanized into becoming a revolutionary,
> which, in part, happens when one is forced to go underground.
> (220–21)

We might wonder how much Amme stylized the diary to fit her own
search for antecedent models, particularly because she justifies her
political inaction by her underground status. The question is finally
a teaser, for we lack the necessary evidence to decide absolutely
(history as the stories we need to tell?). But these tandem stories
click at least two dozen times in the course of the novel, and the
major points help cue us to the more important issues Daitch addresses.

Both Lucienne and Amme are prototypical suburbanites. The
latter describes emerging ideologically from her suburban childhood
in Spartacus, Pennsylvania:

> Born into a small town and tagged with its conventional, tremu-
> lous expectations, codes are maintained, continuity is the thing.
> . . . The malcontent leaves and forms a devoted allegiance to

what the press sees as an extremist point of view. It is a solution to the rebel's vision of social injustice. There is a moment at which the young perpetrator of future crimes recognizes the use of the middle class in consumer society as a deaf and dumb source of exploitable lives, too devout to veer off course except in moments of insanity. ("LAWYER SHOOTS WIFE AND DRIVER.") (222)

Lucienne tells us that "the stations in a woman's life are marked by public ceremony, with guests invited, christenings, weddings, funerals an unalterable chronological sequence" (35). Her father lost at sea, Lucienne sells herself in a profitable marriage so that her sinking family can maintain its provincial gentility. It is after she has married that her brother's student radicalism and her time as Eugène Delacroix's lover expand her thinking beyond the "unalterable" mores of her youth.

Around the wealthy Crozier women, Lucienne feels "so rarely was I addressed directly I was like an inanimate document" (19) and is unable to counter their efforts to write her out of the family history. But revolution offers less of a shift from their conventionality than one might think: it is no simple enabling of the possibility for action. Around the violence and turmoil of the revolution, she freezes: "In a moment that demanded acute attention my mind took odd, undisciplined turns. I was afraid to join the singing. My sense of purpose slipped and I felt hopelessly like an observer, at best an opinionated yet penless journalist" (123). Amme understands Lucienne's paralysis as a species of normalization. As violence fills campus, screen, and newspaper, Amme probes the relationship between media coverage and violent history: "This symbiotic relationship sells newspapers because even if violence doesn't affect some citizens personally, we are fascinated by it, we watch the police snap on the handcuffs and the ambulance workers load bodies on to stretchers. . . . Corporeally distant from the printed page, the screen and the events represented, their distance is curated by the intellect as well, even when confronted by real live victims" (223).

What Amme describes is a modern version of Lucienne in the grip of the Crozier wealth and, later, Lucienne in the grip of the history the men around her have made, for her marginalization leaves her as cut off from action as television viewers in our age. But Amme also describes here the history of Rehnfield, whose relationship to Lucienne's life is a mix of the antiquarian's curated distance and the suburbanite's fascination. Both class and gender hierarchies reduce the subject to a voyeur and make her a citizen of a psychological suburbia that exists across the historical phases of capitalist society.

Nonetheless, Lucienne makes considerable progress, particularly in view of her historical context. Lucienne feels the sheer reality of life while making her way through the barricaded streets, she risks arrest to get food and fuel for herself and Jean de la Tour, and she even walks out of a meeting at which Pierre Joseph Proudhon exhibits his notorious chauvinism. Although the revolution allows her only a modest active role, her affairs first with Delacroix and then with de la Tour bring her to an intellectual awareness. She takes exception to Delacroix's paintings from the first. "I can't reconcile," she writes, "the language of colour and light with these pictures of covert brutality" (48). In his defense, Delacroix "spoke of allegory and as he spoke the paintings become transformed into representatives of Doom and History" (53). But in her rhetoric, one shaped by historical participation rather than abstraction, "the symbol casts events I thought quite complicated into simpler and simpler categories. Perhaps my ability to think critically is no longer up to the job. Symbols are a mental convenience" (146). Symbols and allegory would appear to be antithetical to critical thinking, a strategy of containment which escapes her specific experiences of class and gender and sanitizes them within broadly applicable universals. She even recalls mixing her mother's fables into her father's political discourse as a form of commentary rather than abstraction, a materializing of both discourses that undoes their divisions between morality and politics, narrative and analysis, text and history.

Delacroix and Lucienne see both art and history differently. Delacroix "calls barricaded streets fatal stage sets and argues he is not a stage manager" (79), and Lucienne thinks that "all he wanted to do was paint Homer, Dante, bowls of flowers, compliant women, images to coat gaunt screechy ideologues until they disappear" (133). She is offended by his assumption of Order, Rationality, and Man on the valorized side of "cleanly divided spheres of influence," but "no modern-era patricians or plebeians, no women, no Greek orphans, no barricades" (69). Lucienne is also offended at his refusal to discuss his work seriously with her: "My place is in another room [the bedroom]. I am a human reference point, a footnote positioned in relation to the population of women occupying the studio around the corner. . . . The world of women and the world of ideas are antipodean . . . and between the two ranges his solitary masculine intelligence" (57). "At twenty-six, he wanted to paint his century, but at forty-eight he has yet to do so." Significantly, Lucienne's rejection of Delacroix is on both feminist and political grounds, because he has discounted her life experience altogether.

Amme's intellectual migrations also begin with art, specifically the omission of women's work from her courses. She and her friend Mary make mental lists of the forgotten ones, lists that later become part of a real project. Moreover, Amme's involvement in demonstrations takes away the suburban dialectic of "fascination" and "alienation," a dialectic she describes as "sitting in a warm room. Terrorism can't penetrate it. The dog might carry something nasty in his mouth and drop it on the rug but unpleasantness, politically motivated violence, no. Soldiers don't haul Spartacus citizens out in the middle of the night, picking people off at random" (224). She experiences a link between knowing that "if I stood still I might get shot or blinded," Governor Reagan's role in the violence and in the media's distortions of it, and "a perverse memory: hiding behind the garage from an unpleasant boy, as if it were the same thing" (224). They *are* the same thing, because Daitch's ultimate quarry is the failure of any political activity that does not think its way beyond sexist hierarchies. Reagan and the boy, the radicals and the police, all perpetuate a gender system that is as much a symptom of the old regime as the social injustices Proudhon, de la Tour, and Amme's SDS cronies expound. No wonder that, sitting at a meeting, Lucienne can think of the radicals who, "although living, animated people, . . . remind me of Eugène's painted people": although perhaps on the edge of doing *something*, they were not engaged in *her* history.

Amme knows that "the condition of the suburbs has nothing to do with justice, of people getting what they deserve" and that the American dream mythology is a way of justifying inequities, "a persistent idea, however mistaken and naïve" (225). She understands "it was all about style," whether she is thinking about the media sanitizing history, recalling East Village drug dealers who thought themselves "social rebels" (226), or about the campus radicals she first meets at Berkeley ("a diluted but distinct version of the long-haired boys from East Sixth Street" [230]). She learns early on that history is more about her experience of almost getting knifed when she walks outside a drug house, a woman caught between armed and warring males.

Lucienne knows something of the same as well. When we learn that "after the revolution Jean believes there will be a tremendous erasure of history, public and private" (132), we learn also of her ambivalence to this prospect, a response "rooted in the value of lingering sentiment, fear of slipped memory and the fatal attraction of contradictions" (132). And, unlike Jean, she knows that their life in Algeria will be anything but "a clean slate, a new toy, starting out from the first day as if no others had preceded it" (143). She fears erasing her memories in order to adopt theories, and she preserves the validity of lingering sentiment against an oppressively rationalist mode of thought. She is above all drawn precisely to the tangle of contradiction constituting her experience as a radical woman and that has no place in the master narratives Jean composes in 1848 or Amme's friend Win (Winthrop Auersbach) assembles in 1968. Their elaborate conspiracy treatises on interlocking influence networks contain a considerable proportion of what Lucienne calls the "displaced anger" of frustrated patriarchs, an anger that limits their ability to see the plane of history which Lucienne has experienced. Hence she also rejects the way Rémy Gommereux's realism romanticizes the lives of the poor from a leftist perspective as badly as the more patronizing East Village work of our own day: "Rémy's sentimentality is that of a relatively young man, brush in hand, who sees these women as something they're not. Paintings that shut their eyes tight as Rémy declares, 'I'm only thinking about what is' " (86–87). And she finds the "what is" of history exceeding the clear categories of not only Delacroix but also the male orators: "Clearcut, easily defined sides are like the memory of an infallible innocence, a thing of the past. The innocence turns out to be fallible and shoddy, the sharply defined sides are blurred and turn out to be fake. I used to know how I thought the world should be and now I couldn't tell you anything" (142). She has encountered history at the barricades, as well as from the position of one excluded from shaping it in any direct or incisive way, or even from adding her perspective to that of the reigning ideologues (her ideas, she finds, "are of no interest to him" [129]): she understands the fatal ambiguity of the master's tools.

As we come to see Lucienne's increasingly acute sense of the contradictoriness of things, we can say that one of its aspects is the liberationist fallacy in which the Czars give way to the Stalins, a second is the restrictiveness of categorical logic, and a third is the link between politics and gender. The novel's radical men never understand how much they participate in the same abusive and exploitative power relations they see so clearly in the spheres of class and economics. The kidnapping and dumping of women by the police in 1848, as well as the rapes and murders by wealthy Guy Masterson (whom Amme takes to be Luc Ferrier, an arms maker and powerbroker but also Rehnfield's source for the diary), remain outside the radicals' social analysis. Even the narrators differ over following the implications of the politics of gender once Lucienne reaches the highly chauvinistic Algiers of 1848 and finds her mobility and individuality squelched. Rehnfield has her die from consumption, as if it were impossible to conceive any basis on which Lucienne, having gone so far, could endure. But Amme has her link up with the tough feminist Pascale, who (like the Weatherwomen Amme hears about) broke off conversation with men. For Lucienne, Pascale is an important figure because she has learned to speak and publish, whereas Lucienne still feels only mute frustration. Many of Lucienne's insights, ranging from those on patriarchal logic to her recognition of the covert imperialism of the French radicals in Algeria, derive ultimately from Pascale. Lucienne believes, for example, that women should "work out their own destinies apart from those of men," especially men who call themselves revolutionaries . . . but were, in her mind, replicating the same patriarchal scheme they believed themselves fighting against. Their language recommended different economic remedies but these theories alone were no victory banner as far as she was concerned. She once told me they were all chasing their tails, screwing themselves into the ground. If one were set on packing all the demons into one vast villain, Pascale believes its nomenclature ought to reflect the true enemy. (150–51)

That true enemy is precisely the patriarchal scheme. Lucienne is struck with Pascale's dismissive treatment by the men at the meeting in which she challenges their erasure of women from their political analysis. The experience leads Lucienne to a sharp perception of the contradiction that has the male radicals stuck in a logic circling not only their own egos but also the cultural order they seek to overthrow: "Calculated dismissal and unceremonious condescension make me suspect the two categories: the oppression of women and the struggle of the proletariat represent entirely different sets of circumstances and have little relation to one another" (106). She understands that they are separate but also, for her, interrelated problems. Furthermore, she knows that "whole sub-cities are about to erupt and shatter the everyday Paris, the complacent city. As the fissures appear, it's too late to jump from one side of the fault line to the other" (107). History does not always wait for us to choose channels by the remote control of leisured and encyclopedic analysis.

For Amme, the Berkeley eruptions remain both real and distanced until she is Guy Masterson's rape victim, barely escaping with her life. At that point she and her friend Mary blow up Luc Ferrier, and Amme's confusion of the two men leads to her calling him "Guy Ferrier" (258), as if the difference between Masterson's rape of women and Luc's rape of continents and classes were ultimately inconsequential. Even Rehnfield, according to Amme, "only partially considered a mistake had been made in the victim's identity" (183), knowing enough about Ferrier to suppose him capable of anything: "She knew that under another name he did other things" (262). We do not know, finally, whether Ferrier and Masterson are the same individual, but they are both violent in exploiting their hierarchical privileges. Ironically, two charges go off the same night, it seems; Ferrier's ideological and feminist foes strike simultaneously. Perhaps Daitch means to suggest that these two trails lead ultimately to the same door: Masterson's violence against women and Ferrier's economic exploitation are features of the same face of patriarchy. If so, Daitch's novel belongs on the same shelf

with Acker's and Tillman's highly politicized feminist versions of
suburban ambush.

We need, then, to see how Daitch distinguishes without fully
separating socioeconomic from gender issues, dividing Lucienne,
Rehnfield, and Amme on the former and allying them on the latter.
Daitch makes it clear that the contradiction of gender roles is too
connected with patriarchal logic for radicals to focus exclusively
upon class privileges or industrial wages or interlocking directorates
or colonialism. However, framing one's program on gender issues
alone is not useful either; it is even a species of romantic simplifi-
cation, as in Lucienne's skepticism about her friend Fabienne's irritation: "Fabienne reminds me of Eugène as I think he might have
been at twenty. Voluble and reclusive, an endorser of extremes; all
men are deceivers, all women are victims, all women are flighty, all
men are self-involved, or the other way around in each case. In
another twenty years Fabienne will retreat into her marriage or
whatever her life becomes, just as Eugène retreated into his studio,
rejecting everything and everyone who bewilders him to the point
of irritation or boredom" (108–9).

An inadequate responsiveness to the "attraction of contradictions" leaves us safe within the homogenized, neosuburban retreats
of Fabienne and Eugène, even if embracing these retreats fully, as
Lucienne and Amme have done, leaves us vulnerable to historical
conditions that do not allow a happy ending of the kind offered by
feuilletons, the popular serial stories that Lucienne constantly ridi-
cules as simplistic, arbitrary lines through historical ambiguities.
Sexism and the inability of radical action to displace the power of
wealth appear to stay with us; thus women pay higher costs than
men whether the times are tranquil or revolutionary. If Daitch's
narrative point of view seems here an elaborate and perplexing experience for readers, I suspect it is the price she chooses to pay in
order to shift their relationship to the historical novel. Decidedly
not the Alexandre Dumas feuilletons of Lucienne's day, *L.C.* denies
us a voyeuristic relation to history. It insists that we cope both with
the specificities of its three narrators' circumstances and with what
persists in history as a cultural *langue* out of which their existential
utterances are spoken.

### Judy Lopatin's Modern Romances

Judy Lopatin came to New York in 1976 fresh from the University of Michigan, where, she noted, there were three other people
who also knew who Lou Reed was and why the Velvet Underground
was so important to the new sensibility. Lopatin had gradually
drifted afoul of her creative-writing courses at Michigan, and her

*Village Voice* subscription helped to clarify her reactions to her De-
troit childhood and suburban adolescence. James Wolcott's treatises
on the connection between Lou Reed's early work and the new-wave
scene at C.B.G.B.'s in the mid-seventies made more sense to her
than well-made stories and the protocols of the academic environment. When, after a year in New York retuning her work, she began
Columbia's M.F.A. program, she found encouragement from teachers but, interestingly enough, hostility from other students. "I was
very much not in fashion," she told me. "Most of the students were
interested in naturalism and the well-made story and they kept saying, 'But it doesn't move me!'" She laughs when she tells the tale,
but their hostility meant that "I had to define myself in opposition
to what other students liked or wanted."

This oppositional edge is still there. When I interviewed her,
she was both appreciative of and curious about being grouped with
the writers in this book:

> It's funny, because even though I've inhabited part of the same
> universe they have—I've lived in New York for eleven years and
> I've been downtown a lot and all that—in a certain way I haven't
> been connected with all that has been going on. I only met Cath-
> erine [Texier] recently, and a lot of them I don't know personally,
> some of them I haven't even read. I haven't seen myself as having
> a lot in common with the Soho writers you mentioned [Richard
> Prince and Reese Williams], even with the East Village types. I
> perceive myself as falling in cracks—I'm not mainstream, but I'm
> not in a certain school either.

What we have learned about downtown writing, however, is that it
is less a school than a sensibility, its particular aesthetic strategies
as open as those of the bands Lopatin recalls from C.B.G.B.'s early
days. Lopatin's sensibility is indeed downtown, and it is no accident
that since we talked she has come to know many of the writers in
this book and to publish stories in the *Voice Literary Supplement*
and *Between C & D*.

*Modern Romances* (Fiction Collective, 1986) claims its place in
the present book through its persistent attention to the simultaneity of romance and reality, past and present, fiction and history.
Lopatin's playfulness shows in what passes for an epigraph to the
story collection—Webster's definition of *romance*. The meanings it
tabulates are a reader's guide to the concerns of the collection, and
we would do well to linger over them long enough to set our lineup
cards accordingly. Romance was the medieval vehicle for narratizing
legend, chivalry, and the supernatural, and several of Lopatin's stories follow the efforts of narrators to use these romance motifs as
vehicles for coping with the quotidian present or the disturbing past.
That romance deals with what is "remote in time or place and

usually heroic, adventurous or mysterious" allows Lopatin to explore her interest in the past and its various relations to present awareness. Many of her characters feel romance's "emotional attraction or aura" to particular pasts or ideas of the past. And, finally, it is within (or against) various popular forms of romance that another group of her characters contends with its own "love story" or "passionate love affair."

It is ironic that Lopatin's epigraph should take us back to junior high school and the long-eschewed essay structure that begins with a definition from Webster's. But that return serves to jostle our memory of the multiplicity of ways in which we have used romance at various points in our cultural history. Romance's generic assertion that our ordinary ways of thinking are not sufficient in themselves is very appropriate to the thinking of our era. Against the poverty of the suburban mind-set, character after character resorts to the idyllic, utopian, occasionally supernatural energies of romance, even if those energies are quoted rather than believed. Those who suppose that the romance form can no longer have tangible impact in an age of deconstruction had better know the consequences that publishing *Modern Romances* had for its author. Lopatin allegedly was fired "for fiscal reasons" from the law firm where she worked, and her book hung midair at publication time until the legal rumble subsided among those who felt themselves targeted by one of the stories. Lopatin turns romance from subliterary applications to such penetrating social analysis that the Empire wanted to strike back. Alas, no Jedi appeared, but fortunately, more stories continue to come from Lopatin's pen.

If the Empire took exception to political analysis, Lopatin got into a different sort of trouble with some male members of her audience for the collection's title story. "Modern Romances" is a piece of reportage on love and passion in the new-wave scene circa 1978, when the story was written, and the accent is on the grotesque. "It's one thing when men do it [the grotesque]," Lopatin commented, "but it's another when a woman does. One man I knew said, 'I'm going to have to think again about what kind of girl you are.' And it's not even about me!" She places "Modern Romances" at the "moralistic" extreme of her work. The story's sketch-length segments take snapshots of the most emptied moments of new-wave romance, as if Lopatin were a moral version of the voyeuristic Weegee she writes about in another story. Guy is turned on by Lucie's "cross between FEAR and VIOLENCE," and Lucie is indulgent enough to keep nonverbal her "please be careful with me." "New wave movie: sex scene" shows him holding her down to prevent her masturbating: "You look like a little demented Cleopatra," he tells her. There is blood on the wall after a beer-bottle session, telltale sheets after an infidelity, extra bucks at age fifteen for telling stories to a misogynist who thinks she is "a real nice kid," memories of both her father and her uncle trying to molest her, a boyfriend who covets her nail polish and "adores" her "sleazy image," and another who can be depended upon not actually to kill her when he "wakes up screaming and shaking her in the middle of the night." What holds these bits in line is the utter cool with which they are told, so complete a directness that one hears underground rock 'n' roll backing them. But Lopatin's best comment is in the final segment: "That is the fun of modern romance, nothing can ever be a terrible mistake, so over and over again you can look over your shoulder and see the arms of your past, see them encircle your waist with comfort so cold you don't feel a thing" (14). Lopatin clearly marks her distance from our stereotype of the after-hours sort. Lucie's life—with its mix of violence, power, masochism, rulelessness, quick thrills, and, above all, the utterly detached cool with which its tales are told—is a form of anesthesia.

Perhaps the key lines in "Modern Romances" are when we learn, in "Character of Our Heroine," that "Lucie is a New Wave singer and guitarist. Who (never) reveals herself in her actions and the stories she tells about herself" (10). The parenthetical "never" suggests the ironic status of lives that are styled into the hard smooth surface of the new-wave "heroine" but that become all the more revealing in the process. The lines are reminiscent of "Los Angeles," another 1978 story that skews "Charlie's Angels" into a vaguely feminist sense of how the media estranges its stars from themselves. The Blonde rejects her interviewer's need to see her as a "mysterious woman": "Naah. I am only a perfect woman. Anyone knows there is no mystery in that" (206). Hers is no doubt an imperfect knowledge of the insight's implications, for even the Smart One seems not to have any real relation to the televised product. Asked by her interviewer what she does for fun, she responds: "I watch Los Angeles de Carlos. I'm just like everyone else, you know. I like to watch beautiful girls get into trouble, and get out of it, and imagine that I'm one of those . . . strangers" (209).

Like the rest of the culture, the Smart One finds that her pleasure is cued to the voyeuristic fantasy of identification spiced with sadistic peril to the fetishized female body. There is little distance between Lucie riding the tough new wave and the Smart One or the Blonde perfecting an image that makes her "strangers" to herself, with no mystery remaining from traditional psychological depth. Lucie's beer-bottle violence and the Angels' perils of Pauline mark the same displacement of the experiencing self by the gendered image. If some of Lopatin's male readers object to the grotesque candor of "Modern Romances" it is perhaps a bit of another Pauline peril by which the only thorn in the flesh permitted is a fully sublimated phallogocentric one.

"The Death of Joe Dassin" is a strong story in somewhat the same vein, its narrator aware of the French pun in *"histoires"* between "history" and "affairs" and intent upon seeking out this self-validating form of personal history. But she is stymied by a different twist on the pun—the historical differences that account for different pacing, different mores, different emotional romance frames, which keep her and the Frenchmen she meets at subtle, at times not subtle, odds. That disjunction is what so many of Lopatin's stories explore—the gap between narrative framing and the experience it is designed to contain or, in some cases, displace. We have already seen a pair of stories in which gender typing displaces self for Lucie and the Angels, but this also occurs in Lopatin's stories of voyeurism. "Retrospective on Weegee," Lopatin told me, "is less about a photographer than the desire to know about a recent past that you can't know about because you weren't there. The whole thing is a speculative inquiry about what really happened and trying to piece together the available evidence to satisfy your voyeuristic curiosity." The narrator doubles and intensifies the voyeurism of the photographer with that of the quintessential fiction writer.

"Weegee, simple man that he is, does not bother with ambiguities. He takes his pictures with black-and-white high-contrast film. The critics call it expressionism" (30). Weegee *is* ambiguous, however, in the hands of a narrator whose hypotheses, conjectures, and retractions give the story a pulsing rhythm emphasized by its short segments, its parenthetical reflexive questions, and its mix of fact, evidence, and supposition. Lopatin shares with the critics the game of making Weegee the vicarious medium of their textual existence, and, though she tells us at the end that many topics she must sift through are "not what I was after," she also tells us what she does seek. It is the opposite of Weegee's half-serious, half-showbiz precognition: "There is also something called retrocognition, which as the name implies is knowledge of the past—knowledge of the past one would not ordinarily have" (39). Weegee pulls off a sensational crime prediction, but what our narrator manages is a romance of Weegee's fifties' aura, his slightly seedy, slightly queasy mix of stagecraft and keen observation, and his knowledge of what people do in dark theaters.

In "Trixie Taylor, Hospital Nurse," two sisters try to displace their lives with more interesting ones. Linda doubles her dull career filling out insurance forms at a private practice with that of a lounge lizard dressed in a nightclub singer's gown; she manages to pick up a doctor and things take off from there. But Trixie is more textual than existential, and she is transferred away from "a ward of old women" who complained about all of her personal questions ("What was your secret wish? Your worst nightmare? What games did you play as a child? What did you do in the war?"), and she is dropped by a fiancé who takes exception to her going through his drawers and papers. She wants the retrocognition of their lives, but must vary her narrative strategy when she is placed on a different ward in charge of the paperwork. "She has learned to read between the lines of medical records. Her patients are too young to have real histories, but they have jobs" (110). A narrator-critic, she "puts herself in each bed and thinks about the life she will lead when she leaves the hospital."

Like the doctor who sees mermaids when he looks at Trixie's sister, like Linda who sees excitement when she exits the washroom at the South Seas lounge in sequins, Trixie makes her own life vicarious by trying to realize the narrative pitch of romance in the otherwise flat course of life. The same tone, mostly comic, partly sad, marks several other stories in the collection about, as Lopatin explained in our talk together, "wanting to live your romantic ideas and realizing that they don't translate into real life." In "Nuit Blanche," Lopatin sets a naïve Jilly in Paris wishing for a bit of trouble, even imagining white slavers and almost believing what the predators tell her, but encountering rather routine attempts at seduction (she is promised a movie career) and, appropriately enough, a language she does not understand enough to follow.

"Krystal Goes Mystical" features "the power of the imagination to make what you're seeing a lot more interesting than it really is." Krystal is Lopatin's mostly loving portrait of the blandest character imaginable, a young woman with a safe life, a safe fiancé, a safe future. It is the blandness, perhaps, that drives Krystal to annex just a bit of the romance world that the narrator, her coworker, pursues in her weekend nightlife. When she "goes mystical," it is to tell her "inamorato" on the phone that "I have this funny feeling. I have the feeling we're both facing something dark and mysterious, some force beyond our control. It's as if we're being tested. And if we can get through this we'll be all right" (81). There is, of course, no dark force, just a bland self that "wants to create a dark side where it isn't," Lopatin explained to me, "because it doesn't want to have to think of itself that way."

There is a serious side to such stories, because they suggest that going mystical is our only resource against blandness when we succumb to the culture's inducements toward suburban normality. But these are the comic tales of the collection. The most serious ones catch characters trying to use romance as a form of damage control against a past too powerful or too painful to live with any other way. "A Phantasm, A Bird—" features a divorcée living alone on the beach; for her, a white bird flying low toward her is a dimity frock, a ghost from a past life. The official sighting of this truly "rare and lovely" bird would justify her exile and even, finally, herself as dreamer. As dreamer and as a fiction-maker about her ex-husband

and his girlfriend, she works the materials of her experience into a
romance form that might satisfy her feelings toward them (he self-
destructs as a result of his unruly passion and ugly corporate claws).
Her swirling mix of frames is cued by the dictionary's list of Elements; it begins with aluminum siding, with which she insulated
her bungalow, and includes "the American way of life, and alimony,
and the quest of the Argonauts in search of the Golden Fleece, all
those mythologies; and *Arsenic and Old Lace*" (20). All of them
represent different versions of insulation against the elements, different ways of assimilating disturbing details into fictions that allow
her at least the dream of resolution.

Such efforts at a narrative mode of coping are also in "Visitation
of the Ghost" (which contrasts a romancer with an accomplished
repressor), "The Mystery of Madame Kitten" (in which a woman
changes her life twice by turning the dial on the narrative repertoire), and "Dominica." In the latter story, Nancy manages several
existential shifts through her narratological skills. She first reverses
gender oppression by becoming a dominatrix, then transverses morality by burying her partner's dead client (a bit of fantasy overkill,
literally) during a tropical trip, and finally assuages her mother's
horror at her profession by explaining (whether truthfully or not)
that she has cashed in her whips and become a hairdresser. A seriocomic postmodern gothic with a bit of a feminist cast, "Dominica"
prepares us for the more serious examples of this motif, such as "A
Murder History," in which a killer is so engaged with weaving innocent narratives of his past that he forgets his murder.

Perhaps the most interesting of these gothic tales is "Budapest
Dangereux," not coincidentally one of the latest (1983) stories in
the collection. We hear of Else Berger, a Jewish-Hungarian refugee
who is a fortuneteller; Henny, also of Hungarian descent, who is the
proprietor of a tea shop; and Maria Edge, the mother of a client
whom Else, happily enough, advised to accept a marriage proposal
that led to a contented life in England. Else is tired from overwork,
Maria is a bit nervous about what the future might hold, and Henny
is uneasy about the unsettling faces that appear in her half-waking
states. By the time Lopatin is through with these characters, however, she has woven a complex fabric of memory and desire.

Maria's case is the simplest to understand, as well as the easiest
for Else to contain within her fictions. "Nothing had ever gone
wrong in her life, but despite this Maria had always worried about
the future; and in recent years this worry had metamorphosed into
a reckless, insatiable desire to know the worst" (178). Maria is that
recurrent figure in Lopatin's work whose life is too bland for words
and who needs romance instead. Else has dealt with this need in
Maria before. When Maria explained her feeling that "she had, in
some guise or other, lived in every generation—even her mother's

and father's," Else had convinced her that, because she could not have been both her aunt and herself simultaneously, "it was only the sense of the past she felt," perhaps from the family portrait gallery. It is only some time after losing the fantasy of past lives that Maria develops her compulsion about the future, but it is as pre-packaged in the suburban mode as her portrait-gallery past: "At times Else was tempted to make up horrible fortunes for Maria, to truly scare her; but Else was too reliable to lie. Besides, Maria's vision of the worst was not all that bad, so Else could, in all conscience, tell her quite enough to satisfy her fears" (178). Maria can be handled in Else's soap-opera romance mode because history has been anesthetized for her by wealth and social privilege.

Henny, however, finds her peaceful demeanor as a popular and engaging tea-shop hostess disturbed by two sources of personal guilt. The figure of Miguel is at the center of an early life "before the war was over and she grew up and married Arthur" (188). But it is a life about which she has always been notoriously forgetful until Else's desperate inventions of a past life in gypsy camps trigger Henny's ghosts. Else invents a happy life for Henny, trying to make her feel better with a touch of picturesque costume drama, but Henny sees "dark and brooding" faces rather than happy ones. She becomes frightened of having died in a Nazi death camp, "gassed like Arthur" (who is a narcoleptic and accidentally gassed himself in the garage). By the time Else convinces her that, like Maria, she could not have lived in two places at once, we have come to see that Henny's guilt over not having somehow saved Arthur has crossed plot lines with her repressed affair with Miguel. Else's practice has turned into a form of romance therapy which leads Henny into her unconscious to face her guilt. Finally, "she could feel Miguel's body, a faceless warmth touching her" (188).

Else has the most trouble dealing with herself, because her ghosts are not imagined, like Maria's, or merely personal, like Henny's, but genuinely historical. Else's family died in the Holocaust, and her early ambition to write a historical romance, from which Lopatin's story takes its title, has led only to "a blank book with fleur-de-lis covers" (185):

> Once, long ago, she had meant to write it all down—the dawning
> sense of danger, of not being Hungarian enough; the deportations
> in the countryside; the gangs in the streets of Budapest, the ma-
> chine-gun executions on the shores of the Blue Danube; and then
> traveling, traveling to foreign places, escaping—or not escaping.
> What a romance she would give them! Nobody in America had
> dreamed of what it had been like. And, after a time in America,
> neither did Else Berger, anymore. She buried her memories and
> lived in the future—or, better, a past so distant, so abstract and

impersonal that neither its horrors nor pleasures could be truly felt. (185–86)

Else's problem is that she could not herself live in two places at once, and her life in the New York leaves her guilty over the Nazi camp she escaped. Henny, who strikes Else as looking "a bit like a gypsy" (175), takes her back to these long repressed memories. Henny's face, or its reflection in Else's metal table, becomes other faces now dead, just as Henny's half-seen faces of guilt are those whom Else addresses when, after a reverie, she hisses to Henny in Hungarian to "close the tea shop and go away before it is too late." We can understand why Else turned down her one great marriage proposal, from a psychoanalyst (who might have banished her ghosts sooner) who "had left his homeland before the war, on a premonition" that saved him much of the trauma Else has not exorcised.

"Budapest Dangereux" is an interesting twist on the Holocaust story because it places that horror at three different removes from its characters (the guilty escapee, the American whose family's emigration a generation or more before had saved them all, the aristocrat untouched in any personal way). Else's business of projecting faked futures and inventing Hollywood pasts is the most extreme fictive form of the precognition and retrocognition other characters play with, sometimes on the threshold of believing in their supernatural powers. But, paradoxically, Else's fictions produce perhaps the most telling truth effects in the collection. Maria is turned back into her existentially sedentary ways; Henny, into healthy versions of her memories; Else, into the cruel chances of history that can be known if not resolved.

Romance can lead into the comedy of delusion, the pathos of vicarious and displaced living, and the drama of self-knowledge. But it can also serve the ends of cultural violence, whether on the personal or the cultural level. "Our Perfect Partners" is often comic, making its metaphors suddenly literal, or deflating the monstrous egos of lawyers, contemporary robber barons of our age. But the story also is deadly serious about the class system maintained in a large legal firm, in which moneymaking power leads to social snobbery worse than any titled European ever quite managed to embody. Some of the lawyers are simply buffoons, but Mickey Plotnick, the villain of the piece, is its "vampire," one who snubs the secretaries, cannot even see the functionaries, and derives his well-paid status as a boy wonder from arranging financing for second-rate horror movies. "In a way," Lopatin said of him, "he wants to be better than he is but he's so much a product of his actions that he doesn't really know how to do it; whatever he does is going to be tinged with violence." The story keeps toying with the possibility of a secret life for Mickey because, publicly, he can speak in only "the most mechanical, artificial way." Even when he coerces a bit part in one of the movies, "he just played himself, in the movies, and got paid handsomely for it." The story's last lines are chilling in rendering his readiness to appropriate others' lives: "You never know when Mickey might wake up and see something, or someone, he's never really seen before; you never know when he might realize how much he desires the life of that stranger; you never know what secrets, or tears, might be spilled upon the pillow, along with a certain necessary amount of blood" (156). Despite the gags, then, the story turns into an exposé of the nasty pomposity of corporate culture's bagmen and the callousness and violence with which they exert their privileges.

On the cultural level, "The Etiology of the New War" comes close to serving as a parable of our collective romance of life. It begins innocently enough with a woman at a bank machine, the kind with a phone to report breakdowns. The woman, however, stages a terrorist action: "She leisurely walked up to the 24-hour phone and cried into it, 'Hurry! Bank robbery! Bank robbery!'" (113). Should we become very clever and think that banks are always robbing customers and it is high time somebody said so? Perhaps more interesting is what follows:

> Only two people had any presence of mind. One was the lunatic herself, who then reported the exact location of our bank. The other was a man who came forward immediately to contradict her statement. He said to the phone, "This woman has a problem." Then he turned to the rest of us and said, "There isn't anybody there anyway."
>
> It is no good having presence of mind when there is no presence at the other end of a 24-hour phone. (113–14)

Why, the narrator wonders, does "the *idea* of a bank robbery" leave her "with a distinct impression of horror—similar, I would guess, to the horror people used to feel after a real bank robbery"? Perhaps it is because there is no authority on the line, just a man (of course) stepping forward and labeling the woman a problem and the situation safely unreal (no police will arrive with guns ablaze).

He polices, that is, the customary line between reality and fiction, and he is very relieved that the authorities will not be disturbed by the fiction. However, the woman we are quite easily led to label "crazy" has attempted to stage, through what is to her humor, the simultaneity of the order of reality and that of romance. She is indeed a terrorist, because she foregrounds a New War of culture in which our realities become erased into the romance forms of the media, as when one steps forward in a crisis and heroically restores order, just like in the movies. What the hero fails to appreciate is that the myth of a monitoring agency is just that, a myth: there is

no linear check on the system's logic. Her hoax reveals the larger
hoax that no one is in control, no one is managing authoritatively
the lines between truth and fiction or between reality and romance,
and that even the idea of authority or truth or reality may itself be
our most cherished romance.

The narrator worries whether the New War is "a false alarm,"
"a joke," or something that might "bring excitement into the lives
of potential fools, heroes, voyeurs." Her issue sounds more like the
modes of romance we have been following than like a New War—
the false alarms of Henny and Maria, the jokes in "Our Perfect
Partners" and on the naïve narrators whose illusions wear thin, or
all the fools and voyeurs we have seen. This sense is close to the
mark. The New War is "still only an idea," but its "time has come"
for an age in which the order of signs appears to have displaced that
of the real. For example, what worries her most of all is the way
that, as she ponders such questions, "things creep in from nowhere
and get named before they are even understood" (114). Experience
seems somehow always already assimilated to cultural codings of
one kind or another, as if there were always a narratological agent at
the authoritative end of a twenty-four-hour phone. That there is not
means the woman's "crazy" state outside any rational or meaningful condition is the norm rather than the exception. If, that is, the
culture is a haphazard accumulation of romance motifs running in
all the different serious and comic directions we have seen thus far,
if real human needs and displaced confectionery desires are all
bound up in the same collective narratology, and if no one can pick
up the phone and report breakdowns and hoaxes, then the woman is
anything but "crazy." We are, and the narrator is.

The narrator's question, "What have I got to do with the New
War?" as well as her vague sense that the woman would be useful to
the government if it could enlist her talents at hoaxing, suggests the
cultural free fall of the postmodern era in which storytelling can
have truth effects but not truth, very real consequences but only a
consensual grounding. Ultimately, *Modern Romances* is an arch
survivor's guide to the era of simulation in which many romances
might be sufficient, if none necessary, and in which narratology is a
form of analysis at once ideological, terrorist, tragic, and comic.
"When I was in my more formulaic philosophical period," Lopatin
told me, "I said, 'Yes, I have this theory of simultaneous oppositions.'" She abandoned theory as her fiction matured because
the romance is a richer (because more paradoxical) form in which to
explore such theories. But the idea of "simultaneous oppositions"
is finally what her practice of romance, perhaps any successful practice of romance, achieves—a guerrilla tactic in the New War between the commodity culture's amoral narratology and a postmodern invocation of contraries which ranges from the "moralistic"

quality of "Modern Romances" through the ironies of romance's truth effects to the parabolic curve she throws us in "Etiology."

### Roberta Allen and the Traveling Woman

Roberta Allen's fiction pares away what many consider one of the charms of narrative prose—the mass of encumbering detail and peripheral connections which fosters realism's illusion of a whole world brought forth. If we study the two paintings on the cover of *The Traveling Woman* (Vehicle Editions, 1986)—Allen has for twenty years been a widely exhibited visual artist—we can begin to see what she has kept for her short tales. Although the three stark trees in the paintings have leaves, they stand in a wintry landscape of flat white ground and, over a waving horizon, the sort of bleak sky (these are black-and-white reproductions) to which one tries to grow accustomed during the northern European winter. There are mood and movement but not a profuse texture of associations and details. One painting features a hiking boot midstride, as if airborne; the other, a broad, almost flat hat with a band of ribbon trimmed county-fair blue-ribbon style, the sort that well-mannered adolescent girls wore decades ago. Masculine boot and girlish hat connote the extremes that fail ever to meet fully or comfortably in the tales. Although the narrator's voice maintains the distinctive austerity of these paintings through a variety of locales and relationships, it nonetheless never quite resolves the contradiction between the feminine self from which her art appears to derive and the bootish male world in which, without any of the stabilities money or strong friends might provide, she must make her way. She remains a "traveling woman" whose stability comes in changes that keep her free of the traps of men, desire, and economics.

Each piece stands alone, but together the stories provide a composite view of a life spent in the marginal zones where artists often live and work. The locales shift from Greece to Holland, Morocco to Germany, Portugal to Sweden, Mexico to Yugoslavia, India to America. On assorted ships, boats, and trains, she is in transit between unnamed points, and everywhere the finances are marginal, the marriages and affairs difficult, and her difference as woman, as artist, in disrespect. Each piece exhibits virtually the same structure: in the first phrase a telling movement, comment, or thought is already happening; then the senses sweep through the world in which that moment occurs and return with an overturned wine bottle, an exclamation, a look; finally, a second detail cuts back across the first and ends the piece with a felt epiphany. The ones that work well leave us turning them over and over like a stubborn memory. The less successful ones stir the same embarrassment as an unexpectedly intimate confession, as in "The Suitcase" when a

little girl who sees her father leaving home stops her habit of singing: "Her father doesn't know he took away her song in that suitcase."

Such slips are rare in the collection, and even they make their
contribution, marking those moments at which responses are both
uncontrolled and stereotypical. Most of the time we see the moments when the knife reaches out and splits the quotidian canvas
down the middle, top to bottom, its curling halves like curtains
opening on the flimsiness of the easel holding the frame in place. In
one of the strongest pieces, "The Pact," Allen anatomizes the deal
the narrator strikes repeatedly in her relationships. For our purposes, "The Pact" may serve as something of a kernel for the collection. Much of the story's point may be seen in the first of its four
paragraphs: "Without ever seeing each other they understood how
they would never meet and it was agreed that this would be their
secret. And each one would remain a fantasy; a creation and invention, a daydream of the other." To agree on a pact without meeting
is to jointly subscribe to the culture's lovers' discourse, though with
the unconscious passivity that keeps this subscription a "secret" to
their self-esteem and to their immersion in the image-repertoire.
The mutual projection that prevents seeing or meeting is the constitutive power of that discourse. But that projection slips under the
stress of real experiences and particularly under the inequalities of
gender roles. This slippage energizes the narrator's ability to see her
lover and to meet directly the implications of being *his* invention. It
is at this point that "everything started getting out of hand," for
"what started as an innocent exploit, became rife with accusations,
innuendoes, brutal outbursts, and endless emotional upheavals."

The struggle to coerce each other into the roles invented during
"hours spent in prolonged fantasies" is "not part of the agreement,"
but it happens when the ego fantasy bred by a media culture replaces
"contact" with consumption. Their resolve "to really have it out
with each other" thus becomes a secret decision by both to separate.
"But in truth, each one only fabricated new falsehoods, imagined
new injuries, and created new circumstances for the other." Each,
that is, has it out not with the other as he or she might really be,
but with the created other that he or she has known all the while.
They separate amid a whole fictive reconstruction of their history
which edits memory and personality in appropriate ways. But Allen
gives the whole scene one last twist: "And so it continues." It continues because neither separates from the discursive role and image-
repertoire he or she inhabits, neither revises the lovers' discourse.
To "have it out" means not real change or separation but to play out
this episode in a recycling script of consumer affairs.

"The Pact" suggests that the hold of culture over individual
experience is both insidious and thorough. In "Sand" the romance

script holds well enough that grains of sand do not affect their love-
making and that sweat is processed into his fervent line, "I am
melting into you." But his script's subtext is also spoken: "I want
to find things wrong with you so I can hate you," a self-protective
bit of distancing visible only in his brushing aside her bangs. But its
impact is sufficient to bring history into romance; "why doesn't he
know he deserves her love, she will sigh," knowing that only the
weak or damaged ego needs to protect itself from melting. "At dawn
grains of sand will disturb her sleep," disrupting the dream idyll
with the stubborn grit of difference.

  *The Traveling Woman*'s title piece shows the extent to which
gender affects the narrator's marginal status. One important reason
to be "traveling," rather than "dwelling" in any Heideggerian sense,
is that culture makes it more than a little difficult for her to assume
the role of the active, determining subject. The sketch involves her
meeting a couple; "the man struts like a peacock along the beach
beside his wife," clearly both comfortable and secure in his role. He
is so secure that he approaches "the foreign woman," the narrator,
"as though he already knows her wish; the wish of a woman turned
back in time; recognizing in him, as in a dream, the one who abandoned her, who returns now to make it right." Note how passive she
is, how bound to her daydream of him, how determined by past
abandonment (by the Father?) to repeat endlessly an unempowered
slot in this lovers' discourse. She is "like a child without a will . . .
despite the damage she is dreaming." She has an adult's experience
and desires, but a child's helplessness to effect her ends. She
watches her chance, "lives her forbidden dream—until suddenly he
pulls away," the empowered one who decides. The traveling woman
"sees the old dream without a new end; she can't conquer, can't
shatter, can't send sailing in all directions—smashed—the secret
sharing of the husband and wife. The woman vaguely perceives her
place; she is only a pawn." She is a disposable player in a larger
drama that centers on the domestic hierarchy, and her own notion
of freely experienced desire is a "forbidden dream" in her society.
So many of these sketches involve a father leaving his daughter or
attending her life only for brief visits that the subtext of the collection seems to be the patriarchal fixation in which social patterns
constitute the female ego.

  "The Pact," "Sand," and "The Traveling Woman" suggest the
parameters within which most of the stories operate. One group
follows the lead of "Sand," marking those moments when the narrator's sense of her relationship shifts. Sometimes this shift involves
the discovery of infidelity, as in "Worry," "Reaction," and
"Blinded," among which the guilt shifts from partner to partner but
the freeze-frame effect—Allen's sharply etched details of sound,
smell, or sight—pertains. Other shifts are less sensational, as in

"Ceremony" when both realize they do not want the marriage taking place, in "Sun" when she realizes that she is sorry that he is coming to invade the peacefulness she has experienced alone, or in "Escape" when she remembers why she had wanted a Mexican divorce, but only after living there for three months on the money the divorce would have cost her.

Another group of tales is more in the vein of "The Traveling Woman" and its exposé of gender differences. These stories focus upon an astonishing coldness in the men they portray, as if the Male's primary characteristic were a profound negation of her humanity. In "The Wound," for example, she reads infidelity in the eyes of the woman with whom she finds her husband. He blurts his love for the other woman, but also makes love to his numb victim: "Hardly aware he is inside her body, she digs her fingernails deep into his flesh." "The Doctor" triggers the hasty departure of his wife by contrasting her abandonment of her writing with the narrator's ongoing work and then lamenting his wife's intentional carelessness with birth control. If "The Wound" doubles his emotional with her physical violence, "The Doctor" doubles his wife's marriage trap with his trap of emotional brutality. His response to his wife's departure, in a real testimony to his egoism, is to proposition the artist. "Even if I were perfect, the woman [in 'Ring'] broods, his eagle eyes would find some flaw," a judgmentalism to which she seems not to be privileged. A novelist is less worried about her than the antique she breaks in a fall, a husband devalues his wife by dismissing as unthinkable the sincerity of a friend's proposition, a lover entertains the narrator with complaints about another girl friend.

Another cluster of sketches follows through the economic twists and turns of a husband who is at the least an operator and perhaps a con man, but whose wiles help fund her painting. In "The Painter" he blackmails the manager of an advertising studio who provides her working space but also assaults her. She is uncomfortable; "the money, however, allows the woman to devote all her time to her paintings. She works undisturbed at home while her husband idles away his hours at the pub. Even her husband admires her paintings." This sort of outlaw subsistence is repeated in "The Blow" when he cons their way out of a hotel bill, in "Secret" when he crosses from Holland into Germany to earn a few months' income in three days, and in "Change" when he panhandles for their living expenses in Greece. She has done her share as well, putting up with an art dealer's drunken confessions about a lover in order to get an exhibition. Perhaps these sketches are not the most profoundly moving in *The Traveling Woman*, but they do suggest the expense of anxiety she incurs living well outside the suburban economic margins.

Such encounters with her differences from the norm are at the heart of the most interesting group of stories. In "The Sign" she is so preoccupied with finding her ex-husband's friend that she fails to perform her role as commodity at a dinner with a potential buyer. She "feels free to follow her [sexual] fantasies" now that she is outside the enclosure of marriage. In "Brothel," she acutely feels her difference not only from the owner, who is making the money he needs to leave for India, but also from the working girls: "Who is she here in a Swedish brothel? She envies the girls their distinct purpose. She is undefined in her eyes; a form without function, a visitor on leave from life, empty and aimless in an environment where rules prevail. . . . Her host has an apartment behind the brothel where she sleeps alone. Tonight, however, she feels too lost, too liquid, to refuse the boundaries of his bed." She is "lost" to the suburban world of functional form, "liquid" rather than defined in her identity; the only model of order to which she has access is that of sex object for a man who, although "an expert of eastern religion," seems not to be taken by its ascetic elements. The prevailing rules allow him the privilege of solicitation; they allow her only the illusion of the freedom to refuse.

This outsideness, the fluidity of *The Traveling Woman*, shows itself in many small ways, as when her husband yanks her out of the way of mounted riot police. " 'What's wrong with you?' he says. 'Can't you see what's going on?' " Obviously, they see different things—he sees the normal world of pragmatic survival; she sees "a hundred defiant faces . . . shouting slogans that she doesn't understand," emblematic perhaps of her encounters with the alien tongue of patriarchal politics. In "Language" she understands not the words but the spiritual language of men casually butchering animals; in "Vacation" she finds her elderly art dealer reducing her to the status of a child; in "Young" she walks out on her eighty-year-old aunt, who is going on about how youthful her niece still looks; in "Trespassing" she returns home and finds her English accented, her neighbors hostile and jeering, her husband an alien burden. She withdraws from the narcissism of the youth cult's self-commodification, from mainstream definitions of political action and economic slaughter, and from the fierce energy with which the suburban belittles and normalizes.

As in "Brothel" when she discovers that roles and functions are already deeply instilled within her, the narrator's efforts at withdrawal are always partial and temporary victories at best. The stories in the *Between C & D* anthology are from a different collection and mark the tenuousness with which characters maintain the edge that keeps them from becoming the white noise of suburbia. The title *The Woman in the Shadows* suggests just the degree of shading and sidestepping which is required to balance the breathing room of

marginality against the liquidity of absolute iconoclasm. But that
balancing is difficult, as the "haughty young man" of "Marzipan"
discovers when he runs low on stories and blurts out that his mother
committed suicide. In "The Crisis" a "tall Dutch girl" makes this
sort of abrupt revelation to a stranger, in her case concerning her
pregnancy, and she is frenzied enough to make the startled older
woman "suddenly glad she has lost her youth."

Perhaps the ultimate mood swing is managed by the artist of
"Earthly Pleasures" who, at a lavish seafood dinner prepared to
celebrate her opening, begins to cry, her tears blurring both the toast
and her mascara: "She suddenly remembers an ancient Egyptian
custom at banquets: in order to stimulate the guests to enjoy earthly
pleasures to the full, a coffin containing an imitation skeleton was
sometimes brought in, so that they would appreciate more highly
the good things of life, especially those of the table. As she recalls
this image, she suddenly laughs out loud. The guests look in her
direction, surprised. Embarrassed, she lowers her eyes, but raises
her fork to eat the sumptuous dinner on her plate." Veering from
tears to laughter, she clearly rides an edge from death to pleasure
which makes hers a place apart, even though she shares the feast
with "a number of distinguished guests" from the mainstream. It
is, one suspects, the ironic gap between the Egyptian and the contemporary settings which takes her "terrible sense of loss" after
finishing a hard year's work and replaces it with a renewed energy
of vision. Even an imitation skeleton would devastate rather than
stimulate a culture for which consumption is sufficiently normal as
to need no piquing. A skeleton would reverse the suburban repression of death, just as her wide emotional swing unsettles the even-
ness by which change is neutralized by good manners. Alone at a
dinner of couples, commodified celebrity at a gathering of consumers, she is marked off from them by the humor of death and a creator's postpartum pain. She travels a wider range than that fenced off
by the suburban superego, a mobility of identity and mores which
accounts for both her shaded position and the acuity with which she
can, from such a margin, see.

### Plans for the Night

The most distressing problem in discussing New York writers
is that no limits seem fair to the diversity and sheer numbers of
talented individuals working at varying degrees from the epicenter
of the community *Suburban Ambush* describes. There are books to
be written on writers such as Walter Abish, John Hawkes, Harry
Mathews, and Ursule Molinaro, whose work is essential to the
downtown sensibility and sometimes appears in the same magazines as Acker's and Tillman's. There are figures such as Tom

Ahern, whose work once moved through the New York community and now arrives from Providence via Los Angeles's Sun and Moon Press. And there are unclassifiable cultural forces, such as William S. Burroughs and Richard Kostelanetz, whose New York activities over the last two or three decades have been decisive in facilitating what we now read and write. More extensive involvement in the doings of a David Byrne or a Laurie Anderson, greater time to consider video and film projects, a close reading of paintings whose evocation of the ongoing apocalypse is overlooked by most of us— these are desirable objectives for a book not already testing the economic limits of academic publishing. The following is a gesture in several of the directions we might move in continuing to follow the work of those not already named in this book.

**Michael Kasper** is a Bronx-born bomber of complacencies and unreflective immersion in the media culture, whether we consider his witty pasteups in *Verbo-Visuals* (Left Lane Must Turn Left, 1985) and *All Cotton Briefs* (North American Review Press, 1985), his media burn in *Billy! Turn Down That TV!* (Diana's Bimonthly Press, 1983), or his expertly produced *Plans for the Night* (Benzene Editions, 1987). This last title is a superb example of the "verbo-visual" artist's book combining text and imagery for conceptual impact. Printed to simulate blueprints (white text and graphics on heavy, dark-blue stock), it is a postapocalyptic narrative of survivors who turn the Generals' bomb shelter (Electric, Motors, and Dynamics staff this gleaming hall) into "a refugees' shelter and soup kitchen, a pioneering enterprise in the spiritual regeneration movement" (24). The touch is light—they offer "a sublime lentil goop à la turque, served with a lemon wedge"—but the implications are clear. The idea is almost painfully simple: their plan to shift from defense to survival is not a part of our national-policy blueprints. I suspect that Kasper kept everything simple deliberately, from the fablelike prose to the stylized graphics, in order to make the further point that something is profoundly wrong in a country when so obvious a blueprint is unthinkable.

Kasper's satire of television simulates a mindless sitcom, notes senior citizens watching the closed-circuit security system for entertainment, and recovers memories of John Cameron Swayze television. All the gags are shown in the curiously inflated rectangles of television screens, whose odd shape is the subject of one of Kasper's broadcasts. *All Cotton Briefs* is, next to *Plans for the Night*, Kasper's most appealing book, its one-page bits like a good downtown performer's routines carried out with text and appropriated graphics. Kaspar documents everything from the contradictions in moral posturing to radiation exposure, from postnuclear survival tales to vignettes of South African apartheid, from working conditions in American-owned Third World factories to the mindlessness of congressional processes. Kasper's wit keeps his sketches all half-skewed, and thus we leave few of them with a sense of déjà vu. *Plans for the Night*, for example, ends not with the lentil goop mentioned earlier, but with a (real?) quotation from K. S. Venkataramani: "All life is yearning towards the vegetable, in a higher sense." The ironic spin is and is not there; Kasper hopes we can move away from our vegetable status, but whether we can attain anything like his ideals of ecological harmony, cultural sanity, or coincidence with ourselves seems unlikely, given the gallery of moments at which his sketches catch us amidst wisdom's contrary.

**Allan Pearlman** has published widely in periodicals, including the downtown stalwarts *Appearances* and *Red Tape*. His *Char and Other Stories* (Cheap Review Press, 1987) features remarkable gothic graphics by the highly visible Michael Roman (including a startling hand-screened cover) and three stories that show why Pearlman is often asked to read at all the right places. "Stockings" is perhaps the strongest of the three, a spare parable of East Village spiritual bankruptcy in a woman whose tights, alas, have runs. She slings around the want ads and *Vogue*, occupies a barren apartment furnished with her sleeping bag and an empty refrigerator, and drinks coffee to occupy herself while the rain falls. She laments her lack of job, furniture, television, haircut, and Prince Charming in four-letter staccato recitative. Appropriately enough, absolutely nothing happens for this emptied soul marooned in poverty between an arts scene she lacks any energy to pursue and the commodity sphere in which she would appear to have grown up.

"Woman" is another interesting story; it is akin to "Stockings," only this time Pearlman's target is the fishnet dreams of an arrested adolescent. The socioeconomic facts of life he is learning lead him more to consumer frustration than to political activism: "A ball of lather spattered on the leather of his boots. He knelt and wiped it with his palms and remembered how he hadn't had money to buy shoes—but he had had to have shoes to get a job and he had had to have money to get shoes, and he had had to have a job to get money . . . and he remembered how all that had been one goddamn hard goddamn truth, goddamn" (14). His anxieties rise from resentment over having to work to a vague curiosity over whether his absent roommate will stick him for the whole rent payment; the rest of his thoughts seem to stay within the narrow range of sexual fantasies shading off into sugar-mama reveries.

"Char" catches its protagonist next to a case of spontaneous combustion, a man who leaves behind "an empty blue sport jacket dangling like a deflated zeppelin," a beeping wrist watch that is the only symptom the medics can find to treat, photographers who "swarm around the body like maggots," and crowd-control police who hassle a satirical bum and the blasé crowd that moves on down the street thinking "we'll see this guy in the Post tomorrow." Nothing seems to surprise any more, and Pearlman appears to mix this literal victim with the figurative ones of an internalized cultural apocalypse.

**Mike Topp** is another writer whose fiction is published in numerous downtown magazines, notably *Public Illumination* and *Between C & D*. Equally adept as an editor, he is one of a series of guest editors for *New Observations*; his 1989 issue contained work by such stalwarts of the new writing as Tom Ahern, Peter Cherches, Ron Kolm, and Patrick McGrath. Topp's pieces are witty skewings of narrative and cultural conventions, as we learn quickly by looking at a pair of 1984 privately printed pamphlets. "A Numskull Story" is precisely that, with a "nitwit" throwing himself in front of a train, and a hung-over subway worker handling the third rail. Perhaps the purposelessness of its suicides is a commentary upon some of the more popular urban writing. "Five Stories" belongs to a genre of adult fables that also includes work by writers as diverse as Cherches and Kasper. A porn star tells the papers late in her life that "she'd been drugged by the director in her first movie," and this story finally makes her famous. Only the story that can be told produces fame, one surmises. Another story withholds interpretive filters from the dream matter of an urban refugee: "A man found himself in a strange country many miles from home. He was taken there at night by a large black pig. While traveling they passed a beach full of crabs that had human faces on their backs. He walked around a little, stepped and slipped upon something clammy, and began to scream; his face was tense and pale. When he awoke, cedars laughed in the sunlight, oaks beckoned, and the birches bent far down and waved." Topp's fiction renews the surrealists' love of dream work but seems not to have any sense that ultimate revelations or unmediated selfhood surface in materials this obviously cultural in origin.

Topp's *Between C & D* stories hold resolutely to that hollow zone between culture and self. "Bad Luck" (1.4) lists a long catalog of superstitions ("It is bad luck to sweep the floor before the sun rises. It is bad luck to count the stars"); the only possible point is the absurdity of the maxims by which so much life is actually lived. Grouped pieces so short that they resemble newspaper fillers appear in *Between C & D* 3.1; pieces containing a pair of brothers in the salt and pepper business (respectively), a little boy stuck in a cat door, and a list of 1976 top-ten songs, are obviously spoofs on our appetite for nuggets of information and "human interest." A similar strain of information-age mania is eviscerated by "The Ten Commandments in No Particular Order" (4.2), which offers this as its entire text: "3, 6, 1, 8, 4, 5, 9, 10, 7." Perhaps Topp's wryest joke at our expense, however, is publishing in the strictly pseudonymous

*Public Illumination* under his own name. As one fan remarked to me, "Who would suspect that was a real name!"

**Mark Leyner** collected many of his best darts for *I Smell Esther Williams* (Fiction Collective, 1983), a frustrating book for deep readers raised on realist fiction but a zany parenthesis in the pauses of stand-up routines. The book pursues the illogic of *non sequiturs*, the leaps of quotidian faithlessness, the doo-wahs and uh-huhs of media lyricism. Leyner evidences no belief in continuities that promise to carry us from confusion to illumination, in structures that provide credible contours to experience, in assumptions that presume adequate explanatory powers. Instead, one-liners bounce off every page's margins, collectively forming a matrix of witty distance from the material, sexual, even theological promises of the culture. "The Boston Celtics put me on waivers when I manifested the stigmata of Christ—I couldn't shoot without discomfort" (93), we read in "I'm Writing about Sally." Among other things, the sketch is a compilation of similarly fantasial identities that float through the consciousness of the narrator like anxious bubbles hoping to break over some scene more utopian than the sexual longing sublimated in his need, at the end, "to make way like a smitten redman into each valley and canyon where I'll cup my hands to my mouth and call, 'Yoo-hoo . . . Sally . . . yooo-hoo!'" (98).

Leyner's narrators are the kind who are inventive in deflecting unwanted phone calls. "'I can't talk now,' I said, 'I'm insulating. I've got fiberglass all over me. Bye'" (159). But the beat of the culture continues unabated for them nonetheless: "That department store signal was in my head—Ping Ping Ping Ping" (152). Leyner's work, together with that of Kasper, Pearlman, Topp, and, certainly, Cherches, suggests a genre of writing we could call urban screwball comedy—not because it has the shapeliness and resolution of classic comedy, but precisely because it does not. This genre follows a line of cultural logic that threads through experience rather than along the neat trajectories of theory and myth. Its line lies along the turning threads of cultural devices that fasten without finally taking firm hold of anything, performing the very alogicality of logic, the slapstick of mythology. The genre rarely offers the sweeping analysis of Acker or the delicate dissection of Tillman, but it is a form of diversion that suggests what intelligent readers in a new era might find amusing about our own.

# DOWNTOWN WRITING

This book has focused upon a community of writers working in New York who have, since the mid-seventies, reinvigorated American fiction. Although I have not tried to make the case here, they are part of a much larger national movement with vital centers across the country. At the time I started writing this book, few outside New York much knew about these writers, with some comforting exceptions, and they belonged in fact as well as in spirit to the other book I have been working on, "The Unread Renaissance," a study of what has happened to classic American themes among writers whose primary outlet has been our small presses and little magazines. I began fully sharing Richard Kostelanetz's assumption that multinational corporate ownership of our major publishing houses meant *The End of Intelligent Writing*.

What has amazed me in the time I have been working on *Suburban Ambush* is how the work of writers whom I first encountered in issues of downtown magazines and in the pages of small- and tiny-press offerings has gone on quickly to become important sellers for presses such as Grove, Penguin, and Simon and Schuster's Poseidon imprint. Despite silence or outright antipathy and misunderstanding from much of the major review media, these writers are winning an increasingly large audience, and that victory is one for a vigorous new writing that has escaped from the writing workshops into our streets. These writers are not only talented but also *very* smart, as one learns quickly from talking with them about everything from Reaganomics to what is wrong with the film *Platoon*.

Perhaps no observer understands in more detail the rich history of America's alternative literary tradition(s) than Kostelanetz, as anyone who has followed his writing over the years well knows, and I often find these writers' narratives reminding me of what I take to

be his cardinal principle: "One measure of excellence is the capacity
to inspire in the reader, especially an experienced one, that rare and
humbling awe that here, before one's eyes, is something that is quite
marvelously different from what has gone before, and yet intrinsi-
cally successful and fine" (Kostelanetz 1981, 86). Out of the sheer
intelligence behind these writers' grasp of history and theory, out of
their sensitivity to the implications of the poorly understood world-
wide social revolution of the sixties, and out of their pragmatic
literacy in the countertraditions of writing in this culture comes a
body of writing that satisfies Kostelanetz's criterion more vigorously than any communal outpouring for more than half a century.

"The criticism of contemporary fiction," Jerome Klinkowitz
remarks pointedly, "has been left to partisan sniping over its larger
formal and moral issues, while the specific works themselves are
critically unread" (Klinkowitz 1985, xxxv). Much in agreement
with him, I generally prefer my tactic thus far, letting these writers
speak for themselves through their fiction, their essays, and their
comments in interviews and letters. But I will venture a few pages
here at the end to sketch out my own answers to the three perennial
questions that arise whenever anyone purports to find a new American writing: What is it? Where does it come from? Where is it going?

### Differentiae

To define this new writing verges on high comedy, because the
ethos of definition is part of the problem these writers attack in
their work. It has not been written with the archives and the fresh-
man English reading lists in mind (though I must say that *Haunted
Houses* is only one of the novels covered here that teaches quite well
at any level). It *was* written for people struggling to overcome the
sensation that, if they had a real life at all, somebody else was trying
to live it for them, but a "somebody" who was not a terribly obvious
Sicilian Don or Robber Baron. A "they" lurks behind the specificity
of lived experiences which constitutes this fiction's most literal
referents, but it is one not clearly understood apart from the poststructural acuteness that informs most of it explicitly and the rest
of it at least implicitly. Nonetheless, I will go ahead anyway and cite
my list of traits for separating work that seems truly of its time from
the often beautifully competent summer reruns of (late) modernist
fiction, work that I find quite pleasurable and enriching and with its
own high claims upon our attention but that does not prepare us in
the same way to face the changed world in which we now live. But
readers and reviewers should take this list in an ironic postmodern
way—as an invitation to make their own lists and mail them to my
ever-receptive postal box.

*It is smart about ideological resonances.* In the most innocent modernist and late modernist fiction, writers focusing upon the individual's struggle to achieve a unified and coherent identity amidst the stress of memory, desire, and understanding are at times capable of near-obtuseness about the social, political, and economic resonance of their material and form. A little white girl can invite her little black friend over, and it strikes the writer as a good idea to have towels separately monogrammed just for her friend. The sickly mother and drunken father just *are* that way, no reason. Watch her struggle, say some funny words in her quaintly low-class dialect, be lusted after a bit, and then emerge a female Oliver Twist by novel's end. It is too small a frame for our age, and writers of the new American fiction could not leave those towels alone without marking their residue from the Whites Only era, could not let the mother pine away without their asking why no source of strength is available to her, could not let the father drop his blue work shirt on the floor without their testing the weight of economic determination in its fall. Each detail of experience, each feature of language, each pressure of convention upon the characters or the writer or the reader, and each implication of the context in which the experiences or the writing or the reading take place is part of this fiction's ideological analysis of the culture.

*It is aggressive in pursuing the issues of language and representation.* Ronald Sukenick, one of those writers whose conception of fiction was vital in preparing the possibility for downtown writing, has observed that existing conventions of representation can become "a way of packaging our experience so that we can walk away from it. What we call realism saps our experience of its immediacy and authority, a process tremendously augmented by the electronic media and probably one reason for their great success" (Sukenick 1985, 41). The "novel," he argues, is "an instrument that undercuts official versions of reality in favor of our individual sense of experience, now constantly threatened by the brain wash of politics and the mass market" (ibid., 67). Perhaps no one has worked out the implications of this more persuasively than Brian Wallis in "An Absence of Vision and Drama," a telling review of artists' writings:

> A principal characteristic is their consideration of language as a
> system of representations which constructs its subjects. These
> writings are less concerned with the explanatory (transparent)
> function of language, than with demonstrating its ideological
> function as a structuring discourse. To this end, these new artists'
> writings employ certain formal operations, shared with contem-
> porary visual arts, such as appropriation or reinscription of exist-
> ing images or texts; adoption of nonsequential structure, as in

television or film; privileging a form of writing which is fragmentary, digressive and interpenetrated with other texts; attention to the role of the reader (viewer). The effect to these textual strategies is to call into question the otherwise seamless closure of conventional writing and of representation in general. (Wallis 1985a, 65)

Perhaps it is not surprising that the writer emphasizes experience and the critic emphasizes the issues of language and representation, but what is important about downtown writing is its profound linkage of these two concerns.

*It retains a reflexive edge about the form of fiction.* As Sukenick says with his wonderful directness, "the form of the traditional novel is a metaphor for a society that no longer exists" (Sukenick 1985, 3). Hence the fiction examined in this book has for one of its subtexts a sense almost of betrayal by those who use similar material in traditional form or who write as if everyone went to prep school. The analogy in art criticism might be Benjamin Buchloh's attack upon German neo-expressionism and Arte Cifra as regressions ignoring social and political reality, or Douglas Crimp's assault upon New Image painting as "typical of recent museum exhibitions in its complicity with that art which strains to preserve the modernist aesthetic categories which museums themselves have institutionalized" (Crimp 1984, 187). Much of what I have said about reflexivity in *The Politics of Reflexivity* pertains here, but Raymond Federman, important to a number of the downtown writers, says it succinctly when he envisions "a kind of writing, a kind of discourse whose shape will be an interrogation, an endless interrogation of what it is doing while doing it, and endless denunciation of its fraudulence, of what *it* really is: an illusion (a fiction)" (Federman 1981, 11). The fiction we have explored in the present book constitutes its analytical models of culture, but with a mindfulness of these reflexive issues which registers in its form. As Craig Owens notes concerning the visual art adjacent to this fiction, "its deconstructive thrust is aimed not only against the contemporary myths that furnish its subject matter, but also against the symbolic, totalizing impulse which characterizes modernist art" (Owens 1984, 235). No body of fiction resists totalization more vigorously than downtown writing.

*It is savvy about the role of institutions and discourses.* Although one is unlikely to find a card-carrying Althusserian among this group of writers, institutions such as the family, the church, the schools, and the media are Ideological State Apparatuses skewed out of any totalizing homogeneity by their own histories and interests, but nonetheless potent in their force upon the daily lives of individuals. The discourse systems through which much of their force reaches those individuals, even emerges from their lips as if from within them, might be thought of as the foreign languages we all must learn *if*—a fatal one—there were a "native" language waiting as an alternative. These conventional ways of thinking and speaking *normalize* subjects by structuring their consciousness and channeling their energies. The discourses also *naturalize* the ideological fictions on which they rest. Downtown writing contests normalization and denaturalizes the assumptions of its patterns.

*It is shrewd about the double agent's game.* That there is no "native" language and no alternative to these institutionally sanctioned discourse systems means that to contest their effects one must occupy them from the inside, to become a mole skilled in the cloak of ironic intentions and the dagger of timely thrusts into the heart of their customary functions. Kathy Acker's violent appropriations and rewriting of literary classics is one version of this game, but Lynne Tillman's more subtle appropriation of realism for virtually countercultural ends is another. Catherine Texier writes a book that looks like others in a Penguin series of summer sizzlers, but it is as "hot" ideologically as it is sexually. Ironically exploiting the resources of forms, conventions, and concepts that originated in quite a different cultural paradigm is a dangerous tactic. One is always vulnerable to being reassimilated to the modes of power and knowledge which one seeks to disrupt. But the alternative is silence. As Audrey Lorde once pointed out, "the master's tools will never dismantle the master's house"; if you speak the master's language, you will serve his sentences. But if the master talks doublespeak himself, then a doubled doublespeak proliferates the internal ironic distances to the point at which unexpected spacings open up for the shrewd player.

*It knows there is no outside.* Double agent rather than freedom fighter, it seeks to enlarge liberty rather than dreaming of liberation, especially in a country whose "intelligence community"—surely a misnomer if ever there were one—is allowed to murder whomever it does without most people knowing, let alone seeming to care. Demystified concerning the liberationist fallacy, downtown writers will not be found in the "master's house" composing platforms, treatises in the form of propositional knowledge, or blueprints for the Great Society II. One stages limited guerrilla actions here and there where a space or a branch office or a single book can be made to serve more interests than simply the hegemonic. One makes "orange objects" that resist commodification; one writes books that dye the mindless genres of mass entertainment so as to foreground the ideological superstructure on which they are projected; one shatters the utopian totalizations of another era into shards that can slash open the scrims on the cultural stage; one takes the Bildungsroman that changed Pip into a clerk for a multinational corporation and turns it into an implosion of the disciplinary forces that determine individuality in postindustrial society.

*Its texts are open to play, not mastery.* The lessons of Roland Barthes are well learned. The motifs of mastery, of readerliness, and of an Iserian fill-in-the-blanks system of coauthoring yield to those of playing (the open plotting of games, the performance possibilities of musical instruments, the "give" in pinball machines), of writerliness, of resonances to be heard down constantly shifting hallways and connections to be made by an authorial reader who must acquire this chapter's list of skills in order to play the fiction game. Reading is designed almost as a reeducation camp in the bush country beyond the last suburban cul-de-sac.

*Its formal practice holds no exclusionary rules.* Partisans sometimes write as if plot and character are no longer thinkable. They *are* thinkable, if not in completely familiar ways. What is not thinkable is the disciplinary formalism of a Percy Lubbock. Plot is certainly possible, if not necessary, though not as the sort of metaphysically motivated structuration we are accustomed to in the classic English novel. Acker once said: "I don't live in a world, and I don't think *this* is a world, in which we have the given Aristotelian verities, the nineteenth-century verities of stability, even of the kind of time/space stability that is Newtonian." Plot is not a form homologous with an underlying structure of reality itself, whether Aristotelian or Platonic. Character is not thinkable as the fiction of a univocal and self-present entity. But it can be explored as an amalgam of code systems, whose contradictions agonize individual organisms trying to make it through the near-apocalyptic day of our era. What marks this fiction, in other words, is the extraordinary diversity that includes Michael Kasper's fiction in the form of blueprints, Peter Cherches's SAT question format, Constance DeJong's musically structured recitatives, and Tillman's exquisitely crafted ethnological fiction.

*It is hungry for spirit without theology and the church.* The word *spirit* is loaded with transcendental mysticism, of course, and in that sense it is a poor choice for this point. But new writing does seek to reclaim a nonmaterialistic and activist mode of Being in a market cornered by the organized religion of consumption and television spectatorship. The task requires *materializing* the idea of spirit until spirit itself becomes a viable source of inspiration in an age essentially finished with specifically religious belief as we have known it. Spirit is a concept incompatible with alligator briefcases and Club Med; it takes place outside the arena of leveraged buy outs and organizational politics; it points not to *another* realm elsewhere or after history, but one simultaneous with and accessible to players within history who want a game of healing rather than a winning game. In simplest terms, spirit pulls readers out of specularity into activity with a power that does not look like power to traditionally minded thinkers. As Lucy Lippard states it in her important essay "Trojan Horses: Activist Art and Power," "the power of art is subversive rather than authoritarian, lying in its connection of the ability to make with the ability to see—and then in its power to make others see that they too can make something of what they see . . . and so on" (Lippard 1984, 345). Perhaps *spirit* is entirely too loaded a word, but it signals the seriousness of the venture.

*It privileges feminist elements.* Attentive to the historical particularities of women's place in the culture, fully attentive to the specific sort of talking cure which individual women may pursue in order to escape being the direct object in cultural syntax, downtown writing nonetheless often seems to take feminist critique as its model for analyzing the formation of all subjects in our culture. We would have a messy diagram trying to draw this point, because new writing is the subtlest writing that we have had in following the interaction of gender, race, and class. It is about as sophisticated as possible in keeping straight the material differences in these factors without supposing their operation to be simple within an individual or singular in its effects. The extraordinary fluidity of characters' gender may annoy separatists of one persuasion or another. But it does point to the rarely harmonious interfiling of what we have been pleased to separate as "male" and "female" in the psyches of most, perhaps all, members of society. The conflicts that spring out of the consequences of this fluidity point up many of the most significant cultural contradictions exposed in new writing. Lippard is again helpful, this time for her comments on the general benefits from feminist art, which has

> broadened and deepened the whole notion of "political art" by incorporating the element of the personal, autobiography, consciousness-raising, and social transformation, which led eventually to the still broader notion of "the political is personal"—i.e., an awareness of how local, national, and international events affect our individual lives. (Ibid., 351)

The fiction we have examined constantly measures the political through its impact upon the body, and the incorporated elements Lippard lists are among those we have seen in the specially charged context she cites. For the benefit of speculators, I think this particular trait is one of the most important "growth stocks" as new writing continues to develop.

*It is major.* I would wager that numerous writers who are currently much touted will be lucky to have their names in a list after a hundred years. But there will be Acker Centennial Conferences and Tillman Society Newsletters. This is just my prediction; I may have to help myself out by starting a bit of it. But I think that the quality of fiction discussed in this book is all but unnerving, a striking renaissance that our traditional critical institutions have had enormous difficulty recognizing. When we consider that these writers were born after 1945, we realize how much strong work will likely be forthcoming from this remarkable group.

### Etymologies

Talking about the roots of downtown writing requires us to engage in the very *topos* of filiation from which Barthes so eloquently recoiled in his classic essay "From Work to Text." But it is worth noting that the fiction described in *Suburban Ambush* is not entirely unprecedented, and that it is not only related to work in the adjacent arts, but to that of the generations that preceded it. Kostelanetz deftly summarizes the historian's wisdom:

> In practice, new fiction usually rejects or ignores the recently dominant preoccupations of literature to draw selectively upon unmined or unfashionable strains of earlier work, recording an esthetic indebtedness that may not be immediately apparent. Therefore, thanks to innovative work, certain otherwise forgotten precedents are revived in literature's collective memory. Furthermore, new work tends to draw upon materials and structures previously considered beneath or beyond fiction, as well as upon new developments in the other arts. (Kostelanetz 1981, 86)

My students hear the Futurists here, the Dadaists there, but to these general antecedents (would we not have to begin with Cervantes and Laurence Sterne and end with the *CBEL*?) we could argue some more specific and direct inspirations. Although a fair measure of postmodern irony is again called for, we might say that this downtown writing grows from these roots:

- classic American narrative, though more from Herman Melville's mode than from that of the Brahmins, particularly the polyglot Melville of *Moby Dick* and the ideologically acute author of *The Piazza Tales*;
- modernist masters, though less from Ernest Hemingway than

from Gertrude Stein, particularly (a) her attempt in *The Making of Americans* to understand character as a collection of tendencies and inclinations with a social history and an almost linguistic sort of structure; (b) her sense in essays such as *Composition as Explanation* that it is writing responsively to the *how* of the way people are living, the particular texture and density of ordinary details, that makes a genius truly of her time; and (c) her willingness in *Tender Buttons* and *Lifting Belly* to write from the position of the outsider and to evade the control of syntactic, poetic, and narrative conventions—though we will quickly get into trouble underestimating the impact of Samuel Beckett as well;

- ageless senior figures whose work is protean in its countertraditional energy (such John Cage), or perfectly crafted and attuned to the implications of our evolving present (such as Ursule Molinaro, whose prose style's visual acuity and oral resonance link her to the finer stylists among the downtown set and whose thematic concerns remain strikingly current);

- fifties' Beats, but especially William S. Burroughs, not only because he has stayed active in the New York arts community through Dial-a-Poem and constant readings, but also because his fiction has ventured deep into the repressed territories beyond the suburban lots of the Updikes and Cheevers;

- sixties' radical experimenters, particularly so persistent an agitator for literary difference as Richard Kostelanetz, who is always friendly and helpful to those benefiting from the space his polemical blasts have cleared in literary politics;

- writers who emerged during the sixties and balanced commercial and critical success with remarkable skill, including John Barth (whose reflexive exercises amaze), Donald Barthelme (whose witty appropriations must have encouraged the more politically engaged forms we have seen), Robert Coover (whose narrative experiments in *Pricksongs and Descants* remain highly relevant and suggestive openings), and John Hawkes (whom Patrick McGrath finds crucial among recent novelists);

- seventies' postmoderns, particularly Walter Abish (whose *In the Future Perfect* is an austere venture into the ideological and philosophical heart of cultural logic), Harry Mathews (whose *The Sinking of the Odradek Stadium* has been on everyone's reading list), and Peter Handke (whose *Kaspar* anatomizes the conditioning of the subject and whose *The Left-Handed Woman* is still a favorite fiction title in the East Village);

- reflexive writers half a generation older than the downtown writers whose writing did much of the culture's work in finishing off the remaining naïveté of mainstream fiction, including Raymond Federman (whose ideas about Surfiction and its "word-beings" have influenced a number of downtown writers), Ronald Sukenick (whose sense that "the job of narrative fiction is not to record some preexisting reality but to contribute to the ongoing process of culture building in and through the process of writing itself" [Sukenick 1985, 79–80] has been much extended by younger writers), Steve Katz (whose witty reflexivity has to have been more than merely noticed by the more playful members of the downtown set), and Clarence Major (whose critical edge and resistance to dominant cultural assumptions are highly pertinent);

- the French countertradition, in particular the vital work of Jean Genet (whose plays anatomize power, desire, and the culture of images with deadly acuity, whose novels claim the connectedness of *all* cultural realms and connect postmoderns with the usefulness of the Marquis de Sade's works) and, to a lesser extent, the *nouveau roman*;
- poststructural theory, in particular Michel Foucault's models of history, of power and knowledge, and of questioning *how* forms and institutions have been used in the culture, but also Jean Baudrillard's ideas in *Simulations* and Roland Barthes's essays on film, textuality, and the ideological;
- mass culture, especially the twist given it in the Duchampian tradition rather than the Brylcreem slick given it by Presley's Colonel Parker, and in particular the special note one finds in a group such as the Velvet Underground.

This list is the result of numerous hours of conversation with writers in the lofts, bars, and restaurants of the area and from the resonances I have felt in reading the pages of their novels and of *Bomb*, *Appearances*, *Benzene*, and the like. The list should be longer (where is J. G. Ballard?), much longer if one finds value in a "complete" list of influential cultural figures, but perhaps it provides a start toward the cultural side of the forces shaping downtown writing.

### The Shape of Things to Come

I believe that downtown writing is *postmodern*, but I have been sparing in my use of the term because, thus far, it tells us more about the individual using it than about what is out there. Insofar as the term denotes a period, it suffers the fate of any such label in reducing disparate phenomena to a single word. In our eschatologically minded era, many feel themselves at the end of an epoch that stretches at least into the nineteenth-century, to René Descartes for some, to Saint Augustine for others. We lack adequate distance to be precise about what may have changed and what new cultural regime is displacing it. But our creative artists do seem to have a different feeling about change than, say, the high modernists, who often looked backward for reassurance against change, or the other modernists, the avant-gardists, who frequently enough believed they had exchanged false culture for true reality that their look was often as much backward as forward (whether the exchange in question was for Hugo Ball's transcendental turn, or the "natural" complexity of many Dadaists, or André Breton's Eden of the subconscious).

Our artists seem mostly to feel differently about change, though to argue this requires separating postmoderns from late moderns, who continue enlarging the domain of experience brought under the lens of modernist fiction. Most current fiction is content either to repeat entertainment formulae (whether overtly or under the surge of the trendy) or to continue with modernist formulations of individual identity and more or less liberal humanist instincts about social and political realities. Although both residual and emergent elements are present in the work of the postmoderns, they primarily share Foucault's conclusion in "The Subject and Power"

> that the political, ethical, social, philosophical problem of our
> days is not to try to liberate the individual from the state and from
> the state's institutions but to liberate us both from the state and
> from the type of individualization which is linked to the state. We
> have to promote new forms of subjectivity through the refusal of
> this kind of individuality which has been imposed on us for sev-
> eral centuries. (Foucault 1984, 424)

The individual that downtown writers liberate from the regime they critique is not that liberal humanist self, but one whose "forms of subjectivity" mix many older elements together with a different set of assumptions, the resulting mix a mishmash only to those for whom "the kind of individuality" Foucault eschews still seems "natural."

Nothing is natural for the postmodern, because even "natural catastrophe" is experienced through the cultural framing of dollar damage, insurance coverage, state and federal policies, *things* lost. The natural continues as culture's other, and we are inescapably on *this* side of whatever line you draw between the two (if so old-fashioned a line seems still important). But the larger postmodern sphere of activity consists of enormous energy expended over both Foucault's "refusal" and the effort to "promote new forms" in every sphere. Hal Foster has probed very usefully the whole subject of "(Post)Modern Polemics," noting both Foucault's poststructural pull and the neoconservative appropriation of postmodernism. That is, if one phase of our moment is that of Refusal, then the sort of

parodic engagement with tradition so well explored by Linda Hutcheon can be, by a Charles Jencks, siphoned off into something akin
to T. S. Eliot's effort to revivify the value points of tradition for
modernism. Hutcheon argues that postmodern works

> are all resolutely historical and inescapably political precisely be-
> cause they are parodic. I want to argue that postmodernism is a
> fundamentally contradictory enterprise: its art forms (and its the-
> ory) use and abuse, install and then subvert convention in parodic
> ways, self-consciously pointing both to their own inherent para-
> doxes and provisionality and, of course, to their critical or ironic
> re-reading of the art of the past. (Hutcheon 1986–87, 180)

Hutcheon's *A Poetics of Postmodernism: History, Theory, Fiction*
(published too late to help me here!) is a crucial addition to our
thinking about this subject, expansive enough in its references to
escape Jencks's narrower grasp of postmodernism. That is, although
Jencks answers his question, *What Is Post-Modernism?* by saying
that its "key definers are a pluralism both philosophical and stylistic, and a dialectical or critical relation to a pre-existing ideology"
(Jencks 1986, 23), he reads backward into tradition in a move quite
similar to Eliot's strategy in *The Waste Land*. For Jencks, *The Language of Post-Modern Architecture* "can communicate the values
which are missing and ironically criticise the ones [it] dislikes"
(Jencks 1984, 37), but under dual conditions that are part of the
world Foucault refuses. Referring offhandedly to his rejection of
everyone else's sense of the term, Jencks tells us that he "used the
term to mean the opposite of all this: the end of avant-garde extrem-
ism, the partial return to tradition and the central role of communicating with the public—and architecture is *the* public art"
(ibid., 6).

The language tells us much about Jencks's conservatism, for
tradition brings ideology with it and "communicating" *can* mean
compliance with existing forms. We learn also from Jencks's choice
of heroes, Michael Graves paramount among them. Although this
is not the place to initiate a treatise on architecture, we would want
to look not at Graves's attempt to reassemble the humanist past,
but at those involved in the promotional half of Foucault's mission—at Coop Himmelblau, or Peter Eisenman, or Massimiliano
Fuksas. The kind of postmodernism which we find in downtown
writers has traditional concerns for individual life and for that of the
community, it has a familiar commitment to activism and analysis,
and it is fervent in its hopes to make things better. But the assumptions by which it proceeds are, as we have seen, not traditional, and
again we should turn to Foucault to specify this difference:

Power relations are rooted deep in the social nexus, not reconsti-
tuted "above" society as a supplementary structure whose radical
effacement one could perhaps dream of. . . . Which, be it said in
passing, makes all the more politically necessary the analysis of
power relations in a given society, their historical formation, the
source of their strength or fragility, the conditions which are necessary to transform some or to abolish others. For to say that there
cannot be a society without power relations is not to say either
that those which are established are necessary or, in any case, that
power constitutes a fatality at the heart of societies, such that it
cannot be undermined. Instead, I would say that the analysis,
elaboration, and bringing into question of power relations and the
"agonism" between power relations and the intransitivity of freedom is a permanent political task inherent in all social existence.
(Foucault 1984, 429)

Hence one laments that Brian McHale's ambitious effort to read
*Postmodernist Fiction* places it within ontology (even if it is Pavel's
rather than Plato's) rather than ideology. Attentive to what I have
elsewhere called constitutive poetics, McHale's book is an important contribution to our understanding of postmodern writing, even
though it stops short of considering the generation that comes the
closest to realizing Foucault's dual goals.

Foster makes a distinction in "For a Concept of the Political in
Contemporary Art" which is helpful for understanding the texture
of the postmodernism practiced by downtown writers. He suggests
that "one might distinguish between a 'political art' which, locked
in a rhetorical code, reproduces ideological representations, and an
'art with a politic' which, concerned with the structural positioning
of thought and the material effectivity of practice within the social
totality, seeks to produce a concept of the political relevant to our
present" (Foster 1985a, 155). Although at times Foster phrases this
practice as primarily "resistance or interference" (ibid., 149), we
have seen a variety of strategies for awakening readers to "the structural positioning of thought." Some of those strategies even enable
a "practice within the social totality" that shifts both the individual
and the social in significant ways. That both Refuses and Promotes,
in other words, resisting the "historical amnesia" Fredric Jameson
attributes to the media and going beyond the self-absorption some
find in postmodern work. If one is really to theorize the postmodern—a project beyond the scope of this book—one would follow the
track from Foucault to Baudrillard, as have Arthur Kroker and David
Cook in their remarkable *The Postmodern Scene*. The fiction explored in the present book resonates at many points with their analysis of contemporary social reality, though they are perhaps more
gloomy than most of the downtown writers. But the Shape of Things

to Come, as the postmodern endeavors we see around us move increasingly from Refusal to Promotion, will come to look less and less like neoconservative desires or late modernist nostalgias and more like Kroker and Cook's vision:

> We are living in the age of the death of the social and the triumph of a signifying culture, the violent implosion of gender signs, and the indefinite reversibility and self-liquidation of all the foundational *récits* of contemporary culture. The body is a power grid, tattooed with all the signs of cultural excess on its surface, encoded from within by the language of desire, broken into at will by the ideological interpellation of the subject, and, all the while, held together as a fictive and concrete unity by the illusion of *misrecognition*. (Kroker and Cook 1986, 26)

The replacement of social relations by the passivity and asymmetrical power of the one-way linkup of television, the turbulence of all the categories and narratives by which we form identity, the body's registry of cultural contradiction, and the persistent permutations of our myths of unity all form the crisscrossing network of cultural fictions within which downtown writing finds itself refusing the neoconservative's tradition and struggling to envision what might be promoted as an effective resistance and interference in the gloomy scene that Kroker and Cook assume.

Fortunetelling should perhaps be left to those with kerchiefs rather than a baseball cap, and crystal balls rather than an aging Kaypro, but I believe that a few obvious observations emerge from seeing where this cultural push has taken us. It is safe to say that certain kinds of fiction will come to seem increasingly quaint. Fiction whose only focus is inside the mind of a central character to the exclusion of the external forces that shape that mind will likely be found a bit flat by readers. Fiction not acute about the problematic nature of language and of textuality will seem naïve. Writing narrative without a real critical edge may well come to feel like crafting jeweled eggs for the Romanovs. My first observation is that a redefined realism will dominate the next decade of good novels, one that carries out the Foucauldian program of Refusal and Promotion and that seeks to avoid the Baudrillardian nightmare. The "documentary realism" of which Ian Watt spoke will orient its referents less to the subjective frame of the modernists than to the sociopolitical, radical semiotics of engaged social analysts. Those analysts will seek significant structural change rather than an Augustan confirmation of hierarchy or a Victorian truce between the embattled subject and the omnivorous institutionalization changing what felt like a London still on the human scale into the foundation of our modern bureaucratic Administered Society.

The object of that change, of course, is not only greater social equity but also the ability to contest actively (if not with utopian success) the internalization of the disciplinary network that Foucault finds at the heart of the cultural amalgam. One resource in that contest, and my second observation, is an increasing embrace by "serious" narrative artists of other media. Perhaps Robert Pinsky undertook his *Mindwheel* computer adventure in order to profit from gamers' appetites, but his work with the programmers led him to a fateful interchange with them (Programmers: "Is a scene something that goes on in a place, or a place where something occurs?" Pinsky: "Both." Poets make good narratologists, and the programmers pioneered narratives in which things go on elsewhere in the imagined world whether the player goes there or not, and the scene changes dramatically depending upon when that player finally arrives). Computer narrative will become an important exploration of coauthoring by readers and writers. We have seen DeJong working in video, Tillman in film, Cherches in performance: this list will seem modest and dated in another decade or two when media crossovers are the rule. Recent advances in computer-generated Virtual Reality—one can put on a DataGlove and "feel" an electronic image—might take human beings out of direct experience altogether. But if downtown artists get hold of the equipment, we can imagine not the most reifying of technologies, but one with the most astonishing capacities yet envisioned for shaking a suburbanite out of the "virtual" existence now fostered by the media and for encouraging a bodily tattoo of ideological implications that can follow them to their ultimate conclusion without exterminating the beneficiary of such wisdom.

My third observation is that we are far from the end of the possibilities in ironic play with hybridized genres. Acker mixes narrative, essay, poetry, drawings, and appropriated materials from a myriad of cultural zones. Writers will pursue further the capacity of such mixes to destabilize oppressive alliances among writing, institutions, and ideology. The energy generated by the unsuspected relations found within hybrid structures takes us into Bakhtinian social laboratories where ideologemes are invented and where, however temporarily, social spaces may emerge. At some point the last reader in America will understand that textuality means fiction, and that this is not a loss so much as an opportunity to decide how to shape the imaginative superdome in which we play us and them. At that point, perhaps we will just play us. In the meantime, that is to say in reality, we will need the capacity of hybridization to keep disturbing the pace at which media imagery can fabricate smooth-seamed constructs that seal us off from anything even vaguely resembling direct connection with one another or with the natural and social worlds around us. We will not reach such a zone, of course—it would have to be located entirely outside language and culture, where most of us, at least, are likely to remain—but hybridization may keep the textual membrane thin and supple.

Yet another change is that "our" writing will be more ethnically diverse, just as it has already become distinctly more diverse in authorial gender. This book inadequately reflects Hispanic and black writers engaged in recasting narrative form. It could be argued that these communities do not overlap with the predominantly white postmodern Tanam Press and Lower East Side circles as much as the latter two do with each other. But the real problem is that we have had no way to read nonwhite narrative traditions. They have not been encountered in their own context and in any representative sampling, let alone completeness: we are as untrained in this narrative as we are, say, in our tradition of avant-garde writing. This situation will not instantly improve: the institutional support for publishing new work in these traditions is minimal. In remarks that apply well to the fiction of virtually all minorities, Kurt Hollander argues in the *Latin Americans in NYC* issue of *Portable Lower East Side* (5.1, 2) that many Hispanic authors remain unpublished because of their politics, their portrait of the "hostile, xenophobic society" in which they remain forever "aliens," and their contradiction of the reigning image of Hispanic life which circulates in the entertainment media, the corporate advertisements, and the academic and administrative worlds (158–59). Those Hispanics that do get published, moreover, "can only sit back and watch as their work, often intended to foment social and political change in their country, is packaged here as aesthetic commodities and read only as universal allegories or as exotic travel guides" (158). Hollander's *Portable Lower East Side*, Joel Rose and Catherine Texier's *Between C & D*, and Richard Armijo's Embargo Books Ltd. are among the few places where fiction from different ethnic tributaries mix. I would expect these exceptions to become the rule and that a 1999 *Suburban Ambush* would be strengthened by the richer blend of published work readily available for analysis. I would not expect a narrative melting pot, but a narrative polyphony in which the very strength of difference would be its effective force.

My final observation is a very pleasurable one to make. Downtown writing will continue to be fun, surprising us with the new possibilities it generates out of the poststructural paradigm within which it works. Part of that fun, of course, is its challenge to those of us in academia to get it into our classrooms intelligently and its insights into our theoretical notions and our critical practice. And just as soon as I get the back of my house painted and my shed cleared out, I plan to try a bit of that fun.

# WORKS CITED

Acconci, Vito. 1988. "Television, Furniture, and Sculpture: The Room with the American View." In *ZG: Altered States*, edited by Rosetta Brooks, 30–37. New York: ZG Publications.

Althusser, Louis. 1984. *Essays on Ideology*. London: Verso Editions.

Bakhtin, Mikhail. 1984. *Rabelais and His World*. Trans. Hélène Iswolsky. Bloomington: Indiana University Press.

———. 1985. *The Formal Method in Literary Scholarship*. Trans. Albert J. Wehrle. Cambridge: Harvard University Press.

Barber, Bruce. 1986. "Notes toward an Adequate Interventionist [Performance] Practice." *Act* 1.1 (Winter/Spring): 14–24.

Baskin, Fran. 1986. "Celluloid Theater." *Say! Arts New York*, June, 25.

Baudrillard, Jean. 1983. *Simulations*. Trans. Paul Foss, Paul Patton, and Philip Beitchman. New York: Semiotext(e).

Buchloh, Benjamin H. D. 1984. "Figures of Authority, Ciphers of Regression." In *Art after Modernism: Rethinking Representation*, edited by Brian Wallis, 107–34. New York: New Museum of Contemporary Art.

Cardoni, Edmund. 1986. *Blatant Artifice*. Buffalo, N.Y.: Hallwalls.

Carlin, John. 1988. "Pop Apocalypse: Notes for a Supreme Painting." New York: Gracie Mansion.

Chomsky, Noam. 1984. "Disinformation." In *Disinformation: The Manufacture of Consent*, edited by Geno Rodriguez, 11–18. New York: Alternative Museum.

Cixous, Hélène. 1981. "The Laugh of the Medusa." In *New French Feminisms*, edited by Elaine Marks and Isabelle de Courtivron, 245–64. New York: Schocken Books.

Crimp, Douglas. 1984. "Pictures." In *Art after Modernism: Rethinking Representation*, edited by Brian Wallis, 175–87. New York: New Museum of Contemporary Art.

Deitcher, David. 1985. "Drawing from Memory." In *The Art of Mem-*

ory: *The Loss of History*, edited by William Olander, 15–21. New York: New Museum of Contemporary Art.

Deutsche, Rosalyn, and Cara Gendel Ryan. 1987. "The Fine Art of Gentrification." *Portable Lower East Side* 4.1 (Spring): 33–53. [Reprinted from *October* 31 (Winter 1984).]

Eliot, T. S. 1975. "Tradition and the Individual Talent." In *Selected Prose of T. S. Eliot*, edited by Frank Kermode, 37–44. New York: Harcourt Brace Jovanovich.

*The End of Art Panel*. 1987. New York: B.A.D. Museum. (Accompanies the MetaLanguages/Textual Venues exhibition.)

Federman, Raymond. 1981. "Surfiction—Four Propositions in Form of an Introduction." In *Surfiction: Fiction Now and Tomorrow*. 2d ed., edited by Raymond Federman, 5–15. Chicago: Swallow Press.

Ferrer, Elizabeth, ed. 1985. *The Art of Appropriation*. New York: Alternative Museum.

Foster, Hal. 1985a. "For a Concept of the Political in Contemporary Art." In *Recodings: Art, Spectacle, Cultural Politics*, 139–55. Port Townsend, Wash.: Bay Press.

———. 1985b. "(Post)Modern Polemics." In *Recordings: Art, Spectacle, Cultural Politics*, 121–36. Port Townsend, Wash.: Bay Press.

Foucault, Michel. 1980a. *The History of Sexuality*. Vol. 1, *An Introduction*. Trans. Robert Hurley. New York: Vintage Books.

———. 1980b. *Power/Knowledge: Selected Interviews and Other Writings, 1972–1977*, edited by Colin Gordon. New York: Pantheon Books.

———. 1984. "The Subject and Power." In *Art after Modernism: Rethinking Representation*, edited by Brian Wallis, 417–32. New York: New Museum of Contemporary Art.

Hagenberg, Roland, ed. 1986. *Soho. A Guide. A Documentary*. New York: Egret Publications.

Herman, Edward S. 1984. "Brainwashing under Freedom." In *Disinformation: The Manufacture of Consent*, edited by Geno Rodriguez, 34–36. New York: Alternative Museum.

Hutcheon, Linda. 1986–87. "The Politics of Postmodernism: Parody and History." *Cultural Critique* 5 (Winter): 179–207.

Irigaray, Luce. 1985. *This Sex Which Is Not One*. Ithaca, N.Y.: Cornell University Press.

Jencks, Charles. 1984. *The Language of Post-Modern Architecture*. 4th ed. New York: Rizzoli.

———. 1986. *What Is Post-Modernism?* New York: St. Martin's Press.

Kaprow, Allan. 1986. "Useful Fictions (1975)" and "Postscript to 'Useful Fictions.'" *Act* 1.1 (Winter/Spring): 7–13.

Kardon, Janet, ed. 1984. *The East Village Scene*. Philadelphia: Institute of Contemporary Art.

Kintz, Linda. 1986. "On Learning Deconstruction: Postmodernist Pedagogy."

Klinkowitz, Jerome. 1984. *The Self-Apparent Word: Fiction as Language/Language as Fiction*. Carbondale: Southern Illinois University Press.

———. 1985. *Literary Subversions: New American Fiction and the Practice of Criticism*. Carbondale: Southern Illinois University Press.

Kostelanetz, Richard. 1979. *Twenties in the Sixties*. Westport, Conn.: Greenwood Press.

———. 1981. "New Fiction in America." In *Surfiction: Fiction Now and Tomorrow*. 2d ed., edited by Raymond Federman, 85–100. Chicago: Swallow Press.

Kroker, Arthur, and David Cook. 1986. *The Postmodern Scene: Excremental Culture and Hyper-Aesthetics*. New York: St. Martin's Press, 1986.

Lacan, Jacques. 1970. "Of Structure as an Inmixing of an Otherness Prerequisite to Any Subject Whatever." In *The Structuralist Controversy: The Languages of Criticism and the Sciences of Man*, edited by Richard Macksey and Eugenio Donato, 186–200. Baltimore: Johns Hopkins University Press.

Lawson, Thomas. 1987. "Spies and Watchmen." In *Blasted Allegories*, edited by Brian Wallis, 138–40. New York: New Museum of Contemporary Art.

Linker, Kate. 1983. "Richard Prince's Photographs." *Pamphlet*, 2–6. Lyon: Nouveau Musée.

Lippard, Lucy. 1984. "Trojan Horses: Activist Art and Power." In *Art after Modernism: Rethinking Representation*, edited by Brian Wallis, 341–58. New York: New Museum of Contemporary Art.

McCormick, Carlo. 1984. "Guide to East Village Artists." In *Neo York: Report on a Phenomenon*, edited by Phyllis Plous and Mary Looker. Santa Barbara, Calif.: University Art Museum.

———. 1988. "True Lit." *Paper*, May, 55.

McHale, Brian. 1987. *Postmodernist Fiction*. New York: Methuen.

Moore, Alan, and Marc Miller, eds. 1985. *ABC No Rio Dinero: The Story of a Lower East Side Art Gallery*. New York: ABC No Rio and Collaborative Projects.

Mulvey, Laura. 1984. "Visual Pleasure and Narrative Cinema." In *Art after Modernism: Rethinking Representation*, edited by Brian Wallis, 361–73. New York: New Museum of Contemporary Art.

Musto, Michael. 1986. *Downtown*. New York: Vintage Books.

Olander, William. 1987. "Fake: A Meditation on Authenticity." In *Fake*, edited by William Olander, 6–44. New York: New Museum of Contemporary Art.

Owens, Craig. 1984. "The Allegorical Impulse: Toward a Theory of Postmodernism." In *Art after Modernism: Rethinking Representation*, edited by Brian Wallis, 203–35. New York: New Museum of Contemporary Art.

Plous, Phyllis, and Mary Looker, eds. 1984. *Neo York: Report on a Phenomenon*. Santa Barbara, Calif.: University Art Museum.

Prina, Stephen, and Christopher Williams. 1985. "A Conversation with Lynne Tillman and Sheila McLaughlin." *Journal: A Contemporary Arts Magazine* 5 (Spring): 40–45.

Rian, Jeffrey. 1987. "Social Science Fiction: An Interview with Richard Prince." *Art in America* 75.3 (March): 86–95.

Robinson, Walter, and Carlo McCormick. 1984. "Slouching toward Avenue D." *Art in America* 72.7 (Summer): 135–61.

Ross, David A. 1985. "Nam June Paik's Videotapes." In *Transmission*, edited by Peter D'Agostino, 151–63. New York: Tanam Press.

Sayre, Henry. 1986. "In (the) Place of a Text (Eleanor Antin's *El Desdichado*)." *Act* 1.1 (Winter/Spring): 42–48.

Siegle, Robert. 1986. *The Politics of Reflexivity: Narrative and the Constitutive Poetics of Culture.* Baltimore: Johns Hopkins University Press.

Sukenick, Ronald. 1985. *In Form: Digressions on the Act of Fiction.* Carbondale: Southern Illinois University Press.

Texier, Catherine. n.d. "Le Retour de la Beat Generation." *City Magazine International* 35:58–62.

Vitale, Tom. n.d. "Kathy Acker." *A Movable Feast.* Audiotape.

Wallis, Brian, ed. 1984. *Art after Modernism: Rethinking Representation.* New York: New Museum of Contemporary Art.

———. 1985a. "An Absence of Vision and Drama." *Parkett* 5:63–73.

———. 1985b. "Mindless Pleasure: Richard Prince's Fictions." *Parkett* 6:61–62.

———, ed. 1987. *Blasted Allegories.* New York: New Museum of Contemporary Art.

# INDEX

## to Names and Titles